Concepts

FIFTH EDITION

Strategic Management

Competitiveness and Globalization

FIFTH EDITION

Strategic Management

Competitiveness and Globalization

Concepts

Michael A. Hitt
Arizona State University

R. Duane Ireland
University of Richmond

Robert E. Hoskisson
The University of Oklahoma

Australia · Canada · Mexico · Singapore · Spain · United Kingdom · United States

THOMSON

SOUTH-WESTERN

Strategic Management: Competitiveness and Globalization (Concepts) 5e

Michael A. Hitt, R. Duane Ireland & Robert E. Hoskisson

Editor-in-Chief:
Jack W. Calhoun

Vice President/Team Director:
Michael P. Roche

Executive Editor:
John Szilagyi

Developmental Editor:
Michele Heinz, Elm Street Publishing Services, Inc.

Senior Marketing Manager:
Rob Bloom

Senior Production Editor:
Kara ZumBahlen

Manufacturing Coordinator:
Rhonda Utley

Compositor:
Parkwood Composition

Production House:
Elm Street Publishing Services, Inc.

Printer:
QuebecorWorld, Versailles

Internal Design:
Christy Carr

Cover Designer:
Christy Carr

Cover Images:
© Cartesia Software and © PhotoDisc

Photography Manager:
Deanna Ettinger

Photo Researcher:
Terri Miller

Printed in the United States of America
1 2 3 4 5 05 04 03 02

For more information contact South-Western, 5191 Natorp Boulevard, Mason, Ohio 45040.
Or you can visit our Internet site at: http://www.swcollege.com

Library of Congress Control Number: 2002108281

ISBN: 0-324-11480-X

To my young grandson, Mason. Pa Pa loves you
—Michael A. Hitt

To Mary Ann and to Rebecca and Scott, our children. I love each of you deeply. Always remember that "When you need me, call my name; because without you, my life just wouldn't be the same."
—R. Duane Ireland

To my loving and supportive wife, Kathy Hall Hoskisson, with whom life is much more special, and to my wonderful children, who are uniquely wonderful examples to me.
—Robert E. Hoskisson

Brief Contents

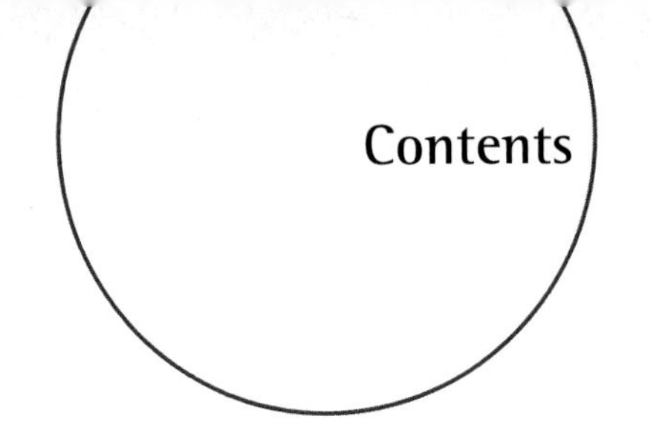

Contents

About This Book

As with the earlier editions of *Strategic Management: Competitiveness and Globalization*, we have carefully integrated "cutting edge" research with practical applications in companies competing in global markets to develop this Fifth Edition. We continue to use this approach because we strongly believe that melding research findings with managerial practices provides you, our readers, with a comprehensive, timely, and accurate explanation of how companies use the strategic management process to successfully compete in the 21st century's dynamic and challenging competitive landscape. Our goals in preparing this edition remain as they were with the first four editions, which are to (1) introduce the strategic management process in a way that illustrates both traditional approaches and the dynamics of strategic change; (2) describe the full set of strategic management tools, techniques, and concepts as well as how firms use them to develop competitive advantages; and (3) present contemporary strategic thinking and issues affecting 21st century firms and the strategic decisions made in those companies. Thus, our major goal in preparing this fifth edition has been to present you, our readers, with a concise, complete, accurate, up-to-date, and interesting explanation of the strategic management process as it is used by firms competing in the global economy.

Using an engaging, action-oriented writing style, we have taken great care to sharpen our presentation of strategic management tools and concepts. We relied on valued feedback from adopters and colleagues to carefully rewrite the chapters to make them clear and concise. Although we fully describe all relevant parts of the strategic, and interesting management process, the chapters in this edition are more succinct. However, the noticeable reduction in chapter length has not come at the expense of informative practical examples. In fact, while reading the chapters, you'll find descriptions of many different types of firms as we explore the strategic management process. These examples are current and show how firms are competing in today's constantly changing global environment.

New Features and Updates

Many new features and updates to this edition enhance the book's value.

- All new chapter *Opening Cases* (13 in total).
- All new *Strategic Focus segments* (three per chapter for a total of 39).
- New *company-specific examples* illustrating each chapter's central themes.
- *Full coverage of strategic issues that are prominent in the 21st century competitive landscape.* Chapter 13, for example, has been rewritten to focus on *Strategic Entrepreneurship*. Important in established firms as well as start-up ventures, strategic entrepreneurship is concerned with combining opportunity seeking behavior with advantage seeking behavior. As we describe in the all-new Chapter 13, firms that learn how to use a strategic perspective to identify and exploit entrepreneurial opportunities increase their ability to outperform their rivals. In Chapter 5, we've sharpened the discussion of paterns of competition that occurs between firms as they try to outperform each other.
- *Discussion of new topics.* In this edition, we discuss the use of profit pools (Chapter 2), activity mapping (Chapter 4), and the use of the balanced scorecard as a means of

measurement and control (Chapter 12). These new tools are gaining importance as parts of an effective strategic management process.

- A continued emphasis on *global coverage* with more emphasis on the international context and issues, both in the chapters and the cases.
- Updated *Review Questions* at the end of each chapter.
- *Experiential exercises* at the end of each chapter. New to this edition, these exercises present real-life strategic management issues and are followed by questions. The exercises can be individual or group-based and are sophisticated, yet simple to use.
- *New full four-color design* with enhanced readability and pedagogical treatment.

These new features and updates provide a unique competitive advantage for this book. With 13 new *Opening Cases* and 39 new *Strategic Focus* segments, we offer 52 major case examples in the chapters. In addition, virtually all of the shorter examples used throughout each chapter are completely new.

This new edition also emphasizes a global advantage with comprehensive coverage of international concepts and issues. In addition to comprehensive coverage of international strategies in Chapter 8, references to and discussions of the international context and issues are included in every chapter. The Opening Cases, Strategic Focus segments, and individual examples in each chapter cover numerous global issues.

Importantly, this new edition solidifies a research advantage for our book. For example, each chapter has more than 100 references. On average, 60 percent of these references are new to this edition. Drawn from the business literature and academic research, the materials in these references are vital to our explanations of how firms use the strategic management process.

The Book's Focus

The strategic management process is our book's focus. Organizations use the strategic management process to understand competitive forces and to develop competitive advantages. The magnitude of this challenge is greater today than it has been in the past. A new competitive landscape exists in the 21st century as a result of the technological revolution (especially in e-commerce) and increasing globalization. The technological revolution has placed greater importance on innovation and the ability to rapidly introduce new goods and services to the marketplace. The global economy, one in which goods and services flow relatively freely among nations, continuously pressures firms to become more competitive. By offering either valued goods or services to customers, competitive firms increase the probability of earning above-average returns. Thus, the strategic management process helps organizations identify *what* they want to achieve as well as *how* they will do it.

The Strategic Management Process

Our discussion of the strategic management process is both traditional and contemporary. In maintaining tradition, we examine important materials that have historically been a part of understanding strategic management. For example, we thoroughly examine how to analyze a firm's external environment (see Chapter 2) and internal environment (see Chapter 3).

Contemporary Treatment

To explain the aforementioned important activities, we try to keep our treatments contemporary. In Chapter 3, for example, we emphasize the importance of identifying and determining the value-creating potential of a firm's resources, capabilities, and core competencies. The strategic actions taken as a result of understanding a firm's resources, capabilities, and core competencies have a direct link with the company's ability to establish a competitive advantage, achieve strategic competitiveness, and earn above-average returns.

Our contemporary treatment is also shown in the chapters on the dynamics of strategic change in the complex global economy. In Chapter 5, for example, we discuss the competitive rivalry between firms and the outcomes of their competitive actions and responses. Chapter 5's discussion suggests a firm's strategic actions are influenced by its competitors' actions and reactions. Thus, competition in the global economy is fluid, dynamic, and fast-paced. Similarly, in Chapter 7, we explain the dynamics of strategic change at the corporate level, specifically addressing the motivation and consequences of mergers, acquisitions, and restructuring (e.g., divestitures) in the global economy.

We also emphasize that the set of strategic actions known as strategy formulation and strategy implementation (see Figure 1.1) must be carefully integrated for the firm to be successful.

Contemporary Concepts

Contemporary topics and concepts are the foundation for our in-depth analysis of strategic actions firms take to implement strategies. In Chapter 10, for example, we describe how different corporate governance mechanisms (e.g., boards of directors, institutional owners, executive compensation, etc.) affect strategy implementation. Chapter 11 explains how firms gain a competitive advantage by effectively using organizational structures that are properly matched to different strategies. The vital contributions of strategic leaders are examined in Chapter 12. In the all-new Chapter 13, we describe the important relationship between the ability to find and exploit entrepreneurial opportunities through competitive advantages.

Key Features

Several features are included in this book to increase its value for you.

Knowledge Objectives

Each chapter begins with clearly stated Knowledge Objectives. Their purpose is to emphasize key strategic management issues you will be able to learn about while studying each chapter. To both facilitate and verify learning, you can revisit the Knowledge Objectives while preparing answers to the Review Questions that are presented at the end of each chapter.

Opening Cases

An Opening Case follows the Knowledge Objectives in each chapter. The Opening Cases describe current strategic issues in modern companies such as Federal Express, Southwest Airlines, eBay, and Dell Computer Corporation, among many others. The purpose of the Opening Cases is to demonstrate how specific firms apply an individual chapter's strategic management concepts. Thus, the Opening Cases serve as a direct and often distinctive link between the theory and application of strategic management in different organizations and industries.

Key Terms

Key Terms that are critical to understanding the strategic management process are boldfaced throughout the chapters. Definitions of the Key Terms appear in chapter margins as well as in the text. Other terms and concepts throughout the text are italicized, signifying their importance.

Strategic Focus Segments

Three all-new Strategic Focus segments are presented in each chapter. As with the Opening Cases, the Strategic Focus segments highlight a variety of high-profile organizations, situations, and concepts. Each segment describes issues that can be addressed by applying a chapter's strategy-related concepts.

End-of-Chapter Summaries

Closing each chapter is a Summary that revisits the concepts outlined in the Knowledge Objectives. The Summaries are presented in a bulleted format to highlight a chapter's concepts, tools, and techniques.

Review Questions

Review Questions are directly tied to each chapter's Knowledge Objectives, prompting readers to reexamine the most important concepts in each chapter.

Experiential Exercises

Developed by Luis Flores, Northern Illinois University, and presented at the end of the chapters, each Experiential Exercise provides an action-oriented opportunity for readers to enhance their understanding of strategic management. Materials come to life as readers use a chapter's materials to answer questions concerned with strategic management issues.

Examples

In addition to the Opening Cases and Strategic Focus segments, each chapter is filled with real-world examples of companies in action. These examples illustrate key strategic management concepts and provide realistic applications of strategic management.

Indices

Besides the traditional end-of-book *Subject Index* and *Name Index,* we offer a *Company Index* as well. The Company Index includes the names of the hundreds of organizations discussed in the text. The three indices help to find where subjects are discussed, a person's name is used, and a company's actions are described.

Full Four-Color Format

Our presentation and discussion of the strategic management process is facilitated by the use of a full four-color format. This format provides the foundation for an interesting and visually appealing treatment of all parts of the strategic management process. Exhibits and photos further enhance the presentation by giving visual insight into the workings of companies competing in the global business environment.

Support Material*

With this edition, we continue our commitment to present you with one of the most comprehensive and quality learning packages available for teaching strategic management. Talented and dedicated people—people who are recognized for their academic achievements and their skill as excellent strategic management teachers—prepared the supplements for this fifth edition. We worked jointly with each person to make certain that all parts of the supplement package are effectively integrated with the text's materials.

*Adopters: Please contact your Thomson Learning sales representative to learn more about the book's supplements or visit http://hitt.swcollege.com.

For the Instructor

Instructor's Resource Manual with Video Guide and Transparency Masters

(ISBN: 0-324-11483-4) Les Palich, Baylor University, prepared a comprehensive *Instructor's Resource Manual.* The Manual provides instructors with a wealth of additional material and presentations that effectively complement the text. Using each chapter's Knowledge Objectives as an organizing principle, the manual has been completely revised to integrate the best knowledge on teaching strategic management to maximize student learning. The Manual includes ideas about how to approach each chapter and how to emphasize essential principles with additional examples that can be used to explain points and to stimulate active discussions in your classrooms. Lecture outlines, detailed answers to the Review Questions at the end of each chapter, guides to the videos, additional assignments, and transparency masters are also included, along with instructions for using each chapter's Experiential Exercise. Flexible in nature, these exercises can be used in class or in other ways, such as homework or as an out-of-the-classroom assignment. The video guide provides information on length, alternative points of usage within the text, subjects to address, and discussion questions to stimulate classroom discussion. Suggested answers to these questions are also provided. The transparency masters are printed from the PowerPoint presentation files and include figures from the text and innovative adaptations.

Test Bank

(ISBN: 0-324-11482-6) The *Test Bank* has been thoroughly revised and enhanced for this edition by Janelle B. Dozier, Ph.D., S.P.H.R., who has also added new questons for each Opening Case and Strategic Focus segment. In addition, Mason Carpenter, Nasgovitz Fellow, University of Wisconsin–Madison, contributed a unique new feature to the test bank: a set of scenario-based questions to each chapter to add an innovative problem-solving dimension to exams. All objective questions are linked to chapter Knowledge Objectives and are ranked by difficulty level, among other measures.

ExamView™ Testing Software

(ISBN: 0-324-11487-7) All of the test questions in the printed *Test Bank* are also available in *ExamView,* a computerized format available in Windows and Macintosh versions. *ExamView* is easy-to-use test-creation software that makes it possible for instructors to easily and efficiently create, edit, store, and print exams.

PowerPoint

(ISBN: 0-324-11485-0) R. Dennis Middlemist, Colorado State University has prepared attractive all-new sets of *PowerPoint* slides that can be downloaded from the Web site designed to be used with this text at http://hitt.swcollege.com. The easily followed presentations include clear figures based on the text and innovative adaptations to illustrate the text concepts. The PowerPoint slides, available both with and without animation, are provided in two versions to allow instructors to choose the most appropriate presentation for their teaching method, whether lecture or discussion.

Transparency Acetates

(ISBN: 0-324-17151-X) For those unable to access PowerPoint, a concise set of transparency acetates adapted from the PowerPoint presentation files is available on request. The transparency acetates include clear figures based on the text.

Instructor's Case Notes

(ISBN: 0-324-11484-2) C. Bradley Shrader, Iowa State University, prepared an all-new *Instructor's Case Notes* for this edition. The all-new case notes provide details about the cases within the framework of case analysis. The structure allows instructors to organize case discussions along common themes and concepts and also feature aspects of the cases that make them unique. The format includes a summary of the case, teaching objectives, discussion questions and answers, and case analysis, and incorporates information from teaching notes prepared by the individual case writers as well. The cases are directly related to appropriate chapters of the text, thus allowing the instructor the opportunity to use and re-use the case for discussion and to make each case an integrative exercise.

Videos

(ISBN: 0-324-17170-6) *Management and Strategy* is a 45-minute video of short clips providing news and information about firms and current strategic management issues that are of particular relevance to students of strategic management, using the resources of Turner Learning/CNN, the world's first 24-hour all-news network. A separate multimedia integration guide, developed by Ross Stapleton-Gray, Ph.D., CISSP, chief university spokesperson on IT security issues for the University of California, accompanies the videotape and provides video descriptions, topical guides, and discussion questions for each clip.

SmallBusinessSchool
the Series on PBS stations and the Web

(ISBN:0-324-26131-4) *Entrepreneurship and Strategy* is a 45-minute video based on the remarkable resources of "Small Business School," the series on PBS stations, Worldnet, and the Web. It looks at seven firms that capitalized on their beginnings and used strategic management to grow market share and create competitive advantage. A resource guide within the *Instructor's Resource Manual* describes each segment and provides discussion questions.

(ISBN: 0-324-11488-5) *Corporate Strategy* is a 45-minute video featuring corporate strategy situations for classroom viewing. A resource guide within the *Instructor's Resource Manual* describes each segment and provides discussion questions.

Instructor's Resource CD-ROM

(ISBN: 0-324-17686-4) Key ancillaries (Instructor's Resource Manual, Instructor's Case Notes, Test Bank, ExamView, and PowerPoint) are provided on CD-ROM, giving instructors the ultimate tool for customizing lectures and presentations.

Simulations

(ISBN: 0-324-16867-5) *Strategic Management in the Marketplace* is a unique and adaptable Web-based simulation that has been tailored to use with our text for the strategic management course. We worked closely with Ernest Cadotte of the University of Tennessee and his colleagues at Innovative Learning Solutions, Inc. to develop this product. Designed around important strategic management tools, techniques, and concepts, the simulation is easy to administer. Visit http://hitt.swcollege.com to learn more.

(ISBN: 0-324-16183-2) *The Global Business Game* simulation challenges students to deal with a host of strategic issues in a global context and make decisions that will lead to the firm's success. We worked with author Joseph Wolfe to prepare the second edition of this simulation, which includes clear operational instructions that closely match topics in the text.

For the Student

Infotrac College Edition

The *Infotrac College Edition* gives students access—anytime, anywhere—to an online database of full-text articles from hundreds of scholarly and popular periodicals, including *Newsweek* and *Fortune.* Fast and easy search tools help you find just what you're looking for from among tens of thousands of articles, updated daily, all at a single site. For more information or to log on, please visit http://www.swcollege. com/infotrac/infotrac.html. Just enter your passcode as provided on the subscription card packaged free with new copies of *Strategic Management.*

Web Tutor™ on WebCT and WebTutor™ on Blackboard

(ISBN: 0-324-15084-9) WebTutor, developed by Craig V. VanSandt of Augustana College to complement *Strategic Management: Competitiveness and Globalization*, provides interactive reinforcement that helps you master complex concepts. Questions and answers for self-study, Internet exercises, useful links to sites relevant to your study of strategic management, InfoTrac resources, and more are included. *WebTutor's* online teaching and learning environment brings together content management, assessment, communication, and collaboration capabilities for enhancing in-class instruction or for delivering distance learning. For more information, including a demonstration, go to http://swcollege.webtutor.com.

For the Student and Instructor

Strategic Management: Competitiveness and Globalization Website

(http://hitt.swcollege.com) This edition's website offers students and instructors access to a wealth of helpful material, including Instructor Resources, Student Resources, Interactive Study Center, and Interactive Quizzes, and links to Strategy Suite, eCoursepacks, and Careers in Management. Resources available on the website include continually updated case information, an Internet index with important strategy URLs, and a section on how to write a case analysis. Additional Experiential Exercises, an online glossary, and the new PowerPoint presentations are also available, as are additional Strategic Focus Applications, Discussion Questions, Ethics Questions, Internet Exercises, and Global Resources. In addition, all Strategic Focus segments from the fourth edition are offered for students and instructors to use as strategy examples, including discussion questions. These are indexed by broad subject categories. The *Strategic Management* website provides information about the authors and allows you to contact the authors and publisher.

The Wall Street Journal

Bring the most up-to-date real-world events into your classroom through *The Wall Street Journal. The Wall Street Journal* is synonymous with the latest word on business, and *Strategic Management,* Fifth Edition, makes it easy for students to apply strategic management concepts to this authoritative publication through a special subscription offer. For a nominal additional cost, *Strategic Management,* Fifth Edition, can be packaged with a card entitling students to a 15-week subscription to both the print and interactive versions of *The Wall Street Journal.* Contact your South-Western/Thomson Learning sales representative for package pricing and ordering information.

e-Coursepack

(ISBN: 0-324-25244-7) Current, interesting, and relevant articles are available to supplement each chapter of *Strategic Management* in an e-Coursepack—the result of a joint effort between the Gale Group, a world leader in e-information publishing for libraries, schools, and businesses, and South-Western. Full-length articles to complement *Strategic Management* are available 24-hours a day, over the Web, from sources such as *Fortune, Across the Board, Management Today,* and the *Sloan Management Review.* Students can also access up-to-date information of key individuals, companies, and textbook cases through predefined searches of Gale databases. For more information, contact your South-Western/Thomson Learning sales representative or call Thomson Custom Publishing at 1-800-355-9983.

Acknowledgments

We want to thank those who helped us prepare the fifth edition. The professionalism, guidance, and support provided by the South-Western editorial and marketing teams of John Szilagyi, Mike Roche, Rob Bloom, and Kara ZumBahlen, and Michele Heinz and Becky Dodson of Elm Street Publishing Services are gratefully acknowledged. We appreciate the excellent work of our supplements author team: Mason Carpenter, Janelle Dozier, Dennis Middlemist, Les Palich, C. Brad Shrader, Ross Stapleton-Gray, and Craig VanSandt. In addition, we owe a debt of gratitude to our colleagues at Arizona State University, University of Richmond, and the University of Oklahoma. Finally, we are sincerely grateful to those who took time to read and provide feedback on drafts of either this fifth edition and previous editions of our book. Their insights and evaluations have enhanced this text, and we list them below with our thanks.

Barbara R. Bartkus, *Old Dominion University*

Tim Blumentritt, *Marquette University*

Denis Collins, *University of Bridgeport*

Anthony F. Chelte, *Western New England College*

Wade Dennis, *Marquette University*

Sam DeMarie, *Iowa State University*

Kimberly M. Ellis, *Michigan State University*

Howard Feldman, *University of Portland*

Walter J. Ferrier, *University of Kentucky*

Luis G. Flores, *Northern Illinois University*

R. Bruce Garrison, *Houston Baptist University*

Jeffrey S. Harrison, *University of Central Florida*

Richard C. Johnson, *University of Missouri*

Alfred L. Kahl, *University of Ottawa*

Vincent P. Luchsinger, *University of Baltimore*

Luis Marino, *University of Alabama*

Catherine A. Maritan, *State University of New York, Buffalo*

David Olson, *California State University, Bakersfield*

Annette L. Ranft, *Wake Forest University*

Wm. Gerard (Gerry) Sanders, *Brigham Young University*

Laszlo Tihanyi, *University of Oklahoma*

Arieh A. Ullman, *Binghamton University*

John J. Villareal, *California State University, Hayward*

Greg Young, *North Carolina State University*

Final Comments

Organizations face exciting and dynamic competitive challenges in the 21st century. These challenges, and effective responses to them, are explored in this fifth edition of *Strategic Management: Competitiveness and Globalization.* The strategic management process conceptualized and described in this text offers valuable insights and knowledge to those committed to successfully meeting the challenge of dynamic competition. Thinking strategically, as this book challenges you to do, increases the likelihood that you will help your company achieve strategic success. In addition, continuous practice with strategic thinking and the use of the strategic management process gives you skills and knowledge that will contribute to career advancement and success. Finally, we want to wish you all the best and nothing other than complete success in all of your endeavors.

Michael A. Hitt

R. Duane Ireland

Robert E. Hoskisson

FIFTH EDITION

Strategic Management

Competitiveness and Globalization

PART ONE

Strategic Management Inputs

1

1

Chapter One

Strategic Management and Strategic Competitiveness

Knowledge Objectives

Studying this chapter should provide you with the strategic management knowledge needed to:

1. Define strategic competitiveness, competitive advantage, and above-average returns.
2. Describe the 21st-century competitive landscape and explain how globalization and technological changes shape it.
3. Use the industrial organization (I/O) model to explain how firms can earn above-average returns.
4. Use the resource-based model to explain how firms can earn above-average returns.
5. Describe strategic intent and strategic mission and discuss their value.
6. Define stakeholders and describe their ability to influence organizations.
7. Describe strategists' work.
8. Explain the strategic management process.

In Bad Times, Good Companies Stand Out

In poor economic times, many firms struggle, as evidenced on a recent cover of *The Economist* titled, "2001 Things to Do in a Recession: 1. Get a Parachute." The accompanying cover photo featured a person on the ledge outside a window of a multistory building. However, some businesses do better in a recession. For example, the weak economic conditions in the United States during 2001 seemed to provide a boost to coffee sales. But, the growth in coffee sales largely occurred in institutional sales to offices. The president of Aramark Corporation suggested that providing coffee is a relatively inexpensive way to keep employees in the office and stimulated. Having this outcome with employees does not necessarily suggest that firms selling coffee are well managed strategically. Rather, they simply benefit from conditions in their external environment.

Other firms perform well even when many of their competitors are suffering from the poor economic conditions. These firms are more likely to have effectively managed strategies. Brinker International, eBay, and the perennially successful Southwest Airlines are three examples of such firms. Why are these firms profitable when many in their industries are not? To paraphrase an old and often-used saying, "It's the strategy and its implementation, stupid!" For example, Brinker, which owns nine restaurant chains, including Chili's, uses a decentralized approach allowing each of its restaurant chains to operate entrepreneurially in local markets. The approach pays off—sales per restaurant have increased by approximately 3.7 percent per year while sales for its competitors, Bennigan's and Houlihan's, have declined. Brinker has also developed new dining concepts such as the popular Eatzi's, a meal-to-go operation that provides gourmet foods for take-out dining.

eBay, one of the few Internet-based firms still profitable in 2000–2001, has enjoyed strong performance when many Internet-based firms are performing poorly and a number of them have ceased operations. eBay provides an online auction service where people can buy and sell personal goods. During the weak economic conditions of 2001, the firm actually forecasted an increase in revenues and earnings, a dream for many Internet firms, such as Amazon.com. eBay's business model is effective, and the firm is the best at what it does. It provides strong consumer value with a brand known for quality and safe transactions on the Internet.

Shown here is the corporate headquarters of Dallas-based Brinker International, which owns and operates restaurants in 48 states and 22 countries. In addition to Chili's and Romano's Macaroni Grill, its largest brands, Brinker has also developed such successful new dining concepts as Maggiano's Little Italy, the Corner Bakery Cafe, and Big Bowl, a new Asian concept.

Because Southwest Airlines has been discussed so much in the past, it may seem passé to comment on its continuing success. Southwest's success is particularly noteworthy in poor economic times and following the retirement of legendary founder and CEO Herb Kelleher. In the first quarter of 2001, when all other major airlines but one suffered net losses, Southwest announced a 65 percent increase in net profits with a 15 percent increase in revenue. Additionally, it also was the only major airline to make a profit in the third quarter of 2001 after the tragic events of September 11.

What accounts for Southwest's success? Southwest is positioned well for poor economic conditions because of its integrated cost leadership/differentiation strategy that results in low fares, but other airlines offer low fares as well. Southwest also has the fewest customer complaints of all major airlines; in contrast, another airline with relatively competitive fares, America West, was rated as the worst airline in the United States. Southwest's well-known positive culture helps it attract the best employees and they treat the customers positively. It also has a high on-time performance. Thus, its cost leadership is not the primary reason for its success. The competitive advantage enjoyed by Southwest results from its highly successful strategy implementation that differentiates the services provided to the customers relative to competitors. Additional comments about Southwest and its successful use of the integrated cost leadership/differentiation strategy appear in Chapter 4.

SOURCES: K. Stewart & K. Hussey, 2001, eBay weathers the dot.com storm, posting solid profits, growth, *Wall Street Journal Interactive,* http://interactive.wsj.com/articles, January 20; 2001, Southwest's net income rises 65%, amid a 15% increase in revenue, *Wall Street Journal Interactive,* http://interactive.wsj.com/articles, April 19; A. Edgecliffe-Johnson, 2001, Bean counters stay smiling, *Financial Times,* http://www.ft.com, April 27; A. Farnham, 2001, America's worst airline? *Forbes,* June 11, 105–115; 2001, Brinker International: Red-hot Chili's, *Forbes,* http://www.forbes.com, June 14.

Although Brinker International, eBay, and Southwest Airlines are highly successful, the reasons for their effective performances differ. Their strategy formulation and implementation actions helped them gain an advantage over their competitors. Brinker International's restaurants offer innovative and quality foods, and Brinker's several restaurant chains are more entrepreneurial than their competitors. eBay provides a high quality unique service allowing access to products through online auctions that others have been unable to imitate. Southwest provides much higher quality customer service for a lower price than its competitors can offer.

Strategic competitiveness is achieved when a firm successfully formulates and implements a value-creating strategy.

A **sustained** or **sustainable competitive advantage** occurs when a firm implements a value-creating strategy and other companies are unable to duplicate it or find it too costly to imitate.

The actions taken by these firms are intended to achieve strategic competitiveness and earn above-average returns. **Strategic competitiveness** is achieved when a firm successfully formulates and implements a value-creating strategy. When a firm implements such a strategy and other companies are unable to duplicate it or find it too costly to imitate,[1] this firm has a **sustained** (or **sustainable) competitive advantage** (hereafter called simply *competitive advantage*). An organization is assured of a competitive advantage only after others' efforts to duplicate its strategy have ceased or failed. In addition, when a firm achieves a competitive advantage, it normally can sustain it only for a certain period.[2] The speed with which competitors are able to acquire the skills needed to duplicate the benefits of a firm's value-creating strategy determines how long the competitive advantage will last.[3]

Above-average returns are returns in excess of what an investor expects to earn from other investments with a similar amount of risk.

Risk is an investor's uncertainty about the economic gains or losses that will result from a particular investment.

Average returns are returns equal to those an investor expects to earn from other investments with a similar amount of risk.

The **strategic management process** is the full set of commitments, decisions, and actions required for a firm to achieve strategic competitiveness and earn above-average returns.

Understanding how to exploit a competitive advantage is important for firms to earn above-average returns.[4] **Above-average returns** are returns in excess of what an investor expects to earn from other investments with a similar amount of risk. **Risk** is an investor's uncertainty about the economic gains or losses that will result from a particular investment.[5] Returns are often measured in terms of accounting figures, such as return on assets, return on equity, or return on sales. Alternatively, returns can be measured on the basis of stock market returns, such as monthly returns (the end-of-the-period stock price minus the beginning stock price, divided by the beginning stock price, yielding a percentage return).

Firms without a competitive advantage or that are not competing in an attractive industry earn, at best, average returns. **Average returns** are returns equal to those an investor expects to earn from other investments with a similar amount of risk. In the long run, an inability to earn at least average returns results in failure. Failure occurs because investors withdraw their investments from those firms earning less-than-average returns.

Dynamic in nature, the **strategic management process** (see Figure 1.1) is the full set of commitments, decisions, and actions required for a firm to achieve strategic competitiveness and earn above-average returns.[6] Relevant strategic inputs derived from analyses of the internal and external environments are necessary for effective strategy formulation and implementation. In turn, effective strategic actions are a prerequisite to achieving the desired outcomes of strategic competitiveness and above-average returns. Thus, the strategic management process is used to match the conditions of an ever-changing market and competitive structure with a firm's continuously evolving resources, capabilities, and competencies (the sources of strategic inputs). Effective strategic actions that take place in the context of carefully integrated strategy formulation and implementation actions result in desired strategic outcomes.[7]

In the remaining chapters of this book, we use the strategic management process to explain what firms should do to achieve strategic competitiveness and earn above-average returns. These explanations demonstrate why some firms consistently achieve competitive success while others fail to do so.[8] As you will see, the reality of global competition is a critical part of the strategic management process.[9]

Several topics are discussed in this chapter. First, we examine the challenge of strategic management. This brief discussion highlights the fact that strategic actions taken to achieve and then maintain strategic competitiveness demand the best efforts of managers, employees, and their organizations on a continuous basis.[10] Second, we describe the 21st-century competitive landscape, created primarily by the emergence of a global economy and rapid technological changes. This landscape provides the context of opportunities and threats within which firms strive to meet the competitive challenge.

We next examine two models that suggest the strategic inputs needed to select strategic actions necessary to achieve strategic competitiveness. The first model (industrial organization) suggests that the external environment is the primary determinant of a firm's strategic actions. The key to this model is identifying and competing successfully in an attractive (i.e., profitable) industry.[11] The second model (resource based) suggests that a firm's unique resources and capabilities are the critical link to strategic competitiveness.[12] Comprehensive explanations in this chapter and the next two chapters show that through the combined use of these models, firms obtain the strategic inputs needed to formulate and implement strategies successfully. Analyses of its external and internal environments provide a firm with the information required to develop its strategic intent and strategic mission (defined later in this chapter). As shown in Figure 1.1, strategic intent and strategic mission influence

Figure 1.1 The Strategic Management Process

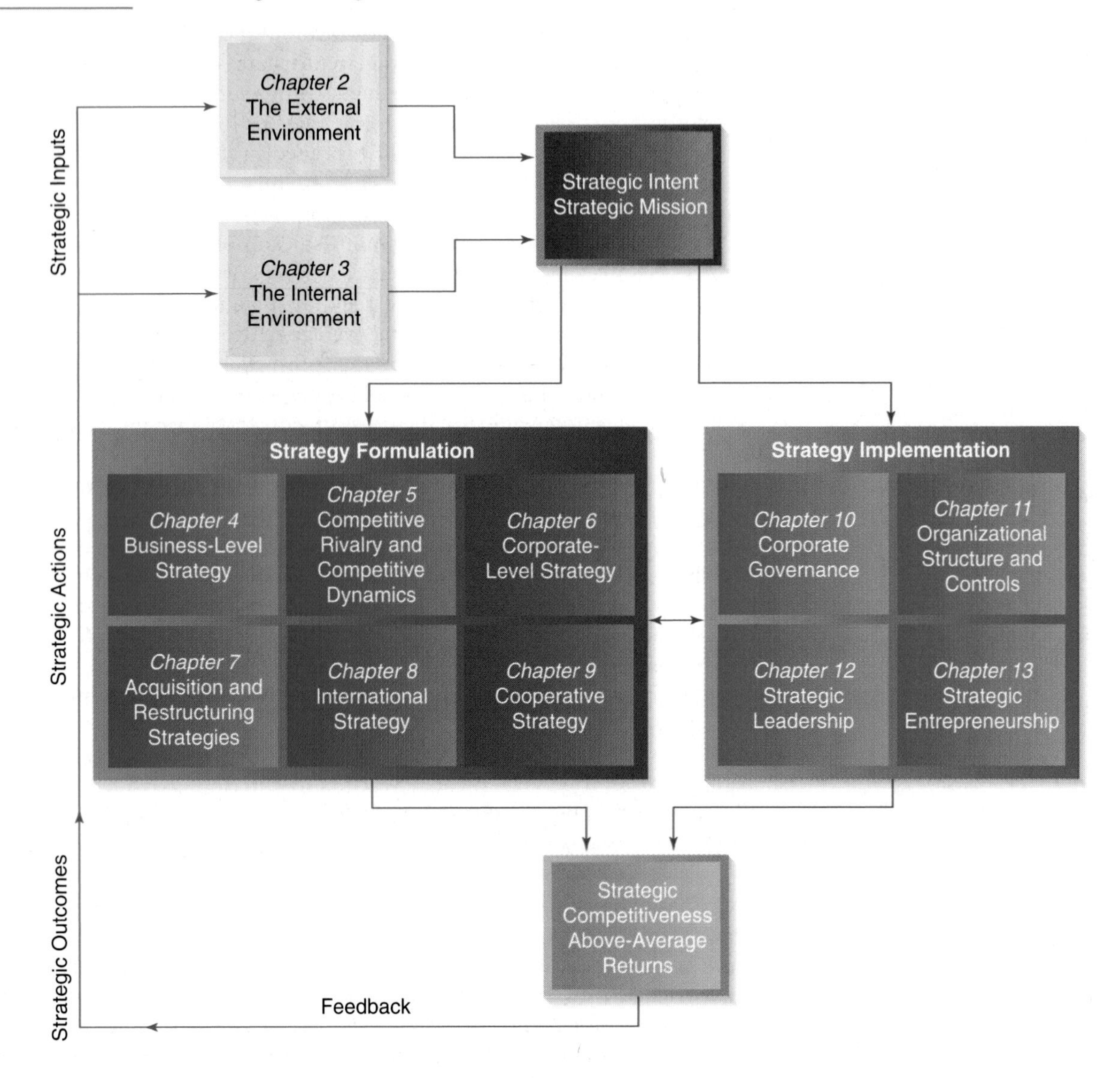

strategy formulation and implementation actions. The chapter's discussion then turns to the stakeholders that organizations serve. The degree to which stakeholders' needs can be met increases directly with enhancements in a firm's strategic competitiveness and its ability to earn above-average returns. Closing the chapter are introductions to organizational strategists and the elements of the strategic management process.

The Challenge of Strategic Management

The goals of achieving strategic competitiveness and earning above-average returns are challenging—not only for large firms such as IBM, but also for those as small as a local computer retail outlet or dry cleaner. As suggested in the Opening Case, the performances of some companies, such as Brinker International, eBay, and Southwest Airlines, have more than met strategic management's challenge to date.

For other firms, the challenges are substantial in the dynamic competitive landscape. Evidence the rapid changes experienced by Cisco Systems. During the 1990s,

Cisco's overall performance was among the best—it was among the top ten firms whose stock price increased over 10,000 percent in that decade. However, in 2001, the firm experienced significant reductions in its stock price. One writer referred to Cisco as a fractured fairy tale.[13] Analysts claim that Cisco managers did not know how to operate in poor economic conditions and did not react effectively or rapidly as conditions changed. Alternatively, Cisco's top management argued that their new strategic actions would, over time, regain the high performance once enjoyed by the firm.[14]

Business failure is rather common. In 2000, for example, 35,325 U.S. businesses filed for bankruptcy, with over 40,000 filing in 2001. Because data about business start-ups and failures are incomplete, the actual number of companies closing their doors exceeds the official count.[15] These statistics suggest that competitive success is transient.[16] Thomas J. Watson, Jr., formerly IBM's chairman, once cautioned people to remember that "corporations are expendable and that success—at best—is an impermanent achievement which can always slip out of hand."[17]

Successful performance may be transient and impermanent, as Levi Strauss found. It was once a highly successful company, with a strong global brand and good financial performance. In the middle of a robust economy in 1997, however, Levi Strauss announced that it was closing 29 plants and laying off over 16,000 employees—the first formal layoff in its history. The firm had made a number of strategic mistakes, but the most serious blunder was that it did not keep up with the changes in the marketplace. As a result, it allowed competitors Gap and Tommy Hilfiger to take away prominent market share. These competitors sold a broader variety of clothing in line with consumer tastes through their new concept retail stores. As shown by this example, a weak or ineffective strategy is a major reason for the impermanence of firm success.

Interestingly, Levi Strauss's major competitor, Gap, has also recently experienced problems after enjoying robust success. Its growth has been driven by new store openings, but sales per store decreased in 2000 and 2001. In 2001, Gap announced that it was laying off up to 7 percent of its workforce and significantly reducing its new store openings.[18]

This same problem of a weak or ineffective strategy is reflected in the substantial decline in performance experienced by such companies as Xerox and eToys. These two companies' difficulties are described in the Strategic Focus on page 10.

It is interesting to note that a survey showed CEOs did not place "strong and consistent profits" as their top priority; in fact, it was ranked fifth. A "strong and well-thought-out strategy" was regarded as the most important factor to make a firm the most respected in the future. Maximizing customer satisfaction and loyalty, business leadership and quality products and services, and concern for consistent profits followed this factor.[19] These rankings are consistent with the view that no matter how good a product or service is, the firm must select the "right" strategy and then implement it effectively.[20]

CEOs' concern for strategy is well founded, as shown by the case of Xerox described in the Strategic Focus. Some firms create their own problems by formulating the wrong strategy or by poorly implementing an effective strategy. Although Xerox clearly had the opportunity to be a dominant corporation with the new technologies it developed, it did not take advantage of them. Furthermore, it squandered its market leadership in copying machines.

Strategy is an integrated and coordinated set of commitments and actions designed to exploit core competencies and gain a competitive advantage.

In recognition of strategic management's challenge, Andrew Grove, Intel's former CEO, observed that only paranoid companies survive and succeed. Firms must continuously evaluate their environments and decide on the appropriate strategy. **Strategy** is an integrated and coordinated set of commitments and actions designed to exploit core competencies and gain a competitive advantage. By choosing a strategy,

Strategic Focus

The Impermanence of Success

There are no guarantees of success. Old, well-established companies such as Xerox can experience problems, as can young but highly successful firms such as eToys, as shown by recent performance outcomes for each.

Xerox is a well-known company with a brand name that is virtually synonymous with copying. Many people may be unaware that the Palo Alto Research Center developed by Xerox in the 1970s was also the birthplace of the personal computer, the laser printer, and the Ethernet, all technologies subsequently exploited by others. Xerox executives did not foresee the potential value of these important new technologies developed in its laboratory. The effects of this lack of foresight are shown by the fact that the Hewlett-Packard division that manufactures and sells laser printers has more total revenue than all of Xerox.

Even with these strategic blunders, Xerox has enjoyed significant success in some areas. For example, in the 1990s, it developed digital presses and copiers, creating lucrative new markets. Digital copiers became a $3 billion-a-year business for Xerox. Unlike its digital copier business, Xerox's diversification into financial services, beginning with its 1983 acquisition of Crum & Forster, was highly unsuccessful. Xerox began exiting the financial services business in 1993. In 1998, it sold Crum & Forster at a major loss and took a $1 billion write-off.

Originally hired from IBM in 1997 to become Xerox's chief operating officer (COO), Rick Thoman was appointed CEO in 1999. Former CEO Paul Allaire remained as chairman of the board. During this time, Thoman and Allaire had conflicting views about the appropriate strategy and changes for the company. As a result, Xerox made more strategic mistakes and began to lose market share in the copier market, its primary business. Although Xerox's stock price reached a high of $64 shortly after Thoman became CEO, he was fired in late 2000 following a bleak financial forecast.

Allaire took the helm again for a short time, but the firm's performance continued to decline. In 2001, the stock price fell as low as $7 per share, eliminating $38 billion in shareholder wealth, and Allaire was replaced by Anne Mulcahy. She immediately announced plans to reduce Xerox's expenses by $1 billion and spoke positively about the company's future, even though it seems unclear to many observers.

eToys was once a highly successful Internet-based retailer of toys. It began operation in 1997 and grew rapidly, soon challenging the market leader, Toys "R" Us. In fact, eToys captured significant market share before Toys "R" Us was able to respond with its own Internet sales operation. Although eToys sales reached a high of $182 million, it accumulated net losses of almost $500 million. Its stock price declined from a high of over $76 to less than 10 cents. In 2001, the firm filed for bankruptcy when analysts described its stock as worthless. Its inventory and other assets were bought at auction by KB Toys, which relaunched the eToys website in the fall of 2001.

SOURCES: 2001, Xerox CEO Mulcahy says company still seeks profitability in 4th period, *The Wall Street Journal Interactive,* http://interactive.wsj.com/articles, August 21; D. Ackman, 2001, For Ford, a Ford; for Xerox, an original, *Forbes,* http://www.forbes.com, July 27; W. Bulkeley & J. S. Lublin, 2001, Xerox names president Mulcahy to succeed Allaire in CEO post, *The Wall Street Journal Interactive,* http://interactive.wsj.com/articles, July 27; M. Sanchanta, 2001, Xerox names Anne Mulcahy as chief executive, *Financial Times,* http://www.ft.com, July 27; A. Bianco & P. L. Moore, 2001, Downfall: The inside story of the management fiasco at Xerox, *Business Week,* March 5, 82–92; http://www.kbtoys.com.

a firm decides to pursue one course of action over others. The firm's executives are thus setting priorities for the firm's competitive actions.

Firms can select effective or ineffective strategies. For example, the choice by Xerox to pursue a strategy other than the development and marketing of the personal computer and laser printers was likely an ineffective one. The purpose of this book is to explain how firms develop and implement effective strategies. Partly because of Grove's approach described above, Intel continuously strives to improve in order to remain competitive. For Intel and others that compete in the 21st century's competitive landscape, Grove believes that a key challenge is to try to do the impossible—namely, to anticipate the unexpected.[21]

The 21st-Century Competitive Landscape[22]

The fundamental nature of competition in many of the world's industries is changing.[23] The pace of this change is relentless and is increasing. Even determining the boundaries of an industry has become challenging. Consider, for example, how advances in interactive computer networks and telecommunications have blurred the definition of the television industry. The near future may find companies such as ABC, CBS, NBC, and HBO competing not only among themselves, but also with AT&T, Microsoft, Sony, and others.

Other characteristics of the 21st-century competitive landscape are noteworthy as well. Conventional sources of competitive advantage, such as economies of scale and huge advertising budgets, are not as effective as they once were. Moreover, the traditional managerial mind-set is unlikely to lead a firm to strategic competitiveness. Managers must adopt a new mind-set that values flexibility, speed, innovation, integration, and the challenges that evolve from constantly changing conditions. The conditions of the competitive landscape result in a perilous business world, one where the investments required to compete on a global scale are enormous and the consequences of failure are severe.[24]

Hypercompetition is a term often used to capture the realities of the 21st-century competitive landscape. Hypercompetition results from the dynamics of strategic maneuvering among global and innovative combatants. It is a condition of rapidly escalating competition based on price-quality positioning, competition to create new know-how and establish first-mover advantage, and competition to protect or invade established product or geographic markets.[25] In a hypercompetitive market, firms often aggressively challenge their competitors in the hopes of improving their competitive position and ultimately their performance.[26]

Several factors create hypercompetitive environments and the 21st-century competitive landscape. The two primary drivers are the emergence of a global economy and technology, specifically rapid technological change.

The Global Economy

A **global economy** is one in which goods, services, people, skills, and ideas move freely across geographic borders.

A **global economy** is one in which goods, services, people, skills, and ideas move freely across geographic borders. Relatively unfettered by artificial constraints, such as tariffs, the global economy significantly expands and complicates a firm's competitive environment.[27] Interesting opportunities and challenges are associated with the emergence of the global economy. For example, Europe, instead of the United States, is now the world's largest single market with 700 million potential customers. The European market also has a gross domestic product (GDP) of $8 trillion, which is comparable to that of the United States.[28] In addition, by 2015, China's total GDP will be greater than Japan's, although its per capita output will likely be lower.[29] In recent years, as the competitiveness rankings in Table 1.1 indicate, the Japanese economy has lagged behind that of the United States and a number of European countries. A few Asian countries, in particular Singapore and Hong Kong (now part of China), have maintained their rankings, which is commendable considering the Asian financial crisis of the latter part of the 1990s.[30] Unfortunately, Japan's economic

Table 1.1 Country Competitiveness Rankings

Country	2001	2000	1999
U.S.	1	1	1
Singapore	2	2	2
Finland	3	4	5
Luxembourg	4	6	3
Netherlands	5	3	4
Hong Kong	6	12	6
Ireland	7	5	8
Sweden	8	14	14
Canada	9	8	10
Switzerland	10	7	7
Australia	11	10	11
Germany	12	11	12
Iceland	13	9	13
Austria	14	15	18
Denmark	15	13	9
Israel	16	21	22
Belgium	17	19	21
Taiwan	18	20	15
U.K.	19	16	19
Norway	20	17	16
New Zealand	21	18	17
Estonia	22	-	-
Spain	23	23	20
Chile	24	25	25
France	25	22	23
Japan	26	24	24
Hungary	27	26	26
Korea	28	28	41
Malaysia	29	27	28
Greece	30	34	32

SOURCE: From *World Competitiveness Yearbook 2001*, IMD, Switzerland. http://www.imd.ch.wcy.esummary, April. Reprinted by permission.

problems have persisted into the 21st century, and these problems continue to affect the economic health of Southeast Asia.[31]

Achieving improved competitiveness allows a country's citizens to have a higher standard of living. Some believe that entrepreneurial activity will continue to influence living standards during the 21st century. For example, a report describing European competitiveness concluded that, "it is only through the creation of more new businesses and more fast-growing businesses that Europe will create more new jobs and achieve higher levels of economic well-being for all of its citizens."[32] The role of entrepreneurship is discussed further in Chapter 13. A country's competitiveness is achieved through the accumulation of individual firms' strategic competitiveness in the global economy. To be competitive, a firm must view the world as its marketplace. For example, Procter & Gamble believes that it still has tremendous potential to grow internationally because the global market for household products is not as mature as it is in the United States.

Although a commitment to viewing the world as a company's marketplace creates a sense of direction, it is not without risks. For example, firms operating in Asian and Latin American countries experienced sales declines at the time the financial crisis began in Asia and spread to Latin America. In 1998, Whirlpool's sales decreased by about 25 percent in Brazil.[33] Large firms such as Whirlpool often commit to competition in the global economy more quickly than do midsize and small firms. Recently, however, U.S. midsize and small firms are demonstrating a strong commitment to competing in the global economy. For example, 60 percent of U.S. firms now exporting goods are defined as small businesses.

The March of Globalization

Globalization is the increasing economic interdependence among countries as reflected in the flow of goods and services, financial capital, and knowledge across country borders.[34] In globalized markets and industries, financial capital might be obtained in one national market and used to buy raw materials in another one. Manufacturing equipment bought from a third national market can then be used to produce products that are sold in yet a fourth market. Thus, globalization increases the range of opportunities for companies competing in the 21st-century competitive landscape.

Wal-Mart, for instance, is trying to achieve boundaryless retailing with global pricing, sourcing, and logistics. Most of Wal-Mart's original international investments were in Canada and Mexico, in close proximity to the United States. However, the company has now moved into several other countries including Argentina, Brazil, Indonesia, and China. By the end of 2000, Wal-Mart was the largest retailer in the world. It changes the structure of business in many countries it enters. For example, in Mexico, it has reduced the prominence of distributors and middlemen with its 520 stores, including Supercenters and Sam's Clubs. By 2001, 25 percent of Wal-Mart's stores were in international locations.[35]

A new German BMW luxury convertible at an outlet in downtown Shanghai draws shoppers. Luxury cars are shattering sales records in China, sharpening the appetite of automobile manufacturers to develop their local production capacity and increase their imports to the country.

AFP/CORBIS

The internationalization of markets and industries makes it increasingly difficult to think of some firms as domestic companies. For example, Daimler Benz, the parent company of Mercedes-Benz, merged with Chrysler Corporation to create DaimlerChrysler. DaimlerChrysler has focused on integrating the formerly independent companies' operations around the world. In a similar move, Ford acquired Volvo's car division. Ford now has six global brands: Ford, Lincoln, Mercury, Jaguar, Mazda, and Aston Martin. It uses these brands to build economies of scale in the purchase and sourcing of components that make up 60 percent of the value of a car.[36]

Unlike the 1980s, when imports increased their sales significantly, today foreign competitors have a 30 percent share of the U.S. auto market. Competition is especially tough for luxury brands, with BMW, Mercedes (DaimlerChrysler), and Lexus (Toyota) increasing their market share against Ford and GM brands. U.S. auto companies are also challenged to be more aware of other nations' cultures, including the languages. Ford, for example, launched a car that it had built in Europe in Japan. Called the Ka, this car's name translated into the word "mosquito" in the Japanese language.[37] These automobile firms should not be thought of as European, Japanese, or American. Instead, they can be more accurately classified as global companies striving to achieve strategic competitiveness in the 21st-century competitive landscape. Some believe that because of the enormous economic benefits it can generate, globalization will not be stopped. It has been predicted that genuine free trade in manufactured goods among the United States, Europe, and Japan would add 5 to 10 percent to the three regions' annual economic output, and free trade in their service sectors would boost aggregate output by another 15 to 20 percent. Realizing these potential gains in economic output requires a commitment from the industrialized nations to cooperatively stimulate the higher levels of trade necessary for global growth. In 2001, global trade in goods and services accounted for approximately 25 percent of the world's GDP.[38]

Evidence suggests that the globalization of some U.S. firms lags behind that of companies in other industrialized countries. Although most large U.S. firms compete in international markets to some degree, not all of them are aggressively responding to global market opportunities.[39] Global competition has increased performance standards in many dimensions, including quality, cost, productivity, product introduction time, and operational efficiency. Moreover, these standards are not static; they are exacting, requiring continuous improvement from a firm and its employees. As they accept the challenges posed by these increasing standards, companies improve their capabilities and individual workers sharpen their skills. Thus, in the 21st-century competitive landscape, only firms capable of meeting, if not exceeding, global standards typically earn strategic competitiveness.[40]

The development of emerging and transitional economies also is changing the global competitive landscape and significantly increasing competition in global markets.[41] The economic development of Asian countries—outside of Japan—is increasing the significance of Asian markets. Firms in the emerging economies of Asia, such as South Korea, however, are becoming major competitors in global industries. Companies such as Cemex are moving more boldly into international markets and are making important investments in Asia. Cemex, a cement producer headquartered in Mexico, also has significant investments in North America and Latin America. Thus, international investments come from many directions and are targeted for multiple regions of the world.

There are risks with these investments (a number of them are discussed in Chapter 8). Some people refer to these risks as the "liability of foreignness."[42] Research suggests that firms are challenged in their early ventures into international markets and can encounter difficulties by entering too many different or challenging international markets. First, performance may suffer in early efforts to globalize until a firm develops the skills required to manage international operations.[43] Additionally, the firm's performance may suffer with substantial amounts of globalization. In this instance, firms may overdiversify internationally beyond their ability to manage these diversified operations.[44] The outcome can sometimes be quite painful to these firms.[45] Thus, entry into international markets, even for firms with substantial experience in them, first requires careful planning and selection of the appropriate markets to enter followed by developing the most effective strategies to successfully operate in those markets.

Global markets are attractive strategic options for some companies, but they are not the only source of strategic competitiveness. In fact, for most companies, even for those capable of competing successfully in global markets, it is critical to remain committed to the domestic market.[46] In the 21st-century competitive landscape, firms are challenged to develop the optimal level of globalization that results in appropriate concentrations on a company's domestic and global operations.

In many instances, strategically competitive companies are those that have learned how to apply competitive insights gained locally (or domestically) on a global scale.[47] These companies do not impose homogeneous solutions in a pluralistic world. Instead, they nourish local insights so that they can modify and apply them appropriately in different regions of the world. Moreover, they are sensitive to globalization's potential effects. Firms with strong commitments to global success evaluate these possible outcomes in making their strategic choices.

New technology such as handheld computers can create a competitive advantage for firms, but once accepted, the technology is subject to almost immediate imitation by competitors.

PHOTODISC, INC.

Technology and Technological Changes

There are three categories of trends and conditions through which technology is significantly altering the nature of competition.

Increasing Rate of Technological Change and Diffusion

Both the rate of change of technology and the speed at which new technologies become available and are used have increased substantially over the last 15 to 20 years. Consider the following rates of technology diffusion:

> It took the telephone 35 years to get into 25 percent of all homes in the United States. It took TV 26 years. It took radio 22 years. It took PCs 16 years. It took the Internet 7 years.[48]

Perpetual innovation is a term used to describe how rapidly and consistently new, information-intensive technologies replace older ones. The shorter product life cycles resulting from these rapid diffusions of new technologies place a competitive premium on being able to quickly introduce new goods and services into the marketplace. In fact, when products become somewhat indistinguishable because of the widespread and rapid diffusion of technologies, speed to market may be the primary source of competitive advantage (see Chapter 5).[49]

There are other indicators of rapid technology diffusion. Some evidence suggests that it takes only 12 to 18 months for firms to gather information about their competitors' research and development and product decisions.[50] In the global economy, competitors can sometimes imitate a firm's successful competitive actions within a few days. Consider, for example, that approximately 75 percent of the product-life gross margins for a typical personal computer are earned within the first 90 days of sales.[51] Once a source of competitive advantage, the protection firms possessed previously through their patents has been stifled by the current rate of technological diffusion. Today, patents are thought by many to be an effective way of protecting proprietary technology only for the pharmaceutical and chemical industries. Indeed, many firms competing in the electronics industry often do not apply for patents to prevent competitors from gaining access to the technological knowledge included in the patent application.

The other factor in technological change is the development of disruptive technologies that destroy the value of existing technology and create new markets.[52] Some have referred to this concept as Schumpeterian innovation, from the work by the famous economist Joseph A. Schumpeter, who suggested that such innovation emerged from a process of creative destruction, in which existing technologies are replaced by new ones. Others refer to this outcome as radical or breakthrough innovation.[53] The development and use of the Internet for commerce is an example of a disruptive technology.

The Information Age

Dramatic changes in information technology have occurred in recent years. Personal computers, cellular phones, artificial intelligence, virtual reality, and massive databases (e.g., Lexis/Nexis) are a few examples of how information is used differently as a result of technological developments. An important outcome of these changes is that the ability to effectively and efficiently access and use information has become an important source of competitive advantage in virtually all industries.

Companies are building electronic networks that link them to customers, employees, vendors, and suppliers. These networks, designed to conduct business over the Internet, are referred to as e-business.[54] e-business is big business. For example, Internet trade in the U. S. reached $251 billion in 2000, up from only $7.8 billion in 1997. It is predicted that e-business will eventually represent 75 to 80 percent of the U.S. gross domestic product. By 2002, 93 percent of firms were expected to conduct some portion of their business on the Internet. While e-business in Europe has taken longer to develop, it is predicted to increase over 300 percent by 2002, up to $67.6 billion.[55]

Both the pace of change in information technology and its diffusion will continue to increase. For instance, the number of personal computers in use is expected to reach 278 million by 2010. The declining costs of information technologies and the increased accessibility to them are also evident in the 21st-century competitive landscape. The global proliferation of relatively inexpensive computing power and its linkage on a global scale via computer networks combine to increase the speed and diffusion of information technologies. Thus, the competitive potential of information technologies is now available to companies of all sizes throughout the world, not only to large firms in Europe, Japan, and North America.

The Internet provides an infrastructure that allows the delivery of information to computers in any location. Access to significant quantities of relatively inexpensive information yields strategic opportunities for a range of industries and companies. Retailers, for example, use the Internet to provide abundant shopping privileges to customers in multiple locations. The pervasive influence of electronic commerce or e-business is creating a new culture, referred to as e-culture, that affects the way managers lead, organize, think, and develop and implement strategies.[56]

Increasing Knowledge Intensity

Knowledge (information, intelligence, and expertise) is the basis of technology and its application. In the 21st-century competitive landscape, knowledge is a critical organizational resource and is increasingly a valuable source of competitive advantage.[57] As a result, many companies now strive to transmute the accumulated knowledge of individual employees into a corporate asset. Some argue that the value of intangible assets, including knowledge, is growing as a proportion of total shareholder value.[58] The probability of achieving strategic competitiveness in the 21st-century competitive landscape is enhanced for the firm that realizes that its survival depends on the ability to capture intelligence, transform it into usable knowledge, and diffuse it rapidly throughout the company.[59] Firms accepting this challenge shift their focus from merely obtaining information to exploiting that information to gain a competitive advantage over rival firms.[60]

To earn above-average returns, firms must be able to adapt quickly to changes in their competitive landscape. Such adaptation requires that the firm develop strategic flexibility. **Strategic flexibility** is a set of capabilities used to respond to various demands and opportunities existing in a dynamic and uncertain competitive environment. Thus, it involves coping with uncertainty and the accompanying risks.[61]

Strategic flexibility is a set of capabilities used to respond to various demands and opportunities existing in a dynamic and uncertain competitive environment.

Firms should develop strategic flexibility in all areas of their operations. To achieve strategic flexibility, many firms have to develop organizational slack—slack resources that allow the firm some flexibility to respond to environmental changes.[62] When larger changes are required, firms may have to undergo strategic reorientations. Such reorientations can drastically change a firm's competitive strategy.[63] Strategic reorientations often result from a firm's poor performance. For example, when a firm earns negative returns, its stakeholders (discussed later in this chapter) are likely to pressure top executives to make major changes.[64]

To be strategically flexible on a continuing basis, a firm has to develop the capacity to learn. Continuous learning provides the firm with new and up-to-date sets of skills, which allow the firm to adapt to its environment as it encounters changes.[65] As illustrated in the Strategic Focus on pages 18–19, new economy firms Excite@Home and PSINet were not able to adapt effectively to their environments. They followed flawed strategies too long and failed. Hewlett-Packard tried to make needed changes but experienced considerable problems with internal resistance and external criticism. As these firms learned, being flexible, learning, and making the necessary changes are difficult, but they are necessary for continued survival.

Next, we describe two models used by firms to generate the strategic inputs needed to successfully formulate and implement strategies and to maintain strategic flexibility in the process of doing so.

The I/O Model of Above-Average Returns

From the 1960s through the 1980s, the external environment was thought to be the primary determinant of strategies that firms selected to be successful.[66] The industrial organization (I/O) model of above-average returns explains the dominant influence of the external environment on a firm's strategic actions. The model specifies that the industry in which a firm chooses to compete has a stronger influence on the firm's performance than do the choices managers make inside their organizations.[67] The firm's performance is believed to be determined primarily by a range of industry properties, including economies of scale, barriers to market entry, diversification, product differentiation, and the degree of concentration of firms in the industry.[68] These industry characteristics are examined in Chapter 2.

Grounded in economics, the I/O model has four underlying assumptions. First, the external environment is assumed to impose pressures and constraints that determine the strategies that would result in above-average returns. Second, most firms competing within a particular industry or within a certain segment of it are assumed to control similar strategically relevant resources and to pursue similar strategies in light of those resources. The I/O model's third assumption is that resources used to implement strategies are highly mobile across firms. Because of resource mobility, any resource differences that might develop between firms will be short lived. Fourth, organizational decision makers are assumed to be rational and committed to acting in the firm's best interests, as shown by their profit-maximizing behaviors.[69] The I/O model challenges firms to locate the most attractive industry in which to compete. Because most firms are assumed to have similar strategically relevant resources that are mobile across companies, competitiveness generally can be increased only when firms find the industry with the highest profit potential and learn how to use their resources to implement the strategy required by the industry's structural characteristics.

The five forces model of competition is an analytical tool used to help firms with this task. The model (explained in Chapter 2) encompasses many variables and tries to capture the complexity of competition. The five forces model suggests that an industry's profitability (i.e., its rate of return on invested capital relative to its cost of capital) is a function of interactions among five forces: suppliers, buyers, competitive rivalry among firms currently in the industry, product substitutes, and potential entrants to the industry.[70] Using this tool, a firm is challenged to understand an industry's profit potential and the strategy necessary to establish a defensible competitive position, given the industry's structural characteristics. Typically, the model

Strategic Focus

Flawed Strategies, Hubris, and Entrenchment

Excite@Home was formed in November 1999 by the $6.7 billion merger of broadband Internet service provider At Home and Excite.com, an Internet portal that competed with Yahoo! The deal combined Excite's content with At Home's high-speed Internet access. Two months later, its stock was trading at almost $60. However, Excite@Home has struggled since that time. A questionable business plan had been implemented without much analysis. The firm was saddled with high debt and substantial competition on the content side from Yahoo! and others. It had service delivery problems, disagreements among its board members, multiple executive departures, and morale problems among its employees. AT&T bought controlling interest in the firm, but its backing provided little help with the major problems.

In April 2001, a new Excite@Home CEO, Patti Hart, was named. She promptly negotiated new debt financing of $100 million, but the debt was short term. By August 2001, the stock price had fallen to 47 cents; one of its lenders demanded repayment of $50 million by the end of the month, claiming that Excite@Home had misrepresented its financial condition at the time of the original loan. Auditor Ernst & Young questioned Excite@Home's viability following its analysis of the firm, which spread bankruptcy fears. Two of its largest distributors, Cox Communications and Comcast, announced they would end their relationship with Excite@Home at the end of their contract. The strategic mistakes of the firm's former managers resulted in a highly uncertain future which culminated in the firm's filing for bankruptcy in the later part of 2001. Subject to the bankruptcy court's approvals, the close of 2001 found Excite@Home selling portions of its assets in order to focus on its core broadband products and services.

Analysts believe that PSINet also used a flawed strategy. At its peak, PSINet provided Internet services to approximately 100,000 companies in 27 countries. Founder and CEO William Schrader's strategy sought growth through acquisitions and building fiber optic networks to serve customers in multiple countries. PSINet financed this growth with substantial debt, often resorting to junk bonds. In four years, the debt increased 3600 percent to $4 billion and annual debt payments reached $400 million. One reporter referred to PSINet's strategy as "half-cocked and fully hocked." A number of the ill-planned acquisitions proved to be overpriced; some were virtually worthless and had to be written off as bad investments. In 2001, the firm defaulted on its debt payments and Schrader was asked to resign.

A third firm trying to implement needed changes to adapt to its new environment but encountering substantial internal retrenchment and external impatience is Hewlett-Packard. In 1999, the firm appointed Carly Fiorina as CEO to make changes that were necessary for it to regain the competitive position it had lost in recent years. Fiorina's planned strategic and structural changes are substantial, and internal managers and professional employees have been highly critical and resistant to them. Not only have they been slow to implement the changes, some have implemented them ineffectively, according to a survey of employees.

While many observers feel that the proposed changes are needed, Hewlett-Packard's financial performance has substantially decreased since Fiorina became CEO. Undoubtedly, some of the downturn in performance is due to the process of changes being made, but the poor strategies and ineffective operational approaches of Fiorina's predecessor are also to blame. Even though the firm's performance is down, Hewlett-Packard's board has provided strong and vocal support for Fiorina's actions. The board publicly stated that she was making the changes it requested and that performance was better than expected. Still, some analysts have been critical, and it is unclear how patient major investors will be for the changes to improve performance. The firm's market capitalization was $40 billion when Fiorina was hired in 1999. By 2001, it had fallen to $31 billion.

Carly Fiorina, Hewlett-Packard CEO, faced internal resistance in her efforts to improve the firm's flexibility and timely response to market demands.

AFP/CORBIS

Hewlett-Packard's latest effort to reverse its decline was to agree to acquire Compaq Computer Corp. The proposed acquisition represents another attempt to change the firm and its culture. As of mid-April 2002, it appeared that HP shareholders approved the decision to acquire Compaq, although the final outcome of the vote hadn't been determined.

SOURCES: M. Richtel, 2001, Excite@Home executive in crisis control at warp speed, *The New York Times,* http://www.nytimes.com, September 2; M. Roman, 2001, More money woes for Excite@Home, *Business Week,* September 10, 56; L. Kehoe, 2001, Hewlett-Packard directors 100% behind Fiorina, *Financial Times,* http://www.ft.com, August 21; M. Noer, 2001, Lights out for Excite@Home? *Forbes,* http://www.forbes.com, August 21; Q. Hardy, 2001, Backstabbing Carly, *Forbes,* June 11, 54–64; S. Woolley, 2001, Digital hubris, *Forbes,* May 28, 66–70; 2001, Why Disney and AT&T went astray, *Knowledge@Wharton,* http://www.knowledge.wharton.upenn.edu, May 14; M. Mangalindan & D. Solomon, 2001, Excite at home is expected to name Patti Hart as its new CEO, *The Wall Street Journal Interactive,* http://interactive.wsj.com/articles, April 17.

suggests that firms can earn above-average returns by manufacturing standardized products or producing standardized services at costs below those of competitors (a cost-leadership strategy) or by manufacturing differentiated products for which customers are willing to pay a price premium (a differentiation strategy, described in depth in Chapter 4).

As shown in Figure 1.2, the I/O model suggests that above-average returns are earned when firms implement the strategy dictated by the characteristics of the general, industry, and competitor environments. Companies that develop or acquire the internal skills needed to implement strategies required by the external environment are likely to succeed, while those that do not are likely to fail. Hence, this model suggests that external characteristics rather than the firm's unique internal resources and capabilities primarily determine returns.

Research findings support the I/O model. They show that approximately 20 percent of a firm's profitability can be explained by the industry. In other words, 20 percent of a firm's profitability is determined by the industry or industries in which it chooses to operate. This research also showed, however, that 36 percent of the variance in profitability could be attributed to the firm's characteristics and actions.[71] The results of the research suggest that both the environment and the firm's characteristics play a role in determining the firm's specific level of profitability. Thus, there is likely a reciprocal relationship between the environment and the firm's strategy, thereby affecting the firm's performance.[72] As the research suggests, successful competition mandates that a firm build a unique set of resources and capabilities. This development should be done within the dynamics of the environment in which a firm operates.

A firm is viewed as a bundle of market activities and a bundle of resources. Market activities are understood through the application of the I/O model. The

Figure 1.2 The I/O Model of Above-Average Returns

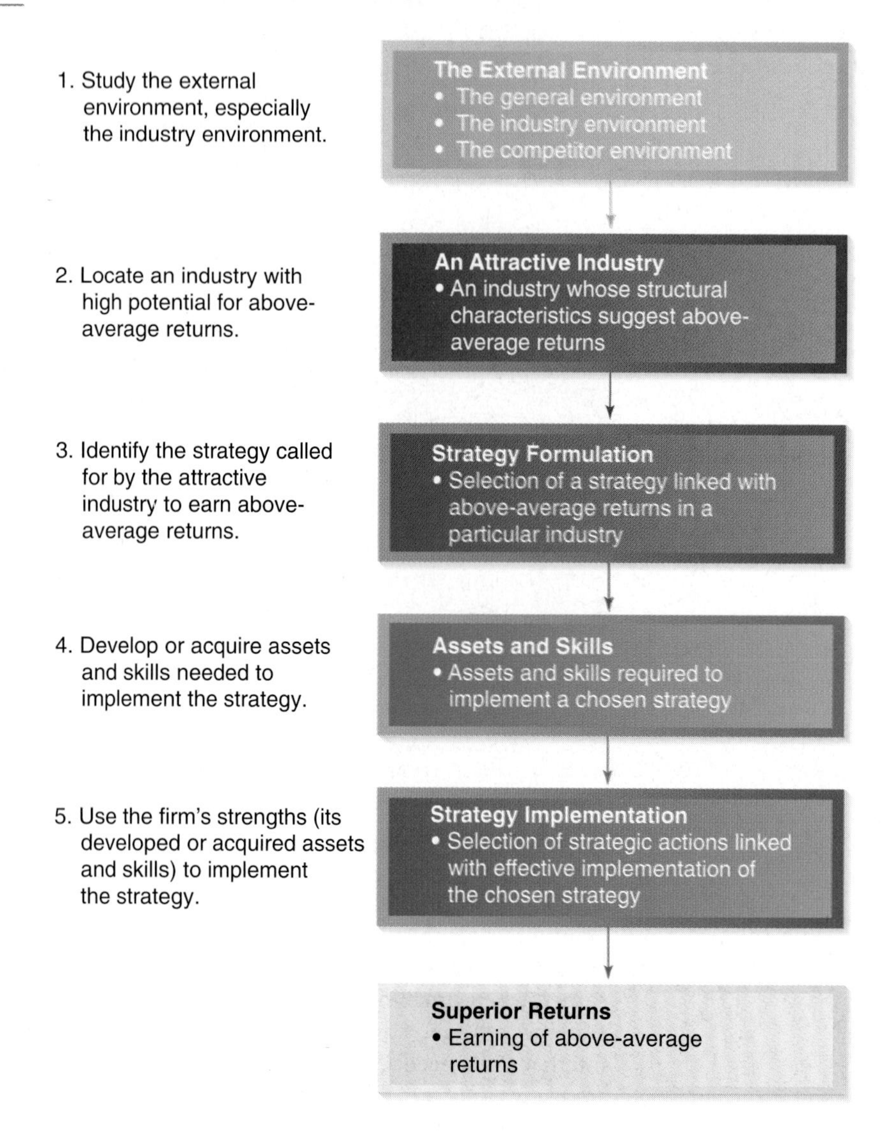

development and effective use of a firm's resources, capabilities, and competencies are understood through the application of the resource-based model. As a result, executives must integrate the two models to develop the most effective strategy.

The Resource-Based Model of Above-Average Returns

The resource-based model assumes that each organization is a collection of unique resources and capabilities that provides the basis for its strategy and that is the primary source of its returns. This model suggests that capabilities evolve and must be managed dynamically in pursuit of above-average returns.[73] According to the model, differences in firms' performances across time are due primarily to their unique resources and capabilities rather than the industry's structural characteristics. This model also assumes that firms acquire different resources and develop unique capabilities. Therefore, not all firms competing within a particular industry possess the same resources and capabilities. Additionally, the model assumes that resources may not be highly mobile across firms and that the differences in resources are the basis of competitive advantage.

Resources are inputs into a firm's production process, such as capital equipment, the skills of individual employees, patents, finances, and talented managers.

Resources are inputs into a firm's production process, such as capital equipment, the skills of individual employees, patents, finances, and talented managers. In general, a firm's resources can be classified into three categories: physical, human, and organizational capital. Described fully in Chapter 3, resources are either tangible or intangible in nature.

A **capability** is the capacity for a set of resources to perform a task or an activity in an integrative manner.

Individual resources alone may not yield a competitive advantage.[74] In general, competitive advantages are formed through the combination and integration of sets of resources. A **capability** is the capacity for a set of resources to perform a task or an activity in an integrative manner. Through the firm's continued use, capabilities become stronger and more difficult for competitors to understand and imitate. As a source of competitive advantage, a capability "should be neither so simple that it is highly imitable, nor so complex that it defies internal steering and control."[75]

The resource-based model of superior returns is shown in Figure 3. Instead of focusing on the accumulation of resources necessary to implement the strategy dictated by conditions and constraints in the external environment (I/O model), the resource-based view suggests that a firm's unique resources and capabilities provide the basis for a strategy. The strategy chosen should allow the firm to best exploit its core competencies relative to opportunities in the external environment.

Not all of a firm's resources and capabilities have the potential to be the basis for competitive advantage. This potential is realized when resources and capabilities are valuable, rare, costly to imitate, and nonsubstitutable.[76] Resources are *valuable* when they allow a firm to take advantage of opportunities or neutralize threats in its external environment. They are *rare* when possessed by few, if any, current and potential competitors. Resources are *costly to imitate* when other firms either cannot obtain them or are at a cost disadvantage in obtaining them compared with the firm that already possesses them. And, they are *nonsubstitutable* when they have no structural equivalents.

Core competencies are resources and capabilities that serve as a source of competitive advantage for a firm over its rivals.

When these four criteria are met, resources and capabilities become core competencies. **Core competencies** are resources and capabilities that serve as a source of competitive advantage for a firm over its rivals. Often related to a firm's functional skills (e.g., the marketing function is a core competence at Philip Morris), core competencies, when developed, nurtured, and applied throughout a firm, may result in strategic competitiveness.

Managerial competencies are important in most firms. For example, they have been shown to be critically important to successful entry into foreign markets.[77] Such competencies may include the capability to effectively organize and govern complex and diverse operations and the capability to create and communicate a strategic vision.[78] Managerial capabilities are important in a firm's ability to take advantage of its resources. For example, as described in the Strategic Focus on page 10, Xerox created the technology for the personal computer and the laser printer. Yet, its management did not have the foresight to develop these technologies and take them to the marketplace. Worse, Xerox essentially gave these technologies to other firms who then successfully exploited them. As shown in the Strategic Focus on page 18, management at Excite@Home and PSINet mismanaged their resources as well.

Another set of important competencies is product related. Included among these competencies is the capability to develop innovative new products and to reengineer existing products to satisfy changing consumer tastes.[79] Firms must also continuously develop their competencies to keep them up to date. This development requires a systematic program for updating old skills and introducing new ones.

Figure 1.3 The Resource-Based Model of Above-Average Returns

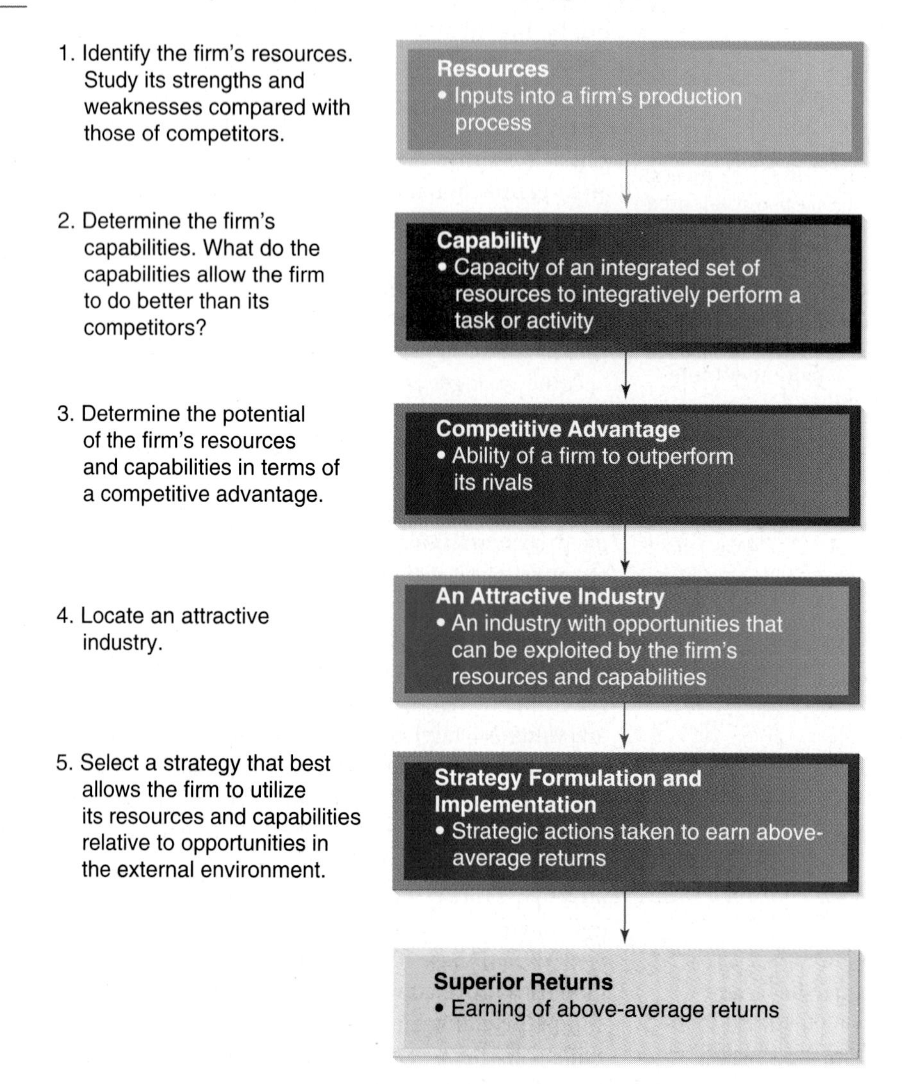

Dynamic core competencies are especially important in rapidly changing environments, such as those that exist in high-technology industries. Thus, the resource-based model suggests that core competencies are the basis for a firm's competitive advantage, its strategic competitiveness, and its ability to earn above-average returns.

Strategic Intent and Strategic Mission

Resulting from analyses of a firm's internal and external environments is the information required to form a strategic intent and develop a strategic mission (see Figure 1.1). Both intent and mission are linked with strategic competitiveness.

Strategic intent is the leveraging of a firm's resources, capabilities, and core competencies to accomplish the firm's goals in the competitive environment.

Strategic Intent

Strategic intent is the leveraging of a firm's resources, capabilities, and core competencies to accomplish the firm's goals in the competitive environment.[80] Strategic

TERRI L. MILLER/E-VISUAL COMMUNICATIONS

Unilever's Dove brand is the top-selling bar soap in the world. The firm capitalized on the brand's popularity by offering personal cleansing products in more than a dozen forms, from facial cleansing cloths to four types of body wash.

intent exists when all employees and levels of a firm are committed to the pursuit of a specific (and significant) performance criterion. Some argue that strategic intent provides employees with the only goal worthy of personal effort and commitment: to unseat the best or remain the best, worldwide.[81] Strategic intent has been effectively formed when employees believe fervently in their company's product and when they are focused totally on their firm's ability to outperform its competitors.

For example, Unilever has stated its strategic intent to make Dove a megabrand—to make Dove to personal care products what Coke is to soft drinks. For 40 years, Dove signified a bar of soap. However, in recent years, Unilever has been developing other personal care products under the Dove brand, including deodorant, vitamins, body wash, facial tissues, and bar soap. Dove helped propel Unilever to become the largest producer of bar soap with more than $330 million in annual sales and a 24 percent share of the U.S. market, and more than $1 billion in sales worldwide.[82]

It is not enough for a firm to know its own strategic intent. Performing well demands that the firm also identify its competitors' strategic intent. Only when these intentions are understood can a firm become aware of the resolve, stamina, and inventiveness (traits linked with effective strategic intents) of those competitors.[83] For example, Unilever must identify and understand Procter & Gamble's strategic intent with its Olay brand. A company's success may be also grounded in a keen and deep understanding of the strategic intent of customers, suppliers, partners, and competitors.[84]

Strategic Mission

As the preceding discussion shows, strategic intent is internally focused. It is concerned with identifying the resources, capabilities, and core competencies on which a firm can base its strategic actions. Strategic intent reflects what a firm is capable of doing with its core competencies and the unique ways they can be used to exploit a competitive advantage.

Strategic mission is a statement of a firm's unique purpose and the scope of its operations in product and market terms.

Strategic mission flows from strategic intent. Externally focused, **strategic mission** is a statement of a firm's unique purpose and the scope of its operations in product and market terms.[85] A strategic mission provides general descriptions of the products a firm intends to produce and the markets it will serve using its core competencies. An effective strategic mission establishes a firm's individuality and is inspiring and relevant to all stakeholders.[86] Together, strategic intent and strategic mission yield the insights required to formulate and implement strategies.

The strategic mission of Johnson & Johnson has a focus on customers, stating that the organization's primary responsibility is to "the doctors, nurses, and patients, mothers and fathers and all others who use our products and services."[87] An effective strategic mission is formed when the firm has a strong sense of what it wants to do and of the ethical standards that will guide behaviors in the pursuit of its goals.[88] Because Johnson & Johnson specifies the products it will offer in particular markets and presents a framework within which the firm operates, its strategic mission is an application of strategic intent.[89]

Research has shown that having an effective intent and mission and properly implementing it has a positive effect on performance as measured by growth in sales, profits, employment, and net worth.[90] When a firm is strategically competitive and earning above-average returns, it has the capacity to satisfy stakeholders' interests.

Stakeholders

Stakeholders are the individuals and groups who can affect, and are affected by, the strategic outcomes achieved and who have enforceable claims on a firm's performance.

Every organization involves a system of primary stakeholder groups with whom it establishes and manages relationships.[91] **Stakeholders** are the individuals and groups who can affect, and are affected by, the strategic outcomes achieved and who have enforceable claims on a firm's performance.[92] Claims on a firm's performance are enforced through the stakeholder's ability to withhold participation essential to the organization's survival, competitiveness, and profitability.[93] Stakeholders continue to support an organization when its performance meets or exceeds their expectations. Also, recent research suggests that firms effectively managing stakeholder relationships outperform those that do not. Stakeholder relationships can therefore be managed to be a source of competitive advantage.[94]

Although organizations have dependency relationships with their stakeholders, they are not equally dependent on all stakeholders at all times; as a consequence, not every stakeholder has the same level of influence. The more critical and valued a stakeholder's participation is, the greater a firm's dependency on it. Greater dependence, in turn, gives the stakeholder more potential influence over a firm's commitments, decisions, and actions. As shown in the Strategic Focus on page 25, managers must find ways to either accommodate or insulate the organization from the demands of stakeholders controlling critical resources.[95]

Cisco changed from being a star to most of its stakeholders to displeasing many of them. In particular, its substantial reduction in stock price concerned shareholders. Its employee layoffs created concern and displeasure among Cisco's workforce, particularly because the need to cut costs was caused by poor strategic decisions that produced large inventories. There seems to be hope but much uncertainty at present among Cisco's stakeholders.

Classification of Stakeholders

The parties involved with a firm's operations can be separated into at least three groups.[96] As shown in Figure 1.4, these groups are the capital market stakeholders (shareholders and the major suppliers of a firm's capital), the product market stakeholders (the firm's primary customers, suppliers, host communities, and unions representing the workforce), and the organizational stakeholders (all of a firm's employees, including both nonmanagerial and managerial personnel).

Each stakeholder group expects those making strategic decisions in a firm to provide the leadership through which its valued objectives will be accomplished.[97] The objectives of the various stakeholder groups often differ from one another, sometimes placing managers in situations where trade-offs have to be made. The most obvious stakeholders, at least in U.S. organizations, are shareholders—those who have invested capital in a firm in the expectation of earning a positive return on their investments. These stakeholders' rights are grounded in laws governing private property and private enterprise.

Shareholders want the return on their investment (and, hence, their wealth) to be maximized. Maximization of returns sometimes is accomplished at the expense of investing in a firm's future. Gains achieved by reducing investment in research and development, for example, could be returned to shareholders, thereby increasing the short-term return on their investments. However, this short-term enhancement of shareholders' wealth can negatively affect the firm's future competitive ability, and

Strategic Focus

Can Cisco Satisfy All of Its Stakeholders?

In the decade of the 1990s, Cisco Systems created more wealth for its shareholders than any other firm. Its stock price increased by 124,825 percent—a $100 investment in Cisco stock in 1990 was worth $1,248,250 by the end of the decade. Cisco was able to satisfy many of its stakeholders during the decade, but with the downturn in the U.S. economy and the poor performance of Internet-based and telecommunications firms (Cisco's major customers), its fortunes turned sour. Its stock price declined by almost 78 percent, from a high of over $71 in 2000 to below $16 in 2001, and Cisco had to lay off employees.

During the earlier strong economy, Cisco experienced delays in obtaining supplies and was unable to meet customers' orders for its systems. As a result, it signed long-term contracts with suppliers to ensure supply. When sales declined significantly, Cisco was faced with large inventories. One analyst suggested that Cisco managers did not know what to do when the economy slowed. Neither shareholders nor employees were pleased with the results.

During this slowdown, CEO John Chambers remained optimistic and vowed to stay the course. He compared the Internet slump to a 100-year flood that had not been anticipated by his team. Such a flood causes considerable destruction, so his analogy was appropriate. Chambers suggested that the firm's focus had changed from revenue growth to profitability, earnings contribution, and growth through internal development rather than acquisitions. He noted that he had learned always to be concerned about profit contribution when entering new markets.

Chambers predicted that brand would become especially important and promised to protect the good brand of Cisco. Chambers also believes that there is a period of consolidation where the strong get stronger and that Cisco is one of the strong. Later in 2001, Chambers announced that Cisco had stabilized and was on track to meet its projections. If so, Cisco should again please many of its stakeholders.

SOURCES: S. Day, 2001, Shares surge after Cisco says its business has stabilized, *The New York Times,* http://www.nytimes.com, August 25; B. Elgin, 2001, A do-it-yourself plan at Cisco, *Business Week,* September 10, 52; G. Anders, 2001, John Chambers after the deluge, *Fast Company,* July, 100–111; S. N. Mehta, 2001, Cisco fractures its own tale, *Fortune,* May 14, 105–112; P. Abrahams, 2001, Cisco chief must sink or swim, *Financial Times,* http://www.ft.com, April 19.

sophisticated shareholders with diversified portfolios may sell their interests if a firm fails to invest in its future. Those making strategic decisions are responsible for a firm's survival in both the short and the long term. Accordingly, it is not in the interests of any stakeholders for investments in the company to be unduly minimized.

In contrast to shareholders, another group of stakeholders—the firm's customers—prefers that investors receive a minimum return on their investments. Customers could have their interests maximized when the quality and reliability of a firm's products are improved, but without a price increase. High returns to customers might come at the expense of lower returns negotiated with capital market shareholders.

Because of potential conflicts, each firm is challenged to manage its stakeholders. First, a firm must carefully identify all important stakeholders. Second, it must prioritize them, in case it cannot satisfy all of them. Power is the most critical criterion in prioritizing stakeholders. Other criteria might include the urgency of satisfying each particular stakeholder group and the degree of importance of each to the firm.[98]

When the firm earns above-average returns, this challenge is lessened substantially. With the capability and flexibility provided by above-average returns, a firm can more easily satisfy multiple stakeholders simultaneously. When the firm is earning only average returns, however, the management of its stakeholders may be more difficult. With average returns, the firm is unable to maximize the interests of all stakeholders. The objective then becomes one of at least minimally satisfying each stakeholder. Trade-off decisions are made in light of how dependent the firm is on the support of its stakeholder groups. A firm earning below-average returns does not have the capacity to minimally satisfy all stakeholders. The managerial challenge in this case is to make trade-offs that minimize the amount of support lost from stakeholders.

Societal values also influence the general weightings allocated among the three stakeholder groups shown in Figure 1.4. Although all three groups are served by firms in the major industrialized nations, the priorities in their service vary because of cultural differences. It is important that those responsible for managing stakeholder relationships in a country outside their native land use a global mind-set. A **global mind-set** is the "capacity to appreciate the beliefs, values, behaviors, and business practices of individuals and organizations from a variety of regions and cultures."[99] Employing a global mind-set allows managers to better understand the realities and preferences existing in the world region and culture in which they are working. Thus, thinking globally means "taking the best [that] other cultures have to offer and blending that into a third culture."[100]

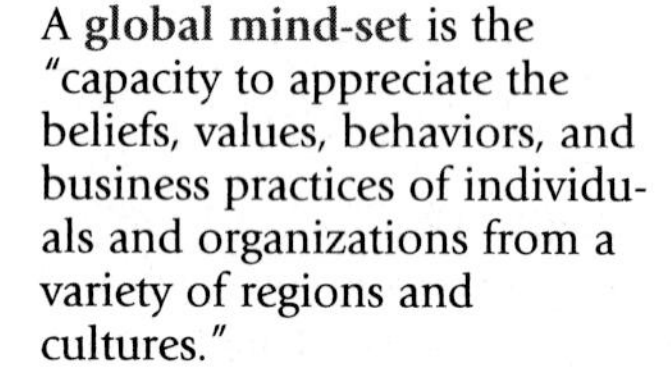
A **global mind-set** is the "capacity to appreciate the beliefs, values, behaviors, and business practices of individuals and organizations from a variety of regions and cultures."

Capital Market Stakeholders

Shareholders and lenders both expect a firm to preserve and enhance the wealth they have entrusted to it. The returns they expect are commensurate with the degree of risk accepted with those investments (that is, lower returns are expected with low-risk investments, and higher returns are expected with high-risk investments). Dissatisfied

Figure 1.4 The Three Stakeholder Groups

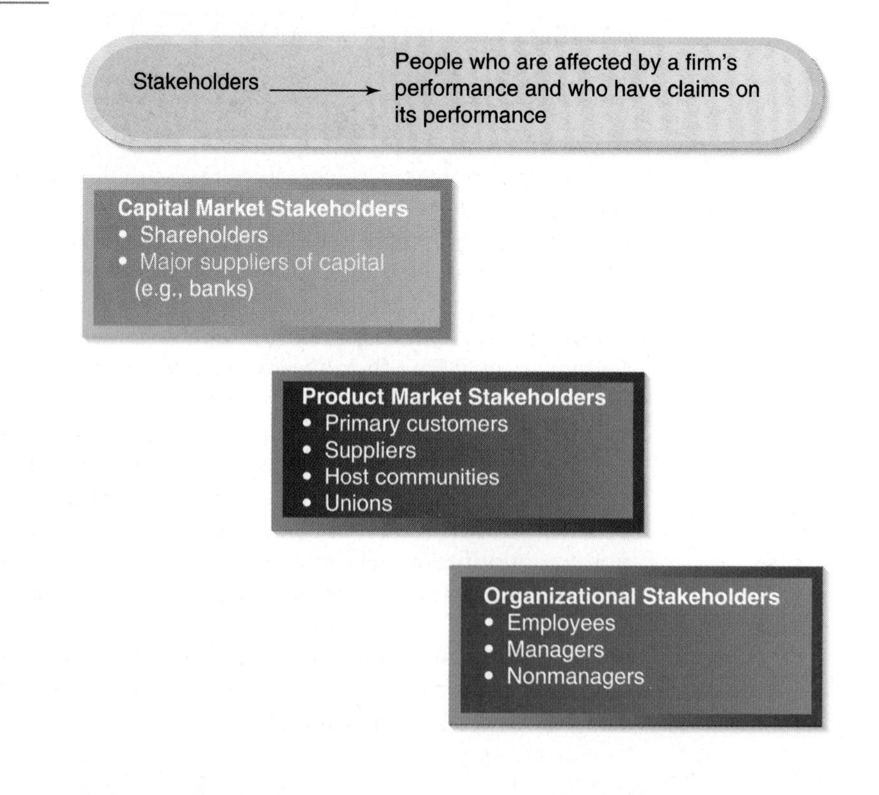

REUTERS NEWMEDIA INC./CORBIS

DaimlerChrysler CEO Juergen Schrempp is shown here addressing shareholders about the firm's three-year plan to increase profitability. The shareholder group of stakeholders expects the firm to preserve and enhance the financial investment the shareholders have made in the firm.

lenders may impose stricter covenants on subsequent borrowing of capital. Dissatisfied shareholders can reflect their dissatisfaction through several means, including selling their stock.

When a firm is aware of potential or actual dissatisfactions among capital market stakeholders, it may respond to their concerns. The firm's response to dissatisfied stakeholders is affected by the nature of its dependency relationship with them (which, as noted earlier, is also influenced by a society's values). The greater and more significant the dependency relationship is, the more direct and significant the firm's response becomes.

As discussed in the Strategic Focus on page 18, capital market stakeholders were displeased with Excite@Home's performance. Questions arose as to the firm's continued viability. Although the company was able to delay a debt payment to one major lender, it had to find the cash to continue, especially while operating under the guidelines associated with its filing for bankruptcy. Likewise, AOL Time Warner invested $100 million in Amazon.com's stock. The cash injection allowed Amazon to continue its plan to expand from retailing to be a services company (supplying services to other firms). The investment by AOL also suggests confidence in the firm's future potential and may encourage other shareholders and potential investors to invest in Amazon.[101]

Product Market Stakeholders

Some might think that there is little commonality among the interests of customers, suppliers, host communities, and unions (product market stakeholders). However, all four groups can benefit as firms engage in competitive battles. For example, depending on product and industry characteristics, marketplace competition may result in lower product prices being charged to a firm's customers and higher prices paid to its suppliers (the firm might be willing to pay higher supplier prices to ensure delivery of the types of goods and services that are linked with its competitive success).

As is noted in Chapter 4, customers, as stakeholders, demand reliable products at the lowest possible prices. Suppliers seek loyal customers who are willing to pay the highest sustainable prices for the goods and services they receive. Host communities want companies willing to be long-term employers and providers of tax revenues without placing excessive demands on public support services. Union officials are interested in secure jobs, under highly desirable working conditions, for employees they represent. Thus, product market stakeholders are generally satisfied when a firm's profit margin yields the lowest acceptable return to capital market stakeholders (i.e., the lowest return lenders and shareholders will accept and still retain their interests in the firm).

All product market stakeholders are important in a competitive business environment, but many firms emphasize the importance of the customer. As the Strategic Focus on page 25 suggests, Cisco experienced problems with consumer demand even before the poor economic conditions at the end of the decade. Some of Cisco's major telecommunications customers were displeased with the firm's practice of allowing them access to its other customers in return for their business. The problem was that Cisco had made the same promise to all telecommunications customers, who are competitors. Thus, low consumer satisfaction was also harmful to Cisco's current sales efforts. The relationship between satisfaction of customers' needs and strategic competitiveness is examined in Chapter 4.

Organizational Stakeholders

Employees—the firm's organizational stakeholders—expect the firm to provide a dynamic, stimulating, and rewarding work environment. They are usually satisfied working for a company that is growing and actively developing their skills, especially those needed to be effective team members and to meet or exceed global work standards. Workers who learn how to use new knowledge productively are critical to organizational success. In a collective sense, the education and skills of a firm's workforce are competitive weapons affecting strategy implementation and firm performance.[102]

Organizational Strategists

Organizational strategists are the people responsible for the design and execution of strategic management processes. These individuals may also be called top-level managers, executives, the top management team, and general managers. Throughout this book, these names are used interchangeably. As discussed in Chapter 12, top-level managers can be a source of competitive advantage as a result of the value created by their strategic decisions.

Small organizations may have a single strategist; in many cases, this person owns the firm and is deeply involved with its daily operations. At the other extreme, large, diversified firms have many top-level managers. In addition to the CEO and other top-level officials (e.g., the chief operating officer and chief financial officer), other managers of these companies are responsible for the performance of individual business units.

Top-level managers play critical roles in a firm's efforts to achieve desired strategic outcomes. In fact, some believe that every organizational failure is actually a failure of those who hold the final responsibility for the quality and effectiveness of a firm's decisions and actions. Failure can stem from changing strategic assumptions, which can cause the strategic mission to become a strategic blunder. This appears to have been a problem at Excite@Home, as described earlier in the Strategic Focus on page 18. Additionally, a firm's method of operating may entail routines that create strategic inertia, where established relationships create shackles that prevent change. Finally, a shared set of beliefs may become dogma that prevents a change in corporate culture.[103] Strategic managers need to ask the right questions to overcome the inertia that success often creates.

Decisions that strategists make include how resources will be developed or acquired, at what price they will be obtained, and how they will be used. Managerial decisions also influence how information flows in a company, the strategies a firm chooses to implement, and the scope of its operations. In making these decisions, managers must assess the risk involved in taking the actions being considered. The level of risk is then factored into the decision.[104] The firm's strategic intent and managers' strategic orientations both affect their decisions. Additionally, how strategists complete their work and their patterns of interactions with others significantly influence the way a firm does business and affect its ability to develop a competitive advantage.

Organizational culture refers to the complex set of ideologies, symbols, and core values that are shared throughout the firm and that influence how the firm conducts business.

Critical to strategic leadership practices and the implementation of strategies, **organizational culture** refers to the complex set of ideologies, symbols, and core values that are shared throughout the firm and that influence how the firm conducts business. Thus, culture is the social energy that drives—or fails to drive—the organization. For example, Southwest Airlines, one of the successful firms discussed in this chapter's Opening Case, is known for having a unique and valuable culture. Its culture encourages employees to work hard but also to have fun while doing so. Moreover, its culture entails respect for others—employees and customers alike. The firm also places a premium on service, as suggested by its commitment to provide POS (Positively Outrageous Service) to each customer. These core values at Southwest Airlines provide a particular type of social energy that drives the firm's efforts. Organizational culture thus becomes a potential source of competitive advantage.

After evaluating available information and alternatives, top-level managers must frequently choose among similarly attractive alternatives. The most effective strategists have the self-confidence necessary to select the best alternatives, allocate the required level of resources to them, and effectively explain to interested parties why certain alternatives were selected.[105] When choosing among alternatives, strategists are accountable for treating employees, suppliers, customers, and others with fairness and respect. Evidence suggests that trust can be a source of competitive advantage, thereby supporting an organizational commitment to treat stakeholders fairly and with respect.[106]

The Work of Effective Strategists

Perhaps not surprisingly, hard work, thorough analyses, a willingness to be brutally honest, a penchant for always wanting the firm and its people to accomplish more, and common sense are prerequisites to an individual's success as a strategist.[107] In addition to possessing these characteristics, effective strategists must be able to think clearly and ask many questions. But, in particular, top-level managers are challenged to "think seriously and deeply . . . about the purposes of the organizations they head or functions they perform, about the strategies, tactics, technologies, systems, and people necessary to attain these purposes and about the important questions that always need to be asked."[108]

Just as the Internet has changed the nature of competition, it is also changing strategic decision making. Speed has become a much more prominent competitive factor, and it makes strategic thinking even more critical. Most high-tech firms operate in hypercompetitive industry environments. As a result of the intense competition in these industries, some product life cycles have decreased from a period of one to two years to a period of six to nine months, leaving less time for a company's products to generate revenue. Speed and flexibility have become key sources of competitive advantage for companies competing in these industries. Thinking strategically, in concert with others, increases the probability of identifying bold, innovative ideas.[109] When these ideas lead to the development of core competencies, they become the foundation for taking advantage of environmental opportunities.

Our discussion highlights the nature of a strategist's work. The work is filled with ambiguous decision situations for which the most effective solutions are not always easily determined. However, the opportunities afforded by this type of work are appealing and offer exciting chances to dream and to act. The following words, given as advice to the late Time Warner chairman and co-CEO Steven J. Ross by his father, describe the opportunities in a strategist's work:

> There are three categories of people—the person who goes into the office, puts his feet up on his desk, and dreams for 12 hours; the person who arrives at 5 A.M. and works for 16 hours, never once stopping to dream; and the person who puts his feet up, dreams for one hour, then does something about those dreams.[110]

The organizational term used for a dream that challenges and energizes a company is strategic intent (discussed earlier in this chapter).[111] Strategists have opportunities to dream and to act, and the most effective ones provide a vision (the strategic intent) to effectively elicit the help of others in creating a firm's competitive advantage.

Predicting Outcomes of Strategic Decisions

Top-level managers attempt to predict the outcomes of strategic decisions they make before they are implemented. In most cases, managers determine the outcomes only after the decisions have been implemented. For example, executives at Montana Power decided to change the firm from a utility company to a high-tech company focusing on broadband services. The firm announced in March 2000 that it would invest $1.6 billion to build a coast-to-coast fiber optic network. Unfortunately for Montana Power, the utility industry began to grow and the broadband industry declined substantially in 2001. As such, the firm's stock price declined from $65 per share in 2000 to less than $8 per share in 2001.

While it may have been difficult for Montana Power to predict the rapid decline in the high-tech businesses, it should have been much easier to predict the growth in the utility business.[112] One means of helping managers understand the potential outcomes of their strategic decisions is to map their industry's profit pools. There are four steps to doing this: (1) define the pool's boundaries, (2) estimate the pool's overall size, (3) estimate the size of the value-chain activity in the pool, and (4) reconcile the calculations.[113]

A **profit pool** entails the total profits earned in an industry at all points along the value chain.

A **profit pool** entails the total profits earned in an industry at all points along the value chain.[114] Analyzing the profit pool in the industry may help a firm see something others are unable to see by helping the firm understand the primary sources of profits in an industry. After these sources have been identified, managers must link the profit potential identified to specific strategies. In a sense, they map the profit potential of their departmental units by linking to the firm's overall profits. They can then better link the strategic actions considered to potential profits.[115]

Mapping profit pools and linking potential profits to strategic actions before they are implemented should be a regular part of the strategic management process. General Motors managers would have done well to take these actions when they decided to continue investing resources in the Oldsmobile brand instead of investing them in their Saturn brand. The firm's investments in Oldsmobile in essence starved Saturn for resources, even though Oldsmobile was no longer a successful product in the market. Finally, after making a decision to stop marketing Oldsmobile, GM decided to invest $1.5 billion in developing a full line of Saturn products.[116]

The Strategic Management Process

As suggested by Figure 1.1, the strategic management process is intended to be a rational approach to help a firm effectively respond to the challenges of the 21st-century competitive landscape. Figure 1.1 also outlines the topics examined in this book to study the strategic management process. Part 1 of this book shows how this process requires a firm to study its external environment (Chapter 2) and internal environment (Chapter 3) to identify marketplace opportunities and threats and determine how to use its core competencies in the pursuit of desired strategic outcomes. With this knowledge, the firm forms its strategic intent to leverage its resources, capabilities, and core competencies and to win competitive battles. Flowing from its strategic intent, the firm's strategic mission specifies, in writing, the products the firm intends to produce and the markets it will serve when leveraging those resources, capabilities, and competencies.

The firm's strategic inputs provide the foundation for its strategic actions to formulate and implement strategies. Both formulating and implementing strategies are critical to achieving strategic competitiveness and earning above-average returns. As suggested in Figure 1.1 by the horizontal arrow linking the two types of strategic actions, formulation and implementation must be simultaneously integrated. In formulating strategies, thought should be given to implementing them. During implementation, effective strategists also seek feedback to improve selected strategies. Only when these two sets of actions are carefully integrated can the firm achieve its desired strategic outcomes.

In Part 2 of this book, the formulation of strategies is explained. First, we examine the formulation of strategies at the business-unit level (Chapter 4). A diversified firm competing in multiple product markets and businesses has a business-level strategy for each distinct product market area. A company competing in a single product market has but one business-level strategy. In all instances, a business-level strategy describes a firm's actions designed to exploit its competitive advantage over rivals. On the other hand, business-level strategies are not formulated and implemented in isolation (Chapter 5). Competitors respond to and try to anticipate each other's actions. Thus, the dynamics of competition are an important input when selecting and implementing strategies.

For the diversified firm, corporate-level strategy (Chapter 6) is concerned with determining the businesses in which the company intends to compete as well as how resources are to be allocated among those businesses. Other topics vital to strategy formulation, particularly in the diversified firm, include the acquisition of other companies and, as appropriate, the restructuring of the firm's portfolio of businesses (Chapter 7) and the selection of an international strategy (Chapter 8). Increasingly important in a global economy, cooperative strategies are used by a firm to gain competitive advantage by forming advantageous relationships with other firms (Chapter 9).

To examine actions taken to implement strategies, we consider several topics in Part 3 of the book. First, the different mechanisms used to govern firms are explained (Chapter 10). With demands for improved corporate governance voiced by various stakeholders, organizations are challenged to satisfy stakeholders' interests and the attainment of desired strategic outcomes. Finally, the organizational structure and actions needed to control a firm's operations (Chapter 11), the patterns of strategic leadership appropriate for today's firms and competitive environments (Chapter 12), and strategic entrepreneurship (Chapter 13) are addressed.

As noted earlier, competition requires firms to make choices to survive and succeed. Some of these choices are strategic in nature, including those of selecting a strategic intent and strategic mission, determining which strategies to implement, choosing an appropriate level of corporate scope, designing governance and organization structures to properly coordinate a firm's work, and, through strategic leadership, encouraging and nurturing organizational innovation.[117] The goal is to achieve and maintain a competitive advantage over rivals.

Primarily because they are related to how a firm interacts with its stakeholders, almost all strategic decisions have ethical dimensions.[118] Organizational ethics are revealed by an organization's culture; that is to say, a firm's strategic decisions are a product of the core values that are shared by most or all of a company's managers and employees. Especially in the turbulent and often ambiguous 21st-century competitive landscape, those making strategic decisions are challenged to recognize that their decisions do affect capital market, product market, and organizational stakeholders differently and to evaluate the ethical implications of their decisions.

As you will discover, the strategic management process examined in this book calls for disciplined approaches to the development of competitive advantage. These approaches provide the pathway through which firms will be able to achieve strategic competitiveness and earn above-average returns in the 21st century. Mastery of this strategic management process will effectively serve readers and the organizations for which they choose to work.

Summary

- Through their actions, firms seek strategic competitiveness and above-average returns. Strategic competitiveness is achieved when a firm has developed and learned how to implement a value-creating strategy. Above-average returns (in excess of what investors expect to earn from other investments with similar levels of risk) allow a firm to simultaneously satisfy all of its stakeholders.
- In the 21st-century competitive landscape, the fundamental nature of competition has changed. As a result, managers making strategic decisions must adopt a new mind-set that is global in nature. Firms must learn how to compete in highly turbulent and chaotic environments that produce disorder and a great deal of uncertainty. The globalization of industries and their markets and rapid and significant technological changes are the two primary factors contributing to the 21st-century competitive landscape.
- There are two major models of what a firm should do to earn above-average returns. The I/O model suggests that the external environment is the primary determinant of the firm's strategies. Above-average returns are earned when the firm locates an attractive industry and successfully implements the strategy dictated by that industry's characteristics.
- The resource-based model assumes that each firm is a collection of unique resources and capabilities that determine its strategy. Above-average returns are earned when the firm uses its valuable, rare, costly-to-imitate, and nonsubstitutable resources and capabilities (i.e., core competencies) as the source of its competitive advantage(s).
- Strategic intent and strategic mission are formed in light of the information and insights gained from studying a firm's internal and external environments. Strategic intent suggests how resources, capabilities, and core competencies will be leveraged to achieve desired outcomes. The strategic mission is an application of strategic intent. The mission is used to specify the product markets and customers a firm intends to serve through the leveraging of its resources, capabilities, and competencies.
- Stakeholders are those who can affect, and are affected by, a firm's strategic outcomes. Because a firm is dependent on the continuing support of stakeholders (shareholders, customers, suppliers, employees, host communities, etc.), they have enforceable claims on the company's performance. When earning above-average returns, a firm can adequately satisfy all stakeholders' interests. However, when earning only average returns, a firm's strategists must carefully manage all stakeholder groups in order to retain their support. A firm earning below-average returns must minimize the amount of support it loses from dissatisfied stakeholders.
- Organizational strategists are responsible for the design and execution of an effective strategic management process. Today, the most effective of these processes are grounded in ethical intentions and conduct. Strategists can be a source of competitive advantage. The strategist's work demands decision trade-offs, often among attractive alternatives. Successful top-level managers work hard, conduct thorough analyses of situations, are brutally and consistently honest, and ask the right questions, of the right people, at the right time.
- Managers must predict the potential outcomes of their strategic decisions. To do so, they must first calculate profit pools in their industry that are linked to the value chain activities. In so doing, they are less likely to formulate and implement an ineffective strategy.

Review Questions

1. What are strategic competitiveness, competitive advantage, and above-average returns?
2. What are the characteristics of the 21st-century landscape? What two factors are the primary drivers of this landscape?
3. According to the I/O model, what should a firm do to earn above-average returns?
4. What does the resource-based model suggest a firm should do to earn above-average returns?
5. What are strategic intent and strategic mission? What is their value for the strategic management process?
6. What are stakeholders? How do the three primary stakeholder groups influence organizations?
7. How would you describe the work of organizational strategists?
8. What are the elements of the strategic management process? How are they interrelated?

Experiential Exercise

Strategic Mission Statements

Strategic intent and strategic mission influence strategy formulation and implementation actions. Following are brief mission statements of some of the firms mentioned in this chapter as they appear on the firms' websites (the firms are identified later in the exercise). Refer to the mission statements to complete this exercise.

a. To leverage the strengths of each member of the . . . team to create a strong, committed, and unified . . . team focused on people, quality and profits.

b. The achievements of an organization are the result of the combined efforts of each individual in the organization working toward common objectives. These objectives should be realistic, should be clearly understood by everyone in the organization and should reflect the organization's basic character and personality.

c. . . . is dedicated to the living spirit of the American dream. We believe the spirit of youth is our greatest inspiration. Resourcefulness is the key to value and excellence. In making quality a priority of our lives and products. By respecting one another we can reach all cultures. By being bold in our vision we continually expand our boundaries.

d. Our mission: To become the world's most respected and valued company by connecting, informing and entertaining people everywhere in innovative ways that will enrich their lives.

e. Our purpose in . . . is to meet the everyday needs of people everywhere—to anticipate the aspirations of our consumers and customers and to respond creatively and competitively with branded products and services which raise the quality of life.

f. Our strategic intent is to be the leader in the global . . . market, providing . . . solutions (hardware, software and services) that enhance business productivity and knowledge sharing.

Break into small groups of three to five students for this exercise.

1. The firm's strategic mission, as defined in the chapter, is a statement of a firm's unique purpose and the scope of its operations in product and market terms. Do the above statements serve as strategic mission statements? As a group, choose a statement you feel best achieves this purpose and one that does not. Be ready to defend your choices to the other groups.
2. As a group, identify an industry for which each statement seems to apply. Do any of the statements seem to apply to several industries? Discuss whether you feel the statements should be broader or narrower across industries to be effective strategic mission statements.

Statement	Industry
a.	
b.	
c.	
d.	
e.	
f.	

3. Now refer to the list below to identify the firms. Based on the material in the text and your everyday knowledge of the firms and their products or services, which statement does your group feel most effectively reflects the firm's strategic intent and mission? Which statement is most closely tied to an individual firm and which to an individual industry?

a. To leverage the strengths of each member of the Brinker team to create a strong, committed, and unified Brinker team focused on people, quality and profits. *(Brinkers International);* b. The achievements of an organization are the result of the combined efforts of each individual in the organization working toward common objectives. These objectives should be realistic, should be clearly understood by everyone in the organization and should reflect the organization's basic character and personality. *(Hewlett-Packard);* c. The Tommy Hilfiger Corporation is dedicated to the living spirit of the American dream. We believe the spirit of youth is our greatest inspiration. Resourcefulness is the key to value and excellence. In making quality a priority of our lives and products. By respecting one another we can reach all cultures. By being bold in our vision we continually expand our boundaries. *(Tommy Hilfiger);* d. Our mission: To become the world's most respected and valued company by connecting, informing and entertaining people everywhere in innovative ways that will enrich their lives. *(AOL Time Warner);* e. Our purpose in Unilever is to meet the everyday needs of people everywhere - to anticipate the aspirations of our consumers and customers and to respond creatively and competitively with branded products and services which raise the quality of life. *(Unilever);* f. Our strategic intent is to be the leader in the global document market, providing document solutions (hardware, software and services) that enhance business productivity and knowledge sharing. *(Xerox)*

Notes

1. C. A. Maritan, 2001, Capital investment as investing in organizational capabilities: An empirically grounded process model, *Academy of Management Journal,* 44: 513–531; C. E. Helfat, 2000, The evolution of firm capabilities, *Strategic Management Journal,* 21(special issue): 955–959; J. B. Barney, 1999, How firms' capabilities affect boundary decisions, *Sloan Management Review,* 40 (3): 137–145.
2. W. Mitchell, 2000, Path-dependent and path-breaking change: Reconfiguring business resources following acquisitions in the U.S. medical sector, 1978–1995, *Strategic Management Journal,* 21(special issue): 1061–1081; K. M. Eisenhardt & S. L. Brown, 1999, Patching: Restitching business portfolios in dynamic markets, *Harvard Business Review,* 77(3): 72–84.
3. E. Bonabeau & C. Meyer, 2001, Swarm intelligence, *Harvard Business Review,* 79(5): 107–114; D. Abell, 1999, Competing today while preparing for tomorrow, *Sloan Management Review,* 40(3): 73–81; D. J. Teece, G. Pisano, & A. Shuen, 1997, Dynamic capabilities and strategic management, *Strategic Management Journal,* 18: 509–533.
4. T. C. Powell, 2001, Competitive advantage: Logical and philosophical considerations, *Strategic Management Journal,* 22: 875–888; R. Coff, 1999, When competitive advantage doesn't lead to performance: The resource-based view and stakeholder bargaining power, *Organization Science,* 10: 119–133.
5. P. Shrivastava, 1995, Ecocentric management for a risk society, *Academy of Management Review,* 20: 119.
6. R. P. Rumelt, D. E. Schendel, & D. J. Teece (eds.), 1994, *Fundamental Issues in Strategy,* Boston: Harvard Business School Press, 527–530.
7. M. J. Epstein & R. A. Westbrook, 2001, Linking actions to profits in strategic decision making, *Sloan Management Review,* 42(3): 39–49.
8. Rumelt, Schendel, & Teece, *Fundamental Issues in Strategy,* 543–547.
9. M. A. Hitt, R. D. Ireland, S. M. Camp, & D. L. Sexton, 2001, Strategic entrepreneurship: Entrepreneurial strategies for wealth creation, *Strategic Management Journal* 22(special issue): 479–491; S. A. Zahra, R. D. Ireland, & M. A. Hitt, 2000, International expansion by new venture firms: International diversity, mode of market entry technological learning and performance, *Academy of Management Journal,* 43: 925-950.
10. M. A. Hitt, L. Bierman, K. Shimizu, & R. Kochhar, 2001, Direct and moderating effects of human capital on strategy and performance in professional service firms, *Academy of Management Journal,* 44: 13–28.
11. A. Nair & S. Kotha, 2001, Does group membership matter? Evidence from the Japanese steel industry, *Strategic Management Journal,* 22: 221–235; A. M. McGahan & M. E. Porter, 1997, How much does industry matter, really? *Strategic Management Journal,* 18(summer special issue): 15–30.
12. J. B. Barney, 2001, Is the resource based "view" a useful perspective for strategic management research? Yes, *Academy of Management Review,* 26: 41–56.
13. S. N. Mehta, 2001, Cisco fractures its own fairy tale, *Fortune,* 105–112.
14. S. Day, 2001, Shares surge after Cisco says its business has stabilized, *The New York Times,* http://www.nytimes.com, August 25.
15. 2001, ABI World, Filing statistics, abiworld.org/stats/newstatsfront.
16. Rumelt, Schendel, & Teece, *Fundamental Issues in Strategy,* 530.
17. C. J. Loomis, 1993, Dinosaurs, *Fortune,* May 3, 36–46.
18. A. Edgecliffe–Johnson, 2001, Gap reins in plans to expand number of stores, *Financial Times,* http://www.ft.com, June 22; N. Monk, 1999, How Levi's trashed a great American brand, *Fortune,* April 12, 83–90.
19. V. Marsh, 1998, Attributes: Strong strategy tops the list, *Financial Times,* http://www.ft.com, November 30.
20. J. Nocera, 1999, Five lessons from Iomega, *Fortune,* August 2, 251–254.
21. A. Reinhardt, 1997, Paranoia, aggression, and other strengths, *Business Week,* October 13, 14; A. S. Grove, 1995, A high-tech CEO updates his views on managing and careers, *Fortune,* September 18, 229–230.
22. This section is based largely on information featured in two sources: M. A. Hitt, B. W. Keats, & S. M. DeMarie, 1998, Navigating in the new competitive landscape: Building competitive advantage and strategic flexibility in the 21st century, *Academy of Management Executive,* 12(4): 22–42; R. A. Bettis & M. A. Hitt, 1995, The new competitive landscape, *Strategic Management Journal,* 16(special summer issue): 7–19.
23. D.Tapscott, 2001, Rethinking strategy in a networked world, *Strategy & Business,* 24 (third quarter), 34–41.
24. R. D. Ireland & M. A. Hitt, 1999, Achieving and maintaining strategic competitiveness in the 21st century: The role of strategic leadership, *Academy of Management Executive,* 13(1): 43–57.
25. R. A. D'Aveni, 1995, Coping with hypercompetition: Utilizing the new 7S's framework, *Academy of Management Executive,* 9(3): 46.
26. W. J. Ferrier, 2001, Navigating the competitive landscape: The drivers and consequences of competitive aggressiveness, *Academy of Management Journal,* 44: 858–877.
27. D. G. McKendrick, 2001, Global strategy and population level learning: The case of hard disk drives, *Strategic Management Journal,* 22: 307–334; T. P. Murtha, S. A. Lenway, & R. Bagozzi, 1998, Global mind-sets and cognitive shifts in a complex multinational corporation, *Strategic Management Journal,* 19: 97–114.
28. S. Koudsi & L. A. Costa, 1998, America vs. the new Europe: By the numbers, *Fortune,* December 21, 149–156.
29. T. A. Stewart, 1993, The new face of American power, *Fortune,* July 26, 70–86.
30. S. Garelli, 2001, Executive summary, *The World Competitiveness Yearbook,* http://www.imd.ch.wcy.esummary.
31. W. Arnold, 2001, Japan's electronics slump takes a toll on Southeast Asia, *The New York Times,* http://www.nytimes.com, September 1.
32. E. Tucker, 1999, More entrepreneurship urged, *Financial Times,* June 22, 2.
33. S. Thurm & M. Tatge, 2000, Whirlpool to launch Internet-ready refrigerator, *The Wall Street Journal,* January 7, B6; I. Katz, 1998, Whirlpool: In the wringer, *Business Week,* December 14, 83–87.
34. V. Govindarajan & A. K. Gupta, 2001, *The Quest for Global Dominance,* San Francisco: Jossey-Bass.
35. D. Luhnow, 2001, Lower tariffs, retail muscle translate into big sales for Wal-Mart in Mexico, *The Wall Street Journal Interactive,* http://www.interactive.wsj.com/articles, September 1; Govindarajan & Gupta, *The Quest for Global Dominance.*
36. 1999, Business: Ford swallows Volvo, *Economist,* January 30, 58.
37. R. McNast, 1999, Tora, tora, taurus, *Business Week,* April 12, 6.
38. Govindarajan & Gupta. *The Quest for Global Dominance;* R. Ruggiero, 1997, The high stakes of world trade, *The Wall Street Journal,* April 28, A18.
39. M. A. Carpenter & J. W. Fredrickson, 2001, Top management teams, global strategic posture, and the moderating role of uncertainty, *Academy of Management Journal,* 44: 533–545.
40. M. Subramaniam & N. Venkataraman, 2001, Determinants of transnational new product development capability: Testing the influence of transferring and deploying tacit overseas knowledge, *Strategic Management Journal,* 22: 359–378; S. A. Zahra, 1999, The changing rules of global competitiveness in the 21st century, *Academy of Management Executive,* 13(1): 36–42; R. M. Kanter, 1995, Thriving locally in the global economy, *Harvard Business Review* 73(5): 151–160.
41. Zahra, Ireland, Gutierrez, & Hitt, 2000, Privatization and entrepreneurial transformation: Emerging issues and a future research agenda, 25: 509–524.
42. S. Zaheer & E. Mosakowski, 1997, The dynamics of the liability of foreignness: A global study of survival in financial services, *Strategic Management Journal,* 18: 439–464.
43. D. Arnold, 2000, Seven rules of international distribution, *Harvard Business Review,* 78(6): 131–137; J. S. Black & H. B. Gregersen, 1999, The right way to manage expats, *Harvard Business Review,* 77(2): 52–63.
44. M. A. Hitt, R. E. Hoskisson, & H. Kim, 1997, International diversification: Effects on innovation and firm performance in product-diversified firms, *Academy of Management Journal,* 40: 767–798.
45. D'Aveni, *Coping with Hypercompetition,* 46.
46. G. Hamel, 2001, Revolution vs. evolution: You need both, *Harvard Business Review,* 79(5): 150–156; T. Nakahara, 1997, Innovation in a borderless world economy, *Research-Technology Management,* May/June, 7–9.
47. J. Birkinshaw & N. Hood, 2001, Unleash innovation in foreign subsidiaries, *Harvard Business Review,* 79(3): 131–137; N. Dawar & T. Frost, 1999, Competing with giants: Survival strategies for local companies in emerging markets, *Harvard Business Review,* 77(2): 119–129.
48. K. H. Hammonds, 2001, What is the state of the new economy? *Fast Company,* September, 101–104.
49. K. H. Hammonds, 2001, How do fast companies work now? *Fast Company,* September, 134–142; K. M. Eisenhardt, 1999, Strategy as strategic decision making, *Sloan Management Review,* 40(3): 65–72.
50. C. W. L. Hill, 1997, Establishing a standard: Competitive strategy and technological standards in winner-take-all industries, *Academy of Management Executive,* 11(2): 7–25.
51. R. Karlgaard, 1999, Digital rules, *Forbes,* July 5, 43.

52. C. M. Christiansen, 1997, *The Innovator's Dilemma,* Boston: Harvard Business School Press.
53. G. Ahuja & C. M. Lampert, 2001, Entrepreneurship in the large corporation: A longitudinal study of how established firms create breakthrough inventions, *Strategic Management Journal,* 22(special issue): 521–543.
54. R. Amit & C. Zott, 2001, Value creation in e-business, *Strategic Management Journal,* 22(special summer issue): 493–520.
55. Ibid.
56. R. M. Kanter, 2001, *e-volve: Succeeding in the Digital Culture of Tomorrow,* Boston: Harvard Business School Press.
57. Hitt, Ireland, Camp, & Sexton, Strategic entrepreneurship, 479–491.
58. F. Warner, 2001, The drills for knowledge, *Fast Company,* September, 186–191; B. L. Simonin, 1999, Ambiguity and the process of knowledge transfer in strategic alliances, *Strategic Management Journal,* 20: 595–624.
59. L. Rosenkopf & A. Nerkar, 2001, Beyond local search: Boundary-spanning, exploration, and impact on the optical disk industry, *Strategic Management Journal,* 22: 287–306; T. H. Davenport & L. Prusak, 1998, *Working Knowledge: How Organizations Manage What They Know,* Boston: Harvard Business School Press.
60. D. F. Kuratko, R. D. Ireland, & J. S. Hornsby, 2001, Improving firm performance through entrepreneurial actions: Insights from Acordia Inc.'s corporate entrepreneurship strategy, *Academy of Management Executive,* 15(4): 60–71; T. K. Kayworth & R. D. Ireland, 1998, The use of corporate IT standards as a means of implementing the cost leadership strategy, *Journal of Information Technology Management,* IX(4): 13–42.
61. K. R. Harrigan, 2001, Strategic flexibility in old and new economies, in M. A. Hitt, R. E. Freeman & J. R. Harrison (eds.), *Handbook of Strategic Management,* Oxford, U.K.: Blackwell Publishers, 97–123.
62. J. L. C. Cheng & I. F. Kesner, 1997, Organizational slack and response to environmental shifts: The impact of resource allocation patterns, *Journal of Management,* 23: 1–18.
63. C. Markides, 1998, Strategic innovation in established companies, *Sloan Management Review,* 39(3): 31–42; V. L. Barker III & I. M. Duhaime, 1997, Strategic change in the turnaround process: Theory and empirical evidence, *Strategic Management Journal,* 18: 13–38.
64. M. A. Hitt, R. D. Ireland, & J. S. Harrison, 2001, Mergers and acquisitions: A value creating or value destroying strategy? In M. A. Hitt, R. E. Freeman, & J. S. Harrison (eds.), *Handbook of Strategic Management,* Oxford, U.K.: Blackwell Publishers, 384–408; W. Boeker, 1997, Strategic change: The influence of managerial characteristics and organizational growth, *Academy of Management Journal,* 40: 152–170.
65. R. T. Pascale, 1999, Surviving the edge of chaos, *Sloan Management Review,* 40(3): 83–94; E. D. Beinhocker, 1999, Robust adaptive strategies, *Sloan Management Review,* 40(3): 95–106; N. Rajagopalan & G. M. Spreitzer, 1997, Toward a theory of strategic change: A multi-lens perspective and integrative framework, *Academy of Management Review,* 22: 48–79.
66. R. E. Hoskisson, M. A. Hitt, W. P. Wan, & D. Yiu, 1999, Swings of a pendulum: Theory and research in strategic management, *Journal of Management,* 25: 417–456.
67. E. H. Bowman & C. E. Helfat, 2001, Does corporate strategy matter? *Strategic Management Journal,* 22: 1–23.
68. A. Seth & H. Thomas, 1994, Theories of the firm: Implications for strategy research, *Journal of Management Studies,* 31: 165–191.
69. Ibid., 169–173.
70. M. E. Porter, 1985, *Competitive Advantage,* New York: Free Press; M. E. Porter, 1980, *Competitive Strategy,* New York: Free Press.
71. A. M. McGahan, 1999, Competition, strategy and business performance, *California Management Review,* 41(3): 74–101; A. M. McGahan & M. E. Porter, 1997, How much does industry matter, really? *Strategic Management Journal,* 18(special summer issue): 15–30.
72. R. Henderson & W. Mitchell, 1997, The interactions of organizational and competitive influences on strategy and performance, *Strategic Management Journal* 18:(special summer issue), 5–14; C. Oliver, 1997, Sustainable competitive advantage: Combining institutional and resource-based views, *Strategic Management Journal,* 18: 697–713; J. L. Stimpert & I. M. Duhaime, 1997, Seeing the big picture: The influence of industry, diversification, and business strategy on performance, *Academy of Management Journal,* 40: 560–583.
73. C. Lee, K. Lee, & J. M. Pennings, 2001, Internal capabilities, external networks, and performance: A study on technology-based ventures, *Strategic Management Journal 22* (special issue): 615–640; C. C. Markides, 1999, A dynamic view of strategy, *Sloan Management Review,* 40(3): 55–72; Abell, Competing today while preparing for tomorrow.
74. R. L. Priem & J. E. Butler, 2001, Is the resource-based "view" a useful perspective for strategic management research? *Academy of Management Review,* 26: 22–40.
75. P. J. H. Schoemaker & R. Amit, 1994, Investment in strategic assets: Industry and firm-level perspectives, in P. Shrivastava, A. Huff, & J. Dutton (eds.), *Advances in Strategic Management,* Greenwich, Conn.: JAI Press, 9.
76. Barney, Is the resource-based "view" a useful perspective for strategic management research? Yes; J. B. Barney, 1995, Looking inside for competitive advantage, *Academy of Management Executive,* 9(4): 56.
77. A. Madhok, 1997, Cost, value and foreign market entry mode: The transaction and the firm, *Strategic Management Journal,* 18: 39–61.
78. W. Kuemmerle, 2001, Go global-or not? *Harvard Business Review,* 79(6): 37–49.
79. Ahuja & Lambert, Entrepreneurship in the large corporation; A. Arora & A. Gambardella, 1997, Domestic markets and international competitiveness: Generic and product specific competencies in the engineering sector, *Strategic Management Journal* 18(special summer issue): 53–74.
80. G. Hamel & C. K. Prahalad, 1989, Strategic intent, *Harvard Business Review,* 67(3): 63–76.
81. Hamel & Prahalad, Strategic intent, 66.
82. J. E. Barnes, 2001, The making (or possible breaking) of a megabrand, *The New York Times,* http://www.nytimes.com, July 22.
83. Hamel & Prahalad, Strategic intent, 64.
84. M. A. Hitt, D. Park, C. Hardee, & B. B. Tyler, 1995, Understanding strategic intent in the global marketplace, *Academy of Management Executive,* 9(2): 12–19.
85. R. D. Ireland & M. A. Hitt, 1992, Mission statements: Importance, challenge, and recommendations for development, *Business Horizons,* 35(3): 34–42.
86. W. J. Duncan, 1999, *Management: Ideas and Actions,* New York: Oxford University Press, 122–125.
87. R. M. Fulmer, 2001, Johnson & Johnson: Frameworks for leadership, *Organizational Dynamics,* 29(3): 211–220.
88. P. Martin, 1999, Lessons in humility, *Financial Times,* June 22, 18.
89. I. M. Levin, 2000, Vision revisited, *Journal of Applied Behavioral Science,* 36: 91–107.
90. I. R. Baum, E. A. Locke, & S. A. Kirkpatrick, 1998, A longitudinal study of the relation of vision and vision communication to venture growth in entrepreneurial firms, *Journal of Applied Psychology,* 83: 43–54.
91. J. Frooman, 1999, Stakeholder influence strategies, *Academy of Management Review,* 24: 191–205.
92. T. M. Jones & A. C. Wicks, 1999, Convergent stakeholder theory, *Academy of Management Review,* 24: 206–221; R. E. Freeman, 1984, *Strategic Management: A Stakeholder Approach,* Boston: Pitman, 53–54.
93. G. Donaldson & J. W. Lorsch, 1983, *Decision Making at the Top: The Shaping of Strategic Direction,* New York: Basic Books, 37–40.
94. A. J. Hillman & G. D. Keim, 2001, Shareholder value, stakeholder management, and social issues: What's the bottom line? *Strategic Management Journal,* 22: 125–139.
95. R. E. Freeman & J. McVea, 2001, A stakeholder approach to strategic management, in M. A. Hitt, R. E. Freeman, & J. S. Harrison (eds.), *Handbook of Strategic Management,* Oxford, U.K.: Blackwell Publishers, 189–207.
96. Ibid.
97. A. McWilliams & D. Siegel, 2001, Corporate social responsibility: A theory of the firm perspective, *Academy of Management Review,* 26: 117–127; D. A. Gioia, 1999, Practicality, paradigms, and problems in stakeholder theorizing, *Academy of Management Review,* 24: 228–232.
98. Freeman & McVea, A stakeholder approach to strategic management; R. K. Mitchell, B. R. Agle, & D. J. Wood, 1997, Toward a theory of stakeholder identification and salience: Defining the principle of who and what really count, *Academy of Management Review,* 22: 853–886.
99. 1995, Don't be an ugly-American manager, *Fortune,* October 16, 225.
100. G. Dutton, 1999, Building a global brain, *Management Review,* May, 23–30.
101. A. Edgecliffe-Johnson, 2001, AOL Time Warner to invest $100m in Amazon stock, *Financial Times,* http://www.ft.com, July 27.
102. Hitt, Bierman, Shimizu, & Kochhar, Direct and moderating effects of human capital.
103. D. N. Sull, 1999, Why good companies go bad, *Harvard Business Review,* 77(4): 42–52.
104. P. Bromiley, K. D. Miller, & D. Rau, 2001, Risk in strategic management research, in M. A. Hitt, R. E. Freeman, & J. S. Harrison (eds.), *Handbook of Strategic Management,* Oxford, U.K.: Blackwell Publishers, 259–288.
105. R. McGrath & I. MacMillan, 2000, *The Entrepreneurial Mindset,* Boston: Harvard Business School Press.

106. J. H. Davis, F. D. Schoorman, R. C. Mayer, & H. H. Tau, 2000, The trusted general manager and business unit performance: Empirical evidence of a competitive advantage, *Strategic Management Journal,* 21: 563–576.
107. W. C. Taylor, 1999, Whatever happened to globalization? *Fast Company,* September, 288–294.
108. T. Leavitt, 1991, *Thinking about Management,* New York: Free Press, 9.
109. K. Lovelace, D. L. Shapiro, & L. R. Weingart, 2001, Maximizing cross-functional new product teams' innovativeness and constraint adherence: A conflict communications perspective, *Academy of Management Journal,* 44: 779–793.
110. M. Loeb, 1993, Steven J. Ross, 1927–1992, *Fortune,* January 25, 4.
111. Hamel & Prahalad, Competing for the Future, 129.
112. B. Richards, 2001, For Montana Power, a broadband dream may turn out to be more of a nightmare, *The Wall Street Journal Interactive,* http://www.interactive.wsj.com/ articles, August 22.
113. O. Gadiesh & J. L. Gilbert, 1998, How to map your industry's profit pool, *Harvard Business Review,* 76(3): 149–162.
114. O. Gadiesh & J. L. Gilbert, 1998, Profit pools: A fresh look at strategy, *Harvard Business Review,* 76(3): 139–147.
115. M. J. Epstein & R. A. Westbrook, 2001, Linking actions to profits in strategic decision making, *Sloan Management Review,* 42(3): 39–49.
116. 2001, Trading places, *Forbes,* http://www.forbes.com, June 14.
117. R. D. Ireland, M. A. Hitt, S. M. Camp, & D. L. Sexton, 2001, Integrating entrepreneurship and strategic management actions to create firm wealth, *Academy of Management Executive,* 15(1): 49–63; Rumelt, Schendel, & Teece, *Fundamental Issues in Strategy,* 9–10.
118. D. R. Gilbert, 2001, Corporate strategy and ethics as corporate strategy comes of age, in M. A. Hitt, R. E. Freeman, & J. S. Harrison (eds.), *Handbook of Strategic Management,* Oxford, U.K.: Blackwell Publishers, 564–582.

2

Chapter Two

The External Environment: Opportunities, Threats, Industry Competition, and Competitor Analysis

Knowledge Objectives

Studying this chapter should provide you with the strategic management knowledge needed to:

1. Explain the importance of analyzing and understanding the firm's external environment.
2. Define and describe the general environment and the industry environment.
3. Discuss the four activities of the external environmental analysis process.
4. Name and describe the general environment's six segments.
5. Identify the five competitive forces and explain how they determine an industry's profit potential.
6. Define strategic groups and describe their influence on the firm.
7. Describe what firms need to know about their competitors and different methods used to collect intelligence about them.

September 11, 2001: The Economic Aftermath

When terrorists flew airplanes into the twin towers of the World Trade Center and the Pentagon and crashed a third plane in Pennsylvania, the world of business was changed forever. However, certain industries were affected more than others. Indeed, firms in the insurance, air travel, financial services, and tourism industries took much of the initial brunt of the economic fallout from the attacks. For example, air travel in the United States was halted for several days after the attacks, and demand was lower for some time following its resumption. Many scheduled conventions were either cancelled or conducted with fewer participants than planned. In the short term, demand for other means of travel, such as trains and buses, increased significantly. In fact, demand for train service was so great that Amtrak applied for emergency federal funding to expand its service.

Firms in the above industries were not the only ones immediately affected—suppliers serving these industries were affected as well. Some airlines cancelled or substantially reduced their contracts with food service providers, partly because of lower demand but also to reduce costs in order to survive. Another supplier to the airlines, Boeing, was also affected when many airlines postponed existing contracts for new aircraft. Boeing executives predicted that their firm might lay off as many as 30,000 employees by the end of 2002 as a direct result of the terrorist attacks. A number of firms have changed their policies on meetings between company personnel who work at different geographical locations. For example, Masimo, a medical-technology company, installed a major videoconferencing system to facilitate meetings without travel.

Firms with manufacturing plants or suppliers located outside their home countries are also experiencing transportation delays in obtaining goods needed for normal operations. As a result, these firms have to maintain more inventory and cannot take advantage of just-in-time systems, thereby increasing costs. Express mail packages between Europe and the United States now require as many as four days for delivery, up from an average of two days before September 11, and have also been slowed as a result of concerns about anthrax attacks by terrorists.

While the U.S. government has tried to reduce September 11's negative effects on the economy in several ways, such as direct payments and

In the wake of the 9/11 terrorism attacks, Amtrak accepted all airline tickets and added capacity to its trains for both passengers and emergency supplies to New York and Washington. Combined ridership on the passenger railway's high-speed Acela Express and Metroliner was about 40 percent higher for the months of October and November 2001 compared to the same period in 2000, and continues slightly over projections in spite of a general travel slowdown in the United States.

JOHNATHAN NOUROK/PHOTOEDIT

loan guarantees to the airlines totaling $15 billion, it cannot buffer most businesses from these effects. For example, it cannot buffer businesses from significant increases in security and insurance costs they are likely to experience for many years.

Few—if any—businesses were prepared for such attacks on the United States and the many changes they brought. They provide a dramatic illustration of the dynamic environment within which firms must operate and to which they must respond. The many significant effects of the external environment suggest the substantial importance both of the strategies firms employ and of their ability to adapt or change those strategies when required to survive and compete in a rapidly changing landscape.

SOURCES: A. Michaels, 2001, Hope for an early deal on WTC insurance, *Financial Times,* http://www.ft.com, December 14; T. Weber, 2001, Companies rethink role of face-to-face, *The Wall Street Journal Interactive,* http://interactive.wsj.com, September 24; J. Fuerbringer, 2001, As the economic ground zero shudders, ripples spread, *The New York Times,* http://www.nytimes.com, September 24; L. Alvarez, 2001, Congress allocates $15 billion to help the airline industry, *The New York Times,* http://www.nytimes.com, September 22; A. Brady & T. Locke, 2001, Cancellation of meetings and conferences deal a heavy blow to convention cities, *The Wall Street Journal,* September 21, A8; J. Lunsford & A. Pasztor, 2001, Boeing Co.'s course in terror's wake seen as a wider U.S. test, *The Wall Street Journal,* September 21, A1, A8; D. Machalaba & C. Tejada, 2001, As demand for train service jumps, Amtrak seeks emergency funding, *The Wall Street Journal Interactive,* http://interactive.wsj.com, September 21.

Companies' experiences and research suggest that the external environment affects firm growth and profitability.[1] Major political events such as the terrorist attacks on September 11, 2001, the strength of different nations' economies at different times, and the emergence of new technologies are a few examples of conditions in the external environment that affect firms in the United States and throughout the world. External environmental conditions such as these create threats to and opportunities for firms that, in turn, have major effects on firms' strategic actions.[2]

Airlines changed their strategies due to the threats in their external environment. They took a number of actions to reduce their costs while simultaneously enticing customers to return to air travel. All airlines but Southwest reduced the number of flights and personnel, and some eliminated routes as well. Southwest Airlines had substantial cash on hand, based on a conscious strategy to have cash available to operate during an emergency or crisis situation. Southwest Airlines' financial resources and human capital, described in Chapter 1 and discussed further in Chapter 4, afforded it strategic flexibility.[3]

This chapter focuses on what firms do to analyze and understand the external environment. As the discussion of September 11, 2001 vividly shows, the external environment influences the firm's strategic options, as well as the decisions made in light of them. The firm's understanding of the external environment is matched with knowledge about its internal environment (discussed in the next chapter) to form its strategic intent, to develop its strategic mission, and to take strategic actions that result in strategic competitiveness and above-average returns (see Figure 1.1).

As noted in Chapter 1, the environmental conditions in the current global economy differ from those previously faced by firms. Technological changes and the continuing growth of information gathering and processing capabilities demand more timely and effective competitive actions and responses.[4] The rapid sociological changes occurring in many countries affect labor practices and the nature of products demanded by increasingly diverse consumers. Governmental policies and laws also affect where and how firms may choose to compete.[5] Deregulation and local government changes, such as those in the global electric utilities industry, affect not only the general competitive environment, but also the strategic decisions made by companies competing globally. To achieve strategic competitiveness, firms must be aware of and understand the different dimensions of the external environment.

Firms understand the external environment by acquiring information about competitors, customers, and other stakeholders to build their own base of knowledge and capabilities.[6] Firms may use this base to imitate the capabilities of their able competitors (and even may imitate successful firms in other industries) and they may use it to build new knowledge and capabilities to achieve a competitive advantage. On the basis of the new information, knowledge, and capabilities, firms may take actions to buffer themselves against environmental effects or to build relationships with stakeholders in their environment.[7] To build their knowledge and capabilities and to take actions that buffer or build bridges to external stakeholders, organizations must effectively analyze the external environment.

The General, Industry, and Competitor Environments

An integrated understanding of the external and internal environments is essential for firms to understand the present and predict the future.[8] As shown in Figure 2.1, a firm's external environment is divided into three major areas: the general, industry, and competitor environments.

The **general environment** is composed of dimensions in the broader society that influence an industry and the firms within it.

The **general environment** is composed of dimensions in the broader society that influence an industry and the firms within it.[9] We group these dimensions into six environmental *segments:* demographic, economic, political/legal, sociocultural, technological, and global. Examples of *elements* analyzed in each of these segments are shown in Table 2.1.

Figure 2.1 The External Environment

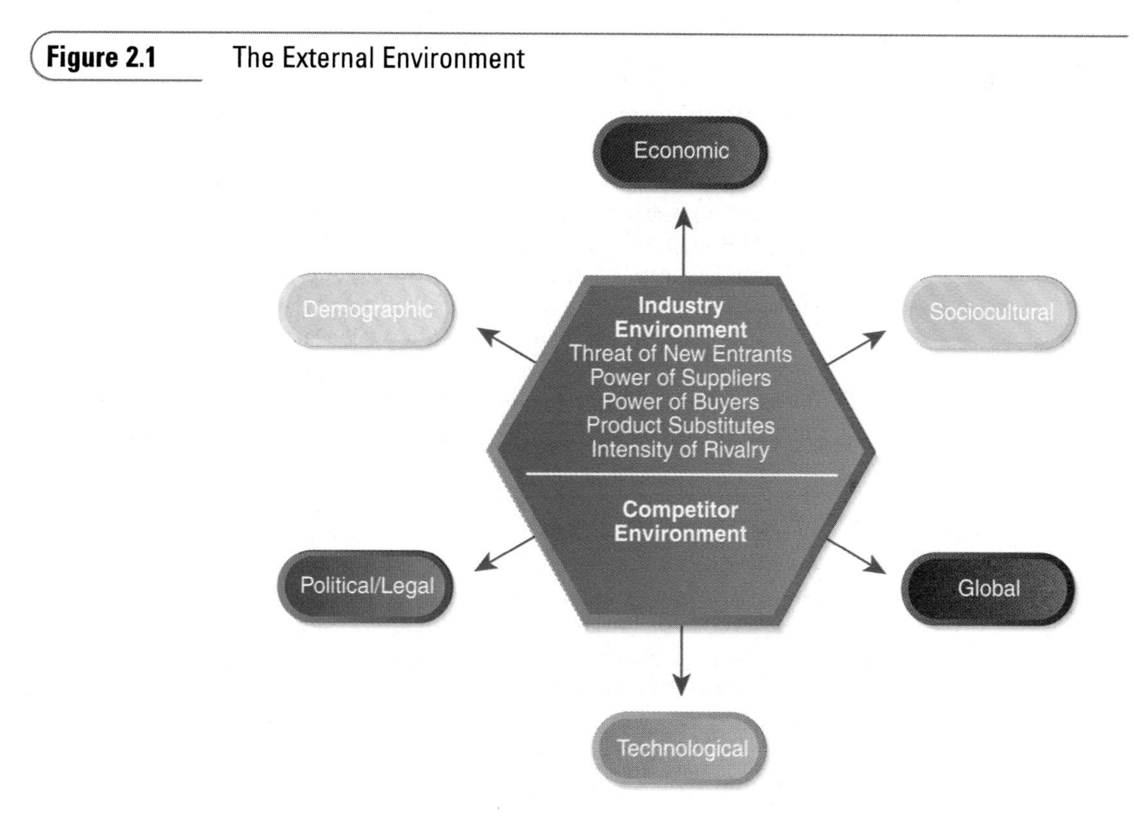

Table 2.1 The General Environment: Segments and Elements

Segment	Elements	
Demographic Segment	• Population size • Age structure • Geographic distribution	• Ethnic mix • Income distribution
Economic Segment	• Inflation rates • Interest rates • Trade deficits or surpluses • Budget deficits or surpluses	• Personal savings rate • Business savings rates • Gross domestic product
Political/Legal Segment	• Antitrust laws • Taxation laws • Deregulation philosophies	• Labor training laws • Educational philosophies and policies
Sociocultural Segment	• Women in the workforce • Workforce diversity • Attitudes about the quality of work life	• Concerns about the environment • Shifts in work and career preferences • Shifts in preferences regarding product and service characteristics
Technological Segment	• Product innovations • Applications of knowledge	• Focus of private and government-supported R&D expenditures • New communication technologies
Global Segment	• Important political events • Critical global markets	• Newly industrialized countries • Different cultural and institutional attributes

Firms cannot directly control the general environment's segments and elements. Accordingly, successful companies gather the information required to understand each segment and its implications for the selection and implementation of the appropriate strategies. For example, the terrorist attacks in the United States on September 11, 2001 surprised most businesses throughout the world. As explained in the Opening Case, this single set of events had substantial effects on the U.S. economy. Although individual firms were affected differently, none could control the U.S. economy. Instead, companies around the globe were challenged to understand the effects of this economy's decline on their current and future strategies.

The **industry environment** is the set of factors that directly influences a firm and its competitive actions and competitive responses: the threat of new entrants, the power of suppliers, the power of buyers, the threat of product substitutes, and the intensity of rivalry among competitors.

The **industry environment** is the set of factors that directly influences a firm and its competitive actions and competitive responses: the threat of new entrants, the power of suppliers, the power of buyers, the threat of product substitutes, and the intensity of rivalry among competitors. In total, the interactions among these five factors determine an industry's profit potential. The challenge is to locate a position within an industry where a firm can favorably influence those factors or where it can successfully defend against their influence. The greater a firm's capacity to favorably influence its industry environment, the greater is the likelihood that the firm will earn above-average returns.

How companies gather and interpret information about their competitors is called *competitor analysis.* Understanding the firm's competitor environment complements the insights provided by studying the general and industry environments.

Analysis of the general environment is focused on the future; analysis of the industry environment is focused on the factors and conditions influencing a firm's profitability within its industry; and analysis of competitors is focused on predicting the dynamics of competitors' actions, responses, and intentions. In combination, the results of the three analyses the firm uses to understand its external environment influence its strategic intent, strategic mission, and strategic actions. Although we discuss each analysis separately, performance improves when the firm integrates the insights provided by analyses of the general environment, the industry environment, and the competitor environment.

External Environmental Analysis

Most firms face external environments that are highly turbulent, complex, and global—conditions that make interpreting them increasingly difficult.[10] To cope with what are often ambiguous and incomplete environmental data and to increase their understanding of the general environment, firms engage in a process called external environmental analysis. The continuous process includes four activities: scanning, monitoring, forecasting, and assessing (see Table 2.2). Those analyzing the external environment should understand that completing this analysis is a difficult, yet significant, activity.[11]

An **opportunity** is a condition in the general environment that if exploited, helps a company achieve strategic competitiveness.

A **threat** is a condition in the general environment that may hinder a company's efforts to achieve strategic competitiveness.

An important objective of studying the general environment is identifying opportunities and threats. An **opportunity** is a condition in the general environment that if exploited, helps a company achieve strategic competitiveness. The fact that 1 billion of the world's total population of 6 billion has cheap access to a telephone is a huge opportunity for global telecommunications companies.[12] And General Electric believes that "e-business represents a revolution that may be the greatest opportunity for growth that [the] Company has ever seen."[13]

A **threat** is a condition in the general environment that may hinder a company's efforts to achieve strategic competitiveness.[14] The once revered firm Polaroid can attest to the seriousness of external threats. Polaroid was a leader in its industry and considered one of the top 50 firms in the United States, but filed for bankruptcy in 2001. When its competitors developed photographic equipment using digital technology, Polaroid was unprepared and never responded effectively. Mired in substantial debt, Polaroid was unable to reduce its costs to acceptable levels (and unable to repay its debt) and eventually had to declare bankruptcy.

Likewise, executives of Enron openly displayed contempt for regulators and consumer groups in its quest for fully deregulated energy markets. Jeffrey Skilling, former CEO of Enron stated, "We are on the side of angels. People want to have open, competitive markets." Unfortunately, Enron's shareholders and employees have been big losers in its meltdown when Enron filed for bankruptcy in 2001, the victim of the economy and reportedly questionable financing practices. Enron executives seemed

Table 2.2 Components of the External Environmental Analysis

Scanning	• Identifying early signals of environmental changes and trends
Monitoring	• Detecting meaning through ongoing observations of environmental changes and trends
Forecasting	• Developing projections of anticipated outcomes based on monitored changes and trends
Assessing	• Determining the timing and importance of environmental changes and trends for firms' strategies and their management

to overlook the reporting of significant losses in the firm's energy trading business and were subject to SEC and Congressional investigations.[15] As these examples indicate, opportunities suggest competitive *possibilities,* while threats are potential *constraints.*

Several sources can be used to analyze the general environment, including a wide variety of printed materials (such as trade publications, newspapers, business publications, and the results of academic research and public polls), trade shows, and suppliers, customers, and employees of public-sector organizations.[16] External network contacts can be particularly rich sources of information on the environment.[17] Much information can be obtained by people in the firm's "boundary-spanning" positions. Salespersons, purchasing managers, public relations directors, and customer service representatives, each of whom interacts with external constituents, are examples of individuals in boundary-spanning positions.[18]

RICHARD CARSON/REUTERS NEWMEDIA INC./CORBIS

Enron became the subject of an SEC investigation at the end of October 2001 after reporting that its third quarter earnings fell by $618 million. In December 2001 Enron entered bankruptcy proceedings, laid off 4000 employees in its Houston headquarters, and saw its share price, once as high as $83, fall to less than $1, and by spring 2002 was also being investigated by the U.S. Justice Department and the FBI.

Scanning

Scanning entails the study of all segments in the general environment. Through scanning, firms identify early signals of potential changes in the general environment and detect changes that are already under way.[19] When scanning, the firm often deals with ambiguous, incomplete, or unconnected data and information. Environmental scanning is critically important for firms competing in highly volatile environments.[20] In addition, scanning activities must be aligned with the organizational context; a scanning system designed for a volatile environment is inappropriate for a firm in a stable environment.[21]

Some analysts expect the pressure brought to bear by the early retirement trend on countries such as the United States, France, Germany, and Japan to be quite significant and challenging. Governments in these countries appear to be offering state-funded pensions to their future elderly populations—but the costs of those pensions cannot be met with the present taxes and social security contribution rates.[22] Firms selling financial planning services and options should analyze this trend to determine if it represents an opportunity for them to help governments find ways to meet their responsibilities.

The Internet provides multiple opportunities for scanning. For example, Amazon.com records significant information about individuals visiting its website, particularly if a purchase is made. Amazon then welcomes them by name when they visit the website again. The firm even sends messages to them about specials and new products similar to those purchased in previous visits. Additionally, many websites and advertisers on the Internet obtain information from those who visit their sites using files called "cookies." These files are saved to the visitors' hard drives, allowing customers to connect more quickly to the website, but also allowing the firm to solicit a variety of information about them. Because cookies are often placed without customers' knowledge, their use can be a questionable practice. A new privacy standard, Platform for Privacy Preferences, has been developed that provides more control over these "digital messengers" and allows users to block the cookies from their hard drives if desired.[23]

Monitoring

When *monitoring,* analysts observe environmental changes to see if an important trend is emerging from among those spotted by scanning.[24] Critical to successful monitoring is the firm's ability to detect meaning in different environmental events and trends. For example, the size of the middle class of African Americans continues to grow in the United States. With increasing wealth, this group of citizens is beginning to more aggressively pursue investment options.[25] Companies in the financial planning sector could monitor this change in the economic segment to determine the degree to which a competitively important trend and a business opportunity are emerging. By monitoring trends, firms can be prepared to introduce new goods and services at the appropriate time to take advantage of the opportunities these trends provide.[26]

Effective monitoring requires the firm to identify important stakeholders. Because the importance of different stakeholders can vary over a firm's life cycle, careful attention must be given to the firm's needs and its stakeholder groups over time.[27] Scanning and monitoring are particularly important when a firm competes in an industry with high technological uncertainty.[28] Scanning and monitoring not only can provide the firm with information, they also serve as a means of importing new knowledge about markets and how to successfully commercialize new technologies that the firm has developed.[29]

Forecasting

Scanning and monitoring are concerned with events and trends in the general environment at a point in time. When *forecasting,* analysts develop feasible projections of what might happen, and how quickly, as a result of the changes and trends detected through scanning and monitoring.[30] For example, analysts might forecast the time that will be required for a new technology to reach the marketplace, the length of time before different corporate training procedures are required to deal with anticipated changes in the composition of the workforce, or how much time will elapse before changes in governmental taxation policies affect consumers' purchasing patterns.

For example, Dow Chemical experienced performance declines between 1999 and 2001. The chemical industry in general has suffered, with the S&P Index down 20 percent during this time. However, Dow forecasted earnings to increase from $2.26 in 2001 to $5.00 in 2004. The positive forecast is partially based on completing its long awaited merger with Union Carbide (announced in 1999), although the U.S. Federal Trade Commission has not yet approved the merger. Part of Dow's forecast is based on increased business it anticipates because of better customer service (the online system it implemented in 2002 includes all customer information, allowing a sales representative to review a customer's account from anywhere in the world).[31]

Assessing

The objective of *assessing* is to determine the timing and significance of the effects of environmental changes and trends on the strategic management of the firm.[32] Through scanning, monitoring, and forecasting, analysts are able to understand the general environment. Going a step further, the intent of assessment is to specify the implications of that understanding for the organization. Without assessment, the firm is left with data that may be interesting but are of unknown competitive relevance.

For example, Ford, General Motors, and DaimlerChrysler sold an increased number of vehicles in the U.S. automobile market in 2001. However, in past years, all three firms lost market share in vehicles to competitors such as Honda, Toyota, Volkswagen, Audi, and BMW. The primary reason for the U.S. firms' increase in sales levels in 2001 was their offers to sell the vehicles at zero percent interest on loans. Without these generous loans, high volume sales are unlikely to persist. Thus, firms must assess the reasons for sales relative to competitors to be able to accurately forecast future sales.

Segments of the General Environment

The general environment is composed of segments (and their individual elements) that are external to the firm (see Table 2.1). Although the degree of impact varies, these environmental segments affect each industry and its firms. The challenge to the firm is to scan, monitor, forecast, and assess those elements in each segment that are of the greatest importance. Resulting from these efforts should be a recognition of environmental changes, trends, opportunities, and threats. Opportunities are then matched with a firm's core competencies (the matching process is discussed further in Chapter 3).

The Demographic Segment

The **demographic segment** is concerned with a population's size, age structure, geographic distribution, ethnic mix, and income distribution.

The **demographic segment** is concerned with a population's size, age structure, geographic distribution, ethnic mix, and income distribution.[33] Demographic segments are analyzed on a global basis because of their potential effects across countries' borders and because many firms compete in global markets.

Population Size

Before the end of 1999, the world's population grew to 6 billion, from 5 billion in 1987. Combined, China and India accounted for one-third of the 6 billion. Experts speculate that the population might stabilize at 10 billion after 2200 if the deceleration in the rate of increase in the world's head count continues. By 2050, India (with over 1.5 billion people projected) and China (with just under 1.5 billion people projected) are expected to be the most populous countries.[34]

Observing demographic changes in populations highlights the importance of this environmental segment. For example, some advanced nations have a negative population growth, after discounting the effects of immigration. In some countries, including the United States and several European nations, couples are averaging fewer than two children. This birthrate will produce a loss of population over time (even with the population living longer on average).[35] However, some believe that a baby boom will occur in the United States during the first 12 years of the 21st century and that by 2012, the annual number of births could exceed 4.3 million. Such a birthrate in the United States would equal the all-time high that was set in 1957.[36] These projections suggest major 21st-century challenges and business opportunities.

Age Structure

In some countries, the population's average age is increasing. In the United States, for example, the percentage of the population aged 65 and older increased less in the 1990s than the population less than 65 years of age. However, in the period 2010–2020, the population of 65 and older is projected to grow by 35.3 percent.[37] Contributing to this growth are increasing life expectancies. This trend may suggest numerous opportunities for firms to develop goods and services to meet the needs of an increasingly older population. For example, GlaxoSmithKline has created a program for low-income elderly people without prescription drug coverage. The program provides drugs to these individuals at a 25 percent reduction in price. In so doing, the firm is able to increase its sales and provide an important service to a population who might not be able to afford the drugs otherwise.[38]

It has been projected that up to one-half of the females and one-third of the males born at the end of the 1990s in developed countries could live to be 100 years old, with some of them possibly living to be 200 or more.[39] Also, the odds that a U.S. baby boomer (a person born between the years 1946 and 1964) will reach age 90 are now one in nine.[40] If these life spans become a reality, a host of interesting business opportunities and societal issues will emerge. For example, the effect on individuals' pension plans will be significant and will create potential opportunities for financial institutions, as well as possible threats to government-sponsored retirement and health plans.[41]

Geographic Distribution

For decades, the U.S. population has been shifting from the north and east to the west and south. Similarly, the trend of relocating from metropolitan to non-metropolitan areas continues and may well accelerate with the terrorist attacks in New York City and Washington, D.C. These trends are changing local and state governments' tax bases. In turn, business firms' decisions regarding location are influenced by the degree of support different taxing agencies offer.

The geographic distribution of populations throughout the world is also affected by the capabilities resulting from advances in communications technology. Through computer technologies, for example, people can remain in their homes, communicating with others in remote locations to complete their work.

Ethnic Mix

The ethnic mix of countries' populations continues to change. Within the United States, the ethnicity of states and their cities varies significantly. For firms, the challenge is to be sensitive to these changes. Through careful study, companies can develop and market products that satisfy the unique needs of different ethnic groups.

Changes in the ethnic mix also affect a workforce's composition. In the United States, for example, the population and labor force will continue to diversify, as immigration accounts for a sizable part of growth. Projections are that the Hispanic and Asian population shares will increase from 14 percent in 1995 to 19 percent in 2020. By 2006, it is expected that (1) 72.7 percent of the U.S. labor force will be white non-Hispanic (down from 75.3 percent in 1996), (2) 11.7 percent will be Hispanic (compared with 9.5 percent in 1996), (3) 11.6 percent will be African-American (up from 11.3 percent in 1996), and (4) 5.4 percent will be Asian (up from 4.3 percent in 1996). By 2020, white non-Hispanic workers will make up only 68 percent of the work force.[42]

As with the U.S. labor force, other countries also are witnessing a trend toward an older workforce. By 2030, the proportion of the total labor force of 45- to 59-year-olds of countries in the Organisation for Economic Co-Operation and Development (industrialized countries) is projected to increase from 25.6 to 31.8 percent; the share of workers aged 60 and over is expected to increase from 4.7 to 7.8 percent. Because a labor force can be critical to competitive success, firms across the globe, including those competing in OECD countries, must learn to work effectively with labor forces that are becoming more diverse and older.[43]

Hispanic Americans are part of an increasingly diverse workforce in the United States. According to a Census Bureau official, "The nation is much more diverse in the year 2000 than it was in 1990, and that diversity is much more complex than we've ever measured before." Hispanic Americans are the fastest growing population group in the United States, with a 58 percent increase from 1990 to 2000, and constitute 12.5 percent of the U.S. population. The group is a significant presence in almost every state, often drawn by employment opportunities.

MICHAEL NEWMAN/PHOTOEDIT

Workforce diversity is also a sociocultural issue. Effective management of a culturally diverse workforce can produce a competitive advantage. For example, heterogeneous work teams have been shown to produce more effective strategic analyses, more creativity and innovation, and higher quality decisions than homogeneous work teams.[44] However, evidence also suggests that diverse work teams are difficult to manage to achieve these outcomes.[45]

Income Distribution

Understanding how income is distributed within and across populations informs firms of different groups' purchasing power and discretionary income. Studies of income distributions suggest that although living standards have improved over time, variations exist within and between nations.[46] Of interest to firms are the average incomes of households and individuals. For instance, the increase in dual-career couples has had a notable effect on average incomes. Although real income has been declining in general, the income of dual-career couples has increased. These figures yield strategically relevant information for firms.

The Economic Segment

The health of a nation's economy affects individual firms and industries. Because of this, companies study the economic environment to identify changes, trends, and their strategic implications.

The **economic environment** refers to the nature and direction of the economy in which a firm competes or may compete.

The **economic environment** refers to the nature and direction of the economy in which a firm competes or may compete.[47] Because nations are interconnected as a result of the global economy, firms must scan, monitor, forecast, and assess the health of economies outside their host nation. For example, many nations throughout the world are affected by the U.S. economy.

The U.S. economy declined into a recession in 2001 that extended into 2002 despite efforts to revive it by the U.S. government. In the summer of 2001, Alan Greenspan, Chairman of the U.S. Federal Reserve, observed that the asset quality of U.S. banks was eroding. Bank loans were becoming riskier because of the economic recession. But, Greenspan cautioned banks not to tighten loan requirements, fearing it would worsen the economy. In the same time period, it was announced that advertising revenue had fallen for most publishers. For example, advertising pages fell by 47.2 percent at *Fast Company* and by 44.3 percent at *Inc* in the first six months of 2001.[48] The economy looked to be on the mend by mid-2002.

DaimlerChrysler's CEO Jurgen E. Schrempp is a strong proponent of completing a transatlantic integration between Europe and North America. Schrempp supports largely unrestricted trade and believes that economic integration between Europe and North America is logical in that "Europe and the United States each account for close to 20 percent of the other's trade in goods while services account for more than 38 percent of bilateral trade." Principles developed by the Transatlantic Business Dialogue (a group of businesspersons and politicians) could support an integration effort. The principles include the removal of all trade barriers and differing regulatory controls and the acceptance of a product in all parts of the transatlantic marketplace once it has been approved.[49] Creating truly "borderless commerce" permitting free trade among nations is a significant challenge, however, because of differing regulations for trade between separate countries.

While bilateral trade can enrich the economies of the countries involved, it also makes each country more vulnerable to negative events. For example, the September 11, 2001 terrorist attacks in the United States have had more than a $100 billion negative effect on the U.S. economy. As a result, the European Union (E.U.) also suffered negative economic effects because of the reduction in bilateral trade between the U.S. and the E.U.[50]

As our discussion of the economic segment suggests, economic issues are intertwined closely with the realities of the external environment's political/legal segment.

The **political/legal segment** is the arena in which organizations and interest groups compete for attention, resources, and a voice of overseeing the body of laws and regulations guiding the interactions among nations.

The Political/Legal Segment

The **political/legal segment** is the arena in which organizations and interest groups compete for attention, resources, and a voice of overseeing the body of laws and regulations guiding the interactions among nations.[51] Essentially, this segment represents how organizations try to influence government and how governments influence them. Constantly changing, the segment influences the nature of competition (see Table 2.1).

Firms must carefully analyze a new political administration's business-related policies and philosophies. Antitrust laws, taxation laws, industries chosen for deregulation, labor training laws, and the degree of commitment to educational institutions are areas in which an administration's policies can affect the operations and profitability of industries and individual firms. Often, firms develop a political strategy to influence governmental policies and actions that might affect them. The effects of global governmental policies on a firm's competitive position increase the importance of forming an effective political strategy.[52]

Business firms across the globe today confront an interesting array of political/legal questions and issues. For example, the debate continues over trade policies. Some believe that a nation should erect trade barriers to protect products manufactured by its companies. Others argue that free trade across nations serves the best interests of individual countries and their citizens. The International Monetary Fund (IMF) classifies trade barriers as restrictive when tariffs total at least 25 percent of a product's price. At the other extreme, the IMF stipulates that a nation has open trade when its tariffs are between 0 and 9 percent. To foster trade, New Zealand initially cut its tariffs from 16 to 8.5 percent and then to 3 percent in 2000. Colombia reduced its tariffs to less than 12 percent. The IMF classifies this percentage as "relatively open."[53] While controversial, a number of countries (including the United States, nations in the European Union, Japan, Australia, Canada, Chile, Singapore, and Mexico) are working together to reduce or eventually eliminate trade barriers.

An interesting debate occurring in the United States concerns the regulation of e-commerce. In part, laws regulating e-commerce attempt to prevent fraud, violations of privacy, and poor service. Some think that governmental policies should also be developed to regulate Internet gambling.[54] Another challenging Internet issue being debated by U.S. government officials is taxation on sales made using Internet sites. A concern of all parties is to develop government policies that will not stifle the legitimate growth of e-commerce.[55] In 2001, the U.S. federal government passed legislation extending the tax-free status of sales over the Internet for several more years. How government agencies can affect business is discussed in the Strategic Focus on page 50.

The Strategic Focus explains some of the effects that governments have on how business is conducted. The regulations related to pharmaceuticals and telecommunications, along with the approval or disapproval of major acquisitions, shows the power of government entities. This power also suggests how important it is for firms to have a political strategy.

The Sociocultural Segment

The **sociocultural segment** is concerned with a society's attitudes and cultural values.

The **sociocultural segment** is concerned with a society's attitudes and cultural values. Because attitudes and values form the cornerstone of a society, they often drive demographic, economic, political/legal, and technological conditions and changes.

Sociocultural segments differ across countries. For example, in the United States, 14 percent of the nation's GDP is spent on health care. This is the highest percentage of any OECD country. Germany allocates 10.4 percent of GDP to health care, while in Switzerland the percentage is 10.2.[56] Countries' citizens have different attitudes about retirement savings as well. In Italy, just 9 percent of the citizenry say that they are saving primarily for retirement, while the percentages are 18 percent in Germany and 48 percent in the United States.[57] Attitudes regarding saving for retirement affect a nation's economic and political/legal segments.

Strategic Focus

Government Can Have a Large Effect on Businesses

Governmental entities can have major effects on businesses. Essentially, government establishes the rules by which business is conducted within the country's boundaries or geographic region it governs. Federal government regulations generally have the most profound effects on business.

Government regulations usually cover many industries and areas of conducting business. For example, the U.S. Food and Drug Administration (FDA) must approve all new drugs sold in the United States. In 2001 the FDA disapproved a new injectable pain relief medicine developed by Pharmacia, asking for additional data before it would consider approving the drug. Similarly, Pfizer received an unfavorable ruling on a new diabetes drug it developed. Likewise, the U.S. Federal Communications Commission must license all telecommunications operators; the Federal Trade Commission and the Justice Department oversee potential mergers and acquisitions.

Regulations are a global phenomenon affecting firms doing business in a country even though their home base may be located in another country. As an example, the European Union's antitrust officials from several different Commissions disapproved the acquisition of Honeywell by GE. Even though the home bases of both firms are in the United States, they have significant operations in Europe. Alternatively, the U.S. Justice Department argued that the proposed alliance between American Airlines (a U.S.-based firm) and British Airways (a U.K.-based firm), be rejected unless they agreed to sell some of their landing and takeoff slots at specific airports to enhance competition on routes between London and the United States.

Firms may also be subject to regulations by more than one government group within a country. For example, Enron had developed a major political strategy designed to encourage deregulation of energy markets. However, the firm's financial problems that became public in 2001 have invited substantial scrutiny and investigations by several government entities to determine if Enron's executives were involved in any wrongdoing. For example, the U.S. Justice Department, the Securities and Exchange Commission, and the U.S. Congress all initiated investigations of Enron activities. The Justice Department's pursuit of the antitrust suit against Microsoft represents another example of the effects government can have on business.

Not all government activity involves controls and regulations. For example, the U.S. Congress passed legislation providing $15 billion of aid for the airlines to reduce the negative effects of the events of September 11, 2001. This package includes $5 billion of direct cash payments and $10 billion of loan guarantees. In some cases, these actions may have allowed some airlines to survive. Governments may take other positive actions, such as reducing taxes, providing advice and support for firms to enter international markets, and promoting tourism, among others.

SOURCES: 2001, Pfizer gets unfavorable ruling in case related to complication of diabetes drug, *The Wall Street Journal Interactive,* http://interactive.wsj.com, December 21; S. Labaton, 2001, U.S. criticizes trans-Atlantic air alliance, *The New York Times,* http://www.nytimes.com, December 18; D. Ackman, 2001, Enron on the Hill, *Forbes,* http://www.forbes.com, December 14; S. Kirchgaessner, 2001, FCC and wireless carriers settle over licences, *Financial Times,* http://www.ft.com, October, 27; D. MacGregor, 2001, Governments act to avert airline industry crisis, *Financial Times,* http://www.ft.com, September, 22; S. Lohr, 2001, States press U.S. to take tough stand on Microsoft, *The New York Times,* http://www.nytimes.com, September 8; B. M. Mantz, 2001, FDA deems Pharmacia pain medication 'not approvable,' seeks additional data, *The Wall Street Journal Interactive,* http://interactive.wsj.com, July 15; P. Shishkin & L. Cohen, 2001, EU antitrust officials recommend blocking GE's Honeywell acquisition, *The Wall Street Journal Interactive,* http://interactive.wsj.com, June 19.

In the United States, boundaries between work and home are becoming blurred, as employees' workweeks continue to be stretched, perhaps because a strong Protestant work ethic is a part of the U.S. culture. Describing a culture's effect on a society, columnist George Will suggested that it is vital for people to understand that a nation's culture has a primary effect on its social character and health.[58] Thus, companies must understand the implications of a society's attitudes and its cultural values to offer products that meet consumers' needs.

A significant trend in many countries is increased workforce diversity. The number of female workers is an important indicator of this, and women are a valuable source of highly productive employees. Some argue, for example, that "educated hard-working women double the talent pool in the U.S. and give the nation a big competitive advantage over countries that deny women full participation in their economies."[59] However, women also comprise an increasing percentage of employees across multiple global workforces. In the United States, women now account for approximately 47 percent of the workforce. In Sweden, they account for roughly 52 percent; in Japan, 44 percent; in France, 40 percent; in Germany, 41 percent; and in Mexico, 37 percent. In the United States, women hold 43 percent of the managerial jobs. In Sweden, women hold 17 percent of managerial positions, while in Japan, the figure is only 9.4 percent.[60]

Because of equal pay and equal opportunity legislation in many countries, relative pay for women is increasing. However, pay differentials between men and women still exist. Among Western European countries, the pay gap between men and women is greatest in the United Kingdom, where men earn 34 percent more than women do, and lowest in Sweden, where a 17 percent gap exists.[61]

An increasing number of women are also starting and managing their own businesses. For example, the U.S. Census Bureau reports that approximately 5.4 million businesses, with $819 billion in annual sales, are owned by women. The National Foundation for Women Business Owners suggests that these figures substantially understate the number of women-owned businesses. The foundation claims that over 9 million businesses were started by women in 2000. Approximately 55 percent of women-owned businesses are in services, with the second largest group (about 18 percent) in some form of retailing. The number of new businesses started by women continues to increase, and thus women own a larger percentage of the total number of businesses.[62]

The growing gender, ethnic, and cultural diversity in the workforce creates challenges and opportunities,[63] including those related to combining the best of both men's and women's traditional leadership styles for a firm's benefit and identifying ways to facilitate all employees' contributions to their firms. Some companies provide training to nurture women's and ethnic minorities' leadership potential. Changes in organizational structure and management practices often are required to eliminate subtle barriers that may exist. Learning to manage diversity in the domestic workforce can increase a firm's effectiveness in managing a globally diverse workforce, as the firm acquires more international operations.

Another manifestation of changing attitudes toward work is the continuing growth of contingency workers (part-time, temporary, and contract employees) throughout the global economy. This trend is significant in several parts of the world, including Canada, Japan, Latin America, Western Europe, and the United States. The fastest growing group of contingency workers is in the technical and professional area. Contributing to this growth are corporate restructurings and a breakdown of lifetime employment practices. Because of tight labor markets for technical and professional workers, agencies providing these contingency workers to companies are offering multiple inducements to those they hire.

Another major sociocultural trend is the continued growth of suburban communities in the United States and abroad. The increasing number of people living in the suburbs has a number of effects. For example, because of the resulting often-longer commute times to urban businesses, there is pressure for better transportation systems and super highway systems (e.g., outer beltways to serve the suburban communities). On the other hand, some businesses are locating in the suburbs closer to their employees. Suburban growth also has an effect on the number of electronic telecommuters, which is expected to increase rapidly in the 21st century. This work-style option is feasible because of changes in the technological segment, including the Internet's rapid growth and evolution.[64]

The Technological Segment

The **technological segment** includes the institutions and activities involved with creating new knowledge and translating that knowledge into new outputs, products, processes, and materials.

Pervasive and diversified in scope, technological changes affect many parts of societies. These effects occur primarily through new products, processes, and materials. The **technological segment** includes the institutions and activities involved with creating new knowledge and translating that knowledge into new outputs, products, processes, and materials.

Given the rapid pace of technological change, it is vital for firms to thoroughly study the technological segment. The importance of these efforts is suggested by the finding that early adopters of new technology often achieve higher market shares and earn higher returns. Thus, executives must verify that their firm is continuously scanning the external environment to identify potential substitutes for technologies that are in current use, as well as to spot newly emerging technologies from which their firm could derive competitive advantage.[65]

Numerous surveys suggest that executives are aware of the potential of a major technological development—the Internet. A survey completed by Booz Allen & Hamilton in partnership with *The Economist* revealed that (1) 92 percent of executives who participated in the survey believed that the Internet would continue to reshape their companies' markets, (2) 61 percent thought that effective use of the Internet would facilitate efforts to achieve their firms' strategic goals, and (3) 30 percent noted that their competitive strategies had already been altered because of the Internet's influence.[66]

The value of the Internet is shown in its use by Staples Inc., the office supply superstores. Staples invested $250 million to create Staples.com to continue its market share leadership in the industry. The firm's online sales reached approximately $1 billion by 2001, up from $99 million in 1999. This accounts for 10 percent of the company's total annual sales. Thomas Steinberg, founder and CEO of Staples, forecasted that sales on the Internet would reach $50 billion annually and represent 25 percent of the office supply industry's total sales in the next few years.[67]

Among its other valuable uses, the Internet is an excellent source of data and information for a firm to use to understand its external environment. Access to experts on topics from chemical engineering to semiconductor manufacturing, to the Library of Congress, and even to satellite photographs is available through the Internet. Other information available through this technology includes Security and Exchange Commission (SEC) filings, Commerce Department data, information from the Bureau of the Census, new patent filings, and stock market updates.

Another use of Internet technology is conducting business transactions between companies, as well as between a company and its customers. According to Dell Computer Corporation's CEO Michael Dell, the Internet also has great potential as a business-organization system. Dell uses this technology to reduce its paperwork flow, to more efficiently schedule its payments, and to coordinate its inventories. Dell accomplishes these tasks by linking personal computers with network servers, which the firm's CEO believes have the potential to revolutionize business processes "in a

A. RAMEY/PHOTOEDIT

Staples Inc., the second-largest office supply firm after Office Depot, showed a profit for 2001 and expects to improve upon it with plans to reduce its prototype to 20,000 square feet, decrease square footage growth without sacrificing convenience, and benefit from smaller investment in fixtures and inventory. The firm is also offering software tools to their customers to integrate their e-procurement systems with Staples for office supplies purchases and will add 200 people to its special sales force to increase catalog and Internet orders at Staples.com.

way that blurs traditional boundaries between supplier and manufacturer, and manufacturer and customer. This will eliminate paper-based functions, flatten organization hierarchies, and shrink time and distance to a degree not possible before."[68] Thus, a competitive advantage may accrue to the company that derives full value from the Internet in terms of both e-commerce activities and transactions taken to process the firm's workflow.

While the Internet was a significant technological advance providing substantial power to companies utilizing its potential, wireless communication technology is predicted to be the next critical technological opportunity. By 2003, handheld devices and other wireless communications equipment will be used to access a variety of network-based services. The use of handheld computers with wireless network connectivity, web-enabled mobile phone handsets, and other emerging platforms (i.e., consumer Internet access devices) is expected to increase substantially, soon becoming the dominant form of communication and commerce.[69]

Clearly, the Internet and wireless forms of communications are important technological developments for many reasons. One reason for their importance, however, is that they facilitate the diffusion of other technology and knowledge critical for achieving and maintaining a competitive advantage.[70] Technological knowledge is particularly important. Certainly on a global scale, the technological opportunities and threats in the general environment have an effect on whether firms obtain new technology from external sources (such as licensing and acquisition) or develop it internally.

The Global Segment

The **global segment** includes relevant new global markets, existing markets that are changing, important international political events, and critical cultural and institutional characteristics of global markets.

The **global segment** includes relevant new global markets, existing markets that are changing, important international political events, and critical cultural and institutional characteristics of global markets.[71] Globalization of business markets creates both opportunities and challenges for firms. For example, firms can identify and enter valuable new global markets. Many global markets (such as those in some South American nations and in South Korea and Taiwan) are becoming borderless and integrated.[72] In addition to contemplating opportunities, firms should recognize potential threats in these markets as well. For instance, companies with home bases in Europe and North America may be subject to terrorist threats in certain parts of the world (such as Middle Eastern regions and parts of Asia).

China presents many opportunities and some threats for international firms. Creating additional opportunities is China's recent admission to the World Trade Organization (WTO). A Geneva-based organization, the WTO establishes rules for global trade. China's membership in this organization suggests the possibility of increasing and less-restricted participation by the country in the global economy.[73] In return for gaining entry to the WTO, China agreed to reduce trade barriers in multiple industries, including telecommunications, banking, automobiles, movies, and professional

ANDREW WONG/AFP/CORBIS

Star TV chairman and CEO James Murdoch (left), China Central Television chairman Zhao Huayong (center), and Guangdong Cable TV Networks chairman Wang Changli (right) toast their December 2001 agreement for a new 24-hour Mandarin language entertainment channel in southern China.

services (for example, the services of lawyers, physicians, and accountants). These reduced barriers are likely part of the reason that Rupert Murdoch realized a major goal of entering the Chinese market. In 2001, Star TV (Murdoch's company), News Corporation, and Chinese television authorities announced an agreement to launch a 24-hour entertainment channel for the wealthy Guangzhou and Zhaoqing cities. The purpose of the channel is to establish a relationship and a track record with the hope of expanding it to other cities and regions of China, a huge potential market.[74]

Moving into international markets extends a firm's reach and potential. Toyota receives almost 50 percent of its total sales revenue from outside Japan, its home country. Over 60 percent of McDonald's sales revenues and almost 98 percent of Nokia's sales revenues are from outside their home countries.[75] Because the opportunity is coupled with uncertainty, some view entering new international markets to be entrepreneurial.[76] Firms can increase the opportunity to sell innovations by entering international markets. The larger total market increases the probability that the firm will earn a return on its innovations. Certainly, firms entering new markets can diffuse new knowledge they have created and learn from the new markets as well.[77]

Firms should recognize the different sociocultural and institutional attributes of global markets. Companies competing in South Korea, for example, must understand the value placed on hierarchical order, formality, and self-control, as well as on duty rather than rights. Furthermore, Korean ideology emphasizes communitarianism, a characteristic of many Asian countries. Korea's approach differs from those of Japan and China, however, in that it focuses on *Inhwa,* or harmony. Inhwa is based on a respect of hierarchical relationships and obedience to authority. Alternatively, the approach in China stresses *Guanxi*—personal relationships or good connections, while in Japan, the focus is on *Wa,* or group harmony and social cohesion.[78] The institutional context of Korea suggests a major emphasis on centralized planning by the government. Indeed, the emphasis placed on growth by many South Korean firms is the result of a government policy to promote economic growth.[79]

Firms based in other countries that compete in these markets can learn from them. For example, the cultural characteristics above suggest the value of relationships. In particular, Guanxi communicates social capital's importance when doing business in China.[80] But, social capital is important for success in most markets around the world.[81]

Global markets offer firms more opportunities to obtain the resources needed for success. For example, the Kuwait Investment Authority is the second largest shareholder of DaimlerChrysler. Additionally, Global Crossing sought financial assistance from potential investors in Europe and Asia. But, it was to no avail as Global Crossing, citing overcapacity in the telecommunications network market as the primary cause of its problems, filed for bankruptcy in 2001.[82] Alternatively, globalization can be threatening. In particular, companies in emerging market countries may be vulnerable to larger, more resource-rich, and more effective competitors from developed markets.

Additionally, there are risks in global markets. A few years ago, Argentina's market was full of promise, but in 2001, Argentina experienced a financial crisis that placed it on the brink of bankruptcy.[83] Thus, the global segment of the general environment is quite important for most firms. As a result, it is necessary to have a top management team with the experience, knowledge, and sensitivity that are necessary to effectively analyze this segment of the environment.[84]

A key objective of analyzing the general environment is identifying anticipated changes and trends among external elements. With a focus on the future, the analysis of the general environment allows firms to identify opportunities and threats. Also critical to a firm's future operations is an understanding of its industry environment and its competitors; these issues are considered next.

Industry Environment Analysis

An **industry** is a group of firms producing products that are close substitutes.

An **industry** is a group of firms producing products that are close substitutes. In the course of competition, these firms influence one another. Typically, industries include a rich mix of competitive strategies that companies use in pursuing strategic competitiveness and above-average returns. In part, these strategies are chosen because of the influence of an industry's characteristics.[85] Some believed that technology-based industries in which e-commerce is a dominant means of competing differ from their more traditional predecessors and that free exchange of information improved the competitiveness of the industries. However, while there were features of the e-commerce and information technology industries that differed from more traditional industries, the economic recession of 2001 and early 2002 showed the vulnerability of these industries as discussed in the Strategic Focus on page 56.

Compared to the general environment, the industry environment has a more direct effect on the firm's strategic competitiveness and above-average returns, as exemplified in the following Strategic Focus. The intensity of industry competition and an industry's profit potential (as measured by the long-run return on invested capital) are a function of five forces of competition: the threats posed by new entrants, the power of suppliers, the power of buyers, product substitutes, and the intensity of rivalry among competitors (see Figure 2.2).

The five forces model of competition expands the arena for competitive analysis. Historically when studying the competitive environment, firms concentrated on companies with which they competed directly. However, firms must search more broadly to identify current and potential competitors by identifying potential customers as well as the firms serving them. Competing for the same customers and thus being influenced by how customers value location and firm capabilities in their decisions is referred to as the market microstructure.[86] Understanding this area is particularly important, because in recent years industry boundaries have become blurred. For example, in the electrical utilities industry, cogenerators (firms that also produce power) are competing with regional utility companies. Moreover, telecommunications companies now compete with broadcasters, software manufacturers provide personal financial services, airlines sell mutual funds, and automakers sell insurance and provide financing.[87] In addition to focusing on customers rather than specific industry boundaries to define markets, geographic boundaries are also relevant. Research suggests that different geographic markets for the same product can have considerably different competitive conditions.[88]

The five forces model recognizes that suppliers can become a firm's competitors (by integrating forward), as can buyers (by integrating backward). Several firms have integrated forward in the pharmaceutical industry by acquiring distributors or wholesalers. In addition, firms choosing to enter a new market and those producing products that are adequate substitutes for existing products can become competitors of a company.

Strategic Focus

Three Industries with Different Experiences in Economic Recession

Firms in the steel industry have experienced substantial rivalry in recent years, even during good economic times. Thus, the steel industry grappled with significant problems in the 2001–2002 economic recession. In this global industry, firms from Asia, Europe, and North America compete against one another. Since 1998, 12 companies have closed their doors and 17 more filed for bankruptcy. LTV, one of the largest steel manufacturers in the United States operated in bankruptcy during 2000–2001. It ceased operations in 2002 and sold its remaining assets. The firm had suffered from more efficient foreign competitors and competition from U.S. mini-mills and could not survive. In an attempt to save large steel manufacturing firms in several countries, the economically most powerful countries agreed to incrementally reduce by 10 percent the output of steel worldwide by 2010. This decision was too late to save LTV but may affect others competing in this struggling industry.

The information technology (IT) industry also has suffered with the economic recession. Actually, the IT industry has multiple segments. While many companies in the IT industry have ceased to operate and others have filed for bankruptcy with hopes of surviving, this industry is quite different than the steel industry. As with others in recent years, the IT industry is consolidating. However, it also has a bright future. Oracle's CEO, Larry Ellison, argues that the industry is maturing but others disagree. Former stars Cisco and Sun Microsystems have retreated but are preparing for improved markets. In fact, GE continued to spend heavily on its IT infrastructure when its competitors were severely reducing their IT spending. GE's intent was to be ahead of its competition as the economy improved. In particular, the firms investing in wireless communications technology may be the future winners. For example, 80 percent of the cell phones sold in 2001 contained Texas Instruments' DSP or analog chip.

For reasons beyond the U.S. or world economy, the U.S. defense industry is again thriving. The industry has many fewer firms than a decade ago. Following a long period of consolidation after the Cold War ended with the crumbling of the Berlin Wall, a few mostly large firms remain active in the industry. Its economic health is due partly to the Bush administration's renewed emphasis on military preparedness, partly to major world events such as September 11, 2001, and partly to unrest in the Middle East. Lockheed Martin, a leader in the industry, won a major $200 billion contract for a new jet fighter plane. Boeing and Lockheed each received $660 million to design and build prototypes of the plane, and Lockheed won the competition for the contract.

SOURCES: R. D. Atlas, 2001, LTV seems on the verge of a shutdown, *The New York Times,* http://www.nytimes.com, December 19; R. G. Matthews, 2001, World steelmakers agree to cut levels, but amount is less than U.S.'s request, *The Wall Street Journal Interactive,* http://interactive.wsj.com, December 19; R. Waters, 2001, Oracle Chief dispels fantasy of young IT sector, *Financial Times,* http://www.ft.com, December 14; 2001, Lockheed wins $200 billion contract from Pentagon to build strike fighters, *The Wall Street Journal Interactive,* http://interactive.wsj.com, October 26; E. Alden, 2001, Lockheed-Martin wins $200 billion fighter contract, *Financial Times,* http://www.ft.com, October 26; S. Lohr, 2001, After the fall, a tech star stays scrappy, *The New York Times,* http://www.nytimes.com, September 30; E. Williams, 2001, Mixed signals, *Forbes,* May 28, 80–89; D. Lyons, 2001, Lion in winter, *Forbes,* April 30, 68–70.

Threat of New Entrants

Evidence suggests that companies often find it difficult to identify new competitors.[89] Identifying new entrants is important because they can threaten the market share of existing competitors. One reason new entrants pose such a threat is that they bring additional production capacity. Unless the demand for a good or service is increasing, additional capacity holds consumers' costs down, resulting in less revenue and lower returns for competing firms. Often, new entrants have a keen interest in gaining a large market share. As a result, new competitors may force existing firms to be more effective and efficient and to learn how to compete on new dimensions (for example, using an Internet-based distribution channel).

The likelihood that firms will enter an industry is a function of two factors: barriers to entry and the retaliation expected from current industry participants. Entry barriers make it difficult for new firms to enter an industry and often place them at a competitive disadvantage even when they are able to enter. As such, high entry barriers increase the returns for existing firms in the industry.[90]

Barriers to Entry

Existing competitors try to develop barriers to entry. In contrast, potential entrants seek markets in which the entry barriers are relatively insignificant. The absence of entry barriers increases the probability that a new entrant can operate profitably. There are several kinds of potentially significant entry barriers.

Economies of Scale. *Economies of scale* are "the marginal improvements in efficiency that a firm experiences as it incrementally increases its size."[91] Therefore, as the quantity of a product produced during a given period increases, the cost of manufacturing each unit declines. Economies of scale can be developed in most business functions, such as marketing, manufacturing, research and development, and purchasing. Increasing economies of scale enhances a firm's flexibility. For example, a firm may choose to reduce its price and capture a greater share of the market. Alternatively, it may keep its price constant to increase profits. In so doing, it likely will increase its free cash flow that is helpful in times of recession, as Radio Shack was able to do in 2001.[92]

New entrants face a dilemma when confronting current competitors' scale economies. Small-scale entry places them at a cost disadvantage. Alternatively, large-scale entry, in which the new entrant manufactures large volumes of a product to gain economies of scale, risks strong competitive retaliation.

Figure 2.2 The Five Forces of Competition Model

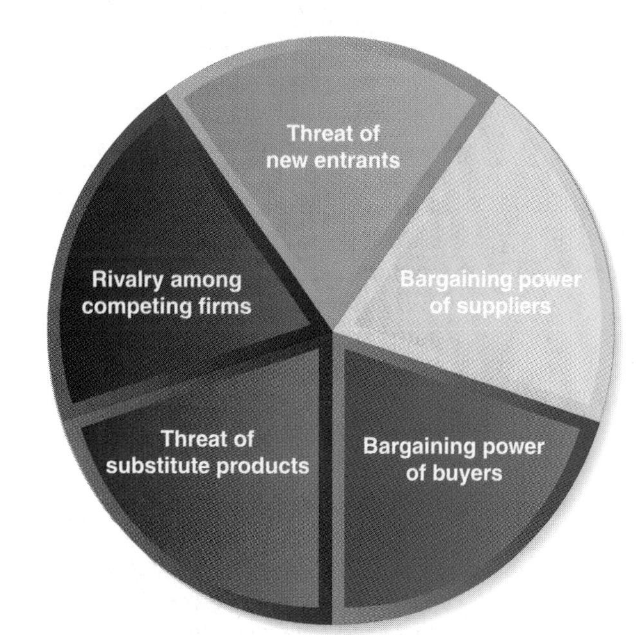

Also important for the firm to understand are instances of current competitive realities that reduce the ability of economies of scale to create an entry barrier. Many companies now customize their products for large numbers of small customer groups. Customized products are not manufactured in the volumes necessary to achieve economies of scale. Customization is made possible by new flexible manufacturing systems (this point is discussed further in Chapter 4). In fact, the new manufacturing technology facilitated by advanced computerization has allowed the development of mass customization in some industries. Mass customized products can be individualized to the customer in a very short time, often within a day. Mass customization is becoming increasingly common in manufacturing products.[93] Companies manufacturing customized products learn how to respond quickly to customers' desires rather than developing scale economies.

Product Differentiation. Over time, customers may come to believe that a firm's product is unique. This belief can result from the firm's service to the customer, effective advertising campaigns, or being the first to market a good or service. Companies such as Coca-Cola, PepsiCo, and the world's automobile manufacturers spend a great deal of money on advertising to convince potential customers of their products' distinctiveness. Customers valuing a product's uniqueness tend to become loyal to both the product and the company producing it. Typically, new entrants must allocate many resources over time to overcome existing customer loyalties. To combat the perception of uniqueness, new entrants frequently offer products at lower prices. This decision, however, may result in lower profits or even losses.

Capital Requirements. Competing in a new industry requires the firm to have resources to invest. In addition to physical facilities, capital is needed for inventories, marketing activities, and other critical business functions. Even when competing in a new industry is attractive, the capital required for successful market entry may not be available to pursue an apparent market opportunity. For example, entering the steel and defense industries would be very difficult because of the substantial resource investments required to be competitive. One way a firm could enter the steel industry, however, is with a highly efficient mini-mill. Alternatively, a firm might enter the defense industry through the acquisition of an existing firm, because of the knowledge requirements.

Switching Costs. Switching costs are the one-time costs customers incur when they buy from a different supplier. The costs of buying new ancillary equipment and of retraining employees, and even the psychic costs of ending a relationship, may be incurred in switching to a new supplier. In some cases, switching costs are low, such as when the consumer switches to a different soft drink. Switching costs can vary as a function of time. For example, in terms of hours toward graduation, the cost to a student to transfer from one university to another as a freshman is much lower than it is when the student is entering the senior year. Occasionally, a decision made by manufacturers to produce a new, innovative product creates high switching costs for the final consumer. Customer loyalty programs, such as airlines awarding frequent flier miles, are intended to increase the customer's switching costs.

If switching costs are high, a new entrant must offer either a substantially lower price or a much better product to attract buyers. Usually, the more established the relationship between parties, the greater is the cost incurred to switch to an alternative offering.

Access to Distribution Channels. Over time, industry participants typically develop effective means of distributing products. Once a relationship with its distributors has been developed, a firm will nurture it to create switching costs for the distributors.

Access to distribution channels can be a strong entry barrier for new entrants, particularly in consumer nondurable goods industries (for example, in grocery stores where shelf space is limited) and in international markets. Thus, new entrants have to persuade distributors to carry their products, either in addition to or in place of those currently distributed. Price breaks and cooperative advertising allowances may be used for this purpose; however, those practices reduce the new entrant's profit potential.

Cost Disadvantages Independent of Scale. Sometimes, established competitors have cost advantages that new entrants cannot duplicate. Proprietary product technology, favorable access to raw materials, desirable locations, and government subsidies are examples. Successful competition requires new entrants to reduce the strategic relevance of these factors. Delivering purchases directly to the buyer can counter the advantage of a desirable location; new food establishments in an undesirable location often follow this practice. Similarly, automobile dealerships located in unattractive areas (perhaps in a city's downtown area) can provide superior service (such as picking up the car to be serviced and then delivering it to the customer) to overcome a competitor's location advantage.

Government Policy. Through licensing and permit requirements, governments can also control entry into an industry. Liquor retailing, banking, and trucking are examples of industries in which government decisions and actions affect entry possibilities. Also, governments often restrict entry into some utility industries because of the need to provide quality service to all and the capital requirements necessary to do so. The European Competition Commission's blocking of GE's acquisition of Honeywell is a prime example of government actions controlling entry to a market.[94] Also, the agreement among governments to restrict the output of steel (as discussed in the Strategic Focus on page 56) places substantial restrictions on new entrants to that industry.

Expected Retaliation

Firms seeking to enter an industry also anticipate the reactions of firms in the industry. An expectation of swift and vigorous competitive responses reduces the likelihood of entry. Vigorous retaliation can be expected when the existing firm has a major stake in the industry (for example, it has fixed assets with few, if any, alternative uses), when it has substantial resources, and when industry growth is slow or constrained. For example, any firms that attempt to enter the steel or IT industries at the current time can expect significant retaliation from existing competitors.

Locating market niches not being served by incumbents allows the new entrant to avoid entry barriers. Small entrepreneurial firms are generally best suited for identifying and serving neglected market segments. When Honda first entered the U.S. market, it concentrated on small-engine motorcycles, a market that firms such as Harley-Davidson ignored. By targeting this neglected niche, Honda avoided competition. After consolidating its position, Honda used its strength to attack rivals by introducing larger motorcycles and competing in the broader market. Competitive actions and competitive responses between firms such as Honda and Harley-Davidson are discussed fully in Chapter 5.

Bargaining Power of Suppliers

Increasing prices and reducing the quality of its products are potential means used by suppliers to exert power over firms competing within an industry. If a firm is unable to recover cost increases by its suppliers through its pricing structure, its profitability is reduced by its suppliers' actions. A supplier group is powerful when

- It is dominated by a few large companies and is more concentrated than the industry to which it sells.
- Satisfactory substitute products are not available to industry firms.
- Industry firms are not a significant customer for the supplier group.

- Suppliers' goods are critical to buyers' marketplace success.
- The effectiveness of suppliers' products has created high switching costs for industry firms.
- It poses a credible threat to integrate forward into the buyers' industry. Credibility is enhanced when suppliers have substantial resources and provide a highly differentiated product.

The automobile manufacturing industry is an example of an industry in which suppliers' bargaining power is relatively low. Actions taken by Nissan and Toyota demonstrate this. Recently these two firms placed significant pressure on their suppliers to provide parts at reduced prices. Toyota, for example, requested price reductions of up to 30 percent. As a result of the success of its requests, Nissan reduced its purchasing costs by $2.25 billion annually. Because they sell their products to a small number of large firms and because they aren't credible threats to integrate forward, auto parts suppliers have little power relative to automobile manufacturers such as Toyota and Nissan.[95]

Bargaining Power of Buyers

Firms seek to maximize the return on their invested capital. Alternatively, buyers (customers of an industry or firm) want to buy products at the lowest possible price—the point at which the industry earns the lowest acceptable rate of return on its invested capital. To reduce their costs, buyers bargain for higher quality, greater levels of service, and lower prices. These outcomes are achieved by encouraging competitive battles among the industry's firms. Customers (buyer groups) are powerful when

- They purchase a large portion of an industry's total output.
- The sales of the product being purchased account for a significant portion of the seller's annual revenues.
- They could switch to another product at little, if any, cost.
- The industry's products are undifferentiated or standardized, and the buyers pose a credible threat if they were to integrate backward into the sellers' industry.

Armed with greater amounts of information about the manufacturer's costs and the power of the Internet as a shopping and distribution alternative, consumers appear to be increasing their bargaining power in the automobile industry. One reason for this shift is that individual buyers incur virtually zero switching costs when they decide to purchase from one manufacturer rather than another or from one dealer as opposed to a second or third one. These realities are forcing companies in the automobile industry to become more focused on the needs and desires of the people actually buying cars, trucks, minivans, and sport utility vehicles. These conditions of the market combined with the recession in 2001 and early 2002 are part of the reasons that Nissan and Toyota are pressuring their suppliers to reduce costs. In so doing, they can better serve and satisfy their customers who have considerable power.

Threat of Substitute Products

Substitute products are goods or services from outside a given industry that perform similar or the same functions as a product that the industry produces. For example, as a sugar substitute, Nutrasweet places an upper limit on sugar manufacturers' prices—Nutrasweet and sugar perform the same function, but with different characteristics. Other product substitutes include fax machines instead of overnight deliveries, plastic containers rather than glass jars, and tea substituted for coffee. Recently firms have introduced to the market several low-alcohol fruit-flavored drinks that many customers substitute for beer. For example, Smirnoff's Ice was introduced with substantial advertising of the type often used for beer. Other firms have introduced lemonade with 5 percent alcohol (e.g., Doc Otis Hard Lemon) and tea and lemon combinations with alcohol (e.g., Bodean's Twisted Tea). These products are increasing in popularity especially among younger people and as product substitutes, have the potential to reduce overall sales of beer.[96]

In general, product substitutes present a strong threat to a firm when customers face few, if any, switching costs and when the substitute product's price is lower or its quality and performance capabilities are equal to or greater than those of the competing product. Differentiating a product along dimensions that customers value (such as price, quality, service after the sale, and location) reduces a substitute's attractiveness.

Intensity of Rivalry among Competitors

Because an industry's firms are mutually dependent, actions taken by one company usually invite competitive responses. Thus, in many industries, firms actively compete against one another. Competitive rivalry intensifies when a firm is challenged by a competitor's actions or when an opportunity to improve its market position is recognized.

Firms within industries are rarely homogeneous; they differ in resources and capabilities and seek to differentiate themselves from competitors.[97] Typically, firms seek to differentiate their products from competitors' offerings in ways that customers value and in which the firms have a competitive advantage. Visible dimensions on which rivalry is based include price, quality, and innovation.

As explained in the Strategic Focus, the rivalry between competitors, such as Fuji and Kodak, Airbus and Boeing, and Sun Microsystems and Microsoft, is intense.

The firms described in the Strategic Focus on page 62 are taking different competitive actions and competitive responses in efforts to be successful. Airbus is using a first mover strategy (explained in Chapter 5), Fuji is buying equity in a local competitor and infusing it with resources, Sun must improve the effectiveness of its Web service to achieve even competitive parity, and Samsung is taking advantage of a major shift in technology to differentiate its products from those of its rivals.

As suggested by the Strategic Focus on page 62, various factors influence the intensity of rivalry between or among competitors. Next, we discuss the most prominent factors that experience shows to affect the intensity of firms' rivalries.

Numerous or Equally Balanced Competitors

Intense rivalries are common in industries with many companies. With multiple competitors, it is common for a few firms to believe that they can act without eliciting a response. However, evidence suggests that other firms generally are aware of competitors' actions, often choosing to respond to them. At the other extreme, industries with only a few firms of equivalent size and power also tend to have strong rivalries. The large and often similar-sized resource bases of these firms permit vigorous actions and responses. The Fuji and Kodak and Airbus and Boeing competitive battles exemplify intense rivalries between pairs of relatively equivalent competitors.

Slow Industry Growth

When a market is growing, firms try to effectively use resources to serve an expanding customer base. Growing markets reduce the pressure to take customers from competitors. However, rivalry in nongrowth or slow-growth markets becomes more intense as firms battle to increase their market shares by attracting competitors' customers.

Typically, battles to protect market shares are fierce. Certainly, this has been the case with Fuji and Kodak. The instability in the market that results from these competitive engagements reduces profitability for firms throughout the industry, as is

Strategic Focus

The High Stakes of Competitive Rivalry

While most industries produce situations where multiple firms compete against each other, there are some industries in which two major competitors compete "head to head" in multiple markets. Among these competitors are Fuji and Kodak, Airbus and Boeing, and Sun Microsystems and Microsoft. Fuji and Kodak have had an almost storied rivalry over the last decade. For example, Kodak invested heavily in developing digital products. Fuji was aware that Kodak was ahead in serving the digital market, so it decided to capture market share in the traditional film market in hopes of changing Kodak's strategy. Fuji engaged in severe price competition in the U.S. market capturing major gains in market share from Kodak. Eventually, Kodak shareholders became dissatisfied, and Kodak had to respond. It reduced its prices and investment in R&D, slowing its move into digital products. Recently, however, Kodak has made major strides in capturing the high potential Chinese film market with approximately 50 percent of the market. To combat Kodak, Fuji, with 30 percent of the Chinese market, is negotiating to acquire equity in Lucky Film, China's only film manufacturer, which has 20 percent of the market. If the acquisition is finalized, Fuji will contribute financial capital, technology, and management while Lucky will provide the manufacturing and distribution.

For a number of years, Airbus and Boeing have competed directly to serve the large airline market. During most of that time, Boeing was the clear winner with a majority of the market with its 700 (including the 727, 737, 747, 757, and 767) series of aircraft. In recent years, Airbus has begun to capture a greater share of this market. Boeing didn't react quickly to these changes, but when Airbus announced that it would produce a new super jumbo jet aircraft, Boeing responded with an announcement that it would develop a larger version of its 747. However, Airbus was the clear winner here, taking all of the contracts in "head to head" competition. Boeing gave up and dropped its plans to develop the larger aircraft. Instead, it announced the development of a smaller and much faster aircraft, but it must invest much time and money to do so. Boeing was not prepared well for the future and seemed to be resting on its laurels. As a result, Airbus has captured leadership of the global large aircraft market.

Scott McNealy, CEO of Sun Microsystems, is wealthy with approximately $668 million in Sun equity and became a success at a relatively young age. Given the economic travails of 2001 and 2002, he considered retiring to a less stressful life, but he still has a major goal. He believes that he must stop Sun's rival Microsoft from dominating the Internet and has stated, "It is mankind against Microsoft." The rivalry between Microsoft and Sun seems to be almost personal between McNealy and Microsoft's Bill Gates. McNealy faces a tough challenge—Microsoft leads Sun in four of six markets in which they compete and executed its Web strategy effectively. Additionally, Sun was not profitable in 2001, while Microsoft was. As a result, Sun's stock price faltered while Microsoft's increased. For Sun to reverse its performance and to successfully challenge Microsoft, it must be effective in providing Web services. While Sun is unlikely to beat Microsoft, it needs to slow down Microsoft's advance to keep it from dominating the Web.

These three competitions are unique, in that in each instance, only two major rivals are involved. In contrast, Samsung faces many competitors in the consumer electronics market, including five with higher market shares (and three of those rivals have more than twice Samsung's annual sales in this market). Nevertheless, Samsung established a goal to become the leader in this market by 2005. Just as Sony became a major player in the consumer electronics market with analog technology and the Trinitron color TV, Samsung is attempting to take the market with digital technology. Samsung executives believe that the change from analog to digital technology leveled the competitive playing field. The current battle is for "mind share" to be followed by the battle for market share.

SOURCES: P. Burrows, 2001, Face-off, *Business Week,* November 19, 104–110; H. Brown, 2001, Look out, Sony, *Forbes,* June 11, 96–101; D. Michaels, Airbus's 'Honest Abe' attitude adds fuel to rivalry with Boeing, *The Wall Street Journal Interactive,* http://interactive.wsj.com, April 3; J. Kynge, 2001, Fuji considers Chinese tie-up to rival Kodak, *Financial Times,* http://www.ft.com, February 27.

demonstrated by the commercial aircraft industry. The market for large aircraft is expected to decline or grow only slightly over the next few years. To expand market share, Boeing and Airbus will compete aggressively in terms of the introduction of new products, and product and service differentiation. Both firms are likely to win some and lose other battles. In early 2002, Airbus seemed to have an edge over Boeing in this market segment.

High Fixed Costs or High Storage Costs

When fixed costs account for a large part of total costs, companies try to maximize the use of their productive capacity. Doing so allows the firm to spread costs across a larger volume of output. However, when many firms attempt to maximize their productive capacity, excess capacity is created on an industry-wide basis. To then reduce inventories, individual companies typically cut the price of their product and offer rebates and other special discounts to customers. These practices, however, often intensify competition. The pattern of excess capacity at the industry level followed by intense rivalry at the firm level is observed frequently in industries with high storage costs. Perishable products, for example, lose their value rapidly with the passage of time. As their inventories grow, producers of perishable goods often use pricing strategies to sell products quickly.

Lack of Differentiation or Low Switching Costs

When buyers find a differentiated product that satisfies their needs, they frequently purchase the product loyally over time. Industries with many companies that have successfully differentiated their products have less rivalry, resulting in lower competition for individual firms.[98] However, when buyers view products as commodities (as products with few differentiated features or capabilities), rivalry intensifies. In these instances, buyers' purchasing decisions are based primarily on price and, to a lesser degree, service. Film for cameras is an example of a commodity. Thus, the competition between Fuji and Kodak is expected to be strong.

The effect of switching costs is identical to that described for differentiated products. The lower the buyers' switching costs, the easier it is for competitors to attract buyers through pricing and service offerings. High switching costs, however, at least partially insulate the firm from rivals' efforts to attract customers. Interestingly, the switching costs—such as pilot and mechanic training—are high in aircraft purchases, yet, the rivalry between Boeing and Airbus remains intense because the stakes for both are extremely high.

High Strategic Stakes

Competitive rivalry is likely to be high when it is important for several of the competitors to perform well in the market. For example, although it is diversified and is a market leader in other businesses, Samsung has targeted market leadership in the consumer electronics market. This market is quite important to Sony and other major competitors such as Hitachi, Matsushita, NEC, and Mitsubishi. Thus, we can expect substantial rivalry in this market over the next few years.

High strategic stakes can also exist in terms of geographic locations. For example, Japanese automobile manufacturers are committed to a significant presence in the U.S. marketplace. A key reason for this is that the United States is the world's single largest market for auto manufacturers' products. Because of the stakes involved in this country for Japanese and U.S. manufacturers, rivalry among firms in the U.S. and the global automobile industry is highly intense. It should be noted that while close proximity tends to promote greater rivalry, physically proximate competition has potentially positive benefits as well. For example, when competitors are located near each other, it is easier for suppliers to serve them and they can develop economies of scale that lead to lower production costs. Additionally, communications with key industry stakeholders such as suppliers are facilitated and more efficient when they are close to the firm.[99]

High Exit Barriers

Sometimes companies continue competing in an industry even though the returns on their invested capital are low or negative. Firms making this choice likely face high exit barriers, which include economic, strategic, and emotional factors causing companies to remain in an industry when the profitability of doing so is questionable. Common exit barriers are

- Specialized assets (assets with values linked to a particular business or location).
- Fixed costs of exit (such as labor agreements).
- Strategic interrelationships (relationships of mutual dependence, such as those between one business and other parts of a company's operations including shared facilities and access to financial markets).
- Emotional barriers (aversion to economically justified business decisions because of fear for one's own career, loyalty to employees, and so forth).
- Government and social restrictions (more common outside the United States, these restrictions often are based on government concerns for job losses and regional economic effects).

Interpreting Industry Analyses

Effective industry analyses are products of careful study and interpretation of data and information from multiple sources. A wealth of industry-specific data is available to be analyzed. Because of globalization, international markets and rivalries must be included in the firm's analyses. In fact, research shows that in some industries, international variables are more important than domestic ones as determinants of strategic competitiveness. Furthermore, because of the development of global markets, a country's borders no longer restrict industry structures. In fact, movement into international markets enhances the chances of success for new ventures as well as more established firms.[100]

Following study of the five forces of competition, the firm can develop the insights required to determine an industry's attractiveness in terms of its potential to earn adequate or superior returns on its invested capital. In general, the stronger competitive forces are, the lower the profit potential for an industry's firms. An unattractive industry has low entry barriers, suppliers and buyers with strong bargaining positions, strong competitive threats from product substitutes, and intense rivalry among competitors. These industry characteristics make it very difficult for firms to achieve

Samsung is competing with many other firms for the cell phone market, even as worldwide sales of new cell phones fell by 3.2 percent, from 412.7 million handsets in 2000 to 399.6 million in 2001—a steep decline from the annual 60 percent growth rate between 1996 and 2000. Sales were up in North America despite a mild recession in the United States. Finland's Nokia led all cell phone makers with a 35 percent market share, followed by Motorola Inc., Siemens AG, Ericcson, and Samsung.

TERRI L.MILLER/E-VISUAL COMMUNICATIONS, INC.

strategic competitiveness and earn above-average returns. Alternatively, an attractive industry has high entry barriers, suppliers and buyers with little bargaining power, few competitive threats from product substitutes, and relatively moderate rivalry.[101]

Strategic Groups

A **strategic group** is a set of firms emphasizing similar strategic dimensions to use a similar strategy.

A set of firms emphasizing similar strategic dimensions to use a similar strategy is called a **strategic group.**[102] The competition between firms within a strategic group is greater than the competition between a member of a strategic group and companies outside that strategic group. Another way of saying this is that intra-strategic group competition is more intense than is inter-strategic group competition.

The extent of technological leadership, product quality, pricing policies, distribution channels, and customer service are examples of strategic dimensions that firms in a strategic group treat similarly. Describing patterns of competition within strategic groups is evidence suggesting that "organizations in a strategic group occupy similar positions in the market, offer similar goods to similar customers, and may also make similar choices about production technology and other organizational features."[103] Thus, membership in a particular strategic group defines the essential characteristics of the firm's strategy.[104]

The notion of strategic groups can be useful for analyzing an industry's competitive structure. Such analyses can be helpful in diagnosing competition, positioning, and the profitability of firms within an industry.[105] Research has found that strategic groups differ in performance, suggesting their importance.[106] Interestingly, research also suggests that strategic group membership remains relatively stable over time, making analysis easier and more useful.[107]

Using strategic groups to understand an industry's competitive structure requires the firm to plot companies' competitive actions and competitive responses along strategic dimensions such as pricing decisions, product quality, distribution channels, and so forth. Doing this shows the firm how certain companies are competing similarly in terms of how they use similar strategic dimensions. For example, there are unique radio markets because consumers prefer different music formats and programming (news radio, talk radio, and so forth). Typically, a radio format is created through choices made regarding music or nonmusic style, scheduling, and announcer style.[108] It is estimated that approximately 30 different radio formats exist, suggesting that there are 30 strategic groups in this industry. The strategies within each of the 30 groups are similar, while the strategies across the total set of strategic groups are dissimilar. Thus, firms could increase their understanding of competition in the commercial radio industry by plotting companies' actions and responses in terms of important strategic dimensions such as those we have mentioned.

Strategic groups have several implications. First, because firms within a group offer similar products to the same customers, the competitive rivalry among them can be intense. The more intense the rivalry, the greater is the threat to each firm's profitability. Second, the strengths of the five industry forces (the threats posed by new entrants, the power of suppliers, the power of buyers, product substitutes, and the intensity of rivalry among competitors) differ across strategic groups. Third, the closer the strategic groups are in terms of their strategies, the greater is the likelihood of rivalry between the groups.

Competitor Analysis

The competitor environment is the final part of the external environment requiring study. Competitor analysis focuses on each company against whom a firm directly competes. For example, Fuji and Kodak, Airbus and Boeing, and Sun Microsystems and Microsoft should be keenly interested in understanding each other's objectives, strategies, assumptions, and capabilities. Furthermore, intense rivalry creates a strong need to understand competitors. In a competitor analysis, the firm seeks to understand

- What drives the competitor, as shown by its *future objectives.*
- What the competitor is doing and can do, as revealed by its *current strategy.*
- What the competitor believes about the industry, as shown by its *assumptions.*
- What the competitor's capabilities are, as shown by its *capabilities* (its strengths and weaknesses).[109]

Information about these four dimensions helps the firm prepare an anticipated response profile for each competitor (see Figure 2.3). Thus, the results of an effective competitor analysis help a firm understand, interpret, and predict its competitors' actions and responses.

Critical to an effective competitor analysis is gathering data and information that can help the firm understand its competitors' intentions and the strategic implications resulting from them.[110] Useful data and information combine to form **competitor intelligence:** the set of data and information the firm gathers to better understand and better anticipate competitors' objectives, strategies, assumptions, and capabilities. In competitor analysis, the firm should gather intelligence not only about its competitors, but also regarding public policies in countries across the world. Intelligence about public policies "provides an early warning of threats and opportunities emerging from the global public policy environment, and analyzes how they will affect the achievement of the company's strategy."[111]

Competitor intelligence is the set of data and information the firm gathers to better understand and better anticipate competitors' objectives, strategies, assumptions, and capabilities.

Figure 2.3 Competitor Analysis Components

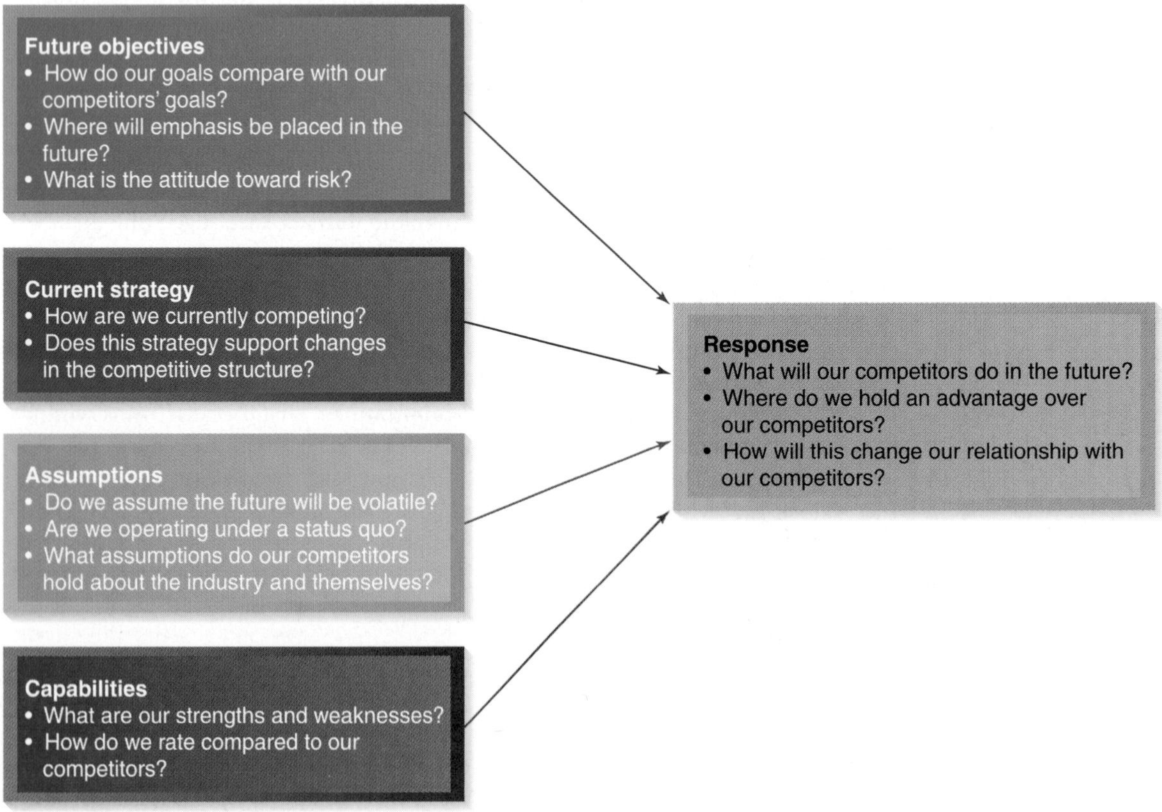

Future objectives
- How do our goals compare with our competitors' goals?
- Where will emphasis be placed in the future?
- What is the attitude toward risk?

Current strategy
- How are we currently competing?
- Does this strategy support changes in the competitive structure?

Assumptions
- Do we assume the future will be volatile?
- Are we operating under a status quo?
- What assumptions do our competitors hold about the industry and themselves?

Capabilities
- What are our strengths and weaknesses?
- How do we rate compared to our competitors?

Response
- What will our competitors do in the future?
- Where do we hold an advantage over our competitors?
- How will this change our relationship with our competitors?

Through effective competitive and public policy intelligence, the firm gains the insights needed to create a competitive advantage and to increase the quality of the strategic decisions it makes when deciding how to compete against its rivals. Claire Hart, CEO of Factiva, a news and information service, believes that competitor intelligence helped her firm to move from the number three to the number two position in her industry. Additionally, she states that competitor intelligence will play an important role in her firm's efforts to reach its objective of becoming the top firm in the industry.[112]

Firms should follow generally accepted ethical practices in gathering competitor intelligence. Industry associations often develop lists of these practices that firms can adopt. Practices considered both legal and ethical include (1) obtaining publicly available information (such as court records, competitors' help-wanted advertisements, annual reports, financial reports of publicly held corporations, and Uniform Commercial Code filings), and (2) attending trade fairs and shows to obtain competitors' brochures, view their exhibits, and listen to discussions about their products.

In contrast, certain practices (including blackmail, trespassing, eavesdropping, and stealing drawings, samples, or documents) are widely viewed as unethical and often are illegal. To protect themselves from digital fraud or theft that occurs through competitors breaking into their employees' PCs, some companies buy insurance to protect against PC hacking. Chubb's new ForeFront plan, for example, offers up to $10 million coverage against digital fraud, theft, and extortion. Cigna's information asset protection division sells anti-hacker policies that cover up to 10 percent of a firm's revenues. The number of clients making claims seems to suggest the value of having one of these policies.[113]

Some competitor intelligence practices may be legal, but a firm must decide whether they are also ethical, given the image it desires as a corporate citizen. Especially with electronic transmissions, the line between legal and ethical practices can be difficult to determine. For example, a firm may develop website addresses that are very similar to those of its competitors and thus occasionally receive e-mail transmissions that were intended for its competitors. According to legal experts, the legality of this "e-mail snagging" remains unclear.[114] Nonetheless, the practice is an example of the challenges companies face when deciding how to gather intelligence about competitors while simultaneously determining what to do to prevent competitors from learning too much about them.

In 2001, Procter & Gamble (P&G) notified Unilever that its own rules regarding gathering intelligence on competitors were violated when obtaining information on Unilever practices. Thus, P&G returned over 80 documents that were taken from Unilever's trash bins. The two firms then negotiated a potential settlement. Unilever wanted P&G to delay several of its planned new product launches, but P&G resisted. Moreover, both firms had to take special care in the negotiations not to violate antitrust laws thereby spurring regulators to take actions. Therefore, for several reasons, competitive intelligence must be handled with sensitivity.[115]

Open discussions of intelligence-gathering techniques can help a firm to ensure that people understand its convictions to follow ethical practices for gathering competitor intelligence. An appropriate guideline for competitor intelligence practices is to respect the principles of common morality and the right of competitors not to reveal certain information about their products, operations, and strategic intentions.[116]

Despite the importance of studying competitors, evidence suggests that only a relatively small percentage of firms use formal processes to collect and disseminate competitive intelligence. Beyond this, some firms forget to analyze competitors' future objectives as they try to understand their current strategies, assumptions, and capabilities, which will yield incomplete insights about those competitors.[117]

Summary

- The firm's external environment is challenging and complex. Because of the external environment's effect on performance, the firm must develop the skills required to identify opportunities and threats existing in that environment.
- The external environment has three major parts: (1) the general environment (elements in the broader society that affect industries and their firms), (2) the industry environment (factors that influence a firm, its competitive actions and responses, and the industry's profit potential, and (3) the competitor environment (in which the firm analyzes each major competitor's future objectives, current strategies, assumptions, and capabilities).
- The external environmental analysis process has four steps: scanning, monitoring, forecasting, and assessing. Through environmental analyses, the firm identifies opportunities and threats.
- The general environment has six segments: demographic, economic, political/legal, sociocultural, technological, and global. For each segment, the firm wants to determine the strategic relevance of environmental changes and trends.
- Compared to the general environment, the industry environment has a more direct effect on the firm's strategic actions. The five forces model of competition includes the threat of entry, the power of suppliers, the power of buyers, product substitutes, and the intensity of rivalry among competitors. By studying these forces, the firm finds a position in an industry where it can influence the forces in its favor or where it can buffer itself from the power of the forces in order to increase its ability to earn above-average returns.
- Industries are populated with different strategic groups. A strategic group is a collection of firms that follow similar strategies along similar dimensions. Competitive rivalry is greater within a strategic group than it is between strategic groups.
- Competitor analysis informs the firm about the future objectives, current strategies, assumptions, and capabilities of the companies with whom it competes directly.
- Different techniques are used to create competitor intelligence: the set of data, information, and knowledge that allows the firm to better understand its competitors and thereby predict their likely strategic and tactical actions. Firms should use only legal and ethical practices to gather intelligence. The Internet enhances firms' capabilities to gather insights about competitors and their strategic intentions.

Review Questions

1. Why is it important for a firm to study and understand the external environment?
2. What are the differences between the general environment and the industry environment? Why are these differences important?
3. What is the external environmental analysis process? What does the firm want to learn as it scans, monitors, forecasts, and assesses its external environment?
4. What are the six segments of the general environment? Explain the differences among them.
5. How do the five forces of competition in an industry affect its profit potential? Explain.
6. What is a strategic group? Of what value is knowledge of the firm's strategic group in formulating that firm's strategy?
7. What is the importance of collecting and interpreting data and information about competitors? What practices should a firm use to gather competitor intelligence and why?

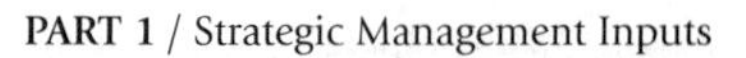

Experiential Exercise

Environmental Analysis

The results of an environmental analysis provide crucial knowledge for the firm's strategic decisions. The following activities can be worked in small groups or individually and then discussed in class.

General Environment Activity. As the manager of environmental analysis for an up-and-coming competitor to Wal-Mart, you've been asked to identify two trends for each of the segments of the general environment and to evaluate the potential impact of those trends on the firm's future strategy. Provide your findings in the table below.

Segment	Trend	Impact on Strategy
Demographic	1.	
	2.	
Economic	1.	
	2.	
Political/legal	1.	
	2.	
Sociocultural	1.	
	2.	
Technological	1.	
	2.	
Global	1.	
	2.	

Industry environment activity. You've also been asked to provide a brief analysis of the industrial environment and the five forces model of competition. Indicate in the following table the strength (high, medium, low) of each force on your industry and its impact on your firm's strategy.

Five Forces Model	Strength	Impact on Strategy
Bargaining power of suppliers		
Bargaining power of buyers		
Threats of substitute products		
Rivalry of competing firms		
Threat of new entrants		

Notes

1. J. Song, 2002, Firm capabilities and technology ladders: Sequential foreign direct investments of Japanese electronics firms in East Asia, *Strategic Management Journal,* 23: 191–210; D. J. Ketchen, Jr. & T. B. Palmer, 1999, Strategic responses to poor organizational performance: A test of competing perspectives, *Journal of Management,* 25: 683–706; V. P. Rindova & C. J. Fombrun, 1999, Constructing competitive advantage: The role of firm-constituent interactions, *Strategic Management Journal,* 20: 691–710.
2. P. Chattopadhyay, W. H. Glick, & G. P. Huber, 2001, Organizational actions in response to threats and opportunities, *Academy of Management Journal,* 44: 937–955.
3. H. Lee & M. A. Hitt, 2002, Top management team composition and characteristics as predictors of strategic flexibility, working paper, University of Connecticut; A. Edgecliffe-Johnson, 2001, Southwest braced to weather trouble, *Financial Times,* http://www.ft.com, October 2; L. Zuckerman, 2001, With seats empty, airlines cut fares to bargain levels, *The New York Times,* http://www.nytimes.com, December 18.
4. R. J. Herbold, 2002, Inside Microsoft: Balancing creativity and discipline, *Harvard Business Review,* 80(1): 73–79; C. M. Grimm & K. G. Smith, 1997, *Strategy As Action: Industry Rivalry and Coordination,* Cincinnati: South-Western; C. J. Fombrun, 1992, *Turning Point: Creating Strategic Change in Organizations,* New York: McGraw-Hill, 13.
5. J. M. Mezias, 2002, Identifying liabilities of foreignness and strategies to minimize their effects: The case of labor lawsuit judgments in the United States, *Strategic Management Journal,* 23: 229–244.
6. R. M. Kanter, 2002, Strategy as improvisational theater, *MIT Sloan Management Review,* 43(2): 76–81; S. A. Zahra, A. P. Nielsen, & W. C. Bogner, 1999, Corporate entrepreneurship, knowledge, and competence development, *Entrepreneurship: Theory and Practice,* 23 (3): 169–189.
7. M. A. Hitt, J. E. Ricart I Costa, & R. D. Nixon, 1998, The new frontier, in M. A. Hitt, J. E. Ricart I Costa, & R. D. Nixon (eds.), *Managing Strategically in an Interconnected World,* Chichester: John Wiley & Sons, 1–12.

8. S. A. Zahra & G. George, 2002, International entrepreneurship: The current status of the field and future research agenda, in M. A. Hitt, R. D. Ireland, S. M. Camp, & D. L. Sexton (eds.), *Strategic Entrepreneurship: Creating a New Mindset,* Oxford, U.K.: Blackwell Publishers, 255–288; W. C. Bogner & P. Bansal, 1998, Controlling unique knowledge development as the basis of sustained high performance, in M. A. Hitt, J. E. Ricart I Costa, & R. D. Nixon (eds.), *Managing Strategically in an Interconnected World,* Chichester: John Wiley & Sons, 167–184.
9. L. Fahey, 1999, *Competitors,* New York: John Wiley & Sons; B. A. Walters & R. L. Priem, 1999, Business strategy and CEO intelligence acquisition, *Competitive Intelligence Review,* 10(2): 15–22.
10. R. D. Ireland & M. A. Hitt, 1999, Achieving and maintaining strategic competitiveness in the 21st century: The role of strategic leadership, *Academy of Management Executive,* 13(1): 43–57; M. A. Hitt, B. W. Keats, & S. M. DeMarie, 1998, Navigating in the new competitive landscape: Building strategic flexibility and competitive advantage in the 21st century, *Academy of Management Executive,* 12(4): 22–42.
11. J. K. Sebenius, 2002, The hidden challenge of cross-border negotiations, *Harvard Business Review,* 80(3): 76–85; J. Kay, 1999, Strategy and the delusion of grand designs, Mastering Strategy (Part One), *Financial Times,* September 27, 2.
12. R. Karlgaard, 1999, Digital rules: Technology and the new economy, *Forbes,* May 17, 43.
13. 2000, GE Overview, General Electric home page, http://www.ge.com, January 12.
14. V. Prior, 1999, The language of competitive intelligence: Part four, *Competitive Intelligence Review,* 10(1): 84–87.
15. A. Berenson & R. A. Oppel, Jr., 2001, Once mighty Enron strains under scrutiny, *The New York Times,* http://www.nytimes.com, October 28; C. H. Deutsch, 2001, Polaroid, deep in debt since 1988, files for bankruptcy, *The New York Times,* http://www.nytimes.com, October 13.
16. G. Young, 1999, "Strategic value analysis" for competitive advantage, *Competitive Intelligence Review,* 10(2): 52–64.
17. M. A. Hitt, R. D. Ireland, S. M. Camp, & D. L. Sexton, 2001, Strategic entrepreneurship: Entrepreneurial strategies for wealth creation, *Strategic Management Journal,* 22(Special Summer Issue): 479–491.
18. L. Rosenkopf & A. Nerkar, 2001, Beyond local search: Boundary-spanning exploration, and impact in the optical disk industry, *Strategic Management Journal,* 22: 287–306.
19. D. F. Kuratko, R. D. Ireland, & J. S. Hornsby, 2001, Improving firm performance through entrepreneurial actions: Acordia's corporate entrepreneurship strategy, *Academy of Management Executive,* 15(4): 60–71; D. S. Elenkov, 1997, Strategic uncertainty and environmental scanning: The case for institutional influences on scanning behavior, *Strategic Management Journal,* 18: 287–302.
20. K. M. Eisenhardt, 2002, Has strategy changed? *MIT Sloan Management Review,* 43 (2): 88–91; I. Goll & A. M. A. Rasheed, 1997, Rational decision-making and firm performance: The moderating role of environment, *Strategic Management Journal,* 18: 583–591.
21. R. Aggarwal, 1999, Technology and globalization as mutual reinforcers in business: Reorienting strategic thinking for the new millennium, *Management International Review,* 39(2): 83–104; M. Yasai-Ardekani & P. C. Nystrom, 1996, Designs for environmental scanning systems: Tests of contingency theory, *Management Science,* 42: 187–204.
22. R. Donkin, 1999, Too young to retire, *Financial Times,* July 2, 9.
23. B. Richards, 2001, Following the crumbs, *The Wall Street Journal,* http:// interactive.wsj. com, October 29.
24. Fahey, *Competitors,* 71–73.
25. P. Yip, 1999, The road to wealth, *Dallas Morning News,* August 2, D1, D3.
26. Y. Luo & S. H. Park, 2001, Strategic alignment and performance of market-seeking MNCs in China, *Strategic Management Journal,* 22: 141–155.
27. I. M. Jawahar & G. L. McLaughlin, 2001, Toward a prescriptive stakeholder theory: An organizational life cycle approach, *Academy of Management Review,* 26: 397–414.
28. M. Song & M. M. Montoya-Weiss, 2001, The effect of perceived technological uncertainty on Japanese new product development, *Academy of Management Journal,* 44: 61–80.
29. H. Yli-Renko, E. Autio, & H. J. Sapienza, 2001, Social capital, knowledge acquisition, and knowledge exploitation in young technologically-based firms, *Strategic Management Journal,* 22(special Summer Issue): 587–613.
30. Fahey, *Competitors.*
31. 2001, Weathering the storm: Dow Chemical, *Forbes,* http://www.forbes.com, June 14.
32. Fahey, *Competitors,* 75–77.
33. L. Fahey & V. K. Narayanan, 1986, *Macroenvironmental Analysis for Strategic Management,* St. Paul, MN: West Publishing Company, 58.
34. D. Fishburn, 1999, *The World in 1999, The Economist* Publications, 9; Six billion . . . and counting, 1999, *Time,* October 4, 16.
35. J. F. Coates, J. B. Mahaffie, & A. Hines, 1997, 2025: *Scenarios of US and Global Society Reshaped by Science and Technology,* Greensboro, NC: Oakhill Press.
36. R. Poe & C. L. Courter, 1999, The next baby boom, *Across the Board,* May, 1; 1999, Trends and forecasts for the next 25 years, World Future Society, 3.
37. 2001, Fewer seniors in the 1990s, *Business Week,* May 28, 30.
38. M. Peterson & M. Freudenheim, 2001, Drug giant to introduce discount drug plan for the elderly, *The New York Times,* http://www.nytimes.com, October 3.
39. D. Stipp, 1999, Hell no, we won't go! *Fortune,* July 19, 102–108; G. Colvin, 1997, How to beat the boomer rush, *Fortune,* August 18, 59–63.
40. J. MacIntyre, 1999, Figuratively speaking, *Across the Board,* November/December, 15.
41. Colvin, How to beat the boomer rush, 60.
42. 1999, U.S. Department of Labor, Demographic change and the future workforce, *Futurework,* November 8, http://www.dol.gov.
43. P. R. Drucker, 2002, They're not employees, they're people, *Harvard Business Review,* 80(2): 70–77.
44. G. Dessler, 1999, How to earn your employees' commitment, *Academy of Management Executive,* 13(2): 58–67; S. Finkelstein & D. C. Hambrick, 1996, *Strategic Leadership: Top Executives and Their Effect on Organizations,* Minneapolis: West.
45. L. H. Pelled, K. M. Eisenhardt, & K. R. Xin, 1999, Exploring the black box: An analysis of work group diversity, conflict, and performance, *Administrative Science Quarterly,* 44: 1–28.
46. E. S. Rubenstein, 1999, Inequality, *Forbes,* November 1, 158-160.
47. Fahey & Narayanan, *Macroenvironmental Analysis,* 105.
48. A. Kutczynski, 2001, Chief abruptly quits magazine group, *The New York Times,* http://www.nytimes.com, August 1; 2001, Update 1-Greenspan says U.S. banks asset quality eroding, *Forbes,* http://www.forbes.com, June 20.
49. J. E. Schrempp, 1999, The world in 1999, Neighbours across the pond, *The Economist,* 28.
50. J. L. Hilsenrath, 2001, Shock waves keep spreading, changing the outlook for cars, hotels—even for cola, *The Wall Street Journal,* http://interactive.wsj.com, October 9.
51. G. Keim, 2001, Business and public policy: Competing in the political marketplace, in M. A. Hitt, R. E. Freeman, J. S. Harrison (Eds.), *Handbook of Strategic Management,* Oxford, U.K.: Blackwell Publishers, 583–601.
52. A. J. Hillman & M. A. Hitt, 1999, Corporate political strategy formulation: A model of approach, participation, and strategy decisions, *Academy of Management Review,* 24: 825–842.
53. M. Carson, 1998, *Global Competitiveness Quarterly,* March 9, 1.
54. R. L. Riley, 1999, Will Uncle Sam trump Internet gamblers? *The Wall Street Journal,* May 14, A14.
55. 1999, Cyberspace: Who will make the rules? *Business Week,* March 22, 30D–30F.
56. J. MacIntyre, 1999, Figuratively speaking, *Across the Board,* May, 11.
57. A. R. Varey & G. Lynn, 1999, Americans save for retirement, *USA Today,* November 16, B1.
58. G. F. Will, 1999, The primacy of culture, *Newsweek,* January 18, 64.
59. 1999, Woman power, *Worth Magazine,* September, 100–101.
60. B. Beck, 1999, The world in 1999, Executive, thy name is woman, *The Economist,* 89; P. Thomas, 1995, Success at a huge personal cost: Comparing women around the world, *The Wall Street Journal,* July 26, B1.
61. R. Taylor, 1999, Pay gap between the sexes widest in W. Europe, *Financial Times,* June 29, 9.
62. J. Raymond, 2001, Defining women: Does the Census Bureau undercount female entrepreneurs? *Business Week Small Biz,* May 21, 12.
63. C. A. Bartlett & S. Ghoshal, 2002, Building competitive advantage through people, *MIT Sloan Management Review,* 43(2): 33–41.
64. 2001,The American metropolis at century's end: Past and future influences, *The Fannie Mae Foundation Survey.*
65. A. Afuah, 2002, Mapping technological capabilities into product markets and competitive advantage: The case of cholesterol drugs, *Strategic Management Journal,* 23: 171–179; X. M. Song, C. A. Di Benedetto, & Y. L. Zhao, 1999, Pioneering advantages in manufacturing and service industries, *Strategic Management Journal,* 20: 811–836.
66. 1999, Business ready for Internet revolution, *Financial Times,* May 21, 17.
67. G. Rifkin, 2001, New economy: Re-evaluating online strategies, *The New York Times,* http://www.nytimes.com, June 25.

68. M. Dell, 1999, The world in 1999, The virtual firm, *The Economist*, 99.
69. 2001, Technology forecast: 2001–2003, PricewaterhouseCoopers, Menlo Park, CA.
70. M. A. Hitt, R. D. Ireland, & H. Lee, 2000, Technological learning, knowledge management, firm growth and performance, *Journal of Technology and Engineering Management*, 17: 231–246.
71. S. Zahra, R. D. Ireland, I. Gutierrez, & M. A. Hitt, 2000, Privatization and entrepreneurial transformation: Emerging issues and a future research agenda, *Academy of Management Review*, 25: 509–524.
72. A. K. Gupta, V. Govindarajan, & A. Malhotra, 1999, Feedback-seeking behavior within multinational corporations, *Strategic Management Journal*, 20: 205–222.
73. 1999, China and the U.S. sign trade deal, clearing hurdle for WTO entry, *The Wall Street Journal*, www.interactive.wsj.com, November 15.
74. J. Kynge, 2001, Murdoch achieves Chinese goal with Star TV deal, *Financial Times*, http://www.ft.com, December 19.
75. R. D. Ireland, M. A. Hitt, S. M. Camp, & D. L. Sexton, 2001, Integrating entrepreneurship and strategic management actions to create firm wealth, *Academy of Management Executive*, 15(1): 49–63.
76. J. W. Lu & P. W. Beamish, 2001, The internationalization and performance of SMEs, *Strategic Management Journal*, 22(special Summer Issue): 565–586.
77. M. Subramaniam & N. Venkatraman, 2001, Determinants of transnational new product development capability: Testing the influence of transferring and deploying tacit overseas knowledge, *Strategic Management Journal*, 22: 359–378; P. J. Lane, J. E. Salk, & M. A. Lyles, 2001, Absorptive capacity, learning and performance in international joint ventures, *Strategic Management Journal*, 22: 1139–1161.
78. S. H. Park & Y. Luo, 2001, Guanxi and organizational dynamics: Organizational networking in Chinese firms, *Strategic Management Journal*, 22: 455–477; M. A. Hitt, M. T. Dacin, B. B. Tyler, & D. Park, 1997, Understanding the differences in Korean and U.S. executives' strategic orientations, *Strategic Management Journal*, 18: 159–167.
79. T. Khanna & K. Palepu, 1999, The right way to restructure conglomerates in emerging markets, *Harvard Business Review*, 77(4): 125–134; Hitt, Dacin, Tyler, & Park, Understanding the differences.
80. Park & Y. Luo, Guanxi and organizational dynamics.
81. M. A. Hitt, H. Lee, & E. Yucel, 2002, The importance of social capital to the management of multinational enterprises: Relational capital among Asian and Western firms, *Asia Pacific Journal of Management*, in press.
82. 2002, Global Crossing denies resemblance to Enron, *Richmond Times Dispatch*, March 22, B15; S. Romero, 2001, Global crossing looks overseas for financing, *The New York Times*, http://www.nytimes.com, December 20; T. Burt, 2001, DaimlerChrysler in talks with Kuwaiti investors, *Financial Times*, http://www.ft.com, February 11.
83. J. Fuerbringer & R. W. Stevenson, 2001, No bailout is planned for Argentina, *The New York Times*, http://www.nytimes.com, July 14; K. L. Newman, 2000, Organizational transformation during institutional upheaval, *Academy of Management Review*, 25: 602–619.
84. M. A. Carpenter & J. W. Fredrickson, 2001, Top management teams, global strategic posture and the moderating role of uncertainty, *Academy of Management Journal*, 44: 533–545.
85. Y. E. Spanos & S. Lioukas, 2001, An examination into the causal logic of rent generation: Contrasting Porter's competitive strategy framework and the resource-based perspective, *Strategic Management Journal*, 22: 907–934.
86. S. Zaheer & A. Zaheer, 2001, Market Microstructure in a global b2b network, *Strategic Management Journal*, 22; 859–873.
87. Hitt, Ricart, Costa, & Nixon, The new frontier.
88. Y. Pan & P. S. K. Chi, 1999, Financial performance and survival of multinational corporations in China, *Strategic Management Journal*, 20: 359–374; G. R. Brooks, 1995, Defining market boundaries, *Strategic Management Journal*, 16: 535–549.
89. P. A. Geroski, 1999, Early warning of new rivals, *Sloan Management Review*, 40(3): 107–116.
90. K. C. Robinson & P. P. McDougall, 2001, Entry barriers and new venture performance: A comparison of universal and contingency approaches, *Strategic Management Journal*, 22(special Summer Issue): 659–685.
91. R. Makadok, 1999, Interfirm differences in scale economies and the evolution of market shares, *Strategic Management Journal*, 20: 935–952.
92. T. McGinnis, 2001, Improving free cash flow, *Forbes*, http://www.forbes.com, December 21.
93. R. Wise & P. Baumgartner, 1999, Go downstream: The new profit imperative in manufacturing, *Harvard Business Review*, 77(5): 133–141; J. H. Gilmore & B. J. Pine, II, 1997, The four faces of mass customization, *Harvard Business Review*, 75(1): 91–101.
94. P. Spiegel, 2001, Senator attacks 'protectionist' EU over GE deal, *Financial Times*, http://www.ft.com, June 21.
95. C. Dawson, 2001, Machete time: In a cost-cutting war with Nissan, Toyota leans on suppliers, *Business Week*, April 9, 42–43.
96. G. Khermouch, 2001, Grown-up drinks for tender taste buds, *Business Week*, March 5, 96.
97. T. Noda & D. J. Collies, 2001, The evolution of intraindustry firm heterogeneity: Insights from a process study, *Academy of Management Journal*, 44: 897–925.
98. D. L. Deephouse, 1999, To be different, or to be the same? It's a question (and theory) of strategic balance, *Strategic Management Journal*, 20: 147–166.
99. W. Chung & A. Kalnins, 2001, Agglomeration effects and performance: Test of the Texas lodging industry, *Strategic Management Journal*, 22: 969–988.
100. W. Kuemmerle, 2001, Home base and knowledge management in international ventures, *Journal of Business Venturing*, 17: 99–122; G. Lorenzoni & A. Lipparini, 1999, The leveraging of interfirm relationships as a distinctive organizational capability: A longitudinal study, *Strategic Management Journal*, 20: 317–338.
101. M. E. Porter, 1980, *Competitive Strategy*, New York: Free Press.
102. M. S. Hunt, 1972, Competition in the major home appliance industry, 1960–1970 (doctoral dissertation, Harvard University); Porter, *Competitive Strategy*, 129.
103. H. R. Greve, 1999, Managerial cognition and the mimetic adoption of market positions: What you see is what you do, *Strategic Management Journal*, 19: 967–988.
104. R. K. Reger & A. S. Huff, 1993, Strategic groups: A cognitive perspective, *Strategic Management Journal*, 14: 103–123.
105. M. Peteraf & M. Shanely, 1997, Getting to know you: A theory of strategic group identity, *Strategic Management Journal*, 18(Special Issue):165–186.
106. A. Nair & S. Kotha, 2001, Does group membership matter? Evidence from the Japanese steel industry, *Strategic Management Journal*, 22: 221–235.
107. J. D. Osborne, C. I. Stubbart, & A. Ramaprasad, 2001, Strategic groups and competitive enactment: A study of dynamic relationships between mental models and performance, *Strategic Management Journal*, 22: 435–454.
108. Greve, Managerial cognition, 972–973.
109. Porter, *Competitive Strategy*, 49.
110. P. M. Norman, R. D. Ireland, K. W. Artz, & M. A. Hitt, 2000, Acquiring and using competitive intelligence in entrepreneurial teams. Paper presented at the Academy of Management, Toronto, Canada.
111. C. S. Fleisher, 1999, Public policy competitive intelligence, *Competitive Intelligence Review*, 10(2): 24.
112. 2001, Fuld & Co., CEO Interview: Claire Hart, President and CEO, Factiva, http://www.dowjones.com, April 4.
113. V. Drucker, 1999, Is your computer a sitting duck during a deal? *Mergers & Acquisitions*, July/August, 25–28; J. Hodges, 1999, Insuring your PC against hackers, *Fortune*, May 24, 280.
114. M. Moss, 1999, Inside the game of e-mail hijacking, *The Wall Street Journal*, November 9, B1, B4.
115. A. Jones, 2001, P&G to seek new resolution of spy dispute, *Financial Times*, http://www.ft.com, September 4.
116. J. H. Hallaq & K. Steinhorst, 1994, Business intelligence methods: How ethical? *Journal of Business Ethics*, 13: 787–794.
117. L. Fahey, 1999, Competitor scenarios: Projecting a rival's marketplace strategy, *Competitive Intelligence Review*, 10(2): 65–85.

3

Chapter Three

The Internal Environment: Resources, Capabilities, and Core Competencies

Knowledge Objectives

Studying this chapter should provide you with the strategic management knowledge needed to:

1. Explain the need for firms to study and understand their internal environment.
2. Define value and discuss its importance.
3. Describe the differences between tangible and intangible resources.
4. Define capabilities and discuss how they are developed.
5. Describe four criteria used to determine whether resources and capabilities are core competencies.
6. Explain how value chain analysis is used to identify and evaluate resources and capabilities.
7. Define outsourcing and discuss the reasons for its use.
8. Discuss the importance of preventing core competencies from becoming core rigidities.

Reputation as a Source of Competitive Advantage

Reputation is defined as the evaluation of a firm by its stakeholders in terms of respect, knowledge or awareness, and emotional or affective regard. A firm's reputation is an intangible resource upon which the company can build capabilities and ultimately core competencies. A company's reputation is also very important in regard to the valuation of the company. The reputation of Coca-Cola, for example, has been valued at $52 billion. Similarly, the reputations of Gillette, Eastman Kodak, Campbell Soup, and Wrigley's Gum have been valued at $12 billion, $11 billion, $9 billion, and $4 billion, respectively.

Because reputation has been such a distinguishing intangible resource, many firms have tried to build perceptual measures of this asset that provide a signal to rivals and stakeholders of the competitive value of their reputations. Each year several periodicals publish rankings of firms based on reputation. For instance, *Fortune* surveys 10,000 executives, directors, and securities analysts to develop its America's Most Admired Companies list (see Table 3.1). The *Financial Times* World's Most Respected Companies survey has an exclusive emphasis on peer evaluation—its ratings are based on evaluations by peer CEOs. Other services, including those provided by Burson-Marsteller, Delahaye Medialink, the Reputation Institute, and Corporate Branding LLC, use various approaches to rank their clients' reputations. Each ranking service maintains that its ranking provides a unique and valuable perspective.

During his two decades as GE's CEO, Jack Welch (left) guided the firm to consistent growth and had a legendary reputation for his leadership style. Jeff Immelt (right) took over from Welch on September 10, 2001, and faced the toughest economy in 20 years, skepticism about financial reporting, and uncertainty. He quickly responded by tightening costs, providing full disclosure in reporting, and reaching out to the customer. "This is not just a job," Immelt says. "This is a passion. This is my life."

Charles Fombrun and colleagues have argued that many ranking services are in the business of public relations rather than academic measurement. In their research, Fombrun and his colleagues use 20 attributes to develop a "reputational quotient." These attributes are divided into six reputation categories: emotional appeal, social responsibility, financial performance, vision and leadership, workplace environment, and products and services.

A firm can develop intangible distinctions between itself from its rivals within each reputational category. These value-creating distinctions help the firm develop the type of reputation that can become a core competence.

Southwest Airlines (further discussed in Chapter 4) has an *emotional appeal* based on its reputation for being a maverick in the rather commodity-like airlines industry. Since cofounder and now retired CEO Herb Kelleher took over in 1978, the company has not lost money in any year. While fare wars, recessions, oil crises, and other disasters have plagued the industry at large and created massive losses for larger airlines such as Delta, United, and American, Southwest's reputation has helped it to sustain its competitive advantage during difficult industry cycles.

Many firms have built their reputations by emphasizing *social responsibility.* The Body Shop, 3M, and DuPont are all firms whose environmental expenditures created an environmentally based competitive advantage. On the other hand, a firm's reputation and image can both suffer when it is involved in a disaster. Exxon lost its reputation in the area of social responsibility following the Valdez oil tanker disaster, for example, and it faced a long road back to regain it. Firestone tire failures on Ford's Explorers hurt the reputations of both Ford and Firestone.

Under former CEO Jack Welch, General Electric (GE) enjoyed consistently high *financial performance* over a number of years and, in the process, built a reputation for steady value creation for its shareholders. It will be interesting to see if GE retains its reputation as a competitive advantage under the leadership of new CEO, Jeffrey Immelt.

Welch also helped GE's reputation for its financial performance with his *vision* and *leadership.* Many of the corporations mentioned above also attribute their success to leaders who produced and communicated a strategic mission (see Chapter 1) to employees, fostering the implementation of the firm's strategic intent. Apple has risen, fallen, and risen again through various leaders, but Steven Jobs, in particular, has had a significant influence on Apple's fortunes over the years, as cofounder and CEO.

If a company can hire better-skilled people because of its reputation for building human capital, it will likely increase its "intellectual capital" (the sum of everything that everybody in the company knows) relative to other firms and enhance its reputation for its *workplace environment.*[1] Intellectual capital can provide competitive advantage for the firm as it competes against its rivals. Merck & Company has been voted as one of America's most admired companies in *Fortune*'s annual survey every year since the list's 1982 inception. Its employees have invented more new medicines than any other American pharmaceutical company. Merck's reputation for supporting the people who bring value-creating intellectual capital to the firm enables it to hire productive researchers, whose work contributes to Merck's success. But without a strong reputation for treating its employees fairly and professionally, it's unlikely that a firm will attract and retain the people required for it to be a leader in intellectual capital.

The most recognized reputational attribute is a firm's brand or trademark. Coca-Cola Company has one of the world's most famous—and some think most valuable—brands. Microsoft also has a strong brand. However, the brands for both companies have recently suffered damage to their reputations. Poor product quality in Europe undermined Coca-Cola's brand; for Microsoft, it's a continuing antitrust case. A strong reputation for a *product* or *service* takes years to develop, but this intangible asset can lose value quickly if the firm does not take care to address reputation threats that might reduce its value. Thus, firms must manage their reputations to build a strong base of value for this important intangible asset. Without appropriate attention to managing this resource, its value can dissipate rapidly.

SOURCES: M. Boyle, 2002, The shiniest reputations in tarnished times, *Fortune,* March 4, 70–72; G. Khermouch, 2002, What makes a boffo brand, *Business Week* (Special Issue), Spring, 20; A. Diba & L. Munoz, 2001, How long can they stay? *Fortune,* February 19, http://www.fortune.com; T. A. Stewart, 2001, Intellectual capital, *Fortune,* May 28, http://www.fortune.com; C. J. Fombrun, N. A. Gardberg, & M. J. Barnett, 2000, Opportunity platforms and safety nets: Corporate citizenship and reputational risk, *Business and Society Review,* 105(1): 85–106; D.L. Deephouse, 2000, Media reputation as a strategic resource: An integration of mass communication and resource-based theories, *Journal of Management,* 26: 1091–1112; C. Eidson & M. Master, 2000, Top ten . . . Most admired . . . Most respected; Who makes the call? *Across the Board,* 37(3): 16–22; P. M. Morgan & J. G. Covin, 2000, Environmental marketing: A source of reputational, competitive and financial advantage, *Journal of Business Ethics,* 23(3): 299–311; J. A. Petrick, R. F. Scherer, J. D. Brodzinski, J. F. Quinn, & M. F. Ainina, 1999, Global leadership skills and reputational capital: Intangible resources of sustainable competitive advantage, *Academy of Management Executive,* 13(1): 58–69.

The firms mentioned in the Opening Case have used their resources and capabilities (see Chapter 1) to create reputation as a source of competitive advantage. Organizations that rely on reputation as a competitive advantage want that advantage to be *sustainable.* Table 3.1 lists several firms that have sustained their reputations and the advantages associated with being rated as America's Most Admired Corporations by *Fortune* magazine. However, as discussed in the first two chapters, several factors in the global economy, including the rapid development of the Internet's capabilities, have made it increasingly difficult for firms to develop a competitive advantage that can be sustained for any period of time.[2] In these instances, firms try to create advantages that can be sustained longer than can others. Regardless of its sustainability, however, a sustainable competitive advantage is developed when firms use the strategic management process to implement strategies that uniquely use a firm's resources, capabilities, and core competencies.

The fact that "competitive advantage continues to provide the central agenda in strategy research"[3] highlights its importance. Competitive advantage research is critical because "resources are the foundation for strategy and (the) unique bundles of resources (that) generate competitive advantages leading to wealth creation."[4] To identify and successfully use their competitive advantages over time, firms think constantly about their strategic management process and how to increase the value it creates.[5] As this chapter's discussion indicates, firms achieve strategic competitiveness and earn above-average returns when their unique core competencies are effectively leveraged to take advantage of opportunities in the external environment.

Increasingly, people are a key source of competitive advantage as organizations compete in the global economy.[6] At Walt Disney Company, for example, the importance of intellectual capital has become increasingly apparent. Walt Disney Studios,

Table 3.1 *Fortune*'s Most Admired Corporate Rankings in 2001, 2000, and 1999

2001 The Top Ten	2000 The Top Ten	1999 The Top Ten
1. General Electric	1. General Electric	1. General Electric
2. Southwest Airlines	2. Cisco Systems	2. Microsoft
3. Wal-Mart Stores	3. Wal-Mart Stores	3. Dell Computer
4. Microsoft	4. Southwest Airlines	4. Cisco Systems
5. Berkshire Hathaway	5. Microsoft	5. Wal-Mart Stores
6. Home Depot	6. Home Depot	6. Southwest Airlines
7. Johnson & Johnson	7. Berkshire Hathaway	7. Berkshire Hathaway
8. FedEx	8. Charles Schwab	8. Intel
9. Citigroup	9. Intel	9. Home Depot
10. Intel	10. Dell Computer	10. Lucent Technologies

SOURCES: M. Boyle, 2002, The shiniest reputations in tarnished times, *Fortune,* March 4, 70–72; A. Diba & L. Munoz, 2001, America's most admired companies, *Fortune,* February 19, 64–66; G. Colvin, 2000, America's most admired companies, *Fortune,* February 21, 108–116.

which in recent years has led the movie industry in market share, is experiencing competitive difficulties. The company's top strategic leaders, Chairman Michael D. Eisner and President Peter Schneider, are focusing on greater financial discipline in the studio at a time when Disney is producing fewer movies and generating less impact on the market. This focus on cost cutting has lead to corporate downsizing and, many believe, the loss of some of the "creative fire" in Disney's animation division. The firm "has become . . . famous in recent years for the people who have left [the studio]." One of the firm's newer animated productions, "Atlantis: The Lost Empire," did not generate as much excitement in the marketplace as past Disney releases, which suggests that Disney's cost cutting and loss of important employees have seriously decreased the quality and quantity of that all-important resource, intellectual capital, and especially the creativity aspect of intellectual capital.[7]

Over time, the benefits of any firm's value-creating strategy can be duplicated by its competitors. In other words, all competitive advantages have a limited life.[8] The question of duplication is not *if* it will happen, but *when.* In general, the sustainability of a competitive advantage is a function of three factors: (1) the rate of core competence obsolescence because of environmental changes, (2) the availability of substitutes for the core competence, and (3) the imitability of the core competence.[9]

The challenge in all firms is to effectively manage current core competencies while simultaneously developing new ones.[10] In the words of Michael Dell, CEO of Dell Computer Corporation, "No [competitive] advantage and no success is ever permanent. The winners are those who keep moving. The only constant in our business is that everything is changing. We have to be ahead of the game."[11] Only when firms develop a continuous stream of competitive advantages do they achieve strategic competitiveness, earn above-average returns, and remain ahead of competitors (see Chapter 5).

In Chapter 2, we examined general, industry, and competitor environments. Armed with this type of knowledge about the realities and conditions of their environments, firms have a better understanding of marketplace opportunities and the goods or services through which they can be pursued. In this chapter, we focus on the firm itself. Through an analysis of its internal environment, a firm determines what it *can do*—that is, the actions permitted by its unique resources, capabilities, and core competencies. As discussed in Chapter 1, core competencies are a firm's source of competitive advantage. The magnitude of that competitive advantage is a function primarily of the uniqueness of the firm's core competencies compared to those of its competitors.[12] Matching what a firm *can do* with what it *might do* (a function of opportunities and threats in the external environment) allows the firm to develop strategic intent, pursue its strategic mission, and select and implement its strategies. Outcomes resulting from internal and external environmental analyses are shown in Figure 3.1.

We examine several topics in this chapter, beginning with the importance and challenge of studying the firm's internal environment. We then discuss the roles of resources, capabilities, and core competencies in developing sustainable competitive advantage. Included in this discussion are the techniques firms can use to identify and evaluate resources and capabilities and the criteria for selecting core competencies from among them. Resources, capabilities, and core competencies are not inherently valuable, but they create value when the firm can use them to perform certain activities that result in a competitive advantage. Accordingly, we also discuss in this chapter the value chain concept and examine four criteria to evaluate core competences that establish competitive advantage.[13]

The Importance of Internal Analysis

In the global economy, traditional factors—such as labor costs, access to financial resources and raw materials, and protected or regulated markets—continue to be sources of competitive advantage, but to a lesser degree than before.[14] One important reason for this decline is that the advantages created by these sources can be overcome through an international strategy (discussed in Chapter 8) and by the relatively free flow of resources throughout the global economy.

Few firms can consistently make the most effective strategic decisions unless they can change rapidly. A key challenge to developing the ability to change rapidly is fostering an organizational setting in which experimentation and learning are expected and promoted.[15] The demands of 21st-century competition require top-level managers to rethink earlier concepts of the firm and competition. For example, Polaroid Corporation sought to accommodate a significant technological shift by changing from analog to digital imaging. Polaroid's managers needed to gain a different understanding of their competitive world and the firm's existing capabilities as well as the new capabilities that were needed. The firm had to overcome the trajectory of its analog imaging capabilities so it could focus on developing and using capabilities required by digital imaging.[16] While the Polaroid story clearly illustrates the importance of managers seeking to direct the firm through a completely new competitive environment, Polaroid's management was not successful and the firm was facing bankruptcy by the end of 2001[17] and preparing to sell major portions of its assets in mid-2002.

Figure 3.1 Outcomes from External and Internal Environmental Analyses

By studying the external environment, firms identify	By studying the internal environment, firms determine
• what they *might* choose to *do*	• what they *can do*

In addition to the firm's ability to change rapidly, a different managerial mind-set is required for firms to be successful in the global economy. Most top-level managers recognize the need to change their mind-sets, but many hesitate to do so. In the words of the European CEO of a major U.S. company, "It is more reassuring for all of us to stay as we are, even though we know the result will be certain failure . . . than to jump into a new way of working when we cannot be sure it will succeed."[18] Jacques Nasser, Ford Motor Company's former CEO, was quite outspoken in his belief that all employees—especially senior-level executives—had to change their mind-set from concentrating on their own area of operation to encompassing a view of the company in its entirety. Nasser felt this change was key to generating the type of rapid decision making required for Ford to be successful in a fast-changing world.[19] Ultimately, however, Nasser may have forced too much change too quickly on Ford employees. One analyst suggested, "I think Ford management is really stretched. There are just too many initiatives going on. Now, they're paying the price for taking their eye off the ball."[20]

Also critical is that managers view the firm as a *bundle* of heterogeneous resources, capabilities, and core competencies that can be used to create an exclusive market position.[21] This perspective suggests that individual firms possess at least some resources and capabilities that other companies do not—at least not in the same combination. Resources are the source of capabilities, some of which lead to the development of a firm's core competencies.[22] Figure 3.2 illustrates the relationships among resources, capabilities, and core competencies and shows how firms use them to create strategic competitiveness. Essentially, the mind-set needed in the global economy requires decision makers to define their firm's strategy in terms of a *unique competitive position*, rather than strictly in terms of operational effectiveness. For instance, Michael Porter argues that quests for productivity, quality, and speed from using a number of management techniques—total quality management (TQM),

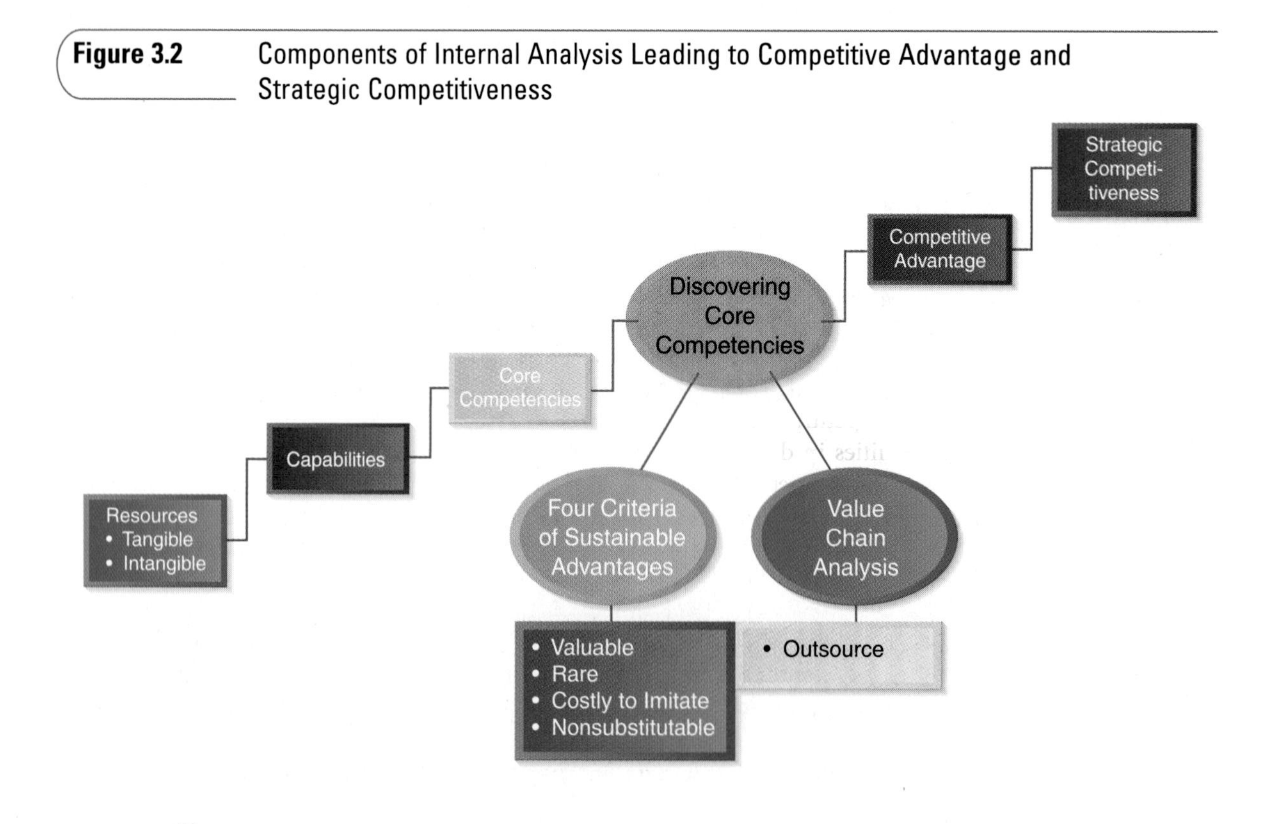

Figure 3.2 Components of Internal Analysis Leading to Competitive Advantage and Strategic Competitiveness

benchmarking, time-based competition, and re-engineering—have resulted in operational efficiency, but have not resulted in strong sustainable strategies.[23] As we discussed in Chapter 1, strategic competitiveness results when the firm satisfies the operational efficiency demands of its external environment while simultaneously using its own unique capabilities to establish a viable strategic position. Because of its importance to business-level strategies, strategic positioning is discussed in greater detail in Chapter 4.

Creating Value

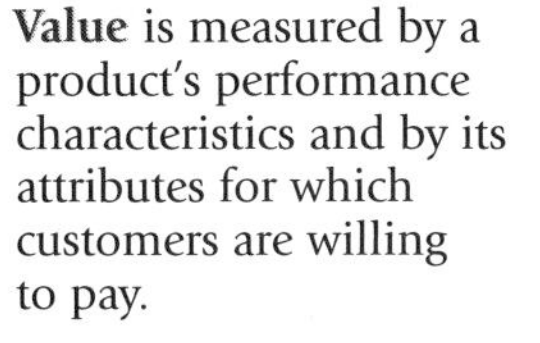
Value is measured by a product's performance characteristics and by its attributes for which customers are willing to pay.

By exploiting core competencies and meeting the demanding standards of global competition, firms create value for customers.[24] **Value** is measured by a product's performance characteristics and by its attributes for which customers are willing to pay.[25]

Sometimes consistency and predictability provide value to customers, such as the type of value Walgreens provides. As noted by a business writer, "Do you realize that from 1975 to today, Walgreens beat Intel? It beat Intel nearly two to one, GE almost five to one. It beat 3M, Coke, Boeing, Motorola."[26] Walgreens was able to do this by using its competencies to offer value desired by its target customer group. Instead of responding to the trends of the day, "During the Internet scare of 1998 and 1999, when slogans of 'Change or Die!' were all but graffitied on the subway, Walgreens obstinately stuck to its corporate credo of 'Crawl, walk, run.' Its refusal to act until it thoroughly understood the implications of e-commerce was deeply unfashionable, but . . . Walgreens is the epitome of the inner-directed company."[27] Thus, Walgreens creates value by focusing on the unique capabilities it has built, nurtured, and continues to improve across time.

Ultimately, creating customer value is the source of a firm's potential to earn above-average returns. What the firm intends regarding value creation affects its choice of business-level strategy (see Chapter 4) and its organizational structure (see Chapter 11).[28] In Chapter 4's discussion of business-level strategies, we note that value is created by a product's low cost, by its highly differentiated features, or by a combination of low cost and high differentiation, compared to competitors' offerings. A business-level strategy is effective only when its use is grounded in exploiting the firm's current core competencies while actions are being taken to develop the core competencies that will be needed to effectively use "tomorrow's" business-level strategy. Thus, successful firms continuously examine the effectiveness of current and future core competencies.[29]

During the last several decades, the strategic management process was concerned largely with understanding the characteristics of the industry in which the firm competed and, in light of those characteristics, determining how the firm should position itself relative to competitors. This emphasis on industry characteristics and competitive strategy may have understated the role of the firm's resources and capabilities in developing competitive advantage. In the current competitive landscape, core competencies, in combination with product-market positions, are the firm's most important sources of competitive advantage.[30] The core competencies of a firm, in addition to its analysis of its general, industry, and competitor environments, should drive its selection of strategies. As Clayton Christensen noted: "Successful strategists need to cultivate a deep understanding of the processes of competition and progress and of the factors that undergird each advantage. Only thus will they be able to see when old advantages are poised to disappear and how new advantages can be built in their stead."[31] By emphasizing core competencies when formulating strategies, companies learn to compete primarily on the basis of firm-specific differences, but they must be very aware of how things are changing as well.

The Challenge of Internal Analysis

The decisions managers make in terms of the firm's resources, capabilities, and core competencies have a significant influence on the firm's ability to earn above-average returns.[32] Making these decisions—identifying, developing, deploying, and protecting resources, capabilities, and core competencies—may appear to be relatively easy. In fact, however, this task is as challenging and difficult as any other with which managers are involved; moreover, it is increasingly internationalized and linked with the firm's success.[33] Managers also face great pressure to pursue only those decisions that help the firm to meet the quarterly earning numbers expected by market analysts.[34] Recognizing the firm's core competencies is essential before the firm can make important strategic decisions, including those related to entering or exiting markets, investing in new technologies, building new or additional manufacturing capacity, or forming strategic partnerships.[35] Patterns of interactions between individuals and groups that occur as strategic decisions affect decision quality as well as how effectively and quickly these decisions are implemented.[36]

The challenge and difficulty of making effective decisions is implied by preliminary evidence suggesting that one-half of organizational decisions fail.[37] Sometimes, mistakes are made as the firm analyzes its internal environment. Managers might, for example, select resources and capabilities as the firm's core competencies that do not create a competitive advantage. When a mistake occurs, decision makers must have the confidence to admit it and take corrective actions.[38] A firm can still grow through well-intended errors—the learning generated by making and correcting mistakes can be important to the creation of new competitive advantages.[39] Moreover, firms can learn from the failure resulting from a mistake; that is, what *not* to do when seeking competitive advantage.[40]

To facilitate the development and use of core competencies, managers must have courage, self-confidence, integrity, the capacity to deal with uncertainty and complexity, and a willingness to hold people accountable for their work and to be held accountable themselves. Thus, difficult managerial decisions concerning resources, capabilities, and core competencies are characterized by three conditions: uncertainty, complexity, and intraorganizational conflicts (see Figure 3.3).[41]

Figure 3.3 Conditions Affecting Managerial Decisions about Resources, Capabilities, and Core Competencies

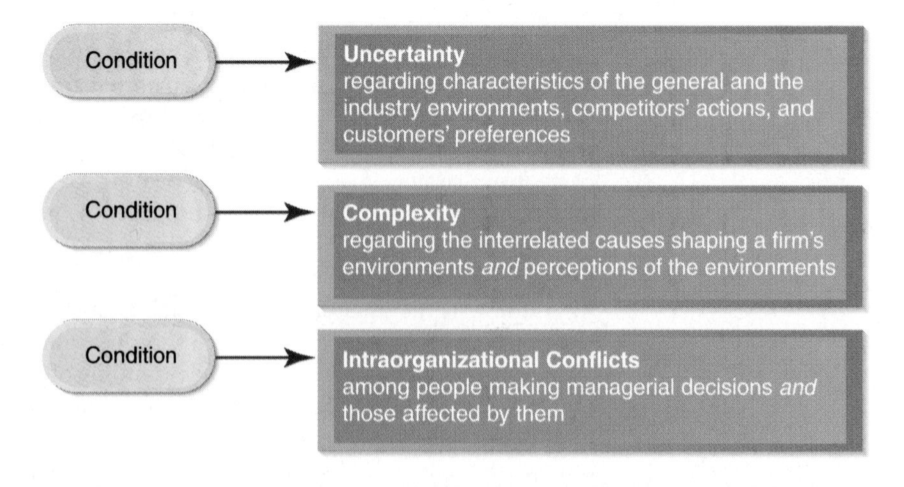

SOURCE: Adapted from R. Amit & P. J. H. Schoemaker, 1993, Strategic assets and organizational rent, *Strategic Management Journal*, 14: 33.

Managers face *uncertainty* in terms of new proprietary technologies, rapidly changing economic and political trends, transformations in societal values, and shifts in customer demands.[42] Environmental uncertainty increases the *complexity* and range of issues to examine when studying the internal environment. Biases about how to cope with uncertainty affect decisions about the resources and capabilities that will become the foundation of the firm's competitive advantage. Finally, *intraorganizational conflict* surfaces when decisions are made about the core competencies to nurture as well as how to nurture them.

In making decisions affected by these three conditions, judgment should be used. *Judgment* is the capability of making successful decisions when no obviously correct model or rule is available or when relevant data are unreliable or incomplete. In this type of situation, decision makers must be aware of possible cognitive biases. Overconfidence, for example, can often lower value when a correct decision is not obvious, such as making a judgment as to whether an internal resource is a strength or a weakness.[43]

When exercising judgment, decision makers demonstrate a willingness to take intelligent risks in a timely manner. In the current competitive landscape, executive judgment can be a particularly important source of competitive advantage. One reason for this is that, over time, effective judgment allows a firm to build a strong reputation and retain the loyalty of stakeholders whose support is linked to above-average returns.[44]

Significant changes in the value-creating potential of a firm's resources and capabilities can occur in a rapidly changing global economy.[45] Because these changes affect a company's power and social structure, inertia or resistance to change may surface. Even though these reactions may happen, decision makers should not deny the changes needed to assure the firm's strategic competitiveness. *Denial* is an unconscious coping mechanism used to block out and not initiate painful changes.[46] For example, Opel was once Germany's number one "everyman's car." Of late, however, the GM-owned European carmaker has suffered operating losses ($429 million in 2000 alone) and poor brand image. Concentrating on making changes in how the firm performs its primary and support activities, Carl-Peter Forster, head of Opel, candidly faced the problem and developed a restructuring plan that should reduce purchasing costs, streamline and modernize the firm's ineffective sales unit, and define new areas of potential growth beyond car sales. These actions, some of which could be painful, may improve the image of the firm's brand and subsequently, its competitive ability.[47]

Because some people have a strong tendency to resist the changes needed to cope with intensely competitive environments, involving a range of individuals and groups is important when making changes in a firm's value-creating abilities.[48]

Resources, Capabilities, and Core Competencies

Resources, capabilities, and core competencies are the characteristics that make up the foundation of competitive advantage. Resources are the source of a firm's capabilities. Capabilities in turn are the source of a firm's core competencies, which are the basis of competitive advantages.[49] As shown in Figure 3.2, combinations of resources and capabilities are managed to create core competencies. In this section we define and provide examples of these building blocks of competitive advantage.

Resources

Broad in scope, resources cover a spectrum of individual, social, and organizational phenomena.[50] Typically, resources alone do not yield a competitive advantage.[51] In

© MARK RICHARDS/PHOTO EDIT

Amazon.com showed a profit for the first time ever in the last quarter of 2001, helped by lucrative fees it earned by selling other firms' products. The world's largest online seller of books, CDs, and DVDs has huge revenues but slender profit margins. It hopes to become the top online resource for electronics, toys, and housewares through partnerships with traditional retailers Target, Toys 'R' Us, Circuit City, and Borders.

fact, a competitive advantage is created through the *unique bundling of several resources.*[52] For example, Amazon.com has combined service and distribution resources to develop its competitive advantages. The firm started as an online bookseller, directly shipping orders to customers. It quickly grew large and established a distribution network through which it could ship "millions of different items to millions of different customers." Compared to Amazon's use of combined resources, traditional bricks-and-mortar companies, such as Toys 'R' Us and Borders, found it hard to establish an effective online presence. These difficulties led them to develop partnerships with Amazon. Through these arrangements, Amazon now handles online presence and the shipping of goods for several firms, including Toys 'R' Us and Borders—which now can focus on sales in their stores. Arrangements such as these are useful to the bricks-and-mortar companies because they are not accustomed to shipping so much diverse merchandise directly to individuals.[53]

Tangible resources are assets that can be seen and quantified.

Intangible resources include assets that typically are rooted deeply in the firm's history and have accumulated over time.

Some of a firm's resources are tangible while others are intangible. **Tangible resources** are assets that can be seen and quantified. Production equipment, manufacturing plants, and formal reporting structures are examples of tangible resources. **Intangible resources** include assets that typically are rooted deeply in the firm's history and have accumulated over time. Because they are embedded in unique patterns of routines, intangible resources are relatively difficult for competitors to analyze and imitate. Knowledge, trust between managers and employees, ideas, the capacity for innovation, managerial capabilities, organizational routines (the unique ways people work together), scientific capabilities, and the firm's reputation for its goods or services and how it interacts with people (such as employees, customers, and suppliers) are all examples of intangible resources.[54]

The four types of tangible resources are financial, organizational, physical, and technological (see Table 3.2). The three types of intangible resources are human, innovation, and reputational (see Table 3.3).

Tangible Resources

As tangible resources, a firm's borrowing capacity and the status of its plant and equipment are visible. The value of many tangible resources can be established through financial statements, but these statements do not account for the value of all of a firm's assets, because they disregard some intangible resources.[55] As such, each of the firm's sources of competitive advantage typically are not be reflected fully on corporate financial statements. The value of tangible resources is also constrained because they are difficult to leverage—it is hard to derive additional business or value from a tangible resource. For example, an airplane is a tangible resource or asset, but: "You can't use the same airplane on five different routes at the same time. You can't put the same crew on five different routes at the same time. And the same goes for the financial investment you've made in the airplane."[56]

Although manufacturing assets are tangible, many of the processes to use these assets are intangible. Thus, the learning and potential proprietary processes associated

Table 3.2 Tangible Resources

Financial Resources	• The firm's borrowing capacity • The firm's ability to generate internal funds
Organizational Resources	• The firm's formal reporting structure and its formal planning, controlling, and coordinating systems
Physical Resources	• Sophistication and location of a firm's plant and equipment • Access to raw materials
Technological Resources	• Stock of technology, such as patents, trademarks, copyrights, and trade secrets

SOURCES: Adapted from J. B. Barney, 1991, Firm resources and sustained competitive advantage, *Journal of Management,* 17: 101; R. M. Grant, 1991, *Contemporary Strategy Analysis,* Cambridge, U.K.: Blackwell Business, 100–102.

with a tangible resource, such as manufacturing equipment, can have unique intangible attributes such as quality, just-in-time management practices, and unique manufacturing processes that develop over time and create competitive advantage.[57]

Intangible Resources

As suggested above, compared to tangible resources, intangible resources are a superior and more potent source of core competencies.[58] In fact, in the global economy, "the success of a corporation lies more in its intellectual and systems capabilities than in its physical assets. [Moreover], the capacity to manage human intellect—and to convert it into useful products and services—is fast becoming the critical executive skill of the age."[59]

There is some evidence that the value of intangible assets is growing relative to that of tangible assets. John Kendrick, a well-known economist studying the main

Table 3.3 Intangible Resources

Human Resources	• Knowledge • Trust • Managerial capabilities • Organizational routines
Innovation Resources	• Ideas • Scientific capabilities • Capacity to innovate
Reputational Resources	• Reputation with customers • Brand name • Perceptions of product quality, durability, and reliability • Reputation with suppliers • For efficient, effective, supportive, and mutually beneficial interactions and relationships

SOURCES: Adapted from R. Hall, 1992, The strategic analysis of intangible resources, *Strategic Management Journal,* 13: 136–139; R. M. Grant, 1991, *Contemporary Strategy Analysis,* Cambridge, U.K.: Blackwell Business, 101–104.

Strategic Focus

Microsoft's Resources and Capabilities

All companies need financial resources to grow and be successful, and there is really no such thing as a firm having too many financial resources, especially if they are used wisely. The firm with excellent access to external and internal funds is in the enviable position of being able to develop in ways that allow it to use its strategies effectively. Microsoft, the world's leading software company, has $30 billion in cash—a figure made even more amazing by the fact that its average growth rate is $1 billion every month. What could Microsoft do with this tangible resource, and what does it actually do with it?

Microsoft is best known for its two main products, Microsoft Windows and Microsoft Office, which generate the bulk of its income. Among numerous other product and market development projects, the company is establishing a presence in the small business market; it is developing an online position through MSN.com, and it is entering the console-game market with a new brand, the Xbox. Many of the markets Microsoft is pursuing are already well established with market leaders and entrenched products. For instance, Xbox competes against Sony's PlayStation 2 and Nintendo's GameCube. Even though it has no competitive advantage in this market, Microsoft has the resources and capabilities to enter it.

Microsoft's cash hoard also allows it to rapidly enter new markets and literally acquire market share by purchasing companies that already have a market presence. For example, in December 2000, Microsoft purchased Great Plains Software Inc. for $1.1 billion. Great Plains is a leader in finance and accounting software for smaller businesses, a market in which Microsoft had not been a serious contender.

Because Microsoft earns above-average returns, it has the financial resources to stimulate continued growth. When MSN.com was first introduced, initial customer reaction wasn't supportive. The brand languished for years. However, through perseverance and Microsoft's purchases of other Internet service providers, MSN.com has emerged as the second-most popular portal on the Web behind AOL. The venture's success was also helped by Microsoft investments of $100 million in Radio Shack Corp. and $200 million in

---

drivers of economic growth, found a general increase in the contribution of intangible assets to U.S. economic growth since the early 1900s: "In 1929, the ratio of intangible business capital to tangible business capital was 30 percent to 70 percent. In 1990, that ratio was 63 percent to 37 percent."[60]

Because intangible resources are less visible and more difficult for competitors to understand, purchase, imitate, or substitute for, firms prefer to rely on them rather than tangible resources as the foundation for their capabilities and core competencies. In fact, the more unobservable (that is, intangible) a resource is, the more sustainable will be the competitive advantage that is based on it. Another benefit of intangible resources is that, unlike most tangible resources, their use can be leveraged. With intangible resources, the larger the network of users, the greater is the benefit to each party.[61] For instance, sharing knowledge among employees does not diminish its value for any one person. To the contrary, two people sharing their individualized knowledge sets often can be leveraged to create additional knowledge that although new to each of them, contributes to performance improvements for the firm.[62]

As illustrated in the Opening Case, the intangible resource of reputation is an important source of competitive advantage for companies such as Coca-Cola, General Electric, and Southwest Airlines. Earned through the firm's actions as well as its words, a value-creating reputation is a product of years of superior marketplace competence as perceived by stakeholders.[63] A well-known and highly valued brand name is an application

Best Buy Co. in exchange for their promotion of MSN's access service. Microsoft's investments were possible only because of Microsoft's tremendous cash flow.

Microsoft's significant financial resources also supported its introduction of the Xbox to an established home video-game market. In addition to the cost of designing and developing the Xbox, Microsoft spent $500 million to market it—an amount of money that few other companies could afford.

A strong financial resource also makes possible Microsoft's competitively superior research and development (R&D) skills. As part of an innovation intangible resource (see Table 3.4), R&D contributes significantly to Microsoft's historic ability to earn above-average returns. In 2000, for example, Microsoft allocated $3.7 billion to R&D, and $4.2 billion in 2001—more than the combined R&D allocations for Microsoft rivals America Online, Sun Microsystems, and Oracle. The integration of a strong tangible resource (financial capacity) with an effective intangible resource (R&D) creates an important competitive advantage for Microsoft.

An old adage says: "You must spend money to make money." Microsoft's robust financial resource allows it to support its intangible resources in ways that can create new competitive advantages or that can support the continuing development of existing advantages. Furthermore, Microsoft uses its resources well. For instance, its purchasing capabilities allowed the firm to recently reduce its annual purchasing costs by $46 million. As discussed later in this chapter, a reduction in a firm's purchasing costs is an example of how value can be created through support activities.

Thus, Microsoft expertly uses a key tangible resource—cash—to foster its intangible resources, including R&D and marketing activities, as well as to build Microsoft's brand name. The result is a powerful capability to develop new products and enter new markets.

SOURCES: S. Avery, 2001, Microsoft cuts buying costs by $46 million, *Purchasing,* January 25, 48–57; 2001, Case vs. Gates: Playing for the web jackpot, *Businessweek Online,* http://www.businessweek.com, June 18; P. Burrows, J. Greene, & A. Park, 2001, SOS: Microsoft to the rescue? *Businessweek Online,* http://www.businessweek.com, June 25; N. Croal, 2001, Game wars 5.0, *Newsweek,* May 28, 65–66; J. DiSabatino, 2001, Microsoft officially launches Office XP, *Computerworld,* June 4, 10; J. Green, 2001, Microsoft: How it became stronger than ever, *Business Week,* June 4, 74–85; A. Hamilton, 2001, Office whizbang, *Time,* June 4, 82; P. Rooney, 2001, Microsoft pushes ahead with Office XP, http://www.CRN.com, June 4; B. Schlender, 2001, Microsoft: The beast is back, *Fortune,* June 11, 75–86.

of reputation as a source of competitive advantage. The Harley-Davidson brand name, for example, has such cachet that it adorns a limited-edition Barbie doll, a popular restaurant in New York City, and a line of L'Oreal cologne. Moreover, Harley-Davidson MotorClothes annually generates over $100 million in revenue for the firm and offers a broad range of clothing items, from black leather jackets to fashions for tots.[64]

Decision makers are challenged to understand fully the strategic value of their firm's tangible and intangible resources. The *strategic value of resources* is indicated by the degree to which they can contribute to the development of capabilities, core competencies, and, ultimately, competitive advantage. For example, as a tangible resource, a distribution facility is assigned a monetary value on the firm's balance sheet. The real value of the facility, however, is grounded in a variety of factors, such as its proximity to raw materials and customers, but also in intangible factors such as the manner in which workers integrate their actions internally and with other stakeholders, such as suppliers and customers.[65]

Capabilities

As a source of capabilities, tangible and intangible resources are a critical part of the pathway to the development of competitive advantage (as shown earlier in Figure 3.2). This is illustrated well in the Strategic Focus on Microsoft on page 84.

Capabilities are the firm's capacity to deploy resources that have been purposely integrated to achieve a desired end state.[66] The glue binding an organization together, capabilities emerge over time through complex interactions among tangible and intangible resources. The discussion of Microsoft in the Strategic Focus demonstrates these complex interactions. Critical to the forming of competitive advantages, capabilities are often based on developing, carrying, and exchanging information and knowledge through the firm's human capital.[67] Because a knowledge base is grounded in organizational actions that may not be explicitly understood by all employees, repetition and practice increase the value of a firm's capabilities.

The foundation of many capabilities lies in the skills and knowledge of a firm's employees and, often, their functional expertise. Hence, the value of human capital in developing and using capabilities and, ultimately, core competencies cannot be overstated. Firms committed to continuously developing their people's capabilities seem to accept the adage that "the person who knows how will always have a job. The person who knows why will always be his boss."[68]

Global business leaders increasingly support the view that the knowledge possessed by human capital is among the most significant of an organization's capabilities and may ultimately be at the root of all competitive advantages. But firms must also be able to utilize the knowledge that they have and transfer it among their operating businesses.[69] For example, researchers have suggested that "in the information age, things are ancillary, knowledge is central. A company's value derives not from things, but from knowledge, know-how, intellectual assets, competencies—all of it embedded in people."[70] Given this reality, the firm's challenge is to create an environment that allows people to fit their individual pieces of knowledge together so that, collectively, employees possess as much organizational knowledge as possible.[71]

To help them develop an environment in which knowledge is widely spread across all employees, some organizations have created the new upper-level managerial position of chief learning officer (CLO). Establishing a CLO position highlights a firm's belief that "future success will depend on competencies that traditionally have not been actively managed or measured—including creativity and the speed with which new ideas are learned and shared."[72] In general, the firm should manage knowledge in ways that will support its efforts to create value for customers.[73]

As illustrated in Table 3.4, capabilities are often developed in specific functional areas (such as manufacturing, R&D, and marketing) or in a part of a functional area (for example, advertising). Research suggests a relationship between capabilities developed in particular functional areas and the firm's financial performance at both the corporate and business-unit levels,[74] suggesting the need to develop capabilities at both levels. Table 3.4 shows a grouping of organizational functions and the capabilities that some companies are thought to possess in terms of all or parts of those functions.

Core Competencies

Defined in Chapter 1, *core competencies* are resources and capabilities that serve as a source of a firm's competitive advantage over rivals. Core competencies distinguish a company competitively and reflect its personality. Core competencies emerge over time through an organizational process of accumulating and learning how to deploy different resources and capabilities. As the capacity to take action, core competencies are "crown jewels of a company," the activities the company performs especially well compared to competitors and through which the firm adds unique value to its goods or services over a long period of time.[75]

Not all of a firm's resources and capabilities are *strategic assets*—that is, assets that have competitive value and the potential to serve as a source of competitive advantage.[76] Some resources and capabilities may result in incompetence, because they represent competitive areas in which the firm is weak compared to competitors. Thus, some resources or capabilities may stifle or prevent the development of a core

Table 3.4 Examples of Firms' Capabilities

Functional Areas	Capabilities	Examples of Firms
Distribution	Effective use of logistics management techniques	Wal-Mart
Human resources	Motivating, empowering, and retaining employees	AEROJET
Management information systems	Effective and efficient control of inventories through point-of-purchase data collection methods	Wal-Mart
Marketing	Effective promotion of brand-name products	Gillette Ralph Lauren Clothing McKinsey & Co.
	Effective customer service	Nordstrom Norwest Solectron Corporation Norrell Corporation
	Innovative merchandising	Crate & Barrel
Management	Ability to envision the future of clothing	Gap, Inc.
	Effective organizational structure	PepsiCo
Manufacturing	Design and production skills yielding reliable products	Komatsu
	Product and design quality	Gap, Inc.
	Production of technologically sophisticated automobile engines	Mazda
	Miniaturization of components and products	Sony
Research & development	Exceptional technological capability	Corning
	Development of sophisticated elevator control solutions	Motion Control
	Rapid transformation of technology into new products and processes	Engineering Inc. Chaparral Steel
	Deep knowledge of silver-halide materials	Kodak
	Digital technology	Thomson Consumer Electronics

competence. Firms with the tangible resource of financial capital, such as Microsoft (see Strategic Focus on page 84), may be able to purchase facilities or hire the skilled workers required to manufacture products that yield customer value. However, firms without financial capital would have a weakness in regard to being able to buy or build new capabilities. To be successful, firms must locate external environmental opportunities that can be exploited through their capabilities, while avoiding competition in areas of weakness.[77]

An important question is "How many core competencies are required for the firm to have a sustained competitive advantage?" Responses to this question vary. McKinsey & Co. recommends that its clients identify three or four competencies around which their strategic actions can be framed.[78] Supporting and nurturing more than four core competencies may prevent a firm from developing the focus it needs to fully exploit its competencies in the marketplace.

Firms should take actions that are based on their core competencies. Recent actions by Starbucks demonstrate this point. Growing rapidly, Starbucks decided that it could use the Internet as a distribution channel to bring about still additional growth. The firm quickly realized that it lacks the capabilities required to successfully

Forbes named Starbucks the world's best food and beverage company for 2002. Pictured here is the firm's original store in Seattle, Washington, opened in 1971.

distribute its products through this channel and that its unique coffee, not the delivery of that product, is its competitive advantage. In part, this recognition caused Starbucks to renew its emphasis on existing capabilities to create more value through its supply chain. Trimming the number of its milk suppliers from 65 to fewer than 25 and negotiating long-term contracts with coffee-bean growers are actions Starbucks has taken to do this. The firm also decided to place automated espresso machines in its busy units. These machines reduce Starbucks' cost while providing improved service to its customers, who can now move through the line much faster. Using its supply chain and service capabilities in these manners allows Starbucks to strengthen its competitive advantages of coffee and the unique venue in which on-site customers experience it.[79]

Of course, not all resources and capabilities are core competencies. The next section discusses two approaches for identifying core competencies.

Building Core Competencies

Two tools help the firm identify and build its core competencies.[80] The first consists of four specific criteria of sustainable advantage that firms can use to determine those resources and capabilities that are core competencies. Because the capabilities shown in Table 3.4 have satisfied these four criteria, they are core competencies. The second tool is the value chain analysis. Firms use this tool to select the value-creating competencies that should be maintained, upgraded, or developed and those that should be outsourced.

Four Criteria of Sustainable Competitive Advantage

As shown in Table 3.5, capabilities that are valuable, rare, costly to imitate, and nonsubstitutable are strategic capabilities. Also called core competencies, strategic capabilities are a source of competitive advantage for the firm over its rivals. Capabilities failing to satisfy the four criteria of sustainable competitive advantage are not core competencies. Thus, as shown in Figure 3.4, every core competence is a capability, but not every capability is a core competence. Operationally, for a capability to be a core competence, it must be "valuable and nonsubstitutable, from a customer's point of view, and unique and inimitable, from a competitor's point of view."[81]

A sustained competitive advantage is achieved only when competitors have failed in efforts to duplicate the benefits of a firm's strategy or when they lack the confidence to attempt imitation. For some period of time, the firm may earn a competitive advantage by using capabilities that are, for example, valuable and rare, but that are imitable.[82] In this instance, the length of time a firm can expect to retain its competitive advantage is a function of how quickly competitors can successfully imitate a good, service, or process. Sustainable competitive advantage results only when all four criteria are satisfied.

Valuable capabilities allow the firm to exploit opportunities or neutralize threats in its external environment.

Valuable

Valuable capabilities allow the firm to exploit opportunities or neutralize threats in its external environment. By effectively using capabilities to exploit opportunities, a firm is able to create value for customers.

Table 3.5 Four Criteria for Determining Strategic Capabilities

Valuable Capabilities	• Help a firm neutralize threats or exploit opportunities
Rare Capabilities	• Are not possessed by many others
Costly-to-Imitate Capabilities	• Historical: A unique and a valuable organizational culture or brand name • Ambiguous cause: The causes and uses of a competence are unclear • Social complexity: Interpersonal relationships, trust, and friendship among managers, suppliers, and customers
Nonsubstitutable Capabilities	• No strategic equivalent

Sometimes, firms' capabilities become valuable only through modifications that improve their ability to satisfy customers' needs. As individuals browse the Web for information, for example, many feel that an insufficient amount of value is created online to make a purchase. About 3 percent of website visitors actually make a purchase, while 97 percent only browse. However, firms are learning to modify their websites to create more value for visitors, thereby turning them into buyers. The results from a recent study suggested that the order-conversion rate increased from 1.8 percent to 3.2 percent in 1999.[83] In this case, a valuable capability converts visitors into buyers. Over time, computer models that analyze website visits of consumers will play an important role in helping firms turn visitors into buyers. Interestingly, the models' real value may be that they make the website more like a human salesperson. "Think of the old-time shoe-store salesman who knew his customers, knew what they had bought for years, and knew who had to try on 11 pairs before one pair would feel right."[84]

Figure 3.4 Core Competence as a Strategic Capability

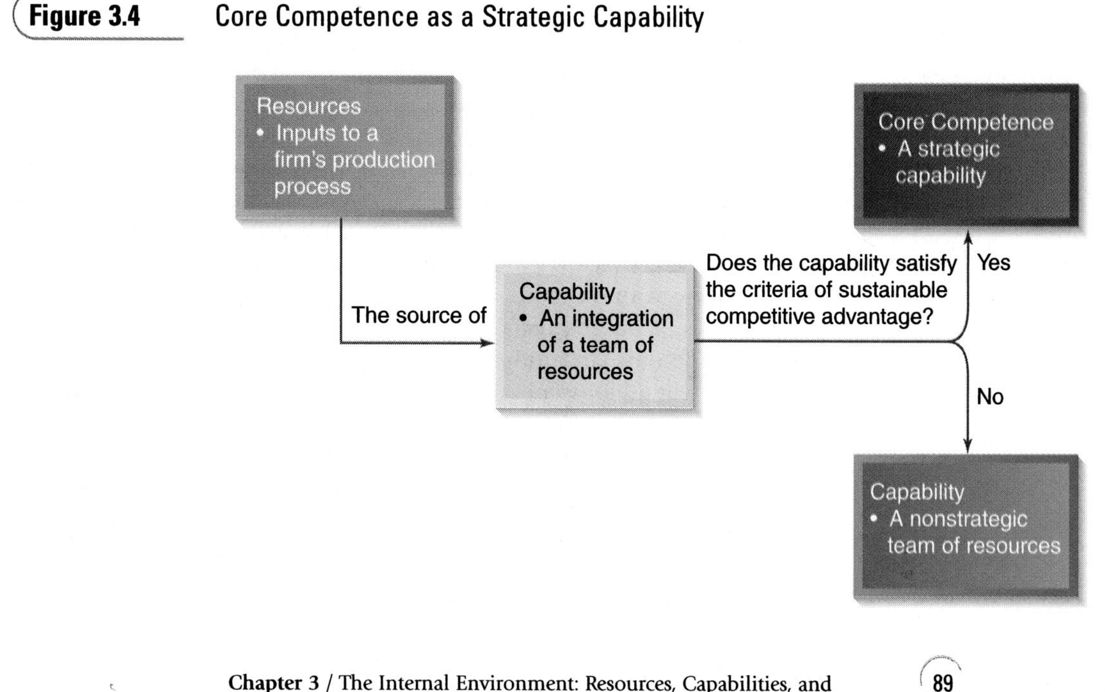

In regard to value creation, e-commerce has a long way to go before a meaningful portion of it behaves like a human salesperson. However, this capability is what most Web businesses such as Amazon.com seek to achieve. In fact, Amazon has amazingly high satisfaction levels among its website visitors as well as buyers. "Customers love Amazon not because it offers the lowest prices—it doesn't—but because the experience has been crafted so carefully that most of us actually enjoy it."[85] Similarly, relying initially on its distribution capabilities to pursue an opportunity, Wal-Mart started its business by offering startlingly low prices on a vast selection of brand-name goods. Analysts believe that Wal-Mart changed the way consumers thought about value, letting them know that they did not have to pay the prices charged by most retailers.[86]

Rare

Rare capabilities are possessed by a few, if any, current or potential competitors.

Rare capabilities are possessed by few, if any, current or potential competitors. A key question managers answer when evaluating this criterion is, "How many rival firms possess these valuable capabilities?" Capabilities possessed by many rivals are unlikely to be a source of competitive advantage for any one of them. Instead, valuable but common (i.e., not rare) resources and capabilities are sources of competitive parity.[87] Competitive advantage results only when firms develop and exploit capabilities that differ from those shared with competitors.

For example, when Palm Computing was established, it had an operating system that was different from its competitors in the PC sector. Palm's software was designed to run on a small handheld device. The first product using the software, Apple's Newton, did not create enough value for consumers and failed. However, funding from US Robotics allowed the founders to create better software and design the hardware as well and incorporate them into the Palm Pilot, and the product was successful. The Palm Pilot sold 350,000 units in 1994, 750,000 in 1995, and one million in 1996. In 1998, 3Com purchased Palm Computing and spun it into a separate corporation in 2000. However, its software is still a rare product and is licensed by 3Com's competitors, such as Handspring. Although Microsoft has a competing operating system, to this point it has not been as successful as the Palm operating system and application software.[88] Thus, Palm's operating system and associated software are still rare.

Costly to Imitate

Costly-to-imitate capabilities are capabilities that other firms cannot easily develop.

Costly-to-imitate capabilities are capabilities that other firms cannot easily develop. Capabilities that are costly to imitate are created because of one or a combination of three reasons (see Table 3.5). First, a firm sometimes is able to develop capabilities because of *unique historical conditions.* "As firms evolve, they pick up skills, abilities and resources that are unique to them, reflecting their particular path through history."[89] Another way of saying this is that firms sometimes are able to develop capabilities because they were in the right place at the right time.[90]

A firm with a unique and valuable *organizational culture* that emerged in the early stages of the company's history "may have an imperfectly imitable advantage over firms founded in another historical period"[91]—one in which less valuable or less competitively useful values and beliefs strongly influenced the development of the firm's culture. This may be the case for the consulting firm McKinsey & Co. "It is that culture, unique to McKinsey and eccentric, which sets the firm apart from virtually any other business organization and which often mystifies even those who engage [its] services."[92] Briefly discussed in Chapter 1, organizational culture is "something that people connect with, feel inspired by, think of as a normal way of operating. It's in their hearts and minds, and its core is voluntary behavior."[93] An organizational culture is a source of advantage when employees are held together tightly by their belief in it.[94]

UPS has been the prototype in many areas of the parcel delivery business because of its excellence in products, systems, marketing, and other operational business capabilities. "Its fundamental competitive strength, however, derives from the organization's unique culture, which has spanned almost a century, growing deeper all along. This culture provides solid, consistent roots for everything the company does, from skills training to technological innovation."[95]

A second condition of being costly to imitate occurs when the link between the firm's capabilities and its competitive advantage is *causally ambiguous.*[96] In these instances, competitors can't clearly understand how a firm uses its capabilities as the foundation for competitive advantage. As a result, firms are uncertain about the capabilities they should develop to duplicate the benefits of a competitor's value-creating strategy. Gordon Forward, CEO of Chaparral Steel, allows competitors to tour his firm's facilities. In Forward's words, competitors can be shown almost "everything and we will be giving away nothing because they can't take it home with them."[97] Contributing to Chaparral Steel's causally ambiguous operations is the fact that workers use the concept of *mentefacturing,* by which manufacturing steel is done by using their minds instead of their hands. "In mentefacturing, workers use computers to monitor operations and don't need to be on the shop floor during production."[98]

Social complexity is the third reason that capabilities can be costly to imitate. Social complexity means that at least some, and frequently many, of the firm's capabilities are the product of complex social phenomena. Interpersonal relationships, trust, and friendships among managers and between managers and employees and a firm's reputation with suppliers and customers are examples of socially complex capabilities. Nucor Steel has been able to create "a hunger for new knowledge through a high-powered incentive system for every employee." This socially complex process has allowed Nucor "to push the boundaries of manufacturing process know-how."[99]

Nonsubstitutable

Nonsubstitutable capabilities are capabilities that do not have strategic equivalents.

Nonsubstitutable capabilities are capabilities that do not have strategic equivalents. This final criterion for a capability to be a source of competitive advantage "is that there must be no strategically equivalent valuable resources that are themselves either not rare or imitable. Two valuable firm resources (or two bundles of firm resources) are strategically equivalent when they each can be separately exploited to implement the same strategies."[100] In general, the strategic value of capabilities increases as they become more difficult to substitute.[101] The more invisible capabilities are, the more difficult it is for firms to find substitutes and the greater the challenge is to competitors trying to imitate a firm's value-creating strategy. Firm-specific knowledge and trust-based working relationships between managers and nonmanagerial personnel are examples of capabilities that are difficult to identify and for which finding a substitute is challenging. However, causal ambiguity may make it difficult for the firm to learn as well and thus may stifle progress because the firm may not know how to improve processes that are not easily codified and thus ambiguous.[102]

For example, competitors are deeply familiar with Dell Computer's successful direct sales model. However, to date, no competitor has been able to imitate Dell's capabilities as suggested by the following comment: "There's no better way to make, sell, and deliver PCs than the way Dell does it, and nobody executes that model better than Dell."[103] Moreover, no competitor has been able to develop and use substitute capabilities that can duplicate the value Dell creates by using its capabilities. Thus, experience suggests that Dell's direct sales model capabilities are nonsubstitutable.

In summary, sustainable competitive advantage is created only by using valuable, rare, costly-to-imitate, and nonsubstitutable capabilities. Table 3.6 shows the competitive consequences and performance implications resulting from combinations of the four criteria of sustainability. The analysis suggested by the table helps managers determine the strategic value of a firm's capabilities. Resources and capabilities falling into the first row in the table (that is, resources and capabilities that are neither valuable nor rare and that are imitable and for which strategic substitutes exist) should not be emphasized by the firm to formulate and implement strategies. Capabilities yielding competitive parity and either temporary or sustainable competitive advantage, however, will be supported. Large competitors such as Coca-Cola and PepsiCo may have capabilities that can yield only competitive parity. In such cases, the firms will nurture these capabilities while simultaneously trying to develop capabilities that can yield either a temporary or sustainable competitive advantage.

Value Chain Analysis

Value chain analysis allows the firm to understand the parts of its operations that create value and those that do not. Understanding these issues is important because the firm earns above-average returns only when the value it creates is greater than the costs incurred to create that value.[104]

Primary activities are involved with a product's physical creation, its sale and distribution to buyers, and its service after the sale.

Support activities provide the support necessary for the primary activities to take place.

The value chain is a template that firms use to understand their cost position and to identify the multiple means that might be used to facilitate implementation of a chosen business-level strategy.[105] As shown in Figure 3.5, a firm's value chain is segmented into primary and support activities. **Primary activities** are involved with a product's physical creation, its sale and distribution to buyers, and its service after the sale. **Support activities** provide the support necessary for the primary activities to take place.

Table 3.6 Outcomes from Combinations of the Criteria for Sustainable Competitive Advantage

Is the Resource or Capability Valuable?	Is the Resource or Capability Rare?	Is the Resource or Capability Costly to Imitate?	Is the Resource or Capability Nonsubstitutable?	Competitive Consequences	Performance Implications
No	No	No	No	Competitive disadvantage	Below-average returns
Yes	No	No	Yes/no	Competitive parity	Average returns
Yes	Yes	No	Yes/no	Temporary competitive advantage	Above-average returns to average returns
Yes	Yes	Yes	Yes	Sustainable competitive advantage	Above-average returns

The value chain shows how a product moves from the raw-material stage to the final customer. For individual firms, the essential idea of the value chain "is to add as much value as possible as cheaply as possible, and, most important, to capture that value." In a globally competitive economy, the most valuable links on the chain tend to belong to people who have knowledge about customers.[106] This locus of value-creating possibilities applies just as strongly to retail and service firms as to manufacturers. Moreover, for organizations in all sectors, the effects of e-commerce make it increasingly necessary for companies to develop value-adding knowledge processes to compensate for the value and margin that the Internet strips from physical processes.[107]

Table 3.7 lists the items to be studied to assess the value-creating potential of primary activities. In Table 3.8, the items to consider when studying support activities are shown. As with the analysis of primary activities, the intent in examining these items is to determine areas where the firm has the potential to create and capture value. All items in both tables should be evaluated relative to competitors' capabilities. To be a source of competitive advantage, a resource or capability must allow the firm (1) to perform an activity in a manner that is superior to the way competitors perform it, or (2) to perform a value-creating activity that competitors cannot complete. Only under these conditions does a firm create value for customers and have opportunities to capture that value.

Sometimes start-up firms create value by uniquely reconfiguring or recombining parts of the value chain. Federal Express (FedEx) changed the nature of the delivery business by reconfiguring outbound logistics (a primary activity) and human

Figure 3.5 The Basic Value Chain

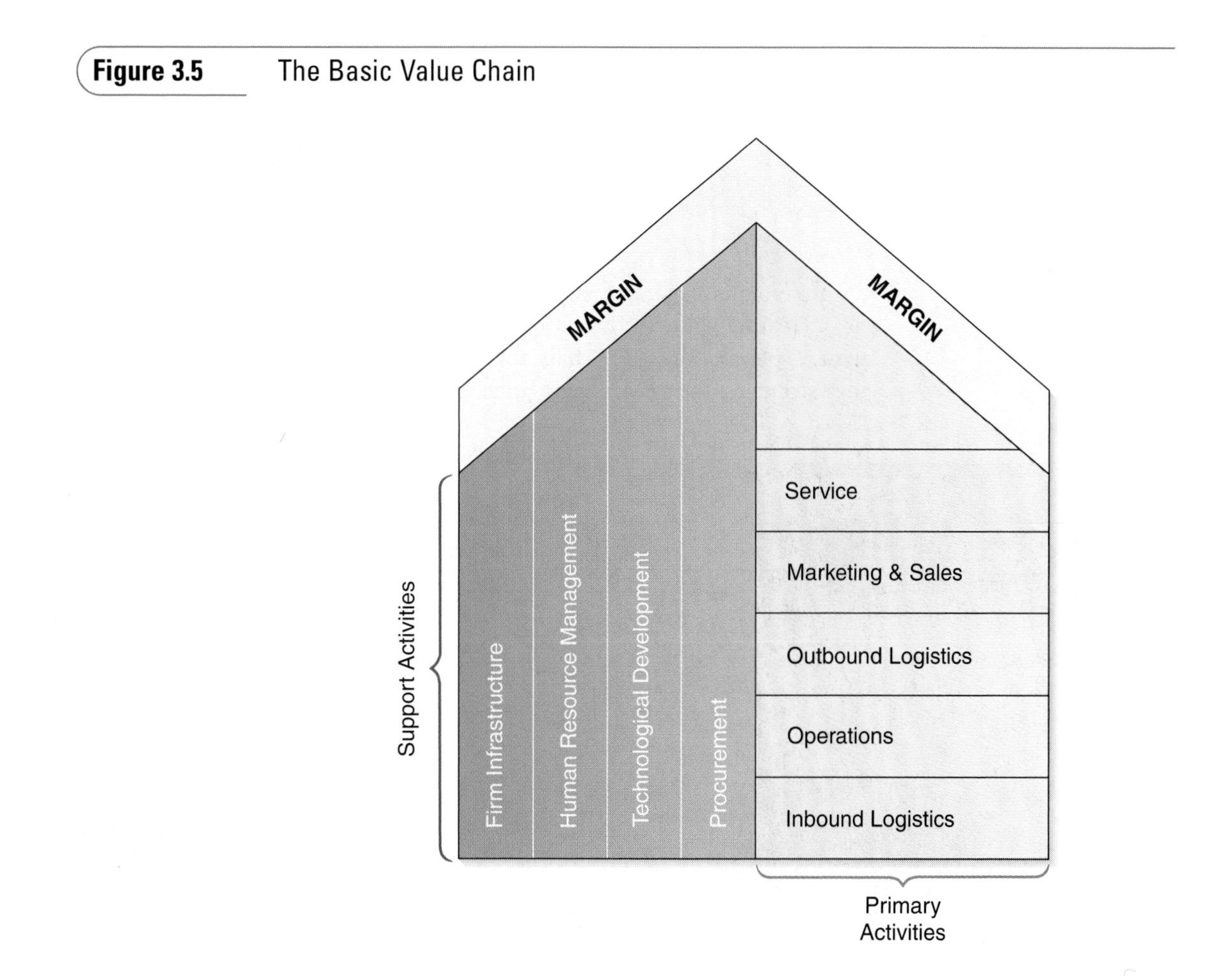

Table 3.7 Examining the Value-Creating Potential of Primary Activities

Inbound Logistics

Activities, such as materials handling, warehousing, and inventory control, used to receive, store, and disseminate inputs to a product.

Operations

Activities necessary to convert the inputs provided by inbound logistics into final product form. Machining, packaging, assembly, and equipment maintenance are examples of operations activities.

Outbound Logistics

Activities involved with collecting, storing, and physically distributing the final product to customers. Examples of these activities include finished-goods warehousing, materials handling, and order processing.

Marketing and Sales

Activities completed to provide means through which customers can purchase products and to induce them to do so. To effectively market and sell products, firms develop advertising and promotional campaigns, select appropriate distribution channels, and select, develop, and support their sales force.

Service

Activities designed to enhance or maintain a product's value. Firms engage in a range of service-related activities, including installation, repair, training, and adjustment.

Each activity should be examined relative to competitors' abilities. Accordingly, firms rate each activity as *superior, equivalent,* or *inferior.*

SOURCE: Adapted with the permission of The Free Press, an imprint of Simon & Schuster Adult Publishing Group, from *Competitive Advantage: Creating and Sustaining Superior Performance,* by Michael E. Porter, pp. 39–40, Copyright © 1985, 1988 by Michael E. Porter.

resource management (a support activity) to originate the overnight delivery business, creating value in the process. As shown in Figure 3.6, the Internet is changing many aspects of the value chain for a broad range of firms. As an example of many of these changes, see the Strategic Focus on page 96 on the upheaval in the value chains of firms in the pharmaceutical industry, creating many entry opportunities for new participants.

Rating a firm's capability to execute its primary and support activities is challenging. Earlier in the chapter, we noted that identifying and assessing the value of a firm's resources and capabilities requires judgment. Judgment is equally necessary when using value chain analysis. The reason is that there is no obviously correct model or rule available to help in the process.

As discussed in the Strategic Focus on page 96, the pharmaceutical industry is undergoing a significant change in its value chain. Millennium Pharmaceuticals has exploited an opportunity to reduce costs in the research and exploration upstream stage in the value chain and has thereby created significant opportunity for itself.

© Mari Tama/AFP/CORBIS

Celera Labs, pictured here, started the biotech rally and expects to map the entire human genome by 2003. In 2001 Celera acquired Axys Pharmaceuticals, which specializes in drug chemistry and early-stage drug testing, to identify and eventually develop new drugs based on genetic research. Until it can develop and market new drugs, however, Celera's database subscriptions and licensing are its main source of revenue.

Table 3.8 Examining the Value-Creating Potential of Support Activities

Procurement

Activities completed to purchase the inputs needed to produce a firm's products. Purchased inputs include items fully consumed during the manufacture of products (e.g., raw materials and supplies, as well as fixed assets—machinery, laboratory equipment, office equipment, and buildings).

Technological Development

Activities completed to improve a firm's product and the processes used to manufacture it. Technological development takes many forms, such as process equipment, basic research and product design, and servicing procedures.

Human Resource Management

Activities involved with recruiting, hiring, training, developing, and compensating all personnel.

Firm Infrastructure

Firm infrastructure includes activities such as general management, planning, finance, accounting, legal support, and governmental relations that are required to support the work of the entire value chain. Through its infrastructure, the firm strives to effectively and consistently identify external opportunities and threats, identify resources and capabilities, and support core competencies.

Each activity should be examined relative to competitors' abilities. Accordingly, firms rate each activity as *superior, equivalent*, or *inferior.*

SOURCE: Adapted with the permission of The Free Press, an imprint of Simon & Schuster Adult Publishing Group., from *Competitive Advantage: Creating and Sustaining Superior Performance*, by Michael E. Porter, pp. 40–43, Copyright © 1985, 1998 by Michael E. Porter.

Furthermore, because larger more established pharmaceutical firms have recognized Millennium's capabilities they have sought partnerships with Millennium to accelerate identifying genetic leads to foster cures using Millennium's platform for genetic exploration. Through partnering with firms such as Eli Lilly and Abbott Laboratories, Millennium has raised $1.8 billion, which, in turn, has helped the firm solidify its R&D platform even further.[108]

What should a firm do about primary and support activities in which its resources and capabilities are not a source of competence and competitive advantage? One solution these firms should consider is outsourcing.

Outsourcing

Outsourcing is the purchase of a value-creating activity from an external supplier.

Concerned with how components, finished goods, or services will be obtained, **outsourcing** is the purchase of a value-creating activity from an external supplier.[109] In multiple global industries, the trend toward outsourcing continues at a rapid pace.[110]

In some industries virtually all firms seek the value that can be captured through effective outsourcing. The automobile manufacturing and more recently the electronics industry are examples of these situations.[111] A number of examples of outsourcing are provided in the Strategic Focus on page 99.

Outsourcing is effective because few, if any, organizations possess the resources and capabilities required to achieve competitive superiority in all primary and support activities. With respect to technologies, for example, research suggests that few companies can afford to develop internally all the technologies that might lead to competitive advantage. By nurturing a smaller number of capabilities, a firm increases

Strategic Focus

Significant Changes in the Value Chains of Pharmaceutical Firms

Over the last few years, significant changes have taken place in the value chains of many pharmaceutical firms. The first medical remedies dated back to herbs and potions that people took to treat illnesses. In the pharmaceutical industry's early history, medical remedies began to be created through chemistry. Companies, especially in Germany, began to systematically isolate ingredients, test them for efficacy, and sell them as pills and serums. Firms such as Pfizer and Eli Lilly began during this phase and used a vertical integration strategy (defined in Chapter 6) along the value chain stages of research, testing, and delivery to the consumer.

In the 1960s, following Crick and Watson's discovery of DNA, biology and genetics became major sources of inputs to pharmaceutical firms. The genetic revolution brought two new *upstream*—or early stage—steps to the industry's value chain: research into genes that cause disease and identification of proteins that those genes produce. Highly specialized biotech firms such as AmGen and Genentech were started through these developments in the upstream research part of the value chain. For the most part, small rather than large companies dominated this new segment of the value chain. With no small firm having market power, this segment was highly fragmented (that is, the segment had a relatively large number of small firms competing against each other but with no firm able to significantly influence the competition among them).

More recently, the mapping of the human genome has further expanded the industry. Firms such as Millennium Pharmaceuticals have been involved in human genome research and mapping. Many of these upstream biopharmaceutical companies are now seeking to move downstream (later stages in the value chain) where larger, more established pharmaceutical companies are positioned with expertise in testing (pre-clinical trials and clinical trials) and delivery (manufacturing and marketing).

To expand downstream, many smaller biopharmaceutical firms have structured partnerships with the larger pharmaceutical firms, who invest in the smaller biotech firms. Biotech firms such as Celera, the major developer of the genome mapping project, and Millennium Pharmaceuticals have research platforms that are attractive to larger downstream pharmaceutical firms because they allow the smaller biotech firms to accelerate the process of identifying genetic leads to develop cures. For example, scientists can now study dozens of experiments in the space of a week, rather than just one experiment, by leveraging information technology in association with gene finding technologies to improve productivity in the discovery stage, one of the early segments of the value chain. Once a lead looks promising, a move to the testing stage is possible.

Because the early testing stages take considerable time, many information and Web-based strategies are employed. In the United States, 15 years and approximately $500 million are needed to develop a drug and bring it to market through both the pre-clinical trials and clinical trials' stages. Any time that can be pared from the 15-year period leads to reduced testing and staging costs. Small specialty online firms using a focus strategy (see Chapter 4) have sought to develop Web-based approaches to help speed up the trial testing phases of the value chain. For instance, Schering-Plough has contracted with Phase Forward Inc., whose system allows clinical investigators (doctors and researchers) to enter patient data directly to a website. This step eliminates error-checking of paper records and "can shave one to two years off getting a drug to market," says Phase Forward CEO Shiv Tasker. Datatrak, another trial contractor, offers online software that is estimated to cut the total trial time by 30 percent. Although these technologies are promising, they account for only a tiny fraction of all trials underway. One consultant suggests that "Everyone is waiting for a Quicken for clinical trials."

Not only does the Internet offer reduced error checking and time during the testing period, a Web-based approach can cost $35 per patient, compared with $350 per person now spent on advertising for patients, phone calls, and other means for the trial period. It also reduces error because the software automatically checks information as it is entered and catches most mistakes. The Web cannot speed up all pharmaceutical research. To determine how many cancer patients survived after two years of treatment, a two-year study is still required.

In regard to the value chain areas of manufacturing and marketing, although Web technologies offer alternative methods of delivery of prescription medicines, 90 percent of customers placing orders on the Web prefer to pick up their orders at a nearby store rather than have them shipped to their homes. A firm like Walgreens with its extensive network of stores has a potent advantage, even as ordering has shifted to the Internet. Accordingly, although online operations such as drugstore.com were forecasted to make brick-and-mortar pharmacies such as Walgreens obsolete and provide cheaper medicines for the consumer more directly from the producer, this has not turned out to be the case.

In summary, the value chain of pharmaceutical firms is changing drastically. In the upstream research stage, computer technologies speed the discovery of useful compounds, and the mapping of human genome project has fostered significant progress. Furthermore, testing has the potential to be shortened through Web-based strategies. Finally, significant changes have occurred in the downstream marketing and delivery of drugs. These changes in the value chain have created significant opportunities for new entrants as well as established producers.

SOURCES: D. Champion, 2001, Mastering the value chain: An interview with Mark Levin of Millennium Pharmaceuticals, *Harvard Business Review,* 79(6): 108–115; E. Licking, J. Carey, & J. Kerstetter, 2001, Bioinformatics, *Business Week,* Spring (Industrial/Technology Edition), 166–170; B. O'Keefe, 2001, Post-genome, Celera now shoots for profits, *Fortune,* February 19, 226; M. E. Porter, 2001, Strategy and the Internet, *Harvard Business Review,* 79(3): 62–78; R. Burcham, 2000, New pharma business model: Can we survive it? *Pharmaceutical Executive,* November, 94–100; J. Carey & E. Licking, 2000, An Rx for drug trials, *Business Week,* December 11, EB66–EB68.

the probability of developing a competitive advantage because it does not become overextended. In addition, by outsourcing activities in which it lacks competence, the firm can fully concentrate on those areas in which it can create value.[112]

Other research suggests that outsourcing does not work effectively without extensive internal capabilities to effectively coordinate external sourcing as well as internal coordination of core competencies.[113] Dell Computer, for example, outsources most of its manufacturing and customer service activities, allowing the firm to concentrate on creating value through its service and online distribution capabilities. However, as the Strategic Focus indicates, a company should exercise caution when most firms in the industry are engaged in outsourcing. Although many firms in the athletic shoe industry (for example, Nike and Reebok) outsource their manufacturing to lower average wage countries, some companies, such as New Balance, have decided not to ship the bulk of their manufacturing overseas. Although the Strategic Focus segment suggests that low-skilled labor and codified technologies logically should be outsourced to countries with lower cost structures and comparative advantage, New Balance has successfully challenged this assumption. Instead of outsourcing all of its production, like most other shoe companies, 20 percent of New Balance's production is kept within the company by upgrading low-skill jobs to improve efficiency. While shoes are still cheaper to produce in China ($1.30 per shoe compared to $4.00 per shoe in the United States), New Balance's domestically produced shoes are made more efficiently (24 minutes per shoe compared with three hours per shoe in China). New Balance believes that the ability to produce domestically, with the advantages of design and quality control that come with it, is worth the extra cost of only 4 percent

Figure 3.6 Prominent Applications of the Internet in the Value Chain

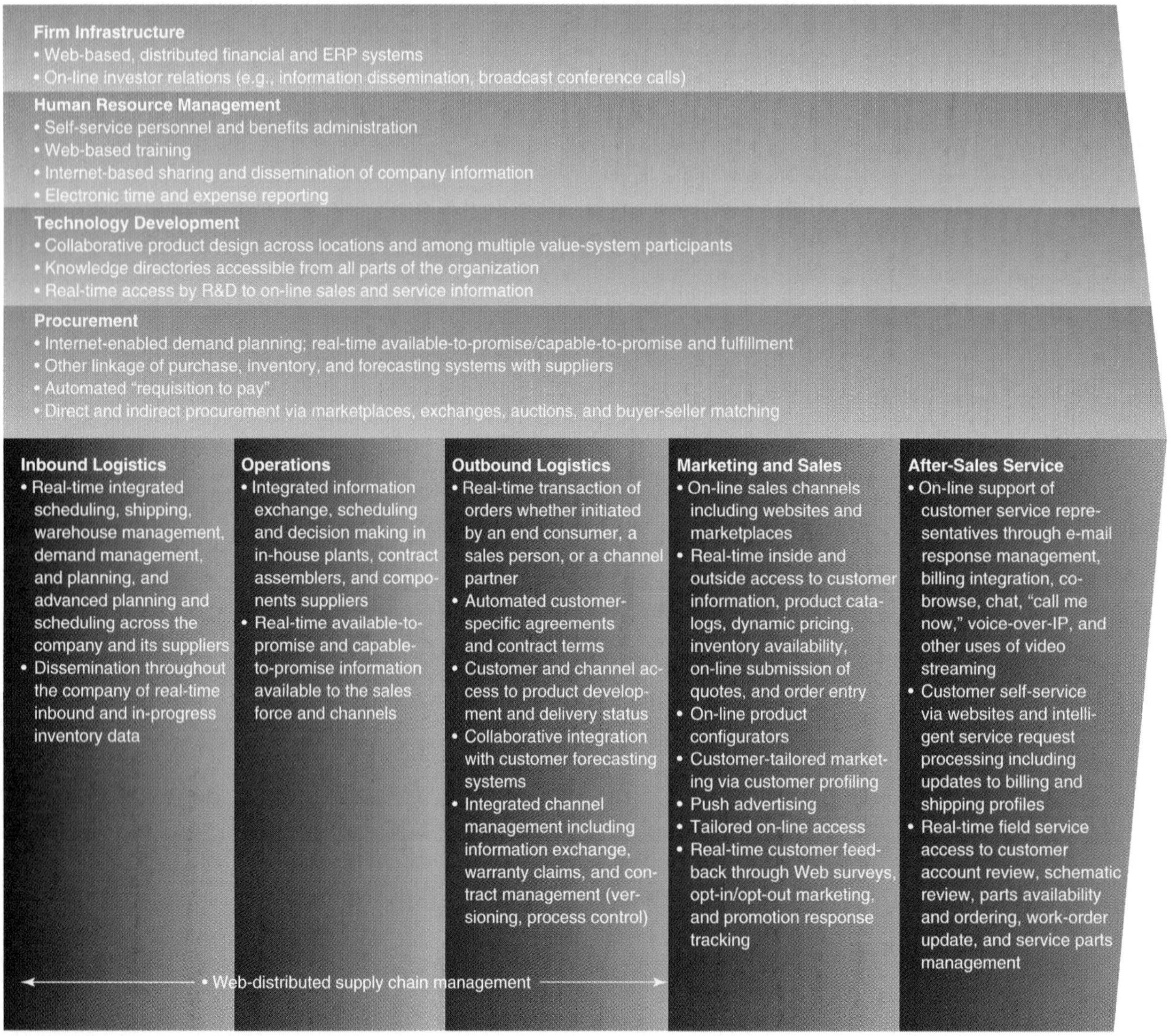

Firm Infrastructure
- Web-based, distributed financial and ERP systems
- On-line investor relations (e.g., information dissemination, broadcast conference calls)

Human Resource Management
- Self-service personnel and benefits administration
- Web-based training
- Internet-based sharing and dissemination of company information
- Electronic time and expense reporting

Technology Development
- Collaborative product design across locations and among multiple value-system participants
- Knowledge directories accessible from all parts of the organization
- Real-time access by R&D to on-line sales and service information

Procurement
- Internet-enabled demand planning; real-time available-to-promise/capable-to-promise and fulfillment
- Other linkage of purchase, inventory, and forecasting systems with suppliers
- Automated "requisition to pay"
- Direct and indirect procurement via marketplaces, exchanges, auctions, and buyer-seller matching

Inbound Logistics
- Real-time integrated scheduling, shipping, warehouse management, demand management, and planning, and advanced planning and scheduling across the company and its suppliers
- Dissemination throughout the company of real-time inbound and in-progress inventory data

Operations
- Integrated information exchange, scheduling and decision making in in-house plants, contract assemblers, and components suppliers
- Real-time available-to-promise and capable-to-promise information available to the sales force and channels

Outbound Logistics
- Real-time transaction of orders whether initiated by an end consumer, a sales person, or a channel partner
- Automated customer-specific agreements and contract terms
- Customer and channel access to product development and delivery status
- Collaborative integration with customer forecasting systems
- Integrated channel management including information exchange, warranty claims, and contract management (versioning, process control)

Marketing and Sales
- On-line sales channels including websites and marketplaces
- Real-time inside and outside access to customer information, product catalogs, dynamic pricing, inventory availability, on-line submission of quotes, and order entry
- On-line product configurators
- Customer-tailored marketing via customer profiling
- Push advertising
- Tailored on-line access
- Real-time customer feedback through Web surveys, opt-in/opt-out marketing, and promotion response tracking

After-Sales Service
- On-line support of customer service representatives through e-mail response management, billing integration, co-browse, chat, "call me now," voice-over-IP, and other uses of video streaming
- Customer self-service via websites and intelligent service request processing including updates to billing and shipping profiles
- Real-time field service access to customer account review, schematic review, parts availability and ordering, work-order update, and service parts management

← • Web-distributed supply chain management →

SOURCE: Reprinted by permission of *Harvard Business Review* from "Strategy and the Internet" by Michael E. Porter, March 2001, p. 75.

of the typical $70 shoe. While not all low-skill jobs could be made more efficient, New Balance raises the question as to which capabilities should be outsourced, even if they seem logical candidates for it.[114] We further study New Balance in Chapter 4 when we describe its use of the focused differentiation business-level strategy to compete against its rivals.

To verify that the appropriate primary and support activities are outsourced, four skills are essential for managers involved in outsourcing programs: strategic thinking; deal making; partnership governance; and managing change.[115] Managers should understand whether and how outsourcing creates competitive advantage within their company—they need to be able to think strategically.[116] To complete effective outsourcing transactions, these managers must also be deal makers, to be

Strategic Focus

Outsourcing Is an International Trend

Because of the significant economic downturn in Japan, many Japanese electronics firms are giving up the cherished dream of keeping everything in a vertically integrated family, where the firms manufacture most of the component parts of the products they ultimately produce. They can no longer ignore the global outsourcing trend. Many of the contract electronic manufacturers (CEMs) are buying Japanese-owned plants in the United States as well as in other countries. Hewlett-Packard, Cisco, IBM, Lucent, EMC, Ericsson, Motorola, and Nortel Networks all outsource to contract electronic manufacturers. One forecast estimated that 9.5 percent of the electronic goods sold throughout the world by original equipment manufacturers (OEMs) are now assembled in CEM plants. This percentage is expected to grow to 17 percent by 2003.

The largest CEMs are Solectron, SCI Systems, Celestica, Flextronics International, and Jabil Circuit. Most provide services besides manufacturing, ranging from product design and testing to supply chain management and even repair of brand-name equipment in the field. OEMs maintain control over critical parts and inbound logistics in regard to design and sourcing. For instance, Nortel uses Solectron and has asked the firm to assume much of the sourcing and procurement responsibilities in the manufacturing processes. Critical and customized components are excluded in order to maintain control over strategic capabilities, as Nortel wants to maintain negotiating power over its "crown jewel components."

Japanese firms are now turning to outsourcing more than in the past. Retailing has been a difficult area for outsourcing because of an archaic distribution system. However, entrepreneur Tadashi Yanaihas pursued a new type of distribution system based on outsourcing, which has allowed significant discounts. His firm, Fast Retailing, sells clothes at a 70 percent discount at its GAP-like Uniqlo stores in Japan. Fast Retailing's business model includes sending craftsmen from Japan to China to teach the latest production technology and styles. The firm contracts with factories in China that operate at 5 percent of the cost of those in Japan and ultra-cheap goods are sent directly to Fast Retailing's retail outlets, completely bypassing Japan's tangled distribution system.

Toys 'R' Us Japan is Japan's largest toy retailer. Since its first store opened in 1989, it is one of the few foreign retailers to have effectively made the transition to the Japanese market. The firm offers low-price toys at 120 stores and reports record profits for fiscal year 2002, outperforming other retailers weakened by the economic slump in Japan.

Although Fast Retailing's approach is unique in Japan, the firm plans to roll out 50 apparel stores in the United Kingdom in late 2001. Firms such as Gap already get 80 percent of their apparel from overseas, with a large portion of these goods coming from China. Fast Retailing may find it difficult to compete with firms that already outsource where cheap labor is available.

Besides electronic and fashion goods, services are also being outsourced. Evalueserve is a firm in New Delhi, India that performs various business processes for clients in Europe and North America. This company offers not only cheaper but also better and faster service than its clients can deliver through their own networks. Firms such as Evalueserve do a lot of back-office work. Their clients electronically send data to them, which is processed in India and then returned to the client in a new, value-added form. A number of services are offered, including medical transcription; rule-set processing, such as whether an airlines' rules allow a passenger to upgrade to business class; problem solving, in which, for instance, the teleworker decides if an insurance claim should be paid; direct customer interaction, in which teleworkers handle transactions with client-customers, such as collecting delinquent payments from credit card customers; and expert knowledge services, where teleworkers predict how credit card users' behavior will change if their credit rating improves.

As broadband capability increases, other services, such as high-level media production for American filmmakers, are expected to grow. These higher end services have already been offered in India's software houses, which have built an $8 billion-dollar business on the quality and the price of Indian programming talent. Similarly, much R&D work is done in India because of India's ability to produce large numbers of hard scientists with PhDs. Much work is now shifting to India in regard to R&D on plastics and other areas of highly skilled manufacturing.

The automobile industry also uses outsourcing. For many years, the large auto manufacturers built vertically integrated systems that included wholly owned auto part suppliers. Recently in the United States, these firms have been spun off into independent parts suppliers, and the auto manufacturers now focus on outsourced supplier networks.

Outsourcing has produced significant savings across many industries, such as autos, electronics, apparel and back-office services. However, it can be carried too far, for instance, if a firm outsources its central areas of core competence. Dell successfully uses outsourcing because the personal computer industry uses standardized modules. Cisco exploited the modular architecture of its routers to compete in the telecommunications switching business from the low end. The firm efficiently outsourced much of its manufacturing to suppliers and much of its new product development to the startups it acquires.

However, once Cisco moved towards optical networks, it was forced to do more integration and perform product design and manufacturing activities internally. Once a firm moves into higher levels of technology where the technology is not solidified, internal sourcing (or vertical integration, as discussed in Chapter 6) constitutes a competitive advantage versus outsourcing. Over time, firms shift back and forth between vertical integration and outsourcing, and managers need to make sure that outsourcing fits their particular situation.

SOURCES: A. Bernstein, 2001, Low-skilled jobs: Do they have to move? *Business Week,* February 26, 94; C. M. Christensen, 2001, The past and future of competitive advantage, *Sloan Management Review* 42(2): 105–109; 2001, Business Special: Back office to the world, *The Economist,* May 5, 59–62; B. Fulford, 2001, One-man restructuring act, *Forbes,* July 9, 106; C. Serant & R. Lamb, 2001, Mega outsourcing deals stall as OEMs re-evaluate demand, *Electronic Business News,* June 18, 12–3; G. Bylinsky, 2000, For sale: Japanese plants in the U.S., *Fortune,* February 21, 240B–240D.

able to secure rights from external providers that can be fully used by internal managers. They must be able to oversee and govern appropriately the relationship with the company to which the services were outsourced. Because outsourcing can significantly change how an organization operates, managers administering these programs must also be able to manage that change, including resolving employee resistance that accompanies any significant change effort.[117]

Core Competencies: Cautions and Reminders

Tools such as outsourcing can help the firm focus on its core competencies. However, evidence shows that the value-creating ability of core competencies should never be taken for granted. Moreover, the ability of a core competence to be a permanent competitive advantage can't be assumed. The reason for these cautions is that all core competencies have the potential to become *core rigidities.* As Leslie Wexner, CEO of The Limited, Inc., says: "Success doesn't beget success. Success begets failure because the more that you know a thing works, the less likely you are to think that it won't work. When you've had a long string of victories, it's harder to foresee your own vulnerabilities."[118] Thus, each competence is a strength and a weakness—a strength because it is the source of competitive advantage and, hence, strategic competitiveness, and a weakness because, if emphasized when it is no longer competitively relevant, it can be a seed of organizational inertia.[119]

Events occurring in the firm's external environment create conditions through which core competencies can become core rigidities, generate inertia, and stifle innovation. "Often the flip side, the dark side, of core capabilities is revealed due to external events when new competitors figure out a better way to serve the firm's customers, when new technologies emerge, or when political or social events shift the ground underneath."[120] However, in the final analysis, changes in the external environment do not cause core capabilities or core competencies to become core rigidities; rather, strategic myopia and inflexibility on the part of managers are the cause.[121]

These shortcomings may be the case at Bavarian Motor Works (BMW). Historically, BMW's unique internal process for designing automobiles has been a competitive advantage that other firms have not been able to duplicate. The firm's design process has required extensive and complex cooperative interactions among a large group of engineers. Recently, to reduce costs, BMW created a system that enables its engineers to use computer simulations to crash-test the cars they have designed and thereby improve them. This technology codifies into a set of algorithms what formerly had been achieved only through complex social interaction among BMW engineers. As such, the firm has codified what had been a complex intangible resource (interactions among design engineers), jeopardizing what had been a competitive advantage. It is much easier for BMW's rivals to imitate a computer simulation than to understand the complex, often unobservable interactions among the firm's engineers. Thus, at least in part, this competitive advantage may not be as valuable as it once was. However, continuous learning by BMW design engineers may allow the firm to maintain its competitive advantage in the long run.[122]

Summary

- In the global landscape, traditional factors (e.g., labor costs and superior access to financial resources and raw materials) can still create a competitive advantage. However, this happens in a declining number of instances. In the new landscape, the resources, capabilities, and core competencies in the firm's internal environment may have a relatively stronger influence on its performance than do conditions in the external environment. The most effective firms recognize that strategic competitiveness and above-average returns result only when core competencies (identified through the study of the firm's internal environment) are matched with opportunities (determined through the study of the firm's external environment).
- No competitive advantage lasts forever. Over time, rivals use their own unique resources, capabilities, and core competencies to form different value-creating propositions that duplicate the value-creating ability of the firm's competitive advantages. In general, the Internet's capabilities are reducing the sustainability of many competitive advantages. Thus, because competitive advantages are not sustainable on a permanent basis, firms must exploit their current advantages while simultaneously using their resources and capabilities to form new advantages that can lead to competitive success in the future.
- Effective management of core competencies requires careful analysis of the firm's resources (inputs to the production process) and capabilities (capacities for teams of resources to perform a task or activity in an integrative manner). To successfully manage core competencies, decision makers must be self-confident, courageous, and willing both to hold others accountable for their work and to be held accountable for the outcomes of their own efforts.
- Individual resources are usually not a source of competitive advantage. Capabilities, which are groupings of tangible and intangible resources, are a more likely source of competitive advantages, especially relatively sustainable ones. A key reason for this is that the firm's nurturing and support of core competencies that are based on capabilities is less visible to rivals and, as such, is harder to understand and imitate.
- Increasingly, employees' knowledge is viewed as perhaps the most relevant source of competitive advantage. To gain maximum benefit from knowledge, efforts are taken to find ways for individuals' unique knowledge sets to be shared throughout the firm. The Internet's capabilities affect both the development and the sharing of knowledge.
- Only when a capability is valuable, rare, costly to imitate, and nonsubstitutable is it a core competence and a source of competitive advantage. Over time, core competencies must be supported, but they cannot be allowed to become core rigidities. Core competencies are a source of competitive advantage only when they allow the firm to create value by exploiting opportunities in the external environment. When this is no longer the case, attention shifts to selecting or forming other capabilities that do satisfy the four criteria of sustainable competitive advantage.
- Value chain analysis is used to identify and evaluate the competitive potential of resources and capabilities. By studying their skills relative to those associated with primary and support activities, firms can understand their cost structure and identify the activities through which they can create value.
- When the firm cannot create value in either a primary or support activity, outsourcing is considered. Used commonly in the global economy, outsourcing is the purchase of a value-creating activity from an external supplier. The firm must outsource only to companies possessing a competitive advantage in terms of the particular primary or support activity under consideration. In addition, the firm must continuously verify that it is not outsourcing activities from which it could create value.

Review Questions

1. Why is it important for a firm to study and understand its internal environment?
2. What is value? Why is it critical for the firm to create value? How does it do so?
3. What are the differences between tangible and intangible resources? Why is it important for decision makers to understand these differences? Are tangible resources linked more closely to the creation of competitive advantages than intangible resources, or is the reverse true? Why?
4. What are capabilities? What must firms do to create capabilities?
5. What are the four criteria used to determine which of a firm's capabilities are core competencies? Why is it important for these criteria to be used?
6. What is value chain analysis? What does the firm gain when it successfully uses this tool?
7. What is outsourcing? Why do firms outsource? Will outsourcing's importance grow in the 21st century? If so, why?
8. What are core rigidities? Why is it vital that firms prevent core competencies from becoming core rigidities?

Experiential Exercise

Organizational Resources

The organizations listed in the table below have different capabilities, core competencies, and competitive advantages.

Part One. In small groups, consider each firm and use logic and consensus to complete the table. Alternatively, complete the table on an individual basis.

Organization	Capabilities	Core Competencies	Competitive Advantage
McDonald's			
NBC			
Post Office			
Microsoft			

Part Two. Based on your responses to the table, now compare each type of firm in terms of its resources and suggest some reasons for the differences.

	Is the Resource or Capability				Competitive consequences: • Competitive disadvantage • Competitive parity • Temporary competitive advantage • Sustainable competitive advantage	Performance implications: • Below-average returns • Average returns • Above-average returns
	Valuable?	Rare?	Costly to Imitate?	Nonsubstitutable?		
McDonald's						
NBC						
Post Office						
Microsoft						

Notes

1. C. A. Bartlett & S. Ghoshal, 2002, Building competitive advantage through people, *MIT Sloan Management Review,* 43(2): 34–41.
2. R. R. Wiggins & T. W. Ruefli, 2002, Sustained competitive advantage: Temporal dynamics and the incidence of persistence of superior economic performance, *Organization Science,* 13: 82–105.
3. M. J. Rouse & U. S. Daellenbach, 1999, Rethinking research methods for the resource-based perspective: Isolating sources of sustainable competitive advantage, *Strategic Management Journal,* 20: 487–494.
4. C. G. Brush, P. G. Greene, & M. M. Hart, 2001, From initial idea to unique advantage: The entrepreneurial challenge of constructing a resource base, *Academy of Management Executive,* 15(1): 64–78.
5. R. Makadok, 2001, Toward a synthesis of the resource-based and dynamic-capability views of rent creation, *Strategic Management Journal,* 22: 387–401; K. M. Eisenhardt & J. A. Martin, 2000, Dynamic capabilities: What are they? *Strategic Management Journal,* 21: 1105–1121.
6. M. A. Hitt, L. Bierman, K. Shimizu, & R. Kochhar, 2001, Direct and moderating effects of human capital on strategy and performance in professional service firms: A resource-based perspective, *Academy of Management Journal,* 44: 13–28; J. Lee & D. Miller, 1999, People matter: Commitment to employees, strategy and performance in Korean firms, *Strategic Management Journal,* 20: 579–593.
7. R. Lyman & G. Fabrikant, 2001, Suddenly, high stakes for Disney's film and TV businesses, *The New York Times Interactive,* http://www.nytimes.com, May 21.
8. E. Autio, H. J. Sapienza, & J. G. Almeida, 2000, Effects of age at entry, knowledge intensity, and imitability on international growth, *Academy of Management Journal,* 43: 909–924.
9. P. L. Yeoh & K. Roth, 1999, An empirical analysis of sustained advantage in the U.S. pharmaceutical industry: Impact of firm resources and capabilities, *Strategic Management Journal,* 20: 637–653.
10. D. F. Abell, 1999, Competing today while preparing for tomorrow, *Sloan Management Review,* 40(3): 73–81; D. Leonard-Barton, 1995, *Wellsprings of Knowledge: Building and Sustaining the Sources of Innovation* (Boston: Harvard Business School Press); R. A.. McGrath, J. C. MacMillan, & S. Venkataraman, 1995, Defining and developing competence: A strategic process paradigm, *Strategic Management Journal,* 16: 251–275.
11. K. M. Eisenhardt, 1999, Strategy as strategic decision making, *Sloan Management Review,* 40(3): 65–72.
12. H. K. Steensma & K. G. Corley, 2000, On the performance of technology-sourcing partnerships: The interaction between partner interdependence and technology attributes, *Academy of Management Journal,* 43: 1045–1067.
13. J. B. Barney, 2001, Is the resource-based "view" a useful perspective for strategic management research? Yes, *Academy of Management Review,* 26: 41–56.

14. J. K. Sebenius, 2002, The hidden challenge of cross-border negotiations, *Harvard Business Review,* 80(3): 76–85; P. W. Liu & X. Yang, 2000, The theory of irrelevance of the size of the firm, *Journal of Economic Behavior & Organization,* 42: 145–165.
15. P. F. Drucker, 2002, They're not employees, they're people, *Harvard Business Review,* 80(2): 70–77; G. Verona, 1999, A resource-based view of product development, *Academy of Management Review,* 24: 132–142.
16. M. Tripsas & G. Gavetti, 2000, Capabilities, cognition, and inertia: Evidence from digital imaging, *Strategic Management Journal,* 21: 1147–1161.
17. D. Whitford, 2001, Polaroid, R.I.P. *Fortune,* November 12, 44.
18. S. Ghoshal & C. A. Bartlett, 1995, Changing the role of top management: Beyond structure to processes, *Harvard Business Review,* 73(1): 96.
19. L. Greenhalgh, 2000, Ford Motor Company's CEO Jac Nasser on transformational change, e-business, and environmental responsibility, *Academy of Management Executive,* 14(3): 46–51.
20. J. Muller, 2001, Ford: Why it's worse than you think, *Business Week,* http://www.businessweek.com, June 25.
21. Barney, Is the resource-based "view" a useful perspective for strategic management research? Yes; V. P. Rindova & C. J. Fombrun, 1999, Constructing competitive advantage: The role of firm-constituent interactions, *Strategic Management Journal,* 20: 691–710; M. A. Peteraf, 1993, The cornerstones of competitive strategy: A resource-based view, *Strategic Management Journal,* 14: 179–191.
22. Barney, Is the resource-based "view" a useful perspective for strategic management research? Yes; T. H. Brush & K. W. Artz, 1999, Toward a contingent resource-based theory: The impact of information asymmetry on the value of capabilities in veterinary medicine, *Strategic Management Journal,* 20: 223–250.
23. M. E. Porter, 1996, What is strategy? *Harvard Business Review,* 74(6): 61–78.
24. S. K. McEvily & B. Chakravarthy, 2002, The persistence of knowledge-based advantage: An empirical test for product performance and technological knowledge, *Strategic Management Journal,* 23: 285–305; P. J. Buckley & M. J. Carter, 2000, Knowledge management in global technology markets: Applying theory to practice, *Long Range Planning,* 33(1): 55–71.
25. 1998, Pocket Strategy, *Value,* The Economist Books, 165.
26. J. Useem, 2001, Most admired: Conquering vertical limits, *Fortune;* February 19, 84–96.
27. Ibid.
28. J. Wolf & W. G. Egelhoff, 2002, A reexamination and extension of international strategy-structure theory, *Strategic Management Journal,* 23: 181–189; R. Ramirez, 1999, Value co-production: Intellectual origins and implications for practice and research, *Strategic Management Journal,* 20: 49–65.
29. S. W. Floyd & B. Wooldridge, 1999, Knowledge creation and social networks in corporate entrepreneurship: The renewal of organizational capability, *Entrepreneurship: Theory and Practice,* 23(3): 123–143; A. Campbell & M. Alexander, 1997, What's wrong with strategy? *Harvard Business Review,* 75(6): 42–51.
30. M. A. Hitt, R. D. Nixon, P. G. Clifford, & K. P. Coyne, 1999, The development and use of strategic resources, in M. A. Hitt, P. G. Clifford, R. D. Nixon, & K. P. Coyne (eds.), *Dynamic Strategic Resources,* Chichester: John Wiley & Sons, 1–14.
31. C. M. Christensen, 2001, The past and future of competitive advantage, *Sloan Management Review,* 42(2): 105–109.
32. T. H. Davenport, 2001, Data to knowledge to results: Building an analytic capability, *California Management Review,* 43(2): 117–138; J. B. Barney, 1999, How a firm's capabilities affect boundary decisions, *Sloan Management Review,* 40(3): 137–145.
33. P. Westhead, M. Wright, & D. Ucbasaran, 2001, The internationalization of new and small firms: A resource-based view, *Journal of Business Venturing* 16(4): 333–358; A. McWilliams, D. D. Van Fleet, & P. M. Wright, 2001, Strategic management of human resources for global competitive advantage, *Journal of Business Strategies* 18(1): 1–24; N. Athanassiou & D. Nigh, 1999, The impact of U.S. company internationalization on top management team advice networks: A tacit knowledge perspective, *Strategic Management Journal,* 20: 83–92.
34. H. Collingwood, 2001, The earnings game: Everyone plays, nobody wins, *Harvard Business Review,* 79(6): 65–74.
35. Eisenhardt, Strategy as strategic decision making.
36. R. S. Dooley & G. E. Fryxell, 1999, Attaining decision quality and commitment from dissent: The moderating effects of loyalty and competence in strategic decision-making teams, *Academy of Management Journal,* 42: 389–402.
37. P. C. Nutt, 1999, Surprising but true: Half the decisions in organizations fail, *Academy of Management Executive,* 13(4): 75–90.
38. M. Keil, 2000, Cutting your losses: Extricating your organization when a big project goes awry, *Sloan Management Review,* 41(3): 55–68.
39. P. G. Audia, E. Locke, & K. G. Smith, 2000, The paradox of success: An archival and a laboratory study of strategic persistence following radical environmental change. *Academy of Management Journal,* 43:837–853; D. A. Aaker & E. Joachimsthaler, 1999, The lure of global branding, *Harvard Business Review,* 77(6): 137–144; R. G. McGrath, 1999, Falling forward: Real options reasoning and entrepreneurial failure, *Academy of Management Review,* 24: 13–30.
40. G. P. West III & J. DeCastro, 2001, The Achilles heel of firm strategy: Resource weaknesses and distinctive inadequacies, *Journal of Management Studies,* 38: 417–442; G. Gavetti & D. Levinthal, 2000, Looking forward and looking backward: Cognitive and experimental search, *Administrative Science Quarterly,* 45: 113–137.
41. R. Amit & P. J. H. Schoemaker, 1993, Strategic assets and organizational rent, *Strategic Management Journal,* 14: 33–46.
42. R. E. Hoskisson & L. W. Busenitz, 2001, Market uncertainty and learning distance in corporate entrepreneurship entry mode choice. In M. A. Hitt, R. D. Ireland, S. M. Camp, & D. L. Sexton (eds.), *Strategic Entrepreneurship: Creating a New Integrated Mindset,* Oxford, U.K.: Blackwell Publishers, 151–172.
43. A. L. Zacharakis & D. L. Shepherd, 2001, The nature of information and overconfidence on venture capitalist's decision making, *Journal of Business Venturing,* 16: 311–332.
44. P. Burrows & A. Park, 2002, What price victory at Hewlett-Packard? *Business Week,* April 1, 36–37.
45. H. Thomas, T. Pollock, & P. Gorman, 1999, Global strategic analyses: Frameworks and approaches, *Academy of Management Executive,* 13(1): 70–82.
46. J. M. Mezias, P. Grinyer, & W. D. Guth, 2001, Changing collective cognition: A process model for strategic change, *Long Range Planning,* 34(1): 71–95.
47. U. Harnischfeger, 2001, Opel limits its ambitions in a grim market, *Financial Times,* http://www.ft.com, June 21.
48. N. Tichy, 1999, The teachable point of view, *Harvard Business Review,* 77(2): 82–83.
49. Brush, Greene, & Hart, From initial idea to unique advantage.
50. Eisenhardt & Martin, Dynamic capabilities: What are they?; M. D. Michalisin, D. M. Kline, & R. D. Smith, 2000, Intangible strategic assets and firm performance: A multi-industry study of the resource-based view, *Journal of Business Strategies,* 17(2): 91–117.
51. West & DeCastro, The Achilles heel of firm strategy: Resource weaknesses and distinctive inadequacies; D. L. Deeds, D. DeCarolis, & J. Coombs, 2000, Dynamic capabilities and new product development in high technology ventures: An empirical analysis of new biotechnology firms, *Journal of Business Venturing,* 15: 211–229; T. Chi, 1994, Trading in strategic resources: Necessary conditions, transaction cost problems, and choice of exchange structure, *Strategic Management Journal,* 15: 271–290.
52. S. Berman, J. Down, & C. Hill, 2002, Tacit knowledge as a source of competitive advantage in the National Basketball Association, *Academy of Management Journal,* 45: 13–31.
53. S. Shepard, 2001, Interview: 'The company is not in the stock', *Business Week,* April 30, 94–96.
54. M. S. Feldman, 2000, Organizational routines as a source of continuous change, *Organization Science,* 11: 611–629; A. M. Knott & B. McKelvey, 1999, Nirvana efficiency: A comparative test of residual claims and routines, *Journal of Economic Behavior & Organization,* 38: 365–383.
55. R. Lubit, 2001, Tacit knowledge and knowledge management: The keys to sustainable competitive advantage, *Organizational Dynamics,* 29(3): 164–178; S. A. Zahra, A. P. Nielsen, & W. C. Bogner, 1999, Corporate entrepreneurship, knowledge, and competence development, *Entrepreneurship: Theory and Practice,* 23(3): 169–189.
56. A. M. Webber, 2000, New math for a new economy, *Fast Company,* January/February, 214–224.
57. R. G. Schroeder, K. A. Bates, & M. A. Junttila, 2002, A resource-based view of manufacturing strategy and the relationship to manufacturing performance, *Strategic Management Journal,* 23: 105–117.
58. Brush & Artz, Toward a contingent resource-based theory.
59. J. B. Quinn, P. Anderson, & S. Finkelstein, 1996, Making the most of the best, *Harvard Business Review,* 74(2): 71–80.
60. Webber, New math, 217.
61. Ibid., 218.
62. R. D. Ireland, M. A. Hitt, & D. Vaidyanath, 2002, Managing strategic alliances to achieve a competitive advantage, *Journal of Management* (in press).
63. D. L. Deephouse, 2000, Media reputation as a strategic resource: An integration of mass communication and resource-based theories, *Journal of Management,* 26: 1091–1112.

64. M. Kleinman, 2001, Harley pushes brand prestige, *Marketing,* May 17, 16; G. Rifkin, 1998, How Harley-Davidson revs its brand, *Strategy & Business,* 9: 31–40.
65. G. Gavetti & D. Levinthal 2000, Looking forward and looking backward: Cognitive and experimental search. *Administrative Science Quarterly,* 45: 113–137; R. W. Coff, 1999, How buyers cope with uncertainty when acquiring firms in knowledge-intensive industries: Caveat emptor, *Organization Science,* 10: 144–161; S. J. Marsh & A. L. Ranft, 1999, Why resources matter: An empirical study of knowledge-based resources on new market entry, in M. A. Hitt, P. G. Clifford, R. D. Nixon, & K. P. Coyne (eds.), *Dynamic Strategic Resources* (Chichester: John Wiley & Sons), 43–66.
66. C. E. Helfat & R. S. Raubitschek, 2000, Product sequencing: Co-evolution of knowledge, capabilities and products, *Strategic Management Journal,* 21: 961–979.
67. Hitt, Bierman, Shimizu, & Kochhar, Direct and moderating effects of human capital on strategy and performance in professional service firms: A resource-based perspective; M. A. Hitt, R. D. Ireland, & H. Lee, 2000, Technological learning, knowledge management, firm growth and performance: An introductory essay, *Journal of Engineering and Technology Management,* 17: 231–246; D. G. Hoopes & S. Postrel, 1999, Shared knowledge: "Glitches," and product development performance, *Strategic Management Journal,* 20: 837–865; J. B. Quinn, 1994, *The Intelligent Enterprise,* New York: Free Press.
68. 1999, Thoughts on the business of life, *Forbes,* May 17, 352.
69. L. Argote & P. Ingram, 2000, Knowledge transfer: A basis for competitive advantage in firms, *Organizational Behavior and Human Decision Processes,* 82: 150–169.
70. G. G. Dess & J. C. Picken, 1999, *Beyond Productivity,* New York: AMACOM.
71. P. Coy, 2002, High turnover, high risk, *Business Week* (Special Issue), Spring, 24.
72. T. T. Baldwin & C. C. Danielson, 2000, Building a learning strategy at the top: Interviews with ten of America's CLOs, *Business Horizons,* 43(6): 5–14.
73. D. F. Kuratko, R. D. Ireland, & J. S. Hornsby, 2001, Improving firm performance through entrepreneurial actions: Acordia's corporate entrepreneurship strategy, *Academy of Management Executive,* 15(4): 60–71; M. T. Hansen, N. Nhoria, & T. Tierney, 1999, What's your strategy for managing knowledge? *Harvard Business Review,* 77(2): 106–116.
74. M. A. Hitt & R. D. Ireland, 1986, Relationships among corporate level distinctive competencies, diversification strategy, corporate structure, and performance, *Journal of Management Studies,* 23: 401–416; M. A. Hitt & R. D. Ireland, 1985, Corporate distinctive competence, strategy, industry, and performance, *Strategic Management Journal,* 6: 273–293; M. A. Hitt, R. D. Ireland, & K. A. Palia, 1982, Industrial firms' grand strategy and functional importance, *Academy of Management Journal,* 25: 265–298; M. A. Hitt, R. D. Ireland, & G. Stadter, 1982, Functional importance and company performance: Moderating effects of grand strategy and industry type, *Strategic Management Journal,* 3: 315–330; C. C. Snow & E. G. Hrebiniak, 1980, Strategy, distinctive competence, and organizational performance, *Administrative Science Quarterly,* 25: 317–336.
75. K. Hafeez, Y. B. Zhang, & N. Malak, 2002, Core competence for sustainable competitive advantage: A structured methodology for identifying core competence, *IEEE Transactions on Engineering Management,* 49(1): 28–35; C. K. Prahalad & G. Hamel, 1990, The core competence of the corporation, *Harvard Business Review,* 68(3): 79–93.
76. C. Bowman & V. Ambrosini, 2000, Value creation versus value capture: Towards a coherent definition of value in strategy, *British Journal of Management,* 11: 1–15; T. Chi, 1994, Trading in strategic resources: Necessary conditions, transaction cost problems, and choice of exchange structure, *Strategic Management Journal,* 15: 271–290.
77. C. Bowman, 2001, "Value" in the resource-based view of the firm: A contribution to the debate, *Academy of Management Review,* 26: 501–502.
78. C. Ames, 1995, Sales soft? Profits flat? It's time to rethink your business, *Fortune,* June 25, 142–146.
79. N. D. Schwartz, 2001, Remedies for an economic hangover, *Fortune,* June 25, 130–138.
80. Barney, How a firm's capabilities; J. B. Barney, 1995, Looking inside for competitive advantage, *Academy of Management Executive,* 9(4): 59–60; J. B. Barney, 1991, Firm resources and sustained competitive advantage, *Journal of Management,* 17: 99–120.
81. C. H. St. John & J. S. Harrison, 1999, Manufacturing-based relatedness, synergy, and coordination, *Strategic Management Journal,* 20: 129–145.
82. Barney, Looking inside for competitive advantage.
83. M. Betts, 2001, Turning browsers into buyers, *Sloan Management Review,* 42(2): 8–9.
84. Ibid.
85. G. Colvin, 2001, Shaking hands on the Web, *Fortune,* May 14, 54.
86. R. Tomkins, 1999, Marketing value for money, *Financial Times,* May 14, 18.
87. Barney, Looking inside for competitive advantage, 52.
88. Brush, Greene, & Hart, From initial idea to unique advantage, 65–67.
89. Barney, Looking inside for competitive advantage, 53.
90. Barney, How a firm's capabilities, 141.
91. Barney, Firm resources, 108.
92. J. Huey, 1993, How McKinsey does it, *Fortune,* November 1, 56–81.
93. J. Kurtzman, 1997, An interview with Rosabeth Moss Kanter, *Strategy & Business,* 16: 85–94.
94. R. Burt, 1999, When is corporate culture a competitive asset? Mastering Strategy (Part Six), *Financial Times,* November 1, 14–15.
95. L. Soupata, 2001, Managing culture for competitive advantage at United Parcel Service, *Journal of Organizational Excellence,* 20(3): 19–26.
96. A. W. King & C. P. Zeithaml, 2001, Competencies and firm performance: Examining the causal ambiguity paradox, *Strategic Management Journal,* 22: 75–99; R. Reed & R. DeFillippi, 1990, Causal ambiguity, barriers to imitation, and sustainable competitive advantage, *Academy of Management Review,* 15: 88–102.
97. Leonard-Barton, *Wellsprings of Knowledge,* 7.
98. A. Ritt, 2000, Reaching for maximum flexibility, *Iron Age New Steel,* January, 20–26.
99. A. K. Gupta & V. Govindarajan, 2000, Knowledge management's social dimension: Lessons from Nucor steel, *Sloan Management Review,* 42(1): 71–80.
100. Barney, Firm resources, 111.
101. Amit & Schoemaker, Strategic assets, 39.
102. S. K. McEvily, S. Das, & K. McCabe, 2000, Avoiding competence substitution through knowledge sharing, *Academy of Management Review,* 25: 294–311.
103. A. Serwer, 2002, Dell does domination, *Fortune,* January 21, 70–75.
104. M. E. Porter, 1985, *Competitive Advantage,* New York: Free Press, 33–61.
105. G. G. Dess, A. Gupta, J.-F. Hennart, & C. W. L. Hill, 1995, Conducting and integrating strategy research at the international corporate and business levels: Issues and directions, *Journal of Management,* 21: 376; Porter, What is strategy?
106. J. Webb & C. Gile, 2001, Reversing the value chain, *Journal of Business Strategy,* 22(2): 13–17; T. A. Stewart, 1999, Customer learning is a two-way street, *Fortune,* May 10, 158–160.
107. R. Amit & C. Zott, 2001, Value creation in E-business, *Strategic Management Journal,* 22(Special Issue): 493–520; M. E. Porter, 2001, Strategy and the Internet, *Harvard Business Review,* 79(3): 62–78.
108. D. Champion, 2001, Mastering the value chain: An interview with Mark Levin of Millennium Pharmaceuticals, *Harvard Business Review,* 79(6): 108–115.
109. J. Y. Murray & M. Kotabe, 1999, Sourcing strategies of U.S. service companies: A modified transaction-cost analysis, *Strategic Management Journal,* 20: 791–809.
110. S. Jones, 1999, Growth process in global market, *Financial Times,* June 22, 17.
111. A. Takeishi, 2001, Bridging inter- and intra-firm boundaries: Management of supplier involvement in automobile product development, *Strategic Management Journal,* 22: 403–433; H. Y. Park, C. S. Reddy, & S. Sarkar, 2000, Make or buy strategy of firms in the U.S., *Multinational Business Review,* 8(2): 89–97
112. Hafeez, Zhang, & Malak, Core competence for sustainable competitive advantage; B. H. Jevnaker & M. Bruce, 1999, Design as a strategic alliance: Expanding the creative capability of the firm, in M. A. Hitt, P. G. Clifford, R. D. Nixon, & K. P. Coyne (eds.). *Dynamic Strategic Resources,* Chichester: John Wiley & Sons, 266–298.
113. A. Takeishi, Bridging inter- and intra-firm boundaries: Management of supplier involvement in automobile product development, 403–433.
114. A Bernstein, 2001, Low-skilled jobs: do they have to move? *Business Week,* February 26, 94.
115. M. Useem & J. Harder, 2000, Leading laterally in company outsourcing, *Sloan Management Review,* 41(2): 25–36.
116. R. C. Insinga & M. J. Werle, 2000, Linking outsourcing to business strategy, *Academy of Management Executive,* 14(4): 58–70.
117. M. Katz, 2001, Planning ahead for manufacturing facility changes: A case study in outsourcing, *Pharmaceutical Technology,* March: 160–164.
118. G. G. Dess & J. C. Picken, 1999, Creating competitive (dis)advantage: Learning from Food Lion's freefall, *Academy of Management Executive,* 13(3): 97–111.
119. M. Hannan & J. Freeman, 1977, The population ecology of organizations, *American Journal of Sociology,* 82: 929–964.
120. Leonard-Barton, *Wellsprings of Knowledge,* 30–31.
121. West & DeCastro, The Achilles heel of firm strategy; Keil, Cutting your losses.
122. Christensen, The past and future of competitive advantage.

PART TWO

Strategic Actions: Strategy Formulation

4

Chapter Four

Business-Level Strategy

Knowledge Objectives

Studying this chapter should provide you with the strategic management knowledge needed to:

1. Define business-level strategies.
2. Discuss the relationship between customers and business-level strategies in terms of *who, what,* and *how.*
3. Explain the differences among business-level strategies.
4. Use the five forces of competition model to explain how above-average returns can be earned through each business-level strategy.
5. Describe the risks of using each of the business-level strategies.

Developing and Using Carefully Designed Strategies: The Key to Corporate Success

Internet technology has a tremendous effect on how firms compete in the 21st century. In Chapter 2, we noted how the Internet affects both industry structures and the potential to operate profitably within them. Internet technology itself, however, is rarely a competitive advantage. It actually makes it more essential for a firm to develop well-designed business-level strategies in order to detail how Internet technology can enable the success of the firm's other strategic actions. According to Michael Porter, many of the companies that succeed in the 21st century ". . . will be ones that use the Internet as a complement to traditional ways of competing, not those that set their Internet initiatives apart from their established operations."

Whatever business-level strategy the firm chooses, it should be carefully developed. Moreover, because of the importance of human capital to a company's competitive success (as discussed in Chapter 3), the ultimate effectiveness of a business-level strategy is strongly influenced by the quality of the people the organization employs. In light of environmental changes and the capabilities of Internet technology, companies across most industries are changing their business-level strategies. For example, an analysis of a number of property-casualty insurers shows that many of these companies have not effectively integrated the Internet into their business-level strategies. However, the competitive pressures within this industry to have an effective on-line presence are influencing the actions many of these firms are taking to establish a competitive advantage while using their business-level strategy.

In mid-2001, networking firms such as Cisco Systems, Nortel Networks, and Lucent Technologies refocused their optical technology strategies in response to dramatically altered conditions in their environments. Cisco decided to place less emphasis on the enterprise market so it could concentrate more on lucrative sales to service providers. Cisco also decided that part of its optical technology business-level strategy of focused differentiation would be to pursue opportunities for fiber-optic related products in metropolitan area networks (MANs). These decisions allowed Cisco to continue its growth-oriented strategies during its mid-2001 decline in sales revenue.

CISCO SYSTEMS, INC.

Senior vice president for Cisco Systems' Internet Switching and Services Group and former chief strategy officer Mike Volpi is responsible for developing products, including Cisco's Catalyst 4000, which allows broadband access over fiber-optic networks.

Lucent's strategy in the core optical technology market is to offer cheaper alternatives, while maintaining at least acceptable levels of differentiation such as quality with each alternative. These actions demonstrate Lucent's use of the cost leadership business-level strategy in this particular product line. Some of Lucent's recent customers are located in nations outside the United States. The firm's strategy appears to have been successful. Belgacom of Belgium and P&T Luxembourg recently chose Lucent to expand the capacity of the two parallel optical network connections between their networks in Belgium and Luxembourg. Lucent has also signed a contract with GNG Networks, one of the leading broadband Internet infrastructure providers in Korea, to provide a high-speed optical networking system for GNG's backbone network.

According to an analyst, Nortel's optical technology strategy is to "... compete in key segments of the industry, such as Internet data centers and broadband, and to dominate the optical market and grow related businesses off that." Nortel's concentration on serving only key segments of an industry demonstrates the use of the focused differentiation business-level strategy. With 75 percent of all North American Internet traffic riding across Nortel's optical network equipment, and more than 750 optical Internet customers worldwide, the firm is now working on making networks that are 20 times faster and capable of handling even more traffic.

Smaller, nimbler companies, such as RedBack Networks, Sycamore Networks, and Ciena, are also creating new optical technology strategies. For the most part, these entrepreneurial ventures competing against Cisco, Lucent, and Nortel are using focused differentiation business-level strategies to serve the needs of particular market segments more effectively than companies with strategies aimed at serving all of a market. However, as will be discussed in the next chapter, one firm's strategies are met with responses from its competitors.

SOURCES: G. Anders, 2001, John Chambers after the deluge, *Fast Company,* July, 100–111; G. Biehn, 2001, Yes, you can profit from e-commerce, *Financial Executive,* May, 26–27; A. P. Burger, 2001, Getting your program back on track. *American Agent & Broker,* May, 69; S. Lee, 2001, Optical titans refocus, *InfoWorld,* April 2, 1, 29; M. E. Porter, 2001, Strategy and the Internet, *Harvard Business Review,* 79(3): 63–78; A. C. Trembly, 2001, Most P-C insurers lack web strategy, *National Underwriter,* February 26, 1, 23; E. Zimmerman, 2001, What are employees worth? *Workforce,* February, 32–36; http://www.lucent.com; http://www.nortel.com.

Strategy is concerned with making choices among two or more alternatives. When choosing a strategy, the firm decides to pursue one course of action instead of others. Indeed, the main point of strategy is to help decision makers choose among the competing priorities and alternatives facing their firm.[1] Business-level strategy is the choice a firm makes when deciding how to compete in individual product markets. The choices are important, as there is an established link between a firm's strategies and its long-term performance.[2] Thus, the choices Cisco, Lucent, and Nortel have made to develop their optical technology strategies will affect the degree to which the firms will be able to earn above-average returns while competing against companies such as RedBack Networks, Sycamore Networks, and Ciena.

Determining the businesses in which the firm will compete is a question of corporate-level strategy and is discussed in Chapter 6. Competition in individual product markets is a question of business-level strategy, which is this chapter's focus. For all types of strategies, companies acquire the information and knowledge needed to make choices as they study external environmental opportunities and threats as well as identify and evaluate their internal resources, capabilities, and core competencies.

In Chapter 1, we defined a *strategy* as an integrated and coordinated set of commitments and actions designed to exploit core competencies and gain a competitive advantage. The different strategies that firms use to gain competitive advantages are shown in Figure 1.1 in Chapter 1. As described in the individual chapters outlined in the figure, the firm tries to establish and exploit a competitive advantage when using each type of strategy. As explained in the Opening Case, Lucent is using a cost leadership strategy while Cisco and Nortel are using the focused differentiation business-level strategy in the optical technology market. Each firm hopes to develop a competitive advantage and exploit it for marketplace success by using the strategy it has chosen.

Every firm needs a business-level strategy.[3] However, every firm may not use all the strategies—corporate-level, acquisition and restructuring, international, and cooperative—that are examined in Chapters 6 through 9. For example, the firm competing in a single-product market area in a single geographic location does not need a corporate-level strategy to deal with product diversity or an international strategy to deal with geographic diversity. Think of a local dry-cleaner with only one location offering a single service (the cleaning and laundering of clothes) in a single storefront. In contrast, a diversified firm will use one of the several types of corporate-level strategies as well as choosing a separate business-level strategy for each product market area in which the company competes (the relationship between corporate-level and business-level strategies is further examined in Chapter 6). Thus, every firm—from the local drycleaner to the multinational corporation—chooses at least one business-level strategy. Business-level strategy can be thought of as the firm's *core* strategy—the strategy that must be formed to describe how the firm will compete.[4]

Not only large corporations rely on strategies to guide their actions. Even a one-person operation, such as this vegetable stand vendor, uses a business-level strategy.

Each strategy the firm uses specifies desired outcomes and how they are to be achieved.[5] Integrating external and internal foci, strategies reflect the firm's theory about how it intends to compete.[6] The fundamental objective of using each strategy is to create value for stakeholders. Strategies are purposeful, precede the taking of actions to which they apply, and demonstrate a shared understanding of the firm's strategic intent and strategic mission.[7] An effectively formulated strategy marshals, integrates, and allocates the firm's resources, capabilities, and competencies so that it will be properly aligned with its external environment.[8] A properly developed strategy also rationalizes the firm's strategic intent and strategic mission along with the actions taken to achieve them.[9]

Information about a host of variables, including markets, customers, technology, worldwide finance, and the changing world economy must be collected and analyzed to properly form and use strategies.[10] As noted in the Opening Case, Internet technology affects how organizations gather and examine information that must be carefully studied when choosing strategies.

A **business-level strategy** is an integrated and coordinated set of commitments and actions the firm uses to gain a competitive advantage by exploiting core competencies in specific product markets.

Business-level strategy, this chapter's focus, is an integrated and coordinated set of commitments and actions the firm uses to gain a competitive advantage by exploiting core competencies in specific product markets.[11] Only firms that continuously upgrade their competitive advantages over time are able to achieve long-term success with their business-level strategy.[12] Key issues the firm must address when choosing a business-level strategy are the good or service to offer customers, how to manufacture or create it, and how to distribute it to the marketplace.[13] Once formed, the business-level strategy reflects where and how the firm has an advantage over its rivals.[14] The essence of a firm's business-level strategy is "choosing to perform activities differently or to perform different activities than rivals."[15]

Customers are the foundation of successful business-level strategies. In fact, some believe that an effective business-level strategy demonstrates the firm's ability to ". . . build and maintain relationships to the best people for maximum value creation, both 'internally' (to firm members) and 'externally' (to customers)."[16] Thus, successful organizations think of their employees as internal customers who produce value-creating products for which customers are willing to pay.

Because of their strategic importance, this chapter opens with a discussion of customers. Three issues are considered in this analysis. In selecting a business-level strategy, the firm determines (1) *who* will be served, (2) *what* needs those target customers have that it will satisfy, and (3) *how* those needs will be satisfied.

Descriptions of five business-level strategies follow the discussion of customers. These five strategies are sometimes called *generic* because they can be used in any business and in any industry.[17] Our analysis of these strategies describes how effective use of each strategy allows the firm to favorably position itself relative to the five competitive forces in the industry (see Chapter 2). In addition, we use the value chain (see Chapter 3) to show examples of the primary and support activities that are necessary to implement each business-level strategy. We also describe the different risks the firm may encounter when using one of these strategies.

Organizational structures and controls that are linked with successful use of each business-level strategy are explained in Chapter 11.

Customers: Who, What, and How

Strategic competitiveness results only when the firm is able to satisfy a group of customers by using its competitive advantages to compete in individual product markets. The most successful companies constantly seek to chart new competitive space in order to serve new customers as they simultaneously try to find ways to better serve existing customers.

Flexibility is important to the firm that emphasizes customers as a vital component of its strategies. For example, Compaq Computer Corp. recently moved away from its "Everything to the Internet" approach, which it had undertaken to compete more successfully against Dell Computer Corp.'s highly successful direct-manufacturing model. However, Compaq did not have the competencies required to maintain pace with Dell's pricing agility. As a result, Compaq changed that approach and recently decided to portray itself as "the leading information technology solutions provider." The firm is targeting large markets such as health care and media as it moves into the lucrative technology services competitive arena.[18] As this example shows, Compaq is flexible enough to change its focus to corporate customers' software needs rather than the personal computer hardware needs of primarily individuals and small businesses. According to Compaq's CEO, service customers' "demand for simplification" is the core need his firm will address as an information technology services provider.[19] However, the degree to which Compaq will be able to satisfy this customer need could be influenced by the transaction between Hewlett-Packard and Compaq. The interest in merging demonstrates flexibility on the part of both of these firms as they seek to become large enough to develop the economies of scale that are necessary to successfully compete against Dell.

A key reason that the firm must satisfy customers with its business-level strategy is that returns earned from relationships with customers are the lifeblood of all organizations.[20] Executives at Motley Fool capture this reality crisply by noting that, "the customer is the person who pays us."[21] The quality of these returns for Internet ventures is dictated by the conversion rate. The conversion rate measures returns by dividing the number of people who visit a site within a particular period by the number of visitors who take action (e.g., purchasing or registering) while visiting.[22]

The Importance of Effectively Managing Relationships with Customers

The firm's relationships with its customers are strengthened when it is committed to offering them superior value. In business-to-business transactions, superior value is often created when the firm's product helps its customers to develop a new competitive advantage or to enhance the value of its existing competitive advantages.[23] Receiving superior value enhances customers' loyalty to the firm that provides it. Evidence suggests that loyalty has a positive relationship with profitability. Ford Motor Company, for example, estimates that each percentage-point increase in customer loyalty—defined as how many Ford owners purchase a Ford product the next time—creates at least $100 million in additional profits annually. MBNA, a credit-card issuer, determined that reducing customer defection rates by 5 percent increases the lifetime profitability of the average customer by 125 percent.[24]

Selecting customers and deciding which of their needs the firm will try to satisfy, as well as how it will do so, are challenging. One reason is competition at the global level, which has created many attractive choices for customers. As discussed in Chapter 2, a large set of what appear to be equally attractive choices increases customers' power and influence relative to companies offering products to them. Some even argue that increased choice and easily accessible information about the functionality of firms' products are creating increasingly sophisticated and knowledgeable customers, making it difficult to earn their loyalty.[25]

Several products are available to firms to help them better understand customers and manage relationships with them. For example, firms can use customer relationship management (CRM) software programs to develop Web-based profiles of their customers and to fully integrate customer communications with back-office activities, such as billing and accounting.[26] Salesforce.com's popular CRM program helps a firm's sales and marketing staffs communicate with customers: "A salesperson can, for instance, quickly check on the status of a customer account, while marketing people can collaborate to plan and execute promotional e-mail campaigns."[27] The unique attribute of Salesforce.com's program is that it is hosted and maintained entirely via the Web. A successful CRM program can be a source of competitive advantage as the firm uses knowledge gained from it to improve strategy implementation processes.

A number of companies have become skilled at the art of *managing* all aspects of their relationship with their customers.[28] In the fast-paced, technologically sophisticated global economy, firms that participate in e-commerce (Internet-based ventures and firms that provide a strong Internet presence along with their storefront operations) can understand their customers as well as manage their relationships with them more effectively than can companies without an Internet presence. As noted in the Opening Case, the probability of successful competition increases even more when the firm carefully integrates Internet technology with its strategy, rather than using Internet technology on a "stand-alone basis."[29]

For example, Amazon.com is an Internet-based venture widely recognized for the quality of information it maintains about its customers and the services it renders. Cemex SA, a major global cement company based in Mexico, uses the Internet to link its customers, cement plants, and main control room, allowing the firm to automate orders and optimize truck deliveries in highly congested Mexico City. Analysts believe that Cemex's integration of Web technology with its cost leadership strategy is helping to differentiate it from competitors.[30] GE's prominent e-commerce position is integrated into its strategies. In fact, this old-economy icon buys and sells more through its private online marketplaces—approximately $20 billion in 2001 alone—than is traded in all the independent business-to-business (B2B) marketplaces combined. GE is using Internet technology to save money and to enhance relationships with its customers by reaching them faster with products of ever-increasing quality.[31]

Reach, Richness, and Affiliation

As the foundation on which e-commerce is linked with the firm's business-level strategy, Internet technology can help the firm establish a competitive advantage through its relationship with customers along the dimensions of *reach, richness,* and *affiliation.*

The *reach* dimension is about the firm's access and connection to customers. For instance, the largest physical retailer in bookstores, Barnes & Noble, carries about 200,000 titles in 900 stores. By contrast, Amazon.com offers some 4.5 million titles and is located on roughly 25 million computer screens, with additional customer connections expected in the future. Thus, Amazon.com's reach is significantly magnified relative to that associated with Barnes & Noble's physical bookstores.[32]

Richness, the second dimension, is concerned with the depth and detail of the two-way flow of information between the firm and the customer. The potential of the richness dimension to help the firm establish a competitive advantage in its relationship with customers led traditional financial services brokers, such as Merrill Lynch, to offer online services in order to better manage information exchanges with their customers. Broader and deeper information-based exchanges allow the firm to better understand its customers and their needs. They also enable customers to become more knowledgeable of how the firm can satisfy them. Internet technology and e-commerce transactions have substantially reduced the costs of meaningful information exchanges with current and possible future customers.

Affiliation, the third dimension, is concerned with facilitating useful interactions with customers. Internet navigators such as Microsoft CarPoint help online clients find and sort information. CarPoint provides data and software to prospective car buyers that enables them to compare car models along 80 objective specifications. The program can supply this information because Internet technology allows a great deal of information to be collected from a variety of sources at a low cost. A prospective buyer who has selected a specific car based on comparisons of different models can then be linked to dealers that meet the customer's needs and purchasing requirements. A company, such as GM, Ford, and DaimlerChrysler, represents its own products, creating a situation in which its financial interests differ substantially from those of consumers. Because its revenues come from sources other than the final customer or end user (such as advertisements on its website, hyperlinks, and associated products and services), CarPoint represents the customer's interests, a service that fosters affiliation.[33]

As we discuss next, effective management of customer relationships, especially in an e-commerce era, helps the firm answer questions related to the issues of *who, what,* and *how* to serve.

Microsoft president Steve Ballmer (right) listens to fomer Ford CEO Jacques Nasser (left) speak at the launch of Microsoft's CarPoint. The Carpoint website increases customer affiliation by allowing users to compare automotive data across all brands and models, to create a profile for their autos, and to choose to be alerted of scheduled maintenance.

© MARK RICHARDS/PHOTOEDIT

Who: Determining the Customers to Serve

A crucial decision at any company related to a business-level strategy is the one made about the target customers for the firm's goods or services *(who)*.[34] To make this decision, companies divide customers into groups based on differences in the customers' needs (needs are defined and further discussed in the next section). Called **market segmentation,** this process clusters people with similar needs into individual and identifiable groups.[35] As part of its business-level strategy, the firm develops a marketing program to effectively sell products to its target customer groups.

Almost any identifiable human or organizational characteristic can be used to subdivide a market into segments that differ from one another on a given characteristic. Common characteristics on which customers' needs vary are illustrated in Table 4.1. Based on their core competencies and opportunities in the external environment, companies choose a business-level strategy to deliver value to target customers and satisfy their specific needs. For example, Rolls-Royce Motor Cars, Ltd. uses a focused differentiation strategy (defined and explained later in this chapter) to manufacture and sell Bentleys and Rolls-Royces. The firm considered both demographic characteristics (e.g., age and income) and socioeconomic characteristics (e.g., social class) (see Table 4.1) to identify its target customers. Customer feedback as well as additional analyses identified psychological factors (e.g., lifestyle choices) that allowed additional

Market segmentation is a process used to cluster people with similar needs into individual and identifiable groups.

Table 4.1 Basis for Customer Segmentation

Consumer Markets

1. Demographic factors (age, income, sex, etc.)
2. Socioeconomic factors (social class, stage in the family life cycle)
3. Geographic factors (cultural, regional, and national differences)
4. Psychological factors (lifestyle, personality traits)
5. Consumption patterns (heavy, moderate, and light users)
6. Perceptual factors (benefit segmentation, perceptual mapping)

Industrial Markets

1. End-use segments (identified by SIC code)
2. Product segments (based on technological differences or production economics)
3. Geographic segments (defined by boundaries between countries or by regional differences within them)
4. Common buying factor segments (cut across product market and geographic segments)
5. Customer size segments

SOURCE: Adapted from S. C. Jain, 2000, *Marketing Planning and Strategy,* Cincinnati: South-Western College Publishing, 120.

segmentation of the firm's core target customer group. Based on this information, the firm further segmented its target customer group into those *who want to drive* an ultra-luxury car themselves and those *who want to be driven* by a chauffeur in their ultra-luxury automobile. The Bentley targets the first individual, while the Rolls Royce satisfies the interests of the chauffeur-driven owner.[36]

Characteristics are often combined to segment a large market into specific groups that have unique needs. For example, McDonald's dominates the fast-food market. However, for college students interested in healthy eating, surveys suggest that Subway is the dominant fast-food choice.[37] This more specific breakdown of the fast-food market for college students is a product of jointly studying demographic, psychological, and consumption-pattern characteristics (see Table 4.1). This knowledge suggests that on a relative basis, Subway's business-level strategy should target college students with a desire for healthier foods more aggressively than should McDonald's.

The Generation X (top left), Swing Generation (top right), Baby Boomer (left in lower photo), and Generation Y (right in lower photo) market segments each have unique needs and interests that firms target.

Demographic characteristics (see the discussion in Chapter 2 and Table 4.1) can also be used to segment markets into generations with unique interests and needs. Evidence suggests, for example, that direct mail is an effective communication medium for the World War II generation (those born before 1932). The Swing generation (those born between 1933 and 1945) values taking cruises and purchasing second homes. Once financially conservative but now willing to spend money, members of this generation seek product information from knowledgeable sources. The Baby Boom generation (born between 1946 and 1964) desires products that reduce the stress generated by juggling career demands and the needs of older parents with those of their own children. Ellen Tracy clothes, known for their consistency of fit and color, are targeted to Baby Boomer women. More conscious of hype, people in Generation X (born between 1965 and 1976) want products that deliver as promised. The Xers use the Internet as a primary shopping tool and expect visually compelling marketing. Members of this group are the fastest growing segment of mutual-fund shareholders, with their holdings overwhelmingly invested in stock funds.[38] Different marketing campaigns and distribution channels (e.g., Internet for Generation X customers as compared to direct mail for the World War II generation) affect the implementation of strategies for those companies interested in serving the needs of different generations.

© BILL VARIE/CORBIS
© WALTER HODGES/CORBIS
© DAVE BARTRUFF/CORBIS

Increasing Segmentation of Markets

Companies frequently use sophisticated systems and programs to gather and interpret information about customers. Using these tools allows firms to gain the insights that are needed to further segment customers into specific groups that have unique needs. For example, many companies segment markets on a global basis. Indeed, because of increasing globalization of the world's economies, global market segmentation has become important to many firms' success. *Global market segmentation* is the process of identifying specific segments—consumer groups across countries—of potential customers with homogeneous attributes who are likely to exhibit similar buying behavior.[39] As discussed later in the chapter, McDonald's understands that customers in different regions in the world prefer slightly different versions of its core food products.

Part of our discussion in the previous section suggests that companies are segmenting markets into increasingly specialized niches of customers with unique needs and interests. Generation Y (born between 1977 and 1984) is a market segment with specific characteristics that affect how firms use business-level strategies to serve these customers' needs. Analysis of purchasing patterns for this customer group shows that this segment prefers to buy in stores rather than online, but that they may use the Internet to study products online prior to visiting a store to make a purchase. This preference suggests that companies targeting this segment might want to combine their storefront operations with a robust and active website.[40] Other examples of targeting specific market segments include New Balance's marketing its shoes to members of the Baby Boom generation (see the Strategic Focus on page 133), Christopher & Banks's focus on working women over the age of 40, and Abercrombie & Fitch's targeting the subgroup of teenagers who demand stylish clothing seen on television shows such as *Dawson's Creek* as well as in music videos.[41]

Once their customer groups have been carefully segmented, companies are also improving their ability to provide individual goods and services with specific functionalities that can satisfy the unique needs of those groups. Sometimes, the needs of domestic and global customers are virtually identical. When customer needs and interests are homogeneous or relatively so across global markets, the firm has a single or only a few target customer groups rather than many.

What: Determining Which Customer Needs to Satisfy

Needs (what) are related to the benefits and features of a good or service.[42] A basic need of all customers is to buy products that create value for them. The generalized forms of value products provide are either low cost with acceptable features or highly differentiated features with acceptable cost.

Successful firms constantly seek new customers as well as new ways to serve existing ones. As a firm decides *who* it will serve, it must simultaneously identify the targeted customer group's needs that its goods or services can satisfy. Top-level managers play a critical role in recognizing and understanding these needs. The valuable insights they gain from listening to and studying customers influence product, technology, distribution, and service decisions. For example, Volkswagen AG planned to base several Volkswagen and Audi models on the same chassis and to use the same transmissions. Upper-level executives at the firm listened to concerns from customers about this decision, who asked why they should pay for the premiere Audi brand when they could obtain much of its technology at a lower cost by purchasing a Volkswagen product. As a result, Volkswagen AG "intends to invest six billion marks ($3.32 billion) during the next few years to ensure that each of its brands retains a separate identity."[43]

Creating separate brand identities, such as Audi and Volkswagen, helps a firm's products convey benefits and features that customers want to purchase. Another way of saying this is that brands can satisfy needs. In late 2000, General Motors (GM) executives concluded that the Oldsmobile brand was no longer crisply differentiated from the company's other major automobile groups (Chevrolet, Pontiac, Buick, and Cadillac). Because it no longer conveyed specific benefits and features that satisfied target customers' needs, GM dropped the Oldsmobile brand from its product lines.[44]

How: Determining Core Competencies Necessary to Satisfy Customer Needs

As explained in Chapters 1 and 3, *core competencies* are resources and capabilities that serve as a source of competitive advantage for the firm over its rivals. Firms use core competencies to implement value-creating strategies and thereby satisfy customers' needs *(how)*. Only those firms with the capacity to continuously improve, innovate, and upgrade their competencies can expect to meet and hopefully exceed customers' expectations across time.[45]

Companies use different core competencies in efforts to produce goods or services that can satisfy customers' needs. IBM, for example, emphasizes its core competence in technology to rapidly develop new service-related products. Beginning in 1993, then newly appointed CEO Lou Gerstner changed IBM by leveraging its ". . . strength in network integration and consulting to transform (the firm) from a moribund maker of mainframe computers to a sexy services company that can basically design, build, and manage a corporation's entire data system."[46]

SAS Institute is the world's largest privately owned software company. Based on over 6.5 million lines of code, SAS programs are used for data warehousing, data mining, and decision support. Allocating over 30 percent of revenues to research and development (R&D), the firm relies on its core competence in R&D to satisfy the data-related needs of such customers as U.S. Census Bureau and a host of consumer goods firms (e.g., hotels, banks, and catalog companies).[47] Vans Inc. relies on its core competencies in innovation and marketing to design and sell skateboards. The firm also pioneered thick-soled, slip-on sneakers that can absorb the shock of five-foot leaps on wheels. Vans uses what is recognized as an offbeat marketing mix to capitalize on its pioneering products. In lieu of mass media ads, the firm sponsors skateboarding events, supported the making of a documentary film that celebrates the "outlaw nature" of the skateboarding culture, and is building skateboard parks at malls around the country.[48]

All organizations, including IBM, SAS and Vans Inc. must be able to use their core competencies (the *how*) to satisfy the needs (the *what*) of the target group of customers (the *who*) the firm has chosen to serve by using its business-level strategy. Next, we discuss the business-level strategies firms use when pursuing strategic competitiveness and above-average returns.

Types of Business-Level Strategy

Business-level strategies are intended to create differences between the firm's position relative to those of its rivals.[49] To position itself, the firm must decide whether it intends to *perform activities differently* or to *perform different activities* as compared to its rivals.[50] Thus, the firm's business-level strategy is a deliberate choice about how it will perform the value chain's primary and support activities in ways that create unique value.

Successful use of a chosen strategy results only when the firm integrates its primary and support activities to provide the unique value it intends to deliver. Value is delivered to customers when the firm is able to use competitive advantages resulting from the integration of activities. Superior fit among primary and support activities forms an activity system. In turn, an effective activity system helps the firm establish and exploit its strategic position. In the Strategic Focus on pages 120–121, we use Southwest Airlines to examine these issues in greater detail.

Favorably positioned firms such as Southwest Airlines have a competitive advantage over their industry rivals and are better able to cope with the five forces of competition (see Chapter 2). Favorable positioning is important in that the universal objective of all companies is to develop and sustain competitive advantages.[51] Improperly positioned firms encounter competitive difficulties and likely will fail to sustain competitive advantages. For example, its ineffective responses to competitors such as Wal-Mart left Sears Roebuck Co. in a weak competitive position for years. These ineffective responses resulted from the inability of Sears to properly implement strategies that were appropriate in light of its external opportunities and threats and its internal competencies. Two researchers describe this situation: "Once a towering force in retailing, Sears spent 10 years vacillating between an emphasis on hard goods and soft goods, venturing in and out of ill-chosen arenas, failing to differentiate itself in any of them, and never building a compelling economic logic."[52] Firms choose from among five business-level strategies to establish and defend their desired strategic position against rivals: *cost leadership, differentiation, focused cost leadership, focused differentiation,* and *integrated cost leadership/differentiation* (see Figure 4.1). Each business-level strategy helps the firm to establish and exploit a competitive advantage within a particular competitive scope.

When selecting a business-level strategy, firms evaluate two types of potential competitive advantage: "lower cost than rivals, or the ability to differentiate and command a premium price that exceeds the extra cost of doing so."[53] Having lower cost derives from the firm's ability to perform activities differently than rivals; being able to differentiate indicates the firm's capacity to perform different (and valuable) activities.[54] Competitive advantage is thus achieved within some scope.

Scope has several dimensions, including the group of product and customer segments served and the array of geographic markets in which the firm competes.

Figure 4.1 Five Business-Level Strategies

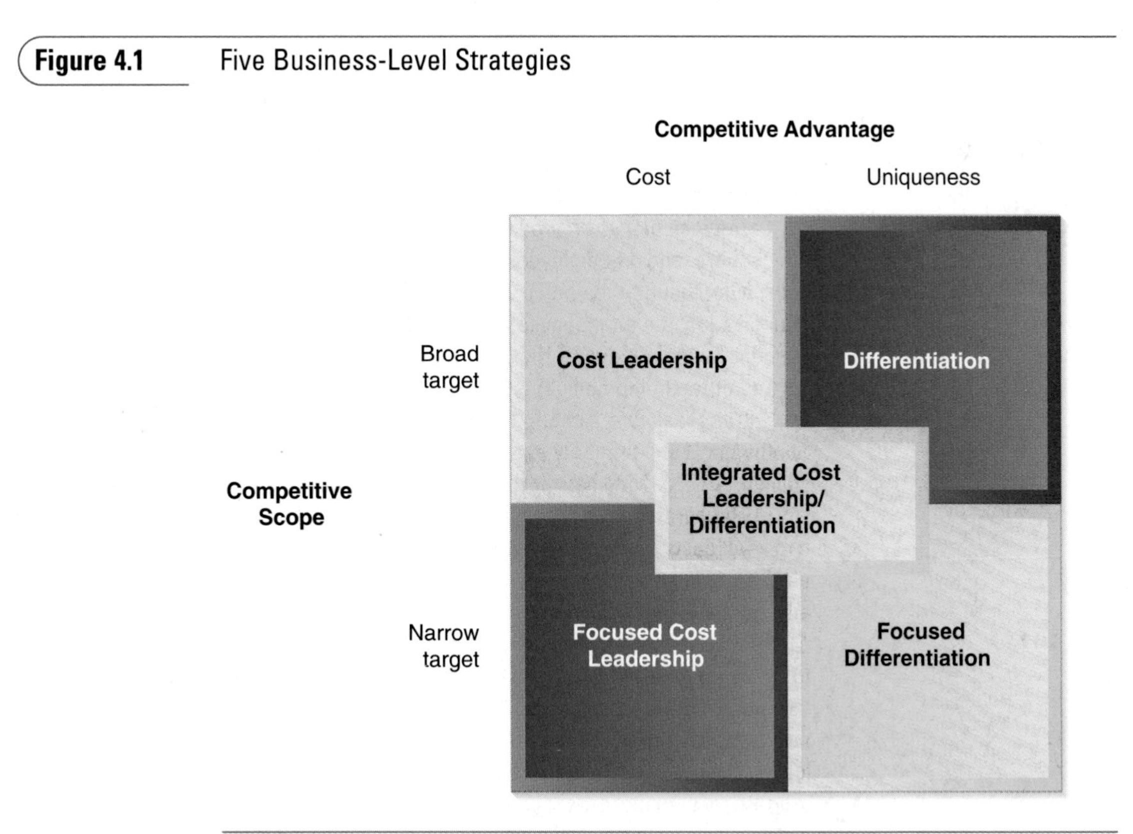

SOURCE: Adapted with the permission of The Free Press, an imprint of Simon & Schuster Adult Publishing Group, from *Competitive Advantage: Creating and Sustaining Superior Performance,* by Michael E. Porter, 12. Copyright © 1985, 1998 by Michael E. Porter.

Strategic Focus

Southwest Airlines' Activity System: Is It Imitable?

Launched in 1971 with service among three Texas cities—Dallas, Houston, and San Antonio—Southwest Airlines has followed its mission of "dedication to the highest quality of customer service delivered with a sense of warmth, friendliness, individual pride, and company spirit." Southwest has become the fifth-largest U.S. carrier and eighth-largest carrier in the world.

Relying on its mission to direct its activities, the company offers short-haul, low-cost, point-to-point service between midsize cities and secondary airports in large cities. It performs its activities in ways that drive the firm's costs lower and lower. According to company officials, Southwest is ". . . always looking for an opportunity to make the lowest even lower." Meals, assigned seating, interline baggage transfers, and premium classes of service are not available on Southwest flights—not offering these services helps the firm keep its costs lower than rivals. What Southwest does offer its customers are low cost, frequent departures to its destinations, and an often entertaining experience while in the air (a form of differentiation).

Because Southwest charges fares as low as 20 percent of those charged by mainstream carriers, the firm's effect on pricing in the markets it serves can be dramatic. Government officials in one city expected many fares to drop by at least half once Southwest's decision to serve their community was implemented. Moreover, because Southwest's low fares tend to attract people who might have driven to their destinations, officials also anticipated that total passenger traffic from the local airport would double within two years of Southwest's entry into their community's market.

According to Southwest, the secrets of its success are simple:

- *Keep costs down.* Throughout its operations, Southwest has maintained a constant focus on keeping costs down. Turning planes around quickly at the gate results in planes being able to log more hours in the air. Using a standardized fleet of Boeing 737 jets reduces maintenance costs and pilot training expenses. Southwest's operating costs are from 25 percent to 80 percent lower than most major carriers.
- *Focus on customers.* Southwest's commitment to customer service and satisfaction is legendary. Some gate agents have even invited stranded passengers to spend the night in their homes.
- *Keep employees happy.* Southwest's culture and benefits create a positive work atmosphere, and its employees are more productive than their counterparts at other airlines, even though their pay is similar. Looking for people who want to serve a cause rather than fill a job, the airline invests significantly in its recruiting and training procedures. Founder Kelleher believes that corporate culture is the most important difference between his and other airline companies.
- *Keep it simple.* Although some longer-haul flights have been added over the years, Southwest is still primarily a point-to-point, short-hop airline. Its destinations are often smaller airports with less air traffic.

The careful fit or integration among Southwest's primary and support activities allows it to keep costs down, focus on customers, keep employees happy, and keep its work simple. This fit is instrumental to the development and use of the firm's two major competitive advantages—organizational culture and customer service. The importance of fit between primary and support activities isn't unique to Southwest, in that fit among activities is a key to the sustainability of competitive advantage for all firms. As Michael Porter comments, "Strategic fit among many activities is fundamental not only to competitive advantage but also to the sustainability of that advantage. It is harder for a rival to match an array of interlocked activities than it is merely to imitate a particular sales-force approach, match a process technology, or replicate a set of product features. Positions built on systems of activities are far more sustainable than those built on individual activities."

An activity system can be mapped to show how individual activities are integrated to achieve fit, as the accompanying map for Southwest's activities shows. Higher-order strategic themes are critical to successful use of the firm's strategy. For Southwest Airlines, these strategic themes are limited passenger service, frequent, reliable departures, lean, highly productive ground and gate crews, high aircraft utilization, very low ticket prices, and short-haul, point-to-point routes between midsize cities and secondary airports. Individual clusters of tightly linked activities make it possible for the outcome of a strategic theme to be achieved. For example, no meals, no seat assignments, and no baggage transfers form a cluster of individual activities that support the strategic theme of limited passenger service.

Southwest Airlines' Activity System

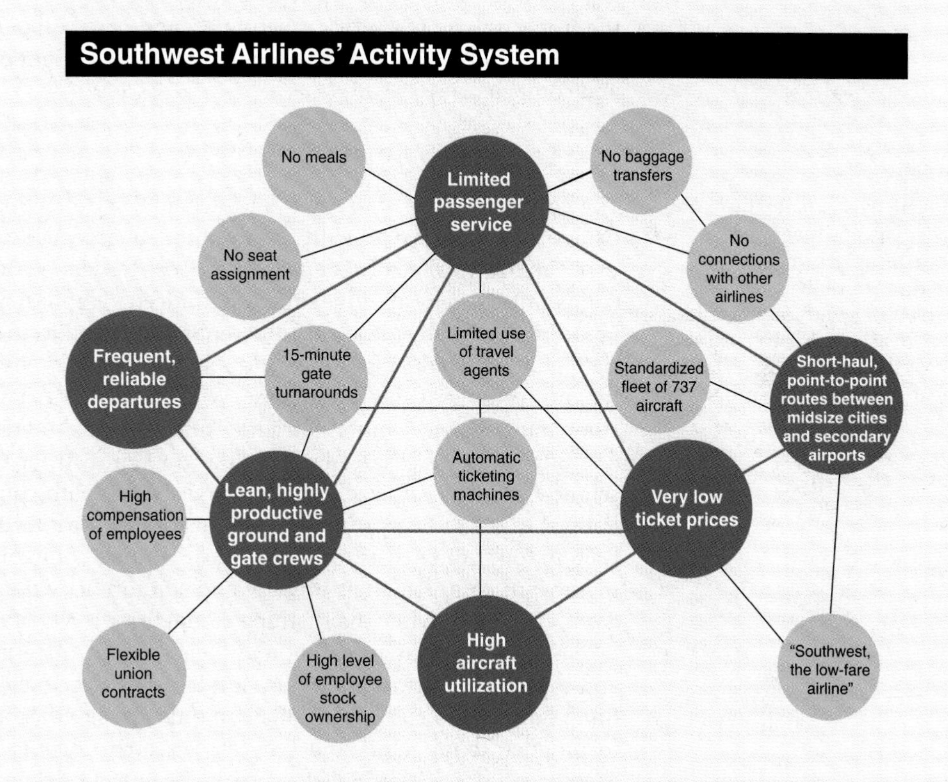

Southwest's tightly integrated primary and support activities make it difficult for competitors to imitate the firm's strategy. The firm's culture influences these activities and their integration. In fact, the firm's unique culture has become a competitive advantage that rivals have not been able to imitate. The firm's executives believe that motivated and dedicated employees and how they work together are the inimitable source of how Southwest develops effective linkages among its activities. This careful integration of *how* Southwest Airlines' employees perform the activities that support the firm's strategic themes reduces the probability that competitors will be able to successfully imitate its activity system.

SOURCES: M. Arndt, 2001, A simple and elegant flight pattern, *Business Week,* June 11, 118; T. Belden, 2001, Southwest Airlines' philosophy keeping it in front of pack now, *Richmond Times-Dispatch,* November 12, D29; J. H. Gittell, 2001, Investing in relationships, *Harvard Business Review,* 79(6): 28–30; C. Jones, 2001, Coming . . . soon? *Richmond Times-Dispatch,* June 22, A1, A9; W. Zellner, 2001, Southwest: After Kelleher, more blue skies, *Business Week,* April 2, 45; 2001, The squeeze on Europe's air fares, *The Economist,* May 26, 57–58; M. E. Porter, 1996, What is strategy? *Harvard Business Review,* 74(6): 61–78; http://www.southwestairlines.com.

Competitive advantage is sought by competing in many customer segments when implementing either the cost leadership or the differentiation strategy. In contrast, when using focus strategies, firms seek a cost competitive advantage or a differentiation competitive advantage in a *narrow competitive scope, segment,* or *niche.* With focus strategies, the firm "selects a segment or group of segments in the industry and tailors its strategy to serving them to the exclusion of others."[55]

None of the five business-level strategies is inherently or universally superior to the others.[56] The effectiveness of each strategy is contingent both on the opportunities and threats in a firm's external environment and on the possibilities provided by the firm's unique resources, capabilities, and core competencies. It is critical, therefore, for the firm to select an appropriate strategy in light of its opportunities, threats, and competencies.

Cost Leadership Strategy

The **cost leadership strategy** is an integrated set of actions designed to produce or deliver goods or services with features that are acceptable to customers at the lowest cost, relative to that of competitors.

The **cost leadership strategy** is an integrated set of actions designed to produce or deliver goods or services with features that are acceptable to customers at the lowest cost, relative to that of competitors.[57] Cost leaders' goods and services must have competitive levels of differentiation. Indeed, emphasizing cost reductions while ignoring competitive levels of differentiation is ineffective. At the extreme, concentrating only on reducing costs could find the firm very efficiently producing products that no customer wants to purchase. When the firm designs, produces, and markets a comparable product more efficiently that its rivals, there is evidence that it is successfully using the cost leadership strategy.[58] Firms using the cost leadership strategy sell no-frills, standardized goods or services (but with competitive levels of differentiation) to the industry's most typical customers. Cost leaders concentrate on finding ways to lower their costs relative to those of their competitors by constantly rethinking how to complete their primary and support activities (see Chapter 2) to reduce costs still further while maintaining competitive levels of differentiation.[59]

As primary activities, inbound logistics (e.g., materials handling, warehousing, and inventory control) and outbound logistics (e.g., collecting, storing, and distributing products to customers) often account for significant portions of the total cost to produce some goods and services. Research suggests that having a competitive advantage in terms of logistics creates more value when using the cost leadership strategy than when using the differentiation strategy.[60] Thus, cost leaders seeking competitively valuable ways to reduce costs may want to concentrate on the primary activities of inbound logistics and outbound logistics.

Cost leaders also carefully examine all support activities to find additional sources of potential cost reductions. Developing new systems for finding the optimal combination of low cost and acceptable quality in the raw materials required to produce the firm's goods or services is an example of how the procurement support activity can facilitate successful use of the cost leadership strategy.

The Vanguard Group, the large mutual-fund company, uses a cost leadership strategy. Facilitating the success of Vanguard's strategy is the tight, effective integration of the activities comprising its activity system.[61] Portraying fees and costs as evil and extolling efficiency, the corporate culture encourages employees' commitment to controlling costs while designing and completing their work. Vanguard's performance outcomes demonstrate the firm's low-cost position. In 1999, for example, the firm incurred average operating costs of 0.27 percent of its assets—less than one-fourth of the estimated average operating costs of 1.31 percent for the mutual fund industry.[62] Vanguard's pioneering index funds, introduced in 1976, help keep the costs down as do its low-cost bond funds with specific maturity ranges (i.e., short, intermediate, and long term). Other cost saving activities include Vanguard's low trading levels and its policy of discouraging ". . . customers from rapid buying and selling because doing so drives up costs and can force a fund manager to trade in order to deploy new capital and raise cash for redemptions."[63] The firm also searches for the least costly, yet still effective, means of providing customer service and of marketing its products.

Vanguard's low cost position for many investment products suggests the quality of its cost control efforts. However, the firm is also committed to providing high quality services (such as the firm's effective and easily navigable website) to its customers. Thus, the firm's products are offered with at least competitive levels of differentiation. Vanguard describes the effectiveness of having the low-cost position with at least competitive levels of differentiation by suggesting that it uses a "lowest reasonable cost" strategy to serve the needs of individual and institutional investors.

Consolidated Stores, Inc., which recently changed its name to Big Lots, Inc., also uses the cost leadership strategy. Committed to the strategic intent of being "The World's Best Bargain Place," Big Lots has become the largest U.S. retailer of closeout merchandise. The company sells goods in over 1,300 locations with positions in 46 states. The firm's stores sell name-brand products at prices that are 15 to 35 percent below those of discount retailers and roughly 70 percent below those of traditional retailers.[64] Big Lots' buyers travel the country looking through manufacturer overruns and discontinued styles, finding goods priced at well below wholesale prices. The firm thinks of itself as the undertaker of the retailing business, purchasing merchandise that others can't sell or don't want.

Having products available to customers at what the firm calls "extreme value" demonstrates the firm's commitment to being the low cost leader. By offering name-brand products in multiple locations and states rather than in only major metropolitan area, Big Lots also provides its target customers (the budget-conscious consumer) with competitive levels of differentiation (e.g., location, convenience). Big Lots captures the essence of the low cost and competitive (but not the most) differentiation position by operating as a "low-cost, value retailer."

As described in Chapter 3, firms use value-chain analysis to determine the parts of the company's operations that create value and those that do not. Figure 4.2 demonstrates the primary and support activities that allow a firm to create value through the cost leadership strategy. Companies unable to link the activities shown in this figure typically lack the resources, capabilities, and core competencies needed to successfully use the cost leadership strategy.

Effective use of the cost leadership strategy allows a firm to earn above-average returns in spite of the presence of strong competitive forces (see Chapter 2). The next sections (one for each of the five forces) explain how firms are able to do this.

Big Lots, Inc. used the cost leadership strategy to become the nation's largest broadline closeout retailer with stores in 46 states. The firm is converting and renaming its Odd Lots, Pic 'N' Save, and MacFrugal's stores to share the Big Lots identity.

© TERRI L. MILLER/E-VISUAL COMMUNICATIONS

Rivalry with Existing Competitors

Having the low-cost position is a valuable defense against rivals. Because of the cost leader's advantageous position, rivals hesitate to compete on the basis of price. Wal-Mart is known for its ability to both control and reduce costs, making it difficult for firms to compete against it on the basis of the price variable. The discount retailer achieves strict cost control in several ways: "Wal-Mart's 660,000-square foot main headquarters, with its drab gray interiors and frayed carpets, looks more like a government building than the home of one of the world's largest corporations. Business often is done in the no-frills cafeteria, and suppliers meet

Figure 4.2 Examples of Value-Creating Activities Associated with the Cost Leadership Strategy

Support Activities	Examples		
Firm Infrastructure	Cost-effective management information systems	Relatively few managerial layers in order to reduce overhead costs	Simplified planning practices to reduce planning costs
Human Resource Management	Consistent policies to reduce turnover costs	Intense and effective training programs to improve worker efficiency and effectiveness	
Technology Development	Easy-to-use manufacturing technologies	Investments in technologies in order to reduce costs associated with a firm's manufacturing processes	
Procurement	Systems and procedures to find the lowest cost (with acceptable quality) products to purchase as raw materials	Frequent evaluation processes to monitor suppliers' performances	

Inbound Logistics	**Operations**	**Outbound Logistics**	**Marketing and Sales**	**Service**
Highly efficient systems to link suppliers' products with the firm's production processes	Use of economies of scale to reduce production costs	A delivery schedule that reduces costs	A small, highly trained sales force	Efficient and proper product installations in order to reduce the frequency and severity of recalls
	Construction of efficient-scale production facilities	Selection of low-cost transportation carriers	Products priced so as to generate significant sales volume	

MARGIN

MARGIN

SOURCE: Adapted with the permission of The Free Press, an imprint of Simon & Schuster Adult Publishing Group, from *Competitive Advantage: Creating and Sustaining Superior Performance,* by Michael E. Porter, p. 47. Copyright © 1985, 1998 by Michael E. Porter.

with managers in stark, cramped rooms. Employees have to throw out their own garbage at the end of the day and double up in hotel rooms on business trips."[65] Saying that it wasn't competitive, Kmart recently initiated a price-cutting initiative. Wal-Mart followed with immediate price reductions. Because of Kmart's higher cost structure and less efficient distribution system, some believed that it was poorly positioned to compete against Wal-Mart on the basis of price even as Kmart attempted to become more efficient by overhauling its product delivery software system and closing at least two aging distribution centers, and restructuring its operations after filing for bankruptcy in 2002.[66]

As noted earlier, research suggests that having a competitive advantage in terms of logistics significantly contributes to the cost leader's ability to earn above-average returns.[67] Because Wal-Mart developed a logistics competitive advantage that has become the world standard, it is unlikely that Kmart can successfully compete against it by engaging in pricing battles.

Bargaining Power of Buyers (Customers)

Powerful customers can force a cost leader to reduce its prices, but not below the level at which the cost leader's next-most-efficient industry competitor can earn average returns. Although powerful customers might be able to force the cost leader to reduce prices even below this level, they probably would not choose to do so. Prices that are low enough to prevent the next-most-efficient competitor from earning average returns would force that firm to exit the market, leaving the cost leader with less competition and in an even stronger position. Customers would thus lose their power and pay higher prices when they are forced to purchase from a single firm operating in an industry without competitive rivals.

Bargaining Power of Suppliers

The cost leader operates with margins greater than those of competitors. Among other benefits, higher margins relative to those of competitors make it possible for the cost leader to absorb its suppliers' price increases. When an industry faces substantial increases in the cost of its supplies, only the cost leader may be able to pay the higher prices and continue to earn either average or above-average returns. Alternatively, a powerful cost leader may be able to force its suppliers to hold down their prices, which would reduce the suppliers' margins in the process.

Potential Entrants

Through continuous efforts to reduce costs to levels that are lower than those of its competitors, a cost leader becomes highly efficient. Because ever-improving levels of efficiency enhance profit margins, they serve as a significant entry barrier to potential competitors. New entrants must be willing and able to accept no better-than-average returns until they gain the experience required to approach the cost leader's efficiency. To earn even average returns, new entrants must have the competencies required to match the cost levels of competitors other than the cost leader. The low profit margins (relative to margins earned by firms implementing the differentiation strategy) make it necessary for the cost leader to sell large volumes of its product to earn above-average returns. However, firms striving to be the cost leader must avoid pricing their products so low that their ability to operate profitability is reduced, even though volume increases.

Product Substitutes

Compared to its industry rivals, the cost leader also holds an attractive position in terms of product substitutes. A product substitute becomes an issue for the cost leader when its features and characteristics, in terms of cost and differentiated features, are potentially attractive to the firm's customers. When faced with possible substitutes, the cost leader has more flexibility than its competitors. To retain customers, it can reduce the price of its good or service. With still lower prices and competitive levels of differentiation, the cost leader increases the probability that customers will prefer its product rather than a substitute.

Competitive Risks of the Cost Leadership Strategy

The cost leadership strategy is not risk free. One risk is that the processes used by the cost leader to produce and distribute its good or service could become obsolete because of innovations by its competitors. These innovations may allow rivals to produce at costs lower than those of the original cost leader, or to provide additional differentiated features without increasing the product's price to customers.

A second risk is that too much focus by the cost leader on cost reductions may occur at the expense of trying to understand customers' perceptions of "competitive levels of differentiation." As noted earlier, Wal-Mart is well known for constantly and aggressively reducing its costs. However, the firm must simultaneously remain focused on understanding when a cost-reducing decision to eliminate differentiated features that can create value in a low-cost environment (e.g., extended shopping hours, increases in the number of check-out counters to reduce waits) in order to reduce costs to still lower levels would create an unattractive value proposition for customers.

A final risk of the cost leadership strategy concerns imitation. Using their own core competencies (see Chapter 3), competitors sometimes learn how to successfully imitate the cost leader's strategy. When this occurs, the cost leader must increase the value that its good or service provides to customers. Commonly, value is increased by selling the current product at an even lower price or by adding differentiated features that customers value while maintaining price.

Even cost leaders must be careful when reducing prices to a still lower level. If the firm prices its good or service at an unrealistically low level (a level at which it will be difficult to retain satisfactory margins), customers' expectations about a reasonable price become difficult to reverse.

Differentiation Strategy

The **differentiation strategy** is an integrated set of actions designed by a firm to produce or deliver goods or services (at an acceptable cost) that customers perceive as being different in ways that are important to them.

The **differentiation strategy** is an integrated set of actions designed by a firm to produce or deliver goods or services (at an acceptable cost) that customers perceive as being different in ways that are important to them.[68] While cost leaders serve an industry's typical customer, differentiators target customers who perceive that value is added by the manner in which the firm's products are differentiated.

Firms must be able to produce differentiated products at competitive costs to reduce upward pressure on the price customers pay for them. When a product's differentiated features are produced through non-competitive costs, the price for the product can exceed what the firm's target customers are willing to pay. When the firm has a thorough understanding of what its target customers value, the relative importance they attach to the satisfaction of different needs, and for what they are willing to pay a premium, the differentiation strategy can be successfully used.[69]

Through the differentiation strategy, the firm produces nonstandardized products for customers who value differentiated features more than they value low cost. For example, superior product reliability and durability and high-performance sound systems are among the differentiated features of Toyota Motor Corporation's Lexus products. The often-used Lexus promotional statement—"The Relentless Pursuit of Perfection"—suggests a strong commitment to overall product quality as a source of differentiation. However, Lexus offers its vehicles to customers at a competitive purchase price. As with Lexus products, a good or service's unique attributes, rather than its purchase price, provide the value for which customers are willing to pay.

Continuous success with the differentiation strategy results when the firm consistently upgrades differentiated features that customers value, without significant cost increases. Because a differentiated product satisfies customers' unique needs, firms following the differentiation strategy are able to charge premium prices. For cus-

The differentiation strategy used by Robert Talbott Inc. to provide high quality dress shirts at a premium price is reflected in founder Robert Talbott's philosophy in 1950—"If you want to be number one in your industry, . . . you must create the finest product, and you must be number one in serving your customers. . . ."

tomers to be willing to pay a premium price, a "firm must truly be unique at something or be perceived as unique."[70] The ability to sell a good or service at a price that substantially exceeds the cost of creating its differentiated features allows the firm to outperform rivals and earn above-average returns.

For example, clothing manufacturer Robert Talbott follows stringent standards of craftsmanship and pays meticulous attention to every detail of production. The firm imports exclusive fabrics from the world's finest mills to make men's dress shirts. Single-needle tailoring is used, and precise collar cuts are made. According to the company, customers purchasing one of its shirts can be assured that they are being provided with the finest quality available.[71] Thus, Robert Talbott's success in shirt making rests on the firm's ability to produce and sell its differentiated shirts at a price significantly higher than the costs of imported fabrics and its unique manufacturing processes.

Rather than costs, a firm using the differentiation strategy always concentrates on investing in and developing features that differentiate a good or service in ways that customers value. Overall, a firm using the differentiation strategy seeks to be different from its competitors on as many dimensions as possible. The less similarity between a firm's goods or services and those of competitors, the more buffered it is from rivals' actions. Commonly recognized differentiated goods include Toyota's Lexus, Ralph Lauren's clothing lines, and Caterpillar's heavy-duty earth-moving equipment. Thought by some to be the world's most expensive and prestigious consulting firm, McKinsey & Co. is a well-known example of a firm that offers differentiated services.

A product can be differentiated in many ways. Unusual features, responsive customer service, rapid product innovations and technological leadership, perceived prestige and status, different tastes, and engineering design and performance are examples of approaches to differentiation. There may be a limited number of ways to reduce costs (as demanded by successful use of the cost leadership strategy). However, virtually anything a firm can do to create real or perceived value is a basis for differentiation. The challenge is to identity features that create value for the customers the firm has chosen to serve.

Firms sometimes introduce a new source of differentiation to test consumer reaction before extending it. H.J. Heinz, for example, recently added color as a source of differentiation for its highly successful ketchup. Green instead of the traditional red, the new color does not change the product's taste. Initial customer reaction was quite favorable, suggesting that color creates perceived value. In response, the company has also introduced purple ketchup and is evaluating orange, yellow, and hot pink as potential new colors.[72]

A firm's value chain can be analyzed to determine whether the firm is able to link the activities required to create value by using the differentiation strategy. Examples of primary and support activities that are commonly used to differentiate a good or service are shown in Figure 4.3. Companies without the core competencies needed to link these activities cannot expect to successfully use the differentiation strategy. Next, we explain how firms using the differentiation strategy can successfully position themselves in terms of the five forces of competition (see Chapter 2) to earn above-average returns.

Figure 4.3 Examples of Value-Creating Activities Associated with the Differentiation Strategy

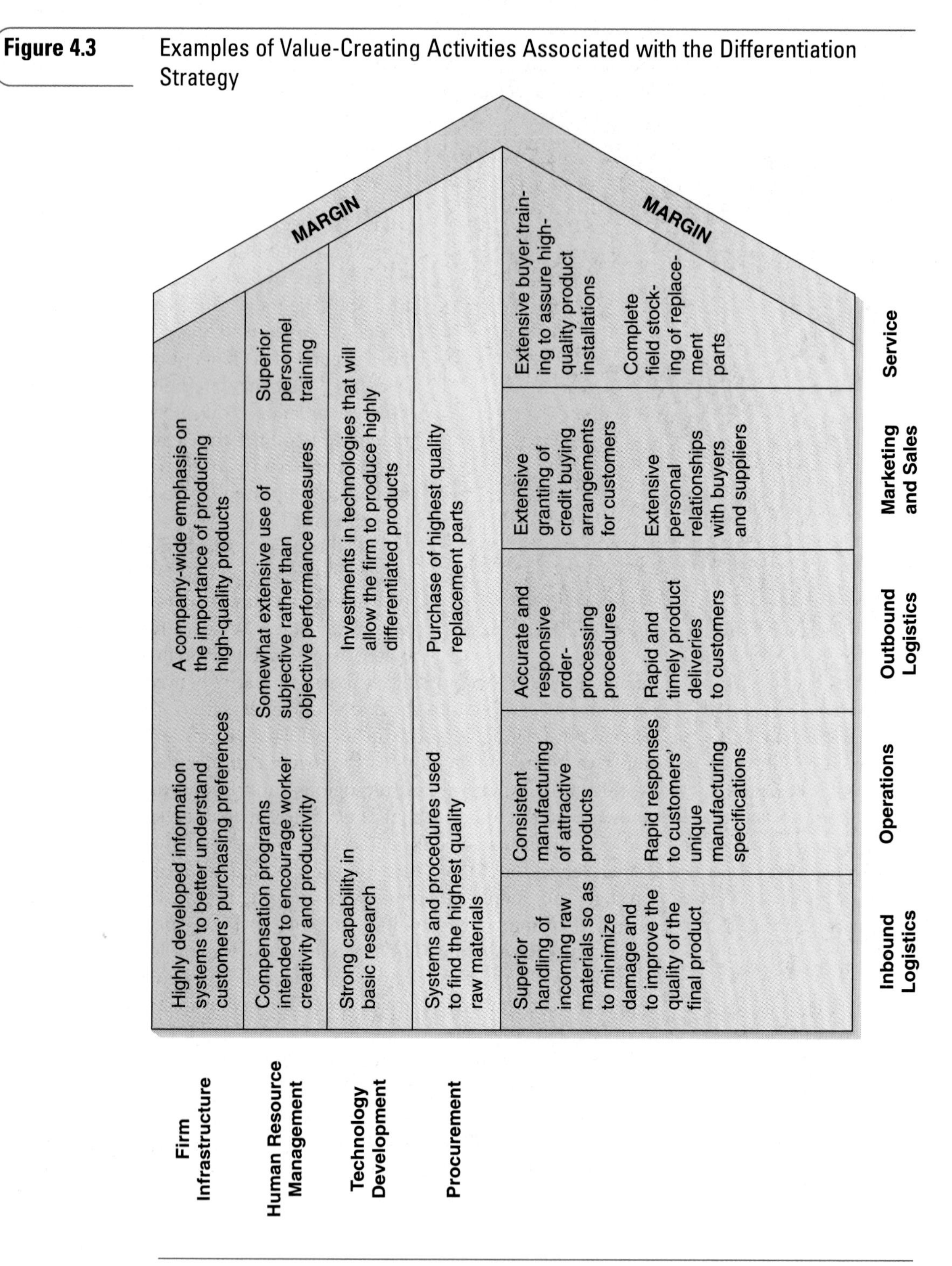

SOURCE: Adapted with the permission of The Free Press, an imprint of Simon & Schuster Adult Publishing Group, from *Competitive Advantage: Creating and Sustaining Superior Performance,* by Michael E. Porter, p. 47. Copyright © 1985, 1998 by Michael E. Porter.

Rivalry with Existing Competitors

Customers tend to be loyal purchasers of products that are differentiated in ways that are meaningful to them. As their loyalty to a brand increases, customers' sensitivity to price increases is reduced. This is especially true of those purchasing high-end, big-ticket items (e.g., luxury automobiles and custom interior design services for the home and office).[73] The relationship between brand loyalty and price sensitivity insulates a firm from competitive rivalry. Thus, McKinsey & Co. is insulated from its competitors, even on the basis of price, as long as it continues to satisfy the differentiated needs of its customer group. Bose is insulated from intense rivalry as long as customers continue to perceive that its stereo equipment offers superior sound quality at a competitive cost.

Heinz's EZ Squirt Blasting Green ketchup, which tastes just like Heinz's traditional ketchup, illustrates the company's effort to be innovative by offering a differentiated product when the firm's research found kids would like to see ketchup in some color other than red. "We wanted to create something where that bottle is pulled out of the fridge more often," a Heinz spokesperson said.

Bargaining Power of Buyers (Customers)

The uniqueness of differentiated goods or services reduces customers' sensitivity to price increases. On the basis of a combination of unique materials and brand image, "L'Oreal has developed a winning formula: a growing portfolio of international brands that has transformed the French company into the United Nations of beauty. Blink an eye, and L'Oreal has just sold 85 products around the world, from Maybelline eye makeup, Redken hair care, and Ralph Lauren perfumes to Helena Rubinstein cosmetics and Vichy skin care." L'Oreal is finding success in markets stretching from China to Mexico as some other consumer product companies falter. L'Oreal's differentiation strategy seeks to convey the allure of different cultures through its many products: "Whether it's selling Italian elegance, New York street smarts, or French beauty through its brands, L'Oreal is reaching out to more people across a bigger range of incomes and cultures than just about any other beauty-products company in the world."[74]

L'Oreal seeks to satisfy customers' unique needs better than its competitors can. One reason that some buyers are willing to pay a premium price for the firm's cosmetic items is that, for these buyers, other products do not offer a comparable combination of features and cost. The lack of perceived acceptable alternatives increases the firm's power relative to that of its customers.

Bargaining Power of Suppliers

Because the firm using the differentiation strategy charges a premium price for its products, suppliers must provide high-quality components, driving up the firm's costs. However, the high margins the firm earns in these cases partially insulate it from the influence of suppliers in that higher supplier costs can be paid through these margins. Alternatively, because of buyers' relative insensitivity to price increases, the differentiated firm might choose to pass the additional cost of supplies on to the customer by increasing the price of its unique product.

Potential Entrants

Customer loyalty and the need to overcome the uniqueness of a differentiated product present substantial entry barriers to potential entrants. Entering an industry under these conditions typically demands significant investments of resources and patience while seeking customers' loyalty.

Product Substitutes

Firms selling brand-name goods and services to loyal customers are positioned effectively against product substitutes. In contrast, companies without brand loyalty face a higher probability of their customers switching either to products that offer differentiated features that serve the same function (particularly if the substitute has a lower price) or to products that offer more features and perform more attractive functions.

Competitive Risks of the Differentiation Strategy

As with the other business-level strategies, the differentiation strategy is not risk free. One risk is that customers might decide that the price differential between the differentiator's product and the cost leader's product is too large. In this instance, a firm may be offering differentiated features that exceed target customers' needs. The firm then becomes vulnerable to competitors that are able to offer customers a combination of features and price that is more consistent with their needs.

Another risk of the differentiation strategy is that a firm's means of differentiation may cease to provide value for which customers are willing to pay. A differentiated product becomes less valuable if imitation by rivals causes customers to perceive that competitors offer essentially the same good or service, but at a lower price. For example, Walt Disney Company operates different theme parks, including The Magic Kingdom, Epcot Center, and the newly developed Animal Kingdom. Each park offers entertainment and educational opportunities. However, Disney's competitors, such as Six Flags Corporation, also offer entertainment and educational experiences similar to those available at Disney's locations. To ensure that its facilities create value for which customers will be willing to pay, Disney continuously reinvests in its operations to more crisply differentiate them from those of its rivals.[75]

A third risk of the differentiation strategy is that experience can narrow customers' perceptions of the value of a product's differentiated features. For example, the value of the IBM name provided a differentiated feature for the firm's personal computers for which some users were willing to pay a premium price in the early life cycle of the product. However, as customers familiarized themselves with the product's standard features, and as a host of other firms' personal computers entered the market, IBM brand loyalty ceased to create value for which some customers were willing to pay. The substitutes offered features similar to those found in the IBM product at a substantially lower price, reducing the attractiveness of IBM's product.

Responding to the effects of this reality, IBM now emphasizes service to drive product sales as a source of differentiation. Through IBM Global Services Inc., the firm is becoming product-service centered rather than remaining true to its origins, when it was product centered.[76] The firm's objective is to sell services to customers, especially when they purchase IBM hardware products.[77] IBM's actions are an example of what a firm can do to offer new, value-creating differentiated features for its current customers as well as to serve new customers.

Counterfeiting is the differentiation strategy's fourth risk. Makers of counterfeit goods—products that attempt to convey differentiated features to customers at significantly reduced prices—are a concern for many firms using the differentiation strategy. For example, Callaway Golf Company's success at producing differentiated products that create value, coupled with golf's increasing global popularity, has created great demand for counterfeited Callaway equipment. Through the U.S. Customs Service's "Project Teed Off" program, agents seized over 110 shipments with a total of more than 100,000 counterfeit Callaway golf club components over a three-year period.[78] Companies such as Callaway also work with government officials in other nations to influence the formation of tighter import regulations to curb the flow of counterfeit products.

Focus Strategies

The **focus strategy** is an integrated set of actions designed to produce or deliver goods or services that serve the needs of a particular competitive segment.

Firms choose a focus strategy when they want their core competencies to serve the needs of a particular industry segment or niche at the exclusion of others. Examples of specific market segments that can be targeted by a focus strategy include a (1) particular buyer group (e.g., youths or senior citizens), (2) different segment of a product line (e.g., products for professional painters or those for "do-it-yourselfers"), or

Callaway Golf Company uses the differentiation strategy for its golf equipment, using top quality materials and incurring considerable research and development costs to create its high-cost clubs. Counterfeiters offer lower-priced imitations, as shown in the photo. The genuine Callaway Big Bertha club is at left, while the club at the right resembles the Big Bertha but is poorly made of low quality materials.

(3) different geographic market (e.g., the east or the west in the United States).[79] Thus, the **focus strategy** is an integrated set of actions designed to produce or deliver goods or services that serve the needs of a particular competitive segment.

Although the breadth of a target is clearly a matter of degree, the essence of the focus strategy "is the exploitation of a narrow target's differences from the balance of the industry."[80] Firms using the focus strategy intend to serve a particular segment of an industry more effectively than can industry-wide competitors. They succeed when they effectively serve a segment whose unique needs are so specialized that broad-based competitors choose not to serve that segment or when they satisfy the needs of a segment being served poorly by industry-wide competitors.[81]

To satisfy the needs of a certain size of company competing in a particular geographic market, Los Angeles-based investment banking firm Greif & Company positions itself as "The Entrepreneur's Investment Bank." Greif & Company is a "leading purveyor of merger and acquisition advisory services to medium-sized businesses based in the Western United States."[82] American Services Group Inc. (ASG) specializes in providing contract health care for prisons and jails. Partly because of costs and liability, governments are outsourcing health care to private companies. Recently, ASG, which has earned the nickname "HMO behind bars," was awarded a three-year contract to care for 13,000 prisoners at New York's Rikers Island facility.[83] Through successful use of the focus strategy, firms such as Greif & Company and ASG gain a competitive advantage in specific market niches or segments, even though they do not possess an industry-wide competitive advantage.[84]

Firms can create value for customers in specific and unique market segments by using the focused cost leadership strategy or the focused differentiation strategy.

Focused Cost Leadership Strategy

Based in Sweden, Ikea, a global furniture retailer, follows the focused cost leadership strategy.[85] Young buyers desiring style at a low cost are Ikea's market segment. For these customers, the firm offers home furnishings that combine good design, function, and acceptable quality with low prices. According to the firm, "low cost is always in focus. This applies to every phase of our activities. The foundation is our range that shall offer good design and function at a low price."[86]

Ikea emphasizes several activities to keep its costs low. For example, instead of relying primarily on third-party manufacturers, the firm's engineers design low-cost, modular furniture ready for assembly by customers. Ikea also positions its products in room-like settings. Typically, competitors' furniture stores display multiple varieties of a single item in separate rooms, and their customers examine living room sofas in one room, tables in another room, chairs in yet another location, and accessories in still another area. In contrast, Ikea's customers can view different living combinations (complete with sofas, chairs, tables, and so forth) in a single setting, which eliminates the need for sales associates or decorators to help the customer imagine how a batch of furniture will look when placed in the customer's home. This approach requires fewer sales personnel, allowing Ikea to keep its costs low. A third practice that helps keep Ikea's costs low is expecting customers to transport their own purchases rather than providing delivery service.

Although a cost leader, Ikea also offers some differentiated features that appeal to its target customers, including in-store playrooms for children, wheelchairs for customer use, and extended hours. Stores outside those in the home country have "Sweden Shops" that sell Swedish specialties such as herring, crisp bread, Swedish caviar, and gingerbread biscuits. Ikea believes that these services and products "are uniquely aligned with the needs of (its) customers, who are young, are not wealthy, are likely to have children (but no nanny), and, because they work for a living, have a need to shop at odd hours."[87] Thus, Ikea's focused cost leadership strategy finds the firm offering some differentiated features with its low cost products.

Focused Differentiation Strategy

Other firms implement the focused differentiation strategy in the pursuit of above-average returns. As noted earlier, firms can differentiate their products in many ways. Consider the following examples of firms using a focused differentiation strategy: The Internet venture Casketfurniture.com targets Generation X people who are interested in using the Internet as a shopping vehicle and who want to buy items with multiple purposes. The firm offers a collection of products including display cabinets, coffee tables, and entertainment centers that can be easily converted into coffins. The $1,975 display cabinet is the company's best selling item. With 16 units on the East Coast, hair salon Cartoon Cuts serves children between the ages of 8 to 14. This age group is a profitable and growing niche in the $50 billion U.S. hair salon industry. Get Well Network Inc. provides products to augment the cable-connected television set found in most hospital rooms. With charges posted to the hospital room bills, patients use the firm's interactive systems to watch pay-per-view movies and to connect to the Internet. StilicForce, a French firm, designed and sells the Trottibasket, a durable plastic basket that slides onto the vertical bar of a Razor scooter. Shaped like a cone, the Trottibasket is used to carry relatively small items the scooter rider needs to transport.[88]

In the Strategic Focus on page 133, we discuss individual sources of differentiation that two firms—New Balance and Maserati (part of Fiat Group)—have created to use the focused differentiation strategy. As described in the Strategic Focus, both New Balance and Maserati use the focused differentiation strategy to target a narrow customer segment. However, the competitive advantages on which the companies rely to serve their unique market segments differ. Technology, R&D capability, managerial creativity, and an empowered and talented workforce are the advantages New Balance uses to offer customers a shoe with an ideal "fit." Relying on its reputation, design skills, and manufacturing expertise, the Maserati Spider appeals to the *emotions* of its target customer group. In both instances, perceived value is created for a narrow segment of broader markets (for athletic shoes and automobiles, respectively).

Firms must be able to complete various primary and support activities in a competitively superior manner to achieve and sustain a competitive advantage and earn above-average returns with a focus strategy. The activities required to use the focused cost leadership strategy are virtually identical to the activities shown in Figure 4.2, and activities required to use the focused differentiation strategy are virtually identical to those shown in Figure 4.3. Similarly, the manner in which each of the two focus strategies allows a firm to deal successfully with the five competitive forces parallel those described with respect to the cost leadership strategy and the differentiation strategy. The only difference is that the competitive scope changes from an industry-wide market to a narrow industry segment. Thus, a review of Figures 4.2 and 4.3 and the text regarding the five competitive forces yields a description of the relationship between each of the two focus strategies and competitive advantage.

Strategic Focus

Satisfying Unique Needs: Of Shoes and Cars

As mentioned earlier, New Balance concentrates on the athletic shoe needs of the Baby Boom generation (born between 1946 and 1964). The high quality "fit" that its shoes provide is the primary source of differentiation, for which the firm's target customer group is willing to pay a premium price.

Early research by New Balance suggested that active Baby Boomers want shoes that fit extremely well rather than shoes that are recognized for their style. A key indicator of the company's commitment to fit is that it is the only shoe manufacturer producing a complete line in a variety of widths—from AA to EEEE. New Balance's philosophy about fit is straightforward: "The better your shoes fit, the more comfortable you will be, the better you will enjoy yourself."

To support the design and manufacture of products with the "best possible fit," New Balance invests significantly in technological research and development (R&D) activities. Several patented technologies resulting from the firm's R&D efforts have been instrumental in the development of some shoes' suspension systems. Well-trained workers use highly sophisticated manufacturing equipment to produce the firm's differentiated products. The differentiation of New Balance's shoes in terms of fit is suggested by the fact that several models have received special recognition by the American Podiatric Medical Association.

Surveys also show that a commitment to provide jobs to U.S. workers is important to Baby Boomers. As mentioned in Chapter 3, New Balance manufactures more of its goods in the United States than do competitors such as Nike Inc. and Reebok International. Company officials observe that, "While most of the footwear industry has moved its production overseas to take advantage of low labor costs and generally cheaper production costs, we have continued to make many of our shoes in the United States and have expanded production substantially." This commitment results in an hourly wage cost disadvantage to the firm. New Balance production employees earn approximately $14 per hour as compared to the 20 cents to 40 cents per hour earned by shoe factory workers in China, Indonesia, and Vietnam—three countries where many U.S. apparel manufacturers, including shoe companies, outsource production of their goods. To counter this cost disadvantage, New Balance cross-trains its employees, allowing them to gain multiple skills that are used in largely self-managed work teams.

In addition, the firm's managers are known for their creative ability to adapt new technologies to shoemaking processes. Self-managed workers, technologically innovative managers, and an award-winning R&D capability are the competitive advantages that allow New Balance to overcome the negative effects of labor cost differentials. Currently, for example, New Balance workers produce a pair of shoes in 24 minutes versus the three hours it takes to make a pair of shoes in China.

Fiat Group, the Italian manufacturer of mass-market cars, owns 90 percent of Ferrari SpA, the famous sports car company with the well-recognized Prancing Horse emblem on its products. Ferrari claims that its highly specialized design and production processes allow it to produce cars that are "unique and unrepeatable." Ferrari's sports car range from $143,000 to $230,000 in price.

In the late 1990s, Ferrari bought Maserati. After a ten-year absence from the U.S. market, a Maserati product was reintroduced in early 2002 after being successfully relaunched earlier in France, Italy, Switzerland, and Germany. Demonstrating precise segmentation of the market for expensive sports cars, Ferrari determined that the Maserati would appeal to wealthy sports car enthusiasts lacking either the resources or the desire to purchase a Ferrari. The target customer was the person with "good taste who is looking for a unique emotion from driving." The narrowness of the competitive scope associated with this target customer is suggested by Ferrari's decision to introduce only 1,200 Maserati cars into the U.S. market in 2002. Priced at approximately $80,000, the two-seater Maserati Spider (the product offered in the United States) competes against the Porsche

911 and the Jaguar XKR. Like its rivals, the Spider travels from zero to 60 miles per hour in roughly 5.3 seconds. Thus, speed is not a dimension on which the Spider is differentiated. Instead, product customization and racing lessons are the intended sources of differentiation of the Maserati.

To emphasize the exclusivity and service that come with the brand, Maserati customers receive a car they helped design, down to the color of the leather stitching in the upholstery, if they so desire. Describing the extent to which Maserati is willing to customize the Spider, the firm's CEO commented that, "If you come to me with denim and want that in the interior, I will do it for you." For customers wanting to sharpen their "race car driving skills," the Master GT driving course is an option. Run by former Formula One driver Ivan Capelli, the course is available to Spider owners to zip around the Varano de Melegari circuit near Parma. Professional instructors guide the learning experience for customers, who leave the experience with a taste of what it is like to drive on a race course and with an improved knowledge of the Spider's performance capabilities.

SOURCES: A. Bernstein, 2001, Low-skilled jobs: Do they have to move? *Business Week,* February 26, 94–95; A. Kirkman, 2001, Zoom! Zoom! *Forbes,* May 14, 208; http://www.ferrari.com; http://www.newbalance.com.

Competitive Risks of Focus Strategies

With either focus strategy, the firm faces the same general risks as does the company using the cost leadership or the differentiation strategy respectively on an industry-wide basis. However, focus strategies have three additional risks.

First, a competitor may be able to focus on a more narrowly defined competitive segment and "outfocus" the focuser. For example, Big Dog Motorcycles is trying to outfocus Harley-Davidson, which is pursuing a broader-focus differentiation strategy. While Harley focuses solely on producing heavyweight motorcycles, Big Dog builds motorcycles that target only the very high end of the heavyweight market—the high-end premium cruiser market—with names such as Pitbull, Wolf, Mastiff, and Bulldog. Big Dog is careful to differentiate its products from those of Harley Davidson, citing its larger motors, fat rear tires, unique state-of-the-art electronics, and 4-piston caliber brakes as examples of value-creating features. With additional value-creating differentiated features (e.g., performance capabilities made possible by larger engines), Big Dog may be able to better serve the unique needs of a narrow customer group.[89]

Second, a company competing on an industry-wide basis may decide that the market segment served by the focus strategy firm is attractive and worthy of competitive pursuit. No longer content with only its traditional customer group, Home Depot now has plans to concentrate on more narrow segments that it has not previously served, such as people who are involved in large-ticket home renovations. In addition, the firm acquired Maintenance Warehouse America Corp. Now called Maintenance Warehouse, this separate Home Depot company is the leading supplier of over 13,000 maintenance repair and replacement products. The owners and managers of multi-housing, lodging, and commercial properties form Maintenance Warehouse's target customer group.[90] Because of its size and capabilities, firms competing in focused market segments (e.g., multi-housing properties only) may be threatened by Home Depot's market segment entrance.

The third risk involved with a focus strategy is that the needs of customers within a narrow competitive segment may become more similar to those of industry-wide customers as a whole. As a result, the advantages of a focus strategy are either reduced or eliminated. At some point, for example, the needs of Ikea's customers for stylish furniture may dissipate, although their desire to buy relatively inexpensive furnishings may not. If this change in needs were to happen, Ikea's customers might buy from large chain stores that sell somewhat standardized furniture at low costs.

Integrated Cost Leadership/Differentiation Strategy

Particularly in global markets, the firm's ability to integrate the means of competition necessary to implement the cost leadership and differentiation strategies may be critical to developing competitive advantages. Compared to firms implementing one dominant business-level strategy, the company that successfully uses an integrated cost leadership/differentiation strategy should be in a better position to (1) adapt quickly to environmental changes, (2) learn new skills and technologies more quickly, and (3) effectively leverage its core competencies while competing against its rivals.

In this chapter's first Strategic Focus (see page 121), the Southwest Airlines activity map demonstrates how a firm gains a competitive advantage by tightly integrating its primary and support activities. Southwest successfully uses the integrated cost leadership/differentiation strategy, allowing the firm to adapt quickly, learn rapidly, and meaningfully leverage its core competencies while competing against its rivals in the airline industry.

Concentrating on the needs of its core customer group (higher-income, fashion-conscious discount shoppers), Target Stores also uses an integrated strategy. Target relies on its relationships with Michael Graves in home, garden, and electronics products, Sonia Kashuk in cosmetics, Mossimo in apparel, and Eddie Bauer in camping and outdoor gear, among others, to offer differentiated products at discounted prices. Committed to presenting a consistent upscale image to its core customer group, the firm carefully studies trends to find new branded items that it believes can satisfy its customers' needs.[91]

Evidence suggests a relationship between successful use of the integrated strategy and above-average returns.[92] Thus, firms able to produce relatively differentiated products at relatively low costs can expect to perform well.[93] Indeed, a researcher found that the most successful firms competing in low-profit-potential industries were integrating the attributes of the cost leadership and differentiation strategies.[94] Other researchers have discovered that "businesses which combined multiple forms of competitive advantage outperformed businesses that only were identified with a single form."[95] The results of another study showed that the highest-performing companies in the Korean electronics industry combined the value-creating aspects of the cost leadership and differentiation strategies.[96] This finding suggests the usefulness of integrated strategy in settings outside the United States.

McDonald's is a global corporation with a strong global brand, offering products at a relatively low cost but with some differentiated features. Its global scale, relationships with franchisees, and rigorous standardization of processes allow McDonald's to lower its costs, while its brand recognition and product consistency are sources of differentiation allowing the restaurant chain to charge slightly higher prices.[97] Thus, the firm uses the integrated cost leadership/differentiation strategy.[98]

The future success of McDonald's has been questioned. One analyst suggests that, "Already in the U.S., competition is eroding its dominance; its great days are probably over. It must now manage a decline which will be bumpy, even violent."[99] Does this comment accurately describe McDonald's future as it uses the integrated strategy? Are the firm's great days "over" as the analyst foresees? We consider these matters in the Strategic Focus on the next page.

Strategic Focus

Global Burgers: Will McDonald's Future Be as Good as Its Past?

McDonald's has a strong and growing global presence, earning more than $9 billion in sales revenue in European countries alone. The firm has over 28,000 restaurants operating in 120 countries. It serves more than 45 million people daily and opens a new store every five hours somewhere in the world.

Committed to stringent standards of product quality, service, and cleanliness, McDonald's uses value pricing (the source of relatively low costs to customers) while offering menu and storefront variety and relying on the power of its brand name (sources of differentiation). Globally, the company seeks to provide its combination of relatively low costs and some levels of differentiation in a culturally sensitive manner. In India, for example, the Maharaja Mac, which is made from lamb, substitutes for the beef-based Big Mac. Popular corn soup is offered on the chain's menu in its Japanese units.

Marketing penetration and expansion plans are based on local customer preferences and cultural practices. In China, for example, early competitive actions concentrated on children as a target market. With a decline in the nation's birth rate and other social and economic changes, some young parents have more money to spend on what is often an only child. McDonald's promotes children's birthdays by aiming advertising at them. Parties with cakes, candles, hats, and gifts are emphasized to young consumers. The party can be hosted in a children's enclosure, sometimes called the Ronald Room. These parties have become popular with upwardly mobile children in Hong Kong, Beijing, and Shanghai. An indicator of the success of this approach is that some parents in Hong Kong take their children to the local McDonald's as a reward for good behavior and academic achievement.

In 1999, McDonald's launched its "Made for You" system. Replacing its historic practice of producing food and storing it in a large tray until purchased, the new system was designed to increase product quality, variety, and delivery speed (sources of differentiation). To do this, new computer equipment and cooking and food preparation machinery were installed in each unit. Crewmembers and managers received extensive training to learn how to maximize efficiency by using the new system. However, after two years and a $1 billion investment, McDonald's moved from "Made for You" to a more simplified system. A primary reason for this change was that the cost of using the "Made for You" system to increase sources of differentiation exceeded acceptable levels for successful use of the integrated cost leadership/differentiation strategy.

To control costs through simplification, McDonald's decided to trim its 36-item core menu, jettisoning various items such as the McFlurry. Simultaneously, the firm intended to introduce new concepts (e.g., "McDonald's with a Diner Inside" and McCafe) as sources of differentiation from competitors. With 300 units already established in 17 countries, the first U.S. McCafe unit opened in Chicago in April, 2001. The U.S. McCafe uses separately trained staff and specialized equipment and features comfortable furniture, including couches. Competition from Starbucks (with 3,300 existing units and 15 new stores opening each week) could affect McCafe's success. McDonald's ruled out the possibility of testing a deli concept because of high labor costs—costs that would exceed those in line with a successful integrated strategy.

Coin changers, double drive-throughs, self-order kiosks, electronic menu boards, and cashless drive-throughs are relatively inexpensive services (and further sources of differentiation) that McDonald's is evaluating for introduction by mid-year 2005. To improve customer frequency and track purchasing behavior, the firm has established the McRewards program. Each purchase earns points that can be used to obtain prizes from several partner firms, including Mattel and Walt Disney Co.

SOURCES: M. Arndt, 2001, McLatte and croissant? *Business Week,* April 2, 14; R. Dzinkowski, 2001, McDonald's Europe, *Strategic Finance,* May, 24–27; K. MacArthur, 2001, McDonald's sees 100%, *Advertising Age,* May/June, 12–134; J. Ettlie, 1999, What the auto industry can learn from McDonald's, *Automotive Manufacturing & Production,* 111(10), 42–43; C. Murphy, 1999, How McDonald's conquered the UK, *Marketing,* February 18, 30–31.

The imitability of many of its newly designed sources of differentiation will affect the degree of success McDonald's can achieve with the integrated cost leadership/differentiation strategy. Major competitors such as Burger King and Wendy's may be able to imitate the value created through McDonald's new products and services, such as double drive-throughs, electronic menu boards, and the McRewards program. Additionally, both competitors have the resources to purchase technologies and equipment that reduce production costs. As a result, McDonald's must simultaneously seek new ways to differentiate its product offerings and storefront concepts and reduce its cost structure to successfully use the integrated strategy. Supporting McDonald's efforts is its commitment to serve the unique needs of customers in different countries. Being able to satisfy country heterogeneity in terms of customers' desires can lead to a competitive advantage.[100]

Will McDonald's efforts to reduce costs through a more simplified menu while offering some additional differentiated features in new storefront formats be sufficient to assure success in the years to come? Time will tell, but history suggests that the firm has the potential to perform well. The rivalry among firms in the fast-food industry is quite intense. As discussed in Chapter 2, this intensity reduces the profitability potential for all companies. However, McDonald's recent actions to enable it to more successfully use a strategy that integrates relatively low costs with some differentiated features may have the potential to contribute to the firm's strategic competitiveness as it competes vigorously with its rivals.

Unlike McDonald's, which uses the integrated cost leadership/differentiation strategy on an industry-wide basis, air-conditioning and heating-systems maker Aaon concentrates on a particular competitive scope. Thus, Aaon is implementing a focused integrated strategy. Aaon manufactures semi-customized rooftop air conditioning systems for large retailers, including Wal-Mart, Target, and Home Depot. Aaon positions its rooftop systems between low-priced commodity equipment and high-end customized systems. The firm's innovative manufacturing capabilities allow it to tailor a production line for units with special heat-recovery options unavailable on low-end systems. Combining custom features with assembly line-production methods results in significant cost savings. Aaon's prices are approximately 5 percent higher than low-end products but are only one-third the price of comparable customized systems.[101] Thus, the firm's narrowly defined target customers receive some differentiated features (e.g., special heat-recovery options) at a low, but not the lowest cost.

A commitment to strategic flexibility (see Chapter 1) is necessary for firms such as McDonald's and Aaon to effectively use the integrated cost leadership/differentiation strategy. Strategic flexibility results from developing systems, procedures, and methods that enable a firm to quickly and effectively respond to opportunities that reduce costs or increase differentiation. Flexible manufacturing systems, information networks, and total quality management systems are three sources of strategic flexibility that facilitate use of the integrated strategy. Valuable to the successful use of each business-level strategy, the strategic flexibility provided by these three tools is especially important to firms trying to balance the objectives of continuous cost reductions and continuous enhancements to sources of differentiation.

Flexible Manufacturing Systems

Modern information technologies have helped make flexible manufacturing systems (FMS) possible. These systems increase the "flexibilities of human, physical, and information resources"[102] that the firm integrates to create differentiated products at low costs. A *flexible manufacturing system* is a computer-controlled process used to produce a variety of products in moderate, flexible quantities with a minimum of manual intervention.[103] Particularly in situations where parts are too heavy for people to handle or when other methods are less effective in creating manufacturing and assembly flexibility, robots are integral to use of an FMS.[104] In spite of their promise, only one in five *Fortune* 1000 companies are using the productive capabilities of an FMS.[105]

The goal of an FMS is to eliminate the "low-cost-versus-product-variety" trade-off that is inherent in traditional manufacturing technologies. Firms use an FMS to change quickly and easily from making one product to making another.[106] Used properly, an FMS allows the firm to respond more effectively to changes in its customers' needs, while retaining low-cost advantages and consistent product quality.[107] Because an FMS also enables the firm to reduce the lot size needed to manufacture a product efficiently, the firm increases its capacity to serve the unique needs of a narrow competitive scope. Thus, FMS technology is a significant technological advance that allows firms to produce a large variety of products at a relatively low cost. Levi Strauss, for example, uses an FMS to make jeans for women that fit their exact measurements. Customers of Andersen Windows can design their own windows using proprietary software the firm has developed. Tire manufacturers Pirelli and Goodyear are turning to robots and other advanced technologies as part of their quest to transform the traditional time-consuming, complex, and costly method of making tires into a more flexible and responsive system.[108]

The effective use of an FMS is linked with a firm's ability to understand the constraints these systems may create (in terms of materials handling and the flow of supporting resources in scheduling, for example) and to design an effective mix of machines, computer systems, and people.[109] In service industries, the processes used must be flexible enough to increase delivery speed and to satisfy changing customer needs. McDonald's, for example, is testing three "vision" stores in three stages to learn how to reduce service times. In addition to installing more automated equipment, the company is experimenting with splitting counter service between two employees—one person taking the order and payment while the other assembles the order.[110] In industries of all types, effective mixes of the firm's tangible assets (e.g., machines) and intangible assets (e.g., people's skills) facilitate implementation of complex competitive strategies, especially the integrated cost leadership/differentiation strategy.[111]

An FMS is a complex engineering project. Some companies use a differentiation strategy to develop and implement flexible manufacturing systems for end users. Generating over $2 billion in annual sales, UNOVA, Inc. follows a differentiation strategy to supply manufacturing technologies and integrated production systems to automotive, aerospace, and heavy equipment producers. In markets throughout the world, the firm provides customers with the most technologically advanced, high-quality systems. To enhance the flexibility its systems provide to end users, UNOVA continuously evaluates its own manufacturing processes to find ways to enhance the sources of value its differentiated features create for customers.[112]

Information Networks

By linking companies with their suppliers, distributors, and customers, information networks provide another source of strategic flexibility. Among other outcomes, these networks facilitate the firm's efforts to satisfy customer expectations in terms of product quality and delivery speed.

As noted earlier, customer relationship management (CRM) is one form of an information-based network process that firms use to better understand customers and their needs. The effective CRM system provides a 360-degree view of the company's relationship with customers, encompassing all contact points, involving all business processes, and incorporating all communication media and sales channels.[113] The firm can then use this information to determine the trade-offs its customers are willing to make between differentiated features and low cost, which is vital for companies using the integrated cost leadership/differentiation strategy.

Information networks are also critical to the establishment and successful use of an enterprise resource planning (ERP) system. ERP is an information system used to identify and plan the resources required across the firm to receive, record, produce, and ship customer orders.[114] For example, salespeople for aircraft parts distributor Aviall use handheld equipment to scan bar-code labels on bins in customers' facilities to determine when parts need to be restocked. Data gathered through this procedure are uploaded via the Web to the Aviall back-end replenishment and ERP system, allowing the order fulfillment process to begin within minutes of scanning.[115] Growth in ERP applications such as the one used at Aviall has been significant.[116] Projections are that the annual sales of ERP software and service will exceed $84 billion before 2003.[117] Full installations of an ERP system are expensive, running into the tens of millions of dollars for large-scale applications.

Improving efficiency on a company-wide basis is a primary objective of using an ERP system. Efficiency improvements result from the use of systems through which financial and operational data are moved rapidly from one department to another. The transfer of sales data from Aviall salespeople to the order entry point at the firm's manufacturing facility demonstrates the rapid movement of information from one function to another. Integrating data across parties that are involved with detailing product specifications and then manufacturing those products and distributing them in ways that are consistent with customers' unique needs enable the firm to respond with flexibility to customer preferences relative to cost and differentiation.

Total Quality Management Systems

In the 1970s and 1980s, executives in Western nations, including the United States, recognized that their firms' success and even survival in some industries (e.g., automobile manufacturing) depended on developing an ability to dramatically improve the quality of their goods and services while simultaneously reducing their cost structures. The relatively low costs of relatively high-quality products from a host of Japanese companies emphasized this message with resounding clarity.[118]

Focused on *doing things right* through efficiency increases, total quality management (TQM) systems are used in firms across multiple nations and economic regions to increase their competitiveness.[119] TQM systems incorporate customer definitions of quality instead of those derived by the firm, and demand that the firm focus on the root causes of a problem rather than its symptoms.[120] Accepted widely as a viable means of improving the firm's competitiveness, TQM systems have been a worldwide movement since the early 1980s.[121]

A key assumption underlying the use of a TQM system is that "the costs of poor quality (such as inspection, rework, lost customers, and so on) are far greater than the costs of developing processes that produce high-quality products and services."[122] This relationship may partially account for financial difficulties Ford Motor Company experienced in mid-2001, when poor product quality and related production delays in the previous year were estimated to have cost Ford over $1 billion in lost profits. A comparison of the estimated warranty costs for Ford and for two of its competitors also demonstrates the competitive disadvantage resulting from poor quality. Deutsche Bank estimated Ford's average warranty cost per vehicle at $650, GM's at $550, and Toyota's at $400.[123] Cost disadvantages such as these make it difficult to compete successfully against rivals (see Chapter 5) and to earn returns that satisfy investors' expectations.

Firms use TQM systems to achieve several specific objectives, including (1) at least meeting customers' expectations while striving to exceed them, especially in terms of quality, (2) focusing on work activities to drive out inefficiencies and waste in all business processes, and (3) incorporating improvements in all parts of the firm while continuously striving for additional improvement opportunities.[124] Achieving these objectives improves a firm's flexibility and facilitates use of all business-level strategies. However, the outcomes suggested by these objectives are particularly important to firms implementing the integrated cost leadership/differentiation strategy. At least meeting (and perhaps exceeding) customers' expectations regarding quality is a differentiating feature, and eliminating process inefficiencies allows the firm to offer that quality at a relatively low cost. Thus, an effective TQM system helps the firm develop the flexibility needed to spot opportunities to simultaneously increase differentiation and/or reduce costs.

Competitive Risks of the Integrated Cost Leadership/ Differentiation Strategy

The potential to earn above-average returns by successfully using the integrated cost leadership/differentiation strategy is appealing. However, experience shows that substantial risk accompanies this potential. Selecting a business-level strategy requires the firm to make choices about how it intends to compete.[125] Achieving the low-cost position in an industry or a segment of an industry by using a focus strategy demands that the firm reduce its costs consistently relative to the costs of its competitors. The use of the differentiation strategy, with either an industry-wide or a focused competitive scope (see Figure 4.1), requires the firm to provide its customers with differentiated goods or services they value and for which they are willing to pay a premium price.

The firm that uses the integrated strategy yet fails to establish a leadership position risks becoming "stuck in the middle."[126] Being in this position prevents the firm from dealing successfully with the competitive forces in its industry and from having a distinguishable competitive advantage. Not only will the firm not be able to earn above-average returns, earning even average returns will be possible only when the structure of the industry in which it competes is highly favorable or if its competitors are also in the same position.[127] Without these conditions, the firm will earn below-average returns. Thus, companies implementing the integrated cost leadership/differentiation strategy, such as McDonald's and Aaon, must be certain that their competitive actions allow them both to offer some differentiated features that their customers value and to provide them with products at a relatively low cost.

There is very little if any research evidence showing that the attributes of the cost leadership and differentiation strategies *cannot* be effectively integrated.[128] The integrated strategy therefore is an appropriate strategic choice for firms with the core competencies required to produce somewhat differentiated products at relatively low costs.

Summary

- A business-level strategy is an integrated and coordinated set of commitments and actions the firm uses to gain a competitive advantage by exploiting core competencies in specific product markets. Five business-level strategies (cost leadership, differentiation, focused cost leadership, focused differentiation, and integrated cost leadership/differentiation) are examined in the chapter. A firm's strategic competitiveness is enhanced when it is able to develop and exploit new core competencies faster than competitors can mimic the competitive advantages yielded by the firm's current competencies.
- Customers are the foundation of successful business-level strategies. When considering customers, a firm simultaneously examines three issues: *who, what,* and *how.* These issues respectively refer to the customer groups to be served, the needs those customers have that the firm seeks to satisfy, and the core competencies the firm will use to satisfy customers' needs. Increasing segmentation of markets throughout the global economy creates opportunities for firms to identify unique customer needs.
- Firms seeking competitive advantage through the cost leadership strategy produce no-frills, standardized products for an industry's typical customer. However, these low cost products must be offered with competitive levels of differentiation. Above-average returns are earned when firms continuously drive their costs lower than those of their competitors, while providing customers with products that have low prices and acceptable levels of differentiated features.
- Competitive risks associated with the cost leadership strategy include (1) a loss of competitive advantage to newer technologies, (2) a failure to detect changes in customers' needs, and (3) the ability of competitors to imitate the cost leader's competitive advantage through their own unique strategic actions.
- The differentiation strategy enables firms to provide customers with products that have different (and valued) features. Differentiated products must be sold at a cost that customers believe is competitive given the product's features as compared to the cost/feature combination available through competitors' offerings. Because of their uniqueness, differentiated goods or services are sold at a premium price. Products can be differentiated along any dimension that some customer group values. Firms using this strategy seek to differentiate their products from competitors' goods or services along as many dimensions as possible. The less similarity with competitors' products, the more buffered a firm is from competition with its rivals.
- Risks associated with the differentiation strategy include (1) a customer group's decision that the differences between the differentiated product and the cost leader's good or service are no longer worth a premium price, (2) the inability of a differentiated product to create the type of value for which customers are willing to pay a premium price, (3) the ability of competitors to provide customers with products that have features similar to those associated with the differentiated product, but at a lower cost, and (4) the threat of counterfeiting, whereby firms produce a cheap "knock-off" of a differentiated good or service.
- Through the cost leadership and the differentiated focus strategies, firms serve the needs of a narrow competitive segment (e.g., a buyer group, product segment, or geographic area). This strategy is successful when firms have the core competencies required to provide value to a narrow competitive segment that exceeds the value available from firms serving customers on an industry-wide basis.
- The competitive risks of focus strategies include (1) a competitor's ability to use its core competencies to "outfocus" the focuser by serving an even more narrowly defined competitive segment, (2) decisions by industry-wide competitors to serve a customer group's specialized needs that the focuser has been serving, and (3) a reduction in differences of the needs between customers in a narrow competitive segment and the industry-wide market.
- Firms using the integrated cost leadership/differentiation strategy strive to provide customers with relatively low-cost products that have some valued differentiated features. The primary risk of this strategy is that a firm might produce products that do not offer sufficient value in terms of either low cost or differentiation. When this occurs, the company is "stuck in the middle." Firms stuck in the middle compete at a disadvantage and are unable to earn more than average returns.

Review Questions

1. What is a business-level strategy?
2. What is the relationship between a firm's customers and its business-level strategy in terms of *who, what,* and *how*? Why is this relationship important?
3. What are the differences among the cost leadership, differentiation, focused cost leadership, focused differentiation, and integrated cost leadership/differentiation business-level strategies?
4. How can each one of the business-level strategies be used to position the firm relative to the five forces of competition in a way that permits the earning of above-average returns?
5. What are the specific risks associated with using each business-level strategy?

Business-Level Strategy

Natural and organic foods are the fastest growing segment of food retailing, and almost every supermarket in America has begun offering at least a limited selection of these products. According to chairman and CEO John Mackey, "Whole Foods is the 'category killer' for natural and organic products, offering the largest selection at competitive prices and the most informed customer service."

The first Whole Foods Markets opened in 1980, in Austin, Texas, and realized $4 million in sales. By 2001 the firm had become the world's largest retailer of natural and organic foods, with 126 stores across the country and the District of Columbia. A strong performer for several years with consistently high same-store sales, cash flow, gross margins, and controlled expansion, the firm's sales grew to $2.27 billion and earnings per share to $1.03 for fiscal 2001, ended in September. Shares are up more than 50 percent over the previous year, and analysts expect the performance to continue, anticipating 18 percent earnings growth in fiscal 2002 and 20 percent growth in 2003.

Whole Foods purchases its products both locally and from all over the world, supporting organic farming on a global level, and prides itself on providing its customer with the highest quality, least processed, most flavorful and naturally preserved foods. While the firm concedes that organic foods generally cost more than conventional foods, it notes that organic farming is not government subsidized and that organic products must meet stricter regulations governing growing, harvesting, transportation, and storage. All of these steps make the process more labor and management intensive.

Whole Foods staff members are encouraged to make their own decisions and play a critical role in helping build the store into a profitable and beneficial part of its community.

Answer the following questions and be prepared to make a short presentation or to discuss your findings with the rest of the class.

1. What type of business-level strategy does Whole Foods appear to follow, based on the above information?
2. What are some of the risks Whole Foods faces with this strategy?
3. Use the following table and show how Whole Foods might apply each strategy to its business activities, based on the information given above (also see Figures 4.2 and 4.3).

Activities	Cost Leadership Strategy	Differentiation Strategy
Inbound Logistics		
Operations		
Outbound Logistics		
Marketing and Sales		
Service		

SOURCES: L. DiCarlo, 2001, The overachievers, *Forbes.com,* http://www.forbes.com, December 5; 2000, Whole Foods Annual Report, Chairman's Letter, http://www.wholefoodsmarket.com/ investor/AR00letter.html.

Notes

1. J. Stopford, 2001, Should strategy makers become dream weavers? *Harvard Business Review,* 79(1): 165–169.
2. C. A. De Kluyver, 2000, *Strategic Thinking,* Upper Saddle River, NJ: Prentice-Hall, 3.
3. E. H. Bowman & C. E. Helfat, 2001, Does corporate strategy matter? *Strategic Management Journal,* 22: 1–23.
4. G. Hamel, 2000, *Leading the Revolution,* Boston: Harvard Business School Press, 71.
5. R. S. Kaplan & D. P. Norton, 2001, *The Strategy-Focused Organization,* Boston: Harvard Business School Press, 90.
6. J. B. Barney, 2002, *Gaining and Sustaining Competitive Advantage,* 2nd ed., Upper Saddle River, NJ.: Prentice-Hall, 6; D. C. Hambrick & J. W. Fredrickson, 2001, Are you sure you have a strategy? *Academy of Management Executive,* 15(4): 48–59.
7. R. D. Ireland, M. A. Hitt, S. M. Camp, & D. L. Sexton, 2001, Integrating entrepreneurship and strategic management actions to create firm wealth, *Academy of Management Executive,* 15(1): 49–63.
8. M. A. Geletkanycez & S .S. Black, 2001, Bound by the past? Experience-based effects on commitment to the strategic status quo, *Journal of Management,* 27: 3–21; C. E. Helfat, 1997, Know-how and asset complementarity and dynamic capability accumulation: The case of R&D, *Strategic Management Journal,* 18: 339–360.
9. D. F. Kuratko, R. D. Ireland, & J. S. Hornsby, 2001, The power of entrepreneurial actions: Insights from Acordia, Inc., *Academy of Management Executive,* 15(4): 60–71; T. J. Dean, R. L. Brown, & C. E. Bamford, 1998, Differences in large and small firm responses to environmental context: Strategic implications from a comparative analysis of business formations, *Strategic Management Journal,* 19: 709–728.
10. L. Tihanyi, A. E. Ellstrand, C. M. Daily, & D. R. Dalton, 2000, Composition of top management team and firm international diversification, *Journal of Management,* 26: 1157–1177; P. F. Drucker, 1999, *Management in the 21st Century,* New York: Harper Business.
11. P. Rindova & C. J. Fombrun, 1999, Constructing competitive advantage: The role of firm-constitute interactions, *Strategic Management Journal,* 20: 691–710; G. G. Dess, A. Gupta, J. F. Hennart, & C. W. L. Hill, 1995, Conducting and integrating strategy research at the international, corporate, and business levels: Issues and directions, *Journal of Management,* 21: 357–393.
12. Hamel, *Leading the Revolution.*
13. De Kluyver, *Strategic Thinking,* 7.
14. S. F. Slater & E. M. Olsen, 2000, Strategy type and performance: The influence of sales force management, *Strategic Management Journal,* 21: 813–829; M. E. Porter, 1998, *On Competition,* Boston: Harvard Business School Press.
15. M. E. Porter, 1996, What is strategy? *Harvard Business Review,* 74(6): 61–78.
16. B. Lowendahl & O. Revang, 1998, Challenges to existing strategy theory in a postindustrial society, *Strategic Management Journal,* 19: 755–773.
17. M. E. Porter, 1980, *Competitive Strategy,* New York: Free Press.
18. P. Burrows & A. Park, 2001, Can Compaq escape from hardware hell? *Business Week,* July 9, 38–39.
19. L. B. Ward, 2001, Compaq changes direction, *Dallas Morning News,* June 26, D1, D12.
20. L. L. Berry, 2001, The old pillars of new retailing, *Harvard Business Review,* 79(4): 131–137; A. Afuah, 1999, Technology approaches for the information age, in Mastering Strategy (Part One), *Financial Times,* September 27, 8.
21. N. Irwin, 2001, Motley Fool branches out, *The Washington Post,* May 22, B5.
22. 2001, Clicking with customers: New challenges in online conversion, *Knowledge@Wharton,* http://www.knowledge.wharton.upenn.edu, May 26.
23. M. Schrage, 2001, Don't scorn your salespeople—you will soon be one, *Fortune,* May 14, 256; D. Peppers, M. Rogers, & B. Dorf, 1999, Is your company ready for one-to-one marketing? *Harvard Business Review,* 77(5): 59–72.
24. T. A. Stewart, 1999, *Intellectual Capital,* New York: Currency Doubleday, 144.
25. K. Ferguson, 2001, Closer than ever, *Business Week Small Biz,* May 21, 14–15; R. S. Winer, 2001, A framework for customer relationship management, *California Management Review,* 43(4): 89–105.
26. Ferguson, Closer than ever, 15.
27. M. Warner, 2001, Salesforce.com, *Fortune,* June 25, 164.
28. P. B. Seybold, 2001, Get inside the lives of your customers, *Harvard Business Review,* 79(5): 81–89.
29. M. E. Porter, 2001, Strategy and the Internet, *Harvard Business Review,* 79(3): 62–78.
30. L. Walker, 2001, Plugged in for maximum efficiency, *The Washington Post,* June 20, G1, G4.
31. 2001, While Welch waited, *The Economist,* May 19, 75–76.
32. 2002, http://www.bn.com, March 15.
33. P. Evans & T. S. Wurster, 1999, Getting real about virtual commerce, *Harvard Business Review,* 77(6): 84–94; S. F. Slater & J. C. Narver, 1999, Market-oriented is more than being customer-led, *Strategic Management Journal,* 20: 1165–1168.
34. 2001, How good, or bad, marketing decisions can make, or break, a company, *Knowledge@Wharton,* http://www.knowledge.wharton.upenn.edu, May 14.
35. W. D. Neal & J. Wurst, 2001, Advances in market segmentation, *Marketing Research,* 13(1): 14–18; S. C. Jain, 2000, *Marketing Planning and Strategy,* Cincinnati: South-Western College Publishing, 104–125.
36. 1999, Associated Press, Rolls Bentley targets U.S. drivers, *Dallas Morning News,* May 2, H5.
37. B. J. Knutson, 2000, College students and fast food-how students perceive restaurant brands, *Cornell Hotel and Restaurant Administration Quarterly,* 41(3): 68–74.
38. C. Burritt, 2001, Aging boomers reshape resort segment, *Lodging Hospitality,* 57(3): 31–32; J. D. Zbar, On a segmented dial, digital cuts wire finer, *Advertising Age,* 72(16): S12; Gen-er-a-tion, *Richmond Times-Dispatch,* April 2, E1–E2; 2001, The America Funds Group, *The American Funds Investor,* Spring/Summer, 24.
39. V. Kumar & A. Nagpal, 2001, Segmenting global markets: Look before you leap, *Marketing Research,* 13(1): 8–13.
40. 2001, Is Gen Y shopping online? *Business Week,* June 11, 16.
41. D. Little, 2001, Hot growth companies, *Business Week,* June 11, 107–110; 2001, http://www.newbalance.com, May 10.
42. D. A. Aaker, 1998, *Strategic Marketing Management,* 5th ed., New York: John Wiley & Sons, 20.
43. S. Miller, 1999, VW sows confusion with common platforms for models, *The Wall Street Journal,* October 25, A25, A38.
44. D. Welch, 2000, GM: 'Out with the Olds' is just the start, *Business Week,* December 25, 57.
45. A. W. King, S. W. Fowler, & C. P. Zeithaml, 2001, Managing organizational competencies for competitive advantage: The middle-management edge, *Academy of Management Executive,* 15(2): 95–106; Porter, Strategy and the Internet, 72.
46. S. N. Mehta, 2001, What Lucent can learn from IBM, *Fortune,* June 25, 40–44.
47. C. A. O'Reilly III & J. Pfeffer, 2000, *Hidden Value: How Great Companies Achieve Extraordinary Results with Ordinary People,* Boston: Harvard Business School Press, 102.
48. A. Weintraub & G. Khermouch, 2001, Chairman of the board, *Business Week,* May 28, 94.
49. M. E. Porter, *Competitive Advantage,* New York: Free Press, 26.
50. Porter, What is strategy?
51. Bowman & Helfat, Does corporate strategy matter?, 1–4; B. McEvily & A. Zaheer, 1999, Bridging ties: A source of firm heterogeneity in competitive capabilities, *Strategic Management Journal,* 20: 133–156.
52. Hambrick & Fredrickson, Are you sure you have a strategy?
53. M. E. Porter, 1994, Toward a dynamic theory of strategy, in R. P. Rumelt, D. E. Schendel, & D. J. Teece (eds.), *Fundamental Issues in Strategy,* Boston: Harvard Business School Press, 423–461.
54. Porter, What is strategy?, 62.
55. Porter, *Competitive Advantage,* 15.
56. G. G. Dess, G. T. Lumpkin, & J. E. McGee, 1999, Linking corporate entrepreneurship to strategy, structure, and process: Suggested research directions, *Entrepreneurship: Theory & Practice,* 23(3): 85–102; P. M. Wright, D. L. Smart, & G. C. McMahan, 1995, Matches between human resources and strategy among NCAA basketball teams, *Academy of Management Journal,* 38: 1052–1074.
57. Porter, *Competitive Strategy,* 35–40.
58. J. A. Parnell, 2000, Reframing the combination strategy debate: Defining forms of combination, *Journal of Management Studies,* 9(1): 33–54.
59. C. Malburg, 2000, Competing on costs, *Industry Week,* October 16, 31.
60. D. F. Lynch, S. B. Keller, & J. Ozment, 2000, The effects of logistics capabilities and strategy on firm performance, *Journal of Business Logistics,* 21(2): 47–68.
61. Porter, What is strategy?, 67.
62. http://www.vanguard.com
63. Porter, What is strategy?, 66.
64. http://www.cnstores.com
65. A. D'Innocenzio, 2001, We are paranoid, *Richmond Times-Dispatch,* June 10, E1, E2.
66. L. Grant, 2001, Kmart, Wal-Mart face off in price-cutting fight, *USA Today,* June 8, B1; A. R. Moses, 2001, Kmart's long road back, *Richmond Times-Dispatch,* November 24, C1, C10.

67. Lynch, Keller, & Ozment, The effects of logistics capabilities.
68. Porter, *Competitive Strategy,* 35–40.
69. Ibid., 65.
70. Porter, *Competitive Advantage,* 14.
71. http://www.roberttalbott.com
72. 2001, Business in Brief, *The Washington Post,* June 20, E2.
73. Joyce, Luxury sales, E1.
74. G. Edmonsdson, E. Neuborne, A. L. Kazmin, E. Thornton, & K. N. Anhalt, 1999, L'Oreal: The beauty of global branding, *Business Week e-biz,* June 28.
75. Barney, *Gaining and Sustaining Competitive Advantage,* 268.
76. Ward, Compaq changes direction.
77. R. More, 2001, Creating profits from integrated product-service strategies, *Ivey Business Journal,* 65(5): 75–81.
78. H. R. Goldstein, A. E. Roth, T. Young, & J. D. Lawrence, 2001, US manufacturers take a swing at counterfeit golf clubs, *Intellectual Property & Technology Law Journal,* May, 23.
79. Porter, *Competitive Strategy,* 98.
80. Porter, *Competitive Advantage,* 15.
81. Ibid., 15–16.
82. 1999, Lloyd Greif Center for Entrepreneurial Studies, Discussion of the Greif Center's founder http://www.marshall.usc.edu.
83. D. Foust & B. Grow, 2001, This company likes it in jail, *Business Week,* June 11, 112.
84. Porter, *Competitive Advantage,* 15.
85. Porter, What is strategy?, 67.
86. http://www.ikea.com
87. Porter, What is strategy?, 65.
88. O. Kharif, 2001, You can take this furniture with you, *Business Week,* April 16, 16; S. Jones, 2001, Cutting a swath in hair care, *The Washington Post,* May 5, E1, E8; E. McCarthy, 2001, Get Well Network enlivens patients' stay at hospital, *The Washington Post,* May 7, E5; A. Overholt, 2001, Basket case, *Fast Company,* July, 60.
89. http://www.bigdog.com
90. http://www.homedepot.com; J. R. Hagerty, 2000, Home Depot strikes at Sears in tool duel, *The Wall Street Journal,* January 10, B1, B4.
91. 2001, The engine that drives differentiation, *DSN Retailing Today,* April 2, 52.
92. Dess, Lumpkin, & McGee, Linking corporate entrepreneurship to strategy, 89.
93. P. Ghemawat, 2001, *Strategy and the Business Landscape,* Upper Saddle River, NJ: Prentice Hall, 56.
94. W. K. Hall, 1980, Survival strategies in a hostile environment, *Harvard Business Review* 58, 5: 75–87.
95. Dess, Gupta, Hennart, & Hill, Conducting and integrating strategy research, 377.
96. L. Kim & Y. Lim, 1988, Environment, generic strategies, and performance in a rapidly developing country: A taxonomic approach, *Academy of Management Journal,* 31: 802–827.
97. Ghemawat, *Strategy and the Business Landscape,* 56.
98. Ibid., 56.
99. M. Naim, 2001, McAtlas shrugged, *Foreign Policy,* May/June, 26–37.
100. A. K. Gupta & V. Govindarajan, 2001, Converting global presence into global competitive advantage, *Academy of Management Executive,* 15(2): 45–56.
101. S. A. Forest, 2001, When cool heads prevail, *Business Week,* June 11, 114.
102. R. Sanchez, 1995, Strategic flexibility in product competition, *Strategic Management Journal,* 16(Summer Special Issue): 140.
103. Ibid., 105.
104. R. Olexa, 2001, Flexible parts feeding boosts productivity, *Manufacturing Engineering,* 126(4): 106–114.
105. I. Mount & B. Caulfield, 2001, The missing link, *Ecompany Now,* May, 82–88.
106. Ibid., 82.
107. 2001, ABB: Integrated drives and process control, *Textile World,* April, 60–61.
108. M. Maynard, 2001, Tiremaking technology is on a roll, *Fortune,* May 28, 148B–148L; J. Martin, 1997, Give 'em exactly what they want, *Fortune,* November 10, 283–285.
109. R. S. Russell & B. W. Taylor III, 2000, *Operations Management,* 3rd ed., Upper Saddle River, NJ: Prentice-Hall, 262–264.
110. K. MacArthur, 2001, McDonald's sees 100% increase in U.S. sales, *AdAge.com,* http://www.adage.com, April 2.
111. J. B. Dilworth, 2000, *Operations Management: Providing Value in Goods and Services,* 3rd ed. (Fort Worth, TX.: The Dryden Press), 286–289; D. Lei, M. A. Hitt, & J. D. Goldhar, 1996, Advanced manufacturing technology, organization design and strategic flexibility, *Organization Studies,* 17: 501–523.
112. R. E. Chalmers, 2001, Assembly systems maximize efficiency, *Manufacturing Engineering,* May, 130–138.
113. S. Isaac & R. N. Tooker, 2001, The many faces of CRM, *LIMRA's MarketFacts Quarterly,* Spring, 20 (1): 84–89.
114. P. J. Rondeau & L. A. Litteral, 2001, The evolution of manufacturing planning and control systems: From reorder point to enterprise resource planning, *Production and Inventory Management,* 42(2): 1–7.
115. M. L. Songini, 2001, Companies test their wireless supply chain wings, *Computerworld,* May 21, 35.
116. N. Checker, 2001, An integrated approach, *Chemical Market Reporter,* June 4, S8–S10.
117. V. A. Mabert, A. Soni, & M. A. Venkataramanan, 2000, Enterprise resource planning survey of U.S. manufacturing firms, *Production and Inventory Management Journal,* Second Quarter, 52–58.
118. D. Chatterji & J. M. Davidson, 2001, Examining TQM's legacies for R&D, *Research Technology Management,* 44(1): 10–12.
119. Kaplan & Norton, *The Strategy-Focused Organization,* 361; M. A. Mische, 2001, *Strategic Renewal: Becoming a High-Performance Organization,* Upper Saddle River, NJ: Prentice-Hall, 15.
120. J. Pfeffer, 1998, *The Human Equation: Building Profits by Putting People First,* Boston: Harvard Business School Press, 156.
121. W. M. Mak, 2000, The Tao of people-based management, *Total Quality Management,* July, 4–6.
122. J. R. Hackman & R. Wageman, 1995, Total quality management: Empirical, conceptual, and practical issues, *Administrative Science Quarterly,* 40: 310.
123. J. Muller, 2001, Ford: Why it's worse than you think, *Business Week,* June 25,
124. Chatterji & Davidson, Examining TQM's legacies, 11.
125. De Kluyver, *Strategic Thinking,* 3; C. H. St. John & J. S. Harrison, 1999, Manufacturing-based relatedness, synergy, and coordination, *Strategic Management Journal,* 20: 129–145.
126. Porter, *Competitive Advantage,* 16.
127. Ibid., 17.
128. Parnell, Reframing the combination strategy debate, 33.

5

Chapter Five

Competitive Rivalry and Competitive Dynamics

Knowledge Objectives

Studying this chapter should provide you with the strategic management knowledge needed to:

1. Define competitors, competitive rivalry, competitive behavior, and competitive dynamics.
2. Describe market commonality and resource similarity as the building blocks of a competitor analysis.
3. Explain awareness, motivation, and ability as drivers of competitive behavior.
4. Discuss factors affecting the likelihood a competitor will take competitive actions.
5. Discuss factors affecting the likelihood a competitor will respond to actions taken against it.
6. Explain competitive dynamics in slow-cycle, fast-cycle, and standard-cycle markets.

Of Trucks and E-commerce: Competitive Rivalry between FedEx and UPS

FedEx and UPS compete directly against each other in several product markets. These competitors are locked in fierce battles to dominate not only package delivery but emerging e-commerce and logistics markets as well. Across time, the rivalry between these firms has resulted in a great deal of competitive behavior (competitive actions and competitive responses taken to build or defend a firm's competitive advantages and improve its market performance).

In 1907, 19-year-old Jim Casey started UPS as a local delivery service. From its founding, strict operational guidelines have been in place at UPS. Even today, drivers are taught 340 steps that are to be precisely followed to successfully deliver a package the "UPS way."

Historically, UPS's rigid culture tended to discourage risk taking and innovation. Nonetheless, in the 1950s, UPS became the first company to use airplanes to deliver packages overnight. However, because of the higher cost compared to package delivery via trucks, UPS decided not to further pursue its innovation of overnight delivery.

In the 1970s, the shipping industry was substantially changed when Frederick Smith founded Federal Express (now called FedEx). Convinced that customers would value not only overnight deliveries but also the ability to electronically track them, FedEx developed a proprietary computerized tracking system called Cosmos. This system introduced computer technology to the shipping industry in previously unheard-of ways and permanently altered the nature of competition within it.

Study of its new competitor convinced UPS that overnight delivery was a market that it couldn't ignore. Thinking of Cosmos as a competitive advantage for FedEx, UPS set out to understand and imitate the system's capabilities. UPS employees even followed FedEx's trucks, partly to understand how Cosmos worked. In 1988, roughly 17 years after FedEx's entry into the overnight market, UPS introduced its rival service. However, it wasn't until 1995 that UPS was able to develop its own electronic tracking system comparable to

Although known for its overnight service, FedEx expected its ground unit to grow by 20 percent in the first quarter of 2002 as companies cutting costs choose this less expensive delivery option. Not only are the firm's gross margins for this service double those of overnight delivery, FedEx hasn't had to cut prices to compete in these markets. The firm's delivery arrangement with the U.S. Postal Service is expected to help both organizations. UPS, the traditional ground service carrier, continues to move in the other direction—its deliveries to and from China have more than doubled its revenue since the firm launched direct flights there. It is opening a new hub in the Philippines to cut transit time and to increase its position against Asia's strongest shipper, DHL.

Cosmos. At that time, many analysts concluded that UPS's slow market entry and inability to duplicate Cosmos's value-creating ability had permanently disadvantaged the firm. This conclusion hasn't proven to be the case. Although FedEx remains dominant in the overnight market, UPS's overnight business grew 8 percent in 2000, compared to 3.6 percent growth for FedEx.

Beyond this, though, UPS decided in the mid-1990s that some of the technological capabilities it had developed to match the sophistication of FedEx's Cosmos system also had commercial applications for Internet-based businesses. This decision was based on experience gained from efforts the firm started in the 1980s to study FedEx's operations methods. During that time period, UPS started applying technology such as tracking software, electronic clipboards, bar codes, and scanners to streamline its operations and cut costs. Efficiencies gained from its technology investments enabled UPS to almost double its operating margins from 8 percent to 15 percent. Study of e-commerce transactions convinced UPS that what it had learned from internal uses of technology could also benefit e-commerce retailers (e-tailers). In short, UPS caught FedEx off guard when it used its internally generated technology skills to offer e-tailers a multitude of shipping options and prices. Additionally, UPS began programming software tools, such as package tracking and returns management, directly into its customers' websites. These tools made it possible for shoppers to track orders with one click of a button and for e-tailers to more efficiently handle returns. Although FedEx and UPS compete for e-tailers' business, UPS remains the shipping partner of choice, as shown by recent market shares for the delivery of online purchases (55 percent for UPS; 10 percent for FedEx).

Encouraged by its success in e-commerce, UPS has initiated other competitive actions to evolve beyond its traditional capital-intensive transportation business. For example, the firm again relied on its technology skills to establish a logistics group in 1994. This unit helps firms such as National Semiconductor and Ford Motor Company learn how to use logistics technology to streamline their supply chains. FedEx competes against UPS in logistics; although both firms help customers better utilize information to track and ship inventory, UPS is pulling ahead of its competitor. Accounting for this success could be UPS's decision to offer warehouse management services. A customer choosing this service outsources its product logistics to UPS, allowing it to then concentrate on its own core competencies. UPS has built a sophisticated central warehouse in Louisville, KY to store, pack, and deliver such products as Samsung cell phones and Nike.com apparel. UPS is even going beyond the handling of physical goods, operating customer service call centers and offering financial products to facilitate e-commerce, such as trade credit and electronic invoicing. The diversity of its logistics business is resulting in an annual growth rate of 40 percent while FedEx tries to reverse a decline in this area.

UPS's competitive actions in logistics seemingly have created an advantageous market position for the firm over its major rival. However, FedEx is responding to UPS's actions. For example, it quietly spent approximately $4 billion to acquire trucking companies and build hubs. In 2000, FedEx directly attacked UPS when it started offering home package delivery by ground. Although UPS still dominates that market with a 77 percent share, FedEx is making strides as its ground shipping business grows by 8 percent to 10 percent annually. Furthermore, FedEx believes that UPS's capital-intensive approach to its logistics business is flawed. According to the head of FedEx's worldwide e-solutions, "the benefit (to customers) is in moving things quickly and coordinating those moves, not in having parts sitting somewhere." This comment reflects FedEx's decision not to warehouse customers' goods, citing the high costs of building warehouses.

SOURCES: 2002, Intrigue on the orient express, *The Economist,* January 19, 55; C. Haddad & J. Ewing, 2001, Ground wars, UPS' rapid ascent leaves FedEx scrambling, *Business Week,* May 21, 64–68; J. Kirby, 2001, An interview with Jim Kelly of UPS, *Harvard Business Review,* 79(10): 116–123; B. Schiffman, 2001, FedEx has guts, *Forbes,* http://www.forbes.com, November 20; E. Schonfeld, 2001, The total package, *eCompany Now,* http://business2.com/articles, June 1; K. G. Smith, W. J. Ferrier, & H. Ndofor, 2001, Competitive dynamics research: Critique and future directions, in M. A. Hitt, R. E. Freeman, & J. S. Harrison (eds.), *Handbook of Strategic Management,* Oxford, U.K.: Blackwell Publishers, 315–361; M. Tagte, 2001, Start the ground war, *Forbes,* http://www.forbes.com, October 26; K. Barron, 2000, Logistics in brown, *Forbes,* http://www.forbes.com, January 10; B. O'Reilly, 2000, They've got mail! The growth of Internet commerce has raised the stakes in the boxing match between UPS and FedEx, *Fortune,* http://www.forbes.com, February 7; M.-J. Chen, 1996, Competitor analysis and interfirm rivalry: Toward a theoretical integration, *Academy of Management Review,* 21: 100–134.

Firms operating in the same market, offering similar products and targeting similar cutomers are **competitors.**

Competitive rivalry is the ongoing set of competitive actions and competitive responses occurring between competitors as they compete against each other for an advantageous market position.

Competitive behavior is the set of competitive actions and competitive responses the firm takes to build or defend its competitive advantages and to improve its market position.

Firms operating in the same market, offering similar products and targeting similar customers are **competitors.**[1] Obviously, FedEx and UPS are competitors. **Competitive rivalry** is the ongoing set of competitive actions and competitive responses occurring between competitors as they compete against each other for an advantageous market position. Competitive rivalry influences an individual firm's ability to gain and sustain competitive advantages.[2] A sequence of firm-level moves, rivalry results from firms initiating their own competitive actions and then responding to actions taken by their competitors.[3] As noted in the Opening Case, **competitive behavior** is the set of competitive actions and competitive responses the firm takes to build or defend its competitive advantages and to improve its market position.[4] Through competitive behavior, the firm tries to successfully position itself relative to the five forces of competition (see Chapter 2) and to defend and use current competitive advantages while building advantages for the future (see Chapter 3). Increasingly, as with FedEx and UPS, competitors engage in competitive actions and responses in more than one market.[5]

All competitive behavior—that is, the total set of actions and responses taken by all firms competing within a market—is called **competitive dynamics.** The relationships among these key concepts are shown in Figure 5.1.

This chapter focuses on competitive rivalry and competitive dynamics. The essence of these important topics is that a firm's strategies are dynamic in nature. Actions taken by one firm elicit responses from competitors that, in turn, typically

Figure 5.1 From Competitors to Competitive Dynamics

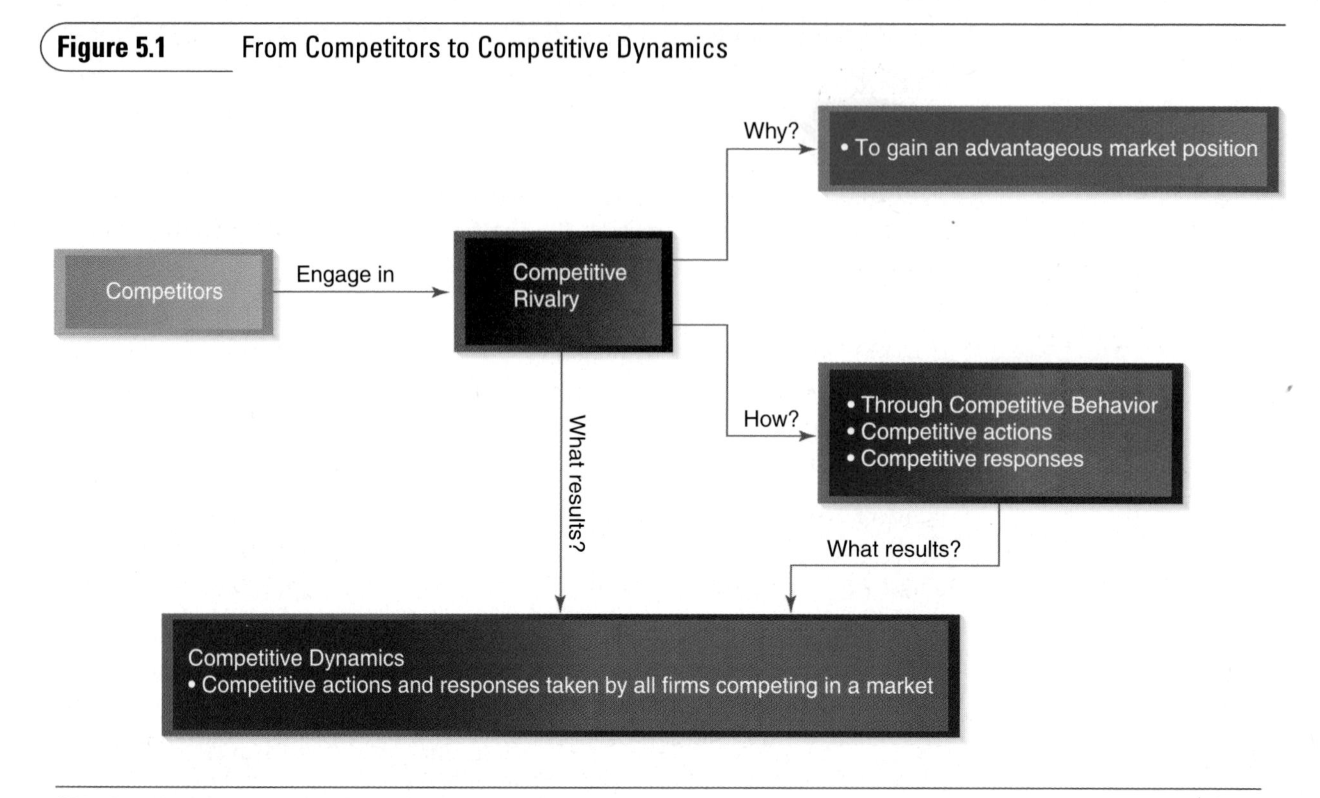

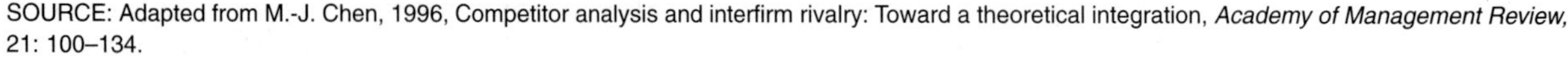

SOURCE: Adapted from M.-J. Chen, 1996, Competitor analysis and interfirm rivalry: Toward a theoretical integration, *Academy of Management Review,* 21: 100–134.

All competitive behavior—that is, the total set of actions and responses taken by all firms competing within a market—is called **competitive dynamics.**

Firms competing against each other in several product or geographic markets are engaged in **multimarket competition.**

result in responses from the firm that took the initial action.[6] This chain of events is illustrated in the Opening Case that describes FedEx and UPS's competitive rivalry as they compete against each other in several markets (e.g., package delivery and logistics services). Firms competing against each other in several product or geographic markets are engaged in **multimarket competition.**[7]

Another way of highlighting competitive rivalry's effect on the firm's strategies is to say that a strategy's success is determined not only by the firm's initial competitive actions but also by how well it anticipates competitors' responses to them *and* by how well the firm anticipates and responds to its competitors' initial actions (also called attacks).[8] Although competitive rivalry affects all types of strategies (for example, corporate-level, acquisition, and international), its most dominant influence is on the firm's business-level strategy or strategies. Recall from Chapter 4 that business-level strategy is concerned with what the firm does to successfully use its competitive advantages in specific product markets.

In the global economy, competitive rivalry is intensifying,[9] meaning that the significance of its effect on firms' business-level strategies is increasing. In the automobile industry, for example, Ford Motor Company CEO William Ford Jr. believes that firms engage in "cutthroat" competition. Companies with strong brand names (such as Coca-Cola, Microsoft, GE, Intel, and IBM) increasingly rely on them as ambassadors to enter new markets or offer new products.[10] This reliance is especially noticeable for firms using a differentiation business-level strategy. Strong brands affect competitive rivalry, in that companies without them must find ways (such as price reductions) to reduce their appeal to customers.[11] A competitor's decision to reduce prices likely will elicit a response from the firm with a strong brand, increasing competitive rivalry as a result.

An expanding geographic scope contributes to the increasing intensity in the competitive rivalry between firms. Some believe, for example, that an aptitude for cross-border management practices and a facility with cultural diversity find European Union firms emerging as formidable global competitors.[12] Similarly, former GE CEO Jack Welch believes that GE's most significant future competitive threats may be from companies not currently in prominent positions on the firm's radar screen, such as those in emerging countries.[13] Thus, the firm trying to predict competitive rivalry should anticipate that in the future it will encounter a larger number of increasingly diverse competitors. This trend also suggests that firms should expect competitive rivalry to have a stronger effect on their strategies' success than historically has been the case.[14]

We offer a model (see Figure 5.2 to show what is involved with competitive rivalry at the firm level).[15] We study rivalry at the firm level because the competitive actions and responses the firm takes are the foundation for successfully building and using its competitive advantages to gain an advantageous market position.[16] Thus, we use the model in Figure 5.2 to help us explain competition between a particular firm and each of its competitors as they compete for the most advantageous market position. Successful use of the model in Figure 5.2 finds companies able to predict competitors' behavior (actions and responses), which, in turn, has a positive effect on the firm's market position and its subsequent financial performance.[17] The sum of all the individual rivalries modeled in Figure 5.2 that are occurring in a particular market reflects the competitive dynamics in that market.

The remainder of the chapter discusses the model shown in Figure 5.2. We first describe market commonality and resource similarity as the building blocks of a competitor analysis. Next, we discuss the effects of three organizational characteristics—awareness, motivation, and ability—on the firm's competitive behavior. We then examine competitive rivalry in detail by describing the factors that affect the likelihood a firm will take a competitive action and the factors that affect the likelihood a firm will respond to a competitor's action. In the chapter's final section, we turn our

Figure 5.2 A Model of Competitive Rivalry

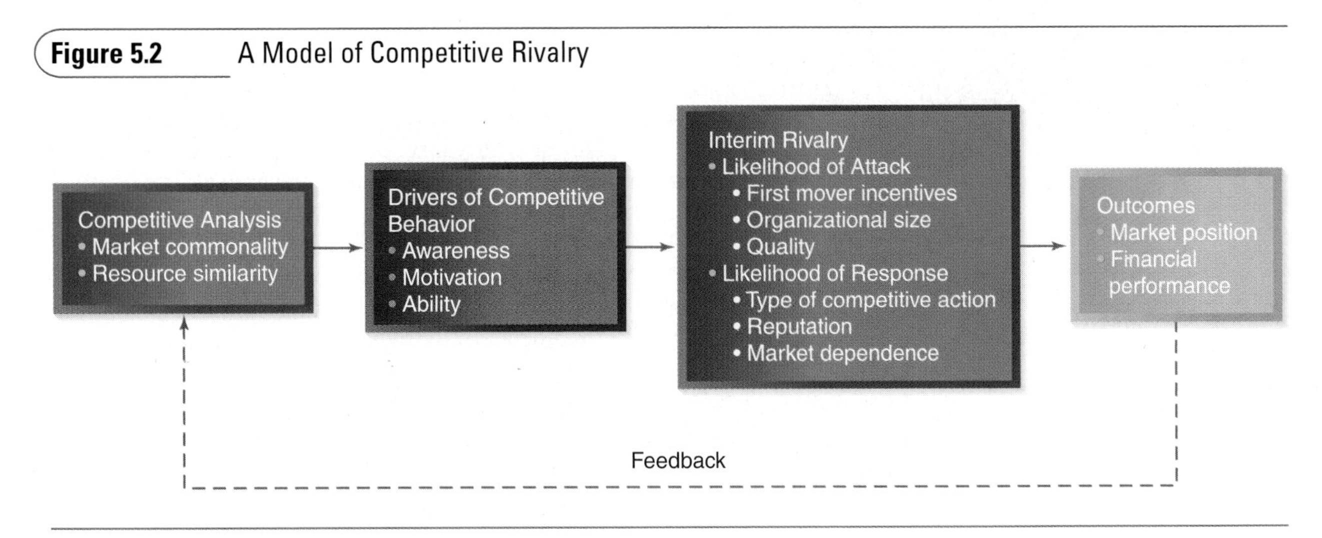

SOURCE: Adapted from M.-J. Chen, 1996, Competitor analysis and interfirm rivalry: Toward a theoretical integration, *Academy of Management Review,* 21: 100–134.

attention to competitive dynamics to describe how market characteristics affect competitive rivalry in slow-cycle, fast-cycle, and standard-cycle markets.

A Model of Competitive Rivalry

Over time, the firm takes many competitive actions and responses.[18] As noted earlier, competitive rivalry evolves from this pattern of actions and responses as one firm's competitive actions have noticeable effects on competitors, eliciting competitive responses from them.[19] This pattern shows that firms are mutually interdependent, that they feel each other's actions and responses, and that marketplace success is a function of both individual strategies and the consequences of their use.[20]

Increasingly too, executives recognize that competitive rivalry can have a major and direct effect on the firm's financial performance.[21] Research findings showing that intensified rivalry within an industry results in decreased average profitability for firms competing in it supports the importance of understanding these effects.[22] Rivalry in the PC market demonstrates these points.

Financial analysts feel that Dell Computer Corp., under founder and CEO Michael Dell (pictured here), has done a great job of exceeding the overall trends in the industry. Dell's policy of direct sales has positioned it well as the low-cost provider, especially when customers want to maximize their computer expenditures both for business computers and home equipment.

In 2001, Dell Computer Corporation launched an intense price war in the PC business, causing prices for PCs as well as servers to drop by as much as 50 percent. Profit margins declined for all firms, including Dell, as noted by analysts who suggested that Dell's action was draining gross profit dollars out of the PC segment for all companies.[23] CEO Michael Dell, however, believed that the direct sales model on which his firm's cost leadership strategy is based would enable it to better survive reduced profitability than its competitors could, in that nimble execution of strategy, which means selling machines directly to consumers, is more important than economies of scale in the PC business.[24]

© BOBBY YIP/REUTERS NEWMEDIA INC./CORBIS

At the core of the intensified rivalry created by Dell's pricing action was the firm's intention of increasing its share of the PC market. Competitors responded to Dell's competitive action, intensifying rivalry in the process. The most dramatic response was Hewlett-Packard's merger with Compaq Computer Corporation.[25] Initially, negative reaction from Walter Hewlett and David Packard, sons of the company's founders, as well as other shareholders, jeopardized the transaction's approval.[26] Although opinions vary, a number of analysts suggest that the new company's competitive position is unattractive compared to Dell's.[27] Further showing the complexity of the merger is the suggestion that Compaq's future would have been shaky had the merger collapsed.[28] Because of its unattractive competitive position, analysts propose that had Compaq remained an independent firm, its competitive position would have been stronger if it were to exit the PC business to concentrate on technology services and the server market.[29]

The intensity of rivalry within a particular market, such as what we described in the PC market, is affected by many factors, including the total number of competitors, market characteristics, and the quality of individual firms' strategies. Firms that develop and use effective business-level strategies tend to outperform competitors in individual product markets, even when experiencing intense competitive rivalry.[30] According to some, Dell's use of an effective business-level strategy may contribute to its ability to frequently outperform its competitors. Indeed, it has been suggested that "Dell sets the standard for the industry, reflecting the strength of its direct sales model (strategy), and its superior cash flow management."[31]

We now turn directly to Figure 5.2 as our foundation for further discussion of competitive rivalry such as that experienced in the PC market.

Competitor Analysis

As noted above, a competitor analysis is the first step the firm takes to be able to predict the extent and nature of its rivalry with each competitor. Recall that a competitor is a firm operating in the same market, offering similar products and targeting similar customers. The number of markets in which firms compete against each other (called market commonality, defined below) and the similarity in their resources (called resource similarity, also defined below) determine the extent to which the firms are competitors. Firms with high market commonality and highly similar resources are ". . . clearly direct and mutually acknowledged competitors."[32] However, being direct competitors does not necessarily mean that the rivalry between the firms will be intense. The drivers of competitive behavior—as well as factors influencing the likelihood that a competitor will initiate competitive actions and will respond to its competitor's competitive actions—influence the intensity of rivalry, even for direct competitors.[33]

In Chapter 2, we discussed competitor analysis as a technique firms use to understand their competitive environment. Along with the general and industry environments, the competitive environment comprises the firm's external environment. In the earlier chapter we described how competitor analysis is used to help the firm *understand* its competitors. This understanding results from studying competitors' future objectives, current strategies, assumptions, and capabilities (see Figure 2.3). In this chapter, the discussion of competitor analysis is extended to describe what firms study as the first step to being able to *predict* competitors' behavior in the form of its competitive actions and responses. The discussions of competitor analysis in Chapter 2 and Chapter 5 are complementary in that firms must first *understand* competitors (Chapter 2) before their competitive actions and competitive responses can be *predicted* (Chapter 5).

Market Commonality

Each industry is composed of various markets. The financial services industry has markets for insurance, brokerage services, banks, and so forth. Denoting an interest to concentrate on the needs of different, unique customer groups, markets can be further subdivided. The insurance market, for example, could be broken into market segments (such as commercial and consumer), product segments (such as health insurance and life insurance), and geographic markets (such as Western Europe and Southeast Asia).

In general, competitors agree about the different characteristics of individual markets that form an industry.[34] For example, in the transportation industry, there is an understanding that the commercial air travel market differs from the ground transportation market that is served by firms such as Yellow Freight System. Although differences exist, most industries' markets are somewhat related in terms of technologies used or core competencies needed to develop a competitive advantage.[35] For example, different types of transportation companies need to provide reliable and timely service. Commercial airline carriers such as Southwest Airlines and Singapore Airlines must therefore develop service competencies to satisfy its passengers, while Yellow Freight System must develop such competencies to serve the needs of those using its fleet to ship their goods.

Firms competing in several or even many markets, some of which may be in different industries, are likely to come into contact with a particular competitor several

© JULIA WATERLOW/EYE UBIQUITOUS/CORBIS

© MENAHEMKAHANA/AFP/CORBIS

While cutting back on expansion in Latin America to boost sales and profitability in existing restaurants in the region, McDonald's plans more stores in China in 2002. Operating in more than 57 countries, Burger King competes with McDonald's in several markets, such as in Israel.

times,[36] a situation bringing forth the issue of market commonality. **Market commonality** is concerned with the number of markets with which the firm and a competitor are jointly involved and the degree of importance of the individual markets to each.[37] Firms competing against one another in several or many markets engage in multimarket competition.[38] For example, McDonald's and Burger King compete against each other in multiple geographic markets across the world,[39] while Prudential and Cigna compete against each other in several market segments (institutional and retail) as well as product markets (such as life insurance and health insurance).[40] Airlines, chemicals, pharmaceuticals, and consumer foods are other industries in which firms often simultaneously engage each other in multiple market competitions.

Firms competing in several markets have the potential to respond to a competitor's actions not only within the market in which the actions are taken, but also in other markets where they compete with the rival. This potential complicates the rivalry between competitors. In fact, recent research suggests that ". . . a firm with greater multimarket contact is less likely to initiate an attack, but more likely to move (respond) aggressively when attacked."[41] Thus, in general, multimarket competition reduces competitive rivalry.[42]

Market commonality is concerned with the number of markets with which the firm and a competitor are jointly involved and the degree of importance of the individual markets to each.

Other research suggests that market commonality and multimarket competition sometimes occur almost by chance.[43] However, once it begins, the rivalry between the unexpected competitors becomes intentional and oftentimes intense. This appears to be the case for AOL and Microsoft. In the Strategic Focus on page 155, we describe the multimarket competition with which these firms are involved as well as some of the competitive actions and responses occurring between them.

As described in the Strategic Focus, the competition between AOL and Microsoft is complex and intense as each firm initiates competitive actions and responds to those of its competitor. The fact that they compete against each other in several markets has the potential to increase the scope and intensity of their rivalry. For example, actions taken by either AOL or Microsoft to improve its market position in instant messaging could result in a competitive response in the online music subscription service market. When predicting their competitor's actions and responses, AOL and Microsoft must consider the strong likelihood that some competitive responses will take place in a market other than the one in which a competitive action was taken.

Resource Similarity

Resource similarity is the extent to which the firm's tangible and intangible resources are comparable to a competitor's in terms of both type and amount.

Resource similarity is the extent to which the firm's tangible and intangible resources are comparable to a competitor's in terms of both type and amount.[44] Firms with similar types and amounts of resources are likely to have similar strengths and weaknesses and use similar strategies.[45] The competition between competitors CVS Corp. and Walgreens to be the largest drugstore chain in the United States demonstrates

Strategic Focus

Internet Wars—A Competition for Dominance between AOL and Microsoft

Companies are sometimes driven to compete in the same markets because of changing conditions. For example, AOL Time Warner and Microsoft traditionally have competed in different markets of the broadly defined technology industry. Microsoft's strength is in software development and sales. Windows, its desktop operating system, runs on 9 out of 10 computers and accounts for approximately 95 percent of Microsoft's operating income. In addition to its thriving online services business, AOL is primarily a media company with HBO, Time Warner, Netscape, and CNN as some of its recognized brands.

With reduced growth in their core businesses, however, AOL and Microsoft find themselves competing to gain dominance of the Internet. Both firms appear to believe that the same set of anywhere, anytime Web services is the key to future success. The desired Web services range from stock quotes to online music to interactive television with delivery being to the office, a customer's living room, or any wireless device. With the common strategic intent of gaining the prominent Web services delivery position via the Internet, the companies increasingly find themselves competing against each other in multiple markets. As an Internet analyst for CIBS World Markets observed, the companies are saying, "I'm keeping my fingers in all of your pies, and you're keeping a finger in all mine."

The key to Internet dominance is gaining online subscribers and then selling products and services to them. With over 31 million subscribers, AOL has a significant size advantage over Microsoft's MSN Online, which has 7 million subscribers. However, the rivalry for customers is becoming more intense. When AOL took the competitive action of increasing its rates for online access by $1.95 per month to $23.90 in July 2001, Microsoft responded by holding its monthly price at $21.95. MSN Online then launched its own competitive action, which was an offer of free service for three months. MSN Online claims that 40 percent of new subscribers in the first few months following this action were former AOL customers. Rivalry for subscribers likely will intensify further as a result of AOL's decision (action) to directly negotiate with PC manufacturers to install AOL on PC desktops.

The scope of competition between AOL and Microsoft is broad, as the firms' multimarket competition finds them competing against each other in online services for entertainment, communication, and information. Commonly free today, many of these services will eventually generate fees for providers. The firms are introducing competing online music subscription services, for example. AOL is partnering with Bertelsmann and EMI to offer its service while Microsoft is offering PressPlay though its partnership with Vivendi Universal and Sony.

Instant messaging is another online market in which both firms compete. AOL pioneered this concept, which allows users to send and receive messages using the Internet when they are simultaneously connected. Instant messaging is vital to customer retention because subscribers are less likely to switch services once they establish a screen name that their friends know and use. AOL currently dominates instant messaging with several million customers using the service during peak times. In an effort to take market share from AOL, Microsoft has bundled MSN Messenger, its instant messaging service, with its newest Windows version. This competitive action is intended to entice all Windows XP purchasers, including AOL subscribers, to switch to MSN Messenger.

SOURCES: 2002, Who's afraid of AOL Time Warner? *The Economist,* January 26, 54–55; 2001, From friends to foes, *The Economist,* June 23, 56–57; J. Angwin & R. Buckman, 2001, AOL, MSN unveil Web-service changes, *The Wall Street Journal,* October 16, B6; A. Borrus, 2001, AOL's point man in the Web war: How CEO Barry Schuler plans to leave Microsoft in the dust, *Business Week,* July 2, 56–57; P. Garcia, 2001, The big fight, *Money,* August 1, 29–33; J. Greene, 2001, Why AOL nixed a Microsoft deal, *Business Week,* July 2, 58; P. Lewis, 2001, AOL vs. Microsoft: Now it's war, *Fortune,* July 23, 88–89; J. Green & A. Borrus, 2001, Case vs. Gates: Playing for the Web jackpot, *Business Week,* June 18, 42; C. Yang, J. Greene & A. Park, 2001, AOL vs. Microsoft: With core operations slowing, both see future growth in the same places, *Business Week,* August 13, 28–30.

these expectations. These firms are using the integrated cost leadership/differentiation strategy to offer relatively low-cost goods with some differentiated features, such as services. Resource similarity, as shown by the firms' recent net income amounts ($746 million for CVS; $776.9 million for Walgreens), suggests that the firms might use similar strategies.[46]

As our discussion shows, in a competitor analysis, the firm analyzes each of its competitors in terms of market commonality and resource similarity. Determining market commonality isn't difficult. CVS and Walgreens, for example, are quite aware of the total number of markets in which they compete against each other as well as the number of storefronts each operates. Recent statistics show that there are 4,133 CVS stores in 34 states and 3,165 Walgreens stores in 43 states. Thus, these firms compete against each other in many markets.

In contrast to market commonality, assessing resource similarity can be difficult, particularly when critical resources are intangible (such as brand name, knowledge, trust, and the capacity to innovate) rather than tangible (for example, access to raw materials and a competitor's ability to borrow capital). As discussed in Chapter 3, a competitor's intangible resources are difficult to identify and understand, making an assessment of their value challenging. CVS and Walgreens know the amount of each other's annual net income (a tangible resource). However, it is difficult for CVS and Walgreens to determine if any intangible resources (such as knowledge and trust among employees) its competitor possesses can lead to a competitive advantage.

The results of the firm's competitor analyses can be mapped for visual comparisons. In Figure 5.3, we show different hypothetical intersections between the firm and individual competitors in terms of market commonality and resource similarity. These intersections indicate the extent to which the firm and those to which it has compared itself are competitors.[47] For example, the firm and its competitor displayed in quadrant I of Figure 5.3 have similar types and amounts of resources and use them to compete against each other in many markets that are important to each. These conditions lead to the conclusion that the firms modeled in quadrant I are direct and mutually acknowledged competitors. In contrast, the firm and its competitor shown in quadrant III share few markets and have little similarity in their resources, indicat-

Figure 5.3 A Framework of Competitor Analysis

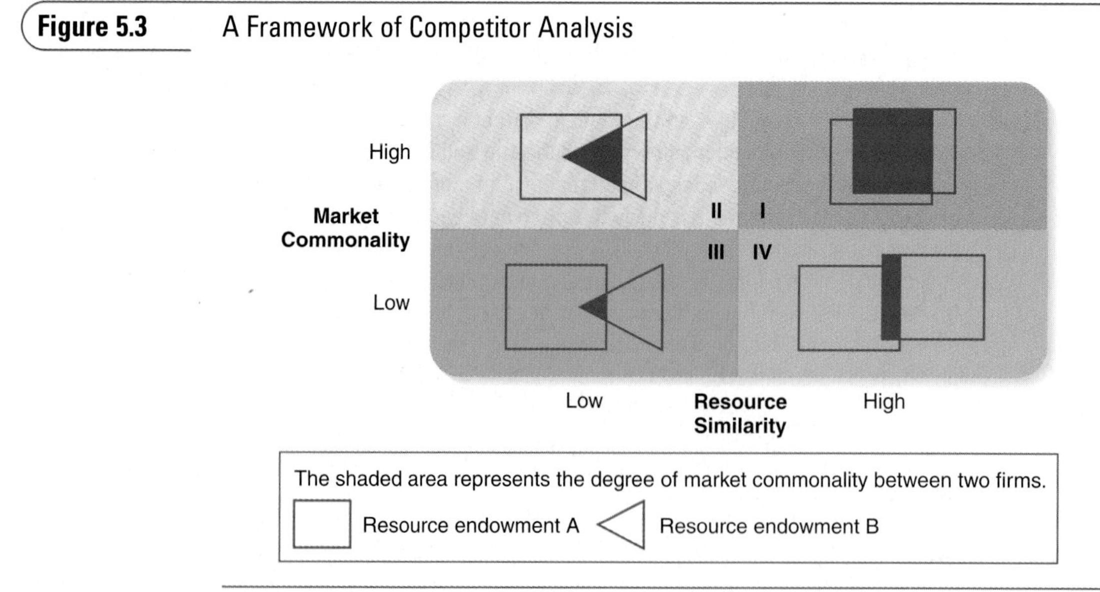

SOURCE: Adapted from M.-J. Chen, 1996, Competitor analysis and interfirm rivalry: Toward a theoretical integration, *Academy of Management Review*, 21: 100–134.

ing that they aren't direct and mutually acknowledged competitors. The firm's mapping of its competitive relationship with rivals is fluid as firms enter and exit markets and as companies' resources change in type and amount. Thus, the companies with whom the firm is a direct competitor change across time.

Drivers of Competitive Actions and Responses

As shown in Figure 5.2, market commonality and resource similarity influence the drivers (awareness, motivation, and ability) of competitive behavior. In turn, the drivers influence the firm's competitive behavior, as shown by the actions and responses it takes while engaged in competitive rivalry.[48]

Awareness, which is a prerequisite to any competitive action or response being taken by the firm or its competitor, refers to the extent to which competitors recognize the degree of their mutual interdependence that results from market commonality and resource similarity.[49] A lack of awareness can lead to excessive competition, resulting in a negative effect on all competitors' performance.[50] Awareness tends to be greatest when firms have highly similar resources (in terms of types and amounts) to use while competing against each other in multiple markets. CVS and Walgreens are fully aware of each other, as are FedEx and UPS, and Wal-Mart and France's Carrefour. The last two firms' joint awareness has increased as they use similar resources to compete against each other for dominant positions in multiple European markets.[51] Awareness affects the extent to which the firm understands the consequences of its competitive actions and responses.

Motivation, which concerns the firm's incentive to take action or to respond to a competitor's attack, relates to perceived gains and losses. Thus, a firm may be aware of competitors but may not be motivated to engage in rivalry with them if it perceives that its position will not improve as a result of doing so or that its market position won't be damaged if it doesn't respond.[52]

Market commonality affects the firm's perceptions and resulting motivation. For example, all else being equal, the firm is more likely to attack the rival with whom it has low market commonality than the one with whom it competes in multiple markets. The primary reason is that there are high stakes involved in trying to gain a more advantageous position over a rival with whom the firm shares many markets. As we mentioned earlier, multimarket competition can find a competitor responding to the firm's action in a market different from the one in which the initial action was taken. Actions and responses of this type can cause both firms to lose focus on core markets and to battle each other with resources that had been allocated for other purposes. Because of the high stakes of competition under the condition of market commonality, there is a high probability that the attacked firm will respond to its competitor's action in an effort to protect its position in one or more markets.[53]

In some instances, the firm may be aware of the large number of markets it shares with a competitor and may be motivated to respond to an attack by that competitor, but it lacks the ability to do so. *Ability* relates to each firm's resources and the flexibility they provide. Without available resources (such as financial capital and people), the firm lacks the ability to attack a competitor or respond to its actions. However, similar resources suggest similar abilities to attack and respond. When a firm faces a competitor with similar resources, careful study of a possible attack before initiating it is essential because the similarly resourced competitor is likely to respond to that action.

Resource *dissimilarity* also influences competitive actions and responses between firms, in that "the greater is the resource imbalance between the acting firm and competitors or potential responders, the greater will be the delay in response"[54] by the firm with a resource disadvantage. For example, Wal-Mart initially used its cost leadership strategy to compete only in small communities (those with a population of 25,000 or less). Using sophisticated logistics systems and extremely efficient purchasing practices as advantages, among others, Wal-Mart created what was at that time a new type of value (primarily in the form of wide selections of products at the lowest competitive prices) for customers in small retail markets. Local stores, facing resource deficiencies relative to Wal-Mart, lacked the ability to marshal resources at the pace required to respond quickly and effectively. However, even when facing competitors with greater resources (greater ability) or more attractive market positions, firms should eventually respond, no matter how daunting doing so seems.[55] Choosing not to respond can ultimately result in failure, as happened with at least some local retailers who didn't respond to Wal-Mart's competitive actions.

Competitive Rivalry

As defined earlier in the chapter, *competitive rivalry* is the ongoing set of competitive actions and competitive responses occurring between competing firms for an advantageous market position. Because the ongoing competitive action/response sequence between a firm and a competitor affects the performance of both firms,[56] it is important for companies to carefully study competitive rivalry to successfully use their strategies. Understanding a competitor's awareness, motivation, and ability helps the firm to predict the likelihood of an attack by that competitor and how likely it is that a competitor will respond to the actions taken against it.

As we described above, the predictions drawn from study of competitors in terms of awareness, motivation, and ability are grounded in market commonality and resource similarity. These predictions are fairly general. The value of the final set of predictions the firm develops about each of its competitor's competitive actions and responses is enhanced by studying the "Likelihood of Attack" factors (such as first-mover incentives and organizational size) and the "Likelihood of Response" factors (such as the actor's reputation) that are shown in Figure 5.2. Studying these factors allows the firm to develop a deeper understanding in order to refine the predictions it makes about its competitors' actions and responses.

A **competitive action** is a strategic or tactical action the firm takes to build or defend its competitive advantages or improve its market position.

A **competitive response** is a strategic or tactical action the firm takes to counter the effects of a competitor's competitive action.

A **strategic action or a strategic response** is a market-based move that involves a significant commitment of organizational resources and is difficult to implement and reverse.

A **tactical action or a tactical response** is a market-based move that is taken to fine-tune a strategy; it involves fewer resources and is relatively easy to implement and reverse.

Strategic and Tactical Actions

Firms use both strategic and tactical actions when forming their competitive actions and competitive responses in the course of engaging in competitive rivalry.[57] A **competitive action** is a strategic or tactical action the firm takes to build or defend its competitive advantages or improve its market position. A **competitive response** is a strategic or tactical action the firm takes to counter the effects of a competitor's competitive action. A **strategic action or a strategic response** is a market-based move that involves a significant commitment of organizational resources and is difficult to implement and reverse. A **tactical action or a tactical response** is a market-based move that is taken to fine-tune a strategy; it involves fewer resources and is relatively easy to implement and reverse. UPS's 1994 decision to establish a logistics group (see the Opening Case) is an example of a strategic action. Hyundai Motor Co.'s expenditures on research and development and plant expansion to support the firm's desire to be one of the world's largest carmakers by 2010[58] also are strategic actions. The Strategic Focus on page 159 describes strategic actions taken by competitors Airbus Industrie and Boeing.

A competitor's strategic action signals that significant amounts of resources are being committed to a project and that once underway, it will be difficult for the action to be reversed. As explained in the Strategic Focus, Boeing and Airbus Industrie are initiating strategic actions that differ based on the companies' interpretations of the future of air travel.

Strategic Focus

Airplane Wars—Airbus and Boeing's Use of Different Strategic Actions

As competitors, Boeing and Airbus Industrie share multiple markets, have relatively similar resources in terms of what is available for the commercial aircraft market, and have pursued similar strategies. However, based on their predictions of the air transport industry's future, they are taking different strategic actions regarding the manufacture of tomorrow's large commercial airliners.

The differences in the firm's strategic actions started to become visible in December 2000 when Airbus launched efforts to build the A380, the world's largest commercial aircraft. The 550-650 seat double-decker superjumbo jet is designed to compete directly against the high end of Boeing's lucrative 747 series. The A380 is a primary challenger to the more than three-decade dominance of the 350-plus seat commercial airliner market Boeing has enjoyed with its 747 series. Airbus has committed $12 billion to the A380's design and development, which is scheduled to make its commercial debut with Singapore Airlines in 2006. Airbus is touting the need for the A380 based on its belief that airline traffic will continue to grow, intensifying problems in already congested airport hubs.

In response to Airbus's A380, Boeing announced plans to build a 520-seat version of the 747 as a competing superjumbo aircraft. In March 2001, after failing to win orders for the 747X, Boeing changed direction and scrapped the project. As part of an evolving strategic action, Boeing made this decision before it committed significant levels of resources to design and build the 747X. Boeing's announcement effectively ceded the superjumbo jet market to Airbus.

Reflecting a radical change, Boeing also indicated that it believed that speed, not size, will be the most important consideration in the future regarding air travel. Rather than the continued dominance of the hub system, Boeing concluded after further analyses that passenger demand for increased point-to-point travel options will result in market fragmentation and a reduction in the importance of hub systems. In fragmented markets, Boeing believes that carriers will need speedy, long-range mid-size planes to bypass major hubs for nonstop service from more remote destinations. In Boeing CEO Alan Mulally's words: "We decided point-to-point routes are the heart of the market. There was a lot of talk on large aircraft, but at the end of the day, after working with airlines, we decided to focus on longer range and increasing speed." Based on these beliefs, Boeing started design development of its futuristic Sonic Cruiser, a 250-passenger jet designed to travel at 95 percent of the speed of sound and to fly above 40,000 feet. The Sonic Cruiser is expected to reduce air travel time by 20 percent as a result of a radical new design, featuring a dramatically swept wing and two wing-mounted jet engines in the rear.

Some analysts believe that the A380 may have a ready market. In the words of one, "There will always be huge amounts of tourist traffic." Boeing's Sonic Cruiser may be a riskier project in terms of consumer acceptance and design feasibility. Indeed, industry experts estimate that because of fuel burn, the Sonic Cruiser's operating costs will be 12 percent to 15 percent higher than the 250-seat 767 that it would replace. Making an airplane travel faster requires using bigger engines, which weigh more and consume additional fuel. In turn, the aircraft body must be made larger to support the bigger engines, which creates more drag and ultimately burns more fuel. To obtain revenues that exceed this higher operating cost would require the Sonic Cruiser to fly mostly business class passengers, who are willing to pay a 20 percent premium over today's fares. Airbus is skeptical of the Sonic Cruiser's viability, as shown by a company official's claim that airline companies' ". . . expectations are economics and environment-friendly aircraft—the Sonic Cruiser is more public relations than engineering."

The reality of September 11, 2001 challenges the viability of Airbus and Boeing's evolving competitive actions regarding next generation commercial jets. Previous predictions that airline traffic will continue to grow 5 percent annually over the next 20 years are being tested. Not only have airlines reduced flights and employees in response to lower passenger levels, they also decreased or are canceling orders for new aircraft. These actions are affecting both Boeing and Airbus. Boeing has laid off 30,000 employees and cut production by 20 percent. Airbus recently received cancellation notices for 73 planes in a single month and halted plans for increasing capacity. This climate of severe uncertainty could potentially derail plans for development of the A380 and the Sonic Cruiser. Airbus requires 250 orders for the A380 project to be profitable. Even before September 11, the company had only 62 firm orders and 40 options to purchase. Boeing may now be less willing to commit substantial resources to the design and potential development of an aircraft that differs radically from current commercial jets. Thus, both firms must think carefully about the viability of their strategic actions in light of a highly uncertain and unpredictable external environment.

SOURCES: C. Matlack, 2002, Earth to Airbus: What's the flight plan? *Business Week,* January 21, 48; 2001, Place your bets, *The Economist,* June 23, 60–61; H. Banks, 2001, Paper plane, *Forbes,* May 28, 52–53; G. Cramb & M. Odell, 2001, Companies and finance Europe: Airbus plans for expansion on hold, *Financial Times,* September 21, 33; S. Holmes, 2001, Boeing's sonic bruiser, *Business Week,* July 2, 64–68; S. Holmes, C. Dawson, & C. Matlack, 2001, Rumble over Tokyo, *Business Week,* April 2, 80–81; C. Matlack & S. Holmes, 2001, Why Airbus could go into a dive, *Business Week,* October 1, 83; S. McClenahen, 2001, Planely different, *Industry Week,* June 11, 68–72; A. Sequeo, 2001, Boeing plans to build smaller, faster jet, *The Wall Street Journal,* March 20, A3; P. Sparaco, 2001, Airbus and Boeing snipe over speed versus size, *Aviation Week & Space Technology,* June 25, 26–27; P. Sparaco, 2001, Airbus thinks bigger, not faster, *Aviation Week & Space Technology,* June 18, 106–112; P. Sparaco, 2001, Airbus' production schedule riding out times, *Aviation Week & Space Technology,* September 24, 33; B. Sweetman, 2001, Three was a crowd, *Air Transport World,* September, 76–80.

Hyundai has become a popular brand in Montgomery, Alabama. The city provided more than $234 million in public incentives to Hyundai to open a plant there (about $117,317 for each of the anticipated 2,000 jobs). The $1 billion plant may help the firm achieve its goal to become one of the world's largest automakers, as Hyundai expects it to produce 300,000 vehicles a year by 2005.

As the discussion in the Strategic Focus indicates, Airbus and Boeing have committed significant amounts of organizational resources to develop the A380 and the Sonic Cruiser, respectively. These actions will be difficult to reverse in that start-up development costs have been incurred and expectations have been established for two customer groups—airline companies and travelers. Disappointing these groups could damage either firm's reputation for being an innovator as well as each company's objective to gain dominance over its major rival. On the other hand, even strategic actions should be reversed when dramatic external environmental changes (such as those caused by September 11) call their viability into serious question.

As we noted earlier, a tactical action or a tactical response is a market-based move that a firm makes to fine-tune a strategy. It involves fewer and more general organizational resources and is relatively easy to implement and reverse, compared to a strategic action or a strategic response. Price changes in particular markets such as those made by airline companies are tactical actions. While reversing their strategic decisions to develop the A380 and Sonic Cruiser is difficult, deciding to reverse a tactical action or response, such as a minor modification to an existing aircraft, is relatively easy for both Airbus and Boeing.

Likelihood of Attack

In addition to market commonality, resource similarity, and the drivers of awareness, motivation, and ability, other factors also affect the likelihood a competitor will use strategic actions and tactical actions to attack its competitors. Three of these factors—first mover incentives, organizational size, and quality—are discussed next.

First-mover Incentives

A **first mover** is a firm that takes an initial competitive action in order to build or defend its competitive advantages or to improve its market position.

A **first mover** is a firm that takes an initial competitive action in order to build or defend its competitive advantages or to improve its market position. The first mover concept has been influenced by the work of the famous economist Joseph Schumpeter, who argued that firms achieve competitive advantage by taking innovative actions[59] (innovation is defined and described in detail in Chapter 13). In general, first movers "allocate funds for product innovation and development, aggressive advertising, and advanced research and development."[60]

The benefits of being a successful first mover can be substantial. Especially in fast-cycle markets (discussed later in the chapter) where changes occur rapidly and where it is virtually impossible to sustain a competitive advantage for any period of time, ". . . a first mover may experience five to ten times the valuation and revenue of a second mover."[61] This evidence suggests that although first mover benefits are never absolute, they are often critical to firm success in industries experiencing rapid technological developments and relatively short product life cycles.[62]

In addition to earning above-average returns until its competitors respond to its successful competitive action, the first mover can gain (1) the loyalty of customers who may become committed to the goods or services of the firm that first made them available and (2) market share that can be difficult for competitors to take during future competitive rivalry. For example, Yahoo! Japan moved first to establish an online auction market service in Japan. Rival eBay entered the market five months later. eBay's delayed response in an industry rife with rapid technological change was a critical mistake, as shown by the fact that first mover Yahoo! Japan recently held 95 percent of the online auction market in Japan while rival eBay's share was only 3 percent. A company official commented about why Yahoo! Japan moved first to establish an online auction market in Japan. The firm wanted to do so because, "We knew catching up with a front-runner is hard, because in auctions, more buyers bring more sellers."[63]

The firm trying to predict its competitors' competitive actions might rightly conclude that the benefits we described above could serve as incentives for many of them to act as first movers. However, while a firm's competitors might be motivated to be first movers, they may lack the ability to do so. First movers tend to be aggressive and willing to experiment with innovation and take higher, yet reasonable levels of risk.[64] To be a first mover, the firm must have readily available the amount of resources that is required to significantly invest in R&D as well as to rapidly and successfully produce and market a stream of innovative products.

Organizational slack makes it possible for firms to have the ability (as measured by available resources) to be first movers. *Slack* is the buffer or cushion provided by actual or obtainable resources that aren't currently in use.[65] Thus, slack is liquid resources that the firm can quickly allocate to support the actions such as R&D investments and aggressive marketing campaigns that lead to first mover benefits. This relationship between slack and the ability to be a first mover allows the firm to predict that a competitor who is a first mover likely has available slack and will probably take aggressive competitive actions to continuously introduce innovative products. Furthermore, the firm can predict that as a first mover, a competitor will try to rapidly gain market share and customer loyalty in order to earn above-average returns until its competitors are able to effectively respond to its first move.

Firms studying competitors should realize that being a first mover carries risk. For example, it is difficult to accurately estimate the returns that will be earned from introducing product innovations to the marketplace.[66] Additionally, the first mover's cost to develop a product innovation can be substantial, reducing the slack available to it to support further innovation. Thus, the firm should carefully study the results a competitor achieves as a first mover. Continuous success by the competitor suggests additional product innovations, while lack of product acceptance over the course of the competitor's innovations may indicate less willingness in the future to accept the risks of being a first mover.

A **second mover** is a firm that responds to the first mover's competitive action, typically through imitation.

A **second mover** is a firm that responds to the first mover's competitive action, typically through imitation. More cautious than the first mover, the second mover studies customers' reactions to product innovations. In the course of doing so, the second mover also tries to find any mistakes the first mover made so that it can avoid the problems resulting from them. Often, successful imitation of the first mover's innovations allows the second mover ". . . to avoid both the mistakes and the huge spending of the pioneers (first movers)."[67] Second movers also have the time to develop processes and technologies that are more efficient than those used by the first mover.[68] Greater efficiencies could result in lower costs for the second mover. Overall, the outcomes of the first mover's competitive actions may provide an effective blueprint for second and even late movers (as described below) as they determine the nature and timing of their competitive responses.[69]

Determining that a competitor thinks of itself as an effective second mover allows the firm to predict that that competitor will tend to respond quickly to first movers' successful, innovation-based market entries. If the firm itself is a first mover, then it can expect a successful second mover competitor to study its market entries and to respond to them quickly. As a second mover, the competitor will try to respond with a product that creates customer value exceeding the value provided by the product that the firm introduced initially as a first mover. The most successful second movers are able to rapidly and meaningfully interpret market feedback to respond quickly, yet successfully to the first mover's successful innovations.[70]

A **late mover** is a firm that responds to a competitive action, but only after considerable time has elapsed after the first mover's action and the second mover's response.

A **late mover** is a firm that responds to a competitive action, but only after considerable time has elapsed after the first mover's action and the second mover's response. Typically, a late response is better than no response at all, although any success achieved from the late competitive response tends to be slow in coming and considerably less than that achieved by first and second movers. Thus, the firm competing against a late mover can predict that that competitor will likely enter a particular market only after both the first and second movers have achieved success by doing so. Moreover, on a relative basis, the firm can predict that the late mover's competitive action will allow it to earn even average returns only when enough time has elapsed for it to understand how to create value that is more attractive to customers than is the value offered by the first and second movers' products. Although exceptions do exist, the firm can predict that as a competitor, the late mover's competitive actions will be relatively ineffective, certainly as compared to those initiated by first movers and second movers.

Organizational Size

An organization's size affects the likelihood that it will take competitive actions as well as the types of actions it will take and their timing.[71] In general, compared to large companies, small firms are more likely to launch competitive actions and tend to be quicker in doing so. Smaller firms are thus perceived as nimble and flexible competitors who rely on speed and surprise to defend their competitive advantages or develop new ones while engaged in competitive rivalry, especially with large companies, to gain an advantageous market position.[72] Small firms' flexibility and nimbleness allow them to develop greater variety in their competitive actions as compared to large firms, which tend to limit the types of competitive actions used when competing with rivals.[73]

Compared to small firms, large ones are likely to initiate more competitive actions as well as strategic actions during a given time period.[74] Thus, when studying its competitors in terms of organizational size, the firm should use a measurement of size such as total sales revenue or total number of employees to compare itself with each competitor. The competitive actions the firm likely will encounter from competitors larger than it is will be different than the competitive actions it will encounter from competitors who are smaller.

The organizational size factor has an additional layer of complexity associated with it. When engaging in competitive rivalry, the firm usually wants to take a large number of competitive actions against its competitors. As we have described, large organizations commonly have the slack resources required to launch a larger number of total competitive actions. On the other hand, smaller firms have the flexibility needed to launch a greater variety of competitive actions. Ideally, the firm would like to have the ability to launch a large number of unique competitive actions. A statement made by Herb Kelleher, former CEO of Southwest Airlines, addresses this matter: "Think and act big and we'll get smaller. Think and act small and we'll get bigger."[75]

In the context of competitive rivalry, Kelleher's statement can be interpreted to mean that relying on a limited number of type of competitive actions (which is the large firm's tendency) can lead to reduced competitive success across time, partly because competitors learn how to effectively respond to what is a limited set of competitive actions taken by a given firm. In contrast, remaining flexible and nimble (which is the small firm's tendency) in order to develop and use a wide variety of competitive actions contributes to success against rivals.

Wal-Mart appears to be an example of a large firm that has the flexibility required to take many types of competitive actions. With $216 billion in sales and a $252 billion market capitalization, Wal-Mart is one of the world's two largest companies in terms of sales revenue along with ExxonMobil. In only six years following its entry into the grocery market, Wal-Mart has become one of the largest grocery retailers in the United States. This accomplishment demonstrates Wal-Mart's ability to successfully compete against its various rivals, even long-established grocers. In spite of its size, the firm remains highly flexible as it takes both strategic actions (such as rapid global expansion) and tactical actions.

Analysts believe that Wal-Mart's tactical actions are critical to its success and show a great deal of flexibility. For example, "every humble store worker has the power to lower the price on any Wal-Mart product if he spots it cheaper elsewhere."[76] Decision-making responsibility and authority have been delegated to the level of the individual worker to make certain that the firm's cost leadership strategy always results in the lowest prices for customers. Managers and employees both spend a good deal of time thinking about additional strategic and tactical actions, respectively, that might enhance the firm's performance. Thus, it is possible that Wal-Mart has met the expectation suggested by Kelleher's statement, in that it is a large firm that ". . . remains stuck to its small-town roots" in order to think and act like the small firm capable of using a wide variety of competitive actions.[77] Wal-Mart's competitors might feel confident in predicting that the firm's competitive actions will be a combination of the tendencies shown by small and large companies.

In the Strategic Focus on page 164, we describe Lehman Brothers' ability to outperform its larger rivals. Although smaller than its primary competitors, its success is resulting in growth, partly at the expense of competitors. The competitive challenge for Lehman will be to continue thinking and acting as a small firm as it becomes a larger organization.

Strategic Focus

Investment Banking Competition: How Lehman Brothers Outperformed Its Larger Rivals

Competing in an industry known for high profile mergers and acquisitions, Lehman Brothers is proving that size is not the most important determinant of competitive success. Its $19 billion market capitalization is relatively small compared to capitalizations of $50 billion for Merrill Lynch and $71 billion for Morgan Stanley. However, Lehman's recent return on equity performances exceed those earned by its peers. Lehman has strong positions in fixed income, equities, and investment banking.

To remain successful, the firm is taking a number of competitive actions, including diversifying into different product markets such as equity issuance and mergers and acquisitions (M&A) advisory work. In 2001, Lehman more than doubled its share of the equity underwriting market from 3 percent to 7 percent. Lehman also is diversifying geographically, with 30 percent of earnings now being generated in Europe. Possibly contributing to Lehman's competitive success is its ability to avoid problems (such as frequent top-level managerial changes) that have affected its competitors.

Lehman's past hasn't been trouble free. The early 1980s saw the company's investment bankers and debt traders in the midst of a bitter battle over compensation and firm strategy. Undercapitalized and demoralized as a result of its internal struggles, Lehman sold itself to American Express in 1984. The two companies' cultures never meshed, resulting in the weakened Lehman's spinoff in 1994.

Making Lehman's current success somewhat impressive is that roughly five years ago, industry analysts were speculating that the firm would either be acquired or be forced to file for bankruptcy. Wall Street's growing belief that smaller, independent investment banks couldn't compete against larger rivals accounted for the dire predictions about Lehman's independence and performance ability. Industry characteristics seem to provide partial support for the predictions, in that investment banks in recent years have faced increasing pressure to offer credit to their corporate customers in addition to traditional advisory services. Most investment banks lack the sizable balance sheets required to lend significant sums of money to support their customers' intended merger or acquisition plans or other business expansions. These pressures resulted in investment banks becoming vulnerable to well-capitalized commercial banks, which succeeded in attracting the investment banks' most lucrative corporate relationships and infringed on their advisory business. In response, boutique investment banks merged with commercial banks and each other, creating industry giants such as J. P. Morgan Chase and Saloman Smith Barney.

Determined to find innovative competitive actions his firm could take to successfully compete against larger rivals, Lehman's current CEO, Richard Fuld, has worked diligently to foster cooperation within the firm. The focus is on being cost efficient and nimble as it competes against its rivals. The company's compensation structure creates incentives for employees to work together to achieve these goals. At the managerial level, for example, division heads are compensated identically based on overall firm performance. "When we line up with a customer, it's about how we approach them as a team," states Fuld, "It's not about the lone rangers. Lone rangers do not live long." Many of Lehman's larger competitors use compensation systems that reward primarily on the basis of individuals' performance.

Additionally, Fuld has fostered an organizational culture that is more open than traditionally is the case with Wall Street companies. He has shunned the executive suite in favor of a centrally located glass office and routinely invites employees to breakfast. As a member of the team, each employee is expected to contribute ideas about competitive actions Lehman can take to continue outperforming its competitors. Employee turnover is lower at Lehman than is the case at many of its competitors. In fact, Lehman's top management team has been together since 1996, and the average tenure of the firm's senior executives is 22 years.

The success attained through some of Lehman's strategic actions (for example, entering and exiting product markets on the basis of strict guidelines) and tactical actions (such as making changes to how services are delivered to customers) is eliciting responses from competitors. For example, Merrill Lynch's new CEO recently noted that his firm will ". . . double up in areas that are high-profit and chop unflinchingly where making money is harder." Merrill Lynch executives believe that actions such as these should improve their firm's ability to successfully compete against Lehman Brothers and its other competitors as well.

SOURCES: 2001, Surviving Wall Street's blues, *The Economist,* September 8, 69; S. Brady, J. Brown, C. Cockerill, A. Currie, A. Helk, P. Lee, J. Marshall, J. Morris, & F. Salmon, 2001, A new global bulge bracket, *Euromoney,* July, 55–68; R. Frank & A. Raghaven, 2001, Rebuilding Wall Street, *The Wall Street Journal,* November 7, C1; C. Gasparino, 2001, Bear Stearns and Lehman push their way past big guns, *The Wall Street Journal,* July 6, C1; G. Silverman & C. Pretzlik, 2001, Interview—Lehman Brothers' Richard Fuld, *Financial Times,* August 16, 16–18; E. Thornton, 2001, Lehman Brothers: So who needs to be big? *BusinessWeek Online,* http://www.businessweek.com, July 16; E. Thornton, A. Tergesen, & D. Welch, 2001, Shaking up Merrill, *Business Week,* November 12, 96–102.

As described in the Strategic Focus, Lehman Brothers has taken a number of competitive actions, such as changing its compensation system and entering new markets, since being spun off in 1994. Moreover, its compensation system contributes to the firm's flexibility and the variety of competitive actions it can take. An outcome of the compensation is the expectation that all employees will offer ideas about what the firm can do to improve its performance. This flexibility should serve Lehman well as some of its competitors (for example, Merrill Lynch) attempt to respond with actions similar to Lehman's.

Quality

Quality exists when the firm's goods or services meet or exceed customers' expectations.

Quality has many definitions, including well-established ones relating it to the production of goods or services with zero defects[78] and seeing it as a never-ending cycle of continuous improvement.[79] From a strategic perspective, we consider quality to be an outcome of how the firm completes primary and support activities (see Chapter 2). Thus, **quality** exists when the firm's goods or services meet or exceed customers' expectations.

In addition to the more traditional manufacturing and service sectors, quality is also important in business-to-business (B2B) transactions.[80] Customers may be interested in measuring the quality of a firm's products against a broad range of dimensions. Sample quality dimensions for goods and services in which customers commonly express an interest are shown in Table 5.1. Thus, in the eyes of customers, quality is about doing the right things relative to performance measures that are important to them.[81] Quality is possible only when top-level managers support it and when its importance is institutionalized throughout the entire organization.[82] When quality is institutionalized and valued by all, employees and managers alike become vigilant about continuously finding ways to improve quality.[83]

Quality is a universal theme in the global economy and is a necessary but not sufficient condition for competitive success. Another way of saying this is that "Quality used to be a competitive issue out there, but now it's just the basic denominator to being in the market."[84] Without quality, a firm's products lack credibility, meaning that customers don't think of them as viable options. Indeed, customers won't consider buying a product until they believe that it can satisfy at least their base level expectations in terms of quality dimensions that are important to them. For years, quality was an issue for Jaguar automobiles as the carmaker endured frequent

Table 5.1 Quality Dimensions of Goods and Services

Product Quality Dimensions

1. *Performance*—Operating characteristics
2. *Features*—Important special characteristics
3. *Flexibility*—Meeting operating specifications over some period of time
4. *Durability*—Amount of use before performance deteriorates
5. *Conformance*—Match with preestablished standards
6. *Serviceability*—Ease and speed of repair
7. *Aesthetics*—How a product looks and feels
8. *Perceived quality*—Subjective assessment of characteristics (product image)

Service Quality Dimensions

1. *Timeliness*—Performed in the promised period of time
2. *Courtesy*—Performed cheerfully
3. *Consistency*—Giving all customers similar experiences each time
4. *Convenience*—Accessibility to customers
5. *Completeness*—Fully serviced, as required
6. *Accuracy*—Performed correctly each time

SOURCES: Adapted from J. W. Dean, Jr., & J. R. Evans, 1994, *Total Quality: Management, Organization and Society,* St. Paul, MN: West Publishing Company; H. V. Roberts & B. F. Sergesketter, 1993, *Quality Is Personal,* New York: The Free Press; D. Garvin, 1988, *Managed Quality: The Strategic and Competitive Edge,* New York: The Free Press.

complaints from drivers about poor quality. As a result of recent actions addressing this issue, quality has improved to the point where customers now view the cars as credible products.[85]

Poor quality also increases costs, which damages the firm's profitability. For example, Ford Motor Company recently ranked worst of the top seven global auto companies in quality. According to former Ford CEO Jacques Nasser, quality problems (which led to higher warranty expenses) and related production delays cost the firm more than $1 billion in lost profits in 2000 alone.[86]

Total quality management (TQM) is a "managerial innovation that emphasizes an organization's total commitment to the customer and to continuous improvement of every process through the use of data-driven, problem-solving approaches based on empowerment of employee groups and teams."

To improve quality or to maintain a focus on it, firms often become involved with total quality management. **Total quality management (TQM)** is a "managerial innovation that emphasizes an organization's total commitment to the customer and to continuous improvement of every process through the use of data-driven, problem-solving approaches based on empowerment of employee groups and teams."[87] Through TQM, firms seek to (1) increase customer satisfaction, (2) cut costs, and (3) reduce the amount of time required to introduce innovative products to the marketplace.[88] Ford is relying on TQM to help "root out" its quality flaws[89] while competitor General Motors is ". . . scrambling to narrow the quality gap that its executives say is the main reason consumers shy away from GM."[90]

Quality affects competitive rivalry. The firm studying a competitor whose products suffer from poor quality can predict that the competitor's costs are high and that its sales revenue will likely decline until the quality issues are resolved. In addition, the firm can predict that the competitor likely won't be aggressive in terms of taking competitive actions, given that its quality problems must be corrected in order to gain credibility with customers. However, once corrected, that competitor is likely to take competitive actions emphasizing significant product quality improvements. Hyundai

Motor Co.'s experiences illustrate these expectations.

Immediately upon becoming CEO of Hyundai Motor Co. in March 1999, Chung Mong Koo started touring the firm's manufacturing facilities. Appalled at what he saw, he told workers and managers alike that, "The only way we can survive is to raise our quality to Toyota's level."[91] To dramatically improve quality, a quality-control unit was established and significant resources (over $1 billion annually) were allocated to research and development (R&D) in order to build cars that could compete on price and deliver on quality. Essentially, Koo introduced Hyundai to TQM through the decisions he made to improve the firm's performance.

Outcomes from Hyundai's focus on quality improvements are impressive. Survey results indicate that Hyundai's quality has improved 28 percent in the last few years as compared to an average 14 percent improvement in the industry. Another indicator of dramatic quality improvements is *Car & Driver*'s rating of Hyundai behind only Nissan, Honda, and Toyota, but ahead of Dodge, Chevrolet, Ford, and Buick in the magazine's recent tests of eight mid-size sedans. Quality was an important criterion used in the tests.[92]

While concentrating on quality improvements, Hyundai didn't launch aggressive competitive actions, as competitors could predict would likely be the case. However, as could also be predicted by firms studying Hyundai as a competitor, improvements to the quality of Hyundai's products has helped the firm to become a more aggressive competitor. Signaling a strong belief in its products' quality, Hyundai now offers a 10-year drive-train warranty in the United States, which the firm has selected as a key market. As a result of improved quality and the innovative outcomes from its R&D investments, Hyundai also introduced the Santa Fe in 2000. A well-conceived sport-utility vehicle (SUV), the Santa Fe was designed and built to outperform Toyota's RAV4 and Honda's CR-V. The Santa Fe's introduction indicates that Hyundai is willing to aggressively attack its competitors in the SUV market with what has turned out to be an innovatively designed and quality-built product.[93]

Likelihood of Response

The success of a firm's competitive action is affected both by the likelihood that a competitor will respond to it as well as by the type (strategic or tactical) and effectiveness of that response. As noted earlier, a competitive response is a strategic or tactical action the firm takes to counter the effects of a competitor's competitive action. FedEx's decision to offer home package delivery by ground is a strategic response to at least one strategic action (establishing a logistics business) taken by UPS (see the Opening Case). In general, a firm is likely to respond to a competitor's action when the consequences of that action are better use of the competitor's competitive advantages or improvement in its market position, or when the action damages the firm's ability to use its advantages or when its market position becomes less defensible.[94]

In addition to market commonality and resource similarity and awareness, motivation, and ability, firms study three other factors—type of competitive action, reputation, and market dependence—to predict how a competitor is likely to respond to competitive actions.

Type of Competitive Action

Competitive responses to strategic actions differ from responses to tactical actions. These differences allow the firm to predict a competitor's likely response to a competitive action that has been launched against it. Of course, a general prediction is that strategic actions receive strategic responses while tactical responses are taken to counter the effects of tactical actions.

In general, strategic actions elicit fewer total competitive responses.[95] The reason is that as with strategic actions, strategic responses, such as market-based moves, involve a significant commitment of resources and are difficult to implement and reverse. Moreover, the time needed for a strategic action to be implemented and its effectiveness assessed delays the competitor's response to that action.[96] The almost 17-year delay for UPS to respond to FedEx's strategic action of establishing the overnight delivery market shows how long it can take for a competitor to launch a response (see the Opening Case). In contrast, a competitor likely will respond quickly to a tactical action, such as when an airline company almost immediately matches a competitor's tactical action of reducing prices in certain markets. And, either strategic actions or tactical actions that target a large number of a rival's customers are likely to be targeted with strong responses.[97]

Actor's Reputation

In the context of competitive rivalry, an actor is the firm taking an action or response while *reputation* is ". . . the positive or negative attribute ascribed by one rival to another based on past competitive behavior."[98] Thus, to predict the likelihood of a competitor's response to a current or planned action, the firm studies the responses that the competitor has taken previously when attacked—past behavior is assumed to be a reasonable predictor of future behavior.

Competitors are more likely to respond to either strategic or tactical actions that are taken by a market leader.[99] For example, Home Depot is the world's largest home improvement retailer and the second largest U.S. retailer (behind Wal-Mart). Known as an innovator in its core home improvement market as well as for having an ability to develop successful new store formats such as its EXPO Design Centers and Villager's Hardware Stores, Home Depot can predict that its competitors carefully study its actions, especially the strategic ones, and that they are likely to respond to them. Lowe's Companies, the second largest U.S. home improvement retailer and Home Depot's major competitor, is aware of Home Depot's actions. Lowe's also has both the motivation and ability to respond to actions by Home Depot. For example, partly in response to Home Depot's consistent focus on updating the retail concept of its core home improvement stores, Lowe's continues to transform ". . . its store base from a chain of small stores into a chain of destination of home improvement warehouses,"[100] increasing the similarity of its store design with Home Depot's as a result of doing so.

Other evidence suggests that commonly successful actions, especially strategic actions, will be quickly imitated, almost regardless of the actor's reputation. For example, although a second mover, IBM committed significant resources to enter the PC market. When IBM was immediately successful in this endeavor, competitors such as Dell, Compaq, and Gateway responded with strategic actions to enter the market. IBM's reputation as well as its successful strategic action strongly influenced entry by these competitors. Thus, in terms of competitive rivalry, IBM could predict that responses would follow its entry to the PC market if that entry proved successful. In addition, IBM could predict that those competitors would try to create value in slightly different ways, such as Dell's legendary decision to sell directly to consumers rather than to use storefronts as a distribution channel.

In contrast to a firm with a strong reputation, such as IBM, competitors are less likely to take responses against companies with reputations for competitive behavior that is risky, complex, and unpredictable. The firm with a reputation as a price predator (an actor that frequently reduces prices to gain or maintain market share) generates few responses to its pricing tactical actions. The reason is that price predators, which typically increase prices once their market share objective is reached, lack credibility with their competitors.[101] The opposite of a price predator in terms of reputation, Wal-Mart is widely recognized for its pricing integrity,[102] giving the firm a great deal of credibility when it launches a tactical action or response around the prices of its goods.

Dependence on the Market

Market dependence denotes the extent to which a firm's revenues or profits are derived from a particular market.[103] In general, firms can predict that competitors with high market dependence are likely to respond strongly to attacks threatening their market position.[104] Interestingly, the threatened firm in these instances tends not to respond quickly, suggesting the importance of an effective response to an attack on the firm's position in a critical market.

A firm such as Wm. Wrigley Company would be expected to respond aggressively, but not necessarily quickly to an attack. With well-known brands such as Spearmint, Doublemint, Juicy Fruit, Big Red, Extra, and Hubba Bubba bubble gum, Wrigley is the world's largest producer of chewing gum, accounting for roughly 50 percent of total chewing gum sales volume worldwide. Through its Amurol Confections subsidiary (which produces several products such as liquid gel candy, suckers, and hard roll candies), Wrigley has a minor amount of diversification. However, chewing gum accounts for more than 90 percent of the firm's total revenue as well as earnings.[105] Wrigley's dominant market position provides the flexibility needed to respond aggressively but carefully to actions that might be taken by a competitor, such as Adams. But, if Adams were to attack Wrigley's sugarless Extra gum through actions related to Adams's Trident, for example, it should understand that Wrigley's dependence on the chewing gum market will induce it to respond aggressively to protect its position in the sugarless gum market.

Competitive Dynamics

Whereas competitive rivalry concerns the ongoing actions and responses between a firm and its competitors for an advantageous market position, competitive dynamics concerns the ongoing actions and responses taking place among *all* firms competing within a market for advantageous positions.

To explain competitive rivalry, we described (1) factors that determine the degree to which firms are competitors (market commonality and resource similarity), (2) the drivers of competitive behavior for individual firms (awareness, motivation, and ability) and (3) factors affecting the likelihood a competitor will act or attack (first mover incentives, organizational size, and quality) and respond (type of competitive action, reputation, and market dependence). Building and sustaining competitive advantages are at the core of competitive rivalry, in that advantages are the link to an advantageous market position.

To explain competitive dynamics, we discuss the effects of varying rates of competitive speed in different markets (called slow-cycle, fast-cycle, and standard-cycle markets, defined below) on the behavior (actions and responses) of all competitors within a given market. Competitive behaviors as well as the reasons or logic for taking them are similar within each market type, but differ across market type.[106] Thus, competitive dynamics differs in slow-cycle, fast-cycle, and standard-cycle markets. The sustainability of the firm's competitive advantages is an important difference among the three market types.

As noted in Chapter 1, firms want to sustain their advantages for as long as possible, although no advantage is permanently sustainable. The degree of sustainability is affected by how quickly competitive advantages can be imitated and how costly it is to do so.

Slow-Cycle Markets

Slow-cycle markets are markets in which the firm's competitive advantages are shielded from imitation for what are commonly long periods of time and where imitation is costly.

Slow-cycle markets are markets in which the firm's competitive advantages are shielded from imitation for what are commonly long periods of time and where imitation is costly.[107] Competitive advantages are sustainable in slow-cycle markets.

Building a one-of-a-kind competitive advantage that is proprietary leads to competitive success in a slow-cycle market. This type of advantage is difficult for competitors to understand. As discussed in Chapter 3, a difficult-to-understand and costly-to-imitate advantage results from unique historical conditions, causal ambiguity, and/or social complexity. Copyrights, geography, patents, and ownership of an information resource are examples of what leads to one-of-a-kind advantages.[108] Once a proprietary advantage is developed, the firm's competitive behavior in a slow-cycle market is oriented to protecting, maintaining, and extending that advantage. Thus, the competitive dynamics in slow-cycle markets involve all firms concentrating on competitive actions and responses that enable them to protect, maintain, and extend their proprietary competitive advantage.

Walt Disney Co. continues to extend its proprietary characters, such as Mickey Mouse, Minnie Mouse, and Goofy. These characters have a unique historical development as a result of Walt and Roy Disney's creativity and vision for entertaining people. Products based on the characters seen in Disney's animated films are sold through Disney's theme park shops as well as self-standing, retail outlets called Disney Stores. The list of character-based products is extensive, including everything from the characters to clothing with the characters' images. Because patents shield it, the proprietary nature of Disney's advantage in terms of animated characters protects the firm from imitation by competitors.

Consistent with another attribute of competition in a slow-cycle market, Disney remains committed to protecting its exclusive rights to its characters and their use as shown by the fact that ". . . the company once sued a day-care center, forcing it to remove the likeness of Mickey Mouse from a wall of the facility."[109] As with all firms competing in slow-cycle markets, Disney's competitive actions (such as building theme parks in France and Japan and other potential locations such as China) and responses (such as lawsuits to protect its right to fully control use of its animated characters) maintain and extend its proprietary competitive advantage while protecting it. Disney has been able to establish through actions and defend through responses an advantageous market position as a result of its competitive behavior.

Patent laws and regulatory requirements such as those in the United States requiring FDA (Federal Drug Administration) approval to launch new products shield pharmaceutical companies' positions. Competitors in this market try to extend patents on their drugs to maintain advantageous positions that they (patents) provide. However, once a patent expires, the firm is no longer shielded from competition, a situation that has financial implications. For example, in describing Merck & Co.'s expected 2002 performance, some analysts observed that in that year, "Merck was expected to get rocked by the loss of revenue as the patent protection for some leading drugs—such as gastroesophageal reflux soother Prilosec, cholesterol drug Mevacor, and hypertension medication Prinivil—expires."[110] Based largely on these patent expirations, Merck announced in late 2001 that its earnings would be lower in 2002 than originally expected. Following the firm's announcement, some analysts lowered their recommendation on Merck stock from "buy" to "hold." In contrast, Pfizer Inc.'s position seemed to be shielded for a period of time according to analysts: "Unlike several of its competitors (including Merck), Pfizer faces little risk to product sales from impending patent expirations and thus for the next 3 to 4 years remains in a growth trajectory."[111]

Research and development (R&D) is the advantage that allows pharmaceutical companies to develop drugs that have the possibility of creating shielded market positions. Because of its importance as a competitive advantage, these firms invest heavily in R&D in hopes that the results of doing so will create additional positions that are shielded from competition. For example, Pfizer intended to increase its 2003 R&D expenditure by roughly 10 percent (from $4.8 billion to $5.3 billion) over 2002's amount. Competitor Merck also intended to increase its R&D expenditure during this time by as much as 16 percent. As with Disney, these actions are being taken to sustain for as long as possible (through patents) and extend in as many ways as possible (through R&D) the firms' proprietary advantages and the shielded market positions resulting from them.

The competitive dynamics generated by firms competing in slow-cycle markets are shown in Figure 5.4. In slow-cycle markets, firms launch a product (e.g., a new drug) that has been developed through a proprietary advantage (e.g., R&D) and then exploit it for as long as possible while the product is shielded from competition. Eventually, competitors respond to the action with a counterattack. In markets for drugs, this counterattack commonly occurs as patents expire, creating the need for another product launch by the firm seeking a shielded market position.

Fast-Cycle Markets

Fast-cycle markets are markets in which the firm's competitive advantages aren't shielded from imitation and where imitation happens quickly and somewhat inexpensively.

Fast-cycle markets are markets in which the firm's competitive advantages aren't shielded from imitation and where imitation happens quickly and somewhat inexpensively. Competitive advantages aren't sustainable in fast-cycle markets.

Reverse engineering and the rate of technology diffusion in fast-cycle markets facilitate rapid imitation. A competitor uses reverse engineering to quickly gain the knowledge required to imitate or improve the firm's products, usually in only a few months. Technology is diffused rapidly in fast-cycle markets, making it available to competitors in a short period of time. The technology often used by fast-cycle competitors isn't proprietary, nor is it protected by patents as is the technology used by

Figure 5.4 Gradual Erosion of a Sustained Competitive Advantage

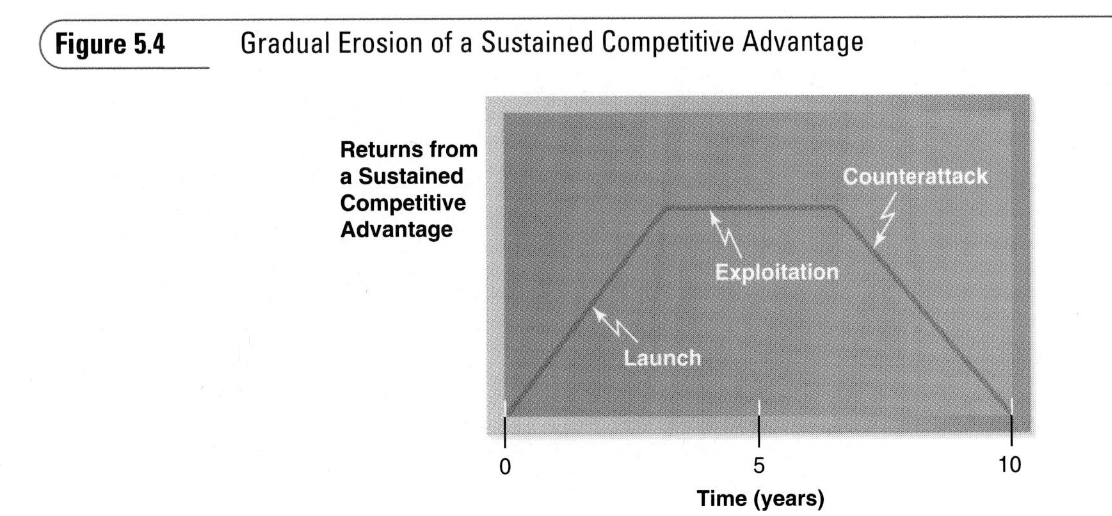

SOURCE: Adapted from I. C. MacMillan, 1988, Controlling competitive dynamics by taking strategic initiative, *Academy of Management Executive*, II(2): 111–118.

firms competing in slow-cycle markets. For example, only a few hundred parts, which are readily available on the open market, are required to build a PC. Patents protect only a few of these parts such as microprocessor chips.[112]

Fast-cycle markets are more volatile than slow-cycle and standard-cycle markets. Indeed, the pace of competition in fast-cycle markets is almost frenzied, as companies rely on ideas and the innovations resulting from them as the engines of their growth. Because prices fall quickly in these markets, companies need to profit quickly from their product innovations. For example, rapid declines in the prices of microprocessor chips produced by Intel and Advanced Micro Devices among others, make it possible for personal computer manufacturers to continuously reduce their prices to end users. Imitation of many fast-cycle products is relatively easy, as demonstrated by Dell and Gateway, along with a host of local PC vendors. All of these firms have partly or largely imitated IBM's initial PC design to create their products. Continuous declines in the costs of parts as well as the fact that the information and knowledge required to assemble a PC isn't especially complicated and is readily available, make it possible for additional competitors to enter this market without significant difficulty.[113]

The fast-cycle market characteristics described above make it virtually impossible for companies in this type of market to develop sustainable competitive advantages. Recognizing this, firms avoid "loyalty" to any of their products, preferring to cannibalize their own before competitors learn how to do so through successful imitation. This emphasis creates competitive dynamics that differ substantially from what is witnessed in slow-cycle markets. Instead of concentrating on protecting, maintaining, and extending competitive advantages as is the case for firms in slow-cycle markets, companies competing in fast-cycle markets focus on learning how to rapidly and continuously develop new competitive advantages that are superior to those they replace. In fast-cycle markets, firms don't concentrate on trying to protect a given competitive advantage because they understand that the advantage won't exist long enough to extend it.

The competitive behavior of firms competing in fast-cycle markets is shown in Figure 5.5. As suggested by the figure, competitive dynamics in this market type finds firms taking actions and responses in the course of competitive rivalry that are oriented to rapid and continuous product introductions and the use of a stream of ever-changing competitive advantages. The firm launches a product as a competitive

Figure 5.5 Obtaining Temporary Advantages to Create Sustained Advantage

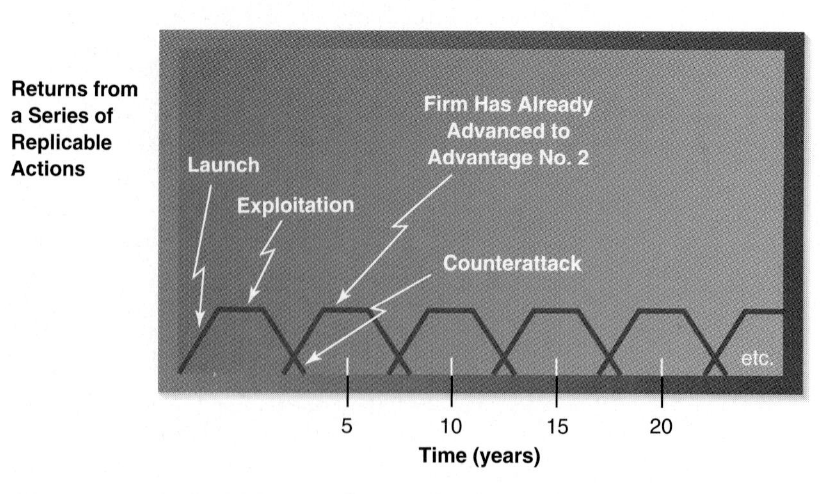

SOURCE: Adapted from I. C. MacMillan, 1988, Controlling competitive dynamics by taking strategic initiative, *Academy of Management Executive,* II(2): 111–118.

action and then exploits the advantage associated with it for as long as possible. However, the firm also tries to move to another temporary competitive before competitors can respond to the first one (see Figure 5.5). Thus, competitive dynamics in fast-cycle markets, in which all firms seek to achieve new competitive advantages before competitors learn how to effectively respond to current ones, often result in rapid product upgrades as well as quick product innovations.[114]

As our discussion suggests, innovation has a dominant effect on competitive dynamics in fast-cycle markets. For individual firms, this means that innovation is a key source of competitive advantage. Through innovation, the firm can cannibalize its own products before competitors' successfully imitate them.

In the fast-cycle semiconductor market, Texas Instruments (TI) and Micron Technology Inc (Micron) both rely on innovation as a competitive advantage. There is evidence to suggest that the two companies are successful in this effort.

Recently *Technology Review Magazine* ranked ". . . Micron number one in the semiconductor market based on quality and quantity of patents and other key indicators including scientific papers cited and the ability to convert cutting edge technology into intellectual property."[115] TI publishes *Technology Innovations* (with subscriptions available through the firm's website) to describe its continuous stream of innovations.[116] Using innovation as the foundation for continuous attacks (launches) and counterattacks, TI increasingly is concentrating on digital signal processors and analog integrated circuits, while Micron is a leading supplier of dynamic random access memory chips, the most widely used semiconductor memory component in PCs.[117] Thus, although they aren't competitors in terms of these particular products, innovation allows each firm to continuously develop temporary competitive advantages that become the foundation for the development of still additional ones.

Standard-Cycle Markets

Standard-cycle markets are markets in which the firm's competitive advantages are moderately shielded from imitation and where imitation is moderately costly.

Standard-cycle markets are markets in which the firm's competitive advantages are moderately shielded from imitation and where imitation is moderately costly. Competitive advantages are partially sustainable in standard-cycle markets, but only when the firm is able to continuously upgrade the quality of its competitive advantages. The competitive actions and responses that form a standard-cycle market's competitive dynamics find firms seeking large market shares, trying to gain customer loyalty through brand names, and carefully controlling their operations to consistently provide the same usage experience for customers without surprises.[118]

Because of large volumes and the size of mass markets, the competition for market share is intense in standard-cycle markets. Procter & Gamble and Unilever compete in standard-cycle markets. A competitor analysis reveals that P&G and Unilever are direct competitors, in that they share multiple markets as they engage each other in competition in over 140 countries and they have similar types and amounts of resources and follow similar strategies. One of the product lines in which these two firms aggressively compete against each other for market share is laundry detergents. The market for these products is large, with an annual sales volume of over $6 billion in the United States alone. The sheer size of this market highlights the importance of market share, as a mere percentage point gain in share translates into a $60 million increase in revenues. As analysts have noted, in a standard-cycle market, "It's a death struggle to incrementally gain share." For P&G and Unilever, this means that the firms must ". . . slog it out for every fraction of every share in every category in every market where they compete."[119]

Standard-cycle companies serve many customers in competitive markets. Because the capabilities on which their competitive advantages are based are less specialized, imitation is faster and less costly for standard-cycle firms than for those competing in slow-cycle markets. However, imitation is less quick and more expensive in these markets than in fast-cycle markets. Thus, competitive dynamics in standard-cycle markets rests midway between the characteristics of dynamics in slow-cycle and fast-cycle markets. The quickness of imitation is reduced and becomes more expensive for standard-cycle competitors when a firm is able to develop economies of scale by combining coordinated and integrated design and manufacturing processes with a large sales volume for its products.

Without scale economies, standard-cycle firms compete at a disadvantage. Recently, for example, some of Britain's well-known retailers such as Marks & Spencer reported continuing declines in sales volume. Entry to Britain by foreign competitors, including Sweden's Hennes & Mauritz, Spain's Zara, Japan's Uniqlo, and United States's Gap, is contributing to this decline. According to analysts, these competitors rely on their global fashion sense and economies of scale to quickly imitate their British competitors. The global presence and resulting sales volumes of these global competitors increase the likelihood that they will develop and benefit from economies of scale. In contrast, Britain's "home-grown retailers" lack the presence and volume required to develop economies of scale and to make imitation of their competitive advantage costly.[120]

Innovation can also drive competitive actions and responses in standard-cycle markets, especially when rivalry is intense. Thus, innovation has a substantial influence on competitive dynamics as it affects the actions and responses of all companies competing within a slow-cycle, fast-cycle, or standard-cycle market. We have emphasized the importance of innovation to the firm's strategic competitiveness in earlier chapters. Our discussion of innovation in terms of competitive dynamics extends the earlier discussions by showing its importance in all types of markets in which firms compete.

Innovation is vital to the competitive behavior of consumer goods competitor General Mills, especially as it competes against manufacturers of generic cereals. The world's largest cereal maker, this firm relies on its brand name as a source of advantage to successfully use the differentiation business-level strategy while competing in its standard-cycle market. Generic cereals, however, are a serious threat to General Mills' advantage as well as the strategy that is based on it. As an analyst noted, "Consumers just will not pay a 50–80 percent premium for General Mills Cheerios, for instance, now that the quality of store brands has become nearly indistinguishable from the original." General Mills is responding to attacks by generic manufacturers with product innovations, including Wheaties Energy Crunch, Milk 'n Cereal Bars, and Chex Morning Mix. To date, innovations have enabled General Mills to retain its sales volume.[121]

General Mills has built on its brand recognition by applying it to new products, and has also countered generic imitators by creating new varieties of its traditional cereals.

Summary

- Competitors are firms competing in the same market, offering similar products and targeting similar customers. Competitive rivalry is the ongoing set of competitive actions and competitive responses occurring between competitors as they compete against each other for an advantageous market position. The outcomes of competitive rivalry influence the firm's ability to sustain its competitive advantages as well as the level (average, below-average, or above-average) of its financial returns.

- For the individual firm, the set of competitive actions and responses it takes while engaged in competitive rivalry is called competitive behavior. Competitive dynamics is the set of actions taken by all firms that are competitors within a particular market.

- Firms study competitive rivalry in order to be able to predict the competitive actions and responses that each of its competitors likely will take. Competitive actions are either strategic or tactical in nature. The firm takes competitive actions to defend or build its competitive advantages or improve its market position. Competitive responses are taken to counter the effects of a competitor's competitive action. A strategic action or a strategic response requires a significant commitment of organizational resources, is difficult to successfully implement, and hard to reverse. In contrast, a tactical action or a tactical response requires fewer organizational resources and is easier to implement and reverse. For an airline company, for example, entering major new markets is an example of a strategic action or a strategic response while changing its prices in a particular market is an example of a tactical action or a tactical response.

- A competitor analysis is the first step the firm takes to be able to predict its competitors' actions and responses. In Chapter 2, we discussed what firms do to *understand* competitors. This discussion is extended further in this chapter as we described what the firm does to *predict* competitors' market-based actions. Thus, understanding precedes prediction. Market commonality (the number of markets with which competitors are jointly involved and their importance to each) and resource similarity (how comparable competitors' resources are in terms of type and amount) are studied to complete a competitor analysis. In general, the greater are market commonality and resource similarity, the more firms acknowledge that they are direct competitors.

- Market commonality and resource similarity shape the firm's awareness (the degree to which it and its competitor understand their mutual interdependence), motivation (the firm's incentive to attack or respond), and ability (the quality of the resources available to the firm to attack and respond). Having knowledge of a competitor in terms of these characteristics increases the quality of the firm's predictions about a competitor's actions and responses.

- In addition to market commonality and resource similarity and awareness, motivation and ability, three more specific factors affect the likelihood a competitor will take competitive actions. The first of these concerns first mover incentives. First movers, those taking an initial competitive action, often earn above-average returns until competitors can successfully respond to their action and gain loyal customers. Not all firms can be first movers in that they may lack the awareness, motivation, or ability required to engage in this type of competitive behavior. Moreover, some firms prefer to be a second mover (the firm responding to the first mover's action). One reason for this is that second movers, especially those acting quickly, can successfully compete against the first mover. By studying the first mover's product, customers' reactions to it and the responses of other competitors to the first mover, the second mover can avoid the early entrant's mistakes and find ways to improve upon the value created for customers by the first mover's good or service. Late movers though (those that respond a long time after the original action was taken), commonly are lower performers and much less competitive.

  Organizational size, the second factor, tends to reduce the number of different types of competitive actions that large firms launch while it results in smaller competitors' using a wide variety of actions. Ideally, the firm would like to initiate a large number of diverse actions when engaged in competitive rivalry.

  The third factor, quality, dampens firms' abilities to take competitive actions, in that product quality is a base denominator to successful competition in the global economy.

- The type of action (strategic or tactical) the firm took, the competitor's reputation for the nature of its competitor behavior, and its dependence on the market in which the action was taken are studied to predict a competitor's response to the firm's action. In general, the number of tactical responses taken exceeds the number of strategic responses. Competitors respond more frequently to the actions taken by the firm with a reputation for predictable and understandable competitive behavior, especially if that firm is a market leader. In general, the firm can predict that when its competitor is highly dependent for its revenue and profitability in the market in which the firm took a competitive action, that competitor is likely to launch a strong response. However, firms that are more diversified across markets are less likely to respond to a particular action that affects only one of the markets in which they compete.

- Competitive dynamics concerns the ongoing competitive behavior occurring among all firms competing in a market for advantageous positions. Market characteristics affect the set of actions and responses firms take while competing in a given market as well as the sustainability of firms' competitive advantages. In slow-cycle markets, where competitive advantages can be maintained, competitive dynamics finds firms taking actions and responses that are intended to protect, maintain, and extend their proprietary advantages. In fast-cycle markets, competition is almost frenzied as firms concentrate on developing a series of temporary competitive advantages. This emphasis is necessary because firms' advantages in fast-cycle markets aren't proprietary and as such, are subject to rapid and relatively inexpensive imitation. Standard-cycle markets are between slow-cycle and fast-cycle markets, in that firms are moderately shielded from competition in these markets as they use competitive advantages that are moderately sustainable. Competitors in standard-cycle markets serve mass markets and try to develop economies of scale to enhance their profitability. Innovation is vital to competitive success in each of the three types of markets. Firms should recognize that the set of competitive actions and responses taken by all firms differs by type of market.

Review Questions

1. Who are competitors? How are competitive rivalry, competitive behavior, and competitive dynamics defined in the chapter?
2. What is market commonality? What is resource similarity? What does it mean to say that these concepts are the building blocks for a competitor analysis?
3. How do awareness, motivation, and ability affect the firm's competitive behavior?
4. What factors affect the likelihood a firm will take a competitive action?
5. What factors affect the likelihood a firm will initiate a competitive response to the action taken by a competitor?
6. How is competitive dynamics in slow-cycle markets described in the chapter? In fast-cycle markets? In standard-cycle markets?

Experiential Exercise

Competitive Rivalry

Part One. Define first mover and second mover, and provide examples of firms for each category.

First mover:

Second mover:

Part Two. In the following table, list the advantages and disadvantages of being the first mover and of being the second mover.

First Mover		Second Mover	
Advantages	Disadvantages	Advantages	Disadvantages

Part Three. Based on the above information, what are the most important issues that you feel first and second movers must consider before initiating a competitive move?

Notes

1. M.-J. Chen, 1996, Competitor analysis and interfirm rivalry: Toward a theoretical integration, *Academy of Management Review,* 21: 100–134.
2. S. Jayachandran, J. Gimeno, & P. R. Varadarajan, 1999, Theory of multimarket competition: A synthesis and implications for marketing strategy, *Journal of Marketing,* 63(3): 49–66.
3. R. E. Caves, 1984, Economic analysis and the quest for competitive advantage. In *Papers and Proceedings of the 96th Annual Meeting of the American Economic Association,* 127–132.
4. G. Young, K. G. Smith, C. M. Grimm, & D. Simon, 2000, Multimarket contact and resource dissimilarity: A competitive dynamics perspective, *Journal of Management,* 26: 1217–1236; C. M. Grimm & K. G. Smith, 1997, *Strategy as Action: Industry Rivalry and Coordination,* Cincinnati: South-Western College Publishing, 53–74.
5. H. A. Haveman & L. Nonnemaker, 2000, Competition in multiple geographic markets: The impact on growth and market entry, *Administrative Science Quarterly,* 45: 232–267.
6. G. Young, K. G. Smith, & C. M. Grimm, 1996, "Austrian" and industrial organization perspectives on firm-level competitive activity and performance, *Organization Science,* 73: 243–254.
7. K. G. Smith, W. J. Ferrier, & H. Ndofor, 2001, Competitive dynamics research: Critique and future directions, in M. A. Hitt, R. E. Freeman, & J. S. Harrison (eds.), *Handbook of Strategic Management,* Oxford, U.K.: Blackwell Publishers, 326.
8. G. S. Day & D. J. Reibstein, 1997, The dynamic challenges for theory and practice, in G. S. Day & D. J. Reibstein (eds.), *Wharton on Competitive Strategy,* New York: John Wiley & Sons, 2.
9. D. L. Deeds, D. DeCarolis, & J. Coombs, 2000, Dynamic capabilities and new product development in high technology adventures: An empirical analysis of new biotechnology firms, *Journal of Business Venturing,* 15: 211–299.
10. G. Khermouch, S. Holmes, & M. Iklwan, 2001, The best global brands, *Business Week,* August 6, 50–57.
11. C. Lederer & S. Hill, 2001, See your brands through your customers' eyes, *Harvard Business Review,* 79(6): 125–133.
12. S. Crainer, 2001, And the new economy winner is . . . . Europe, *Strategy & Business,* Second Quarter, 40–47.
13. J. E. Garten, 2001, The wrong time for companies to beat a global retreat, *Business Week,* December 17, 22.
14. Young, Smith, Grimm, & Simon, Multimarket contact and resource dissimilarity, 1230–1233.
15. D. R. Gnyawali & R. Madhavan, 2001, Cooperative networks and competitive dynamics: A structural embeddedness perspective, *Academy of Management Review,* 26: 431–445.
16. Young, Smith, Grimm, & Simon, Multimarket contact and resource dissimilarity, 1217; M. E. Porter, 1991, Towards a dynamic theory of strategy, *Strategic Management Journal,* 12: 95–117.
17. S. Godin, 2002, Survival is not enough, *Fast Company,* January, 90–94.
18. S. J. Marsh, 1998, Creating barriers for foreign competitors: A study of the impact of anti-dumping actions on the performance of U.S. firms, *Strategic Management Journal,* 19: 25–37; K. G. Smith, C. M. Grimm, G. Young, & S. Wally, 1997, Strategic groups and rivalrous firm behavior: Toward a reconciliation, *Strategic Management Journal,* 18: 149–157.
19. W. J. Ferrier, 2001, Navigating the competitive landscape: The drivers and consequences of competitive aggressiveness, *Academy of Management Journal,* 44: 858–877; M. E. Porter, 1980, *Competitive Strategy,* New York: Free Press.
20. Smith, Ferrier, & Ndofor, Competitive dynamics research, 319.
21. K. Ramaswamy, 2001, Organizational ownership, competitive intensity, and firm performance: An empirical study of the Indian manufacturing sector, *Strategic Management Journal,* 22: 989–998.
22. K. Cool, L. H. Roller, & B. Leleux, 1999, The relative impact of actual and potential rivalry on firm profitability in the pharmaceutical industry, *Strategic Management Journal,* 20: 1–14.
23. I. Sager, F. Keenan, C. Edwards, & A. Park, 2001, The mother of all price wars, *Business Week,* July 30, 32–35.
24. 2001, In the family's way, *The Economist,* December 15, 56.
25. Sager, Keenan, Edwards, & Park, The mother of all price wars, 33.
26. M. Williams, 2001, David Packard supports Hewlett family in opposing H-P's Compaq acquisition, *The Wall Street Journal Interactive,* http://www.interactive.wsj.com/articles, November 7; 2001, Hewlett deal launches family, board spats, *Reuters,* http://activequote100.fidelity.com, December 13.
27. P. Burrows, 2001, Carly's last stand? *Business Week,* December 24, 63–70.
28. A. Park, 2001, Can Compaq survive as a solo act? *Business Week,* December 24, 71.
29. C. Harrison, 2001, Compaq should discontinue its PC line, analysts say, *Dallas Morning News,* December 16, D1, D16.
30. W. P. Putsis, Jr., 1999, Empirical analysis of competitive interaction in food product categories, *Agribusiness,* 15(3): 295–311.
31. 2001, Dell Computer, *Standard & Poor's Stock Report,* http://www.standard&poor.com, December 8.
32. Chen, Competitor analysis, 108.
33. Ibid., 109.
34. E. Abrahamson & C. J. Fombrun, 1994, Macrocultures: Determinants and consequences. *Academy of Management Review,* 19: 728–755.
35. C. Salter, 2002, On the road again, *Fast Company,* January, 50–58.
36. Young, Smith, Grimm, & Simon, Multimarket contact, 1219.
37. Chen, Competitor analysis, 106.
38. J. Gimeno & C. Y. Woo, 1999, Multimarket contact, economies of scope, and firm performance. *Academy of Management Journal,* 42: 239–259.
39. K. MacArthur, 2001, McDonald's flips business strategy, *Advertising Age,* April 2, 1 & 36.
40. 2001, Prudential Financial Inc., *Standard & Poor's Stock Report,* http://www.standard&poor.com, December 27.
41. Young, Smith, Grimm, & Simon, Multimarket contact and resource dissimilarity, 1230.
42. J. Gimeno, 1999, Reciprocal threats in multimarket rivalry: Staking out 'spheres of influence' in the U.S. airline industry, *Strategic Management Journal,* 20: 101–128; N. Fernanez & P. L. Marin, 1998, Market power and multimarket contact: Some evidence from the Spanish hotel industry, *Journal of Industrial Economics,* 46: 301–315.
43. H. J. Korn & J. A. C. Baum, 1999, Chance, imitative, and strategic antecedents to multimarket contact, *Academy of Management Journal,* 42: 171–193.
44. Jayachandran, Gimeno, & Varadarajan, Theory of multimarket competition, 59; Chen, Competitor analysis, 107.
45. J. Gimeno & C. Y. Woo, 1996, Hypercompetition in a multimarket environment: The role of strategic similarity and multimarket contact on competitive de-escalation, *Organization Science,* 7: 322–341.
46. R. Berner, 2001, CVS: Will its growth elixir work? *Business Week,* July 9, 50–53.
47. Chen, Competitor analysis, 107–108.
48. Ibid., 110.
49. Ibid., 110; W. Ocasio, 1997, Towards an attention-based view of the firm, *Strategic Management Journal,* 18(Summer Special Issue): 187–206; Smith, Ferrier, & Ndofor, Competitive dynamics research, 320.
50. G. P. Hodgkinson & G. Johnson, 1994, Exploring the mental models of competitive strategists: The case for a processual approach, *Journal of Management Studies,* 31: 525–551; J. F. Porac & H. Thomas, 1994, Cognitive categorization and subjective rivalry among retailers in a small city, *Journal of Applied Psychology,* 79: 54–66.

51. 2001, Wal around the world, *The Economist,* December 8, 55–56.
52. Smith, Ferrier, & Ndofor, Competitive dynamics research, 320.
53. Chen, Competitor analysis, 113.
54. Grimm & Smith, *Strategy as Action,* 125.
55. 2002, Blue light blues, *The Economist,* January 29, 54; D. B. Yoffie & M. Kwak, 2001, Mastering strategic movement at Palm, *MIT Sloan Management Review,* 43(1): 55–63.
56. K. G. Smith, W. J. Ferrier & C. M. Grimm, 2001, King of the hill: Dethroning the industry leader, *Academy of Management Executive,* 15(2): 59–70.
57. G. S. Day, 1997, Assessing competitive arenas: Who are your competitors? In G. S. Day & D. J. Reibstein (eds.), *Wharton on Competitive Strategy,* New York: John Wiley & Sons, 25–26.
58. M. Ihlwan, L. Armstrong, & K. Kerwin, 2001, Hyundai gets hot, *Business Week,* December 17, 84–86.
59. J. Schumpeter, 1934, *The Theory of Economic Development,* Cambridge, MA.: Harvard University Press.
60. J. L. C. Cheng & I. F. Kesner, 1997, Organizational slack and response to environmental shifts: The impact of resource allocation patterns, *Journal of Management,* 23: 1–18.
61. F. Wang, 2000, Too appealing to overlook, *America's Network,* December, 10–12.
62. G. Hamel, 2000, *Leading the Revolution,* Boston: Harvard Business School Press, 103.
63. K. Belson, R. Hof, & B. Elgin, 2001, How Yahoo! Japan beat eBay at its own game, *Business Week,* June 4, 58.
64. Smith, Ferrier, & Ndofor, Competitive dynamics research, 331.
65. L. J. Bourgeois, 1981, On the measurement of organizational slack, *Academy of Management Review,* 6: 29–39.
66. M. B. Lieberman & D. B. Montgomery, 1988, First-mover advantages, *Strategic Management Journal,* 9: 41–58.
67. 2001, Older, wiser, webbier, *The Economist,* June 30, 10.
68. M. Shank, 2002, Executive strategy report, IBM business strategy consulting, http://www.ibm.com, March 14; W. Boulding & M. Christen, 2001, First-mover disadvantage, *Harvard Business Review,* 79(9): 20–21.
69. K. G. Smith, C. M. Grimm, & M. J. Gannon, 1992, *Dynamics of Competitive Strategy,* Newberry Park, CA.: Sage Publications.
70. H. R. Greve, 1998, Managerial cognition and the mimetic adoption of market positions: What you see is what you do, *Strategic Management Journal,* 19: 967–988.
71. Smith, Ferrier, & Ndofor, Competitive dynamics research, 327.
72. M.-J. Chen & D. C. Hambrick, 1995, Speed, stealth and selective attack: How small firms differ from large firms in competitive behavior, *Academy of Management Journal,* 38: 453–482.
73. D. Miller & M.-J. Chen, 1996, The simplicity of competitive repertoires: An empirical analysis, *Strategic Management Journal,* 17: 419–440.
74. Young, Smith, & Grimm, "Austrian" and industrial organization perspectives.
75. B. A. Melcher, 1993, How Goliaths can act like Davids, *Business Week,* Special Issue, 193.
76. 2001, Wal around the world, 55.
77. Ibid., 55.
78. P. B. Crosby, 1980, *Quality Is Free,* New York: Penguin.
79. W. E. Deming, 1986, *Out of the Crisis,* Cambridge, MA.: MIT Press.
80. T. Laseter, B. Long, & C. Capers, 2001, B2B benchmark: The state of electronic exchanges, *Strategy & Business,* Fourth Quarter, 32–42.
81. R. S. Kaplan & D. P. Norton, 2001, *The Strategy-Focused Organization,* Boston: Harvard Business School Press.
82. R. Cullen, S. Nicholls, & A. Halligan, 2001, Measurement to demonstrate success, *British Journal of Clinical Governance,* 6(4): 273–278.
83. K. E. Weick & K. M. Sutcliffe, 2001, *Managing the Unexpected,* San Francisco: Jossey-Bass, 81–82.
84. J. Aley, 1994, Manufacturers grade themselves, *Fortune,* March 21, 26.
85. J. Green & D. Welch, 2001, Jaguar may find it's a jungle out there, *Business Week,* March 26, 62.
86. J. Muller, 2001, Ford: Why it's worse than you think, *Business Week,* June 25, 80–89.
87. J. D. Westhpal, R. Gulati, & S. M. Shortell, 1997, Customization or conformity: An institutional and network perspective on the content and consequences of TQM adoption, *Administrative Science Quarterly,* 42: 366–394.
88. S. Sanghera, 1999, Making continuous improvement better, *Financial Times,* April 21, 28.
89. Muller, Ford, 82.
90. J. White, G. L. White, & N. Shirouzu, 2001, Soon, the big three won't be, as foreigners make inroads, *The Wall Street Journal,* August 13, A1, A12.
91. Ihlwan, Armstrong, & Kerwin, Hyundai gets hot, 84.
92. J. Hyde, 2001, In Detroit, a new definition of 'quality,' *Reuters Business News,* http://www.reuters.com, December 22.
93. Ihlwan, Armstrong, & Kerwin, Hyundai gets hot, 85.
94. J. Schumpeter, 1950, *Capitalism, Socialism and Democracy,* New York: Harper; Smith, Ferrier & Ndofor, Competitive dynamics research, 323.
95. M.-J. Chen & I. C. MacMillan, 1992, Nonresponse and delayed response to competitive moves, *Academy of Management Journal,* 35: 539–570; Smith, Ferrier, & Ndofor, Competitive dynamics research, 335.
96. M.-J. Chen, K. G. Smith, & C. M. Grimm, 1992, Action characteristics as predictors of competitive responses, *Management Science,* 38: 439–455.
97. M.-J. Chen & D. Miller, 1994, Competitive attack, retaliation and performance: An expectancy-valence framework, *Strategic Management Journal,* 15: 85–102.
98. Smith, Ferrier, & Ndofor, Competitive dynamics research, 333.
99. W. J. Ferrier, K. G. Smith, & C. M. Grimm, 1999, The role of competitive actions in market share erosion and industry dethronement: A study of industry leaders and challengers, *Academy of Management Journal,* 42: 372–388.
100. 2001, Lowe's Companies, *Standard & Poor's Stock Reports,* http://www.standard&poor.com, December 26.
101. Smith, Grimm, & Gannon, *Dynamics of Competitive Strategy.*
102. 2001, Retail Update 2001, *Argus Market Digest,* http://www.argusresearch.com, December 28.
103. A. Karnani & B. Wernerfelt, 1985, Research note and communication: Multiple point competition, *Strategic Management Journal,* 6: 87–97.
104. Smith, Ferrier, & Ndofor, Competitive dynamics research, 330.
105. 2001, Wrigley (Wm.) Jr., *Standard & Poor's Stock Report,* http://www.standard&poor.com, December 26.
106. J. R. Williams, 1999, *Renewable Advantage: Crafting Strategy through Economic Time,* New York: Free Press.
107. J. R. Williams, 1992, How sustainable is your competitive advantage? *California Management Review* 34(3): 29–51.
108. Ibid., 6.
109. Ibid., 57.
110. 2001, Fool take: Merck lurks, *Richmond Times-Dispatch,* December 30, D7.
111. 2001, Pfizer Inc., *Argus Company Report,* http://www.argusresearch. com, December 29.
112. Williams, *Renewable Advantage,* 8.
113. Ibid., 8.
114. R. Sanchez, 1995, Strategic flexibility in production competition, *Strategic Management Journal,* 16(Summer Special Issue): 9–26.
115. 2001, Industry awards, Micron Technology Inc. Home page, http://www.micron.com, December 30.
116. 2001, Technology innovations, Texas Instruments Home page, http://www.ti.com, December 30.
117. 2001, Micron Technology, *Standard & Poor's Stock Reports,* http://www.standard&poors.com, December 22; 2001, Texas Instruments, *Standard & Poor's Stock Reports,* http://www.standard&poors.com, December 22.
118. Williams, *Renewable Advantage,* 7.
119. K. Brooker, 2001, A game of inches, *Fortune,* February 5, 98–100.
120. 2001, High street woes, *The Economist,* July 28, 56.
121. 2001, General Mills Inc., *Argus Market Digest,* http:www.argusresearch.com, December 28.

6

Chapter Six

Corporate-Level Strategy

Knowledge Objectives

Studying this chapter should provide you with the strategic management knowledge needed to:

1. Define corporate-level strategy and discuss its importance to the diversified firm.
2. Describe the advantages and disadvantages of single- and dominant-business strategies.
3. Explain three primary reasons why firms move from single- and dominant-business strategies to more diversified strategies.
4. Describe how related diversified firms create value by sharing or transferring core competencies.
5. Explain the two ways value can be created with an unrelated diversification strategy.
6. Discuss the incentives and resources that encourage diversification.
7. Describe motives that can encourage managers to overdiversify a firm.

Cendant: A Diversified Service Conglomerate

Cendant Corporation was created in December 1997 by a merger between HFS, Inc., and CUC International. The merger combined a marketing company (CUC) with HFS, a diversified firm with franchising operations in several industries, including real estate, hospitality, and vehicle services. Henry Silverman, CEO of the former HFS, was appointed as chairman of the merged company. Massive accounting irregularities in CUC's businesses caused Cendant's shares to lose nearly half their market value four months after the merger and resulted in criminal charges against some of CUC's former executives.

Cendant Corporation owns a diversified set of services businesses, including its fee-for-services businesses—hotel, real estate, tax preparation, rental cars, fleet and fuel cards, mortgage origination, employee location, and vacation exchange and rental services. Cendant grows through acquisitions as well as through internal means, such as development of new product lines, to implement its related-linked corporate-level diversification strategy. Discussed in detail in the chapter, this strategy mixes related and unrelated diversification. Cendant also uses joint ventures and franchising (types of cooperative strategies that we discuss further in Chapter 9) to reach its growth objectives.

The focus of Cendant's corporate-level strategy is rapid growth through buying strong brands that are effectively positioned in the fee-for-service business area. Its businesses usually have low to moderate capital requirements but generate high margins and provide growing returns on capital and strong cash flows. Furthermore, Cendant seeks productivity improvements to lower costs by employing newer technologies.

Cendant Corporation implemented its strategic growth plan in 2001 and ended the year with revenues of $8.9 billion, a 90 percent increase over the previous year, and an increase in its share price by more than 100 percent. Cendant's real estate services, including Coldwell Banker Commercial Real Estate Services, with approximately 100 franchise offices and 1,000 U.S. sales agents, provided 21 percent of the firm's revenue for 2001.

Cendant's real estate franchises include Century 21, Coldwell Banker Commerce, and ERA—some of the most well-known franchises in the commercial and residential real estate brokerage market. Furthermore, it is one of the largest real estate retail mortgage originators in the United States. It also has a relocation service called Cendant Mobility. Real estate services generate approximately 40 percent of revenues for this diversified company.

In travel services, Cendant has a vast array of lodging franchises, including Days Inn, Howard Johnson's, Ramada Inn, Super 8, and Travel Lodge, among others. In fact, one in four customers in the budget segment stay in a Cendant franchised property. Because its customer base is budget conscious, the September 11, 2001 strikes on the United States were expected to have less of an effect on Cendant's revenues than on highly differentiated and more expensive lodging facilities. Cendant also owns Fairfield Communities, Inc., which operates a business through which vacation ownership interests are sold. To complement its travel business, it acquired Galileo International, a distributor of electronic global distribution services for the travel industry. Customers in 115 countries use Galileo's services to access schedule and fare information, make reservations, and issue tickets. Another recent Cendant acquisition, CheapTickets.com, provides additional opportunity in the online travel reservation segment. With the capability formed through its acquisitions, Cendant feels that it can effectively compete with online travel companies such as Travelocity.com and Priceline.com. Travel services generate approximately 28 percent of Cendant's revenues.

Cendant has a vehicle service division and is the leader in providing fleet and fuel management service cards. Avis Rental Service, National Car Parts, and Right Express form the core of this division. In total, this group of businesses accounts for roughly 17 percent of Cendant's sales revenue.

In regard to financial services, Cendant owns Jackson Hewitt Tax Service, the second largest U.S. tax preparation company, as well as Benefit Consultants, FISI-Madison Financial, and Long Term Preferred Care in the insurance and loyalty marketing area. On a combined basis, Cendant's financial services business unit contributes approximately 15 percent to the firm's total revenues.

Part of Cendant's related-linked diversification strategy is to acquire companies that complement its prestigious branded businesses. For instance, Galileo International, originally United Airlines' Apollo reservation system, has the second largest share of the electronic travel reservation business. Sabre Holdings Corporation, a competitor that operates the Sabre computer reservation system and also controls Travelocity.com, holds the largest share of this market. The Galileo network connects 43,000 travel agency sites to 550 airlines, 37 car rental companies, 47,000 hotel properties, 368 tour operators, and three major cruise lines. Thus, this acquisition creates a stronger link between its travel businesses.

A key objective of Cendant's acquisition strategy is to add companies that augment growth, strengthening the various businesses or segments where the firm has competitive advantages. Its best success with cross marketing has been in its array of real estate franchises. Although Cendant's businesses within each service type demonstrate some degree of relatedness, it has yet to realize the potential synergy between service categories. For example, Cendant hasn't developed a strong, value-creating relationship between car rentals and lodging. However, its acquisition of Galileo may provide more opportunity to exploit interrelatedness across Cendant's major strategic business units of travel, lodging, and vehicle service businesses. As is the case for all diversified business, Cendant must provide clear and transparent reports of its operations so investors and other stakeholders can fairly judge the value being created by exploiting interrelationships among the firm's business units.

SOURCES: 2002, Cendant Corp., *Standard & Poor's Stock Reports*, http://www.fidelity.com, April 1; A. Serwer, 2002, Dirty rotten numbers, *Fortune*, February 18, 74–84; A. Barrett & D. Brady, 2001, Just when it seems on the mend, *Business Week*, October 15, 75–76; 2001, Cendant home page, http://www.cendant.com; D. Colarusso, 2001, Wall Street is pondering Cendant's fresh start, *The New York Times*, http://www.nytimes.com, April 22; M. Rich, 2001, Cendant agrees to buy cheap tickets, *The Wall Street Journal*, August 14, B6; C. Rosen, 2001, Cendant ventures into travel, *Information Week*, June 25, 24; R. Sorkin & B. J. Feder, 2001, Owner of Avis and Day's Inn seen buying travel service, *The New York Times*, http://www.nytimes.com, June 18; A. Barrett, S. A. Forest, & T. Lowry, 2000, Henry Silverman's long road back, *Business Week*, February 28, 126–136.

Our discussions of business-level strategies (Chapter 4) and the competitive rivalry and competitive dynamics associated with them (Chapter 5) concentrate on firms competing in a single industry or product market.[1] When a firm chooses to diversify beyond a single industry and to operate businesses in several industries, it uses a corporate-level strategy of diversification. As explained in the Opening Case, Cendant operates in multiple industries while using a related-linked corporate-level strategy. A corporate-level strategy of diversification allows the firm to use its core competencies to pursue opportunities in the external environment.[2]

Diversification strategies play a major role in the behavior of large firms.[3] Strategic choices regarding diversification are, however, fraught with uncertainty.[4] The decision to merge CUC International with HFS seemed to have potential for improving the marketing capabilities of the merged firm, Cendant. However, because of accounting irregularities in some CUC businesses, the merger created significant difficulties, resulting in an initial precipitous decline in Cendant's market value.

A diversified company has two levels of strategy: business (or competitive) and corporate (or companywide).[5] Each business unit in the diversified firm chooses a business-level strategy as its means of competing in individual product markets. The firm's corporate-level strategy is concerned with two key questions: what businesses the firm should be in, and how the corporate office should manage the group of businesses.[6] Defined formally, **corporate-level strategy** specifies actions taken by the firm to gain a competitive advantage by selecting and managing a group of different businesses competing in several industries and product markets. In the current global environment, top executives should view their firm's businesses as a portfolio of core competencies when they select new businesses and decide how to manage them.[7] As with other strategic decisions that may not be as complex, speed is critical when executives make changes to this portfolio.[8]

Corporate-level strategy specifies actions taken by the firm to gain a competitive advantage by selecting and managing a group of different businesses competing in several industries and product markets.

A corporate-level strategy is expected to help the firm earn above-average returns by creating value, just as with the diversified firm's business-level strategies.[9] Some suggest that few corporate-level strategies actually create value.[10] A corporate-level strategy's value is ultimately determined by the degree to which "the businesses in the portfolio are worth more under the management of the company than they would be under any other ownership."[11] Thus, the effective corporate-level strategy creates, across all business units, aggregate returns that exceed what those returns would be without the strategy[12] and contributes to the firm's strategic competitiveness and its ability to earn above-average returns.[13]

Product diversification, a primary corporate-level strategy, concerns the scope of the industries and markets in which the firm competes as well as ". . . how managers buy, create and sell different businesses to match skills and strengths with opportunities presented to the firm."[14] Successful diversification is expected to reduce variability in the firm's profitability in that its earnings are generated from several different business units.[15] Because firms incur development and monitoring costs when diversifying, the ideal business portfolio balances diversification's costs and benefits.[16] Increasingly, a number of "traditional" economy firms are diversifying into Internet and e-commerce businesses in attempts to develop a properly balanced portfolio.[17]

Diversification requires the crafting of a multibusiness or corporate-level strategy. Multibusiness strategies often involve the firm with many different industry environments and product markets and, as explained in Chapter 11, require unique organizational structures. In the Opening Case, we describe Cendant's use of a multibusiness strategy to compete in the real estate, hospitality, travel, and vehicle services markets. The prevailing logic of diversification suggests that the firm should diversify into additional markets when it has excess resources, capabilities, and core competencies with multiple value-creating uses.[18] The probability of success increases when top-level managers verify that the firm has excess, value-creating resources, capabilities, and core competencies before choosing and trying to implement a corporate-level strategy.

We begin the chapter by examining different levels (from low to high) of diversification. Value-creating reasons for firms to use a corporate-level strategy are explored next. When diversification results in companies simultaneously competing against each other in multiple markets, they are engaging in multipoint competition.[19] For instance, the merger between Hewlett-Packard and Compaq Computer Corporation is expected to create a new firm that will be able to compete against IBM simultaneously in the attractive services market as well as in the PC and server markets.[20]

The chapter also describes using the vertical integration strategy as a means to gain power over competitors. Two types of diversification strategies denoting moderate to very high levels of diversification—related and unrelated—are then examined. The chapter also explores value-neutral incentives to diversify as well as managerial motives for diversification, which can be value destructive.

Levels of Diversification

Diversified firms vary according to their level of diversification and the connections between and among their businesses. Figure 6.1 lists and defines five categories of businesses according to increasing levels of diversification. In addition to the single- and dominant-business categories, more fully diversified firms are classified into related and unrelated categories. A firm is related through its diversification when there are several links between its business units; for example, units may share products or services, technologies, or distribution channels. The more links among businesses, the more "constrained" is the relatedness of diversification. Unrelatedness refers to the absence of direct links between businesses.

Low Levels of Diversification

A firm pursing a *low level of diversification* uses either a single or a dominant corporate-level diversification strategy. A single business diversification strategy is a corporate-level strategy wherein the firm generates 95 percent or more of its sales revenue from its core business area.[21] For example, focusing on the chewing-gum market, Wm. Wrigley Jr. Company uses a single business strategy while operating in relatively few product markets.[22] Wrigley's trademark chewing-gum brands include Spearmint, Doublemint, and Juicy Fruit. Sugarfree gums Hubba Bubba, Orbit, and Ice White were added in the 1990s. Its collaboration with Procter & Gamble to produce a dental chewing gum causes Wrigley to become slightly more diversified than it has been historically, although it is still using the single business diversification strategy. The dental chewing gum will be marketed under P&G's Crest brand.[23]

With the dominant business corporate-level diversification strategy, the firm generates between 70 and 95 percent of its total revenue within a single business area. Smithfield Foods uses the dominant business diversification strategy as shown by the fact that the majority of its sales are generated from raising and butchering hogs. Recently, however, Smithfield diversified into beef packing by acquiring Moyer Packing Co., a smaller beef processor. Smithfield also attempted to acquire IBP, the largest beef packer, but was outbid by Tyson Foods.[24] Although it is still using the dominant business diversification strategy, the firm's addition of beef packing operations suggests that its portfolio of businesses is becoming more diversified. If Smithfield were to

Figure 6.1 Levels and Types of Diversification

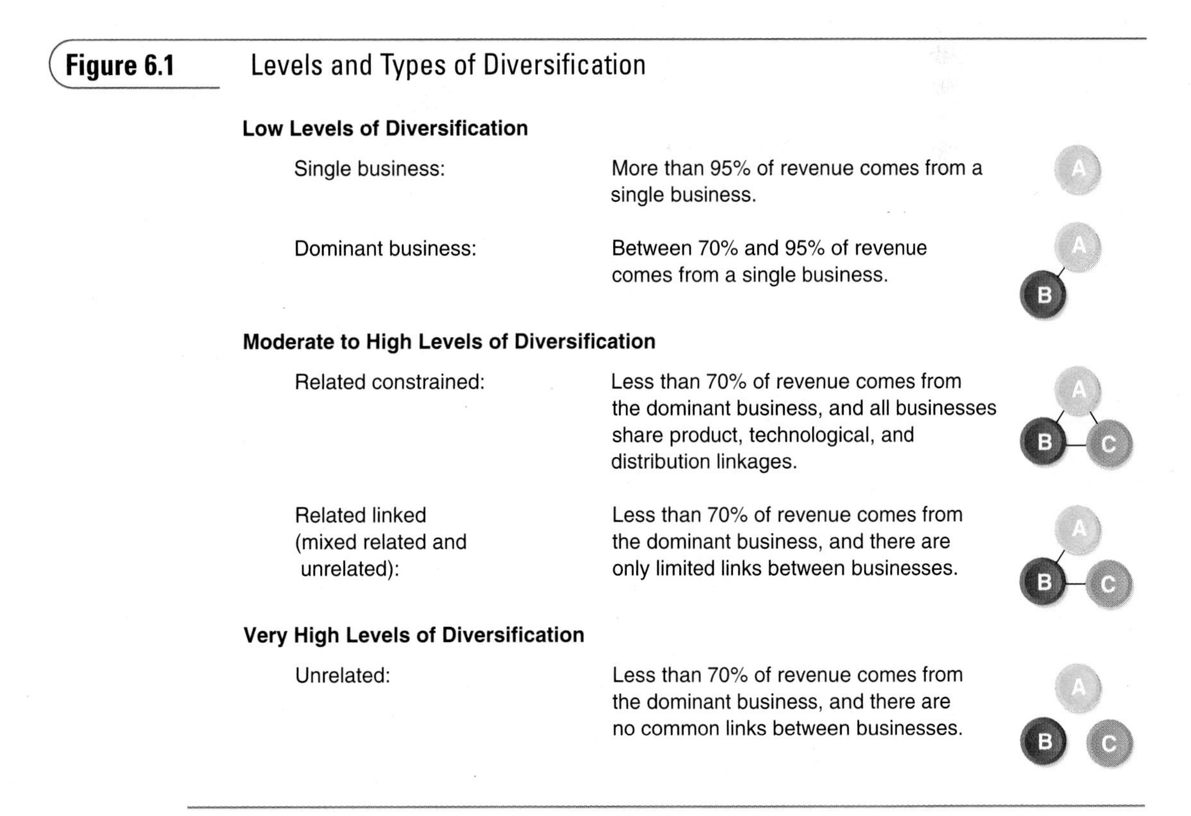

SOURCE: Adapted from R. P. Rumelt, 1974, *Strategy, Structure and Economic Performance,* Boston: Harvard Business School.

TERRI MILLER /E-VISUAL COMMUNICATIONS, INC.

According to Wrigley CEO Bill Wrigley Jr., the firm's fourth-generation family leader, investments in new products "and other investments in sales infrastructure and global systems capability are consistent with our focus on long-term growth." In addition to the firm's typical products shown here, X-Cite, a combination chewing gum and mint, will be available throughout much of Europe and the Pacific region in 2003, and Eclipse Flash Strips—a dissolvable breath film, or mint strip—was introduced in the United States in 2002.

become even more diversified, its corporate-level strategy could find the firm more accurately described as one that is moderately diversified.

Moderate and High Levels of Diversification

A firm generating more than 30 percent of its sales revenue outside a dominant business and whose businesses are related to each other in some manner uses *a related diversification corporate-level strategy.* When the links between the diversified firm's businesses are rather direct, *a related constrained diversification strategy* is being used. Campbell Soup, Procter & Gamble, Xerox, and Merck & Company all use a related constrained strategy. A related constrained firm shares a number of resources and activities between its businesses.

The diversified company with a portfolio of businesses with only a few links between them is called a mixed related and unrelated firm and is using the *related linked diversification strategy* (see Figure 6.1). Johnson & Johnson, General Electric, and Schlumberger follow this corporate-level diversification strategy. Compared to related constrained firms, related linked firms share fewer resources and assets between their businesses, concentrating on transferring knowledge and competencies between the businesses instead.

A highly diversified firm, which has no relationships between its businesses, follows an unrelated diversification strategy. United Technologies, Textron, and Samsung are examples of firms using this type of corporate-level strategy.[25] Although many U.S. firms using the unrelated diversification strategy have refocused to become less diversified, a number continue to have high levels of diversification. In Latin America and other emerging economies such as China, Korea, and India, conglomerates (firms following the unrelated diversification strategy) continue to dominate the private sector.[26] For instance, in Taiwan, "the largest 100 groups produced one third of the GNP in the past 20 years."[27] Typically family controlled, these corporations account for the greatest percentage of private firms in India.[28] Similarly, the largest business groups in Brazil, Mexico, Argentina, and Colombia are family-owned, diversified enterprises.[29] However, questions are being raised as to the viability of these large diversified business groups, especially in developed economies such as Japan.[30]

Reasons for Diversification

There are many reasons firms use a corporate level diversification strategy (see Table 6.1). Typically, a diversification strategy is used to increase the firm's value by improving its overall performance. Value is created either through related diversification or through unrelated diversification when the strategy allows a company's business units to increase revenues or reduce costs while implementing their business-level strategies. Another reason for diversification is to gain market power relative to competitors. Often, this is achieved through vertical integration (see the discussion later in the chapter).

Other reasons for using a diversification strategy may not increase the firm's value; in fact, diversification could have neutral effects, increase costs, or reduce a firm's revenues and its value. These reasons include diversification to match and

Table 6.1 Motives, Incentives, and Resources for Diversification

Motives to Enhance Strategic Competitiveness

- Economies of scope (related diversification)
  Sharing activities
  Transferring core competencies
- Market power (related diversification)
  Blocking competitors through multipoint competition
  Vertical integration
- Financial economies (unrelated diversification)
  Efficient internal capital allocation
  Business restructuring

Incentives and Resources with Neutral Effects on Strategic Competitiveness

- Antitrust regulation
- Tax laws
- Low performance
- Uncertain future cash flows
- Risk reduction for firm
- Tangible resources
- Intangible resources

Managerial Motives (Value Reduction)

- Diversifying managerial employment risk
- Increasing managerial compensation

thereby neutralize a competitor's market power (such as to neutralize another firm's advantage by acquiring a distribution outlet similar to its rival) and to expand a firm's portfolio of businesses to reduce managerial employment risk (if one of the businesses in a diversified firm fails, the top executive of the firm remains employed). Because diversification can increase a firm's size and thus managerial compensation, managers have motives to diversify a firm to a level that reduces its value. Diversification rationales that may have a neutral or negative effect on the firm's value are discussed in a later section.

To provide an overview of value-creating diversification strategies, Figure 6.2 illustrates operational relatedness and corporate relatedness. Study of these independent relatedness dimensions shows the importance of resources and key competencies.[31] The figure's vertical dimension indicates sharing activities (operational relatedness) while its horizontal dimension depicts corporate capabilities for transferring knowledge (corporate relatedness). The firm with a strong capability in managing operational synergy, especially in sharing assets between its businesses, falls in the upper left quadrant, which also represents vertical sharing of assets through vertical integration. The lower right quadrant represents a highly developed corporate capability for transferring a skill across businesses. This capability is located primarily in the corporate office. The use of either operational relatedness or corporate relatedness is based on a knowledge asset that the firm can either share or transfer.[32] Unrelated diversification is also illustrated in Figure 6.2 in the lower left quadrant. As shown, the unrelated diversification strategy creates value through financial economies rather than through either operational relatedness or corporate relatedness among business units.

Figure 6.2 Value-creating Strategies of Diversification: Operational and Corporate Relatedness

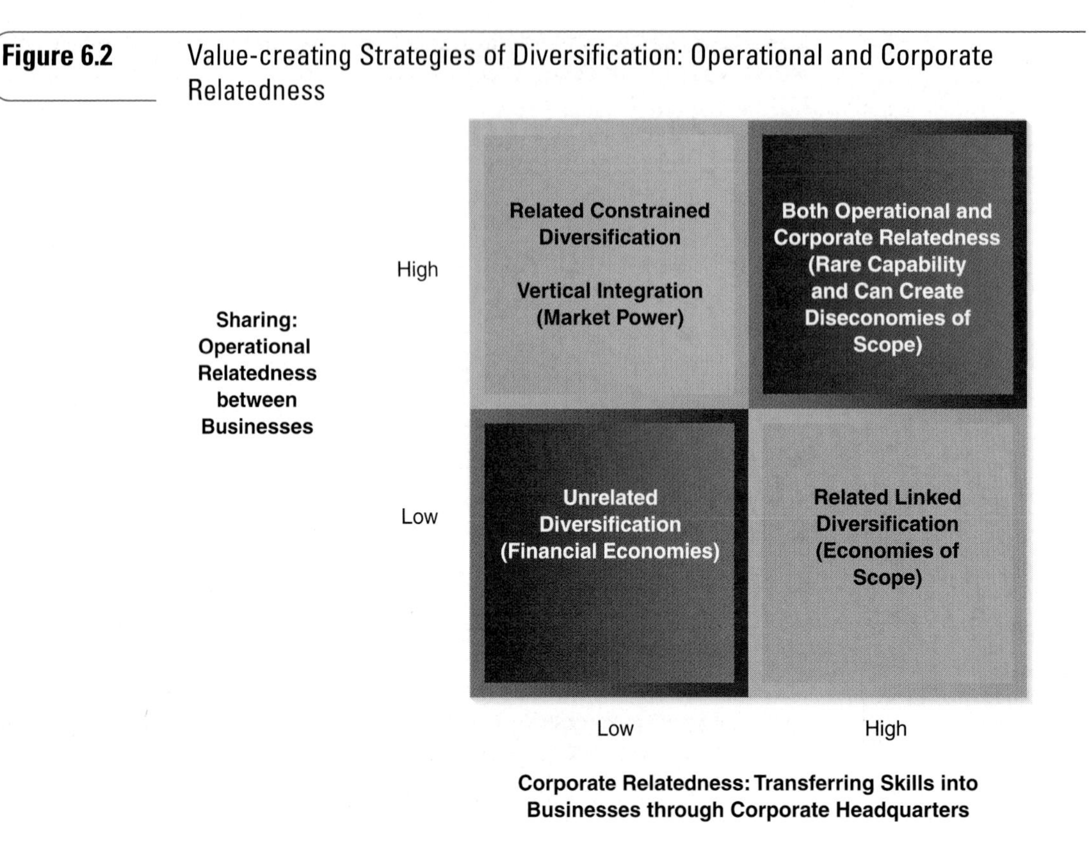

Related Diversification

With the related diversification corporate-level strategy, the firm builds upon or extends its resources, capabilities, and core competencies to create value.[33] The company using the related diversification strategy wants to develop and exploit economies of scope between its business units. Available to companies operating in multiple industries or product markets,[34] **economies of scope** are cost savings that the firm creates by successfully transferring some of its capabilities and competencies that were developed in one of its businesses to another of its businesses.

Economies of scope are cost savings that the firm creates by successfully transferring some of its capabilities and competencies that were developed in one of its businesses to another of its businesses.

As illustrated in Figure 6.2, firms seek to create value from economies of scope through two basic kinds of operational economies: sharing activities (operational relatedness) and transferring skills or corporate core competencies (corporate relatedness). The difference between sharing activities and transferring competencies is based on how separate resources are jointly used to create economies of scope. Tangible resources, such as plant and equipment or other business-unit physical assets, often must be shared to create economies of scope. Less tangible resources, such as manufacturing know-how, also can be shared. However, when know-how is transferred between separate activities and there is no physical or tangible resource involved, a corporate core competence has been transferred as opposed to operational sharing of activities having taken place.

Operational Relatedness: Sharing Activities

Firms can create operational relatedness by sharing either a primary activity (such as inventory delivery systems) or a support activity (for example, purchasing practices) (see Chapter 3's discussion of the value chain). Sharing activities is quite common, especially among related constrained firms. Procter & Gamble's paper towel business and baby diaper business both use paper products as a primary input to the manufacturing process. The firm's joint paper production plant that produces inputs for the two divisions is an example of a shared activity. In addition, these two businesses are likely to share distribution channels and sales networks, because they both produce consumer products.

Firms expect activity sharing among units to result in increased strategic competitiveness and improved financial returns. For example, PepsiCo purchased Quaker Oats for $12 billion on August 10, 2001. Pepsi has done well in the recent past, but sales growth in carbonated beverages—a staple for PepsiCo—may have reached a point of market saturation and could even decline, because medical studies have linked soft drink consumption to childhood obesity. With the purchase of Quaker Oats, the maker of sports drink Gatorade, Pepsi hopes it has found a reliable growth driver. Gatorade is the market leader in sports drinks and experienced a 13 percent annual growth rate in sales revenue between 1998 and 2001. Pepsi is integrating Gatorade into its distribution channels, partly to increase Gatorade's market share outside the United States. Thus, Pepsi soft drinks, such as Pepsi Cola and Mountain Dew, and Gatorade are sharing the firm's outbound logistics activity. Similarly, the same distribution channels could be used to distribute Quaker Oats' healthy snacks and Frito Lay's salty snacks.[35]

Other issues affect the degree to which activity sharing creates positive outcomes. For example, activity sharing requires sharing strategic control over business units. Moreover, one business unit manager may feel that another unit is receiving a disproportionate share of the gains. Such a perception could create conflicts between division managers.

Activity sharing also is risky because business-unit ties create links between outcomes. For instance, if demand for one business's product is reduced, there may not be sufficient revenues to cover the fixed costs required to operate the facilities being shared. Organizational difficulties such as these can prevent activity sharing success.[36]

Although activity sharing across business units isn't risk free, research shows that it can create value. For example, studies that examined acquisitions of firms in the same industry (called horizontal acquisitions), such as the banking industry, have found that sharing resources and activities and thereby creating economies of scope contributed to post-acquisition increases in performance and higher returns to shareholders.[37] Additionally, firms that sold off related units in which resource sharing was a possible source of economies of scope have been found to produce lower returns than those that sold off businesses unrelated to the firm's core business.[38] Still other research discovered that firms with more related units had lower risk.[39] These results suggest that gaining economies of scope by sharing activities across a firm's businesses may be important in reducing risk and in creating value. Further, more attractive results are obtained through activity sharing when a strong corporate office facilitates it.[40]

Corporate Relatedness: Transferring of Core Competencies

Over time, the firm's intangible resources, such as its know-how, become the foundation of core competencies. As suggested by Figure 6.2, corporate core competencies are complex sets of resources and capabilities that link different businesses, primarily through managerial and technological knowledge, experience, and expertise.[41]

Related linked firms often transfer competencies across businesses, thereby creating value in at least two ways. First, the expense of developing a competence has been incurred in one unit. Transferring it to a second business unit eliminates the need for the second unit to allocate resources to develop the competence. Resource intangibility is a second source of value creation through corporate relatedness. Intangible resources are difficult for competitors to understand and imitate. Because of this difficulty, the unit receiving a transferred competence often gains an immediate competitive advantage over its rivals.

Currently, McDonald's is attempting to create value by transferring an intangible resource among businesses it has acquired. Chipotle Mexican Grill (a small Colorado chain of Mexican food restaurants), Donatos Pizza (a pizza restaurant chain), Boston Market (a nationally known chain specializing in home-style cooking), and Prêt à Manger (a London chain with an eclectic food offering, such as sushi and salmon sandwiches) are now owned by McDonald's. Efforts are underway from the corporate level to transfer McDonald's knowledge about all phases of the fast food industry and restaurant operations to its newly acquired businesses. These actions demonstrate that McDonald's executives believe that the knowledge the company has gained from operating its core business can also create value in its other food venues—venues attracting customers who do not frequent McDonald's units. Interestingly, McDonald's stock price declined in early 2002 with questions surfacing about the firm's ability to maintain its historic growth and performance rates (this issue is further discussed in the Strategic Focus on page 136). Although all of these acquired businesses are small, McDonald's believes that each can profitably grow by applying its knowledge in their unique settings. Estimates are that the new units could add 2 percent to McDonald's growth rate within a few years.[42]

A number of firms have successfully transferred some of their resources and capabilities across businesses. Virgin Industries transferred its marketing skills across travel, cosmetics, music, drinks, and a number of other businesses. Thermo Electron uses its entrepreneurial skills to start new ventures and maintain a new-venture network. Coopers Industries manages a number of manufacturing-related businesses. Honda has developed and transferred its expertise in small and now larger engines for different types of vehicles, from motorcycles and lawnmowers to its range of automotive products.[43]

One way managers facilitate the transfer of competencies is to move key people into new management positions. However, a business-unit manager of an older division may be reluctant to transfer key people who have accumulated knowledge and experience critical to the business unit's success. Thus, managers with the ability to facilitate the transfer of a core competence may come at a premium, or the key people involved may not want to transfer. Additionally, the top-level managers from the transferring division may not want the competencies transferred to a new division to fulfill the firm's diversification objectives. Research suggests that transferring expertise in manufacturing-based businesses often does not result in improved performance.[44] Businesses in which performance does improve often demonstrate a corporate passion for pursuing skill transfer and appropriate coordination mechanisms for realizing economies of scope.

Market Power

Related diversification can also be used to gain market power. Market power exists when a firm is able to sell its products above the existing competitive level or to reduce the costs of its primary and support activities below the competitive level, or both.[45]

One approach to gaining market power through diversification is *multipoint competition*. Multipoint competition exists when two or more diversified firms simultaneously compete in the same product areas or geographic markets.[46] As mentioned earlier, the actions taken by Hewlett-Packard (HP) in its merger with Compaq Computer Corporation demonstrate multipoint competition. This merger allows the combined firm to compete with other larger companies, such as IBM and Sun

Microsystems. For example, HP and Compaq are now coordinating their efforts in PCs, servers, and services. The combined revenues of the two companies almost equal those of IBM. The merged firm will most likely compete directly with IBM in the server market and will continue to increase its services division as well.[47]

The preceding example illustrates the potential dynamics of multipoint competition. As a strategic action (see Chapter 5), HP and Compaq's decision to merge is partly a competitive response to IBM's success in servers and services.[48] Counterattacks are not common in multipoint competition because the threat of a counterattack may prevent strategic actions from being taken, or, more likely, firms may retract their strategic actions when faced with the threat of counterattack.[49] Using a matching strategy, where the responding firm takes the same strategic action as the attacker, is a prominent form of response because it signals a commitment to defend the status quo without escalating rivalry.[50] This can be seen in the responses of media firms to the AOL Time Warner merger, as illustrated in the Strategic Focus on page 192 about Disney and other media firms.

Vertical integration exists when a company produces its own inputs (backward integration) or owns its own source of distribution of outputs (forward integration).

Some firms choose to create value by using vertical integration to gain market power (see Figure 6.2). **Vertical integration** exists when a company produces its own inputs (backward integration) or owns its own source of distribution of outputs (forward integration). In some instances, firms partially integrate their operations, producing and selling their products by using both company units and outside sources.

Vertical integration is commonly used in the firm's core business to gain market power over rivals. Market power is gained as the firm develops the ability to save on its operations, avoid market costs, improve product quality, and, possibly, protect its technology from imitation by rivals. Market power also is created when firms have strong ties between their assets for which no market prices exist. Establishing a market price would result in high search and transaction costs, so firms seek to vertically integrate rather than remaining separate businesses.[51]

Smithfield Foods, mentioned earlier, is a vertically integrated company with hog processing as its core business. Smithfield has vertically integrated backward by raising the hogs that it later processes in its plants. Most packaging plants operate profitably when the price of meat is low and suffer with high meat prices. In contrast, Smithfield can better control its costs because it owns facilities that provide the raw materials required for its core processing operations. This control often results in Smithfield having market power over its competitors because it typically produces products at below the average industry production cost. Recent acquisitions of ten U.S. and a few international meat-packaging companies are intended to support the firm's use of vertical integration to yield competitively attractive options to consumers.[52]

There are also limits to vertical integration. For example, an outside supplier may produce the product at a lower cost. As a result, internal transactions from vertical integration may be expensive and reduce profitability relative to competitors. Also, bureaucratic costs may occur with vertical integration. And, because vertical integration can require substantial investments in specific technologies, it may reduce the firm's flexibility, especially when technology changes quickly. Finally, changes in demand create capacity balance and coordination problems. If one division is building a part for another internal division, but achieving economies of scale requires the first division to manufacture quantities that are beyond the capacity of the internal buyer to absorb, it would be necessary to sell the parts outside the firm as well as to the internal division. Thus, although vertical integration can create value, especially through market power over competitors, it is not without risks and costs.

Many manufacturing firms no longer pursue vertical integration.[53] In fact, deintegration is the focus of most manufacturing firms, such as Intel and Dell, and even among large automobile companies, such as Ford and General Motors, as they develop independent supplier networks.[54] Solectron Corp., a contract manufacturer,

Strategic Focus

Multipoint Competition among Media Firms: Content Is King at Disney

Following the announcement of the AOL Time Warner merger, other content-oriented media firms felt pressure to pursue distribution businesses. The merger provided a content company (AOL) with several distribution outlets (Time Warner). Time Warner already had distribution assets through its cable TV operations, and the merger with AOL added the largest Internet service provider (ISP). Vivendi Universal (discussed in a later Strategic Focus), created through the merger of French utility conglomerate Vivendi with Seagrams, which owned Universal Studios and Universal Music, is seeking to match the content and distribution strategy developed by AOL Time Warner.

Walt Disney Company, however, has resisted the pressure to imitate these competitive actions. The firm has been a strong force in the business of entertaining consumers for decades. True to its beginnings, Disney has grown to be one of the largest moviemakers in the industry—consistently producing hit movies. As the company grew and the media industry consolidated, it brought ABC and its affiliates under its corporate umbrella, becoming a major competitor in the television network business. The diversified entertainment behemoth also built theme parks all over the world. According to Disney CEO Michael Eisner, all of the firm's business segments focus on one main product offering: content. In his view, Disney provides content—an actual, intellectual product made for consumption by the consumer.

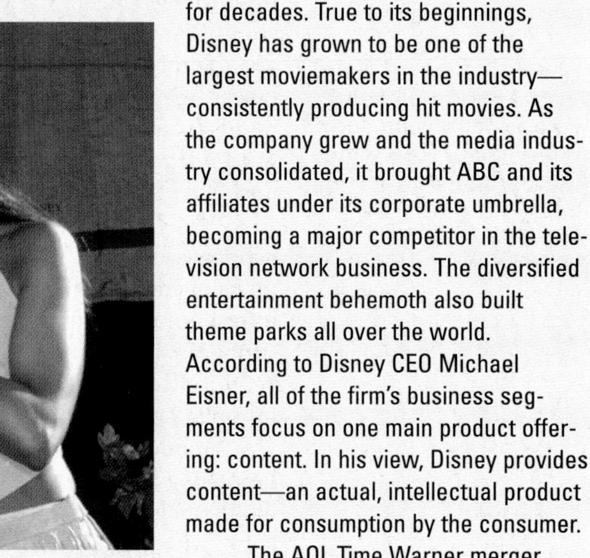

According to Walt Disney corporate website (http://disney.go.com), the firm's key objective is to be the world's premier family entertainment company through the ongoing development of its powerful brand and character franchises. Shown here are performers Lebo M and Paulette Ivory from a production of the musical play, "The Lion King," which builds on the company's movie characters by the same name. Walt Disney once remarked about his company, "I only hope we don't lose sight of one thing—that it was all started by a mouse."

The AOL Time Warner merger resulted in a battle in which AOL Time Warner cut Disney-owned ABC off from 3.5 million subscribers for 39 hours because of disputes between the two companies. There is much pressure, both from outside investors and inside executives, to expand Disney's distribution options. Some content producers have approached the company about bidding for AT&T Broadband, but it has not done so. Disney hopes that its content offerings will be so strong that consumers would complain if the Disney-owned channels were taken off the air, as was the case during the disagreement with AOL Time Warner.

To support "content is king" as the foundation for its competition position, Disney completed a transaction with News Corporation and Saban Entertainment Inc. to buy Fox Family Worldwide. This acquisition added over 100 million subscribers to Disney's already vast cable operations, which include the Disney Channel, Toon Disney, SoapNet, and ESPN. Fox Family Worldwide also provides Disney with a rich library of content, including 6,500 episodes of animated shows such as *Digimon, Spider-Man,* and *Mighty Morphin Power Rangers.* The company plans to integrate the Fox Family Channel with ABC's operations to air reruns of shows originally aired on the ABC Network or other Disney-owned channels. This "repurposing" will allow viewers to see their favorite shows outside of the normal viewing time. It will also allow Disney to make extra revenue from the shows and the firm should be able to spread the cost across several outlets.

Disney sees itself as a creator of entertainment content rather than as a distribution channel for it. Consistent with its vision, Disney continues to diversify in ways that add content to its substantial library, such as its acquisition of Fox Family Worldwide, and resists the temptation to add distribution capabilities, such as cable businesses like AT&T

Broadband. Because of the multipoint competition for advertising, Disney may have to respond to the pressures for distribution assets. However, Disney encountered difficulties in its past attempts to do so, such as the go.com Internet portal. Thus, Disney feels pressure to move beyond its emphasis on content into new areas of competence to meet the competition, which is developing distribution channel capabilities.

SOURCES: B. Carter, 2001, Disney discusses strategy behind buying Fox Family, *The New York Times,* http://www.nytimes.com, July 24; N. Deogun, S. Beatty, B. Orwall, & J. Lippman, 2001, Disney plans to acquire Fox Family for $3 billion and debt assumption, *The Wall Street Journal Interactive,* http://www.interactive.wsj.com, July 23; G. Fabrikant & A. R. Sorkin, 2001, Disney is said to be close to acquiring Fox Family, *The New York Times,* http://www.nytimes.com, July 23; J. Flint & B. Orwall, 2001, 'ABC Family' cable channel will recycle network fare, *The Wall Street Journal Interactive,* http://www.interactive.wsj.com, July 24; R. Grover, 2001, Fox Family enters the Mouse House, *Business Week Online,* http://www.businessweek.com, July 24; J. Guyon, 2001, Can Messier make cash flow like water? *Fortune,* September 3, 148–150; R. Linnett, Leap frog, *Advertising Age,* 2001, July 30, S12; S. Schiesel, 2001, For Disney's Eisner, the business is content, not conduits, *The New York Times,* http://www.nytimes.com, July 2.

represents a new breed of large contract manufacturers that is helping to foster this revolution in supply-chain management. Such firms often manage their customers' entire product lines, and offer services ranging from inventory management to delivery and after-sales service. Performing business through e-commerce also allows vertical integration to be changed into "virtual integration."[55] Thus, closer relationships are possible with suppliers and customers through virtual integration or electronic means of integration, allowing firms to reduce the costs of processing transactions while improving their supply-chain management skills and tightening the control of their inventories. "The longer the supply chain, the bigger the potential gains from B2B e-commerce, since it allows firms to eliminate the many layers of middlemen that hamper economic efficiency."[56]

Simultaneous Operational Relatedness and Corporate Relatedness

As Figure 6.2 suggests, some firms simultaneously seek operational and corporate forms of economies of scope.[57] Because simultaneously managing two sources of knowledge is very difficult, such efforts often fail, creating diseconomies of scope.[58] For example, USA Networks Inc. has focused primarily on TV entertainment, owning networks such as USA, the Sci Fi channel, and the Home Shopping Network. CEO Barry Diller seeks to make the company a leader in the interactive-commerce market. In 2001, USA Networks bought a controlling interest in Expedia, the online travel website, from Microsoft and announced its intention of buying National Leisure Group, a small travel company. The firm plans to innovate by combining its acquired firms' travel capabilities with its current cable TV capabilities. Resulting from this integration of capabilities will be a new cable network that provides a travel-shopping channel allowing viewers to buy travel services over the phone. Thus, the firm will share the phone capabilities already in place for its shopping channels and also transfer its TV capabilities to its newly acquired online travel and travel service assets. The online-travel market was seen as having tremendous growth potential before the terrorist acts of September 11, and USA Networks wanted to establish a first-mover advantage in this market in combination with its TV capability.[59] Although this strategy is difficult to implement, if the firm is successful, it could create value that is hard for competitors to imitate.

Vivendi is trying to achieve both operational relatedness and corporate relatedness in the media business. Vivendi's strategy, as illustrated in the Strategic Focus on page 194, may be difficult to achieve because its distribution of content is focused on mobile web technology.

Strategic Focus

Vivendi: From Water Treatment to Media Might

With a foundation in the water treatment business, the French firm Vivendi has diversified into various media businesses. This movement into media became more pronounced with Vivendi's announcement of its merger with Seagram's Universal Studios and Universal Music Group. At the time of this transaction, Vivendi CEO, Jean-Marie Messier described his vision of the future. The vision is one in which consumers could use either their cellular telephones or handheld computers to purchase music through an online music site and view movies through broadband subscription services. To realize this vision, Vivendi Universal acquired MP3.com, an online music-sharing website. Messier asserted that it was "a big step forward for Vivendi Universal's priority to develop an aggressive, legitimate and attractive offering of our content to consumers." To overcome the powerful middlemen, such as Blockbuster video-rental chain and HBO cable network and to reach his vision, Vivendi Universal has formed a joint venture with other studios (including Sony Pictures, AOL Time Warner's Warner Brothers, Viacom's Metro-Goldwyn-Mayer) to create a digital video on demand platform. This service will allow direct broadband delivery of digital video to
consumers.

When Vivendi Universal purchased Houghton Mifflin, a U.S. educational publisher, Messier asserted that it was "another step forward for Vivendi Universal to achieve world leadership in key content segments." He also said that leveraging the acquired content and technologies assets of Houghton Mifflin would allow Vivendi Universal "to capitalize on the growth of the education sector" and to match the publishing and content assets of AOL Time Warner.

In June 2001, Vivendi Universal further extended its reach by acquiring a larger stake in Elektrim Telekomunikacja, the telecommunication assets of Polish conglomerate Elektrim, which gave it control over that company, and, in effect, control over Polska Telefonia Cyfrowa (PTC), Eastern Europe's largest mobile-telephone operator. Vivendi already is one of the largest providers of mobile phone service in Europe. Earlier, Vivendi joined forces with British telecommunications leader Vodafone to create Vizzavi, which was launched in France in June 2000. "Vizzavi would be Messier's distribution arm in Europe, beaming content over the wireless Web to Vivendi's eight million and Vodafone's 48 million mobile-phone customers." This additional acquisition gave Vivendi Universal a strong foothold into the mobile phone market in Eastern Europe, which fits nicely with its vision of the future.

The acquisition of MP3.com brought a number of things to Vivendi Universal. First, even though Vivendi had fought with the online music distributors, MP3.com gave it a well-known online brand. More importantly for Vivendi, however, is the technology and know-how that the acquisition provides. Vivendi Universal and Sony Music have announced that they will also enter into the online music distribution business through a music service named Pressplay. The purchase of MP3.com brings into the company the demonstrated technology and experience that will be essential to Pressplay's success.

Vivendi Universal's acquisitions have extended the company's content and distribution network. The merger with Universal and the acquisition of Houghton Mifflin provided the company with well-known brands to produce content. By purchasing an online music distributor, Vivendi expanded its ability to put its content in front of the consumer for purchase. The procurement of a controlling stake in PTC gives the company a high performing cellular phone company and is a step into the future where people "see a trailer for a film on [their] . . . mobile phone." By diversifying into different content and distribution areas, Vivendi Universal is building for a future in which it hopes to be a one-stop media outlet. In content businesses, it shares activities to produce movies, movie themes in its theme parks, and movie sound tracks. Additionally, it has the knowledge through its phone acquisitions and alliances and the MP3.com acquisition to transfer this expertise to improve distribution. However, because Vivendi's distribution is more dependent on mobile online technology than other large media firms, the success of Vivendi's approach remains an open question. Furthermore, it is hard to tell how the acquisitions are doing relative to the basic water treatment assets, given that the income streams from these assets are hard to distinguish in the accounting reports. The increased emphasis on transparency regarding how a firm is generating its revenue and profits suggests that this could become an important issue.

SOURCES: C. Matlack, 2002, Memo to Jean-Marie Messier, *Business Week,* March 4, 56; 2001, Associated Press, MP3.com adds 1 millionth song; launches new subscriber service, *The Detroit News Online,* http://www.detnews.com, June 14; D. Leonard, 2001, Mr. Messier is ready for his close-up, *Fortune,* September 3, 136–148; 2001, Dow Jones Newswire, France's Vivendi appears to win battle for mobile operator PTC in Poland, *The Wall Street Journal Interactive,* http://www.wsj.com, June 28; B. Orwall, 2001, Five Hollywood studios enter venture to offer feature films of the Internet, *The Wall Street Journal Interactive,* http://www.wsj.com, August 17; M. Richtel, 2001, Vivendi deal for MP3.com highlights trend, *The New York Times,* http://www.nytimes.com, May 22; S. Schiesel, 2001, Vivendi will acquire Houghton Mifflin for $1.7 billion, *The New York Times,* http://www.nytimes.com, June 2; A. R. Sorkin, 2001, Vivendi in deal to acquire MP3.com, *The New York Times,* http://www.nytimes.com, May 21; A. Weintraub, R. Grover, & C. Matlack, 2001, Vivendi faces the music on the Web, *Business Week,* June 4, 43.

As illustrated in the Strategic Focus about Vivendi, a critical aspect of achieving both operational relatedness and corporate relatedness is how well a firm manages the sharing of activities *and* the transferring of knowledge. Disney, another media firm, has been successful in using both operational relatedness and corporate relatedness, although it has not developed distribution capabilities.

Pictured here are Vivendi CEO Jean-Marie Messier (left) with USA Networks CEO Barry Diller.

Disney's strategy is especially successful compared to Sony when measured by revenues generated from successful movies. By using operational relatedness and corporate relatedness, Disney made $3 billion on the 150 products that were marketed with its movie, *The Lion King.* Sony's *Men in Black* was a super hit at the box office and earned $600 million, but box-office and video revenues were practically the entire success story. Disney was able to accomplish its great success by sharing activities regarding the *Lion King* theme within its movie and theme parks, music and retail products divisions, while at the same time transferring knowledge into these same divisions, creating a music CD, *Rhythm of the Pride Lands,* and producing a video, *Simba's Pride.* In addition, there were *Lion King* themes at Disney resorts and Animal Kingdom parks.[60] However, as is the case with Vivendi Universal, it is difficult for analysts from outside the firm to fully assess the value-creating potential of the firm pursuing both operational relatedness and corporate relatedness. As such, Disney's and Vivendi Universal's assets have been discounted somewhat because "the biggest lingering questions is whether multiple revenue streams will outpace multiple-platform overhead."[61]

Unrelated Diversification

Firms do not seek either operational relatedness or corporate relatedness when using the unrelated diversification corporate-level strategy. An unrelated diversification strategy (see Figure 6.2) can create value through two types of financial economies.

Financial economies are cost savings realized through improved allocations of financial resources based on investments inside or outside the firm.

Financial economies are cost savings realized through improved allocations of financial resources based on investments inside or outside the firm.[62]

The first type of financial economy results from efficient internal capital allocations. This approach seeks to reduce risk among the firm's business units—for example, through the development of a portfolio of businesses with different risk profiles. The approach thereby reduces business risk for the total corporation. The second type of financial economy is concerned with purchasing other corporations and restructuring their assets. This approach finds the diversified firm buying other companies, restructuring their assets in ways that allows the purchased company to operate more profitably, and then selling the company for a profit in the external market.

Efficient Internal Capital Market Allocation

In a market economy, capital markets are thought to efficiently allocate capital. Efficiency results from investors' purchasing of firm equity shares (ownership) that have high future cash-flow values. Capital is also allocated through debt as shareholders and debtholders try to improve the value of their investments by taking stakes in businesses with high growth prospects.

In large diversified firms, the corporate office distributes capital to business divisions to create value for the overall company. Such an approach may provide gains from internal capital market allocation relative to the external capital market.[63] This happens because while managing the firm's portfolio of businesses, the corporate office may gain access to detailed and accurate information regarding those businesses' actual and prospective performance.

The corporate office needs to convey its ability to create value in this manner to the market. One way firms have been doing this is through tracking stocks, as General Motors has done for its Hughes Aerospace division.[64] GM created a new stock listing for the Hughes assets that conveyed better information to the market about this additional asset. This approach allows more scrutiny by the market and thus more transparency of increasingly complex and diversified internal operations.

Compared with corporate office personnel, investors have relatively limited access to internal information and can only estimate divisional performance and future business prospects. Although businesses seeking capital must provide information to potential suppliers (such as banks or insurance companies), firms with internal capital markets may have at least two informational advantages. First, information provided to capital markets through annual reports and other sources may not include negative information, instead emphasizing positive prospects and outcomes. External sources of capital have limited ability to understand the dynamics inside large organizations. Even external shareholders who have access to information have no guarantee of full and complete disclosure.[65] Second, although a firm must disseminate information, that information also becomes simultaneously available to the firm's current and potential competitors. With insights gained by studying such information, competitors might attempt to duplicate a firm's competitive advantage. Thus, an ability to efficiently allocate capital through an internal market may help the firm protect its competitive advantages.

If intervention from outside the firm is required to make corrections to capital allocations, only significant changes are possible, such as forcing the firm into bankruptcy or changing the top management team. Alternatively, in an internal capital market, the corporate office can fine-tune its corrections, such as choosing to adjust managerial incentives or suggesting strategic changes in a division. Thus, capital can be allocated according to more specific criteria than is possible with external market allocations. Because it has less accurate information, the external capital market may fail to allocate resources adequately to high-potential investments compared with corporate office investments. The corporate office of a diversified company can more effectively perform tasks such as disciplining underperforming management teams through resource allocations.[66]

Research suggests, however, that in efficient capital markets, the unrelated diversification strategy may be discounted.[67] "For years, stock markets have applied a 'conglomerate discount': they value diversified manufacturing conglomerates at 20 percent less, on average, than the value of the sum of their parts. The discount still applies, in good economic times and bad. Extraordinary manufacturers (like GE) can defy it for a while, but more ordinary ones (like Philips and Siemens) cannot."[68]

Some firms still use the unrelated diversification strategy.[69] These large diversified business groups are found in many European countries and throughout emerging economies as well. For example, research indicates that the conglomerate or unrelated diversification strategy has not disappeared in Europe, where the number of firms using it has actually increased.[70] Although many conglomerates, such as ITT and Hansen Trust, have refocused, other unrelated diversified firms have replaced them.

The Achilles heel of the unrelated diversification strategy is that conglomerates in developed economies have a fairly short life cycle because financial economies are more easily duplicated than are the gains derived from operational relatedness and corporate relatedness. This is less of a problem in emerging economies, where the absence of a "soft infrastructure" (including effective financial intermediaries, sound regulations, and contract laws) supports and encourages use of the unrelated diversification strategy.[71] In fact, in emerging economies such as those in India and Chile, diversification increases performance of firms affiliated with large diversified business groups.[72]

Restructuring

Financial economies can also be created when firms learn how to create value by buying and selling other companies' assets in the external market.[73] As in the real estate business, buying assets at low prices, restructuring them, and selling them at a price exceeding their cost generates a positive return on the firm's invested capital.

Under CEO Dennis L. Kozlowski, Tyco International, Ltd., gains financial economies through restructuring. Tyco focuses on two types of acquisitions: platform, which represent new bases for future acquisitions, and add-on, in markets Tyco currently has a major presence. As with many unrelated diversified firms, Tyco acquires mature product lines. "In Tyco's entrepreneurial culture, managers have enormous autonomy. Kozlowski relies on a computerized reporting system that gives him a detailed snapshot of how each business is performing. It's updated several times a week with information including sales, profit margins, and order backlog sliced by geography and product area. If he spots a problem, Kozlowski invariably uses the phone rather than e-mail."[74]

During Kozlowski's tenure, Tyco has created a significant amount of value by acquiring companies, restructuring their assets, and then selling them in the external market for a gain. Nonetheless, in the wake of the Enron disaster, Tyco's accounting has been called into question along with many other complex firms including GE. Large unrelated diversified firms creating value by buying, restructuring, and selling other companies' assets often complete a significant number of transactions. For example, "During the past decade Tyco has acquired hundreds of humdrum businesses—an astounding 700 in the past three years alone [1999–2001]."[75] Completing large numbers of complex transactions has resulted in accounting practices that aren't as transparent as stakeholders now demand. Actions being taken in 2002 suggest that firms creating value through financial economies are responding to the demand for greater transparency in their practices. Responding in this manner will provide the transparent information the market requires to more accurately estimate the value the diversified firm is creating when using the unrelated diversification strategy.[76]

Selling underperforming divisions and placing the rest under rigorous financial controls such as those described for Tyco increases a unit's value. Rigorous controls require divisions to follow strict budgets and account regularly for cash inflows and outflows to corporate headquarters. A firm creating financial economies at least partly through rigorous controls may have to use hostile takeovers or tender offers, because target firm managers often do not find this environment attractive and are less willing to be acquired. Hostile takeovers have the potential to increase the resistance of the target firm's top-level managers.[77] In these cases, corporate-level managers often are discharged, while division managers are retained, depending on how important each is to future operational success.

Creating financial economies by acquiring and restructuring other companies' assets requires an understanding of significant trade-offs. Success usually calls for a focus on mature, low-technology businesses because of the uncertainty of demand for high-technology products. Otherwise, resource allocation decisions become too complex, creating information-processing overload on the small corporate staffs of unrelated diversified firms. Service businesses with a client orientation are also difficult to buy and sell in this way, because of their client-based sales orientation.[78]

Sales staffs of service businesses are more mobile than those of manufacturing-oriented businesses and may seek jobs with a competitor, taking clients with them.[79] This is especially so in professional service businesses such as accounting, law, advertising, consulting, and investment banking. Sears, Roebuck & Co. discovered this problem after its 1981 diversification into financial services by acquiring Coldwell Banker and Dean Witter Reynolds, Inc. The anticipated synergies in financial services did not materialize, and Sears' retail performance deteriorated. In 1992, Sears announced the divestiture of financial services and a refocusing on retail operations.[80]

Diversification: Incentives and Resources

The economic reasons given in the last section summarize conditions under which diversification strategies can increase a firm's value. Diversification, however, is also often undertaken with the expectation that it will prevent reductions in firm value. Thus, there are reasons to diversify that are value neutral. In fact, some research suggests that all diversification leads to tradeoffs and some suboptimization.[81] Nonetheless, as we explain next, several incentives may lead a firm to pursue further diversification.

Incentives to Diversify

Incentives to diversify come from both the external environment and a firm's internal environment. The term "incentive" implies that managers have choices. External incentives include antitrust regulations and tax laws. Internal incentives include low performance, uncertain future cash flows, and an overall reduction of risk for the firm. Several of the incentives are illustrated in the Strategic Focus on page 199, where we highlight actions being taken at Boeing, PepsiCo, and Procter & Gamble.

As the discussion in the Strategic Focus indicates, there are incentives for the firm to use a diversification strategy. Diversification strategies taken in light of various incentives (such as PepsiCo's need to diversify its beverage line) sometimes increase the firm's ability to create value. Currently, it seems that Boeing and PepsiCo's diversification strategies are helping those firms create value. However, when a particular diversification strategy isn't creating the expected amount of value, which was determined to be the case by P&G upper-level decision makers, the firm must take corrective action to either reduce or increase the degree to which it is diversified.

Strategic Focus

Diversification Incentives Don't Always Lead to Success

Boeing was in trouble in the late 1990s after it acquired McDonnell Douglas. Besides performance problems associated with integrating the acquisition, Boeing's dominant segment—its civil-jet business—had slowed; the commercial jet market was only expanding by 5 percent per year. In response to these issues, Boeing decided to diversify.

In 2001, Boeing felt the effects of the airline industry's performance declines. Among other actions taken, the firm made the decision to lay off at least 30,000 employees before the end of 2002. However, because of the earlier performance problems and continuing uncertainty regarding the civilian airline industry, Boeing had already diversified over several years. Accordingly, the firm expects to benefit through its strong position as a space program supplier and particularly through its military and communications supply units. Because Boeing is a large producer of AWACS and C-17s for the U.S. Air Force, Boeing could benefit from the United States decision to enhance its air power after the September 11, 2001 terrorist attacks. Boeing expects that military sales could increase 10 percent and account for as much as 75 percent of sales increases in 2002 across its various business units. The company announced that no defense-related workers would be affected by the planned lay-offs.

Instead of focusing only on building jets and rockets, Boeing had also decided to move into services. In 2001, the firm won a $4 billion order from the U.S. Air Force to upgrade avionics on existing C-130 aircraft, which rival Lockheed Martin had built. Boeing recently entered the aircraft maintenance and services market and believes that it has significant growth potential in these two areas.

Boeing also released its plans for building air-traffic management systems, which it hopes to develop with the Federal Aviation Administration when the agency overhauls the air-traffic control system. If the FAA partners with Boeing, the company believes that the market may be worth $70 billion annually. Boeing is also delving into the broadband communications market, hoping to provide airline passengers with live television and high-speed data links. In addition, the company recently opened an office in Europe to facilitate expansion of its financing company. Because of the terrorist crisis, many of the airlines have asked Boeing to refinance their current accounts, which will increase the returns from the firm's financing unit.

Some firms diversify, as did Boeing, because of unexpected poor performance. Others diversify because they expect future growth to slow. As mentioned earlier, PepsiCo, maker of Pepsi, acquired Quaker Oats in order to gain access to the increased growth associated with Gatorade in the sports drink segment. Thus, there are a number of incentives for firms to diversify beyond their successful business areas. However, not all of these efforts create value.

Procter & Gamble (P&G) has been divesting its non-core brands. In recent years, P&G diversified in an effort to boost sales, because many of its products, such as Pantene shampoo, compete in mature markets. Some of the products resulting from the diversification, such as its Olay line of cosmetics and artificial cooking fat Olestra, have failed. New CEO A. G. Lafley has decided to sell off the performing poorly brands and refocus on P&G's core, higher-profit businesses by backing the company out of the food product business and other failed undertakings.

SOURCES: S. Holmes & S. Crock, 2002, The fortunes—and misfortunes—of war, *Business Week*, January 14, 90–91; 2001, Hard man Harry, *The Economist*, June 9, 68; S. Jaffe, 2001, Do Pepsi and Gatorade mix? *Business Week Online*, http://www.businessweek.com, August 14; J. Lunsford & A. Pasztor, 2001, Boeing Co.'s course in terror's wake seen as a wider U.S. test, *The Wall Street Journal*, September 20, A1, A8; E. Nelson, 2001, P&G expects to restore growth; Will pull the plug on failed projects, *The Wall Street Journal Interactive*, http://www.wsj.com, June 18.

Antitrust Regulation and Tax Laws

Government antitrust policies and tax laws provided incentives for U.S. firms to diversify in the 1960s and 1970s.[82] Antitrust laws to mergers that created increased market power (via either vertical or horizontal integration) were stringently enforced during that period.[83] As a result, many of the mergers during that time were unrelated, involving companies pursuing different lines of business. Thus, the merger wave of the 1960s was "conglomerate" in character. Merger activity that produced conglomerate diversification was encouraged primarily by the Celler-Kefauver Act, which discouraged horizontal and vertical mergers. For example, in the 1973–1977 period, 79.1 percent of all mergers were conglomerate.[84]

During the 1980s, antitrust enforcement lessened, resulting in more and larger horizontal mergers (acquisitions of target firms in the same line of business, such as a merger between two oil companies).[85] In addition, investment bankers became more open to the kinds of mergers they tried to facilitate; as a consequence, hostile takeovers increased to unprecedented numbers.[86] The conglomerates or highly diversified firms of the 1960s and 1970s became more "focused" in the 1980s and early 1990s as merger constraints were relaxed and restructuring was implemented.[87]

In the late 1990s and early 2000s, antitrust concerns emerged again with the large volume of mergers and acquisitions (see Chapter 7).[88] Thus, mergers are now receiving more scrutiny than they did in the 1980s and through the early 1990s.

The tax effects of diversification stem not only from individual tax rates, but also from corporate tax changes. Some companies (especially mature ones) generate more cash from their operations than they can reinvest profitably. Some argue that *free cash flows* (liquid financial assets for which investments in current businesses are no longer economically viable) should be redistributed to shareholders as dividends.[89] However, in the 1960s and 1970s, dividends were taxed more heavily than ordinary personal income. As a result, before 1980, shareholders preferred that firms use free cash flows to buy and build companies in high-performance industries. If the firm's stock value appreciated over the long term, shareholders might receive a better return on those funds than if they had been redistributed as dividends, because they would be taxed more lightly under capital-gains rules than dividends when they sell their stock.

Under the 1986 Tax Reform Act, however, the top individual ordinary income tax rate was reduced from 50 to 28 percent, and the special capital-gains tax was also changed, treating capital gains as ordinary income. These changes created an incentive for shareholders to stop encouraging firms to retain funds for purposes of diversification. These tax law changes also influenced an increase in divestitures of unrelated business units after 1984. Thus, while individual tax rates for capital gains and dividends created a shareholder incentive to increase diversification before 1986, they encouraged less diversification after 1986, unless it was funded by tax-deductible debt. The elimination of personal-interest deductions, as well as the lower attractiveness of retained earnings to shareholders, might prompt the use of more leverage by firms, for which interest expense is tax deductible.

Corporate tax laws also affect diversification. Acquisitions typically increase a firm's depreciable asset allowances. Increased depreciation (a non-cash-flow expense) produces lower taxable income, thereby providing an additional incentive for acquisitions. Before 1986, acquisitions may have been the most attractive means for securing tax benefits,[90] but the 1986 Tax Reform Act diminished some of the corporate tax advantages of diversification.[91] The recent changes recommended by the Financial Accounting Standards Board (FASB) regarding the elimination of the "pooling of interests" method for accounting for the acquired firm's assets and the elimination of the write-off for research and development in process reduce some of the incentives to make acquisitions, especially related acquisitions in high technology industries (these changes are discussed further in Chapter 7).[92]

Although there was a loosening of federal regulations in the 1980s and a retightening in the late 1990s, a number of industries have experienced increased merger activity due to industry specific deregulation activity, including banking, telecommunications, oil and gas, and electric utilities, among others. For example, the electric utilities industry is deregulating throughout the developed world.[93] German utility companies such as RWE are finding deregulation challenging, in that it has produced lower electricity prices and limited profit growth. RWE, which easily raised $17 billion for acquisitions, hoped to diversify into utility markets in the United States and Europe to buffer deregulation's effects. CFO Klaus Sturany explained that the company was looking to purchase firms in the company's "core businesses: electricity, gas, water, and waste management . . . [that] fit strategically."[94] Important to RWE is whether the acquisition is in a growth market, whether the quality of management is good, and whether existing profitability is high. RWE plans to find the most growth with water companies, but is also considering unregulated companies in the electricity generation sector. Such moves will require significant learning because most utilities have traditionally operated in slow-cycle markets.[95]

Low Performance

Some research shows that low returns are related to greater levels of diversification.[96] If "high performance eliminates the need for greater diversification,"[97] as in the case of Wm. Wrigley Jr. Co., then low performance may provide an incentive for diversification. Firms plagued by poor performance often take higher risks.[98] Poor performance may lead to increased diversification as it did with Boeing described in the Strategic Focus on page 199, especially if resources exist to do so.[99] Continued poor returns following additional diversification, however, may slow its pace and even lead to divestitures. Thus, an overall curvilinear relationship, as illustrated in Figure 6.3, may exist between diversification and performance.[100]

As mentioned in the Strategic Focus, Procter & Gamble may have diversified beyond its capabilities to manage the diversification. The company has had strong historical success in its consumer soaps, including Tide and Ivory, and in toothpaste (Crest). However, its Olay cosmetics and artificial cooking fat, Olestra, have not been

Figure 6.3 The Curvilinear Relationship between Diversification and Performance

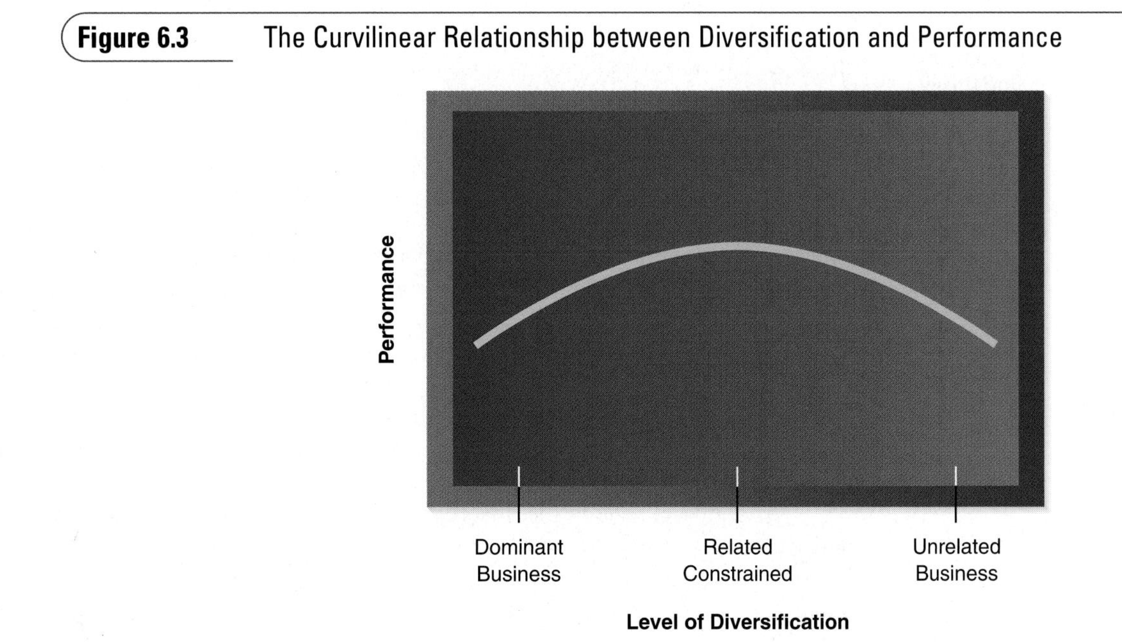

successful, resulting in the firm's recent decision to refocus on its "core" brands. P&G's refocusing may suggest that its diversification level was producing poor returns (see diversification-performance curve in Figure 6.3).

Uncertain Future Cash Flows

As a firm's product line matures or is threatened, diversification may be taken as an important defensive strategy.[101] Small firms and companies in mature or maturing industries sometimes find it necessary to diversify for long-term survival.[102] Certainly, this was one of the dominant reasons for diversification among railroad firms during the 1960s and 1970s. Railroads diversified primarily because the trucking industry was perceived to have significant negative effects for rail transportation and thus created demand uncertainty. Uncertainty, however, can be derived from supply, demand, and distribution sources. As explained earlier, PepsiCo acquired Quaker Oat to fortify its growth with Gatorade and healthy snacks. These products are projected to experience greater growth rates than Pepsi's soft drinks.

Tupperware also wanted to diversify its distribution due to uncertainty about demand for its products. Historically, Tupperware products were sold by independent sales agents sponsoring "Tupperware parties." Because more women have entered the workforce, the firm's traditional customer base—women in their homes—has eroded. Tupperware's response over the past few years has been to sell its products to new customers through different distribution channels. For example, in July 2001, the company reached an agreement with retailer Target to display Tupperware products in SuperTarget stores. To prevent problems with the traditional sales channel, Tupperware's independent sales agents staff the displays of the firm's products in SuperTarget stores. Tupperware products are also available through Target's website. Company officials estimated that 40 percent of sales would come from this and similar ventures (such as television, Internet, and mall ventures) within five years.[103] Thus, Tupperware is diversifying its distribution channels in order to reduce the uncertainty of its future cash flows.

Firm Risk Reduction

Synergy exists when the value created by business units working together exceeds the value those same units create working independently.

Diversified firms pursuing economies of scope often have investments that are too inflexible to realize synergy between business units. As a result, a number of problems may arise. **Synergy** exists when the value created by business units working together exceeds the value those same units create working independently. But, as a firm increases its relatedness between business units, it also increases its risk of corporate failure, because synergy produces joint interdependence between business units and the firm's flexibility to respond is constrained. This threat may force two basic decisions.

First, the firm may reduce its level of technological change by operating in more certain environments. This behavior may make the firm risk averse and thus uninterested in pursuing new product lines that have potential, but are not proven. Alternatively, the firm may constrain its level of activity sharing and forego synergy's benefits. Either or both decisions may lead to further diversification. The former would lead to related diversification into industries in which more certainty exists. The latter may produce additional, but unrelated, diversification.[104] Research suggests that a firm using a related diversification strategy is more careful in bidding for new businesses, whereas a firm pursuing an unrelated diversification strategy may be more likely to overprice its bid, because an unrelated bidder may not have full information about the acquired firm.[105]

For example, StarTek Inc. historically has generated its revenues by packaging and shipping software for Microsoft, by providing technical support to AOL Time Warner and AT&T, and by maintaining communications systems for AT&T. Because StarTek was so dependent on a small number of large customers, especially Microsoft,

it chose to diversify to reduce its dependence risk. In 1999, StarTek spent $12.4 million to acquire a 20 percent interest in Gifts.com, an online retailer selling gifts, home furnishings, and other merchandise. Reader's Digest Association Inc. also has an ownership position in Gifts.com, a firm that continues to lose money. If this doesn't soon change, StarTek could lose its investment in the venture. StarTek also invested in a mortgage-financing firm that has since been accused of defrauding investors, forcing StarTek to take a $3 million charge in 2001. Moreover, these problems were coming at a time when sales of software that StarTek handles for Microsoft, its biggest customer, were declining.[106] As the StarTek example shows, firms seeking to reduce risk by diversifying should fully understand the nature of the businesses they are entering through their diversification efforts.

Resources and Diversification

Although a firm may have incentives to diversify, it must also possess the resources required to create value through diversification.[107] As mentioned earlier, tangible, intangible, and financial resources all facilitate diversification. Resources vary in their utility for value creation, however, because of differences in rarity and mobility—that is, some resources are easier for competitors to duplicate because they are not rare, valuable, costly to imitate, and nonsubstitutable (see Chapter 3). For instance, free cash flows are a financial resource that may be used to diversify the firm. Because financial resources are more flexible and common, they are less likely to create value compared with other types of resources and less likely to be a source of competitive advantage.[108]

However, as a financial resource, cash can be used to invest in other resources that can lead to more valuable and less imitable advantages. For example, Microsoft had $30 billion in cash reserves in 2001, generated largely by its Windows and Office monopolies. Its cash reserves were growing by $1 billion every month.[109] With this much cash in reserve (more, by far, than any other company), Microsoft is able to invest heavily in R&D, to gradually build a market presence with products such as Xbox, Microsoft's video game machine, and to make diversifying acquisitions of other companies and new business ventures. This level of cash creates significant flexibility, allowing Microsoft to invest in R&D so that it has the support required for it to possibly become a competitive advantage. But, as this example suggests, excess cash can be the conduit the firm needs to create more sustainable advantages.[110]

Tangible resources usually include the plant and equipment necessary to produce a product and tend to be less flexible assets: Any excess capacity often can be used only for closely related products, especially those requiring highly similar manufacturing technologies. Excess capacity of other tangible resources, such as a sales force, can be used to diversify more easily. Again, excess capacity in a sales force is more effective with related diversification, because it may be utilized to sell similar products. The sales force would be more knowledgeable about related-product characteristics, customers, and distribution channels.[111] Tangible resources may create resource interrelationships in production, marketing, procurement, and technology, defined earlier as activity sharing. Intangible resources are more flexible than tangible physical assets in facilitating diversification. Although the sharing of tangible resources may induce diversification, intangible resources such as tacit knowledge could encourage even more diversification.[112]

Managerial Motives to Diversify

Managerial motives for diversification may exist independently of incentives and resources and include managerial risk reduction and a desire for increased compensation.[113] For instance, diversification may reduce top-level managers' employment risk (the risk of job loss or income reduction). That is, corporate executives may diversify a firm in order to diversify their own employment risk, as long as profitability does not suffer excessively.[114]

Diversification also provides an additional benefit to managers that shareholders do not enjoy. Diversification and firm size are highly correlated, and as size increases, so does executive compensation.[115] Large firms are more complex and difficult to manage; thus managers of larger firms usually receive more compensation.[116] Higher compensation may serve as a motive for managers to engage in greater diversification. Governance mechanisms, such as the board of directors, monitoring by owners, executive compensation, and the market for corporate control, may limit managerial tendencies to overdiversify. These mechanisms are discussed in more detail in Chapter 10.

On the other hand, governance mechanisms may not be strong, and in some instances managers may diversify the firm to the point that it fails to earn even average returns.[117] The loss of adequate internal governance may result in poor relative performance, thereby triggering a threat of takeover. Although takeovers may improve efficiency by replacing ineffective managerial teams, managers may avoid takeovers through defensive tactics, such as "poison pills," or may reduce their own exposure to them with "golden parachute" agreements. Therefore, an external governance threat, although restraining managers, does not flawlessly control managerial motives for diversification.[118]

Most large publicly held firms are profitable because managers are positive stewards of firm resources and many of their strategic actions (e.g., diversification strategies) contribute to the firm's success. As mentioned, governance devices should be designed to deal with exceptions to the norms of achieving strategic competitiveness and increasing shareholder wealth. Thus, it is overly pessimistic to assume that managers usually act in their own self-interest as opposed to their firm's interest.[119]

Managers may also be held in check by concerns for their reputation. If positive reputation facilitates power, a poor reputation may reduce it. Likewise, a strong external market for managerial talent may deter managers from pursuing inappropriate diversification.[120] In addition, a diversified firm may police other diversified firms to acquire those poorly managed firms in order to restructure its own asset base. Knowing that their firms could be acquired if they are not managed successfully encourages managers to use value-creating strategies.

Even when governance mechanisms cause managers to correct a problem of poorly implemented diversification or overdiversification, these moves are not without trade-offs. For instance, firms that are spun off may not realize productivity gains, even though spinning them off is in the best interest of the divesting firm.[121] Accordingly, the assumption that managers need disciplining may not be entirely correct, and sometimes governance may create consequences that are worse than those resulting from overdiversification. Governance that is excessive may cause a firm's managers to be overly cautious and risk averse.[122]

As shown in Figure 6.4, the level of diversification that can be expected to have the greatest positive effect on performance is based partly on how the interaction of resources, managerial motives, and incentives affects the adoption of particular diversification strategies. As indicated earlier, the greater the incentives and the more flexible the resources, the higher is the level of expected diversification. Financial resources (the most flexible) should have a stronger relationship to the extent of diversification than either tangible or intangible resources. Tangible resources (the most inflexible) are useful primarily for related diversification.

As discussed in this chapter, firms can create more value by effectively using diversification strategies. However, diversification must be kept in check by corporate governance (see Chapter 10). Appropriate strategy implementation tools, such as

Figure 6.4 Summary Model of the Relationship between Firm Performance and Diversification

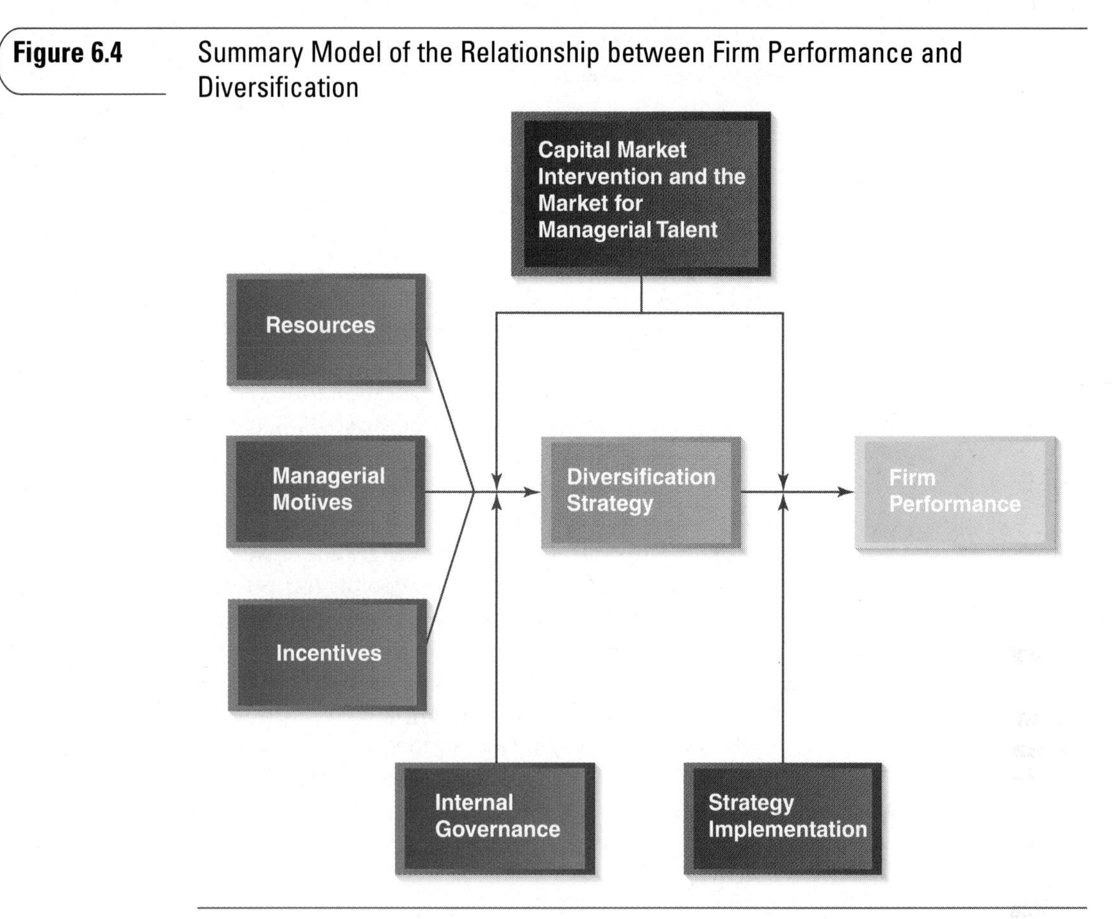

SOURCE: R. E. Hoskisson & M. A. Hitt, 1990, Antecedents and performance outcomes of diversification: A review and critique of theoretical perspectives, *Journal of Management,* 16: 498.

organizational structures, are also important (see Chapter 11), as shown by the experiences of a number of Internet-based firms.

CMGI Inc. is a diversified Internet company incubator that "bought up Internet businesses willy-nilly during the delirious days of hyperinflated dot.com stock prices, but has since failed to figure out a way to make its many companies work together for profits."[123] When this happens, the firm's board of directors must act decisively, in that the board of directors is largely responsible for making certain that its firm's top-level managers are making decisions that have a high probability of leading to competitive success and that are in shareholders' best interests. Unfortunately, because their boards tend to be fairly weak in terms of their composition, this isn't likely to happen in a fairly large number of new Internet-based ventures, especially those in which the CEO is also the firm's founder. In slightly different words, a weak board of directors working with strong top-level managers may result in decisions that aren't in shareholders best interests.[124] This might be the case at Internet Capital Group. An SEC investigation of this firm found that while many retail investors were still buying shares in the firm, managers and inside board members were selling their shares. Thus, top-level managers and board members may have benefited from information that was available to them but not to outside investors.[125]

We have described corporate-level strategies in this chapter. In the next one, we discuss the use of mergers and acquisitions as a prominent means of firms to diversify. These trends toward more diversification through acquisitions, which have been partially reversed due to restructuring (see Chapter 7), indicate that learning has taken place regarding corporate-level diversification strategies.[126] Firms performing well in their dominant business may not want to diversify, as shown by the effect of the U.S. economy in 2001 and 2002. Moreover, firms that diversify should do so cautiously, choosing to focus on a relatively few, rather than many, businesses.[127] In fact, research suggests that although unrelated diversification has decreased, related diversification has increased, possibly due to the restructuring that continued into the 1990s and early 21st century.[128]

Both in some emerging economies as well as in many industrialized countries, such as Germany, Italy and France, diversification has become the norm for the most successful firms. Subsequently, though, many of these diversified firms began to restructure. This sequence of diversification followed by restructuring mirrors actions of firms in the United States and the United Kingdom.[129]

In Europe, for example, many of the largest conglomerates are restructuring as a result of two elements' effects. First, deregulation across Europe is creating more competition, and the emergence of the European Union is causing firms to pursue pan-European strategies. Second, the realities of global competition are becoming prominent in Europe, resulting in corporate restructurings, and firms in several industries sectors are responding by restructuring to encourage long-term growth in both sales revenue and profitability.

As in the United States, these firms are finding that strategic competitiveness can be increased when they pursue a level of diversification that is appropriate for their resources (especially financial resources) and core competencies and the opportunities and threats in their external environment.[130]

Summary

- Using a single- or dominant-business corporate-level strategy may be preferable to seeking a more diversified strategy, unless a corporation can develop economies of scope or financial economies between businesses, or unless it can obtain market power through additional levels of diversification. These economies and market power are the main sources of value creation when the firm diversifies.
- Related diversification creates value through the sharing of activities or the transfer of core competencies.
- Sharing activities usually involves sharing tangible resources between businesses. Transferring core competencies involves transferring core competencies developed in one business to another one. It also may involve transferring competencies between the corporate office and a business unit.
- Sharing activities is usually associated with the related constrained diversification corporate-level strategy. Activity sharing is costly to implement and coordinate, may create unequal benefits for the divisions involved in the sharing, and may lead to fewer managerial risk-taking behaviors.
- Transferring core competencies is often associated with related linked (or mixed related and unrelated) diversification, although firms pursuing both sharing activities and transferring core competencies can use it.
- Efficiently allocating resources or restructuring a target firm's assets and placing them under rigorous financial controls are two ways to accomplish successful unrelated diversification. These methods focus on obtaining financial economies.
- The primary reason a firm diversifies is to create more value. However, diversification is sometimes pursued because of incentives from tax and anti-trust government policies, performance disappointments, uncertainties about future cash flow, or to reduce risk.
- Managerial motives to diversify (including to increase compensation) can lead to overdiversification and a reduction in the firm's value-creating ability. On the other hand, managers can also be good stewards of the firm's assets.
- Managers need to pay attention to their firm's internal environment and its external environment when making decisions about the optimum level of diversification for their company. Of course, internal resources are important determinants of the direction that diversification should take. However, conditions in the firm's external environment may facilitate additional levels of diversification as might unexpected threats from competitors.

Review Questions

1. What is corporate-level strategy? Why is it important to the diversified firm?
2. What are the advantages and disadvantages of single- and dominant-business strategies, compared with those of firms with higher levels of diversification?
3. What are three reasons that firms choose to become more diversified by moving away from either a single- or a dominant-business corporate-level strategy?
4. How do firms share activities or transfer core competencies to obtain economies of scope when using a related diversification strategy?
5. What are the two ways to obtain financial economies when using an unrelated diversification strategy?
6. What incentives and resources encourage diversification?
7. What motives might encourage managers to diversify the firm beyond an appropriate level?

Experiential Exercise

Diversification

As a member of the strategic management team for a very successful sporting goods firm that specializes in the manufacturing and marketing of soccer equipment, you have been asked to provide your thoughts as to whether the firm should diversify and to what extent.

Part One. List the advantages and disadvantages of diversification in the following table.

Part Two. Provide examples of related and unrelated diversification areas that you feel might be appropriate for the firm, including some specific advantages and disadvantages that the firm might find for each.

Advantages	Disadvantages

Notes

1. M. E. Porter, 1980, *Competitive Strategy*, New York: The Free Press, xvi.
2. R. E. Hoskisson, R. A. Johnson, D. Yiu, & W. P. Wan, 2001, Restructuring strategies of diversified business groups: Differences associated with country institutional environments. In M. A. Hitt, R. E. Freeman, J. S. Harrison (eds.), *Handbook of Strategic Management*, Oxford, U.K.: Blackwell Publishers, 433–463; Y. Luo, 2001, Determinants of entry in an emerging economy: A multilevel approach, *Journal of Management Studies*, 38: 443–472; T. B. Palmer & R. M. Wiseman, 1999, Decoupling risk taking from income stream uncertainty: A holistic model of risk, *Strategic Management Journal*, 20: 1037–1062.
3. E. H. Bowman & C. E. Helfat, 2001, Does corporate strategy matter? *Strategic Management Journal*, 22: 1–23; M. A. Hitt, R. E. Hoskisson, & H. Kim, 1997, International diversification: Effects on innovation and firm performance in product-diversified firms, *Academy of Management Journal*, 40: 767–798.
4. R. L. Simerly & M. Li, 2000, Environmental dynamism, capital structure and performance: A theoretical integration and an empirical test, *Strategic Management Journal*, 21: 31–49; D. D. Bergh & M. W. Lawless, 1998, Portfolio restructuring and limits to hierarchical governance: The effects of environmental uncertainty and diversification strategy, *Organization Science*, 9: 87–102.
5. M. E. Porter, 1987, From competitive advantage to corporate strategy, *Harvard Business Review*, 65(3): 43–59.
6. Porter, From competitive advantage to corporate strategy; C. A. Montgomery, 1994, Corporate diversification, *Journal of Economic Perspectives*, 8: 163–178.
7. G. H. Stonehouse, J. D. Pemberton, & C. E. Barber, 2001, The role of knowledge facilitators and inhibitors: Lessons from airline reservations systems, *Long Range Planning*, 34(2): 115–138; B. Wysocki, Jr., 1999, Corporate America confronts the meaning of a "core" business, *The Wall Street Journal*, November 9, A1, A4.
8. C. Meyer, 2001, The second generation of speed, *Harvard Business Review*, 79(4): 24–25.
9. M. Kwak, 2002, Maximizing value through diversification, *MIT Sloan Management Review*, 43(2): 10; R. A. Burgelman & Y. L. Doz, 2001, The power of strategic integration, *MIT Sloan Management Review*, 42(3): 28–38; C. C. Markides, 1997, To diversify or not to diversify, *Harvard Business Review*, 75(6): 93–99.
10. P. Wright, M. Kroll, A. Lado, & B. Van Ness, 2002, The structure of ownership and corporate acquisition strategies, *Strategic Management Journal*, 23: 41–53; C. C. Markides & P. J. Williamson, 1996, Corporate diversification and organizational structure: A resource-based view, *Academy of Management Journal*, 39: 340–367.
11. A. Campbell, M. Goold, & M. Alexander, 1995, Corporate strategy: The question for parenting advantage, *Harvard Business Review*, 73(2): 120–132.
12. T. H. Brush, P. Bromiley, & M. Hendrickx, 1999, The relative influence of industry and corporate on business segment performance: An alternative estimate, *Strategic Management Journal*, 20: 519–547; T. H. Brush & P. Bromiley, 1997, What does a small corporate effect mean? A variance components simulation of corporate and business effects, *Strategic Management Journal*, 18: 825–835.
13. J. B. Barney, 2002, *Gaining and Sustaining Competitive Advantage*, 2nd ed., Upper Saddle River, NJ.: Prentice-Hall.
14. D. D. Bergh, 2001, Diversification strategy research at a crossroads: Established, emerging and anticipated paths. In M. A. Hitt, R. E. Freeman, & J. S. Harrison (eds.), *Handbook of Strategic Management*, Oxford, UK: Blackwell Publishers, 363.
15. C. Kim, S. Kim, & C. Pantzalis, 2001, Firm diversification and earnings volatility: An empirical analysis of U.S.-based MNCs, *American Business Review*, 19(1): 26–38; W. Lewellen, 1971, A pure financial rationale for the conglomerate merger, *Journal of Finance*, 26: 521–537.
16. J. D. Fisher & Y. Liang, 2000, Is sector diversification more important than regional diversification? *Real Estate Finance*, 17(3): 35–40.
17. H. von Kranenburg, M. Cloodt, & J. Hagedoorn, 2001, An exploratory story of recent trends in the diversification of Dutch publishing companies in the multimedia and information industries, *International Studies of Management & Organization*, 31(10): 64–86.
18. B. S. Silverman, 1999, Technological resources and the direction of corporate diversification: Toward an integration of the resource-based view and transaction cost economics, *Administrative Science Quarterly*, 45: 1109–1124; D. Collis & C. A. Montgomery, 1995, Competing on resources: Strategy in the 1990s, *Harvard Business Review*, 73(4): 118–128; M. A. Peteraf, 1993, The cornerstones of competitive advantage: A resource-based view, *Strategic Management Journal*, 14: 179–191.
19. Bergh, Diversification strategy research at a crossroads, 369.
20. N. Deogun, G. McWilliams, & M. Williams, 2001, Hewlett-Packard nears pact to buy Compaq for 26 Billion in Stock, *The Wall Street Journal*, September 4, A1, A6.
21. R. P. Rumelt, *Strategy, Structure, and Economic Performance*, Boston: Harvard Business School, 1974; L. Wrigley, 1970, *Divisional autonomy and diversification* (Ph.D. dissertation), Harvard Business School.
22. W. Heuslein, 2001, Wm. Wrigley Jr. Co.: Getting unstuck, *Forbes*, January 8, 138–139.

23. T. Mason, 2001, Can gum and dental care mix? *Marketing,* August 23, 21.
24. S. Killman, 2001, Smithfield foods CEO welcomes backlash over its hog farms, *The Wall Street Journal,* August 21, B4; J. Forster, 2001, Who's afraid of a little mud? *Business Week,* May 21, 112–113.
25. M. Ihlwan, P. Engardio, I. Kunii, & R. Crockett, 1999, Samsung: How a Korean electronics giant came out of the crisis stronger than ever, *Business Week Online,* http://www.businessweek.com, December 20.
26. L. A. Keister, 2000, *Chinese Business Groups: The Structure and Impact of Inter-Firm Relations During Economic Development,* New York: Oxford University Press; T. Khanna & K. Palepu, 1997, Why focused strategies may be wrong for emerging markets, *Harvard Business Review,* 75(4): 41–50.
27. C. Chung, 2001, Markets, culture and institutions: The emergence of large business groups in Taiwan, 1950s–1970s, *Journal of Management Studies,* 38: 719–745.
28. S. Manikutty, 2000, Family business groups in India: A resource-based view of the emerging trends, *Family Business Review,* 13: 279–292.
29. 1997, Inside story, *The Economist,* December 6, 7–9.
30. K. Dewenter, W. Novaes, & R. H. Pettway, 2001, Visibility versus complexity in business groups: Evidence from Japanese keiretsus, *Journal of Business,* 74: 79–100.
31. M. Farjoun, 1998, The independent and joint effects of the skill and physical bases of relatedness in diversification, *Strategic Management Journal,* 19: 611–630.
32. R. E. Hoskisson & L.W. Busenitz, 2002, Market uncertainty and learning distance in corporate entrepreneurship entry mode choice. In M. A. Hitt, R. D. Ireland, S. M. Camp, & D. L. Sexton (eds.), *Strategic Entrepreneurship: Creating a New Mindset,* Oxford, U.K.: Blackwell Publishers, 150–172; R. Morck & B. Yeung, 1999, When synergy creates real value, Mastering Strategy (Part 7), *Financial Times,* November 8, 6–7.
33. B. Garette & P. Dussauge, 2000, Alliances versus acquisitions: Choosing the right option, *European Management Journal,* 18(1): 63–69; L. Capron, 1999, The long term performance of horizontal acquisitions, *Strategic Management Journal,* 20: 987–1018.
34. M. E. Porter, 1985, *Competitive Advantage,* New York: The Free Press, 328.
35. S. Jaffe, 2001, Do Pepsi and Gatorade mix? *Business Week Online,* http://www.businessweek.com, August 14.
36. M. L. Marks & P. H. Mirvis, 2000, Managing mergers, acquisitions, and alliances: Creating an effective transition structure, *Organizational Dynamics,* 28(3): 35–47.
37. G. Delong, 2001, Stockholder gains from focusing versus diversifying bank mergers, *Journal of Financial Economics,* 2: 221–252; T. H. Brush, 1996, Predicted change in operational synergy and post-acquisition performance of acquired businesses, *Strategic Management Journal,* 17: 1–24; H. Zhang, 1995, Wealth effects of U.S. bank takeovers, *Applied Financial Economics,* 5: 329–336.
38. D. D. Bergh, 1995, Size and relatedness of units sold: An agency theory and resource-based perspective, *Strategic Management Journal,* 16: 221–239.
39. M. Lubatkin & S. Chatterjee, 1994, Extending modern portfolio theory into the domain of corporate diversification: Does it apply? *Academy of Management Journal,* 37: 109–136.
40. A. Van Oijen, 2001, Product diversification, corporate management instruments, resource sharing, and performance, *Academy of Management Best Paper Proceedings* (on CD-ROM Business Policy and Strategy Division); T. Kono, 1999, A strong head office makes a strong company, *Long Range Planning,* 32(2): 225.
41. M. Y. Brannen, J. K. Liker, & W. M. Fruin, 1999, Recontextualization and factory-to-factory knowledge transfer from Japan to the US: The Case of NSK, In J. K. Liker, W. M. Fruin, & P. Adler (eds.) *Remade in America: Transplanting and Transforming Japanese Systems,* New York: Oxford University Press, 117–153; L. Capron, P. Dussauge, & W. Mitchell, 1998, Resource redeployment following horizontal acquisitions in Europe and the United States, 1988–1992, *Strategic Management Journal,* 19: 631–61; A. Mehra, 1996, Resource and market based determinants of performance in the U.S. banking industry, *Strategic Management Journal,* 17: 307–322; S. Chatterjee & B. Wernerfelt, 1991, The link between resources and type of diversification: Theory and evidence, *Strategic Management Journal,* 12: 33–48.
42. B. Horovitz, 2001, McDonald's tries a new recipe to revive sales, *USA Today,* July 10, 1–2.
43. M. Maremont, 2000, For plastic hangers, you almost need to go to Tyco International, *The Wall Street Journal,* February 15, A1, A10; R. Whittington, 1999, In praise of the evergreen conglomerate, Mastering Strategy (Part 6), *Financial Times,* November 1, 4–6; W. Ruigrok, A. Pettigrew, S. Peck, & R. Whittington, 1999, Corporate restructuring and new forms of organizing: Evidence from Europe, *Management International Review,* 39(Special Issue): 41–64.
44. C. St. John & J. S. Harrison, 1999, Manufacturing-based relatedness, synergy, and coordination, *Strategic Management Journal,* 20: 129–145.
45. W. G. Shepherd, 1986, On the core concepts of industrial economics, in H. W. deJong & W. G. Shepherd (eds.), *Mainstreams in Industrial Organization,* Boston: Kluwer Publications.
46. D. Genesove & W. P. Mullin, 2001. Rules, communication, and collusion: Narrative evidence from the Sugar Institute Case, *American Economic Review,* 91: 379–398; J. Gimeno & C. Y. Woo, 1999, Multimarket contact, economies of scope, and firm performance, *Academy of Management Journal,* 42: 239–259.
47. S. Lohr & S. Gaither, 2002, Hewlett Packard declares victory on the merger, *The New York Times,* http://www.nytimes.com, March 20; N. Deogun, G. McWilliams, & M. Williams, 2001 Hewlett-Packard nears pact to buy Compaq for $26 billion in stock, *The Wall Street Journal,* September 4: A1, A6.
48. A. Karnani & B. Wernerfelt, 1985, Multipoint competition, *Strategic Management Journal,* 6: 87–96.
49. H. A. Haveman & L. Nonnemaker, 2000, Competition in multiple geographic markets: The impact on growth and market entry, *Administrative Science Quarterly,* 45: 232–267.
50. Genesove & Mullin, Rules, communication, and collusion.
51. O. E. Williamson, 1996, Economics and organization: A primer, *California Management Review,* 38(2): 131–146.
52. S. Killman, 2001, Smithfield foods CEO welcomes backlash over its hog farms, *The Wall Street Journal,* August 21, B4.
53. K. R. Harrigan, 2001, Strategic flexibility in the old and new economies. In M. A. Hitt, R. E. Freeman, & J. S. Harrison (eds.) *Handbook of Strategic Management,* Oxford, U.K.: Blackwell Publishers, 97–123.
54. R. E. Kranton, & D. F. Minehart, 2001, Networks versus vertical integration, *The Rand Journal of Economics,* 3: 570–601.
55. P. Kothandaraman & D. T. Wilson, 2001, The future of competition: Value-creating networks, *Industrial Marketing Management,* 30: 379–389.
56. D. Stapleton, P. Gentles, J. Ross, & K. Shubert, 2001, The location-centric shift from marketplace to marketspace: Transaction cost-inspired propositions of virtual integration via an e-commerce model, *Advances in Competitiveness Research,* 9: 10–41.
57. K. M. Eisenhardt & D. C. Galunic, 2000, Coevolving: At last, a way to make synergies work, *Harvard Business Review,* 78(1): 91–111.
58. R. Schoenberg, 2001, Knowledge transfer and resource sharing as value creation mechanisms in inbound continental European acquisitions, *Journal of Euro-Marketing,* 10: 99–114.
59. M. Peers, 2001, USA Networks agrees to acquire control of Expedia from Microsoft, *The Wall Street Journal Interactive,* http://www.wsj.com, July 16.
60. Eisenhardt & Galunic, Coevolving, 94.
61. M. Freeman, 2002, Forging a model for profitability, *Electronic Media,* January 28, 1, 13.
62. Bergh, Predicting divestiture of unrelated acquisitions; C. W. L. Hill, 1994, Diversification and economic performance: Bringing structure and corporate management back into the picture, in R. P. Rumelt, D. E. Schendel, & D. J. Teece (eds.), *Fundamental Issues in Strategy,* Boston: Harvard Business School Press, 297–321.
63. O. E. Williamson, 1975, *Markets and Hierarchies: Analysis and Antitrust Implications,* New York: Macmillan Free Press.
64. M. T. Billet & D. Mauer, 2001, Diversification and the value of internal capital markets: The case of tracking stock, *Journal of Banking & Finance,* 9: 1457–1490.
65. R. Kochhar & M. A. Hitt, 1998, Linking corporate strategy to capital structure: Diversification strategy, type, and source of financing, *Strategic Management Journal,* 19: 601–610.
66. Ibid.; P. Taylor & J. Lowe, 1995, A note on corporate strategy and capital structure, *Strategic Management Journal,* 16: 411–414.
67. M. Kwak, 2001, Spinoffs lead to better financing decisions, *MIT Sloan Management Review,* 42(4): 10; O. A. Lamont & C. Polk, 2001, The diversification discount: Cash flows versus returns, *Journal of Finance,* 56: 1693–1721; R. Rajan, H. Servaes, & L. Zingales, 2001, The cost of diversity: The diversification discount and inefficient investment, *Journal of Finance,* 55: 35–79.
68. 2001, Spoilt for choice, *The Economist,* http://www.economist.com, July 5.
69. D. J. Denis, D. K. Denis, & A. Sarin, 1999, Agency theory and the reference of equity ownership structure on corporate diversification strategies, *Strategic Management Journal,* 20: 1071–1076; R. Amit & J. Livnat, 1988, A concept of conglomerate diversification, *Journal of Management,* 14: 593–604.
70. Whittington, In praise of the evergreen conglomerate, 4.

71. T. Khanna & J. W. Rivkin, 2001. Estimating the performance effects of business groups in emerging markets, *Strategic Management Journal,* 22: 45–74.
72. T. Khanna & K. Palepu, 2000, Is group affiliation profitable in emerging markets? An analysis of diversified Indian business groups, *Journal of Finance,* 55: 867–892; T. Khanna & K. Palepu, 2000, The future of business groups in emerging markets: Long-run evidence from Chile, *Academy of Management Journal,* 43: 268–285.
73. R. E. Hoskisson, R. A. Johnson, D. Yiu, & W. P. Wan, 2001. Restructuring strategies and diversified business groups: Differences associated with country institutional environments. In M. A. Hitt, R. E. Freeman & J. S. Harrison (eds.), *Handbook of Strategic Management,* Oxford, UK: Blackwell Publishers, 433–463; S. J. Chang & H. Singh, 1999, The impact of entry and resource fit on modes of exit by multibusiness firms, *Strategic Management Journal,* 20: 1019–1035.
74. W. C. Symonds & P. L. Moore, 2001, The most aggressive CEO, *Business Week,* May 28: 68–77.
75. H. Greenberg, 2002, Does Tyco play accounting games? *Fortune,* April 1, 83–86.
76. Ibid.
77. J. S. Harrison, H. M. O'Neill, & R. E. Hoskisson, 2000, Acquisition strategy and target resistance: A theory of countervailing effects of pre-merger bidding and post-merger integration. In C. Cooper & A. Gregory (eds.) *Advances in Mergers and Acquisitions,* Vol. 1, Greenwich, CT: JAI/Elsevier, Inc, 157–182.
78. T. A. Doucet & R. M. Barefield, 1999, Client base valuation: The case of a professional service firm, *Journal of Business Research,* 44: 127–133.
79. S. Nambisan, 2001, Why service businesses are not product businesses, *MIT Sloan Management Review,* 42(4): 72–80.
80. S. L. Gillan, J. W. Kensinger, & J. D. Martin, 2000, Value creation and corporate diversification: The case of Sears, Roebuck & Co., *Journal of Financial Economics,* 55: 103–137.
81. E. Stickel, 2001, Uncertainty reduction in a competitive environment, *Journal of Business Research,* 51: 169–177; S. Chatterjee & J. Singh, 1999, Are tradeoffs inherent in diversification moves? A simultaneous model for type of diversification and mode of expansion decisions, *Management Science,* 45: 25–41.
82. M. Lubatkin, H. Merchant, & M. Srinivasan, 1997, Merger strategies and shareholder value during times of relaxed antitrust enforcement: The case of large mergers during the 1980s, *Journal of Management,* 23: 61–81.
83. D. P. Champlin & J. T. Knoedler, 1999, Restructuring by design? Government's complicity in corporate restructuring, *Journal of Economic Issues,* 33(1): 41–57.
84. R. M. Scherer & D. Ross, 1990, *Industrial Market Structure and Economic Performance,* Boston: Houghton Mifflin.
85. A. Shleifer & R. W. Vishny, 1994, Takeovers in the 1960s and 1980s: Evidence and implications, in R. P. Rumelt, D. E. Schendel, & D. J. Teece (eds.), *Fundamental Issues in Strategy,* Boston: Harvard Business School Press, 403–422.
86. Lubatkin, Merchant, & Srinivasan, Merger strategies and shareholder value; D. J. Ravenscraft & R. M. Scherer, 1987, *Mergers, Sell-Offs and Economic Efficiency,* Washington, DC: Brookings Institution, 22.
87. D. A. Zalewski, 2001, Corporate takeovers, fairness, and public policy, *Journal of Economic Issues,* 35: 431–437; P. L. Zweig, J. P. Kline, S. A. Forest, & K. Gudridge, 1995, The case against mergers, *Business Week,* October 30, 122–130; J. R. Williams, B. L. Paez, & L. Sanders, 1988, Conglomerates revisited, *Strategic Management Journal,* 9: 403–414.
88. E. J. Lopez, 2001, New anti-merger theories: A critique, *Cato Journal,* 20: 359–378; 1998, The trustbusters' new tools, *The Economist,* May 2, 62–64.
89. M. C. Jensen, 1986, Agency costs of free cash flow, corporate finance, and takeovers, *American Economic Review,* 76: 323–329.
90. R. Gilson, M. Scholes, & M. Wolfson, 1988, Taxation and the dynamics of corporate control: The uncertain case for tax motivated acquisitions, in J. C. Coffee, L. Lowenstein, & S. Rose-Ackerman (eds.), *Knights, Raiders, and Targets: The Impact of the Hostile Takeover,* New York: Oxford University Press, 271–299.
91. C. Steindel, 1986, Tax reform and the merger and acquisition market: The repeal of the general utilities, *Federal Reserve Bank of New York Quarterly Review,* 11(3): 31–35.
92. M. A. Hitt, J. S. Harrison, & R. D. Ireland, 2001, *Mergers and Acquisitions: A Guide to Creating Value for Stakeholders,* New York: Oxford University Press.
93. R. F. Hirsh, 2000, *Power Loss: The Origins of Deregulation and Restructuring in the American Electric Power Industry,* Cambridge: MIT Press.
94. J. Ewing, 2001, Guten tag, America, *Business Week Online,* http://www.businessweek.com, July 27.
95. A. Lomi & E. Larsen, 2000, Strategic implications of deregulation and competition in the electricity industry *European Management Journal,* 17(2): 151–163.
96. Y. Chang & H. Thomas, 1989, The impact of diversification strategy on risk-return performance, *Strategic Management Journal,* 10: 271–284; R. M. Grant, A. P. Jammine, & H. Thomas, 1988, Diversity, diversification, and profitability among British manufacturing companies, 1972–1984, *Academy of Management Journal,* 31: 771–801.
97. Rumelt, *Strategy, Structure and Economic Performance,* 125.
98. M. N. Nickel & M. C. Rodriguez, 2002, A review of research on the negative accounting relationship between risk and return: Bowman's paradox, *Omega,* 30(1): 1–18; R. M. Wiseman & L. R. Gomez-Mejia, 1998, A behavioral agency model of managerial risk taking, *Academy of Management Review,* 23: 133–153; E. H. Bowman, 1982, Risk seeking by troubled firms, *Sloan Management Review,* 23: 33–42.
99. J. G. Matsusaka, 2001, Corporate diversification, value maximization, and organizational capabilities, *Journal of Business,* 74: 409–432.
100. L. E. Palich, L. B. Cardinal, & C. C. Miller, 2000, Curvilinearity in the diversification-performance linkage: An examination of over three decades of research, *Strategic Management Journal,* 21: 155–174.
101. Simerly & Li, Environmental dynamism, capital structure and performance.
102. J. C. Sandvig & L. Coakley, 1998, Best practices in small firm diversification, *Business Horizons,* 41(3): 33–40; C. G. Smith & A. C. Cooper, 1988, Established companies diversifying into young industries: A comparison of firms with different levels of performance, *Strategic Management Journal,* 9: 111–121.
103. S. Day, 2001, Tupperware to sell products in SuperTarget stores, *The New York Times,* http://www.nytimes.com, July 18.
104. N. M. Kay & A. Diamantopoulos, 1987, Uncertainty and synergy: Towards a formal model of corporate strategy, *Managerial and Decision Economics,* 8: 121–130.
105. R. W. Coff, 1999, How buyers cope with uncertainty when acquiring firms in knowledge-intensive industries: Caveat emptor, *Organization Science,* 10: 144–161.
106. M. Selz, 2001, StarTek expands beyond core services as falling demand halts financial growth, *The Wall Street Journal Interactive,* http://www.wsj.com, June 26.
107. Chatterjee & Singh, Are tradeoffs inherent in diversification moves?; S. J. Chatterjee & B. Wernerfelt, 1991, The link between resources and type of diversification: Theory and evidence, *Strategic Management Journal,* 12: 33–48.
108. Kochhar & Hitt, Linking corporate strategy to capital structure.
109. J. Greene, 2001, Microsoft: How it became stronger than ever, *Business Week,* June 4, 75–85.
110. K. Haanes & O. Fjeldstad, 2000, Linking intangible resources and competition, *European Management Journal,* 18(1): 52–62.
111. L. Capron & J. Hulland, 1999, Redeployment of brands, sales forces, and general marketing management expertise following horizontal acquisitions: A resource-based view, *Journal of Marketing,* 63(2): 41–54.
112. R. D. Smith, 2000, Intangible strategic assets and firm performance: A multi-industry study of the resource-based view, *Journal of Business Strategies,* 17(2): 91–117.
113. M. A. Geletkanycz, B. K. Boyd, & S. Finklestein, 2001, The strategic value of CEO external directorate networks: Implications for CEO compensation, *Strategic Management Journal,* 9: 889–898; W. Grossman & R. E. Hoskisson, 1998, CEO pay at the crossroads of Wall Street and Main: Toward the strategic design of executive compensation, *Academy of Management Executive,* 12(1): 43–57; S. Finkelstein & D. C. Hambrick, 1996, *Strategic Leadership: Top Executives and Their Effects on Organizations,* St. Paul, MN: West Publishing Company.
114. P. J. Lane, A. A. Cannella, Jr., & M. H. Lubatkin, 1998, Agency problems as antecedents to unrelated mergers and diversification: Amihud and Lev reconsidered, *Strategic Management Journal,* 19: 555–578; D. L. May, 1995, Do managerial motives influence firm risk reduction strategies? *Journal of Finance,* 50: 1291–1308; Y. Amihud and B. Lev, 1981, Risk reduction as a managerial motive for conglomerate mergers, *Bell Journal of Economics,* 12: 605–617.
115. S. R. Gray & A. A. Cannella, Jr., 1997, The role of risk in executive compensation, *Journal of Management,* 23: 517–540; H. Tosi & L. Gomez-Mejia, 1989, The decoupling of CEO pay and performance: An agency theory perspective, *Administrative Science Quarterly,* 34: 169–189.
116. R. Bliss & R. Rosen, 2001, CEO compensation and bank mergers, *Journal of Financial Economics,* 1:107–138; S. Finkelstein & R. A. D'Aveni, 1994, CEO duality as a double-

edged sword: How boards of directors balance entrenchment avoidance and unity of command, *Academy of Management Journal,* 37: 1070–1108.

117. J. W. Lorsch, A. S. Zelleke, & K. Pick, 2001, Unbalanced boards, *Harvard Business Review,* 79(2): 28–30; R. E. Hoskisson & T. Turk, 1990, Corporate restructuring: Governance and control limits of the internal market, *Academy of Management Review,* 15: 459–477.
118. R. C. Anderson, T. W. Bates, J. M. Bizjak, & M. L. Lemmon, 2000, Corporate governance and firm diversification, *Financial Management,* 29(1): 5–22; J. D. Westphal, 1998, Board games: How CEOs adapt to increases in structural board independence from management. *Administrative Science Quarterly,* 43: 511–537; J. K. Seward & J. P. Walsh, 1996, The governance and control of voluntary corporate spin offs, *Strategic Management Journal,* 17: 25–39; J. P. Walsh & J. K. Seward, 1990, On the efficiency of internal and external corporate control mechanisms, *Academy of Management Review,* 15: 421–458.
119. W. G. Rowe, 2001, Creating wealth in organizations: The role of strategic leadership, *Academy of Management Executive,* 15(1): 81–94; Finkelstein & D'Aveni, CEO duality as a double-edged sword.
120. E. F. Fama, 1980, Agency problems and the theory of the firm, *Journal of Political Economy,* 88: 288–307.
121. R. A. Johnson, 1996, Antecedents and outcomes of corporate refocusing, *Journal of Management,* 22: 439–483; C. Y. Woo, G. E. Willard, & U. S. Dallenbach, 1992, Spin-off performance: A case of overstated expectations, *Strategic Management Journal,* 13: 433–448.
122. M. Wright, R. E. Hoskisson, & L. W. Busenitz, 2001, Firm rebirth: Buyouts as facilitators of strategic growth and entrepreneurship, *Academy of Management Executive,* 15(1): 111–125; H. Kim & R. E. Hoskisson, 1996, Japanese governance systems: A critical review, in S. B. Prasad (ed.), *Advances in International Comparative Management,* Greenwich, CT: JAI Press, 165–189.
123. D. Lewis, 2000, CMGI ventures into the red, *Internetweek,* December 18, 34.
124. A. L. Ranft & H. M. O'Neill, 2001, Board composition and high-flying founders: Hints of trouble to come? *Academy of Management Executive,* 15(1): 126–138; P. Buxbaum, 2000, The trouble with dot-com boards, *Chief Executive,* October, 50–51.
125. A. Serwer & J. Boorstin, 2001, Following the money, *Fortune,* September 17, 102–114.
126. L. Capron, W. Mitchell, & A. Swaminathan, 2001, Asset divestiture following horizontal acquisitions: A dynamic view, *Strategic Management Journal,* 22: 817–844.
127. Bergh, Diversification strategy: Research at a crossroads, 370–371; W. M. Bulkeley, 1994, Conglomerates make a surprising come-back—with a '90s twist, *The Wall Street Journal,* March 1, A1, A6.
128. J. P. H. Fan & L. H. P. Lang, 2000, The measurement of relatedness: An application to corporate diversification, *Journal of Business,* 73: 629–660.
129. Khanna & Palepu, The future of business groups in emerging markets, 268–285; P. Ghemawat & T. Khanna, 1998, The nature of diversified business groups: A research design and two case studies, *Journal of Industrial Economics,* 46: 35–61.
130. W. P. Wan & R. E. Hoskisson, 2002, Home country environments, corporate diversification strategies, and firm performance, *Academy of Management Journal,* in press.

7

Chapter Seven

Acquisition and Restructuring Strategies

Knowledge Objectives

Studying this chapter should provide you with the strategic management knowledge needed to:

1. Explain the popularity of acquisition strategies in firms competing in the global economy.
2. Discuss reasons firms use an acquisition strategy to achieve strategic competitiveness.
3. Describe seven problems that work against developing a competitive advantage using an acquisition strategy.
4. Name and describe attributes of effective acquisitions.
5. Define the restructuring strategy and distinguish among its common forms.
6. Explain the short- and long-term outcomes of the different types of restructuring strategies.

Hewlett-Packard's Acquisition of Compaq: IBM Envy or Good Business Acumen?

In the summer of 2001, CEO Carly Fiorina of Hewlett-Packard (HP) and Compaq CEO Michael Capellas agreed that HP should acquire Compaq. In the following months this decision was debated on several fronts. In many ways, the decision represents classic arguments regarding the value of acquisitions. At the time of the acquisition announcement both firms were experiencing performance problems, although Compaq's problems were more severe than those of HP, which raised another question: can merging two poorly performing firms create one high performing firm?

There were several arguments in favor of the acquisition. First, because both firms compete in some of the same markets, their integration would create economies of scale and produce estimated cost savings of at least $2.5 billion. Second, merging the two companies would generate annual revenues of approximately $87 billion and a strong cash flow, providing the combined firm with financial and market power similar to IBM. Third, HP and Compaq also offer some different products, which could be sold to the other's customers. Finally, the companies have complementary technological capabilities, such as HP in Internet systems and Compaq in highly reliable servers and clustering software.

Shown here answering questions at the firm's headquarters, Walter Hewlett, Hewlett-Packard board member and son of founder William Hewlett, led a bitter eight-month public battle against the firm's merger with Compaq. When Hewlett filed a lawsuit after the merger was approved by shareholders, the company did not renominate him to the board because of his "ongoing adversarial relationship with the company" and "concerns about his lack of candor and issues of trust," according to an HP statement.

Arguments about the potential problems and disadvantages of the acquisition were also strong. Both firms operate in the highly competitive, volatile, and low margin personal computer market. The combined firm would derive about 25 percent of its revenues from this business. Moreover, the acquisition would require integrating two massive firms, a highly challenging task. Some analysts questioned Fiorina's ability to effectively integrate the businesses. Not only would the acquisition cost HP over $20-plus billion (with the final price determined by the firms' value when the transaction is finalized), there are concerns that it would cause HP to lose focus of its highly successful printer and other supplemental computing equipment businesses. For these reasons, a number of industry analysts and major shareholders of HP questioned the wisdom of the acquisition. Walter Hewlett and other members of the founders' families were particularly outspoken in their opposition.

HP's goal is to develop its services and software businesses to compete with IBM. IBM's services produce over $26 billion in annual revenue, but HP generates a little over $11 billion in annual revenue from its services business. Thus, HP is unlikely to challenge IBM in this arena, and the acquisition of Compaq is unlikely to help much. While Compaq does provide more services capabilities, additional capabilities are still needed for HP to compete effectively with IBM.

The stakes are high both for HP and for Fiorina. The acquisition will be expensive, and Fiorina's job may be on the line. In a close vote, the acquisition was approved by HP's shareholders at their March 2002 meeting, followed by Walter Hewlett's lawsuit against the results of the vote. Had a few major stockholders been able to stop the acquisition, Fiorina might have lost her job. Both U.S. and European regulators have approved the proposed transaction, eliminating one hurdle to its completion.

SOURCES: C. Gaither, 2002, Hewlett heir files lawsuit to overturn merger vote, *The New York Times Interactive*, http://www.nytimes.com, March 29; 2002, The new HP: The pros and cons of the merger, *BusinessWeek Online*, http://www.businessweek.com, December 24; R. Sidel & M. Williams, 2001, Hewlett's fight on Compaq turns heads; HP director's stance is unusually strong, *The Wall Street Journal*, December 31, C1, C13; S. Morrison, 2001, HP talks up Compaq computer revenue potential, *Financial Times*, http://www.ft.com, December 19; L. DiCarlo, 2001, HP's IBM envy, *Forbes*, http://www.forbes.com, December 14; 2001, Hewlett-Packard chief executive says integration process is key, *The Wall Street Journal Interactive*, http://interactive.wsj.com, September 4; R. Sidel & J. Wilke, 2001, Hewlett-Packard nears pact to buy Compaq for $26 billion, *The Wall Street Journal*, September 4.

In Chapter 6, we studied corporate-level strategies, focusing on types and levels of product diversification strategies that can build core competencies and create competitive advantage. As noted in that chapter, diversification allows a firm to create value by productively using excess resources.[1] In this chapter, we explore mergers and acquisitions, often combined with a diversification strategy, as a prominent strategy employed by firms throughout the world. The acquisition of Compaq by Hewlett-Packard (HP) is a horizontal acquisition, as Compaq competed with HP in several markets. Still, each firm markets some different products and has different strengths. As such, combining the two firms creates an opportunity for synergy to be developed beyond economies of scope as described in the chapter's Opening Case.

In the latter half of the 20th century, acquisitions became a prominent strategy used by major corporations. Even smaller and more focused firms began employing acquisition strategies to grow and enter new markets. However, acquisition strategies are not without problems; a number of acquisitions fail. Thus, we focus on how acquisitions can be used to produce value for the firm's stakeholders.[2] Before describing attributes associated with effective acquisitions, we examine the most prominent problems companies experience with an acquisition strategy. For example, when acquisitions contribute to poor performance, a firm may deem it necessary to restructure its operations. Closing the chapter are descriptions of three restructuring strategies, as well as the short- and long-term outcomes resulting from their use. Setting the stage for these topics is an examination of the popularity of mergers and acquisitions and a discussion of the differences among mergers, acquisitions, and takeovers.

The Popularity of Merger and Acquisition Strategies

Acquisitions have been a popular strategy among U.S. firms for many years. Some believe that this strategy played a central role in an effective restructuring of U.S. businesses during the 1980s and 1990s.[3] Increasingly, acquisition strategies are becoming more popular with firms in other nations and economic regions, including Europe. In fact, about 40–45 percent of the acquisitions in recent years have been made across country borders (i.e., a firm headquartered in one country acquiring a firm headquartered in another country).[4]

There were five waves of mergers and acquisitions in the 20th century with the last two in the 1980s and 1990s. There were 55,000 acquisitions valued at $1.3 trillion in the 1980s, but acquisitions in the 1990s exceeded $11 trillion in value.[5] World economies, particularly the U.S. economy, slowed in the new millennium, reducing the number of mergers and acquisitions completed.[6] The annual value of mergers and acquisitions peaked in 2000 at about $3.4 trillion and fell to about $1.75 trillion in 2001.[7] Slightly more than 15,000 acquisitions were announced in 2001 compared to over 33,000 in 2000.[8] The acquisition of Compaq by HP was the second largest acquisition announced in 2001.

Although acquisitions have slowed, their number remains high. In fact, an acquisition strategy is sometimes used because of the uncertainty in the competitive landscape. A firm may make an acquisition to increase its market power because of a competitive threat, to enter a new market because of the opportunity available in that market, or to spread the risk due to the uncertain environment.[9] In addition, a firm may acquire other companies as options that allow the firm to shift its core business into different markets as the volatility brings undesirable changes to its primary markets.[10]

The strategic management process (see Figure 1.1) calls for an acquisition strategy to increase a firm's strategic competitiveness as well as its returns to shareholders. Thus, an acquisition strategy should be used only when the acquiring firm will be able to increase its economic value through ownership and the use of an acquired firm's assets.[11]

Evidence suggests, however, that at least for acquiring firms, acquisition strategies may not result in these desirable outcomes. Studies by academic researchers have found that shareholders of acquired firms often earn above-average returns from an acquisition, while shareholders of acquiring firms are less likely to do so, typically earning returns from the transaction that are close to zero.[12] In approximately two-thirds of all acquisitions, the acquiring firm's stock price falls immediately after the intended transaction is announced. This negative response is an indication of investors' skepticism about the likelihood that the acquirer will be able to achieve the synergies required to justify the premium.[13] For example, some analysts question the value of the AOL Time Warner merger creating the world's largest media company. The firm's market value has continued to decline since the merger was announced. Executives at AOL Time Warner also predicted that the company would continue to be harmed by a major decline in advertising, a current market trend.[14]

A **merger** is a strategy through which two firms agree to integrate their operations on a relatively co-equal basis.

An **acquisition** is a strategy through which one firm buys a controlling, or 100 percent, interest in another firm with the intent of making the acquired firm a subsidiary business within its portfolio.

A **takeover** is a special type of an acquisition strategy wherein the target firm did not solicit the acquiring firm's bid.

Mergers, Acquisitions, and Takeovers: What Are the Differences?

A **merger** is a strategy through which two firms agree to integrate their operations on a relatively co-equal basis. There are not many true mergers, because one party is usually dominant. Entergy executives halted the planned merger between the FPL GROUP INC. and Entergy Corporation in 2001. They claimed that FPL was trying to dilute the leadership roles of Entergy managers in the planned integrated firm and thus would not be a merger of equals.[15]

An **acquisition** is a strategy through which one firm buys a controlling, or 100 percent, interest in another firm with the intent of making the acquired firm a subsidiary business within its portfolio. In this case, the management of the acquired firm reports to the management of the acquiring firm. While most mergers are friendly transactions, acquisitions include unfriendly takeovers. A **takeover** is a special type of an acquisition strategy wherein the target firm did not solicit the acquiring firm's bid.

Oftentimes, takeover bids spawn bidding wars. For example, TMP Worldwide thought it had an agreement to acquire HotJobs.com, but Yahoo! offered $81 million more and acquired HotJobs. The number of unsolicited takeover bids increased in the economic downturn in 2001–2002, a common activity in economic recessions, because the poorly managed firms that are undervalued relative to their assets are more easily identified.[16]

Many takeover attempts are not desired by the target firm's managers and are referred to as hostile. In a few cases, unsolicited offers may come from parties familiar to the target firm. For example, financier Kirk Kerkorian, who specializes in takeovers, has acquired Metro-Goldwyn-Mayer (MGM) five separate times. The value of his investment in MGM has grown considerably as well, outperforming the Standard & Poor's 500. Still, MGM has struggled against fierce competition in recent years, and Kerkorian is trying to sell it (again).[17]

On a comparative basis, acquisitions are more common than mergers and takeovers. Accordingly, this chapter focuses on acquisitions.

Reasons for Acquisitions

In this section, we discuss reasons that support the use of an acquisition strategy. Although each reason can provide a legitimate rationale for an acquisition, the acquisition may not necessarily lead to a competitive advantage.

Increased Market Power

A primary reason for acquisitions is to achieve greater market power.[18] Defined in Chapter 6, *market power* exists when a firm is able to sell its goods or services above competitive levels or when the costs of its primary or support activities are below those of its competitors. Market power usually is derived from the size of the firm and its resources and capabilities to compete in the marketplace.[19] It is also affected by the firm's share of the market. Therefore, most acquisitions designed to achieve greater market power entail buying a competitor, a supplier, a distributor, or a business in a highly related industry to allow exercise of a core competence and to gain competitive advantage in the acquiring firm's primary market. One goal in achieving market power is to become a market leader.[20] For example, the acquisition of Compaq by HP will result in the combined firm having 25 percent of the personal computer market and revenues comparable to IBM, a major competitor in technical (computer-based) services.

Firms use horizontal, vertical, and related acquisitions to increase their market power.

Horizontal Acquisitions. The acquisition of a company competing in the same industry in which the acquiring firm competes is referred to as a *horizontal acquisition.* Horizontal acquisitions increase a firm's market power by exploiting cost-based and revenue-based synergies.[21] Research suggests that horizontal acquisitions of firms with similar characteristics result in higher performance than when firms with dissimilar characteristics combine their operations. Examples of important similar characteristics include strategy, managerial styles, and resource allocation patterns. Similarities in these characteristics make the integration of the two firms proceed more smoothly.[22]

As shown in the Strategic Focus on page 218, horizontal acquisitions are often most effective when the acquiring firm integrates the acquired firm's assets with its assets, but only after evaluating and divesting excess capacity and assets that do not complement the newly combined firm's core competencies.[23] However, as also described in the following Strategic Focus, horizontal acquisitions do not guarantee success. Some are successful, such as McDonald's acquisition of Boston Market, but it seems to have been partially based on luck because McDonald's originally intended to close and convert all Boston Market restaurants. Some require a long time to achieve success, such as Daimler-Benz's acquisition of Chrysler. The potential success of others has been questioned, such as the Coors' acquisition of Bass Brewers and Amgen's acquisition of Immunex. It will take time to determine if the managers of Coors and Amgen can produce positive returns from these acquisitions.

Vertical Acquisitions. A *vertical acquisition* refers to a firm acquiring a supplier or distributor of one or more of its goods or services. A firm becomes vertically integrated through this type of acquisition, in that it controls additional parts of the value chain (see Chapter 3). Walt Disney Company's acquisition of Fox Family Worldwide is an example of vertical integration. This acquisition expands Disney's cable network while Disney remains focused on its core business of creating content. Thus, it has purchased important new distribution for the content it develops. Disney is also launching a new cable television channel targeting young children called Playhouse Disney. The downside for Disney relates to the cost ($5.3 billion) and new debt it had to assume to make the purchase.[24]

Related Acquisitions. The acquisition of a firm in a highly related industry is referred to as a *related acquisition.* The proposed acquisition of Honeywell by GE (see the Strategic Focus on page 230) can be classified as a highly related acquisition. Both firms operate businesses in the aerospace industry: GE is a major manufacturer of jet engines, while Honeywell manufactures other avionics equipment. Thus, they have complementary products. GE also has powerful businesses in aircraft leasing and financing. Jack Welch, CEO of GE at the time of the proposed acquisition, stated that "This is the cleanest deal you'll ever see . . . there is no product overlap. Everything is complementary."[25]

Acquisitions intended to increase market power are subject to regulatory review, as well as to analysis by financial markets. For example, Compaq suffered in the financial markets as a result of the fallout among HP investors, posing serious threats to the proposed acquisition.[26] Likewise as we know from the Strategic Focus on page 230, European regulators did not approve the GE acquisition of Honeywell, dooming this strategic action. Thus, firms seeking growth and market power through acquisitions must understand the political/legal segment of the general environment (see Chapter 2) in order to successfully use an acquisition strategy.

Overcoming Entry Barriers

Barriers to entry (introduced in Chapter 2) are factors associated with the market or with the firms currently operating in it that increase the expense and difficulty faced by new ventures trying to enter that particular market. For example, well-established competitors may have substantial economies of scale in the manufacture of their products. In addition, enduring relationships with customers often create product loyalties that are difficult for new entrants to overcome. When facing differentiated products, new entrants typically must spend considerable resources to advertise their goods or services and may find it necessary to sell at a price below competitors' to entice customers.

Facing the entry barriers created by economies of scale and differentiated products, a new entrant may find the acquisition of an established company to be more effective than entering the market as a competitor offering a good or service that is unfamiliar to current buyers. In fact, the higher the barriers to market entry, the greater the probability that a firm will acquire an existing firm to overcome them. Although an acquisition can be expensive, it does provide the new entrant with immediate market access.

Firms trying to enter international markets often face quite steep entry barriers.[27] In response, acquisitions are commonly used to overcome those barriers.[28] At

Strategic Focus

The Good, the Bad, and the Lucky of Horizontal Acquisitions

Internet-based startups experienced a high rate of failure at the turn of the 21st century. In fact, many of them faced an imperative of combine or fail—they had to merge in order to have adequate resources to survive. These horizontal acquisitions were largely involuntary. Although biotechnology firms Amgen and Immunex are also similar, Amgen's acquisition of Immunex for approximately $18 billion was not necessary, and many analysts questioned its value. The acquisition should allow the resulting firm to capture economies of scale, particularly in selling each of the firm's major arthritis drugs, but the two firms are so similar that they are unlikely to capture synergies other than the efficiencies from economies of scale. Moreover, the acquisition and the similarity in the two firms' products may actually confuse the market. Additionally, Amgen may not be able to recapture the substantial premium it had to pay for the acquisition because of the lack of potential synergy.

Many analysts have questioned Adolph Coors Company's horizontal acquisition of Bass Brewers, a firm with major operations in the United Kingdom. Their concern is that the acquisition does little to help Coors compete in the much larger U.S. market and may, in fact, take its focus off this important market. Moreover, because of the physical distance between the two firms, some economies of scale, such as purchasing agricultural ingredients for the manufacture of the beer, may not be great.

DaimlerChrysler offerings range from the Mercedes SL (shown here with board member Juergen Hubbert in the driver's seat) to the Dodge pickup truck (pictured with DaimlerChrysler design executive Trevor Creed).

least for large multinational corporations, another indicator of the importance of entering and then competing successfully in international markets is the fact that five emerging markets (China, India, Brazil, Mexico, and Indonesia) are among the 12 largest economies in the world, with a combined purchasing power that is already one-half that of the Group of Seven industrial nations (United States, Japan, Britain, France, Germany, Canada, and Italy).[29]

Cross-Border Acquisitions. Acquisitions made between companies with headquarters in different countries are called *cross-border acquisitions.* These acquisitions are often made to overcome entry barriers. In Chapter 9, we examine cross-border alliances and the reason for their use. Compared to a cross-border alliance, a firm has more control over its international operations through a cross-border acquisition.[30]

Historically, U.S. firms have been the most active acquirers of companies outside their domestic market. However, in the global economy, companies throughout

The Daimler-Benz acquisition of Chrysler Corporation began with great promise because of the potentially complementary core businesses of the two firms—Chrysler's mid-priced autos and minivans and Daimler's luxury autos. However, because of major differences in the two firms' corporate cultures and operating processes, integration was difficult, and the performance of the merged firm suffered. But in 2001, DaimlerChrysler showed signs of producing more positive results and realizing its initial promise, following the total replacement of the top management of the firm's U.S. operations.

A major success story is McDonald's acquisition of Boston Market. McDonald's acquired the firm for its locations, intending to close the Boston Market restaurants and build other types of restaurants in their place. McDonald's named Jeffrey Kindler to oversee Boston Market as its CEO. While about 100 of the stores were closed and almost 60 were converted, Kindler also saw unrealized opportunities in a loyal clientele and managers with good ideas, and he negotiated a 10-year contract with Heinz to produce and market frozen dinners with the Boston Market brand. In 2001, Boston Market had sales of over $700 million and is now consistently profitable. As a result, McDonald's is keeping the remaining 700 plus Boston Market restaurants.

SOURCES: D. Ackman, 2002, Not much fizz in Coors deal, *Forbes*, http://www.forbes.com, January 2; P. T. Larson, 2001, Amgen agrees to buy Immunex for $16 billion, *Financial Times*, http://www.ft.com, December 12; A. Pollack & A. R. Sorkin, 2001, Amgen is said to make offer of $18 billion for Immunex, *The New York Times Interactive*, http://www.nytimes.com, December 17; M. Herper, 2001, Why Amgen should not buy Immunex, *Forbes*, http://www.forbes.com, December 15; M Arndt, 2001, There's life in the old bird yet, *Business Week*, May 14, 77–78; G. Anders, 2001, Weak companies, strong mergers, *Fast Company*, February, 182–186; J. Muller, J. Green, & C. Tierney, 2001, Chrysler's rescue team, *Business Week*, January 15, 49–50; J. Ball, J. B. White, & S. Miller, 2000, Earnings at DaimlerChrysler fall as trouble at U.S. division piles up, *The Wall Street Journal Interactive*, http://interactive.wsj.com, October 27.

the world are choosing this strategic option with increasing frequency. In recent years, cross-border acquisitions have represented as much as 45 percent of the total number of acquisitions made annually.[31] The Daimler-Benz acquisition of Chrysler Corporation provides an example of this activity. Because of relaxed regulations, the amount of cross-border activity among nations within the European community also continues to increase. Accounting for this growth in a range of cross-border acquisitions, some analysts believe, is the fact that many large European corporations have approached the limits of growth within their domestic markets and thus seek growth in other markets. Additionally, they are trying to achieve market power to compete effectively throughout the European Union and thus have made acquisitions in other European countries.

Firms in all types of industries are completing cross-border acquisitions. For example, in the cosmetics industry, Japan's Shiseido created a new division to pursue mergers and acquisitions. With its growth long fueled by acquisitions, the firm is now committed to emphasizing the cross-border variety, especially with European companies. In another segment of the consumer goods industry, Kimberly-Clark, the world's largest producer of tissue products, intends to acquire primarily non-U.S. companies to expand its disposable medical products lines and tissue and diaper businesses.[32]

Cost of New-Product Development and Increased Speed to Market

Developing new products internally and successfully introducing them into the marketplace often require significant investments of a firm's resources, including time, making it difficult to quickly earn a profitable return.[33] Also of concern to firms' managers is achieving adequate returns from the capital invested to develop and commercialize new products—an estimated 88 percent of innovations fail to achieve adequate returns. Perhaps contributing to these less-than-desirable rates of return is the successful imitation of approximately 60 percent of innovations within four years after the patents are obtained. Because of outcomes such as these, managers often perceive internal product development as a high-risk activity.[34]

Acquisitions are another means a firm can use to gain access to new products and to current products that are new to the firm. Compared to internal product development processes, acquisitions provide more predictable returns as well as faster market entry. Returns are more predictable because the performance of the acquired firm's products can be assessed prior to completing the acquisition.[35] For these reasons, extensive bidding wars and acquisitions are more frequent in high technology industries.[36]

Acquisition activity is also extensive throughout the pharmaceutical industry, where firms frequently use acquisitions to enter markets quickly, to overcome the high costs of developing products internally, and to increase the predictability of returns on their investments. Interestingly, Merck & Co. has chosen not to acquire new drugs but to develop them internally, a strategy that has been beneficial for most of the last 20 years as it became the world's largest and most successful pharmaceutical firm. However, in the new millennium, Merck has experienced problems and now trails Pfizer and GlaxoSmithKline in the industry. Some analysts suggest that Merck may be unable to return to its number one ranking unless it acquires another large successful pharmaceutical firm.[37]

© BOB KRIST/CORBIS

Merck spent approximately $2.45 billion on research and development in 2001. In 2000 Merck began collaborating with Schering-Plough in what the companies call "a flexible, creative partnership." One group in this arrangement plots strategies for combining ezetimibe (under study for reduction of cholesterol) and Zocor, Merck's leading cholesterol-reducer. Another group oversees the development combining Singulair, the leading asthma drug in the United States, and Claritin to combat allergic rhinits. Pictured here is a researcher in a Merck lab.

As indicated previously, compared to internal product development, acquisitions result in more rapid market entries.[38] Acquisitions often represent the fastest means to enter international markets and help firms overcome the liabilities associated with such strategic moves.[39] Acquisitions provide rapid access both to new markets and to new capabilities. Using new capabilities to pioneer new products and to enter markets quickly can create advantageous market positions.[40] Pharmaceutical firms, for example, access new products through acquisitions of other drug manufacturers. They also acquire biotechnology firms both for new products and for new technological capabilities. Pharmaceutical firms often provide the manufacturing and marketing capabilities to take the new products developed by biotechnology firms to the market.[41]

Lower Risk Compared to Developing New Products

Because an acquisition's outcomes can be estimated more easily and accurately compared to the outcomes of an internal product development process, managers may view acquisitions as lowering risk.[42] The difference in risk between an internal product development process and an acquisition can be seen in the results of Merck's strategy and its competitors described above.

As with other strategic actions discussed in this book, the firm must exercise caution when using a strategy of acquiring new products rather than developing them internally. While research suggests that acquisitions have become a common means of avoiding risky internal ventures (and therefore risky R&D investments), they may

also become a substitute for innovation.[43] Thus, acquisitions are not a risk-free alternative to entering new markets through internally developed products.

Increased Diversification

Acquisitions are also used to diversify firms. Based on experience and the insights resulting from it, firms typically find it easier to develop and introduce new products in markets currently served by the firm. In contrast, it is difficult for companies to develop products that differ from their current lines for markets in which they lack experience. Thus, it is uncommon for a firm to develop new products internally to diversify its product lines.[44] Using acquisitions to diversify a firm is the quickest and, typically, the easiest way to change its portfolio of businesses.[45]

Both related diversification and unrelated diversification strategies can be implemented through acquisitions. For example, Tyco International has been very aggressive in using acquisitions and building a conglomerate—a highly unrelated diversified firm.[46] Tyco's companies manufacture products as diverse as valves and garbage bags. In 2001, Tyco acquired a large commercial finance company, CIT Group, Inc. However, Tyco experienced problems in 2002 for making a number of acquisitions without reporting them or the debt they obtained to finance them.

Research has shown the more related the acquired firm is to the acquiring firm, the greater is the probability that the acquisition will be successful.[47] Thus, horizontal acquisitions (through which a firm acquires a competitor) and related acquisitions tend to contribute more to the firm's strategic competitiveness than acquiring a company that operates in quite different product markets from those in which the firm competes.[48] For example, firms in the financial services industry have become more diversified over time, often through acquisitions. One study suggests that these firms are diversifying not only to provide a more complete line of products for their customers but also to create strategic flexibility. In other words, they diversify into some product lines to provide options for future services they may wish to emphasize. As noted earlier, such acquisitions are a means of dealing with an uncertain competitive environment.[49]

Reshaping the Firm's Competitive Scope

As discussed in Chapter 2, the intensity of competitive rivalry is an industry characteristic that affects the firm's profitability.[50] To reduce the negative effect of an intense rivalry on their financial performance, firms may use acquisitions to reduce their dependence on one or more products or markets. Reducing a company's dependence on specific markets alters the firm's competitive scope.

One of the arguments against HP's acquisition of Compaq, described in the Opening Case, is that it increases the firm's dependence on the highly competitive and volatile personal computer market. Thus, rather than using acquisitions to avoid competition, HP is increasing its emphasis in a market characterized by substantial competitive rivalry. Some major shareholders and analysts believe that HP should emphasize its printers and computer accessories businesses.

GE reduced its emphasis in the electronics markets many years ago by making acquisitions in the financial services industry. Today, GE is considered a service firm because a majority of its revenue now comes from services instead of industrial products.[51]

Learning and Developing New Capabilities

Some acquisitions are made to gain capabilities that the firm does not possess. For example, acquisitions may be used to acquire a special technological capability. Research has shown that firms can broaden their knowledge base and reduce inertia through acquisitions.[52] Therefore, acquiring other firms with skills and capabilities that differ from its own helps the acquiring firm to learn new knowledge and remain agile. Of course, firms are better able to learn these capabilities if they share some similar properties with the firm's current capabilities. Thus, firms should seek to acquire companies with different but related and complementary capabilities in order to build their own knowledge base.[53]

One of Cisco System's primary goals in its acquisitions is to gain access to capabilities that it does not currently possess. Cisco executives emphasize the importance of learning throughout the organization.[54] Cisco has developed an intricate process to quickly integrate the acquired firms and their capabilities (knowledge) after an acquisition is completed. Cisco's processes account for its phenomenal success in the latter half of the 1990s and being named one of the top ten most admired firms by *Fortune* in 2000.[55] While it suffered in the collapsing value of Internet-based companies in 2001 and early 2002, Cisco is expected to bounce back strongly as the U.S. economy recovers.

Problems in Achieving Acquisition Success

Acquisition strategies based on legitimate reasons described in this chapter can increase strategic competitiveness and help firms to earn above-average returns. However, acquisition strategies are not risk-free. Reasons for the use of acquisition strategies and potential problems with such strategies are shown in Figure 7.1.

Research suggests that perhaps 20 percent of all mergers and acquisitions are successful, approximately 60 percent produce disappointing results, and the last 20 percent are clear failures.[56] Successful acquisitions generally involve a well-conceived strategy in selecting the target, avoiding paying too high a premium, and an effective integration process.[57] As shown in Figure 7.1, several problems may prevent successful acquisitions.

Integration Difficulties

Integrating two companies following an acquisition can be quite difficult. Integration challenges include melding two disparate corporate cultures, linking different financial and control systems, building effective working relationships (particularly when management styles differ), and resolving problems regarding the status of the newly acquired firm's executives.[58]

The importance of a successful integration should not be underestimated. Without it, an acquisition is unlikely to produce positive returns. Thus, as suggested by a researcher studying the process, "managerial practice and academic writings show that the post-acquisition integration phase is probably the single most important determinant of shareholder value creation (and equally of value destruction) in mergers and acquisitions."[59]

Integration is complex and involves a large number of activities. For instance, Intel acquired Digital Equipment Corporation's semiconductors division. Successful integration was crucial—on the day Intel began to merge the acquired division into its operations, hundreds of employees working in dozens of different countries needed to complete 6,000 deliverables.[60]

It is important to maintain the human capital of the target firm after the acquisition. Much of an organization's knowledge is contained in its human capital.[61] Turnover of key personnel from the acquired firm can have a negative effect on the performance of the merged firm.[62] The loss of key personnel, such as critical managers, weakens the acquired firm's capabilities and reduces its value.

If implemented effectively, the integration process can have a positive effect on target firm managers and reduce the probability that they will leave.[63] Cisco Systems, as noted earlier, has been highly effective in making acquisitions, partly because of its

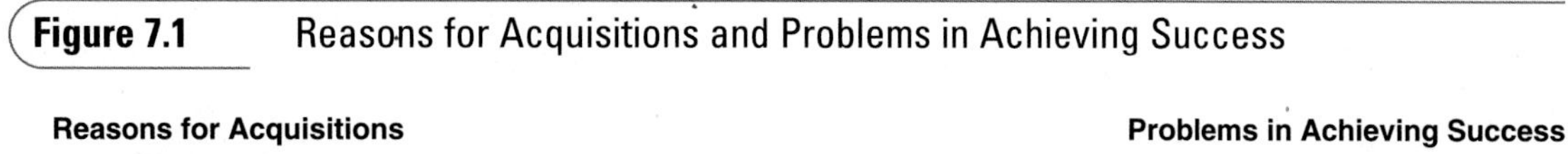
Figure 7.1 Reasons for Acquisitions and Problems in Achieving Success

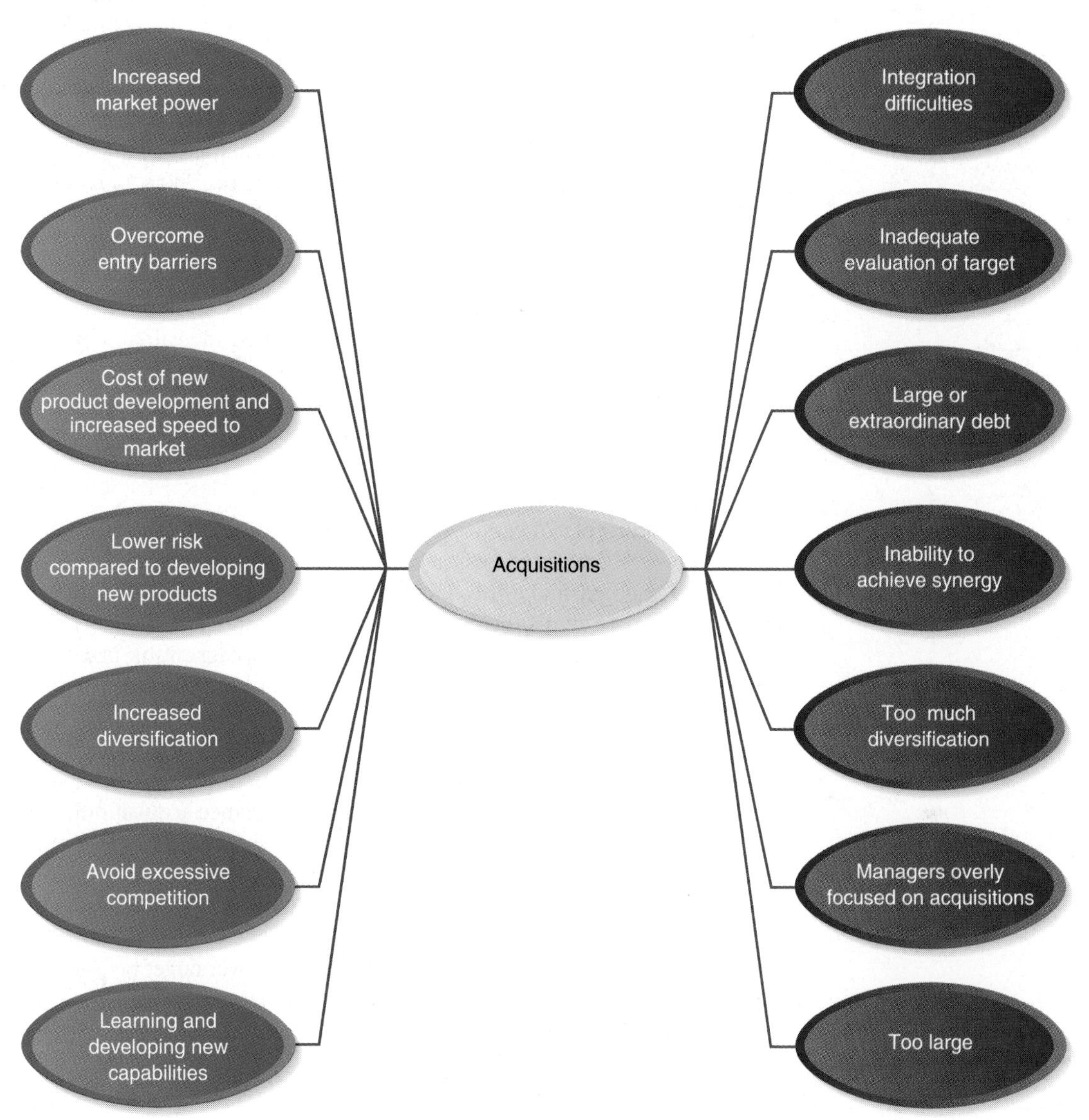

ability to quickly integrate its acquisitions into its existing operations. Focusing on small companies with products and services related closely to its own, Cisco uses a relatively large team charged with the responsibility to integrate key target firm personnel and processes into the firm. An important goal of the team is to make the acquired firm employees feel ownership in Cisco.[64]

Inadequate Evaluation of Target

Due diligence is a process through which a potential acquirer evaluates a target firm for acquisition. In an effective due-diligence process hundreds of items are examined in areas as diverse as the financing for the intended transaction, differences in cultures between the acquiring and target firm, tax consequences of the transaction, and actions that would be necessary to successfully meld the two workforces. Due diligence is commonly performed by investment bankers, accountants, lawyers, and management consultants specializing in that activity, although firms actively pursuing acquisitions may form their own internal due-diligence team.

The failure to complete an effective due-diligence process may easily result in the acquiring firm paying an excessive premium for the target company. In fact, research shows that without due diligence, "the purchase price is driven by the pricing of other 'comparable' acquisitions rather than by a rigorous assessment of where, when, and how management can drive real performance gains. [In these cases], the price paid may have little to do with achievable value."[65] As shown in the Strategic Focus on page 225, an effective due-diligence process may have revealed the true value of Enron to Dynegy, Inc., the firm that had agreed to acquire it.

In fact, as we discussed, Dynegy could have lost considerable value if it had completed the acquisition of Enron. It was saved because investors and lenders expressed concerns. Furthermore, Dynegy obtained the valuable pipeline assets for $1.5 billion. Under normal circumstances, effective due diligence would have identified Enron's problems, and Dynegy would not have entered into an agreement to acquire the company.

Large or Extraordinary Debt

To finance a number of acquisitions completed during the 1980s and 1990s, some companies significantly increased their levels of debt. A financial innovation called junk bonds helped make this increase possible. *Junk bonds* are a financing option through which risky acquisitions are financed with money (debt) that provides a large potential return to lenders (bondholders). Because junk bonds are unsecured obligations that are not tied to specific assets for collateral, interest rates for these high-risk debt instruments sometimes reached between 18 and 20 percent during the 1980s.[66] Some prominent financial economists viewed debt as a means to discipline managers, causing them to act in shareholders' best interests.[67]

Junk bonds are now used less frequently to finance acquisitions, and the conviction that debt disciplines managers is less strong. Nonetheless, some firms still take on significant debt to acquire companies. For example, Disney increased its total debt by $5.3 billion to approximately $15 billion to acquire Fox Family Worldwide. This action caused Moody's Investors Service to review Disney's debt condition.[68] Furthermore, some analysts believe that Disney is a potential takeover target because of its poor performance.[69] Analysts also question the amount of debt taken on by International Paper to finance several acquisitions. The firm built its total debt to $15.5 billion, equal to approximately 50 percent of its capital and 400 percent of its annual cash flow.[70]

High debt can have several negative effects on the firm. For example, because high debt increases the likelihood of bankruptcy, it can lead to a downgrade in the firm's credit rating by agencies such as Moody's and Standard & Poor's.[71] In addition, high debt may preclude needed investment in activities that contribute to the firm's long-term success, such as R&D, human resource training, and marketing.[72] Still, use of leverage can be a positive force in a firm's development, allowing it to take advantage of attractive expansion opportunities. However, too much leverage (such as extraordinary debt) can lead to negative outcomes, including postponing or eliminating investments, such as R&D expenditures, that are necessary to maintain strategic competitiveness over the long term.

Inability to Achieve Synergy

Derived from "synergos," a Greek word that means "working together," *synergy* exists when the value created by units working together exceeds the value those units could create working independently (see Chapter 6). That is, synergy exists when assets are

Strategic Focus

Dynegy Should Thank Its Lucky Stars

In November 2001 Dynegy, Inc., agreed to acquire its former rival Enron, the once highly successful, then highly troubled energy trading company. Only months before the merger was announced, Enron's market value was approximately $70 billion. When the firm announced that it had overstated earnings for several years, however, investors lost confidence. Dynegy accordingly agreed to purchase Enron for only $9 billion—far less than anticipated. In the next two weeks, serious financial problems continued to be revealed, and Enron's market value fell to less than $270 million. Dynegy claimed that Enron had failed to fully disclose the scope of its financial woes and withdrew its offer to acquire Enron. The U.S. Justice Department and Congress announced investigations into Enron's potential managerial improprieties, and the firm filed for bankruptcy shortly thereafter.

Enron also filed a lawsuit against Dynegy for withdrawing from the acquisition agreement, demanding $10 billion in damages. Dynegy countersued to acquire Enron's largest pipeline asset for $1.5 billion—an amount agreed upon earlier even if the acquisition was not consummated—and eventually received the asset.

Dynegy came out of the transaction the clear winner—the firm obtained a valued asset and dodged a bullet by not acquiring Enron. It is unclear, however, whether Dynegy conducted effective due diligence. If it had done so, it probably would not have agreed to buy Enron for $9 billion—or any other price. As it turned out, concerned major investors and lenders who forced Enron's disclosure of questionable financial practices helped Dynegy.

Enron executives likely created the firm's financial problems partially out of hubris, an exaggerated self-confidence. Its former CEO Jeffrey Skilling once remarked, "We're on the side of angels." Enron had built an envious energy trading operation and annual revenues of over $100 billion, but it experienced substantial losses in some trades when the economy turned sour in 2001 (such as its losses of over $127 million in trading of fiber-optic capacity). Substantial criticism has been aimed at Enron's auditor and board of directors for allowing unacceptable financial practices to occur. The full story of Enron's problems and practices may take years to discover.

SOURCES: N. Weinberg & D. Fisher, 2001, Power play, *Forbes*, December 24, 53–58; G. Robinson, 2001, Congressional probe into Enron intensifies, *Financial Times*, http://www.ft.com, December 17; R. Abelson, 2001, Enron board comes under a storm of criticism, *The New York Times Interactive*, http://www.nytimes.com, December 16; D. Ackman, 2001, Enron's mysterious, troubled core, *Forbes*, http://www.forbes.com, December 15; J. R. Emshwiller & R. Smith, 2001, Behind Enron's fall, a culture of secrecy which cost the firm its investors' trust, *The Wall Street Journal Interactive*, http://interactive.wsj.com, December 5; R. A. Opper, Jr. & A. R. Sorkin, 2001, Enron files largest U.S. claim for bankruptcy, *The New York Times Interactive*, http://www.nytimes.com, December 3; F. Norria, 2001, Gas pipeline is prominent as Dynegy seeks Enron, *The New York Times Interactive*, http://www.nytimes.com, November 13.

worth more when used in conjunction with each other than when they are used separately.[73] For shareholders, synergy generates gains in their wealth that they could not duplicate or exceed through their own portfolio diversification decisions.[74] Synergy is created by the efficiencies derived from economies of scale and economies of scope and by sharing resources (e.g., human capital and knowledge) across the businesses in the merged firm.[75]

A firm develops a competitive advantage through an acquisition strategy only when a transaction generates private synergy. *Private synergy* is created when the combination and integration of the acquiring and acquired firms' assets yield capabilities and core competencies that could not be developed by combining and integrating either firm's assets with another company. Private synergy is possible when firms' assets are complementary in unique ways; that is, the unique type of asset complementarity is not possible by combining either company's assets with another firm's assets.[76] Because of its uniqueness, private synergy is difficult for competitors to understand and imitate. However, private synergy is difficult to create.

A firm's ability to account for costs that are necessary to create anticipated revenue- and cost-based synergies affects the acquisition's success. Firms experience several expenses when trying to create private synergy through acquisitions. Called transaction costs, these expenses are incurred when firms use acquisition strategies to create synergy.[77] Transaction costs may be direct or indirect. Direct costs include legal fees and charges from investment bankers who complete due diligence for the acquiring firm. Indirect costs include managerial time to evaluate target firms and then to complete negotiations, as well as the loss of key managers and employees following an acquisition.[78] Firms tend to underestimate the sum of indirect costs when the value of the synergy that may be created by combining and integrating the acquired firm's assets with the acquiring firm's assets is calculated.

Too Much Diversification

© PETER MORGAN/REUTERS NEWMEDIA INC./CORBIS

Former Tyco CEO L. Dennis Kozolowski, center, answers questions following an investors' meeting. The firm had announced that it would split into four publicly traded companies to boost shareholder value and to erase $11 billion in debt. The firm's strategy of growth through acquisitions resulted in investors questioning its failure to fully disclose information about 700 acquisitions from 1998 to 2001, although the firm had accounted for their net cost. Tyco's later decision not to split into four separate companies shows the complexity of managing acquisition strategies.

As explained in Chapter 6, diversification strategies can lead to strategic competitiveness and above-average returns. In general, firms using related diversification strategies outperform those employing unrelated diversification strategies. However, conglomerates, formed by using an unrelated diversification strategy, also can be successful. For example, Virgin Group, the U.K. firm with interests ranging from cosmetics to trains, is successful. Tyco International, a highly diversified U.S. firm, has also been successful. Tyco was ranked by *Forbes* as the 25th-highest performing firm over the five-year period of 1997–2001, the highest ranking by a conglomerate firm. During this period, its stock price increased 341 percent.[79] However, Tyco's performance suffered in 2002, after it revealed unreported acquisitions and accumulated debt over the previous three years.

At some point, firms can become overdiversified. The level at which overdiversification occurs varies across companies because each firm has different capabilities to manage diversification. Recall from Chapter 6 that related diversification requires more information processing than does unrelated diversification. The need for related diversified firms to process more information of greater diversity is such that they become overdiversified with a smaller number of business units, compared to firms using an unrelated diversification strategy.[80] Regardless of the type of diversification strategy implemented, however, declines in performance result from overdiversification, after which business units are often divested.[81] The pattern of excessive diversification followed by divestments of underperforming business units acquired earlier was frequently observed among U.S. firms during the 1960s through the 1980s.[82]

Even when a firm is not overdiversified, a high level of diversification can have a negative effect on the firm's long-term performance. For example, the scope created by additional amounts of diversification often causes managers to rely on financial rather than strategic controls to evaluate business units' performances (financial and strategic controls are defined and explained in Chapters 11 and 12). Top-level executives often rely on financial controls to assess the performance of business units when they do not have a rich understanding of business units' objectives and strategies. Use of financial controls, such as return on investment (ROI), causes individual business-unit managers to focus on short-term outcomes at the expense of long-term investments. When long-term investments are reduced to increase short-term profits, a firm's overall strategic competitiveness may be harmed.[83]

Another problem resulting from too much diversification is the tendency for acquisitions to become substitutes for innovation. Typically, managers do not intend acquisitions to be used in that way. However, a reinforcing cycle evolves. Costs associated with acquisitions may result in fewer allocations to activities, such as R&D, that are linked to innovation. Without adequate support, a firm's innovation skills begin to atrophy. Without internal innovation skills, the only option available to a firm is to complete still additional acquisitions to gain access to innovation. Evidence suggests that a firm using acquisitions as a substitute for internal innovations eventually encounters performance problems.[84]

Managers Overly Focused on Acquisitions

Typically, a fairly substantial amount of managerial time and energy is required for acquisition strategies to contribute to the firm's strategic competitiveness. Activities with which managers become involved include (1) searching for viable acquisition candidates, (2) completing effective due-diligence processes, (3) preparing for negotiations, and (4) managing the integration process after the acquisition is completed.

Top-level managers do not personally gather all data and information required to make acquisitions. However, these executives do make critical decisions on the firms to be targeted, the nature of the negotiations, and so forth. Company experiences show that participating in and overseeing the activities required for making acquisitions can divert managerial attention from other matters that are necessary for long-term competitive success, such as identifying and taking advantage of other opportunities and interacting with important external stakeholders.[85]

For example, Case Corporation acquired New Holland to create CNH Global with annual sales of almost $11 billion, resulting in the second highest market share in the agricultural and construction equipment industry. However, the executives became preoccupied with integrating the two firms and largely ignored external economic events and competitors. The company's markets were rapidly changing and its competitors were taking away its customers. As a result, CNH's annual revenues in 2000 declined by $2.5 billion from the combined 1998 revenues of the two separate companies.[86] Thus, upper-level executives should avoid focusing on an acquisition strategy at the expense of the firm's long-term strategic competitiveness.

Acquisitions can consume significant amounts of managerial time and energy in both the acquiring and target firms. In particular, managers in target firms may operate in a state of virtual suspended animation during an acquisition.[87] Although the target firm's day-to-day operations continue, most of the company's executives are hesitant to make decisions with long-term consequences until negotiations have been completed. Evidence suggests that the acquisition process can create a short-term perspective and a greater aversion to risk among top-level executives in a target firm.[88]

Too Large

Most acquisitions create a larger firm that should help increase its economies of scale. These economies can then lead to more efficient operations—for example, the two sales organizations can be integrated using fewer sales reps because a sales rep can sell the products of both firms (particularly if the products of the acquiring and target firms are highly related).

Many firms seek increases in size because of the potential economies of scale and enhanced market power (discussed earlier). For example, when Daniel Brewster took the job as CEO of Gruner+Jahr USA Publishing, he announced that he had been given a mandate by the parent company, Bertelsmann, to double the firm's size in five years. With the resources provided by Bertelsmann, Brewster made $600 million in acquisitions in a six-month period, including the $342 million acquisition of *Fast Company*. Essentially, the goal given to Brewster by Bertelsmann was for Gruner+Jahr USA to become number one or two in the markets served. Thus, Brewster is trying to gain economies of scale and market power simultaneously.[89]

At some level, the additional costs required to manage the larger firm will exceed the benefits of the economies of scale and additional market power. In addition, the complexities generated by the larger size often lead managers to implement more bureaucratic controls to manage the combined firm's operations. Bureaucratic controls are formalized supervisory and behavioral rules and policies designed to ensure consistency of decisions and actions across different units of a firm. However, through time, formalized controls often lead to relatively rigid and standardized managerial behavior. Certainly, in the long run, the diminished flexibility that accompanies rigid and standardized managerial behavior may produce less innovation. Because of innovation's importance to competitive success, the bureaucratic controls resulting from a large organization (that is, built by acquisitions) can have a detrimental effect on performance.[90]

Effective Acquisitions

Earlier in the chapter, we noted that acquisition strategies do not consistently produce above-average returns for the acquiring firm's shareholders. Nonetheless, some companies are able to create value when using an acquisition strategy.[91] Results from a research study shed light on the differences between unsuccessful and successful acquisition strategies and suggest that there is a pattern of actions that can improve the probability of acquisition success.[92]

The study shows that when the target firm's assets are complementary to the acquired firm's assets, an acquisition is more successful. With complementary assets, integrating two firms' operations has a higher probability of creating synergy. In fact, integrating two firms with complementary assets frequently produces unique capabilities and core competencies.[93] With complementary assets, the acquiring firm can maintain its focus on core businesses and leverage the complementary assets and capabilities from the acquired firm. Oftentimes, targets were selected and "groomed" by establishing a working relationship sometime prior to the acquisition. As discussed in Chapter 9, strategic alliances are sometimes used to test the feasibility of a future merger or acquisition between the involved firms.[94]

The study's results also show that friendly acquisitions facilitate integration of the firms involved in an acquisition. Through friendly acquisitions, firms work together to find ways to integrate their operations to create synergy. In hostile takeovers, animosity often results between the two top-management teams, a condition that in turn affects working relationships in the newly created firm. As a result, more key personnel in the acquired firm may be lost, and those who remain may resist the changes necessary to integrate the two firms.[95] With effort, cultural clashes can be overcome, and fewer key managers and employees will become discouraged and leave.[96]

Additionally, effective due-diligence processes involving the deliberate and careful selection of target firms and an evaluation of the relative health of those firms (financial health, cultural fit, and the value of human resources) contribute to successful acquisitions. Financial slack in the form of debt equity or cash, in both the acquiring and acquired firms, also has frequently contributed to success in acquisitions. While financial slack provides access to financing for the acquisition, it is still important to maintain a low or moderate level of debt after the acquisition to keep debt costs low. When substantial debt was used to finance the acquisition, companies with successful acquisitions reduced the debt quickly, partly by selling off assets from the acquired firm, especially non-complementary or poorly performing assets. For these firms, debt costs do not prevent long-term investments such as R&D, and managerial discretion in the use of cash flow is relatively flexible.

Another attribute of successful acquisition strategies is an emphasis on innovation, as demonstrated by continuing investments in R&D activities. Significant R&D investments show a strong managerial commitment to innovation, a characteristic that is increasingly important to overall competitiveness, as well as acquisition success.

Flexibility and adaptability are the final two attributes of successful acquisitions. When executives of both the acquiring and the target firms have experience in managing change and learning from acquisitions, they will be more skilled at adapting their capabilities to new environments.[97] As a result, they will be more adept at integrating the two organizations, which is particularly important when firms have different organizational cultures.

Efficient and effective integration may quickly produce the desired synergy in the newly created firm. Effective integration allows the acquiring firm to keep valuable human resources in the acquired firm from leaving.[98]

The attributes and results of successful acquisitions are summarized in Table 7.1. Managers seeking acquisition success should emphasize the seven attributes that are listed.

As explained in the Strategic Focus on page 230, the attempted acquisition of Honeywell by GE had some but not all of the attributes of successful acquisitions summarized in Table 7.1.

Table 7.1 Attributes of Successful Acquisitions

Attributes	Results
1. Acquired firm has assets or resources that are complementary to the acquiring firm's core business	1. High probability of synergy and competitive advantage by maintaining strengths
2. Acquisition is friendly	2. Faster and more effective integration and possibly lower premiums
3. Acquiring firm conducts effective due diligence to select target firms and evaluate the target firm's health (financial, cultural, and human resources)	3. Firms with strongest complementarities are acquired and overpayment is avoided
4. Acquiring firm has financial slack (cash or a favorable debt position)	4. Financing (debt or equity) is easier and less costly to obtain
5. Merged firm maintains low to moderate debt position	5. Lower financing cost, lower risk (e.g., of bankruptcy), and avoidance of trade-offs that are associated with high debt
6. Sustained and consistent emphasis on R&D and innovation	6. Maintain long-term competitive advantage in markets
7. Has experience with change and is flexible and adaptable	7. Faster and more effective integration facilitates achievement of synergy

Strategic Focus

Was GE's Attempted Acquisition of Honeywell a Correct Strategy?

In 2001, Honeywell International agreed to be acquired by General Electric (GE). Even though the transaction was subject to approval by the European Union, GE and Honeywell executives likened the merger of these two firms to "a match made in heaven."

Analysts questioned the value of the acquisition by GE, however. The current Honeywell resulted from a previous acquisition of Honeywell by AlliedSignal. The integration of Honeywell and AlliedSignal had not gone well, and the firm's performance was suffering. United Technology made an offer to acquire Honeywell, but Honeywell executives and its board of directors rejected the offer.

Some considered GE as a "white knight" rescuing Honeywell from United Technologies. United Technologies had the last laugh—as it was one of four major firms that lobbied against the acquisition that was eventually disapproved by the European Union anti-trust regulators.

There seemed to be potential synergy between GE and Honeywell, especially in the aerospace businesses with GE's jet engines and Honeywell's avionic equipment. However, concern over potential dominance of this market is what led European regulators to disapprove the acquisition. It is unclear how much due diligence GE conducted prior to making its offer to acquire Honeywell. The fact that Honeywell and AlliedSignal had been unable to achieve an effective integration of their operations should have caused concerns for GE. Jack Welch, CEO of GE at the time, and Lawrence Bossidy, former CEO of AlliedSignal, were friends, but their two firms did not have major working relationships. GE also overlooked the possibility of disapproval by European regulators, conceding that its negotiated deal with Honeywell was completed so rapidly that no time had been allowed for consulting European lawyers on the regulatory concerns.

The deal had the trappings of managerial hubris. Welch was planning to retire, and some analysts touted this acquisition as his last great strategic move. In fact, he was writing a book planned for publication immediately after his retirement, and the last chapter was slated to cover the Honeywell acquisition. When the acquisition was disapproved, the last chapter of the book was hurriedly rewritten. When Bossidy came out of retirement to become CEO of Honeywell immediately after the deal fell through, speculation grew that he and Welch had an informal agreement to make the acquisition, with GE outbidding United Technologies.

Jeffrey Immelt, the new CEO of GE, predicted that although 2001 had not been a great year for the company, GE would continue to grow through acquisitions and that profits would increase by as much as 18 percent in 2002. There was no such positive prediction for Honeywell.

SOURCES: A. Hill, 2001, GE pins expansion plans on acquisitions, *Financial Times,* http://www.ft.com, December 19; D. Jones, 2001, Welch book trips on merger hurdle, *The Wall Street Journal,* July 24, D3; D. Hargreaves & A. Hill, 2001, GE accused of cold feet on Honeywell deal, *Financial Times,* http://www.ft.com, July 6; 2001, European foes stall merger with GE: Focus is misplaced in Honeywell deal, *Arizona Republic,* June 20, V4; L. Zuckerman & A. R. Sorkin, 2001, G.E. calls its $45 billion bid for Honeywell all but dead, *The New York Times Interactive,* http://www.nytimes.com, June 17; M. Murray, P. Shiskin, B. Davis, & A. Raghavan, 2001, As Honeywell deal goes awry for GE, fallout may be global, *The Wall Street Journal Interactive,* http://interactive.wsj.com, June 14.

It is unclear whether GE's acquisition of Honeywell would have succeeded if it had been approved. While it had some of the characteristics of effective acquisitions, such as potential complementary capabilities, and a friendly acquisition, reports suggest that the due diligence process was inadequate. Some analysts were concerned that it would have been difficult to integrate Honeywell into GE, and GE did not foresee the regulatory challenges.

As we have learned, some acquisitions enhance strategic competitiveness. However, the majority of acquisitions that took place from the 1970s through the 1990s did not enhance firms' strategic competitiveness. In fact, "history shows that anywhere between one-third [and] more than half of all acquisitions are ultimately divested or spun-off."[99] Thus, firms often use restructuring strategies to correct for the failure of a merger or an acquisition.

Restructuring

Restructuring is a strategy through which a firm changes its set of businesses or financial structure.

Defined formally, **restructuring** is a strategy through which a firm changes its set of businesses or financial structure.[100] From the 1970s into the 2000s, divesting businesses from company portfolios and downsizing accounted for a large percentage of firms' restructuring strategies. Restructuring is a global phenomenon.[101]

The failure of an acquisition strategy often precedes a restructuring strategy. Among the famous restructurings taken to correct for an acquisition failure are (1) AT&T's $7.4 billion purchase of NCR and subsequent spin-off of the company to shareholders in a deal valued at $3.4 billion, (2) Novell's purchase of WordPerfect for stock valued at $1.4 billion and its sale of the company to Corel for $124 million in stock and cash, and (3) Quaker Oats acquisition of Snapple Beverage Company for $1.7 billion, only to sell it three years later for $300 million.[102]

In other instances, however, firms use a restructuring strategy because of changes in their external and internal environments. For example, opportunities sometimes surface in the external environment that are particularly attractive to the diversified firm in light of its core competencies. In such cases, restructuring may be appropriate to position the firm to create more value for stakeholders, given the environmental changes.

As discussed next, there are three restructuring strategies that firms use: downsizing, downscoping, and leveraged buyouts.

Downsizing

Once thought to be an indicator of organizational decline, downsizing is now recognized as a legitimate restructuring strategy. *Downsizing* is a reduction in the number of a firm's employees and, sometimes, in the number of its operating units, but it may or may not change the composition of businesses in the company's portfolio. Thus, downsizing is an intentional proactive management strategy, whereas "decline is an environmental or organizational phenomenon that occurs involuntarily and results in erosion of an organization's resource base."[103]

In the late 1980s, early 1990s, and early 2000s, thousands of jobs were lost in private and public organizations in the United States. One study estimates that 85 percent of Fortune 1000 firms have used downsizing as a restructuring strategy.[104] Moreover, *Fortune* 500 firms laid off more than one million employees, or 4 percent of their collective workforce, in 2001 and into the first few weeks of 2002.[105]

Firms use downsizing as a restructuring strategy for different reasons. The most frequently cited reason is that the firm expects improved profitability from cost reductions and more efficient operations. For example, Ford announced a major downsizing and restructuring plan in 2002 that the company predicts will increase its operating profits by as much as $9 billion over the next few years. To reach this goal, Ford will lay off 35,000 employees worldwide, closing five manufacturing plants and cutting production at the remaining plants by an average of 16 percent. Because four of the five plants scheduled for closure are in the United States and the fifth is in

Canada, North American operations will be hit particularly hard. Ford executives felt forced to take this action because of poor financial performance and a loss of market share to competitors.[106]

Downscoping

Compared to downsizing, downscoping has a more positive effect on firm performance.[107] *Downscoping* refers to divestiture, spin-off, or some other means of eliminating businesses that are unrelated to a firm's core businesses. Commonly, downscoping is described as a set of actions that causes a firm to strategically refocus on its core businesses.

A firm that downscopes often also downsizes simultaneously. However, it does not eliminate key employees from its primary businesses in the process, because such action could lead to a loss of one or more core competencies. Instead, a firm that is simultaneously downscoping and downsizing becomes smaller by reducing the diversity of businesses in its portfolio.

By refocusing on its core businesses, the firm can be managed more effectively by the top management team. Managerial effectiveness increases because the firm has become less diversified, allowing the top management team to better understand and manage the remaining businesses.[108]

In general, U.S. firms use downscoping as a restructuring strategy more frequently than do European companies. In general, the trend in Europe, Latin America, and Asia has been to build conglomerates. In Latin America, these conglomerates are called *grupos.* Many Asian and Latin American conglomerates have begun to adopt Western corporate strategies in recent years and have been refocusing on their core businesses. This downscoping has occurred simultaneously with increasing globalization and with more open markets that have greatly enhanced the competition. By downscoping, these firms have been able to focus on their core businesses and improve their competitiveness.[109]

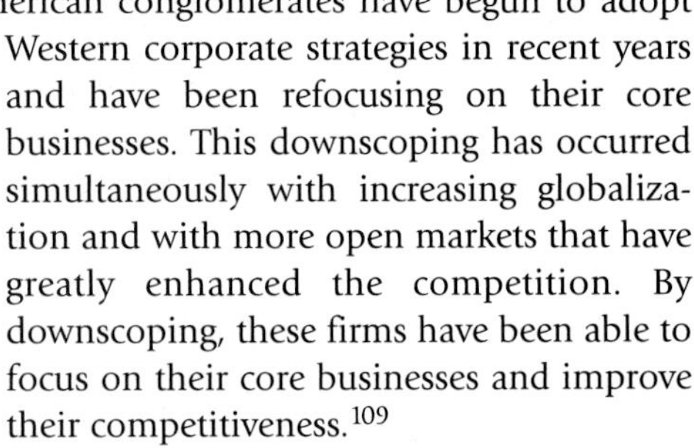

Among the U.S.-based firms using downscoping as a restructuring strategy, AT&T has refocused twice in the last ten years. Poor performance was the primary reason for both restructuring actions. In the first action, AT&T completed a trivestiture by spinning off Lucent Technologies and NCR. When AT&T's core long distance business began to lose market share, CEO Michael Armstrong diversified by acquiring cable companies at too high a price. He then provided high-speed Internet access and local telephone service over the cable-television network, but these services could not compensate for the poor performance in the core business. Therefore, in what is called "Armstrong's last stand," the downscoping restructuring was announced.[110]

In 2001, as part of his restructuring plan, AT&T CEO C. Michael Armstrong oversaw the auction of AT&T's cable television business, unwound an international joint venture with BT Group, and cut debt by $22 billion. Further cost-cutting measures in 2002 included the sale of AT&T's New Jersey headquarters property.

Leveraged Buyouts

Leveraged buyouts are commonly used as a restructuring strategy to correct for managerial mistakes or because the firm's managers are making decisions that primarily serve their own interests rather than those of shareholders.[111] A *leveraged buyout* (LBO) is a restructuring strategy whereby a party buys all of a firm's assets in order to take the firm private. Once the transaction is completed, the company's stock is no longer traded publicly.

Usually, significant amounts of debt are incurred to finance the buyout, hence the term "leveraged" buyout. To support debt payments and to downscope the company to concentrate on the firm's core businesses, the new owners may immediately sell a number of assets.[112] It is not uncommon for those buying a firm through an LBO to restructure the firm to the point that it can be sold at a profit within a five-year to eight-year period.

Management buyouts (MBOs), employee buyouts (EBOs), and whole-firm buyouts, in which one company or partnership purchases an entire company instead of a part of it, are the three types of LBOs. In part because of managerial incentives, MBOs, more so than EBOs and whole-firm buyouts, have been found to lead to downscoping, an increased strategic focus, and improved performance.[113] Research has shown that management buyouts can also lead to greater entrepreneurial activity and growth.

While there may be different reasons for a buyout, one is to protect against a capricious financial market, allowing the owners to focus on developing innovations and bringing them to the market.[114] As such, buyouts can represent a form of firm rebirth to facilitate entrepreneurial efforts and stimulate strategic growth.[115]

Restructuring Outcomes

The short-term and long-term outcomes resulting from the three restructuring strategies are shown in Figure 7.2. As indicated, downsizing does not commonly lead to a higher firm performance. Still, in free-market-based societies at large, downsizing has generated a host of entrepreneurial new ventures as individuals who are laid off start their own businesses.

Research has shown that downsizing contributed to lower returns for both U.S. and Japanese firms. The stock markets in the firms' respective nations evaluated downsizing negatively. Investors concluded that downsizing would have a negative

Figure 7.2 Restructuring and Outcomes

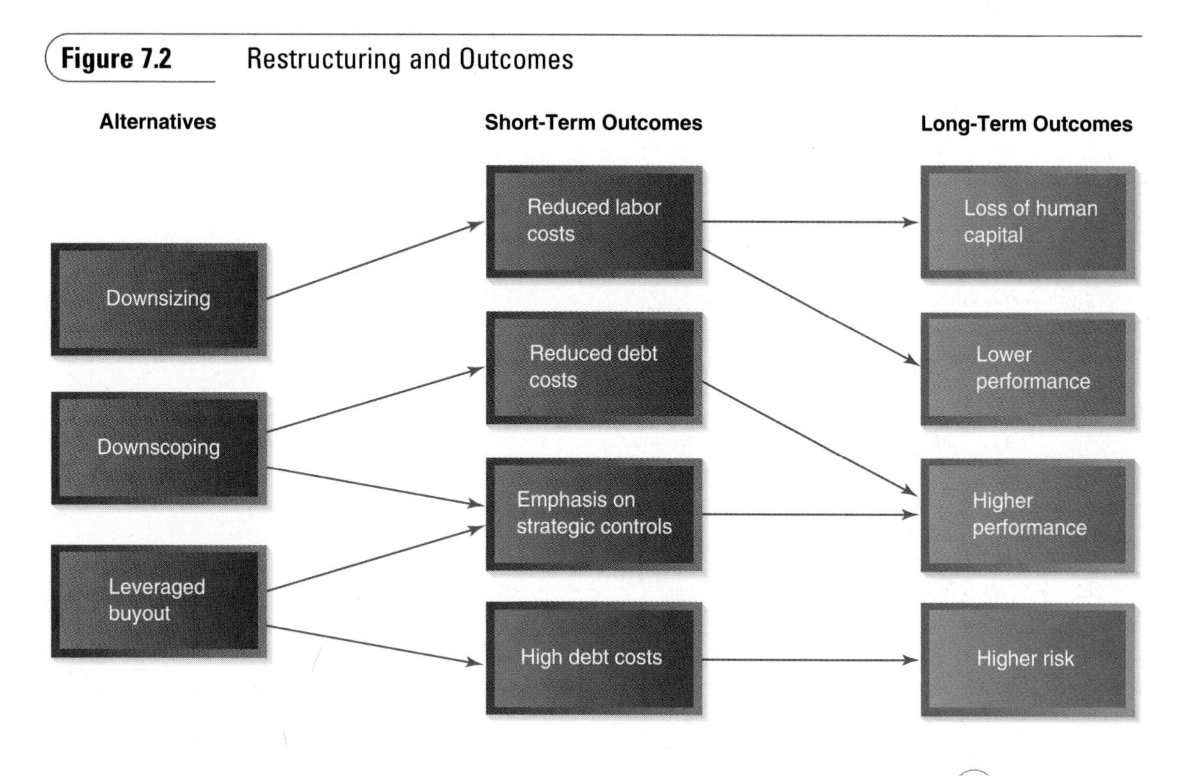

effect on companies' ability to achieve strategic competitiveness in the long term. Investors also seem to assume that downsizing occurs as a consequence of other problems in a company.[116] Ford's announcement in 2002 that it was downsizing by eliminating 35,000 jobs exemplifies this situation. Ford is experiencing significant performance problems due to its lack of competitiveness in the markets in which it competes.[117]

As shown in Figure 7.2, downsizing tends to result in a loss of human capital in the long term. Losing employees with many years of experience with the firm represents a major loss of knowledge. As noted in Chapter 3, knowledge is vital to competitive success in the global economy.[118] Thus, in general, research evidence and corporate experience suggest that downsizing may be of more tactical (or short-term) value than strategic (or long-term) value.

As Figure 7.2 indicates, downscoping generally leads to more positive outcomes in both the short and the long term than does downsizing or engaging in a leveraged buyout. Downscoping's desirable long-term outcome of higher performance is a product of reduced debt costs and the emphasis on strategic controls derived from concentrating on the firm's core businesses. In so doing, the refocused firm should be able to increase its ability to compete.

While whole-firm LBOs have been hailed as a significant innovation in the financial restructuring of firms, there can be negative trade-offs. First, the resulting large debt increases the financial risk of the firm, as is evidenced by the number of companies that filed for bankruptcy in the 1990s after executing a whole-firm LBO. Sometimes, the intent of the owners to increase the efficiency of the bought-out firm and then sell it within five to eight years creates a short-term and risk-averse managerial focus. As a result, these firms may fail to invest adequately in R&D or take other major actions designed to maintain or improve the company's core competence.[119] However, research also suggests that in firms with an entrepreneurial mind-set, buyouts can lead to greater innovation, especially if the debt load is not too great.[120] In a more recent action, AT&T was broken into four separate businesses: wireless, broadband, business services, and consumer service. Research has shown that refocusing is usually not successful unless the firm has adequate resources to have the flexibility to formulate the necessary strategies to compete effectively.[121] Thus, only time will tell if AT&T's latest restructuring efforts will be successful.

Summary

- Acquisition strategies are increasingly popular. Because of globalization, deregulation of multiple industries in many different economies, and favorable legislation, etc., the number and size of domestic and cross-border acquisitions continues to increase.
- Firms use acquisition strategies to (1) increase market power, (2) overcome entry barriers to new markets or regions, (3) avoid the costs of developing new products and increase the speed of new market entries, (4) reduce the risk of entering a new business, (5) become more diversified, (6) reshape their competitive scope by developing a different portfolio of businesses, and (7) enhance their learning, thereby adding to their knowledge base.
- Among the problems associated with the use of an acquisition strategy are (1) the difficulty of effectively integrating the firms involved, (2) incorrectly evaluating the target firm's value, (3) creating debt loads that preclude adequate long-term investments (e.g., R&D), (4) overestimating the potential for synergy, (5) creating a firm that is too diversified, (6) creating an internal environment in which managers devote increasing amounts of their time and energy to analyzing and completing the acquisition, and (7) developing a combined firm that is too large, necessitating extensive use of bureaucratic, rather than strategic, controls.
- Effective acquisitions have the following characteristics: (1) the acquiring and target firms have complementary resources that can be the basis of core competencies in the newly created firm, (2) the acquisition is friendly thereby facilitating integration of the two firms' resources, (3) the target firm is selected and purchased based on thorough due diligence, (4) the acquiring and target firms have considerable slack in the form of cash or debt capacity, (5) the merged firm maintains a low or moderate level of debt by selling off portions of the acquired firm or some of the acquiring firm's poorly performing units, (6) the acquiring and acquired firms have experience in terms of adapting to change, and (7) R&D and innovation are emphasized in the new firm.
- Restructuring is used to improve a firm's performance by correcting for problems created by ineffective management. Restructuring by downsizing involves reducing a number of employees and hierarchical levels in the firm. Although it can lead to short-term cost reductions, they may be realized at the expense of long-term success, because of the loss of valuable human resources (and knowledge).
- The goal of restructuring through downscoping is to reduce the firm's level of diversification. Often, the firm divests unrelated businesses to achieve this goal. Eliminating unrelated businesses makes it easier for the firm and its top-level managers to refocus on the core businesses.
- Leveraged buyouts (LBOs) represent an additional restructuring strategy. Through an LBO, a firm is purchased so that it can become a private entity. LBOs usually are financed largely through debt. There are three types of LBOs: management buyouts (MBOs), employee buyouts (EBOs), and whole-firm LBOs. Because they provide clear managerial incentives, MBOs have been the most successful of the three. Oftentimes, the intent of a buyout is to improve efficiency and performance to point where the firm can be sold successfully within five to eight years.
- Commonly, restructuring's primary goal is gaining or reestablishing effective strategic control of the firm. Of the three restructuring strategies, downscoping is aligned the most closely with establishing and using strategic controls.

Review Questions

1. Why are acquisition strategies popular in many firms competing in the global economy?
2. What reasons account for firms' decisions to use acquisition strategies as one means of achieving strategic competitiveness?
3. What are the seven primary problems that affect a firm's efforts to successfully use an acquisition strategy?
4. What are the attributes associated with a successful acquisition strategy?
5. What is the restructuring strategy and what are its common forms?
6. What are the short- and long-term outcomes associated with the different restructuring strategies?

Experiential Exercise

Mergers and Acquisitions

You are on the executive board of an information technology firm that provides trafficking software to the trucking industry. One of the firm's managers feels the company should grow and has suggested expanding by creating trafficking software for rail shipments or by offering trucking trafficking services online. You know your firm is in a position to expand but are not sure about the best way to do so.

Part One. Should the firm consider a merger with or an acquisition of a firm that offers the suggested services, or should it develop them internally? List the advantages and disadvantages of each strategic option.

Part Two. Based on your findings and other information, assume that your firm decides to obtain trafficking software for rail shipments through an acquisition of an existing firm. Predict some general problems your firm might encounter in an acquisition and how they might be resolved.

Notes

1. R. Whittington, 1999, In praise of the evergreen conglomerate, Mastering Strategy (Part Six), *Financial Times*, November 1, 4–6; P. Moran & S. Ghoshal, 1999, Markets, firms, and the process of economic development, *Academy of Management Review*, 24: 390–412; M. A. Hitt, R. E. Hoskisson, R. D. Ireland, & J. S. Harrison, 1991, Effects of acquisitions on R&D inputs and outputs, *Academy of Management Journal*, 34: 693–706.
2. M. A. Hitt, J. S. Harrison, & R. D. Ireland, 2001, *Mergers and Acquisitions: A Guide to Creating Value for Stakeholders*, New York: Oxford University Press.
3. 2000, How M&As will navigate the turn into a new century, *Mergers & Acquisitions*, January, 29–35.
4. J. A. Schmidt, 2002, Business perspective on mergers and acquisitions, in J. A. Schmidt (ed.), *Making Mergers Work*, Alexandria, VA: Society for Human Resource Management, 23–46.
5. M. A. Hitt, R. D. Ireland, & J. S. Harrison, 2001, Mergers and acquisitions: A value creating or a value destroying strategy? In M. A. Hitt, R. E. Freeman, & J. S. Harrison, *Handbook of Strategic Management*, Oxford, U.K.: Blackwell Publishers, 385–408.
6. L. Saigol, 2002, Thin pickings in dismal year for dealmaking, *Financial Times*, http://www.ft.com, January 2; 2001, Waiting for growth, *The Economist*, http://www.economist.com, April 27.
7. 2002, Mergers Snapshot: 2001 deal volume, *The Wall Street Journal*, January 4, C12; 2001, The great merger wave breaks, *The Economist*, January 27, 59–60.
8. R. Sidel, 2002, Volatile U.S. markets and global slowdown cool corporate desire to merge, *The Wall Street Journal*, January 2, R10.
9. P. Chattopadhyay, W. H. Glick, & G. P. Huber, 2001, Organizational actions in response to threats and opportunities, *Academy of Management Journal*, 44: 937–955.
10. H. T. J. Smit, 2001, Acquisition strategies as option games, *Journal of Applied Corporate Finance*, 14 (2): 79–89.
11. J. Anand, 1999, How many matches are made in heaven, Mastering Strategy (Part Five), *Financial Times*, October 25, 6–7.
12. M. C. Jensen, 1988, Takeovers: Their causes and consequences, *Journal of Economic Perspectives*, 1(2): 21–48.
13. A. Rappaport & M. L. Sirower, 1999, Stock or cash? *Harvard Business Review*, 77(6): 147–158.
14. C. Grimes, 2002, AOL Time Warner offers conservative 2002 outlook, *Financial Times*, http://www.ft.com, January 8; C. Yang, R. Grover, & A. T. Palmer, 2001, Show time for AOL Time Warner, *Business Week*, January 15, 57–64.
15. R. Sidel, 2001, FPL, Entergy blame each other as they call off $8 billion merger, *The Wall Street Journal Interactive*, http://www.interactive.wsj.com, April 2.
16. E. Thorton, F. Keesnan, C. Palmeri, & L. Himelstein, 2002, It sure is getting hostile, *Business Week*, January 14, 28–30.
17. J. Harding & C. Grimes, 2002, MGM owner sounds out possible suitors, *Financial Times*, http://www.ft.com, January 16; B. Pulley, 2001, The wizard of MGM, *Forbes*, 122–128.
18. P. Haspeslagh, 1999, Managing the mating dance in equal mergers, Mastering Strategy (Part Five), *Financial Times*, October 25, 14–15.
19. P. Wright, M. Kroll, & D. Elenkov, 2002, Acquisition returns, increase in firm size and chief executive officer compensation: The moderating role of monitoring, *Academy of Management Journal*, 45: in press.
20. G. Anders, 2002, Lessons from WaMU's M&A playbook, *Fast Company*, January, 100–107.
21. L. Capron, 1999, Horizontal acquisitions: The benefits and risks to long-term performance, *Strategic Management Journal*, 20: 987–1018.
22. M. Lubatkin, W. S. Schulze, A. Mainkar, & R. W. Cotterill, 2001, Ecological investigation of firm effects in horizontal mergers, *Strategic Management Journal*, 22: 335–357; K. Ramaswamy, 1997, The performance impact of strategic similarity in horizontal mergers: Evidence from the U.S. banking industry, *Academy of Management Journal*, 40: 697–715.
23. L. Capron, W. Mitchell, & A. Swaminathan, 2001, Asset divestiture following horizontal acquisitions: A dynamic view, *Strategic Management Journal*, 22: 817–844.
24. C. Parkes, 2001, Disney's debt climbs to $15 billion on Fox Family buy, *Financial Times*, http://www.ft.com, July 24; N. Deogun, B. Orwall, & J. Lippman, 2001, Disney plans to acquire Fox Family for $3 billion and debt assumption, *The Wall Street Journal Interactive*, http://interactive.wsj.com, July 23; N. Deogun & J. Lippman, 2001, Disney nears deal to buy Fox Family but AOL, Viacom continue talks, *The Wall Street Journal Interactive*, http://interactive.wsj.com, July 21.
25. M. Murray, P. Shiskin, B. Davis, & A. Raghavan, 2001, As Honeywell deal goes awry for GE, fallout may be global, *The Wall Street Journal Interactive*, http://interactive.wsj.com, June 14.
26. Q. Hardy, 2002, Compaq with the devil, *Forbes*, January 7, 40.
27. M. Lerner, 2001, Israeli Antitrust Authority's general director David Tadmor on corporate mergers, *Academy of Management Executive*, 15(1): 8–11.
28. S. J. Chang & P. M. Rosenzweig, 2001, The choice of entry mode in sequential foreign direct investment, *Strategic Management Journal*, 22: 747–776.
29. J. A. Gingrich, 1999, Five rules for winning emerging market consumers, *Strategy & Business*, 15: 19–33.
30. Hitt, Harrison, & Ireland, *Mergers and Acquisitions*, Chapter 10; D. Angwin & B. Savill, 1997, Strategic perspectives on European cross–border acquisitions: A view from the top European executives, *European Management Review*, 15: 423–435.
31. Schmidt, Business perspective on mergers and acquisitions.
32. 1999, Bloomberg News, Kimberly-Clark planning acquisitions, *Dallas Morning News*, December 1, D2; E. Robinson, 1999, Shiseido pursues M&A, *Financial Times*, July 27, 14.
33. J. K. Shank & V. Govindarajan, 1992, Strategic cost analysis of technological investments, *Sloan Management Review*, 34(3): 39–51.
34. Hitt, Harrison, & Ireland, *Mergers and Acquisitions*.
35. M. A. Hitt, R. E. Hoskisson, R. A. Johnson, & D. D. Moesel, 1996, The market for corporate control and firm innovation, *Academy of Management Journal*, 39: 1084–1119.
36. R. Coff, 2002, Bidding wars over R&D intensive firms: Knowledge, opportunism and the market for corporate control, *Academy of Management Journal*, 45: in press.
37. R. Langreth, 2002, Betting on the brain, *Forbes*, January 7, 57–59.
38. K. F. McCardle & S. Viswanathan, 1994, The direct entry versus takeover decision and stock price performance around takeovers, *Journal of Business*, 67: 1–43.
39. J. W. Lu & P. W. Beamish, 2001, The internationalization and performance of SMEs, *Strategic Management Journal*, 22(Special Issue): 565–586.
40. G. Ahuja & C. Lampert, 2001, Entrepreneurship in the large corporation: A longitudinal study of how established firms create breakthrough inventions, *Strategic Management Journal*, 22(Special Issue): 521–543.
41. F. Rothaermel, 2001, Incumbent's advantage through exploiting complementary assets via Interfirm cooperation, *Strategic Management Journal*, 22(Special Issue): 687–699.
42. G. Ahuja & R. Katila, 2001, Technological acquisitions and the innovation performance of acquiring firms: A longitudinal study, *Strategic Management Journal*, 22: 197–220. M. A. Hitt, R. E. Hoskisson, & R. D. Ireland, 1990, Mergers and acquisitions and managerial commitment to innovation in M-form firms, *Strategic Management Journal*, 11(Special Summer Issue): 29–47.
43. Hitt, Hoskisson, Johnson, & Moesel, The market for corporate control.
44. Hitt, Hoskisson, Ireland, & Harrison, Effects of acquisitions on R&D inputs and outputs, 693–706.
45. D. D. Bergh, 1997, Predicting divestiture of unrelated acquisitions: An integrative model of ex ante conditions, *Strategic Management Journal*, 18: 715–731.
46. P. L. Moore, 2001, The most aggressive CEO, *Business Week*, May 28, 67–77.
47. Hitt, Harrison, & Ireland, *Mergers and Acquisitions*.
48. J. Anand & H. Singh, 1997, Asset redeployment, acquisitions and corporate strategy in declining industries, *Strategic Management Journal*, 18(Special Summer Issue): 99–118.
49. M. Raynor, 2001, *Strategic Flexibility in the Financial Services Industry*, report published by Deloitte Consulting and Deloitte & Touche, Toronto, Canada.
50. W. J. Ferrier, 2001, Navigating the competitive landscape: The drivers and consequences of competitive aggressiveness, *Academy of Management Journal*, 44: 858–877.
51. 2002, General Electric, *Standard & Poor's Stock Report*, http://www.fidelity.com, April 4; R. E. Hoskisson & M. A. Hitt, 1994, *Downscoping: How to Tame the Diversified Firm*, New York: Oxford University Press.
52. F. Vermeulen & H. Barkema, 2001, Learning through acquisitions, *Academy of Management Journal*, 44: 457–476.
53. J. S. Harrison, M. A. Hitt, R. E. Hoskisson, & R. D. Ireland, 2001, Resource complementarities in business combinations: Extending the logic to organizational alliances, *Journal of Management*, 27: 679–690.

54. M. Killick, I. Rawoot, & G. J. Stockport, 2001, *Cisco Systems Inc–Growth Through Acquisitions,* case in the European Case Clearing House Collection; A. Muoio, 2000, Cisco's quick study, *Fast Company,* October, 287–295.
55. G. Colvin, 2000, America's most admired companies, *Fortune,* February 21, 108–111.
56. Schmidt, Business perspective on mergers and acquisitions.
57. Hitt, Harrison, & Ireland, *Mergers and Acquisitions.*
58. A. J. Viscio, J. R. Harbison, A. Asin, & R. P. Vitaro, 1999, Post-merger integration: What makes mergers work? *Strategy & Business,* 17: 26–33; D. K. Datta, 1991, Organizational fit and acquisition performance: Effects of post-acquisition integration, *Strategic Management Journal,* 12: 281–297.
59. M. Zollo, 1999, M&A—the challenge of learning to integrate, Mastering Strategy (Part Eleven), *Financial Times,* December 6, 14–15.
60. Ibid., 14.
61. M. A. Hitt, L. Bierman, K. Shimizu, & R. Kochhar, 2001, Direct and moderating effects of human capital on strategy and performance in professional service firms, *Academy of Management Journal,* 44: 13–28.
62. G. G. Dess & J. D. Shaw, 2001. Voluntary turnover, social capital and organizational performance, *Academy of Management Review,* 26: 446–456.
63. J. A. Krug & H. Hegarty, 2001, Predicting who stays and leaves after an acquisition: A study of top managers in multinational firms, *Strategic Management Journal,* 22: 185–196.
64. K. Ohmae, 1999, The Godzilla companies of the new economy, *Strategy & Business,* 18: 130–139.
65. Rappaport & Sirower, Stock or cash? 149.
66. G. Yago, 1991, Junk Bonds: How High Yield Securities Restructured Corporate America, New York: Oxford University Press, 146–148.
67. M. C. Jensen, 1986, Agency costs of free cash flow, corporate finance, and takeovers, *American Economic Review,* 76: 323–329.
68. C. Parkee, 2001, Disney's debt climbs to $15 billion on Fox Family buy, *Financial Times,* http://www.ft.com, July 24.
69. C. Grimes, 2002, Takeover talk grows at Disney amid frustration, *Financial Times,* http://www.ft.com, January 16.
70. N. Byrnes & M. Arndt, 2001, John Dillion's high-risk paper chase, *Business Week,* January 22, 58–60.
71. M. A. Hitt & D. L. Smart, 1994, Debt: A disciplining force for managers or a debilitating force for organizations? *Journal of Management Inquiry,* 3: 144–152.
72. Hitt, Harrison, & Ireland, *Mergers and Acquisitions.*
73. T. N. Hubbard, 1999, Integration strategies and the scope of the company, Mastering Strategy (Part Eleven), *Financial Times,* December 6, 8–10.
74. Hitt, Harrison, & Ireland, *Mergers and Acquisitions.*
75. Ibid.
76. Harrison, Hitt, Hoskisson, & Ireland, Resource complementarity; J. B. Barney, 1988, Returns to bidding firms in mergers and acquisitions: Reconsidering the relatedness hypothesis, *Strategic Management Journal,* 9(Special Summer Issue): 71–78.
77. O. E. Williamson, 1999, Strategy research: Governance and competence perspectives, *Strategic Management Journal,* 20: 1087–1108.
78. Hitt, Hoskisson, Johnson, & Moesel, The market for corporate control.
79. 2002, Forbes 400 best big companies, *Forbes,* http://www.forbes.com, January 14.
80. C. W. L. Hill & R. E. Hoskisson, 1987, Strategy and structure in the multiproduct firm, *Academy of Management Review,* 12: 331–341.
81. R. A. Johnson, R. E. Hoskisson, & M. A. Hitt, 1993, Board of director involvement in restructuring: The effects of board versus managerial controls and characteristics, *Strategic Management Journal,* 14(Special Issue): 33–50; C. C. Markides, 1992, Consequences of corporate refocusing: Ex ante evidence, *Academy of Management Journal,* 35: 398–412.
82. D. Palmer & B. N. Barber, 2001, Challengers, elites and families: A social class theory of corporate acquisitions, *Administrative Science Quarterly,* 46: 87–120.
83. Hitt, Harrison, & Ireland, *Mergers and Acquisitions.*
84. Ibid.
85. Hitt, Johnson, & Moesel, The market for corporate control.
86. M. Arndt, 2001, A merger's bitter harvest, *Business Week,* February 5, 112–114.
87. Hitt, Harrison, & Ireland, *Mergers and Acquisitions;* Hitt, Hoskisson, Ireland, & Harrison, The effects of acquisitions.
88. R. E. Hoskisson, M. A. Hitt, & R. D. Ireland, 1994, The effects of acquisitions and restructuring (strategic refocusing) strategies on innovation, in G. von Krogh, A. Sinatra, and H. Singh (eds.), *Managing Corporate Acquisitions,* London: Macmillan Press, 144–169.
89. T. Lowry, 2001, How many magazines did we buy today? *Business Week,* January 22, 98–99.
90. Hitt, Harrison, & Ireland, *Mergers and Acquisitions.*
91. Ibid.
92. M. A. Hitt, R. D. Ireland, J. S. Harrison, & A. Best, 1998, Attributes of successful and unsuccessful acquisitions of U.S. firms, *British Journal of Management,* 9: 91–114.
93. Harrison, Hitt, Hoskisson, & Ireland, Resource complementarity.
94. J. Reuer, 2001, From hybrids to hierarchies: Shareholder wealth effects of joint venture partner buyouts, *Strategic Management Journal,* 22: 27–44.
95. D. D. Bergh, 2001, Executive retention and acquisition outcomes: A test of opposing views on the influence of organizational tenure, *Journal of Management,* 27: 603–622; J. P. Walsh, 1989, Doing a deal: Merger and acquisition negotiations and their impact upon target company top management turnover, *Strategic Management Journal,* 10: 307–322.
96. M. L. Marks & P. H. Mirvis, 2001, Making mergers and acquisitions work: Strategic and psychological preparation, *Academy of Management Executive,* 15(2): 80–92.
97. Hitt, Harrison, & Ireland, *Mergers and Acquisitions;* Q. N. Huy, 2001, Time, temporal capability and planned change, *Academy of Management Review,* 26: 601–623; L. Markoczy, 2001, Consensus formation during strategic change, *Strategic Management Journal,* 22: 1013–1031.
98. R. W. Coff, 2002, Human capital, shared expertise, and the likelihood of impasse in corporate acquisitions, *Journal of Management,* in press.
99. Anand, How many matches, 6.
100. R. A. Johnson, 1996, Antecedents and outcomes of corporate refocusing, *Journal of Management,* 22: 437–481; J. E. Bethel & J. Liebeskind, 1993, The effects of ownership structure on corporate restructuring, *Strategic Management Journal,* 14(Special Issue, Summer): 15–31.
101. R. E. Hoskisson, R. A. Johnson, D. Yiu, & W. P. Wan, 2001, Restructuring strategies of diversified groups: Differences associated with country institutional environments, in M. A. Hitt, R. E. Freeman, and J. S. Harrison (eds.), *Handbook of Strategic Management,* Oxford, UK: Blackwell Publishers, 433–463; S. R. Fisher & M. A. White, 2000, Downsizing in a learning organization: Are there hidden costs? *Academy of Management Review,* 25: 244–251; A. Campbell & D. Sadtler, 1998, Corporate breakups, *Strategy & Business,* 12: 64–73; E. Bowman & H. Singh, 1990, Overview of corporate restructuring: Trends and consequences, in L. Rock & R. H. Rock (eds.), *Corporate Restructuring,* New York: McGraw-Hill.
102. Hitt, Harrison, & Ireland, *Mergers and Acquisitions.*
103. W. McKinley, J. Zhao, & K. G. Rust, 2000, A sociocognitive interpretation of organizational downsizing, *Academy of Management Review,* 25: 227–243.
104. W. McKinley, C. M. Sanchez, & A. G. Schick, 1995, Organizational downsizing: Constraining, cloning, learning, *Academy of Management Executive,* IX(3): 32–44.
105. P. Patsuris, 2002, Forbes.com layoff tracker surpasses 1M mark, *Forbes,* http://www.forbes.com, January 16.
106. 2002, Ford to cut 35,000 jobs, close five plants, slash production in broad restructuring, *The Wall Street Journal Interactive,* http://interactive.wsj.com, January 13.
107. Hoskisson & Hitt, *Downscoping.*
108. Johnson, Hoskisson, & Hitt, Board of directors' involvement; R. E. Hoskisson & M. A. Hitt, 1990, Antecedents and performance outcomes of diversification: A review and critique of theoretical perspectives, *Journal of Management,* 16: 461–509.
109. Hoskisson, Johnson, Yiu, & Wan, Restructuring strategies.
110. S. Rosenbush, 2001, Armstrong's last stand, *Business Week,* February 5, 88–96.
111. D. D. Bergh & G. F. Holbein, 1997, Assessment and redirection of longitudinal analysis: Demonstration with a study of the diversification and divestiture relationship, *Strategic Management Journal,* 18: 557–571; C. C. Markides & H. Singh, 1997, Corporate restructuring: A symptom of poor governance or a solution to past managerial mistakes? *European Management Journal,* 15: 213–219.
112. M. F. Wiersema & J. P. Liebeskind, 1995, The effects of leveraged buyouts on corporate growth and diversification in large firms, *Strategic Management Journal,* 16: 447–460.
113. A. Seth & J. Easterwood, 1995, Strategic redirection in large management buyouts: The evidence from post-buyout restructuring activity, *Strategic Management Journal,* 14: 251–274; P. H. Phan & C. W. L. Hill, 1995, Organizational restructuring and economic performance in leveraged buyouts: An ex-post study, *Academy of Management Journal,* 38: 704–739.
114. M. Wright, R. E. Hoskisson, L. W. Busenitz, & J. Dial, 2000, Entrepreneurial growth through privatization: The upside of management buyouts, *Academy of Management Review,* 25: 591–601.

115. M. Wright, R. E. Hoskisson, & L. W. Busenitz, 2001, Firm rebirth: Buyouts as facilitators of strategic growth and entrepreneurship, *Academy of Management Executive*, 15 (1): 111–125.
116. P. M. Lee, 1997, A comparative analysis of layoff announcements and stock price reactions in the United States and Japan, *Strategic Management Journal*, 18: 879–894.
117. Ford to cut 35,000 jobs.
118. Fisher & White, Downsizing in a learning organization.
119. W. F. Long & D. J. Ravenscraft, 1993, LBOs, debt, and R&D intensity, *Strategic Management Journal*, 14(Special Summer Issue): 119–135.
120. Wright, Hoskisson, Busenitz, & Dial, Entrepreneurial growth through privatization.
121. D. D. Dawley, J. J. Hoffman, & B. T. Lamont, 2002, Choice situation, refocusing and post-bankruptcy performance, *Journal of Management*, in press.

8

Chapter Eight

International Strategy

Knowledge Objectives

Studying this chapter should provide you with the strategic management knowledge needed to:

1. Explain traditional and emerging motives for firms to pursue international diversification.
2. Explore the four factors that lead to a basis for international business-level strategies.
3. Define the three international corporate-level strategies: multidomestic, global, and transnational.
4. Discuss the environmental trends affecting international strategy, especially liability of foreignness and regionalization.
5. Name and describe the five alternative modes for entering international markets.
6. Explain the effects of international diversification on firm returns and innovation.
7. Name and describe two major risks of international diversification.
8. Explain why the positive outcomes from international expansion are limited.

China Enters the World Trade Organization

On September 17, 2001, just a few days after the September 11 terrorist attacks, Beijing and its Chinese leaders formally accepted the requirements to enter the World Trade Organization (WTO). Over the next five years, this agreement portends to create a more open market and lower tariffs for importing and exporting goods into and out of China as the country increases its world trade and has more trading partners. Because of the size of the Chinese market, the agreement's effect on globalization is expected to be significant.

China's orientation toward increased trade actually began in 1979 when the late Chinese leader Deng Xiaoping introduced reforms leading towards a market economy. This change was phased in through a decentralization process, during which most enterprises were turned over to local government officials. At the same time, state-owned enterprises were gradually introduced to a market economy. Thus, Chinese leaders have been preparing for entrance into the WTO for over the last 20 years. However, because most Chinese firms are still all or partially state-owned, significant changes must occur in these firms as they encounter more efficient and competitive foreign firms in the global marketplace. In fact, Premier Zhu Rongji, the current leader of the reforms, said that to meet the competition, state-owned enterprises would need to reduce their work forces by "two-thirds." This reduction would result in 25 million people being added to China's unemployment rolls by 2006.

On the one hand, China seeks to compete strongly in high tech industries. For instance, the country hopes to supplant India as the number two software producer in the world after the United States. Currently, India holds this position, but like India, China also offers a well-educated, hard-working technology and engineering work force, but India exports $6.2 billion worth of software, while China has not yet reached the $1 billion mark.

To learn more about the Indian approach, the Chinese minister of higher education recently visited India's Bangalore software district, where Chinese software firm Huawei Technologies has a center. The firm's biggest operation outside of China, Huawei's Bangalore operation employs 536 people—180 Chinese workers work alongside Indian programmers to learn how the Indian employees approach the

In November 2001, China's Shi Guangsheng signed an agreement to join the World Trade Organization, which describes its purpose as "the only global international organization dealing with the rules of trade between nations. At its heart are the WTO agreements, negotiated and signed by the bulk of the world's trading nations and ratified in their parliaments. The goal is to help producers of goods and services, exporters, and importers conduct their business."

development of software code. As a professor from China says, "They are learning how Indian programmers work together, how they coordinate."

On the other hand, however, China has a number of state-owned firms that are not competitive in world markets. Even though many firms have made significant changes during previous reforms, more change is necessary for them to be competitive. For instance, Angang Iron & Steel was listed in 1997 as a "red chip" firm on the Hong Kong exchange (only the best state-owned firms have qualified to be listed on Hong Kong or Shanghai stock exchanges). Since 1995, to make improvements in productivity, Angang has cut 30,000 people from its employment rolls (it still employs a total of 165,000). However, relative to South Korean steel producer Posco, Angang still needs to be more competitive. Posco produces 26 million tons of steel with 20,000 workers, while Angang produces 9.3 million tons with 43,000 workers—meaning that Posco is six times as productive as Angang. Even though Chinese wages are lower than those in South Korea, this example indicates that many of China's more productive employers have a long way to go to be competitive in world markets.

Still, China is a magnet for foreign direct investment and has an economy that has grown 8 percent per year in the recent past. In 2000, China's foreign direct investment was up 20 percent to a total of $27.4 billion, more than the combined investment received by the rest of Asia

As the Opening Case indicates, China's entry into the World Trade Organization (WTO) has put significant focus on this huge potential market. While more firms will enter China in the coming years, many foreign firms who have entered China have found it difficult to establish legitimacy.[1] This is most likely due to China's recent history.

"Collective property party" is the Chinese translation of the term *communist party.* Although law has established property rights, many Chinese (still under a Communist regime) do not share this mind-set. Their opposition to property rights is mainly of two types: ideological and practical. First, many local government and communist party officials feel that private enterprise is undermining the socialist ideal. As a result, many of the local policies (such as taxes, license fees, and so on) towards private firms are punitive. Second, as pointed out in the Opening Case, many officials fear that foreign private domestic competitors will undermine state-owned enterprises, which provide social, educational, medical, and retirement benefits to their employees. Although China's reforms include funds for social programs, there may be uncertainty as to how they will be distributed locally. Thus, private firms and those that are becoming more market oriented must work hard to establish legitimacy with local government officials, suppliers, and customers.

China and its entrance into the WTO clearly illustrate how entering international markets features both opportunities and threats for firms that choose to compete in global markets. This chapter examines opportunities facing firms as they seek to develop and exploit core competencies by diversifying into global markets. In (not including Japan). Although the country should grow and develop a strong middle class because of the direct foreign investment and its economic growth, it will also suffer from market liberalization. Thus, China's entrance into the WTO creates both a challenge and an opportunity for the country.

China will pursue its typical incremental strategy of change as it moves into world markets and is not likely to follow the WTO rules as strictly as preferred for new foreign entrants. In fact, China's decentralization from 1979 to the present will likely make implementation of the WTO rules somewhat difficult. Because local Chinese governments have more control now, the implementation will largely fall to local government officials, making the process of change more incremental than revolutionary. These local barriers are likely to facilitate an increase in foreign direct investment, however, because foreign firms will have to invest to overcome them. Consequently, although change represents an important opportunity with a significant risk of social upheaval, it will lead to more globalization both for China and for those investing in the nation's future.

SOURCES: S. Rai, 2002, Chinese race to supplant India software, *The New York Times,* http://www.nytimes.com, January 5; 2001, Asia: Ready for the competition? China and the WTO, *The Economist,* September 15, 35–36; B. Einhorn, C. Dawson, I. Kunii, D. Roberts, A. Webb, & P. Engardio, 2001, China: Will its entry into the WTO unleash new prosperity or further destabilize the world economy? *Business Week,* October 29, 38; 2001, Finance and economics: China's economy, celebration, and concern, *The Economist,* November 10, 102; D. Murphy, 2001, Riding the tiger of trade, *Far Economic Eastern Review,* November 22, 38–44; B. Powell, 2001, China's great step forward, *Fortune,* September 17, 128–142; A. Tanzer, 2001, Chinese walls, *Forbes,* November 12, 74–75.

addition, we discuss different problems, complexities, and threats that might accompany use of the firm's international strategies. Although national boundaries, cultural differences, and geographical distances all pose barriers to entry into many markets, significant opportunities draw businesses into the international arena. A business that plans to operate globally must formulate a successful strategy to take advantage of these global opportunities.[2] Furthermore, to mold their firms into truly global companies, managers must develop global mind-sets. Especially in regard to managing human resources, traditional means of operating with little cultural diversity and without global sourcing are no longer effective.[3]

As firms move into international markets, they develop relationships with suppliers, customers, and partners, and then learn from these relationships. Selling its products in 190 countries, Siemens, for example, uses 31 websites in 38 languages to facilitate development and use of relationships as well as opportunities to learn from them. Firms also learn from their competitors in international markets. In essence, they begin to imitate each other's policies in order to compete more effectively.[4] Such activity is evident in the pharmaceuticals industry as firms compete against each other in global markets.[5]

In this chapter, as illustrated in Figure 1.1, we discuss the importance of international strategy as a source of strategic competitiveness and above-average returns. The chapter focuses on the incentives to internationalize. Once a firm decides to compete internationally, it must select its strategy and choose a mode of entry into international markets. It may enter international markets by exporting from domestic-based operations, licensing some of its products or services, forming joint ventures with international partners, acquiring a foreign-based firm, or establishing a new subsidiary. Such international diversification can extend product life cycles, provide incentives for more innovation, and produce above-average returns. These benefits are tempered by political and economic risks and the problems of managing a complex international firm with operations in multiple countries.

Figure 8.1 provides an overview of the various choices and outcomes. The relationships among international opportunities, and the exploration of resources and capabilities that result in strategies and modes of entry that are based on core competencies, are explored in this chapter.

Identifying International Opportunities: Incentives to Use an International Strategy

An **international strategy** is a strategy through which the firm sells its goods or services outside its domestic market.

An **international strategy** is a strategy through which the firm sells its goods or services outside its domestic market.[6] One of the primary reasons for implementing an international strategy (as opposed to a strategy focused on the domestic market) is that international markets yield potential new opportunities.

Raymond Vernon captured the classic rationale for international diversification.[7] He suggested that, typically, a firm discovers an innovation in its home-country market, especially in an advanced economy such as that of the United States. Some demand for the product may then develop in other countries, and exports are provided by domestic operations. Increased demand in foreign countries justifies direct foreign investment in production capacity abroad, especially because foreign competitors also organize to meet increasing demand. As the product becomes standardized, the firm may rationalize its operations by moving production to a region with low manufacturing costs.[8] Vernon, therefore, suggests that firms pursue international diversification to extend a product's life cycle.

Another traditional motive for firms to become multinational is to secure needed resources. Key supplies of raw material—especially minerals and energy—are

Figure 8.1 Opportunities and Outcomes of International Strategy

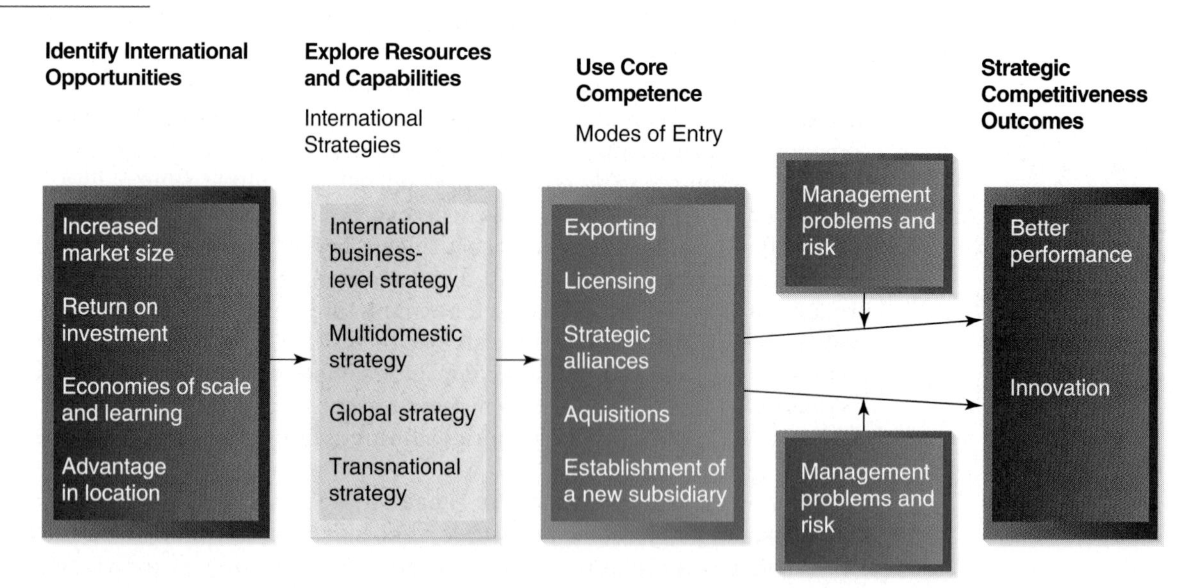

important in some industries. For instance, aluminum producers need a supply of bauxite, tire firms need rubber, and oil companies scour the world to find new petroleum reserves. Other industries, such as clothing, electronics, watch making, and many others, seek low-cost factors of production, and have moved portions of their operations to foreign locations in pursuit of lower costs.

Research on China found that reasons for investing in China differ by the type of firm.[9] Large multinational firms invest primarily to gain access to the large demand potential of China's domestic market. Smaller firms from newly industrializing economies, such as Hong Kong, that use more mundane technologies are more interested in low-cost sources of inputs such as labor and land, to maintain their cost advantages.

Although these traditional motives persist, other emerging motivations also drive international expansion (see Chapter 1). For instance, pressure has increased for a global integration of operations, mostly driven by more universal product demand. As nations industrialize, the demand for some products and commodities appears to become more similar. This "nation-less," or borderless, demand for globally branded products may be due to similarities in lifestyle in developed nations. Increases in global communication media also facilitate the ability of people in different countries to visualize and model lifestyles in different cultures. Benetton, an Italian casual-wear apparel company, has used its global brand and well-established worldwide retail presence as the foundation needed to more effectively manage its supply and manufacturing networks with improved communications technology.[10]

In some industries, technology drives globalization because economies of scale necessary to reduce costs to the lowest level often require an investment greater than that needed to meet domestic market demand. The major Korean car manufacturers Daewoo and Hyundai certainly found this to be true.[11] There is also pressure for cost reductions, achieved by purchasing from the lowest-cost global suppliers. For instance, research and development expertise for an emerging business start-up may not exist in the domestic market.[12]

New large-scale, emerging markets, such as China and India, provide a strong internationalization incentive because of the potential demand in them.[13] Because of currency fluctuations, firms may also choose to distribute their operations across many countries, including emerging ones, in order to reduce the risk of devaluation in one country.[14] However, the uniqueness of emerging markets presents both opportunities and challenges.[15] While China, for example, differs from Western countries in many respects, including culture, politics, and the precepts of its economic system,[16] it also offers a huge potential market. Many international firms perceive Chinese markets as almost untouched markets, without exposure to many modern and sophisticated products. Once China is exposed to these products, these firms believe that demand will develop. However, the differences between China and Western countries pose serious challenges to Western competitive paradigms that emphasize the skills needed to manage financial, economic, and political risks.

A large majority of U.S.-based companies' international business is in European markets, where 60 percent of U.S. firms' assets that are located outside the domestic market are invested. Two-thirds of all foreign R&D spending by U.S. affiliates also takes place in Europe.[17] Companies seeking to internationalize their operations in Europe, as elsewhere, need to understand the pressure on them to respond to local, national, or regional customs, especially where goods or services require customization because of cultural differences or effective marketing to entice customers to try a different product.[18]

Of course, all firms encounter challenges when using an international strategy. For example, Unilever is a large European-centered global food and consumer products firm that adapts its products to local tastes as it moves into new national markets.

Its investors expect Unilever executives to create global mega-brands, which have the most growth potential and margins, even though most of Unilever's growth has come through acquisition and the selling of the acquired, unique local brands. Establishing mega-brands while also dealing with the forces for localization is difficult. As noted in Chapter 11, Unilever is restructuring to meet these challenges.[19]

Local repair and service capabilities are another factor influencing an increased desire for local country responsiveness. This localization may even affect industries that are seen as needing more global economies of scale, for example, white goods (home appliances, such as refrigerators). Alternatively, suppliers often follow their customers, particularly large ones, into international markets, which eliminates the firm's need to find local suppliers.[20] The transportation costs of large products and their parts, such as heavy earthmoving equipment, are significant, which may preclude a firm's suppliers following the firm to an international market.

Employment contracts and labor forces differ significantly in international markets. For example, it is more difficult to lay off employees in Europe than in the United States because of employment contract differences. In many cases, host governments demand joint ownership, which allows the foreign firm to avoid tariffs. Also, host governments frequently require a high percentage of procurements, manufacturing, and R&D to use local sources. These issues increase the need for local investment and responsiveness compared to seeking global economies of scale.[21]

We've discussed incentives influencing firms to use international strategies. When successful, firms can derive four basic benefits from using international strategies: (1) increased market size; (2) greater returns on major capital investments or on investments in new products and processes; (3) greater economies of scale, scope, or learning; and (4) a competitive advantage through location (for example, access to low-cost labor, critical resources, or customers). We examine these benefits in terms of both their costs (such as higher coordination expenses and limited access to knowledge about host country political influences[22]) and their managerial challenges.

Increased Market Size

Firms can expand the size of their potential market—sometimes dramatically—by moving into international markets. As part of its expansion efforts, Whirlpool learned how to be successful in emerging markets. In India, the firm conducted 14 months of research on local tastes and values. The company also provided incentives to Indian retailers to stock its products, and it uses local contractors to collect payments and deliver appliances throughout India. Since implementing this strategy in 1996, Whirlpool's sales in India had grown 80 percent by 2001. The ability to market its appliances overseas is important to Whirlpool because U.S. demand is forecast to stay flat through 2009, but international demand should grow 17 percent, to 293 million units.[23]

Although changing consumer tastes and practices linked to cultural values or traditions is not simple, following an international strategy is a particularly attractive option to firms (such as Whirlpool) competing in domestic markets that have limited growth opportunities. For example, the U.S. soft-drink industry is relatively saturated. Coca-Cola's case volume grew just about 1 percent per quarter in 2001 in North America, its largest market, but about 5 percent internationally.[24] PepsiCo hopes it has found a reliable growth driver with its purchase of Quaker Oats, the maker of the market leading sports drink Gatorade. PepsiCo plans to integrate Gatorade into its distribution systems and hopefully build market share outside of the United States.[25] Because most changes in domestic market share for any single firm come at the expense of competitors' shares, rivals Coca-Cola and PepsiCo entered international markets to take advantage of new growth opportunities instead of focusing on competing directly against each other to increase their share of their domestic, core soft drink market.[26]

The size of an international market also affects a firm's willingness to invest in R&D to build competitive advantages in that market. Larger markets usually offer higher potential returns and thus pose less risk for a firm's investments. The strength of the science base in the country in question also can affect a firm's foreign R&D investments. Most firms prefer to invest more heavily in those countries with the scientific knowledge and talent to produce value-creating products and processes from their R&D activities. However, research indicates that simultaneously pursuing R&D and collaborative foreign R&D joint ventures reduces effectiveness.[27]

Return on Investment

Large markets may be crucial for earning a return on significant investments, such as plant and capital equipment or R&D. Therefore, most R&D-intensive industries such as electronics are international. For example, significant R&D expenditures by multinational firms in Singapore's electronics industry must meet return on investment requirements. Besides meeting these requirements, the R&D project must also be "consistent with [regional] customer demands, the achievement of time-based competitiveness, the training of R&D manpower and the development of conducive innovation environments."[28] Thus, most firms investing in the Singapore electronics industry use approaches framed around the need to satisfy multiple project outcome requirements.

In addition to the need for a large market to recoup heavy investment in R&D, the development pace for new technology is increasing. As a result, new products become obsolete more rapidly. Therefore, investments need to be recouped more quickly. Moreover, firms' abilities to develop new technologies are expanding, and because of different patent laws across country borders, imitation by competitors is more likely. Through reverse engineering, competitors are able to take apart a product, learn the new technology, and develop a similar product that imitates the new technology. Because their competitors can imitate the new technology relatively quickly, firms need to recoup new-product development costs even more rapidly. Consequently, the larger markets provided by international expansion are particularly attractive in many industries such as computer hardware, because they expand the opportunity for the firm to recoup a large capital investment and large-scale R&D expenditures.[29]

Regardless of any other reason, however, the primary reason for making investments in international markets is to generate above-average returns on investments. For example, with domestic growth in the low single digits, Tricon Global Restaurants, owner of Kentucky Fried Chicken (KFC), Pizza Hut, and Taco Bell, has increased its overall growth by expanding globally. Tricon has around 5,000 KFC restaurants in the United States currently and has opened over 6,000 internationally. Overall the company operates more than 30,000 restaurants in over 100 countries worldwide—more than any other restaurant company. Even though the firm focused on growth, its global expansion realized an improved return on investment. Tricon's margin on its investments was up to just over 15 percent in 2001 from 11.6 percent in 1997, and the company's stock value doubled in 2001 compared to August of 2000. This success has come from the company's strategy of adapting to local tastes and preferences.[30]

Expected returns from the investments represent a primary predictor of firms moving into international markets. Still, firms from different countries have different expectations and use different criteria to decide whether to invest in international markets.[31]

KFC Corporation, based in Louisville, Kentucky, is the world's most popular chicken restaurant chain. Every day, nearly eight million customers are served around the world, choosing from the company's Original Recipe® chicken and also choosing among menu items tailored to the country, such as a salmon sandwich in Japan. Pictured here is one of the firm's restaurants in Quebec, Canada.

Economies of Scale and Learning

By expanding their markets, firms may be able to enjoy economies of scale, particularly in their manufacturing operations. To the extent that a firm can standardize its products across country borders and use the same or similar production facilities, thereby coordinating critical resource functions, it is more likely to achieve optimal economies of scale.[32]

Economies of scale are critical in the global auto industry. China's decision to join the World Trade Organization will allow carmakers from other countries to enter the country and lower tariffs to be charged (in the past Chinese carmakers have had an advantage over foreign carmakers due to tariffs). Ford, Honda, General Motors, and Volkswagen are each producing an economy car to compete with the existing cars in China. Because of global economies of scale all of these companies are likely to obtain market share in China.[33] As a result, Chinese carmakers will have to change the way they do business to compete with foreign carmakers.

Firms may also be able to exploit core competencies in international markets through resource and knowledge sharing between units across country borders.[34] This sharing generates synergy, which helps the firm produce higher-quality goods or services at lower cost. In addition, working across international markets provides the firm with new learning opportunities. Multinational firms have substantial occasions to learn from the different practices they encounter in separate international markets. Even firms based in developed markets can learn from operations in emerging markets.[35]

Location Advantages

Firms may locate facilities in other countries to lower the basic costs of the goods or services they provide.[36] These facilities may provide easier access to lower-cost labor, energy, and other natural resources. Other location advantages include access to critical supplies and to customers.

Once positioned favorably with an attractive location, firms must manage their facilities effectively to gain the full benefit of a location advantage.[37] In Eastern Europe, Hungary is a prime location for many manufacturers. Flextronics, a large electronics contract manufacturer, is locating critical resources there. Hungary has good safety regulations and rapidly approves new projects. This small country borders seven nations and connects Europe to the emerging economies east of it. In 2001, 57 percent of Hungary's exports were in electronics equipment, providing a strong and growing market for Flextronics. Furthermore, it has lower labor costs than Ireland, another important electronic components producing country in Europe.[38]

In North America, Mexico has well-developed infrastructures and a skilled, though inexpensive, labor force, and it has received significant amounts of foreign direct investment. The costs of locating in Mexico are significantly lower than other countries regionally.[39] Flextronics found the country's reasonably low labor rate and proximity to its customers in North America ideal. As such, it located a 124-acre industrial park in Guadalajara, Mexico, where everything from handheld computers to routers is manufactured.

International Strategies

Firms choose to use one or both of two basic types of international strategies: business-level international strategy and corporate-level international strategy. At the business level, firms follow generic strategies: cost leadership, differentiation, focused cost leadership, focused differentiation, or integrated cost leadership/differentiation. There are three corporate-level international strategies: multidomestic, global, or transnational (a combination of multidomestic and global). To create competitive advantage, each strategy must realize a core competence based on difficult-to-duplicate resources and capabilities.[40] As discussed in Chapters 4 and 6, firms expect to create value through the implementation of a business-level strategy and a corporate-level strategy.[41]

International Business-Level Strategy

Each business must develop a competitive strategy focused on its own domestic market. We discuss business-level generic strategies in Chapter 4 and competitive rivalry and competitive dynamics in Chapter 5. International business-level strategies have some unique features. In an international business-level strategy, the home country of operation is often the most important source of competitive advantage.[42] The resources and capabilities established in the home country frequently allow the firm to pursue the strategy into markets located in other countries. However, as a firm continues its growth into multiple international locations, research indicates that the country of origin diminishes in importance as the dominant factor.[43]

Michael Porter's model, illustrated in Figure 8.2, describes the factors contributing to the advantage of firms in a dominant global industry and associated with a specific country or regional environment.[44] The first dimension in Porter's model is *factors of production*. This dimension refers to the inputs necessary to compete in any industry—labor, land, natural resources, capital, and infrastructure (such as transportation, postal, and communication systems). There are basic (for example, natural and labor resources) and advanced (such as digital communication systems and a highly educated workforce) factors. Other production factors are generalized (highway systems and the supply of debt capital) and specialized (skilled personnel in a specific industry, such as the workers in a port that specialize in handling bulk chemicals). If a country has both advanced and specialized production factors, it is likely to serve an industry well by spawning strong home-country competitors that also can be successful global competitors.

Ironically, countries often develop advanced and specialized factors because they lack critical basic resources. For example, some Asian countries, such as South Korea, lack abundant natural resources but offer a strong work ethic, a large number of engineers, and systems of large firms to create an expertise in manufacturing. Similarly, Germany developed a strong chemical industry, partially because Hoechst and BASF spent years creating a synthetic indigo dye to reduce their dependence on imports, unlike Britain, whose colonies provided large supplies of natural indigo.[45]

The second dimension in Porter's model, *demand conditions,* is characterized by the nature and size of buyers' needs in the home market for the industry's goods or services. The sheer size of a market segment can produce the demand necessary to create scale-efficient facilities. This efficiency could also lead to domination of the industry in other countries. Specialized demand may also create opportunities beyond national

Figure 8.2 Determinants of National Advantage

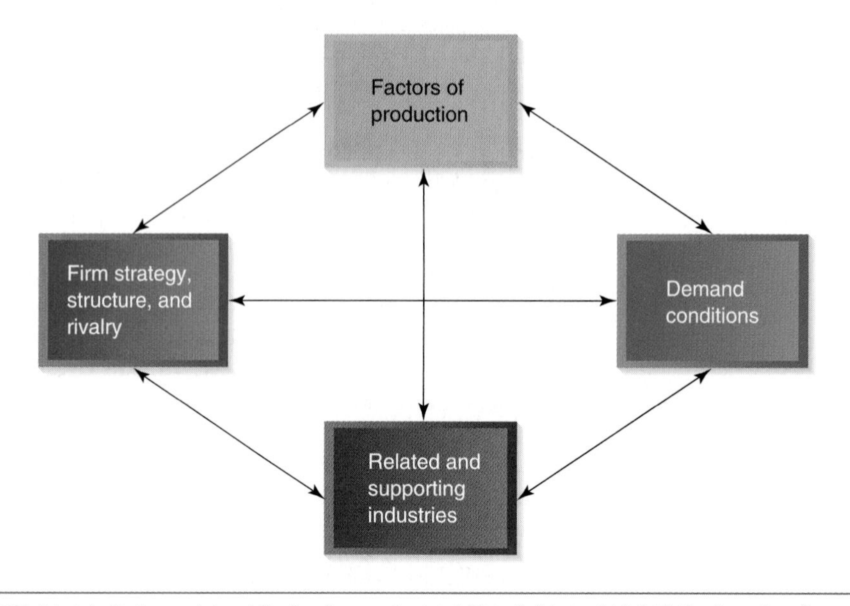

SOURCE: Adapted with the permission of The Free Press, an imprint of Simon & Schuster Adult Publishing Group, from *Competitive Advantage of Nations,* by Michael E. Porter, p. 72. Copyright ©1990, 1998 by Michael E. Porter.

boundaries. For example, Swiss firms have long led the world in tunneling equipment because of the need to tunnel through mountains for rail and highway passage in Switzerland. Japanese firms have created a niche market for compact, quiet air conditioners, which are important in Japan because homes are often small and located closely together.[46]

Related and supporting industries are the third dimension in Porter's model. Italy has become the leader in the shoe industry because of related and supporting industries; a well-established leather-processing industry provides the leather needed to construct shoes and related products. Also, many people travel to Italy to purchase leather goods, providing support in distribution. Supporting industries in leather-working machinery and design services also contribute to the success of the shoe industry. In fact, the design services industry supports its own related industries, such as ski boots, fashion apparel, and furniture. In Japan, cameras and copiers are related industries. Denmark's dairy products industry is related to an industry focused on food enzymes.

Firm strategy, structure, and rivalry make up the final country dimension and also foster the growth of certain industries. The dimension of strategy, structure, and rivalry among firms varies greatly from nation to nation. Because of the excellent technical training system in Germany, there is a strong emphasis on methodical product and process improvements. In Japan, unusual cooperative and competitive systems have facilitated the cross-functional management of complex assembly operations. In Italy, the national pride of the country's designers has spawned strong industries in sports cars, fashion apparel, and furniture. In the United States, competition among computer manufacturers and software producers has favored the development of these industries.

The four basic dimensions of the "diamond" model in Figure 8.2 emphasize the environmental or structural attributes of a national economy that contribute to national advantage. Government policy also clearly contributes to the success and failure of many firms and industries, as exemplified by the Turkish construction industry.[47] Relatively lower wages, the country's geographic and cultural proximity to several promising markets, the existence of a rivalrous home market and the accompanying pressures to continuously upgrade their capabilities have helped Turkish contractors achieve international success. Turkish government policy, however, has created financing difficulties for foreign projects. Related industries, such as the weak Turkish design, engineering, and consultant service industries, have also weakened Turkey's international position versus other international competitors.

Although each firm must create its own success, not all firms will survive to become global competitors—not even those operating with the same country factors that spawned the successful firms. The actual strategic choices managers make may be the most compelling reason for success or failure. Accordingly, the factors illustrated in Figure 8.2 are likely to produce competitive advantages only when the firm develops and implements an appropriate strategy that takes advantage of distinct country factors. Thus, these distinct country factors are necessary to consider when analyzing the business-level strategies (i.e., cost leadership, differentiation, focused cost leadership, focused differentiation, and integrated cost leadership/differentiation discussed in Chapter 4) in an international context.

International Corporate-Level Strategy

The international business-level strategies are based at least partially on the type of international corporate-level strategy the firm has chosen. Some corporate strategies give individual country units the authority to develop their own business-level strategies; other corporate strategies dictate the business-level strategies in order to standardize the firm's products and sharing of resources across countries.[48]

International corporate-level strategy focuses on the scope of a firm's operations through both product and geographic diversification.[49] International corporate-level strategy is required when the firm operates in multiple industries and multiple countries or regions.[50] The headquarters unit guides the strategy, although business or country-level managers can have substantial strategic input, given the type of international corporate level strategy followed. The three international corporate-level strategies are multidomestic, global, and transnational, as shown in Figure 8.3.

Multidomestic Strategy

A **multidomestic strategy** is an international strategy in which strategic and operating decisions are decentralized to the strategic business unit in each country so as to allow that unit to tailor products to the local market.

A **multidomestic strategy** is an international strategy in which strategic and operating decisions are decentralized to the strategic business unit in each country so as to allow that unit to tailor products to the local market.[51] A multidomestic strategy focuses on competition within each country. It assumes that the markets differ and therefore are segmented by country boundaries. In other words, consumer needs and desires, industry conditions (e.g., the number and type of competitors), political and legal structures, and social norms vary by country. With multidomestic strategies, the firm can customize its products to meet the specific needs and preferences of local customers. Therefore, these strategies should maximize a firm's competitive response to the idiosyncratic requirements of each market.[52]

The use of multidomestic strategies usually expands the firm's local market share because the firm can pay attention to the needs of the local clientele.[53] However, the use of these strategies results in more uncertainty for the corporation as a whole, because of the differences across markets and thus the different strategies employed by local country units.[54] Moreover, multidomestic strategies do not allow for the achievement of economies of scale and can be more costly. As a result, firms employing a multidomestic strategy decentralize their strategic and operating decisions to the

Figure 8.3 International Corporate-Level Strategies

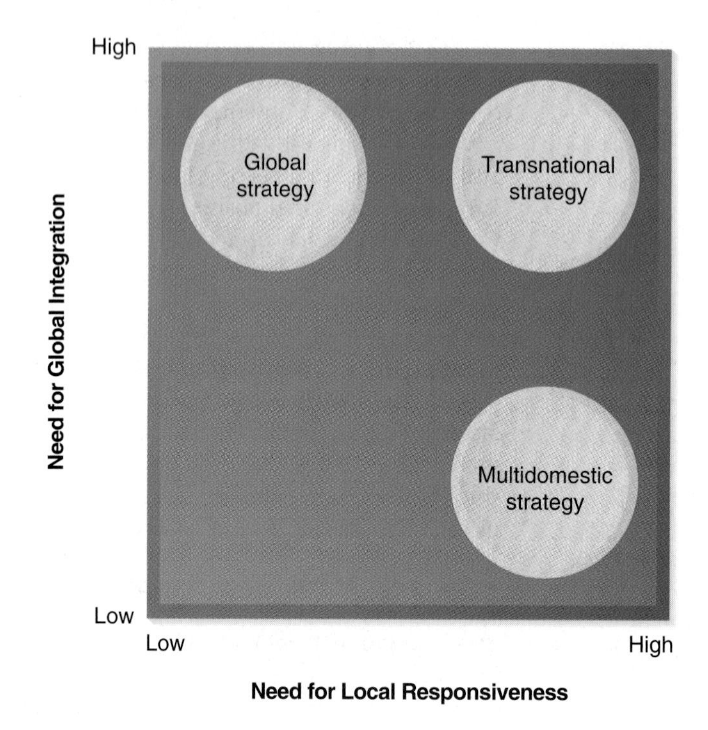

business units operating in each country. The multidomestic strategy has been more commonly used by European multinational firms because of the variety of cultures and markets found in Europe.

As mentioned earlier, Tricon has a strong incentive to compete internationally with its restaurant concepts (KFC, Taco Bell, and Pizza Hut). Tricon pursues a multidomestic strategy by trying to localize as much as possible. The firm does not open restaurants based solely on the U.S. model. It consistently adapts to local tastes and negotiates well when cultural and political climates change. "In Japan, for instance, KFC sells tempura crispy strips. In northern England, KFC stresses gravy and potatoes, while in Thailand it offers fresh rice with soy or sweet chili sauce. In Holland the company makes a potato-and-onion croquette. In France it sells pastries alongside chicken. And in China the chicken gets spicier the farther inland you travel. More and more, if it's only an American brand without a regional appeal, it's going to be difficult to market."[55] However, Tricon examines the distance from its American culture base and does better in those countries where it factors in how far its base culture is from the foreign culture it is considering to enter.[56] Thus, it sticks to high population areas, where American culture has some appeal as well.

A **global strategy** is an international strategy through which the firm offers standardized products across country markets, with competitive strategy being dictated by the home office.

Global Strategy

In contrast to a multidomestic strategy, a global strategy assumes more standardization of products across country markets.[57] As a result, a global strategy is centralized and controlled by the home office. The strategic business units operating in each country are assumed to be interdependent, and the home office attempts to achieve integration across these businesses. A **global strategy** is an international strategy through which the firm offers standardized products across country markets, with competitive strategy being dictated by the home office. Thus, a global strategy emphasizes economies of scale and offers greater opportunities to utilize innovations developed at the corporate level or in one country in other markets.

While a global strategy produces lower risk, the firm may forgo growth opportunities in local markets, either because those markets are less likely to identify opportunities or because opportunities require that products be adapted to the local market.[58] The global strategy is not as responsive to local markets and is difficult to manage because of the need to coordinate strategies and operating decisions across country borders. Consequently, achieving efficient operations with a global strategy requires sharing of resources and coordination and cooperation across country boundaries, which in turn require centralization and headquarters control. Many Japanese firms have successfully used the global strategy.[59]

Executives from Cemex opened the session of the New York Stock Exchange when the firm's initial listing of its shares took place in 1999. Cemex CEO Lorenzo Zambrano is fourth from the left.

Cemex, a Monterrey, Mexico-based cement maker, is the world's third largest cement manufacturer. Cemex acquired Southdown, the U.S. cement company for $3 billion at the end of 2001 and began to consolidate this operation with its other U.S. assets. Cemex has the leading market position in Spain with around 72 percent of the production capacity in the Spanish cement industry. Besides its significant assets in North and South America and southern Europe, the firm is also making inroads in Asia through acquisitions.

To integrate its businesses globally, Cemex uses the Internet as one way of increasing revenue and lowering its cost structure. The firm takes advantage of its dominant presence in Mexico and other Latin American locations by providing over 3,000 points of distribution through the Internet. Through its e-business subsidiary CxNetworks, Cemex launched the construction materials website Arkio.com; it expects to recoup the cost of implementation within a year and to add an additional $45 million in revenue by the end of 2002.

By using the Internet to improve logistics and manage an extensive supply network, Cemex can significantly reduce costs. With the savings derived from its Internet supply chain management efforts and by consolidating operations such as the Southdown acquisition into its existing U.S. operations, Cemex expects to cut $100 million from operating costs in the United States alone by 2003. Thus, Cemex is using a global strategy to integrate many aspects of its worldwide operations.[60]

Transnational Strategy

A **transnational strategy** is an international strategy through which the firm seeks to achieve both global efficiency and local responsiveness.

A **transnational strategy** is an international strategy through which the firm seeks to achieve both global efficiency and local responsiveness. Realizing these goals is difficult: one requires close global coordination while the other requires local flexibility. "Flexible coordination"—building a shared vision and individual commitment through an integrated network—is required to implement the transnational strategy.[61] In reality, it is difficult to successfully use the transnational strategy because of the conflicting goals (see Chapter 11 for more on implementation of this and other corporate-level international strategies). On the positive side, effective implementation of a transnational strategy often produces higher performance than does implementation of either the multidomestic or global international corporate-level strategies.[62]

The Strategic Focus on page 255 on the global automobile industry suggests that many large automobile manufacturers choose the transnational strategy to deal with global trends. DaimlerChrysler employed a transnational strategy to design and manufacture The Crossfire, a new product that is to be produced in 2003. The Crossfire has a sleek Chrysler design, but 40 percent of its components are from Mercedes-Benz. This global integration has facilitated lower costs for the vehicle—already engineered components were adapted from elsewhere and design enhancements produced a potentially attractive car for the U.S. market.[63] Thus, both General Motors (as described in the Strategic Focus) and DaimlerChrysler are using the transnational strategy to improve their competitiveness in the global automobile industry.

Environmental Trends

Although the transnational strategy is difficult to implement, emphasis on global efficiency is increasing as more industries begin to experience global competition. To add to the problem, there is also an increased emphasis on local requirements: global goods and services often require some customization to meet government regulations within particular countries or to fit customer tastes and preferences. In addition, most multinational firms desire coordination and sharing of resources across country markets to hold down costs, as illustrated by the Cemex example above. Furthermore, some products and industries may be more suited than others for standardization across country borders.

As a result, most large multinational firms with diverse products employ a multidomestic strategy with certain product lines and a global strategy with others. Many multinational firms may require this type of flexibility if they are to be strategically competitive, in part due to trends that change over time. Two important trends are the liability of foreignness which has increased after the terrorist attacks on September 11, 2001 and the trend towards regionalization.

Liability of Foreignness

The dramatic success of Japanese firms such as Toyota and Sony in the United States and other international markets in the 1980s was a powerful jolt to U.S. managers and awakened them to the importance of international competition in what were rapidly becoming global markets. In the 1990s, Eastern Europe and China represented potential major international market opportunities for firms from many countries, including the United States, Japan, Korea, and European nations.[64] However, as described in the Strategic Focus on page 257, there are legitimate concerns about the relative attractiveness of global strategies. Research showing that global strategies are not as prevalent as once thought and are very difficult to implement, even when using Internet based strategies,[65] as well as the September 11, 2001 attacks are sample explanations for these concerns.

In the 21st century, firms may focus less on truly global markets and more on regional adaptation. Although parallel developments in the Internet and mobile telecommunication facilitate communications across the globe, the implementation of web-based strategies also requires local adaptation.

The globalization of businesses with local strategies is demonstrated by the online operation of Lands' End, Inc., using local Internet portals to offer its products for sale. Lands' End, formally a direct-mail catalog business and now a part of Sears Roebuck and Company, launched its web-based business in 1995. The firm established websites in the U.K. and Germany in 1999, and in France, Italy, and Ireland in 2000 prior to initiating a catalog business in those countries. Not only are catalogs very expensive to print and mail outside the United States, they must also be sent to the

Strategic Focus

Large U.S. Auto Manufacturers and the Transnational Strategy

The Big Three automobile manufacturers—General Motors, Ford, and Chrysler (now part of DaimlerChrysler)—found their sales, market share, and revenues were hurt so much by the globalization of competition that their dominance in the crucial North American market was significantly diminished. For 60 years these three companies controlled the American car market, shaping consumer preferences as to which cars would be purchased and the price that would be paid for the cars. As recently as the late 1990s, these companies were earning record profits. However, the market shares of foreign car manufacturers have grown from their original, anemic level, and these firms are now serious competitors to domestic U.S. dominance. Toyota is close to the 13.8 percent market share held by Chrysler-branded products of DaimlerChrysler in the United States, and, as a group, Asian automakers hold 32 percent of the market.

Ford struggled when its main profit driver, the Explorer, received a reputation as being prone to roll over. Even as the firm attempted to fix this deficiency, problems on the production line forced a recall of the new Explorers that were supposed to be safer than the older models. General Motors has long fought an image that it does not build quality vehicles. Despite its ranking in a recent survey as being the most reliable domestic car maker in the 90 days after sales, GM still placed behind Toyota, Honda, and Nissan. For many consumers, quality is one of the major factors affecting their car purchase.

Although domestic companies are improving, some foreign car makers already have a good reputation and a known reliability rating. At the low end of the market, companies such as Hyundai and Kia are capturing market share. As price competition increases, domestic automakers have seen their market share shrink proportionately. Another problem is the cost of manufacturing. Even though in 2001 domestic carmakers had 61.2 percent of the American market and remained the largest auto sellers, this combined market share had fallen from the 73.5 percent share they held in 1995. Furthermore, profitability is down compared to Japanese carmakers, whose factories are more efficient than those of the U.S. firms.

In response to this situation, U.S. firms and other large automakers are using international corporate-level strategies. For example, General Motors has invested billions of dollars in foreign car companies, moving towards a more transnational strategy for its automobiles. The company owns Saab and Opel and also owns stakes in Fiat, Subaru, and Suzuki Motor. In the past, GM used a multidomestic strategy, where its foreign business units were managed in a decentralized way and each unit could decide what cars to design and build. This laissez-faire management approach resulted in poor financial results—GM's international operations lost almost $900 million in 2000, and its revenue remained flat at $35 billion.

GM CEO G. Richard Wagoner, Jr. decided to overcome this problem by implementing a transnational strategy. The senior managers from its partners' headquarters and product development centers now report directly to a top-ranking GM executive in the relevant region of the world. Thus, GM's top management team has more control over what happens in each of its foreign car companies but can continue to be responsive to regional or country needs. The result has been some successful products, such as the Suzuki-designed Opel Agila sold in Europe.

SOURCES: J. Ball, 2001, DaimlerChrysler sees net fall 58 percent, but says restructuring is on track, *The Wall Street Journal Interactive*, http://www.wsj.com, July 23; S. Freeman, 2001, Auto makers post slower sales in July amid continued economic uncertainty, *The Wall Street Journal Interactive*, http://www.wsj.com, August 2; S. Freeman, 2001, Auto sales rise despite Big Three as foreign brands gain ground, *The Wall Street Journal Interactive*, http://www.wsj.com, July 5; J. Muller, 2001, Ford, GM, and . . .Toyota, *Business Week*, January 14, 86–87; N. Shirouzu, 2001, Ford's loss widens in quarter due to sales incentives, recall, *The Wall Street Journal Interactive*, http://www.wsj.com, July 18; D. Welch, 2001, GM tries to show who's boss, *Business Week*, March 12, 54–55; G. L. White, 2001, GM net income tumbles 73 percent on weaker sales and prices, *The Wall Street Journal Interactive*, http://www.wsj.com, July 18; J. B. White, G. L. White, & N. Shirouzu, 2001, Soon, the Big Three won't be, as foreigners make inroads, *The Wall Street Journal Interactive*, http://www.wsj.com, August 13.

right people, and buying mailing lists is expensive. With limited online advertising and word-of-mouth, a website business can be built in a foreign country without a lot of initial marketing expenses. Once the online business is large enough, a catalog business can be launched with mailing targeted to customers who have used the business online.

Sam Taylor, vice president of international operations for Lands' End, suggested, "We've got a centralized Internet team based in Dodgeville, Wisconsin—all of our development, our designers. But you do need some local presence, so we have our local Internet manager . . . designers, marketing people and all that . . . because we don't know the nuances of the local markets."[66] He also indicated that each additional website was cheaper to implement. "Launching Ireland, France and Italy, we took the U.K. site, cloned it and partnered with Berlitz to translate it into French and into Italian. It was very cost effective. To launch the French site, it cost us 12 times less than the U.K. site, and to launch Italy, it cost us 16 times less."[67] Lands' End now derives 16 percent of its total revenues from Internet sales and ships to 185 countries, primarily from its Dodgeville, Wisconsin, corporate headquarters. Thus, even smaller companies can sell their goods and services globally when facilitated by electronic infrastructure without having significant (brick-and-mortar) facilities outside of their home location. But significant local adaptation is still needed in each country or region.

Regionalization

Regionalization is a second trend that has become more common in global markets. Because a firm's location can affect its strategic competitiveness,[68] it must decide whether to compete in all or many global markets, or to focus on a particular region or regions. Competing in all markets provides economies that can be achieved because of the combined market size. Research suggests that firms that compete in risky emerging markets can also have higher performance.[69]

However, a firm that competes in industries where the international markets differ greatly (in which it must employ a multidomestic strategy) may wish to narrow its focus to a particular region of the world. In so doing, it can better understand the cultures, legal and social norms, and other factors that are important for effective competition in those markets. For example, a firm may focus on Far East markets only rather than competing simultaneously in the Middle East, Europe, and the Far East. Or, the firm may choose a region of the world where the markets are more similar and some coordination and sharing of resources would be possible. In this way, the firm may be able not only to better understand the markets in which it competes, but also to achieve some economies, even though it may have to employ a multidomestic strategy. This is the case with Tricon, as we explained earlier.

Countries that develop trade agreements to increase the economic power of their regions may promote regional strategies. The European Union (EU) and South America's Organization of American States (OAS) in South America are country associations that developed trade agreements to promote the flow of trade across country boundaries within their respective regions.[70] Many European firms acquire and integrate their businesses in Europe to better coordinate pan-European brands as the EU creates more unity in European markets.

The North American Free Trade Agreement (NAFTA), signed by the United States, Canada, and Mexico, facilitates free trade across country borders in North America and may be expanded to include other countries in South America, such as Argentina, Brazil, and Chile.[71] NAFTA loosens restrictions on international strategies within a region and provides greater opportunity for international strategies. NAFTA does not exist for the sole purpose of U.S. businesses moving across its borders. In

Strategic Focus

Globalization Subsequent to Terrorist Attacks

The openness of economic policies that foster globalization in the post-Cold War era is counter to the increased concern for security after the terrorist attacks of September 11, 2001 in New York and Washington, D.C. Higher risks suggest higher cost of capital, and investors will not lend capital unless they get a higher return for foreign investment because the risks of such investments have increased. For instance, insurance and risk management costs will result in increased production prices, forcing e companies to reanalyze the risks of doing business in countries where security risks are higher.

Tighter immigration policies have also developed in the wake of the war on terrorism. For instance, these policies will increase labor costs that previously were reduced through foreign immigration. In the 1990s, two-thirds of the record inflow of 14 million nationals was legal immigrants, who accounted for 30 percent of the growth of the U.S. work force over the decade. Ethnic Chinese or Indians—who have been the backbone of new economy software innovations—founded 30 percent of Silicon Valley start-ups in the 1990s. "It is likely that the economic boom of the 1990s would not have happened if it had not been for immigrant flows," stated Mark M. Zandi, chief economist at the consulting firm Economy.com Inc.

Globalization helped disseminate investment capital, technology, and entrepreneurial ideas across borders. In globalization's wake, consumer goods manufacturers boosted productivity with just-in-time supply chains and pools of technical talent that immigrated into Silicon Valley. "Now, there is sand in the gears of cross border connectivity. That is a huge tectonic change in the global landscape," said Morgan Stanley Dean Witter's chief global economist, Steven S. Roach.

Although the events of September 11 created uncertainty about the progress of globalization, research also suggests that globalization is not as pervasive as once believed. In only a few sectors, such as consumer electronics, is a global strategy as defined above economically viable. For most manufacturing (such as automobiles), national responsiveness and implementation of the transnational strategy are increasingly important. In fact, even in a service sector such as banking, the more successful multinationals design their strategies on a regional basis, while the less successful multinationals pursue global strategies.

Business may need to rethink the globalization that was emphasized in the 1990s, not only as a result of events such as the terrorist attacks, but also because research on multinational firm strategy suggests that the global strategy isn't leading to competitive success in many industries. Stanley Fischer, a former executive at the International Monetary Fund, says, "It's hard to see that this [terrorism] is going to be a permanent setback." In fact, many have noted that the terrorists were themselves models of globalization, "using its tools—satellite telecommunications, the passenger jet—to turn the system on itself." Although Internet commerce has reduced the need for local sales outlets, research suggests that geography still matters in regard to competition and rivalry of firms who use the Internet. Thus, the events of September 11 are likely to slow the process of globalization—but not to reverse it.

SOURCES: S. R. Miller & A. Parkhe, 2002, Is there a liability of foreignness in global banking? An empirical test of banks' x-efficiency, *Strategic Management Journal,* 23: 55–75; P. Engardio, R. Miller, G. Smith, D. Brady, M. Kripalani, A. Borrus, & D. Foust, 2001, What's at stake: How terrorism threatens the global economy, *Business Week,* October 22, 34–37; K. Macharzina, 2001, Editorial: The end of pure global strategies? *Management International Review,* 41(2): 105; A. Rugman & R. Hodgetts, 2001, The end of global strategy, *European Management Journal,* 19(4): 333–343; S. Zaheer & A. Zaheer, 2001, Market microstructure in a global B2B network, *Strategic Management Journal,* 22: 859–873; J. Useem, 2001, Is it a small world after all? Terrorist attacks have ravaged our spirit, but not our global economy, *Fortune,* October 15, 38–42.

fact, Mexico is the number-two trading partner of the United States, and NAFTA greatly increased Mexico's exports to this country. In December 1999, the U.S. trade deficit with Mexico increased to its highest level, $1.7 billion; the catalyst for Mexico's export boom was NAFTA.[72] Although Vicente Fox's election as president of Mexico and Mexico's new spirit of democracy have created opportunity for change, the poor U.S. economy and the September 11, 2001 attacks have lowered the economic outlook for Mexico. Fox promised 1.3 million new export-led jobs annually, but Mexican employment instead was reduced by 500,000 jobs in 2001 because its trade was so closely tied to the U.S. economy.[73]

Most firms enter regional markets sequentially, beginning in markets with which they are more familiar. They also introduce their largest and strongest lines of business into these markets first, followed by their other lines of business once the first lines are successful.[74]

After the firm selects its international strategies and decides whether to employ them in regional or world markets, it must choose a market entry mode.[75]

Choice of International Entry Mode

International expansion is accomplished by exporting products, licensing arrangements, strategic alliances, acquisitions, and establishing new wholly owned subsidiaries. These means of entering international markets and their characteristics are shown in Table 8.1. Each means of market entry has its advantages and disadvantages. Thus, choosing the appropriate mode or path to enter international markets affects the firm's performance in those markets.[76]

Exporting

Many industrial firms begin their international expansion by exporting goods or services to other countries.[77] Exporting does not require the expense of establishing operations in the host countries, but exporters must establish some means of marketing and distributing their products. Usually, exporting firms develop contractual arrangements with host-country firms.

The disadvantages of exporting include the often high costs of transportation and possible tariffs placed on incoming goods. Furthermore, the exporter has less

Table 8.1 Global Market Entry: Choice of Entry Mode

Type of Entry	Characteristics
Exporting	High cost, low control
Licensing	Low cost, low risk, little control, low returns
Strategic alliances	Shared costs, shared resources, shared risks, problems of integration (e.g., two corporate cultures)
Acquisition	Quick access to new market, high cost, complex negotiations, problems of merging with domestic operations
New wholly owned subsidiary	Complex, often costly, time consuming, high risk, maximum control, potential above-average returns

control over the marketing and distribution of its products in the host country and must either pay the distributor or allow the distributor to add to the price to recoup its costs and earn a profit. As a result, it may be difficult to market a competitive product through exporting or to provide a product that is customized to each international market.[78] However, evidence suggests that cost leadership strategies enhance the performance of exports in developed countries, whereas differentiation strategies are more successful in emerging economies.[79]

Firms export mostly to countries that are closest to their facilities because of the lower transportation costs and the usually greater similarity between geographic neighbors. For example, U.S. NAFTA partners Mexico and Canada account for more than half of the goods exported from Texas. The Internet has also made exporting easier. Even small firms can access critical information about foreign markets, examine a target market, research the competition, and find lists of potential customers. Governments also use the Internet to facilitate applications for export and import licenses. Although the terrorist threat is likely to slow its progress, high-speed technology is still the wave of the future.[80]

Small businesses are most likely to use the exporting mode of international entry.[81] Currency exchange rates are one of the most significant problems small businesses face. While larger firms have specialists that manage the exchange rates, small businesses rarely have this expertise. On January 1, 2002, 12 countries began using Euro notes and coins for the first time. This change to a common currency in Europe is helpful to small businesses operating in European markets. Instead of 12 different exchange rates, these firms exporting to EU countries only have to obtain information on one, which should relieve tension and facilitate exports.[82]

Licensing

Licensing is one of the forms of organizational networks that are becoming common, particularly among smaller firms.[83] A licensing arrangement allows a foreign firm to purchase the right to manufacture and sell the firm's products within a host country or set of countries.[84] The licenser is normally paid a royalty on each unit produced and sold. The licensee takes the risks and makes the monetary investments in facilities for manufacturing, marketing, and distributing the goods or services. As a result, licensing is possibly the least costly form of international expansion.

Licensing is also a way to expand returns based on previous innovations. Even if product life cycles are short, licensing may be a useful tool. For instance, because the toy industry faces relentless change and an unpredictable buying public, licensing is used and contracts are often completed in foreign markets where labor may be less expensive.[85]

Licensing also has disadvantages. For example, it gives the firm very little control over the manufacture and marketing of its products in other countries. In addition, licensing provides the least potential returns, because returns must be shared between the licenser and the licensee. Worse, the international firm may learn the technology and produce and sell a similar competitive product after the license expires. Komatsu, for example, first licensed much of its technology from International Harvester, Bucyrus-Erie, and Cummins Engine to compete against Caterpillar in the earthmoving equipment business. Komatsu then dropped these licenses and developed its own products using the technology it had gained from the U.S. companies.[86]

In addition, if a firm wants to move to a different ownership arrangement, licensing may create some inflexibility. Thus, it is important that a firm thinks ahead and considers sequential forms of entry in international markets.[87]

Strategic Alliances

In recent years, strategic alliances have become a popular means of international expansion.[88] Strategic alliances allow firms to share the risks and the resources required to enter international markets.[89] Moreover, strategic alliances can facilitate the development of new core competencies that contribute to the firm's future strategic competitiveness.[90]

Most strategic alliances are formed with a host-country firm that knows and understands the competitive conditions, legal and social norms, and cultural idiosyncrasies of the country, which should help the expanding firm manufacture and market a competitive product. In return, the host-country firm may find its new access to the expanding firm's technology and innovative products attractive. Each partner in an alliance brings knowledge or resources to the partnership.[91] Indeed, partners often enter an alliance with the purpose of learning new capabilities. Common among those desired capabilities are technological skills.[92]

H.J. Heinz Co., for example, sought growth in the Asia-Pacific market as well as a way to reduce its operating costs there. The company decided to form an alliance with Japanese food company Kagome Co. The partners planned to use Heinz's existing retail network to enhance distribution of products, while Kagome would take the lead in research and production. For Kagome, whose food division had been struggling, the alliance could possibly help since Heinz has many strong food products, such as Boston Market frozen dinners and Ore-Ida frozen potatoes. Both companies felt that the alliance would help them cut operating costs as well as expand sales.[93]

Attracted by the huge Chinese market, Pearson PLC—the British education and publishing company that publishes the *Financial Times* and *The Economist,* among others—formed an alliance with CCTV, a unit of China State Television. The venture, named CTV Media Ltd., will provide "conversational English in an entertaining setting" to more than one billion viewers reached each day by CCTV. This venture opens up the Chinese television viewing market to Pearson and also to many international advertisers looking to promote their products in China.[94]

Not all alliances are successful; in fact, many fail. The primary reasons for failure include incompatible partners and conflict between the partners.[95] International strategic alliances are especially difficult to manage.[96] Several factors may cause a relationship to sour. Trust between the partners is critical and is affected by at least four fundamental issues: the initial condition of the relationship, the negotiation process to arrive at an agreement, partner interactions, and external events.[97]

Research has shown that equity-based alliances, over which a firm has more control, tend to produce more positive returns[98] (strategic alliances are discussed in greater depth in Chapter 9). However, if conflict in a strategic alliance or joint venture will not be manageable, an acquisition may be a better option. Research suggests that alliances are more favorable in the face of high uncertainty and where cooperation is needed to bring out the knowledge dispersed between partners and where strategic flexibility is important; acquisitions are better in situations with less need for strategic flexibility and when the transaction is used to maintain economies of scale or scope.[99]

Acquisitions

As free trade has continued to expand in global markets, cross-border acquisitions have also been increasing significantly. In recent years, cross-border acquisitions have comprised more than 45 percent of all acquisitions completed worldwide.[100] As explained in Chapter 7, acquisitions can provide quick access to a new market. In fact, acquisitions may provide the fastest, and often the largest, initial international expansion of any of the alternatives.

Although acquisitions have become a popular mode of entering international markets, they are not without costs. International acquisitions carry some of the disadvantages of domestic acquisitions (see Chapter 7). In addition, they can be expensive and often require debt financing, which also carries an extra cost. International negotiations for acquisitions can be exceedingly complex and are generally more complicated than for domestic acquisitions. For example, it is estimated that only 20 percent of the cross-border bids made lead to a completed acquisition, compared to 40 percent for domestic acquisitions.[101] Dealing with the legal and regulatory requirements in the target firm's country and obtaining appropriate information to negotiate an agreement frequently present significant problems. Finally, the problems of merging the new firm into the acquiring firm often are more complex than in domestic acquisitions. The acquiring firm must deal not only with different corporate cultures, but also with potentially different social cultures and practices. Therefore, while international acquisitions have been popular because of the rapid access to new markets they provide, they also carry with them important costs and multiple risks.

SERGIO DORANTES/CORBIS

Wal-Mart entered the international market for the first time in 1991 when it opened a store in Mexico City. In 1994, the Mexico City store pictured here was the firm's largest unit in the world.

Wal-Mart, the world's largest retailer, has used several entry modes to globalize its operations. For example, in China, the firm used a joint venture mode of entry. To begin its foray into Latin American countries, Wal-Mart also used joint ventures. But in some cases, such as in Mexico, it acquired its venture partner after entering the host country's market.

In Germany, Wal-Mart acquired a 21-store hypermarket chain in 1997 and acquired 74 Interspar stores in 1998. There were many problems with these acquisitions. None of these stores were profitable when Wal-Mart acquired them, and the amount of money needed to update them had been underestimated. The firm also encountered cultural problems. In the first year, the stores suffered significant losses, and it is expected to take many years before they show a profit—or break even—in Germany.

Wal-Mart learned from the German experience. When the firm bought a chain of British supermarket stores, it gave the managers running them the freedom to make necessary changes. Wal-Mart has learned that to be successful in foreign markets, it must have people in charge who understand the local culture and customers' needs.[102]

New Wholly Owned Subsidiary

The establishment of a new wholly owned subsidiary is referred to as a **greenfield venture.**

The establishment of a new wholly owned subsidiary is referred to as a **greenfield venture.** This process is often complex and potentially costly, but it affords maximum control to the firm and has the most potential to provide above-average returns. This potential is especially true of firms with strong intangible capabilities that might be leveraged through a greenfield venture.[103]

The risks are also high, however, because of the costs of establishing a new business operation in a new country. The firm may have to acquire the knowledge and expertise of the existing market by hiring either host-country nationals, possibly from competitors, or consultants, which can be costly. Still, the firm maintains control over the technology, marketing, and distribution of its products. Alternatively, the company must build new manufacturing facilities, establish distribution networks, and learn and implement appropriate marketing strategies to compete in the new market.

When British American Tobacco (BAT) decided to increase its market share in South Korea, a very tough market for imported cigarettes, it resolved to build a new greenfield cigarette factory there. The South Korean market is very protected, with a state-run monopoly, Korea Tobacco and Ginseng Corporation, controlling most of the market. Also, South Korea has said that it would impose increasingly high tariffs on imported tobacco, and there is a strong sentiment of antiforeignism among consumers. John Taylor, president of BAT Korea, hoped that its maneuver, which would produce cigarettes "made in Korea, by Koreans and for Koreans," would increase British American Tobacco's market share from 3.7 percent to 10 percent.[104]

Dynamics of Mode of Entry

A firm's choice of mode of entry into international markets is affected by a number of factors.[105] Initially, market entry will often be achieved through export, which requires no foreign manufacturing expertise and investment only in distribution. Licensing can facilitate the product improvements necessary to enter foreign markets, as in the Komatsu example. Strategic alliances have been popular because they allow a firm to connect with an experienced partner already in the targeted market. Strategic alliances also reduce risk through the sharing of costs. All three modes therefore are best for early market development tactics. Also, the strategic alliance is often used in more uncertain situations such as an emerging economy.[106] However, if intellectual property rights in the emerging economy are not well protected, the number of firms in the industry is growing fast, and the need for global integration is high, the wholly owned entry mode is preferred.[107]

To secure a stronger presence in international markets, acquisitions, or greenfield ventures may be required. Many Japanese automobile manufacturers, such as Honda, Nissan, and Toyota, have gained a presence in the United States through both greenfield ventures and joint ventures.[108] Toyota has particularly strong intangible production capabilities that it has been able to transfer through greenfield ventures.[109] Both acquisitions and greenfield ventures are likely to come at later stages in the development of an international strategy. In addition, both strategies tend to be more successful when the firm making the investment possesses valuable core competencies.[110] Large diversified business groups, often found in emerging economies, not only gain resources through diversification, but also have specialized abilities in managing differences in inward and outward flows of foreign direct investment. In particular, Korean *chaebols* have been adept at making acquisitions in emerging economies.[111]

Thus, to enter a global market, a firm selects the entry mode that is best suited to the situation at hand. In some instances, the various options will be followed sequentially, beginning with exporting and ending with greenfield ventures.[112] In other cases, the firm may use several, but not all, of the different entry modes, each in different markets. As explained above, this is how Wal-Mart has entered various international markets. The decision regarding which entry mode to use is primarily a result of the industry's competitive conditions, the country's situation and government policies, and the firm's unique set of resources, capabilities, and core competencies.

Strategic Competitiveness Outcomes

Once its international strategy and mode of entry have been selected, the firm turns its attention to implementation issues. It is important to do this, because as explained next, international expansion is risky and may not result in a competitive advantage (see Figure 8.1). The probability the firm will achieve success by using an international strategy increases when that strategy is effectively implemented.

International Diversification and Returns

International diversification is a strategy through which a firm expands the sales of its goods or services across the borders of global regions and countries into different geographic locations or markets.

As noted earlier, firms have numerous reasons to diversify internationally. **International diversification** is a strategy through which a firm expands the sales of its goods or services across the borders of global regions and countries into different geographic locations or markets. Because of its potential advantages, international diversification should be related positively to firms' returns. Research has shown that, as international diversification increases, firms' returns increase.[113] In fact, the stock market is particularly sensitive to investments in international markets. Firms that are broadly diversified into multiple international markets usually achieve the most positive stock returns.[114] There are also many reasons for the positive effects of international diversification, such as potential economies of scale and experience, location advantages, increased market size, and the opportunity to stabilize returns. The stabilization of returns helps reduce a firm's overall risk.[115] All of these outcomes can be achieved by smaller and newer ventures, as well as by larger and established firms. New ventures can also enjoy higher returns when they learn new technologies from their international diversification.[116]

Firms in the Japanese automobile industry (as indicated in the Strategic Focus on page 255) have found that international diversification may allow them to better exploit their core competencies, because sharing knowledge resources between operations can produce synergy. Also, a firm's returns may affect its decision to diversify internationally. For example, poor returns in a domestic market may encourage a firm to expand internationally in order to enhance its profit potential. In addition, internationally diversified firms may have access to more flexible labor markets, as the Japanese do in the United States, and may thereby benefit from global scanning for competition and market opportunities. Also, through global networks with assets in many countries, firms can develop more flexible structures to adjust to changes that might occur.[117]

Benetton, an Italian casual-wear company, developed a network structure over the years that has allowed it to improve its performance. "Without giving up the strongest aspects of its networked model, it is integrating and centralizing, instituting direct control over key processes throughout the supply chain. The company is also diversifying into sportswear, sports equipment and communications."[118] To manage the network, the firm has instituted state-of-the-art technology for communication and managing the supply chain. Accordingly, multinational firms with efficient and competitive operations are more likely to produce above-average returns for their investors and better products for their customers than are solely domestic firms. However, as explained later, international diversification can be carried too far.

International Diversification and Innovation

In Chapter 1, we note that the development of new technology is at the heart of strategic competitiveness. As noted in Porter's model (see Figure 8.2), a nation's competitiveness depends, in part, on the capacity of its industry to innovate. Eventually and inevitably, competitors outperform firms that fail to innovate and improve their operations and products. Therefore, the only way to sustain a competitive advantage is to upgrade it continually.[119]

International diversification provides the potential for firms to achieve greater returns on their innovations (through larger or more numerous markets) and lowers the often substantial risks of R&D investments. Therefore, international diversification provides incentives for firms to innovate.[120]

In addition, international diversification may be necessary to generate the resources required to sustain a large-scale R&D operation. An environment of rapid technological obsolescence makes it difficult to invest in new technology and the capital-intensive operations required to take advantage of such investment. Firms operating solely in domestic markets may find such investments problematic because of the length of time required to recoup the original investment. If the time is extended, it may not even be possible to recover the investment before the technology becomes obsolete.[121] As a result, international diversification improves a firm's ability to appropriate additional and necessary returns from innovation before competitors can overcome the initial competitive advantage created by the innovation. In addition, firms moving into international markets are exposed to new products and processes. If they learn about those products and processes and integrate this knowledge into their operations, further innovation can be developed.[122]

The relationship among international diversification, innovation, and returns is complex. Some level of performance is necessary to provide the resources to generate international diversification, which in turn provides incentives and resources to invest in research and development. The latter, if done appropriately, should enhance the returns of the firm, which then provides more resources for continued international diversification and investment in R&D.[123]

Because of the potential positive effects of international diversification on performance and innovation, such diversification may even enhance returns in product-diversified firms. International diversification would increase market potential in each of these firm's product lines, but the complexity of managing a firm that is both product diversified and internationally diversified is significant. Research suggests that firms in less developed countries gain from being product diversified when partnering with multinational firms from a more developed country that are looking to enter a less developed country in pursuit of increased international diversification.[124]

© HENNY RAY ABRAMS/AFP/CORBIS

Another firm joins the New York Stock Exchange—executives from ABB open the session to celebrate their firm's listing on the exchange. ABB CEO Jorgen Cenerman is second from the left.

Asea Brown Boveri (ABB) demonstrates these relationships. This firm's operations involve high levels of both product and international diversification, yet ABB's performance is strong. Some believe that the firm's ability to effectively implement the transnational strategy contributes to its strategic competitiveness. One of ABB's latest moves was in North Korea; it had signed in Pyongyang (the capital of North Korea) "a wide-ranging, long-term co-operation agreement aimed at improving the performance of the country's electricity transmission network and basic industries."[125] To manage itself, ABB assembled culturally diverse corporate and divisional management teams that facilitated the simultaneous achievement of global integration and local responsiveness.

Evidence suggests that more culturally diverse top-management teams often have a greater knowledge of international markets and their idiosyncrasies[126] (top-management teams are discussed further in Chapter 12). Moreover, an in-depth understanding of diverse markets among top-level managers facilitates intrafirm coordination and the use of long-term, strategically relevant criteria to evaluate the performance of managers and their units.[127] In turn, this approach facilitates improved innovation and performance.[128]

Complexity of Managing Multinational Firms

Although firms can realize many benefits by implementing an international strategy, doing so is complex and can produce greater uncertainty.[129] For example, multiple risks are involved when a firm operates in several different countries. Firms can grow only so large and diverse before becoming unmanageable, or the costs of managing them exceed their benefits. Other complexities include the highly competitive nature of global markets, multiple cultural environments, potentially rapid shifts in the value of different currencies, and the possible instability of some national governments.

Risks in an International Environment

International diversification carries multiple risks.[130] Because of these risks, international expansion is difficult to implement, and it is difficult to manage after implementation. The chief risks are political and economic. Taking these risks into account, highly internationally diversified firms are accustomed to market conditions yielding competitive situations that differ from what was predicted. Sometimes, these situations contribute to the firm's strategic competitiveness; on other occasions, they have a negative effect on the firm's efforts.[131] Specific examples of political and economic risks are shown in Figure 8.4.

Political Risks

Political risks are risks related to instability in national governments and to war, both civil and international. Instability in a national government creates numerous problems, including economic risks and uncertainty created by government regulation; the existence of many, possibly conflicting, legal authorities; and the potential nationalization of private assets. For example, as illustrated in the Strategic Focus on page 267 about Argentina, foreign firms that invest in another country may have concerns about the stability of the national government and what might happen to their investments or assets because of unrest and government instability.

Economic Risks

As illustrated in the Strategic Focus on page 267 about Argentina, economic risks are interdependent with political risks. Foremost among the economic risks of international diversification are the differences and fluctuations in the value of different currencies.[132] The value of the dollar relative to other currencies determines the value of the international assets and earnings of U.S. firms; for example, an increase in the value of the U.S. dollar can reduce the value of U.S. multinational firms' international assets and earnings in other countries. Furthermore, the value of different currencies can also, at times, dramatically affect a firm's competitiveness in global markets because of its effect on the prices of goods manufactured in different countries.

An increase in the value of the dollar can harm U.S. firms' exports to international markets because of the price differential of the products. It can also affect economies of other countries as in the case of Argentina, which had pegged its currency, the peso, one-for-one with the U.S. dollar. The devaluation caused a significant recession, 18 percent unemployment, and not many options for emerging from this morass.[133]

Limits to International Expansion: Management Problems

Firms tend to earn positive returns on early international diversification, but the returns often level off and become negative as the diversification increases past some point.[134] There are several reasons for the limits to the positive effects of international

Figure 8.4 Risk in the International Environment

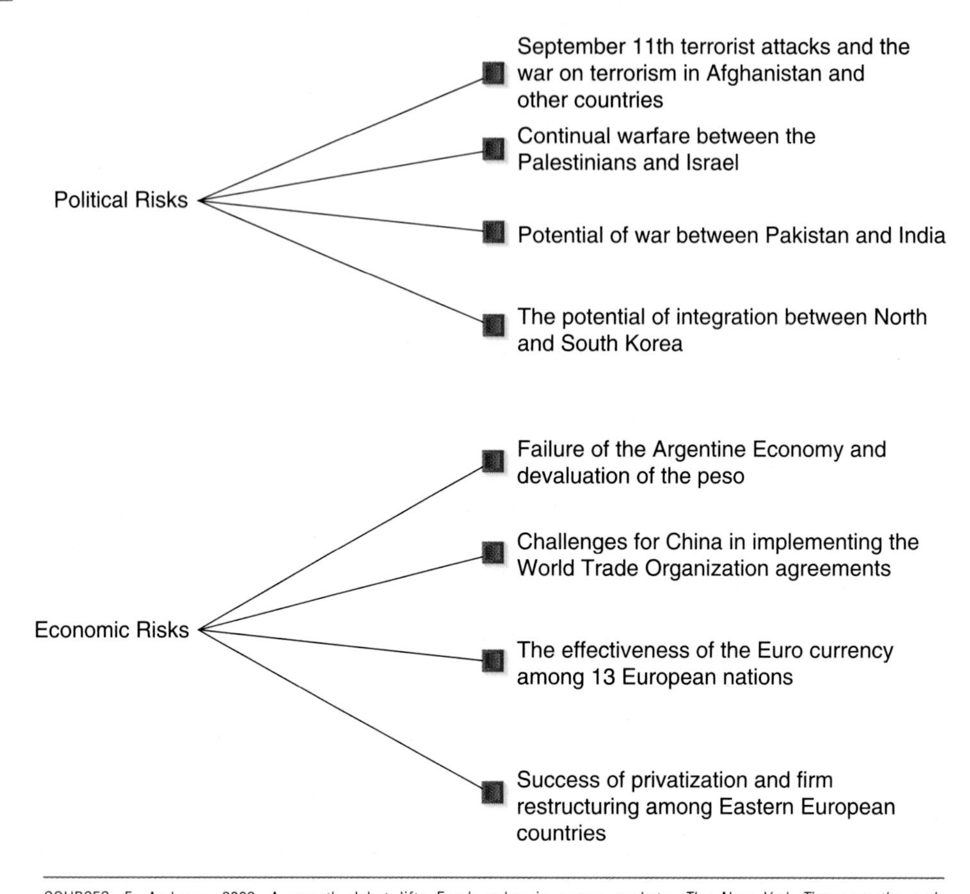

SOURCES: E. Andrews, 2002, A smooth debut lifts Euro's value in money markets, *The New York Times on the web,* http://www.nytimes.com, January 3; M. Kripalani, N. Mangi, F. Balfour, P. Magnusson, & R. Brady, 2002, Now, will India and Pakistan get serious about peace? *Business Week,* January 14, 51; M. Wallin, 2002, Argentina grapples with postdevaluation, *The Wall Street Journal,* January 10, A8; B. Einhorn, C. Dawson, I. Kunii, D. Roberts, A. Webb, & P. Engardio, 2001, China: Will its entry into the WTO unleash new prosperity or further destabilize the world economy? *Business Week,* October 29, 38; P. Engardio, R. Miller, G. Smith, D. Brady, M. Kripalani, A. Borrus, & D. Foust, 2001, What's at stake: How terrorism threatens the global economy, *Business Week,* October 22, 33–34; D. Eisenberg, 2001, Arafat's dance of death, *Time,* December 24, 64–65; B. Fulford, 2001, Another enemy, *Forbes;* October 29, 117; K. E. Myer, 2001, Institutions, transaction costs, and entry model choice in Eastern Europe, *Journal of International Business Studies,* 32: 357–367.

diversification. First, greater geographic dispersion across country borders increases the costs of coordination between units and the distribution of products. Second, trade barriers, logistical costs, cultural diversity, and other differences by country (e.g., access to raw materials and different employee skill levels) greatly complicate the implementation of an international diversification strategy.[135]

Institutional and cultural factors can present strong barriers to the transfer of a firm's competitive advantages from one country to another. Marketing programs often have to be redesigned and new distribution networks established when firms expand into new countries. In addition, firms may encounter different labor costs and capital charges. In general, it is difficult to effectively implement, manage, and control a firm's international operations.[136]

Wal-Mart made significant mistakes in some Latin American markets. For example, its first Mexican stores carried ice skates, riding lawn mowers, fishing tackle—even

Strategic Focus

Currency Devaluation in Argentina

Since the early 1990s, the value of the Argentine peso had been an even exchange with the U.S. dollar. In January 2002, however, Argentina was forced to devalue the peso by approximately 40 percent after the country had defaulted on its $141 billion public debt. The devaluation created significant chaos for the people of Argentina. President Fernando de la Rúa had resigned on December 20, 2001, two years after being elected. Adolfo Rodrígues Saá replaced de la Rúa, but lasted only eight days in office. Eduardo Duhalde became Argentina's president on January 1, 2002.

Argentina policy makers, with the devaluation, changed the peso's association with the U.S. dollar. For the ten years before the devaluation, many foreign banks had invested over $10 billion in Argentina. After the devaluation, the Fleetwood Boston Financial Corporation showed an estimated $140 million loss and CitiGroup Chairman Sanford I. Weill indicated that his firm also would experience a significant loss. These losses may take place because the contracts for the firms allow their investments to be repaid in pesos rather than in U.S. dollars. In contrast, AES Corporation, a U.S. corporation that builds power plants in Argentina, had stipulated in its contracts that it must be paid in U.S. dollars.

Although many firms earn only a small percentage of their annual income from Argentina, such as Coca-Cola, their earnings will be decreased not only because of the devaluation but also because Argentina's economy has been in recession and will get worse due to the devaluation. Consumers will have less buying power due to the devaluation.

The one-to-one ratio of the peso for the U.S. dollar policy had been implemented in the early 1990s as a solution to the hyperinflation that Argentina experienced throughout the 1980s. Because the two currencies were linked, however, as the dollar increased in value in open currency markets, Argentina's exports also became more expensive. Thus, although the even exchange of pesos for dollars had blunted the earlier inflation problem, it contributed to the country's recession in the late 1990s.

In addition, Argentina's politics have not helped its economic situation. Although privatization of water, petroleum, airline firms, and other state-owned corporations presented an opportunity for increased economic growth, the patronage-based political system allowed top politicians to give the country's privatized assets to those which were not the best managers, leading to the dissipation of the value of the privatized firms. Thus, the privatization process did not lead Argentina's privatized firms to be competitive in world markets, and the politics involved did not facilitate improved economic growth.

The politicians also pursued policies that increased government spending. When significant deficits resulted, the International Monetary Fund (IMF), which oversees lending to emerging market countries, forced stringent fiscal policies on the Argentine government, further increasing Argentina's recessionary environment. Rather than being able to increase government spending at a critical juncture, the government was forced to tighten fiscal policy, which did not allow the country to emerge from recession quickly.

Although there are a number of causes for the economic and political crisis that resulted in the currency devaluation, all are hurt by the circumstance: the people of Argentina, the government, and the foreign investors who committed significant capital to build businesses in Argentina.

SOURCES: J. Fox, 2002, Argentina, *Fortune,* January 7, 26; 2002, Between the creditors and the streets, *The Economist,* January 5, 29–30; G. Smith, J. Goodman, C. Lindblad, & A. Robinson, 2002, A wrong turn in Argentina, *Business Week Online,* http://www.businessweek.com, January 21; K. A. Dolan, 2001, Tails we win, *Forbes,* August 20, 54; J. Goodman, 2001, Thinking the unthinkable; Argentina could be forced to cut the peso's peg to the dollar, *Business Week,* November 19, 58; M. Wallin, Argentine leaders declare state of emergency, *The Wall Street Journal,* December 20, A8, A12.

clay pigeons for skeet shooting. To get rid of the clay pigeons they would be radically discounted "only to have automated inventory systems linked to Wal-Mart's corporate headquarters in Bentonville, Arkansas, order a fresh batch." Once Wal-Mart began to get the right mix of products, the Mexican currency was devalued in 1994. However, over time, Wal-Mart has become very successful in Latin America, especially Mexico. It has been able to increase its market share by taking advantage of local sourcing, especially by taking advantage of the lower wages in Mexico through NAFTA.[137]

The amount of international diversification that can be managed will vary from firm to firm and according to the abilities of each firm's managers. The problems of central coordination and integration are mitigated if the firm diversifies into more friendly countries that are geographically close and have cultures similar to its own country's culture. In that case, there are likely to be fewer trade barriers, the laws and customs are better understood, and the product is easier to adapt to local markets.[138] For example, U.S. firms may find it less difficult to expand their operations into Mexico, Canada, and Western European countries than into Asian countries.

Management must also be concerned with the relationship between the host government and the multinational corporation.[139] Although government policy and regulations are often barriers, many firms, such as Toyota and General Motors, have turned to strategic alliances to overcome those barriers. By forming interorganizational networks, such as strategic alliances, firms can share resources and risks but also build flexibility.[140]

Summary

- The use of international strategies is increasing not only because of traditional motivations, but also for emerging reasons. Traditional motives include extending the product life cycle, securing key resources, and having access to low-cost labor. Emerging motivations focus on the combination of the Internet and mobile telecommunications, which facilitates global transactions. Also, there is increased pressure for global integration as the demand for commodities becomes borderless, and yet pressure is also increasing for local country responsiveness.
- An international strategy usually attempts to capitalize on four benefits: increased market size; the opportunity to earn a return on large investments; economies of scale and learning; and advantages of location.
- International business-level strategies are usually grounded in one or more home-country advantages, as Porter's diamond model suggests. The diamond model emphasizes four determinants: factors of production; demand conditions; related and supporting industries; and patterns of firm strategy, structure, and rivalry.
- There are three types of international corporate-level strategies. A multidomestic strategy focuses on competition within each country in which the firm competes. Firms using a multidomestic strategy decentralize strategic and operating decisions to the business units operating in each country, so that each unit can tailor its goods and services to the local market. A global strategy assumes more standardization of products across country boundaries; therefore, competitive strategy is centralized and controlled by the home office. A transnational strategy seeks to combine aspects of both multidomestic and global strategies in order to emphasize both local responsiveness and global integration and coordination. This strategy is difficult to implement, requiring an integrated network and a culture of individual commitment.
- Although the transnational strategy's implementation is a challenge, environmental trends are causing many multinational firms to consider the need for both global efficiency and local responsiveness. Many large multinational firms—particularly those with many diverse products—use a multidomestic strategy with some product lines and a global strategy with others.
- The threat of terrorist attacks increases the risks and costs of international strategies. Furthermore, research suggests that the liability of foreignness is more difficult to overcome than once thought.
- Some firms decide to compete only in certain regions of the world, as opposed to viewing all markets in the world as potential opportunities. Competing in regional markets allows firms and managers to focus their learning on specific markets, cultures, locations, resources, etc.
- Firms may enter international markets in one of several ways, including exporting, licensing, forming strategic alliances, making acquisitions, and establishing new wholly owned subsidiaries, often referred to as greenfield ventures. Most firms begin with exporting or licensing, because of their lower costs and risks, but later may expand to strategic alliances and acquisitions. The most expensive and risky means of entering a new international market is through the establishment of a new wholly owned subsidiary. On the other hand, such subsidiaries provide the advantages of maximum control by the firm and, if they are successful, the greatest returns.
- International diversification facilitates innovation in a firm, because it provides a larger market to gain more and faster returns from investments in innovation. In addition, international diversification may generate the resources necessary to sustain a large-scale R&D program.
- In general, international diversification is related to above-average returns, but this assumes that the diversification is effectively implemented and that the firm's international operations are well managed. International diversification provides greater economies of scope and learning, which, along with greater innovation, help produce above-average returns.
- Several risks are involved with managing multinational operations. Among these are political risks (e.g., instability of national governments) and economic risks (e.g., fluctuations in the value of a country's currency).
- There are also limits to the ability to manage international expansion effectively. International diversification increases coordination and distribution costs, and management problems are exacerbated by trade barriers, logistical costs, and cultural diversity, among other factors.

Review Questions

1. What are the traditional and emerging motives that cause firms to expand internationally?
2. What four factors provide a basis for international business-level strategies?
3. What are the three international corporate-level strategies? How do they differ from each other? What factors lead to their development?
4. What environmental trends are affecting international strategy?
5. What five modes of international expansion are available, and what is the normal sequence of their use?
6. What is the relationship between international diversification and innovation? How does international diversification affect innovation? What is the effect of international diversification on a firm's returns?
7. What are the risks of international diversification? What are the challenges of managing multinational firms?
8. What factors limit the positive outcomes of international expansion?

Experiential Exercise

International Strategy

Coca-Cola's first international bottling plants opened in 1906 in Canada, Cuba, and Panama. Today the firm produces nearly 300 brands in almost 200 countries, and more than 70 percent of its income comes from outside the United States.

Coca-Cola's German operation began in 1929. Germany—Coke's first marketing success outside North America—is the firm's fifth-largest market. Nine bottlers with a total of 24 production plants serve Germany's population of 82 million people; and the firm has 13,000 German employees, and by 1939 was selling 4.5 million cases annually. Popular Coca-Cola products in Germany include Fanta (first introduced as a substitute to Coke during World War II) in several flavors, Mezzo Mix (a cola and orange-flavored beverage), Bonaqa table water, and Lift Apfelsaftschorle (apple juice with carbonated water).

Coca-Cola was introduced in Chile in 1941 with the opening of plants in Santiago and Valparaiso. Brands marketed in Chile include Coca-Cola, Coca-Cola Light, Sprite, Sprite Light, Fanta, Fanta Sabores, Lift, Vital mineral water, Nordic Mist Ginger Ale, and Nordic Mist Tonic Water. Juice brands are Kapo, Andifrut, and Nectar Andina. The Coca-Cola system in Chile has 11 bottling plants and employs more than 4,000 people.

1. Based on the above information, the cultural differences between Germany and Chile (as well as the obvious differences among the other countries in which Coca-Cola operates), and the type of product offered by the firm, compare and contrast the three generic international corporate level strategies illustrated in Figure 8.3 as they apply to Coca-Cola. Which strategy is best for this firm, and why?
2. Describe how Coca-Cola's country operations might be affected by the environmental trends of liability of foreignness and regionalization.

Notes

1. D. Ahlstrom & G. D. Bruton, 2001, Learning from successful local private firms in China: Establishing legitimacy, *Academy of Management Executive,* 15(4): 72–83.
2. A. K. Gupta & V. Govindarajan, 2001, Converting global presence into global competitive advantage, *Academy of Management Executive,* 15(2): 45–57.
3. A. McWilliams, D. D. Van Fleet, & P. M. Wright, 2001, Strategic management of human resources for global competitive advantage, *Journal of Business Strategies,* 18(1): 1–24; B. L. Kedia & A. Mukherji, 1999, Global managers: Developing a mindset for global competitiveness, *Journal of World Business,* 34(3): 230–251.
4. B. R. Koka, J. E. Prescott, & R. Madhaven, 1999, Contagion influence on trade and investment policy: A network perspective, *Journal of International Business Studies,* 30: 127–148.
5. G. Bottazzi, G. Dosi, M. Lippi, F. Pammolli, & M. Riccaboni, 2001, Innovation and corporate growth in the evolution of the drug industry, *International Journal of Industrial Organization,* 19: 1161–1187.
6. S. Tallman, 2001, Global strategic management, in M. A. Hitt, R. E. Freeman, & J. S. Harrison (eds.), *Handbook of Strategic Management,* Oxford, U.K.: Blackwell Publishers, 462–490; C. W. L. Hill, 2000, *International Business: Competing in the Global Marketplace,* 3d ed., Boston: Irwin/McGraw Hill, 378–380.
7. R. Vernon, 1996, International investment and international trade in the product cycle, *Quarterly Journal of Economics,* 80: 190–207.
8. H. F. Lau, C. C. Y. Kwok, & C. F. Chan, 2000, Filling the gap: Extending international product life cycle to emerging economies, *Journal of Global Marketing,* 13(4): 29–51.
9. Y. Shi, 2001, Technological capabilities and international production strategy of firms: The case of foreign direct investment in China, *Journal of World Business,* 18(4): 523–532.
10. A. Camuffo, P. Romano, & A. Vinelli, 2001, Back to the future: Benetton transforms its global network, *Sloan Management Review,* 43(1): 46–52.
11. B. Kim & Y. Lee, 2001, Global capacity expansion strategies: Lessons learned from two Korean carmakers, *Long Range Planning,* 34(3): 309–333.
12. K. Macharzina, 2001, The end of pure global strategies? *Management International Review,* 41(2): 105; W. Kuemmerle, 1999, Foreign direct investment in industrial research in the pharmaceutical and electronics industries—Results from a survey of multinational firms, *Research Policy,* 28:(2/3), 179–193.
13. Y. Luo, 2000, Entering China today: What choices do we have? *Journal of Global Marketing,* 14(2): 57–82.
14. C. C. Y. Kwok & D. M. Reeb, 2000, Internationalization and firm risk: An upstream-downstream hypothesis, *Journal of International Business Studies,* 31: 611–629; J. J. Choi & M. Rajan, 1997, A joint test of market segmentation and exchange risk factor in international capital markets, *Journal of International Business Studies,* 28: 29–49.
15. R. E. Hoskisson, L. Eden, C. M. Lau, & M. Wright, 2000, Strategy in emerging economies, *Academy of Management Journal,* 43: 249–267; D. J. Arnold & J. A. Quelch, 1998, New strategies in emerging markets, *Sloan Management Review,* 40: 7–20.
16. M. W. Peng, Y. Lu, O. Shenkar, & D. Y. L. Wang, 2001, Treasures in the China house: A review of management and organizational research on Greater China, *Journal of Business Research,* 52(2): 95–110; S. Lovett, L. C. Simmons, & R. Kali, 1999, Guanxi versus the market: Ethics and efficiency, *Journal of International Business Studies,* 30: 231–248.
17. J. P. Quinlan, 1998, Europe, not Asia, is corporate America's key market, *The Wall Street Journal,* January 12, A20.
18. W. Kuemmerle, 2001, Go global—or not? *Harvard Business Review,* 79(6): 37–49; Y. Luo & M. W. Peng, 1999, Learning to compete in a transition economy: Experience, environment and performance, *Journal of International Business Studies,* 30: 269–295.
19. R. Gray, 2001, Local on a global scale, *Marketing,* September 27, 22–23.
20. X. Martin, A. Swaminathan, & W. Mitchell, 1999, Organizational evolution in the interorganizational environment: Incentives and constraints on international expansion strategy, *Administrative Science Quarterly,* 43: 566–601.
21. P. Ghemawat, 2001, Distance still matters: The hard reality of global expansion, *Harvard Business Review,* 79(8): 137–147.
22. S. R. Miller & A. Parkhe, 2002. Is there a liability of foreignness in global banking? An empirical test of banks' x-efficiency, *Strategic Management Journal,* 23: 55–75; T. Kostova & S. Zaheer, 1999, Organizational legitimacy under conditions of complexity: The case of the multinational enterprise, *Academy of Management Review,* 24: 64–81; S. Zaheer & E. Mosakowski, 1997, The dynamics of the liability of foreignness: A global study of survival in financial services, *Strategic Management Journal,* 18: 439–464.
23. P. Engardio, 2001, Smart Globalization, *Business Week Online,* http://www.businessweek.com, August 27.
24. 2002, Coca-Cola, *Standard & Poor's Stock Report,* http://www.fidelity.com, March 28; H. Chura & R. Linnett, 2001, Coca-Cola readies global assault, *Advertising Age,* April 2, 1, 34.
25. S. Jaffe, 2001, Do Pepsi and Gatorade mix? *Business Week Online,* http://www.businessweek.com, August 14.
26. B. Morris & P. Sellers, 2000, What really happened at Coke? *Fortune,* January 10, 114–116.
27. R. C. Shrader, 2001, Collaboration and performance in foreign markets: The case of young high-technology manufacturing firms, *Academy of Management Journal,* 44: 45–60; W. Kuemmerle, 1999, The drivers of foreign direct investment into research and development: An empirical investigation, *Journal of International Business Studies,* 30: 1–24.
28. Z. Liao, 2001, International R&D project evaluation by multinational corporations in the electronics and IT industry of Singapore, *R & D Management,* 31: 299–307.
29. W. Shan & J. Song, 1997, Foreign direct investment and the sourcing of technological advantage: Evidence from the biotechnology industry, *Journal of International Business Studies,* 28: 267–284.
30. B. O'Keefe, 2001, Global brands, *Fortune,* November 26, 102–110.
31. W. Chung, 2001, Identifying technology transfer in foreign direct investment: Influence of industry conditions and investing firm motives, *Journal of International Business Studies,* 32: 211–229.
32. A. J. Mauri & A. V. Phatak, 2001, Global integration as inter-area product flows: The internalization of ownership and location factors influencing product flows across MNC units, *Management International Review,* 41(3): 233–249.
33. D. Roberts & A. Webb, 2001, China's carmakers: Flattened by falling tariffs, *Business Week,* December 3, 51.
34. W. Kuemmerle, 2002, Home base and knowledge management in international ventures, *Journal of Business Venturing,* 2: 99–122; H. Bresman, J. Birkinshaw, & R. Nobel, 1999, Knowledge transfer in international acquisitions, *Journal of International Business Studies,* 30: 439–462; J. Birkinshaw, 1997, Entrepreneurship in multinational corporations: The characteristics of subsidiary initiatives, *Strategic Management Journal,* 18: 207–229.
35. Ahlstrom & Bruton, Learning from successful local private firms in China; S. A. Zahra, R. D. Ireland, & M. A. Hitt, 2000, International expansion by new venture firms: International diversity, mode of market entry, technological learning, and performance, *Academy of Management Journal,* 43: 925–950.
36. Mauri & Phatak, Global integration as inter-area product flows.
37. J. Bernstein & D. Weinstein, 2002, Do endowments predict the location of production? Evidence from national and international data, *Journal of International Economics,* 56(1): 55–76.
38. D. Wilson, 2001, Turns to Diamond—Hungary glitters as Central Europe's choice manufacturing site, *Ebn,* January 29, 46.
39. R. Robertson & D. H. Dutkowsky, 2002, Labor adjustment costs in a destination country: The case of Mexico, *Journal of Development Economics,* 67: 29–54.
40. D. A. Griffith & M. G. Harvey, 2001, A resource perspective of global dynamic capabilities, *Journal of International Business Studies,* 32: 597–606; D. J. Teece, G. Pisano, & A. Shuen, 1997, Dynamic capabilities and strategic management, *Strategic Management Journal,* 18: 509–533.
41. Y. Luo, 2000, Dynamic capabilities in international expansion, *Journal of World Business,* 35(4): 355–378.
42. L. Nachum, 2001, The impact of home countries on the competitiveness of advertising TNCs, *Management International Review,* 41(1): 77–98.
43. Ibid.
44. M. E. Porter, 1990, *The Competitive Advantage of Nations,* New York: The Free Press.
45. Ibid., 84.
46. Ibid., 89.
47. O. Oz, 2001, Sources of competitive advantage of Turkish construction companies in international markets, *Construction Management and Economics,* 19(2): 135–144.
48. J. Birkinshaw, 2001, Strategies for managing internal competition, *California Management Review,* 44(1): 21–38.
49. W. P. Wan & R. E. Hoskisson, 2002, Home country environments, corporate diversification strategies and firm performance, *Academy of Management Journal,* in press;

J. M. Geringer, S. Tallman, & D. M. Olsen, 2000, Product and international diversification among Japanese multinational firms, *Strategic Management Journal,* 21: 51–80.

50. M. A. Hitt, R. E. Hoskisson, & R. D. Ireland, 1994, A mid-range theory of the interactive effects of international and product diversification on innovation and performance, *Journal of Management,* 20: 297–326.
51. A.-W. Harzing, 2000, An empirical analysis and extension of the Bartlett and Ghoshal typology of multinational companies, *Journal of International Business Studies,* 32: 101–120; S. Ghoshal, 1987, Global strategy: An organizing framework, *Strategic Management Journal,* 8: 425–440.
52. J. Sheth, 2000, From international to integrated marketing, *Journal of Business Research,* 51(1): 5–9; J. Taggart & N. Hood, 1999, Determinants of autonomy in multinational corporation subsidiaries, *European Management Journal,* 17: 226–236.
53. Y. Luo, 2001, Determinants of local responsiveness: Perspectives from foreign subsidiaries in an emerging market, *Journal of Management,* 27: 451–477.
54. M. Carpenter & J. Fredrickson, 2001, Top management teams, global strategic posture, and the moderating role of uncertainty, *Academy of Management Journal,* 44: 533–545; T. T. Herbert, 1999, Multinational strategic planning: Matching central expectations to local realities, *Long Range Planning,* 32: 81–87.
55. O'Keefe, Global brands.
56. Ghemawat, Distance still matters, 147.
57. Harzing, An empirical analysis and extension of the Bartlett and Ghoshal typology.
58. D. G. McKendrick, 2001, Global strategy and population level learning: The case of hard disk drives, *Strategic Management Journal,* 22: 307–334.
59. M. W. Peng, S. H. Lee, & J. J. Tan, 2001, The keiretsu in Asia: Implications for multilevel theories of competitive advantage, *Journal of International Management,* 7: 253–276; A. Bhappu, 2000, The Japanese family: An institutional logic for Japanese corporate networks and Japanese management. *Academy of Management Review,* 25: 409–415; J. K. Johaansson & G. S. Yip, 1994, Exploiting globalization potential: U.S. and Japanese strategies, *Strategic Management Journal,* 15: 579–601.
60 D. Ilott, 2002, Success story—Cemex: The cement giant has managed concrete earnings in a mixed year, *Business Mexico,* January(Special Edition), 34; 2001, Business: The Cemex way, *The Economist,* June 16, 75–76.
61. C. A. Bartlett & S. Ghoshal, 1989, *Managing Across Borders: The Transnational Solution,* Boston: Harvard Business School Press.
62. J. Child & Y. Yan, 2001, National and transnational effects in international business: Indications from Sino-foreign joint ventures, *Management International Review,* 41(1): 53–75.
63. J. Muller & C. Tierney, 2002, Daimler and Chrysler have a baby, *Business Week,* January 14, 36–37.
64. T. Isobe, S. Makino, & D. B. Montgomery, 2000, Resource commitment, entry timing and market performance of foreign direct investments in emerging economies: The case of Japanese international joint ventures in China, *Academy of Management Journal,* 43: 468–484.
65. S. Zaheer & A. Zaheer, 2001, Market microstructure in a global B2B network, *Strategic Management Journal,* 22: 859–873.
66. C. Sliwa, 2001, Clothing retailer finds worldwide business on the Web, *Computerworld,* April 30, 40–44.
67. Ibid.
68. F. X. Molina-Morales, 2001, European industrial districts: Influence of geographic concentration on performance of the firm, *Journal of International Management,* 7: 277–294; M. E. Porter & S. Stern, 2001, Innovation: Location matters, *Sloan Management Review,* 42(4): 28–36.
69. C. Pantzalis, 2001, Does location matter? An empirical analysis of geographic scope and MNC market valuation, *Journal of International Business Studies,* 32: 133–155.
70. R. D. Ludema, 2002, Increasing returns, multinationals and geography of preferential trade agreements, *Journal of International Economics,* 56: 329–358; L. Allen & C. Pantzalis, 1996, Valuation of the operating flexibility of multinational corporations, *Journal of International Business Studies,* 27: 633–653.
71. J. I. Martinez, J. A. Quelch, & J. Ganitsky, 1992, Don't forget Latin America, *Sloan Management Review,* 33(Winter): 78–92.
72. H. Przybyla, 2000, Strong U.S. economy pushing trade deficit with Latin America, *Houston Chronicle,* January 21, C1, C4.
73. C. Lindblad, 2001, Mexico: The Fox revolution is spinning its wheels, *Business Week,* December 10, 51.
74. J. Chang & P. M. Rosenzweig, 1998, Industry and regional patterns in sequential foreign market entry, *Journal of Management Studies,* 35: 797–822.
75. S. Zahra, J. Hayton, J. Marcel, & H. O'Neill, 2001, Fostering entrepreneurship during international expansion: Managing key challenges, *European Management Journal,* 19: 359–369.
76. Zahra, Ireland, & Hitt, International expansion by new venture firms.
77. M. W. Peng, C. W. L. Hill, & D. Y. L. Wang, 2000, Schumpeterian dynamics versus Williamsonian considerations: A test of export intermediary performance, *Journal of Management Studies,* 37: 167–184.
78. Luo, Determinants of local responsiveness.
79. M. A. Raymond, J. Kim, & A. T. Shao, 2001, Export strategy and performance: A comparison of exporters in a developed market and an emerging market, *Journal of Global Marketing;* 15(2): 5–29; P. S. Aulakh, M. Kotabe, & H. Teegen, 2000, Export strategies and performance of firms from emerging economies: Evidence from Brazil, Chile and Mexico. *Academy of Management Journal,* 43: 342–361.
80. B. Walker & D. Luft, 2001, Exporting tech from Texas, *Texas Business Review,* August, 1–5.
81. P. Westhead, M. Wright, & D. Ucbasaran, 2001, The internationalization of new and small firms: A resource-based view, *Journal of Business Venturing,* 16: 333–358.
82. D. Fairlamb & R. McNatt, 2002, The Euro: A shopper's best friend, *Business Week,* January 14, 8.
83. M. A. Hitt & R. D. Ireland, 2000, The intersection of entrepreneurship and strategic management research, in D. L. Sexton & H. Landstrom (eds.) *Handbook of Entrepreneurship,* Oxford, U.K.: Blackwell Publishers, 45–63.
84. A. Arora & A. Fosfuri, 2000, Wholly owned subsidiary versus technology licensing in the worldwide chemical industry, *Journal of International Business Studies,* 31: 555–572.
85. M. Johnson, 2001, Learning from toys: Lessons in managing supply chain risk from the toy industry, *California Management Review,* 43(3): 106–124.
86. C. A. Bartlett & S. Rangan, 1992, Komatsu limited, in C. A. Bartlett & S. Ghoshal (eds.), *Transnational Management: Text, Cases and Readings in Cross-Border Management,* Homewood, IL: Irwin, 311–326.
87. B. Petersen, D. E. Welch, & L. S. Welch, 2000, Creating meaningful switching options in international operations, *Long Range Planning,* 33(5): 688–705.
88. J. W. Lu & P. W. Beamish, 2001, The internationalization and performance of SMEs, *Strategic Management Journal,* 22(Special Issue): 565–586; M. Koza & A. Lewin, 2000, Managing partnerships and strategic alliances: Raising the odds of success, *European Management Journal,* 18(2): 146–151.
89. J. S. Harrison, M. A. Hitt, R. E. Hoskisson, & R. D. Ireland, 2001, Resource complementarity in business combinations: Extending the logic to organization alliances, *Journal of Management,* 27: 679–690; T. Das & B. Teng, 2000, A resource-based theory of strategic alliances, *Journal of Management.* 26: 31–61.
90. M. Peng, 2001. The resource-based view and international business, *Journal of Management,* 27: 803–829.
91. P. J. Lane, J. E. Salk, & M. A. Lyles, 2002, Absorptive capacity, learning, and performance in international joint ventures, *Strategic Management Journal,* 22: 1139–1161; B. L. Simonin, 1999, Transfer of marketing know-how in international strategic alliances: An empirical investigation of the role and antecedents of knowledge ambiguity, *Journal of International Business Studies,* 30: 463–490; M. A. Lyles & J. E. Salk, 1996, Knowledge acquisition from foreign parents in international joint ventures: An empirical examination in the Hungarian context, *Journal of International Business Studies,* 27(Special Issue): 877–903.
92. Shrader, Collaboration and performance in foreign markets; M. A. Hitt, M. T. Dacin, E. Levitas, J. L. Arregle, & A. Borza, 2000, Partner selection in emerging and developed market contexts: Resource based and organizational learning perspectives, *Academy of Management Journal,* 43: 449–467.
93. J. Eig, 2001, H.J. Heinz and Japan's Kagome are expected to form alliance, *The Wall Street Journal Interactive,* http://www.wsj.com, July 26.
94. C. Grande, 2001, Pearson plans to teach English on Chinese TV, *Financial Times,* November 20, 27.
95. Y. Gong, O. Shenkar, Y. Luo, & M-K. Nyaw, 2001, Role conflict and ambiguity of CEOs in international joint ventures: A transaction cost perspective, *Journal of Applied Psychology,* 86: 764–773.
96. D. C. Hambrick, J. Li, K. Xin, & A. S. Tsui, 2001, Compositional gaps and downward spirals in international joint venture management groups, *Strategic Management Journal,* 22: 1033–1053; M. T. Dacin, M. A. Hitt, & E. Levitas, 1997, Selecting partners for successful international alliances: Examination of U.S. and Korean Firms, *Journal of World Business,* 32: 3–16.
97. A. Arino, J. de la Torre, & P. S. Ring, 2001, Relational quality: Managing trust in corporate alliances, *California Management Review,* 44(1): 109–131.
98. Y. Pan & D. K. Tse, 2000, The hierarchical model of market entry modes, *Journal of International Business Studies,* 31: 535–554; Y. Pan, S. Li, & D. K. Tse, 1999, The

impact of order and mode of market entry on profitability and market share, *Journal of International Business Studies,* 30: 81–104.
99. W. H. Hoffmann & W. Schaper-Rinkel, 2001, Acquire or ally? A strategy framework for deciding between acquisition and cooperation, *Management International Review,* 41(2): 131–159.
100. M. A. Hitt, J. S. Harrison, & R. D. Ireland, 2001, *Creating Value through Mergers and Acquisitions,* New York: Oxford University Press.
101. 1999, French Dressing, *The Economist,* July 10, 53–54.
102. W. Zellner, K. A. Schimdt, M. Ihlwan, H. Dawley, 2001, How well does Wal-Mart travel? *Business Week,* September 3, 82–84.
103. A.-W. Harzing, 2002, Acquisitions versus greenfield investments: International strategy and management of entry modes, *Strategic Management Journal,* 23: 211–227; K. D. Brouthers & L. E. Brouthers, 2000, Acquisition or greenfield start-up? Institutional, cultural and transaction cost influences, *Strategic Management Journal,* 21: 89–97.
104. D. Kirk, 2001, British American Tobacco finds opening in South Korea, *The New York Times,* http://www.nytimes.com, August 9.
105. S.-J. Chang & P. Rosenzweig, 2001, The choice of entry mode in sequential foreign direct investment, *Strategic Management Journal,* 22: 747–776.
106. K. E. Myer, 2001, Institutions, transaction costs, and entry mode choice in Eastern Europe, *Journal of International Business Studies,* 32: 357–367.
107. Y. Luo, 2001, Determinants of entry in an emerging economy: A multilevel approach, *Journal of Management Studies,* 38: 443–472.
108. A. Takeishi, 2001, Bridging inter- and intra-firm boundaries: Management of supplier involvement in automobile product development, *Strategic Management Journal,* 22: 403–433.
109 D. K Sobek, II, A. C. Ward, & J. K. Liker, 1999, Toyota's principles of set-based concurrent engineering, *Sloan Management Review,* 40(2): 53–83.
110. H. Chen, 1999, International performance of multinationals: A hybrid model, *Journal of World Business,* 34: 157–170.
111. S.-J. Chang & J. Hong, 2002, How much does the business group matter in Korea? *Strategic Management Journal,* 23: 265–274.
112. J. Song, 2002, Firm capabilities and technology ladders: Sequential foreign direct investments of Japanese electronics firms in East Asia, *Strategic Management Journal,* 23: 191–210.
113. M.Ramirez-Aleson & M. A. Espitia-Escuer, 2001, The effect of international diversification strategy on the performance of Spanish-based firms during the period 1991–1995, *Management International Review,* 41(3): 291–315; A. Delios & P. W. Beamish, 1999, Geographic scope, product diversification, and the corporate performance of Japanese firms, *Strategic Management Journal,* 20: 711–727.
114. C. Pantzalis, 2001, Does location matter? An empirical analysis of geographic scope and MNC market valuation, *Journal of International Business Studies,* 32: 133–155; C. Y. Tang & S. Tikoo, 1999, Operational flexibility and market valuation of earnings, *Strategic Management Journal,* 20: 749–761.
115. J. M. Geringer, P. W. Beamish, & R. C. daCosta, 1989, Diversification strategy and internationalization: Implications for MNE performance, *Strategic Management Journal,* 10: 109–119; R. E. Caves, 1982, *Multinational Enterprise and Economic Analysis,* Cambridge, MA: Cambridge University Press.
116. Zahra, Ireland, & Hitt, International expansion by new venture firms.
117. T. W. Malnight, 2002, Emerging structural patterns within multinational corporations: Toward process-based structures, *Academy of Management Journal,* 44: 1187–1210.
118. Camuffo, Romano, & Vinelli, Back to the future: Benetton transforms its global network.
119. G. Hamel, 2000, *Leading the Revolution,* Boston: Harvard Business School Press.
120. L. Tihanyi, R. A. Johnson, R. E. Hoskisson, & M. A. Hitt, 2002. Institutional ownership differences and international diversification: The effects of board of directors and technological opportunity, *Academy of Management Journal,* in press.
121. F. Bradley & M. Gannon, 2000, Does the firm's technology and marketing profile affect foreign market entry?, *Journal of International Marketing,* 8(4): 12–36; M. Kotabe, 1990, The relationship between off-shore sourcing and innovativeness of U.S. multinational firms: An empirical investigation, *Journal of International Business Studies,* 21: 623–638.
122. I. Zander & O. Solvell, 2000, Cross border innovation in the multinational corporation: A research agenda, *International Studies of Management and Organization,* 30(2): 44–67; Y. Luo, 1999, Time-based experience and international expansion: The case of an emerging economy, *Journal of Management Studies,* 36: 505–533.
123. Z. Liao, 2001, International R&D project evaluation by multinational corporations in the electronics and IT industry of Singapore, *R & D Management,* 31: 299–307; M. Subramaniam & N. Venkartraman, 2001, Determinants of transnational new product development capability: Testing the influence of transferring and deploying tacit overseas knowledge, *Strategic Management Journal,* 22: 359–378.
124. Wan & Hoskisson, Home country environments, corporate diversification strategies and firm performance.
125. 2001, Business as usual, or for real? *Business Asia,* January 8, 3–5.
126. M. Carpenter & J. Fredrickson, 2001, Top management teams, global strategic posture, and the moderating role of uncertainty, *Academy of Management Journal,* 44: 533–545; S. Finkelstein & D. C. Hambrick, 1996, *Strategic Leadership: Top Executives and Their Effects on Organizations,* St. Paul, MN: West Publishing Company.
127. A. McWilliams, D. D. Van Fleet, & P. M. Wright, 2001, Strategic management of human resources for global competitive advantage, *Journal of Business Strategies,* 18(1): 1–24.
128. M. A. Hitt, R. E. Hoskisson, & H. Kim, 1997, International diversification: Effects on innovation and firm performance in product-diversified firms, *Academy of Management Journal,* 40: 767–798.
129. D. Rondinelli, B. Rosen, & I. Drori, 2001, The struggle for strategic alignment in multinational corporations: Managing readjustment during global expansion, *European Management Journal,* 19: 404–405; Carpenter & Fredrickson, Top management teams, global strategic posture, and the moderating role of uncertainty.
130. D. M. Reeb, C. C. Y. Kwok, & H. Y. Baek, 1998, Systematic risk of the multinational corporation, *Journal of International Business Studies,* 29: 263–279.
131. C. Pompitakpan, 1999, The effects of cultural adaptation on business relationships: Americans selling to Japanese and Thais, *Journal of International Business Studies,* 30: 317–338.
132. L. L. Jacque & P. M. Vaaler, 2001, The international control conundrum with exchange risk: An EVA framework, *Journal of International Business Studies,* 32: 813–832.
133. 2002, Argentina's ugly economic choices: No good options, *The Economist,* January 5, 30–31.
134. Wan & Hoskisson, Home country environments, corporate diversification strategies and firm performance; Hitt, Hoskisson, & Kim, International diversification; S. Tallman & J. Li, 1996, Effects of international diversity and product diversity on the performance of multinational firms, *Academy of Management Journal,* 39: 179–196; Hitt, Hoskisson, & Ireland, A mid-range theory of interactive effects; Geringer, Beamish, & daCosta, Diversification strategy.
135. A. K. Rose & E. van Wincoop, 2001, National money as a barrier to international trade: The real case for currency union, *American Economic Review,* 91: 386–390.
136. I. M. Manev & W. B. Stevenson, 2001, Nationality, cultural distance, and expatriate status: Effects on the managerial network in a multinational enterprise, *Journal of International Business Studies,* 32: 285–303.
137. D. Luhnow, 2001, How NAFTA helped Wal-Mart transform the Mexican market, *The Wall Street Journal,* August 31, A1, A2.
138. D. E. Thomas & R. Grosse, 2001, Country-of-origin determinants of foreign direct investment in an emerging market: The case of Mexico, *Journal of International Management,* 7: 59–79.
139. J. Feeney & A. Hillman, 2001, Privatization and the political economy of strategic trade policy, *International Economic Review,* 42: 535–556; R. Vernon, 2001, Big business and national governments: Reshaping the compact in a globalizing economy, *Journal of International Business Studies,* 32: 509–518; B. Shaffer & A. J. Hillman, 2000, The development of business-government strategies by diversified firms, *Strategic Management Journal,* 21: 175–190.
140. B. Barringer & J. Harrison, 2000, Walking the tightrope: Creating value through interorganizational relationships, *Journal of Management,* 26: 367–404.

9

Chapter Nine

Cooperative Strategy

Knowledge Objectives

Studying this chapter should provide you with the strategic management knowledge needed to:

1. Define cooperative strategies and explain why firms use them.
2. Define and discuss three types of strategic alliances.
3. Name the business-level cooperative strategies and describe their use.
4. Discuss the use of corporate-level cooperative strategies in diversified firms.
5. Understand the importance of cross-border strategic alliances as an international cooperative strategy.
6. Describe cooperative strategies' risks.
7. Describe two approaches used to manage cooperative strategies.

The S-92 Helicopter: A Product of a Cross-Border Alliance

Several factors, including product complexity and research and development costs, make it very difficult for a firm to undertake major projects on its own while competing in the 21st-century competitive landscape. A business analyst speaking about the nature of competition in the aerospace industry said, "If an aerospace company is not good at alliances, it's not in business." Similarly, the chief information officer of international food processor and distributor Cargill believes that successful product innovations require alliances: "To bring something new to the marketplace requires so much cooperation and integration of knowledge that you just can't get it done unless you pick partners."

Cross-border alliances are one type of cooperative strategy used to deal with the realities of the 21st-century competitive landscape and to develop product innovations. As discussed later in the chapter, a cross-border strategic alliance is a partnership formed between firms with headquarters in different nations. Firms use a cross-border alliance to uniquely combine their value-creating resources and capabilities to develop a competitive advantage that neither partner could form on its own.

Aerospace is one of the industries in which highly diversified United Technologies competes. The firm is involved with over 100 worldwide cooperative strategies, including cross-border alliances and joint ventures (defined later in the chapter). One of United Technologies' cooperative strategies is the cross-border alliance formed by the firm's Sikorsky business unit to produce the S-92 helicopter. Five firms from four continents joined with Sikorsky to form this alliance. Using its unique resource and capabilities, each partner assumed different responsibilities for the design and production of the S-92. The combination of the partners' resources and capabilities is thought to have resulted in a competitive advantage for the alliance.

The Sikorski S-92 demonstrates cooperation both in its creation and also in the end product. Following Canadian firm Cougar Helicopter's launch order, firms around the world have placed orders, including HeliJet of Vancouver, Aircontactgruppen AS of Norway, Copterline of Finland, and East Asia Airlines/Helicopter Hong Kong. The Irish Air Corps has ordered three S-92 SAR (search and rescue) variant helicopters and has an option for two more military transport variants. The craft also met Hollywood's demands—the Sikorski S-92 plays a part in *Mr. Deeds*, a 2002 comedy feature film, as a world-class executive transport helicopter owned by a fictional multimillion-dollar media firm.

COURTESY OF RICHARD ZELLNER/SIKORSKY AIRCRAFT

Called "Team S-92," this alliance's partners and their responsibilities are: (1) Japan's Mitsubishi Heavy Industries (main cabin section), (2) Jingdezhen Helicopter Group/CATIC of the People's Republic of China (vertical tail fin and stabilizer), (3) Spain's Gamesa Aeronautica (main rotor pylon, engine nacelles AFT tail, transition section, and cabin interior), (4) Aerospace Industrial Development Corporation of Taiwan (the electrical harness, flight controls, hydraulic lines, and environmental controls forming the cockpit), and (5) Embraer of Brazil (main landing gear and fuel system). As the sixth member of the alliance, Sikorsky is responsible for the main and tail rotor head components and the S-92's transmissions. The "International Wide Area Network" connects alliance members via satellite. This connection enables real-time interactions among partners as they integrate their work.

Sikorsky has alliance responsibilities beyond those described above, including the final assembly of the S-92 and its certification as launch-ready. Following final assembly, the production program to commercially launch the S-92 was initiated in 1999. Commenting about the craft's potential, Sikorsky president Dean Borgman stated that, "The S-92 will be tops in its class in terms of cost and performance. We have numerous opportunities with this aircraft to sell to civil and government operators."

In 2000, Sikorsky, representing the Team S-92 alliance, formed a strategic relationship (called a launch agreement) with Canadian offshore operator Cougar Helicopters, which intends to use the S-92 to support its offshore operations in St. John's, Newfoundland and Halifax, Nova Scotia. Sikorsky formed a strategic relationship with Cougar to facilitate the S-92's successful commercial launch. Through cooperative interactions with Cougar, Sikorsky is discovering possible S-92 modifications that it and its alliance partners may need to initiate for the project's long-term success.

Describing the benefits of this strategic relationship, a Sikorsky official stated that, "Cougar is an ideal launch customer. They are extremely professional and innovative. Further, they will put the aircraft to the test with very high utilization, actual icing conditions, and a requirement for the high service levels we have designed in. Sikorsky and our other customers will benefit greatly from the S-92's entry into service with Cougar." Cougar is scheduled to take delivery of the first two production runs of the S-92 in late 2002 and early 2003. Thus, Sikorsky formed a cross-border alliance to produce the S-92 and a strategic relationship (which essentially was another strategic alliance) to facilitate the product's commercial launch.

SOURCES: 2002, The S-92 program, United Technologies, http://www.utc.com; 2002, Cougar and Sikorsky work accord to launch S-92, Cougar Helicopters, http://www.cougar.com, March 14; D. Donovan, 2001, United Technologies, *Forbes Best of the Web,* May 21, 66; J. Fahey, 2001, Cargill, *Forbes Best of the Web,* May 21, 66.

Pursuing internal opportunities (doing better than competitors through strategic execution or innovation) and merging with or acquiring other companies are the two primary means by which firms grow that we have discussed to this point in the book. In this chapter, we examine cooperative strategies, which are the third major alternative firms use to grow, develop value-creating competitive advantages, and create differences between them and competitors.[1] Defined formally, a **cooperative strategy** is a strategy in which firms work together to achieve a shared objective.[2] Thus, cooperating with other firms is another strategy that is used to create value for a customer that exceeds the cost of constructing that value in other ways[3] and to establish a favorable position relative to competition (see Chapters 2, 4, 5, and 8).[4] The increasing importance of cooperative strategies as a growth engine shouldn't be underestimated. In fact, some believe that "in a global market tied together by the Internet, corporate partnerships and alliances are proving a more productive way to keep companies growing."[5] This means that effective competition in the 21st-century landscape results when the firm learns how to cooperate with as well as compete against competitors.[6]

A **cooperative strategy** is a strategy in which firms work together to achieve a shared objective.

Increasingly, cooperative strategies are formed by firms competing against one another,[7] as shown by the fact that more than half of the strategic alliances (a type of cooperative strategy) established within a recent two-year period were between competitors.[8] In an alliance between FedEx and the U.S. Postal Service (USPS), for example, FedEx transports roughly 3.5 million pounds of USPS packages daily on its planes and is allowed to place its drop boxes in post offices. ". . . . The seven-year deal will earn [FedEx] more than $7 billion—$6.3 billion in transportation charges and $900 million in increased drop-box revenue."[9]

Because they are the primary type of cooperative strategy that firms use, strategic alliances (defined in the next section) are this chapter's focus. Although not frequently used, collusive strategies are another type of cooperative strategy discussed in this chapter. In a *collusive strategy,* two or more firms cooperate to raise prices above the fully competitive level.[10]

We examine several topics in this chapter. First, we define and offer examples of different strategic alliances as primary types of cooperative strategies. Next, we discuss the extensive use of cooperative strategies in the global economy and reasons for this use. In succession, we then describe business-level (including collusive strategies), corporate-level, international, and network cooperative strategies—most in the form of strategic alliances. The chapter closes with discussions of the risks of using cooperative strategies as well as how effective management of them can reduce those risks.

Strategic Alliances as a Primary Type of Cooperative Strategy

Strategic alliances are increasingly popular. Two researchers describe this popularity by noting that an "unprecedented number of strategic alliances between firms are being formed each year. [These] strategic alliances are a logical and timely response to intense and rapid changes in economic activity, technology, and globalization, all of which have cast many corporations into two competitive races: one for the world and the other for the future."[11]

A **strategic alliance** is a cooperative strategy in which firms combine some of their resources and capabilities to create a competitive advantage.[12] Thus, as linkages between them, strategic alliances involve firms with some degree of exchange and sharing of resources and capabilities to co-develop or distribute goods or services.[13] Strategic alliances let firms leverage their existing resources and capabilities while

A **strategic alliance** is a cooperative strategy in which firms combine some of their resources and capabilities to create a competitive advantage.

A key element in Polo Ralph Lauren's growth strategy is extending its Polo Ralph Lauren brands and creating new brands while maintaining a consistent global image. The firm controls its brands by opening new specialty stores, improving the merchandising in its existing specialty stores, and strategically acquiring select licensees. CEO and chairman Ralph Lauren, pictured here during the 2002 presentation of his men's fashion collection, started by designing ties in 1967; his firm's gross global sales in 2001 reached $4.8 billion.

ANTONIO CALANNI/ASSOCIATED PRESS

working with partners to develop additional resources and capabilities as the foundation for new competitive advantages.[14]

Many firms, especially large global competitors, establish multiple strategic alliances. General Motors' alliances, for example, ". . . include collaboration with Honda on internal combustion engines, with Toyota on advanced propulsion, with Renault on medium- and heavy-duty vans for Europe and, in the U.S., with AM General on the brand and distribution rights for the incomparable Hummer."[15] Focusing on developing advanced technologies, Lockheed Martin has formed over 250 alliances with firms in more than 30 countries as it concentrates on its primary business of defense modernization.[16] In general, strategic alliance success requires cooperative behavior from all partners. Actively solving problems, being trustworthy, and consistently pursuing ways to combine partners' resources and capabilities to create value are examples of cooperative behavior known to contribute to alliance success.[17]

A competitive advantage developed through a cooperative strategy often is called a collaborative or relational advantage.[18] As previously discussed, particularly in Chapter 4, competitive advantages significantly influence the firm's marketplace success.[19] Rapid technological changes and the global economy are examples of factors challenging firms to constantly upgrade current competitive advantages while they develop new ones to maintain strategic competitiveness.[20]

The firms mentioned in the Opening Case combined their resources and capabilities to develop competitive advantages while working together as the Team S-92 alliance. No individual member of the alliance could have developed the *design* and *manufacturing* competitive advantages that were instrumental to the design and production of the S-92 helicopter—a product with size and cost benefits over competing helicopters.

Three Types of Strategic Alliances

There are three major types of strategic alliances—joint venture, equity strategic alliance, and nonequity strategic alliance.

A **joint venture** is a strategic alliance in which two or more firms create a legally independent company to share some of their resources and capabilities to develop a competitive advantage.

A **joint venture** is a strategic alliance in which two or more firms create a legally independent company to share some of their resources and capabilities to develop a competitive advantage. Joint ventures are effective in establishing long-term relationships and in transferring tacit knowledge. Because it can't be codified, tacit knowledge is learned through experiences[21] such as those taking place when people from partner firms work together in a joint venture. As discussed in Chapter 3, tacit knowledge is an important source of competitive advantage for many firms.[22]

Typically, partners in a joint venture own equal percentages and contribute equally to its operations. Sprint and Virgin Group's joint venture, called Virgin Mobile USA, targets 15- to 30-year-olds as customers for pay-as-you-go wireless phone service. Brand (from Virgin) and service (from Sprint) are the primary capabilities the firms contribute to this joint venture.[23] In another example, Sony Pictures Entertainment, Warner Bros., Universal Pictures, Paramount Pictures, and Metro-Goldwyn-Mayer Inc. each have a 20 percent stake in a joint venture to use the Internet to deliver feature films on demand to customers.[24] Overall, evidence suggests that a joint venture may be the optimal alliance when firms need to combine their resources and capabilities to create a competitive advantage that is substantially different from any they possess individually and when the partners intend to enter highly uncertain markets.[25]

An **equity strategic alliance** is an alliance in which two or more firms own different percentages of the company they have formed by combining some of their resources and capabilities to create a competitive advantage.

An **equity strategic alliance** is an alliance in which two or more firms own different percentages of the company they have formed by combining some of their resources and capabilities to create a competitive advantage. Many foreign direct investments such as those made by Japanese and U.S. companies in China are completed through equity strategic alliances.[26]

In another example, Cott Corporation, the world's largest retailer brand soft drink supplier, recently formed an equity strategic alliance with J. D. Iroquois Enterprises Ltd. to strengthen its reach into the spring water segment of its markets. With a 49 percent stake in the new venture, Cott gained exclusive supply rights for Iroquois' private label spring water products. Iroquois president Dan Villeneuve believes that the alliance ". . . will expand the Iroquois branded business in the West and Far East,"[27] which is the benefit his firm gains from its equity strategic alliance with Cott.

A **nonequity strategic alliance** is an alliance in which two or more firms develop a contractual relationship to share some of their unique resources and capabilities to create a competitive advantage.

A **nonequity strategic alliance** is an alliance in which two or more firms develop a contractual relationship to share some of their unique resources and capabilities to create a competitive advantage. In this type of strategic alliance, firms do not establish a separate independent company and therefore don't take equity positions. Because of this, nonequity strategic alliances are less formal and demand fewer partner commitments than joint ventures and equity strategic alliances.[28] The relative informality and lower commitment levels characterizing nonequity strategic alliances make them unsuitable for complex projects where success requires effective transfers of tacit knowledge between partners.[29]

However, firms today increasingly use this type of alliance in many different forms such as licensing agreements, distribution agreements, and supply contracts.[30] For example, Ralph Lauren Company uses licensing agreements extensively. To support its flagship Polo brand, the firm currently uses 29 domestic licensing agreements, including West Point Stevens (bedding), Reebok (casual shoes), and ICI Paints (Ralph Lauren Home Products).[31] A key reason for the growth in types of cooperative strategies, as indicated by the Opening Case, is the complexity and uncertainty that characterize most global industries and make it difficult for firms to be successful without some sort of partnerships.[32]

Typically, outsourcing commitments take the form of a nonequity strategic alliance.[33] Discussed in Chapter 3, *outsourcing* is the purchase of a value-creating primary or support activity from another firm. Magna International Inc., a leading global supplier of technologically advanced automotive systems, components, and modules, has formed many nonequity strategic alliances with automotive manufacturers who have outsourced work to it. Magna's effectiveness with nonequity strategic alliances is suggested by the awards honoring the quality of its work that Magna has received from many of its customers, including General Motors, Ford Motor Company, Honda, DaimlerChrysler, and Toyota.[34]

Reasons Firms Develop Strategic Alliances

As previously noted, the use of cooperative strategies as a path to strategic competitiveness is on the rise[35] in for-profit firms of all sizes as well as in public organizations.[36] Thus, cooperative strategies are becoming more important to companies.[37] For example, recently surveyed executives of technology companies stated that strategic alliances are central to their firms' success.[38] Speaking directly to the issue of technology acquisition and development for these firms, a manager noted that, "You have to partner today or you will miss the next wave. You cannot possibly acquire the technology fast enough, so partnering is essential."[39]

Some even suggest that strategic alliances ". . . may be the most powerful trend that has swept American business in a century."[40] Among other benefits, strategic alliances allow partners to create value that they couldn't develop by acting independently[41] and to enter markets more quickly.[42] Moreover, most (if not virtually all) firms lack the full set of resources and capabilities needed to reach their objectives, which indicates that partnering with others will increase the probability of reaching them.[43]

The effects of the greater use of cooperative strategies—particularly in the form of strategic alliances—are noticeable. In large firms, for example, alliances now account for more than 20 percent of revenue.[44] Booz Allen Hamilton, Inc., predicted that by the end of 2002, alliances would account for as much as 35 percent of revenue for the one thousand largest U.S. companies.[45] Supporting this expectation is the belief of many senior-level executives that alliances are a prime vehicle for firm growth.[46]

In some industries, alliance versus alliance is becoming more prominent than firm against firm as a point of competition. In the global airline industry, for example, ". . . competition increasingly is between . . . alliances rather than between airlines."[47] This increased use of cooperative strategies and its results are not surprising in that the mid-1990s saw predictions that cooperative strategies were the wave of the future.[48]

The individually unique competitive conditions of slow-cycle, fast-cycle, and standard-cycle markets[49] find firms using cooperative strategies to achieve slightly different objectives (see Table 9.1). We discuss these three market types in Chapter 5 where we study competitive rivalry and competitive dynamics. *Slow-cycle markets* are markets where the firm's competitive advantages are shielded from imitation for relatively long periods of time and where imitation is costly. These markets are close to monopolistic conditions. Railroads and historically, telecommunications, utilities, and financial services are examples of industries characterized as slow-cycle markets. In *fast-cycle markets,* the firm's competitive advantages aren't shielded from imitation, preventing their long-term sustainability. Competitive advantages are moderately shielded from imitation in *standard-cycle markets,* typically allowing them to be sustained for a longer period of time compared to fast-cycle market situations, but for a shorter period of time than in slow-cycle markets.

Table 9.1 Reasons for Strategic Alliances by Market Type

Market	Reason
Slow-Cycle	• Gain access to a restricted market • Establish a franchise in a new market • Maintain market stability (e.g., establishing standards)
Fast-Cycle	• Speed up development of new goods or services • Speed up new market entry • Maintain market leadership • Form an industry technology standard • Share risky R&D expenses • Overcome uncertainty
Standard-Cycle	• Gain market power (reduce industry overcapacity) • Gain access to complementary resources • Establish better economies of scale • Overcome trade barriers • Meet competitive challenges from other competitors • Pool resources for very large capital projects • Learn new business techniques

Slow-Cycle Markets

Firms in slow-cycle markets often use strategic alliances to enter restricted markets or to establish franchises in new markets. For example, Paris-based steelmaker Usinor Group formed an equity strategic alliance with Dofasco, Canada's second-largest mill, to build a plant to supply car bodies for Honda, Toyota, General Motors, Ford, and DaimlerChrysler. For its 20 percent stake in the new venture, Usinor contributed $22 million in cash and technological know-how. Dofasco operates the North American–based plant and distributes its products. Through this alliance, Usinor and Dofasco were able to establish a new franchise ". . . in the import-averse U.S." steel market.[50]

In another example, the restricted entry to India's insurance market prompted American International Group (AIG) to form a joint venture—Tata AIG—with Mumbai-based Tata Group, ". . . which is one of the country's largest conglomerates and a trusted Indian brand name."[51] AIG executives believed that cooperative strategies were the only viable way for their firm to enter a market in which state-operated insurers had played a monopolistic role for decades.

Utility companies also use strategic alliances as a means of competing in slow-cycle markets. In the petrochemical industry, for example, Petróleos de Venezuela and Petrobras of Brazil formed a joint venture that calls for cross-investments between the partners. The eventual goal of this cooperative strategy is to form a pan–Latin American energy cooperative with firms in other countries. To reach the goal, the initial partners seek to expand the venture to add other state-owned oil companies in the region, including Colombia's Ecopetrol and Petróleos Mexicanos.[52]

Slow-cycle markets are becoming rare in the 21st-century competitive landscape for several reasons, including the privatization of industries and economies, the rapid expansion of the Internet's capabilities in terms of the quick dissemination of information, and the speed with which advancing technologies make quickly imitating even complex products possible.[53] Firms competing in slow-cycle markets should recognize the future likelihood that they'll encounter situations in which their competitive advantages become partially sustainable (in the instance of a standard-cycle market) or unsustainable (in the case of a fast-cycle market). Cooperative strategies can be helpful to firms making the transition from relatively sheltered markets to more competitive ones.

President of Polish Airlines LOT Jan Litwinski (left) and Lufthansa President Jan Weber (center) shake hands after signing a preliminary agreement in April 2002 for LOT to become a member of Star Alliance.

©AFP/CORBIS/LESZEK WROBLEWSKI

Fast-Cycle Markets

Fast-cycle markets tend to be unstable, unpredictable, and complex.[54] Combined, these conditions virtually preclude the establishment of long-lasting competitive advantages, forcing firms to constantly seek sources of new competitive advantages while creating value by using current ones. Alliances between firms with current excess resources and capabilities and those with promising capabilities help companies competing in fast-cycle markets to make an effective transition from the present to the future and also to gain rapid entry to new markets.

Sometimes, companies establish venture capital programs to facilitate these efforts.[55] Visa International formed a venture capital program to ". . . scout technologies and capabilities that will affect the future of financial services and the payments industry and enable (the firm) to deliver value to its more than 21,000 member institutions."[56] Visa International forms strategic alliances with firms that it believes have promising technologies and skills that, when shared with Visa's own resources and capabilities, have the potential to create new competitive advantages, providing the foundation for successfully entering new markets. In particular, Visa seeks partners to help create what it believes is the next generation of commerce—u-commerce, which is the ". . . merging and integration over time of the physical and the virtual world,

where you may not be face-to-face, but still have the levels of trust, convenience, protection and security in addition to the ease in performing transactions even though you are physically far apart."[57]

Standard-Cycle Markets

In standard-cycle markets, which are often large and oriented toward economies of scale (e.g., commercial aerospace), alliances are more likely to be made by partners with complementary resources and capabilities. For example, Lufthansa (Germany) and United Airlines (United States) initially formed the Star Alliance in 1993. Since then, 13 other airlines have joined this alliance. Star Alliance partners share some of their resources and capabilities to serve almost 900 global airports. The goal of the Star Alliance is to ". . . combine the best routes worldwide and then offer seamless world travel through shared booking."[58]

Companies also may cooperate in standard-cycle markets to gain market power. As discussed in Chapter 6, market power allows the firm to sell its product above the existing competitive level or to reduce its costs below the competitive level, or both. Goodyear Tire recently spent $120 million to expand the tire plant in Dalian, China that was created through a 1994 joint venture between Goodyear and Dalian Rubber General Factory. The partners in the already successful venture want to expand the manufacturing facility to continue pursuing ". . . what is clearly destined to be one of the world's biggest long-term business opportunities."[59] Goodyear's investment is expected to increase plant efficiency and to provide even more differentiated and attractive products to those who demand top quality high performance tires and are willing to pay an above-average competitive price for them.

Business-Level Cooperative Strategy

A **business-level cooperative strategy** is used to help the firm improve its performance in individual product markets.

A **business-level cooperative strategy** is used to help the firm improve its performance in individual product markets. As discussed in Chapter 4, business-level strategy details what the firm intends to do to gain a competitive advantage in specific product markets. Thus, the firm forms a business-level cooperative strategy when it believes that combining its resources and capabilities with those of one or more partners will create competitive advantages that it can't create by itself and that will lead to success in a specific product market. There are four business-level cooperative strategies (see Figure 9.1).

Complementary Strategic Alliances

Complementary strategic alliances are business-level alliances in which firms share some of their resources and capabilities in complementary ways to develop competitive advantages.

Complementary strategic alliances are business-level alliances in which firms share some of their resources and capabilities in complementary ways to develop competitive advantages.[60] There are two types of complementary strategic alliances—vertical and horizontal (see Figure 9.1).

Vertical Complementary Strategic Alliance

In a *vertical complementary strategic alliance,* firms share their resources and capabilities from different stages of the value chain to create a competitive advantage (see Figure 9.2). McDonald's has formed vertical complementary alliances with major oil companies and independent store operators. With units located in these firms' storefronts, the customer can ". . . fill up (his or her) car, buy a meal, and pick up items for the home, with just one stop."[61] In another example, Boeing Company formed a vertical complementary alliance that included several partners to design and build the 777 plane, partly because of the project's scale and size. The partners, each of whom

Figure 9.1 Business-Level Cooperative Strategies

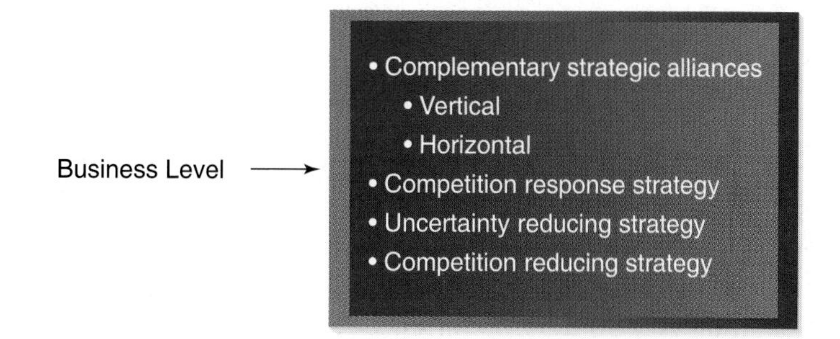

had superior resources and capabilities in a different part of the value chain, included United Airlines and five Japanese companies. According to an alliance partner, "The development of the 777 was the fastest and most efficient construction of a new commercial aircraft ever."[62]

Horizontal Complementary Alliance

A *horizontal complementary strategic alliance* is an alliance in which firms share some of their resources and capabilities from the same stage of the value chain to create a competitive advantage (see Figure 9.2). Commonly, firms use this type of alliance to focus on long-term product development and distribution opportunities.[63] Shin Caterpillar Mitsubishi Ltd. (SCM), for example, is a joint venture between Caterpillar Inc. and Mitsubishi Heavy Industries Ltd. that celebrates its 40th anniversary in 2003. These partners continue to share resources and capabilities to produce innovative products that neither firm could design and produce by itself. SCM is a leading supplier of earthmoving and construction equipment in Japan and also sells the products it produces on a global basis to other Caterpillar units.[64]

Two auto parts suppliers formed a horizontal complementary alliance to create a competitive advantage in terms of linking "bricks and clicks." CSK Auto Inc., which operates Checker Auto Parts, Shuck's Auto Supply, Kragen Auto Parts, and Advance Auto Parts, whose stores are called Advance Auto, joined forces to establish a separate company. Called PartsAmerica.com, the Web-based venture was launched in September 2000. The venture provides customers with easy access to nearly $1.5 billion in inventory and 3,000 locations in all 50 states. Customers can use either company's local stores to pick up and return parts ordered online.[65] The alliance's partners believe that sharing some of their resources and capabilities allows them to provide the "ultimate bricks and clicks" model in their industry.[66]

Competition Response Strategy

As discussed in Chapter 5, competitors initiate competitive actions to attack rivals and launch competitive responses to their competitors' actions. Strategic alliances can be used at the business level to respond to competitors' attacks. Because they can be

Figure 9.2 Vertical and Horizontal Complementary Strategic Alliances

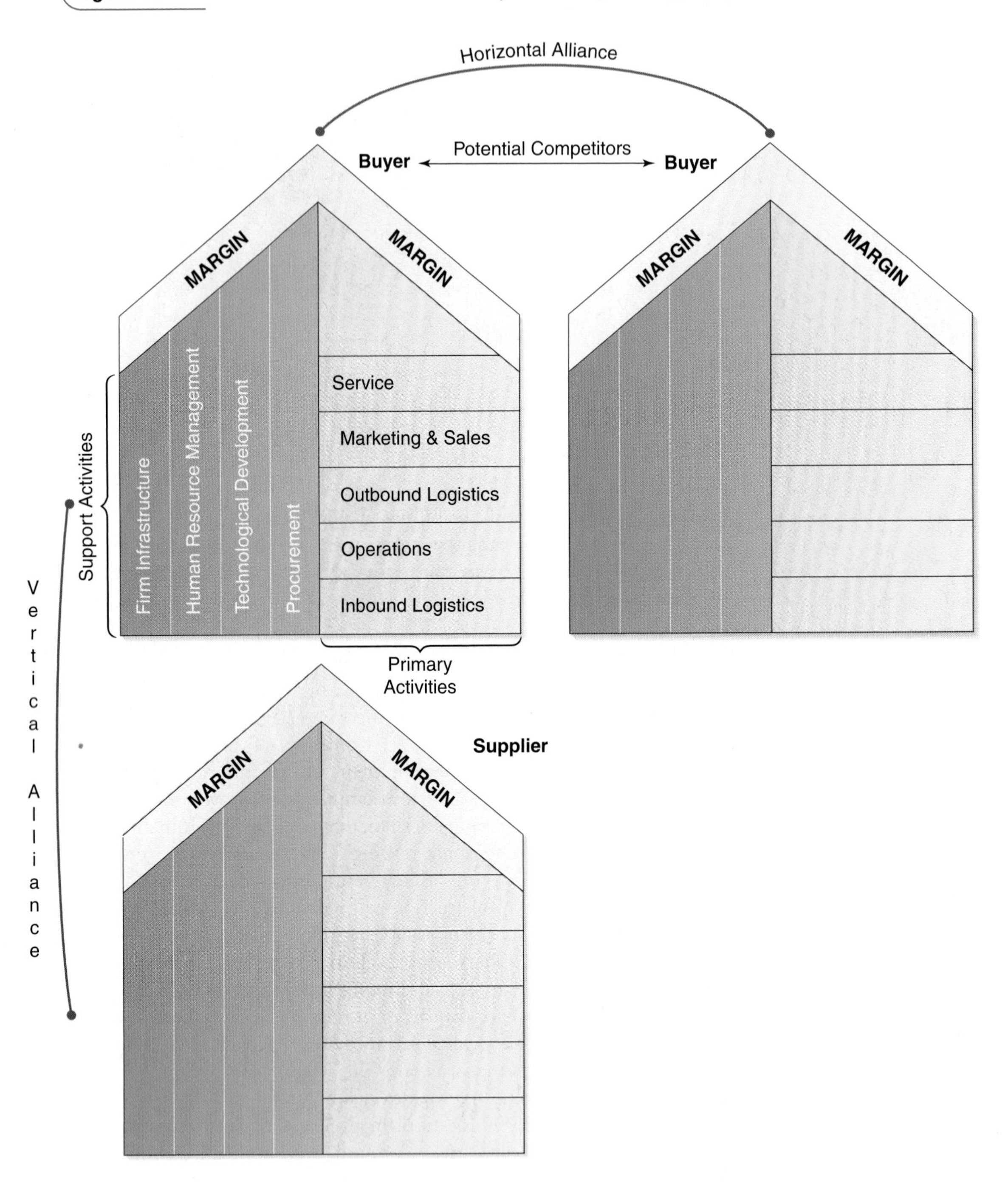

difficult to reverse and expensive to operate, strategic alliances are primarily formed to respond to strategic rather than tactical actions.

Recall from Chapter 5's Opening Case that UPS established its logistics business in 1994. Main rival FedEx responded to this strategic action by UPS when it too entered the logistics business. However, in 2002, UPS seemed to be outperforming its rival in this business area, at least as measured by sales growth. To improve its competitive position by responding to UPS, FedEx took several actions, including forming a strategic alliance with worldwide professional services firm KPMG. The alliance's intent is to deliver total, end-to-end supply-chain solutions to large and mid-sized companies. To reach this objective, the partners are combining some of their resources and capabilities to help firms improve their supply-chain planning and execution processes that connect suppliers and manufacturers with their end-customers. To form this alliance, FedEx committed what it believes are its industry-leading supply-chain-focused consulting, information-management systems, and transportation and logistics expertise. For its part, KPMG agreed to provide its supply-chain consulting and e-integration services.[67]

Strategic alliances are also sometimes used in the global oil industry to respond to competitors' actions, especially when those actions are strategic and were themselves products of strategic alliances. Recently, for example, Marathon Oil Co. (formerly a part of USX Corp.) completed a strategic alliance with Yukos, Russia's second largest oil company. The alliance was formed both to promote the two firms' international growth goals and as a response to the multitude of alliances formed by these companies' global competitors.[68] As a newly formed independent company, Marathon seeks to become recognized as a pacesetting firm in terms of sustainable growth for shareholders. According to company documents, unique cooperative partnerships such as the one with Yukos are critical to its efforts to reach this objective.[69]

COURTESY OF FUJITSU SIEMENS COMPUTERS

"Powering the Information Age" is Fujitsu Siemens Computers vision. The vision combines the strength and innovation of its parent companies, Fujitsu Limited and Siemens AG. Fujitsu Siemens offers business customers products from PDAs, notebooks, PCs, and workstations to servers, mainframes, and enterprise storage solutions, and is the top supplier of computers for home users in Europe.

Uncertainty Reducing Strategy

Particularly in fast-cycle markets, business-level strategic alliances are used to hedge against risk and uncertainty.[70] Global overcapacity and cost competition affected the capabilities of Siemens and Fujitsu to independently reach their objectives in the global PC market. To reduce the risk and uncertainty associated with their PC operations, the two firms formed a joint venture. Called Fujitsu Siemens Computers, this company was formally established on October 1, 1999. Evidence suggests that the formerly independent Fujitsu Computers (Europe) and Siemens Computer Systems are effectively sharing their technological resources and capabilities to create their joint venture. By uniquely combining what Fujitsu Siemens Computers believes is leading-edge technology from Fujitsu with manufacturing, marketing and logistics capabilities from Siemens, the joint venture has become Europe's top supplier of PCs for home users and small business firms.[71]

In other instances, firms form business-level strategic alliances to reduce the uncertainty associated with developing new product or technology standards. In the global automobile industry, for example, GM and Toyota formed a five-year R&D alliance that essentially makes the "no. 1 U.S. auto maker and the no. 1 Japanese auto maker partners in the competition to develop alternative-power green cars" for the 21st century. Through this alliance, the two firms expect to be able to set the industry standard for environmentally friendly vehicles.[72] At the same time, GM and Toyota joined Ford, DaimlerChrysler, and Renault SA in an alliance to develop an industrywide standard for accommodating communications and entertainment equipment being developed by automobile manufacturers.[73] Thus, the uncertainty and risk of the 21st-century landscape finds firms, such as those competing in the global automobile industry, forming multiple strategic alliances to increase their strategic competitiveness.

Competition Reducing Strategy

Collusive strategies are an often-illegal type of cooperative strategy, separate from strategic alliances, that are used to reduce competition. There are two types of collusive strategies—explicit collusion and tacit collusion.

Explicit collusion ". . . exists when firms directly negotiate production output and pricing agreements in order to reduce competition."[74] Explicit collusion strategies are illegal in the United States and most developed economies (except in regulated industries).

Firms that use explicit collusion strategies may face litigation and may be found guilty of non-competitive actions. In a 1995 price-fixing scandal, for example, three Archer Daniels Midland (ADM) executives were convicted and sentenced to jail terms for cooperating with competitors to fix prices on farm commodity products.[75] Similarly, prominent toy retailer Toys 'R' Us was found in violation of U.S. federal trade laws for colluding with toy manufacturers to not sell their popular toy lines to Toys 'R' Us's primary competitors, such as Costco and Sam's Club warehouse clubs.[76]

Tacit collusion exists when several firms in an industry indirectly coordinate their production and pricing decisions by observing each other's competitive actions and responses. Tacit collusion results in below fully competitive production output and prices that are above fully competitive levels. Unlike explicit collusion, firms engaging in tacit collusion do not directly negotiate output and pricing decisions.

Discussed in Chapter 6, *mutual forbearance* is a form of tacit collusion ". . . in which firms avoid competitive attacks against those rivals they meet in multiple markets."[77] Rivals learn a great deal about each other when engaging in multimarket competition, including how to deter the effects of their rival's competitive attacks and responses. Given what they know about each other as a competitor, firms choose not to engage in what could be destructive competitions in multiple product markets.

Tacit collusion tends to be used as a business-level competition reducing strategy in highly concentrated industries, such as breakfast cereals. Firms in these industries recognize that they are interdependent and that their competitive actions and responses significantly affect competitors' behavior toward them. Understanding this interdependence and carefully observing competitors because of it tend to lead to tacit collusion.

Four firms (Kellogg, General Mills, Post, and Quaker) recently accounted for 84 percent of sales volume in the ready-to-eat segment of the U.S. cereal market. Some believe that this high degree of concentration results in ". . . prices for branded cereals that are well above (the) costs of production."[78] Prices above the competitive level in this industry suggest the possibility that the dominant firms were using a tacit collusion cooperative strategy.

At a broad level in free-market economies, governments need to determine how rivals can collaborate to increase their competitiveness without violating established regulations.[79] Reaching this determination is challenging when evaluating collusive strategies, particularly tacit ones. For example, the European Commission recently initiated an investigation of "suspicious price fixing" by the world's largest music producers and a few large retailers. A Commission spokesperson said, "We're trying to assess whether companies are trying to keep prices higher. It's sufficiently important to consumers to justify an investigation."[80] For individual companies, the issue is to understand the effect of a competition reducing strategy on their performance and competitiveness.

Assessment of Business-Level Cooperative Strategies

Firms use business-level strategies to develop competitive advantages that can contribute to successful positioning and performance in individual product markets. For a competitive advantage to be developed by using an alliance, the particular set of resources and capabilities that is combined and shared in a particular manner through the alliance must be valuable, rare, imperfectly imitable, and nonsubstitutable (see Chapter 3).

Evidence suggests that complementary business-level strategic alliances, especially vertical ones, have the greatest probability of creating a sustainable competitive advantage.[81] Strategic alliances designed to respond to competition and to reduce uncertainty can also create competitive advantages. However, these advantages tend to be more temporary than those developed through complementary (both vertical and horizontal) strategic alliances. The primary reason is that complementary alliances have a stronger focus on the creation of value compared to competition reducing and uncertainty reducing alliances, which tend to be formed to respond to competitors' actions rather than to attack competitors.

Of the four business-level cooperative strategies, the competition reducing strategy has the lowest probability of creating a sustainable competitive advantage. In the ready-to-eat breakfast cereal market, for example, annual household purchases of ready-to-eat cereals declined roughly 1.5 pounds between 1993 and 1997.[82] Even if the four largest cereal makers did use tacit collusion as a competition reducing strategy, the results likely failed to meet their performance expectations. The company using competition reducing business-level strategic alliances should carefully monitor them as to the degree to which they are facilitating the firm's efforts to develop and successfully use value-creating competitive advantages.

Corporate-Level Cooperative Strategy

A **corporate-level cooperative strategy** is used by the firm to help it diversify in terms of the products it offers or the markets it serves or both.

A **corporate-level cooperative strategy** is used by the firm to help it diversify in terms of the products it offers or the markets it serves or both. Diversifying alliances, synergistic alliances, and franchising are the most commonly used corporate-level cooperative strategies (see Figure 9.3).

Firms use diversifying alliances and synergistic alliances to grow and diversify their operations through a means other than a merger or acquisition.[83] When a firm seeks to diversify into markets in which the host nation's government prevents mergers and acquisitions, alliances become an especially appropriate option. Corporate-level strategic alliances are also attractive compared to mergers and particularly acquisitions, because they require fewer resource commitments[84] and permit greater flexibility in terms of efforts to diversify partners' operations.[85] An alliance can be used as well to determine if the partners might benefit from a future merger or acquisition

Figure 9.3 Corporate-Level Cooperative Strategies

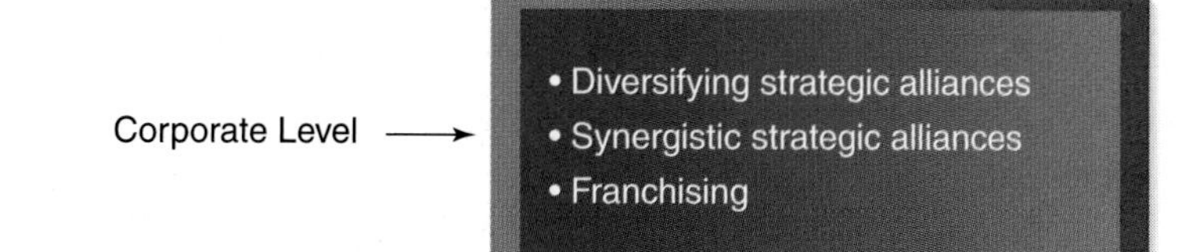

between them. This "testing" process often characterizes alliances completed to combine firms' unique technological resources and capabilities.[86]

The collaboration that Wal-Mart, Seiyu Ltd. (a Japanese retail chain), and Sumitomo Corporation (a Japanese trading company) recently formed is partly an attempt to determine if there is a compelling reason for the firms to become more closely aligned in the future. Initially, Wal-Mart took a 6.1 percent interest in Seiyu, with Sumitomo owning 15.6 percent of the company. The firms intend to work together to study and develop retail business opportunities in Japan. If the collaboration is successful, Wal-Mart has the option of increasing its stake in Seiyu across time to as much as 66.7 percent.[87]

Diversifying Strategic Alliance

A **diversifying strategic alliance** is a corporate-level cooperative strategy in which firms share some of their resources and capabilities to diversify into new product or market areas.

A **diversifying strategic alliance** is a corporate-level cooperative strategy in which firms share some of their resources and capabilities to diversify into new product or market areas. Boeing Company, for example, recently formed an alliance with the Insitu Group to develop a prototype for an unmanned aerial vehicle system to be called Scan Eagle. Insitu will incorporate Boeing's systems integration, communications technologies, and payload technologies into a version of its Seascan aircraft. Insitu is committed to designing and producing low-cost, long-endurance unmanned aerial vehicles—an earlier prototype of the Seascan flew 2,000 miles using 1.5 gallons of gasoline. Boeing's interest is gaining access to a product that can help it to further diversify into government and commercial markets. Involvement with some of Boeing's technological resources and capabilities is the benefit of this alliance for the Insitu Group.[88]

Synergistic Strategic Alliance

A **synergistic strategic alliance** is a corporate-level cooperative strategy in which firms share some of their resources and capabilities to create economies of scope.

A **synergistic strategic alliance** is a corporate-level cooperative strategy in which firms share some of their resources and capabilities to create economies of scope. Similar to the business-level horizontal complementary strategic alliance, synergistic strategic alliances create synergy across multiple functions or multiple businesses between partner firms.

Cisco Systems, Inc. has formed many synergistic strategic alliances in the pursuit of profitable growth. Its synergistic alliance with Hewlett-Packard (HP) is intended to provide an optimized computing environment for Internet commerce players, such as telecom service operators and enterprise users. Synergy is expected from this alliance as HP integrates its state-of-the-art telecommunications management solutions with Cisco's industry-leading networking solutions. Working together through this alliance, the two firms anticipate melding ". . . the worlds of computing and networking, data and voice, and Unix and Windows NT."[89]

In the financial services sector, Rabobank and DG Bank, the Dutch and German cooperative institutions, have formed a joint venture as a synergistic strategic alliance. Called DG-Rabo International, this equally owned venture combines the unique resources and capabilities of each bank in the corporate and investment-banking business areas. Viewed by some as "one of the most important cross-border partnerships yet seen in European banking," the organizations intend to further meld their skills to cooperate in other areas (e.g., asset management transactions) in the future.[90] Thus, this synergistic strategic alliance is different from a complementary business-level alliance in that it diversifies both banks into a new business, but in a synergistic way.

Franchising

Franchising is a corporate-level cooperative strategy in which a firm (the franchisor) uses a franchise as a contractual relationship to describe and control the sharing of its resources and capabilities with partners (the franchisees).

Franchising is a corporate-level cooperative strategy in which a firm (the franchisor) uses a franchise as a contractual relationship to describe and control the sharing of its resources and capabilities with partners (the franchisees).[91] A *franchise* is a "contractual agreement between two legally independent companies whereby the franchisor grants the right to the franchisee to sell the franchisor's product or do business under its trademarks in a given location for a specified period of time."[92]

Franchising is a popular strategy: companies using it account for $1 trillion in annual U.S. retail sales and compete in more than 75 industries. As the Cendant strategy outlined in Chapter 6 indicates, franchising can be used successfully across a number of businesses. Cendant has used franchising in real estate, for example, through its Century 21 and ERA brands. Already frequently used in developed nations, franchising is expected to account for significant portions of growth in emerging economies in the 21st century's first two decades.[93] As with diversifying and synergistic strategic alliances, franchising is an alternative to pursuing growth through mergers and acquisitions.

McDonald's, Hilton International, and Krispy Kreme are well-known examples of firms that use the franchising corporate-level cooperative strategy. Although franchising is its dominant corporate-level cooperative strategy, McDonald's also forms diversifying strategic alliances, such as its partnership with a Swiss firm to develop a Golden Arches Hotel.[94]

In the most successful franchising strategy, the partners (the franchiser and the franchisees) closely work together.[95] A primary responsibility of the franchisor is to develop programs to transfer to the franchisees the knowledge and skills that are needed to successfully compete at the local level.[96] In return, franchisees should provide feedback to the franchisor regarding how their units could become more effective and efficient.[97] Working cooperatively, the franchisor and its franchisees find ways to strengthen the core company's brand name, which is often the most important competitive advantage for franchisees operating in their local markets.[98]

Franchising is a particularly attractive strategy to use in fragmented industries, such as retailing and commercial printing. In fragmented industries, a large number of small and medium-sized firms compete as rivals; however, no firm or small set of firms has a dominant share, making it possible for a company to gain a large market share by consolidating independent companies through contractual relationships.[99] Recently La Quinta Inns decided to use franchising as a corporate-level cooperative strategy in order to increase its market share. Even though the lodging industry isn't as fragmented as it once was, La Quinta's decision to franchise has been viewed favorably. As one analyst observed, "La Quinta is in a situation where they don't have the ability to invest a lot of capital for growth, so finding franchisees is a lower-risk strategy of trying to grow the brand."[100]

Assessment of Corporate-Level Cooperative Strategies

Costs are incurred with each type of cooperative strategy.[101] Compared to those at the business-level, corporate-level cooperative strategies commonly are broader in scope and more complex, making them relatively more costly. Those forming and using cooperative strategies, especially corporate-level ones, should be aware of alliance costs and carefully monitor them.

In spite of these costs, firms can create competitive advantages and value when they effectively form and use corporate-level cooperative strategies.[102] The likelihood of this being the case increases when successful alliance experiences are internalized.

In other words, those involved with forming and using corporate-level cooperative strategies can also use them to develop useful knowledge about how to succeed in the future. To gain maximum value from this knowledge, firms should organize it and verify that it is always properly distributed to those involved with the formation and use of alliances.[103]

We explain in Chapter 6 that firms answer two questions to form a corporate-level strategy—the businesses in which the diversified firm will compete and how those businesses will be managed. These questions are also answered as firms form corporate-level cooperative strategies. Thus, firms able to develop corporate-level cooperative strategies and manage them in ways that are valuable, rare, imperfectly imitable and nonsubstitutable (see Chapter 3) develop a competitive advantage that is in addition to advantages gained through the activities of individual cooperative strategies. Later in the chapter, we further describe alliance management as a source of competitive advantage.

A **cross-border strategic alliance** is an international cooperative strategy in which firms with headquarters in different nations combine some of their resources and capabilities to create a competitive advantage.

International Cooperative Strategy

A **cross-border strategic alliance** is an international cooperative strategy in which firms with headquarters in different nations combine some of their resources and capabilities to create a competitive advantage. Taking place in virtually all industries, the number of cross-border alliances being completed continues to increase,[104] in some cases at the expense of mergers and acquisitions.[105] This type of cooperative strategy is critical to Citigroup's positions in global markets: "If it wasn't for cross-border alliances with entities like the Japanese postal system, which gave the bank entry into the otherwise locked-up consumer banking market, Citi wouldn't be a highly regarded local operator with 100 million customers in 100 countries."[106]

There are several reasons for the increasing use of cross-border strategic alliances. In general, multinational corporations outperform firms operating on only a domestic basis,[107] so a firm may form cross-border strategic alliances to leverage core competencies that are the foundation of its domestic success to expand into international markets.[108] At Coca-Cola, efforts are underway to cut across the firm's geographic units to identify opportunities to leverage existing brands and competitive advantages. One result from these efforts was the decision to expand the firm's alliance with Nestlé. Called Beverage Partners Worldwide, this cross-border strategic alliance will add herbal beverages to its product line, which already includes Nestea and Nescafé, and will expand into additional global markets.[109]

Pictured here is Sony's nine-floor showroom in downtown Tokyo. Sony provides entertainment and electronic products and services to consumers around the world through its partnerships. Its major products are cutting-edge technology in audio components and systems, video equipment, televisions, information and communications products (including computer products), and other electronic components. Its principal US businesses include Sony Electronics Inc., Sony Pictures Entertainment, Sony Music Entertainment Inc., and Sony Computer Entertainment of America.

ASSOCIATED PRESS/TSUGUFUMI MATSUMOTO

Limited domestic growth opportunities is another reason firms use cross-border alliances. Diversified and globally oriented Sony Corporation, for example, has long relied on cross-border alliances (more than 100) to pursue growth objectives greater than its home market can support. One of the firm's recent alliances is with Ericsson to make cell phones.[110] In a different industry, General Mills formed Cereal Partners Worldwide with Nestlé partly in response to stagnating growth in General Mills' core breakfast cereal market in the United States. This joint venture (much like Coca-Cola and Nestlé's alliance) combines General Mills' cereal expertise with ". . . Nestlé's brand recognition and distribution throughout Europe."[111]

Another reason for forming cross-border alliances is government economic policies. As discussed in Chapter 8, local ownership is an important national policy objective in some nations. In India, for example, governmental policies reflect a strong preference to license local companies. Only recently did the South Korean government increase the ceiling on foreign investment in South Korean firms.[112] Thus, in some countries, the full range of entry mode choices that we describe in Chapter 8 may not be available to firms wishing to internationally diversify. Indeed, investment by foreign firms in these instances may be allowed only through a partnership with a local firm, such as in a cross-border alliance. A cross-border strategic alliance can also be helpful to foreign partners from an operational perspective, because the local partner has significantly more information about factors contributing to competitive success such as local markets, sources of capital, legal procedures, and politics.[113]

Firms also use cross-border alliances to help transform themselves or to better use their competitive advantages to take advantage of opportunities surfacing in the rapidly changing global economy. For example, GEC, a U.K.-based company, seeks to move from "a broadly focused group deriving much of its revenues from the defence budget to a full range telecommunications and information systems manufacturer." The uncertainty characterizing many nations' defense budgets is influencing GEC's decision to develop cross-border alliances such as the one it formed with NEC, the Japanese electronics giant. The alliance has both a commercial and technological focus—NEC distributes GEC products through its extensive marketing channels and the two companies collaborate in their R&D efforts to develop new technologies.[114]

In general, cross-border alliances are more complex and risky than domestic strategic alliances. However, the fact that firms competing internationally tend to outperform domestic-only competitors suggests the importance of learning how to diversify into international markets. Compared to mergers and acquisitions, cross-border alliances may be a better way to learn this process, especially in the early stages of the firms' geographic diversification efforts. Careful and thorough study of a proposed cross-border alliance contributes to success[115] as do precise specifications of each partner's alliance role.[116] These points are explored later in our discussion of how to best manage alliances.

Network Cooperative Strategy

Increasingly, firms are involved with more than one cooperative strategy. Procter & Gamble (P&G), for instance, has formed over 120 strategic alliances. In a recent year, P&G ". . . teamed with Dana Undies to make Pampers cotton underwear, with Magla to make Mr. Clean disposable gloves and mops, and with GM to distribute its Tempo car clean-up towels" and agreed to partner with Whirlpool to develop a new "clothes refresher" product and appliance.[117]

A **network cooperative strategy** is a cooperative strategy wherein several firms agree to form multiple partnerships to achieve shared objectives.

In addition to forming their own alliances with individual companies, a growing number of firms are joining forces in multiple cooperative strategies. A **network cooperative strategy** is a cooperative strategy wherein several firms agree to form multiple partnerships to achieve shared objectives.

A network cooperative strategy is particularly effective when it is formed by firms clustered together,[118] as with Silicon Valley in California and Singapore's Silicon Island.[119] Effective social relationships and interactions among partners while sharing their resources and capabilities make it more likely that a network cooperative strategy will be successful,[120] as does having a productive *strategic center firm* (discussed further in Chapter 11). As explained in the Strategic Focus on page 292, Johnson Controls is a strategic center firm in its network cooperative strategy that the firm calls "Peer Partnering."[121]

From a financial perspective, Johnson Controls has been successful. Fiscal year 2001 was the firm's ". . . 55th consecutive year of sales increases and the 26th year of increased dividends. It was also the 11th consecutive year of increased income. (And), dividends have been paid consecutively since 1887."[122] The early evidence suggests that as a network cooperative strategy, Peer Partnering will be an increasingly important contributor to the 21st-century success of Johnson Controls. It is likely that the network resulting from the Peer Partnering strategy will grow as initial members identify other capabilities that the network needs.

Strategic Focus

Integrating Partners' Resources and Capabilities through a Network Cooperative Strategy

By emphasizing innovation to produce products and provide service exceeding customers' expectations, Johnson Controls, Inc. (JCI) has become a leading manufacturer of automotive interior systems, automotive batteries, and automated building control systems. A wide range of cooperative strategies has served as the engine of its growth. In its brand partnerships with LEGO InMotion, for example, it designs, develops, and engineers new co-branded products for vehicle interiors, offering 50 new LEGO-related features targeting active families. In its Packmate partnership with Jansport, JCI integrates a variety of Jansport luggage packs into the rear of fold-flat seats.

Given its success with other cooperative strategies such as co-branding and its belief in the value that can be achieved through collaboration, JCI established Peer Partnering—a network cooperative strategy—in 2000. JCI and its partners in the program (Gentex Corporation, Jabil Circuit, Inc., Microchip Technology, Inc. Royal Philips Electronics, SAGEM, Tokai Rika, and Yazaki North America) view vehicle interiors as an important source of differentiation for auto manufacturers and work with each other to develop and use advanced electronics as the foundation for innovative products to integrate into vehicle interiors. A JCI spokesperson says that through the Peer Partnering strategy, ". . . we deliver vehicle-integrated electronics that surprise and delight customers, and enable automakers to differentiate their products. This strategy, which accelerates the development process, increases innovation and reduces costs, is a winning one for our customers, our partners and for us as well." BMW, DaimlerChrysler, Ford, General Motors, Honda, Mazda, Mitsubishi, Nissan, Renault, Rover, Toyota, and Volkswagen are customers for JCI's automotive systems group (interiors and batteries) and also buy the products produced through the network cooperative strategy.

Headquartered in several nations (for example, SAGEM in France, Tokai Rika in Japan), the Peer Partnering members share some of their resources and capabilities. As the strategic center firm, JCI manages the relationships among all partners and holds each accountable in terms of the commitments it made to the network strategy and verifies that each firm benefits from its participation in the collaborative effort. The core contributions to the network are JCI's innovation and integration capabilities and its partners' capabilities in advanced, electronic-based technologies. The partners work through different combinations of their resources and capabilities with the shared objective of producing value-creating products for auto and truck interiors. A digital compass, upgraded audio equipment, and interior switches with optimized user interface capabilities are some of the first products from the Peer Partnering network.

The Peer Partnering network can also benefit as its members participate in other cooperative strategies. Tokai Rika, for example, has a strategic alliance with Toyoda Gosei to collaborate on the development, manufacture, and sale of automotive safety systems (such as air bags and seat belts) and components. Some of the skills Tokai Rika forms through this relationship may enhance the value of its contributions to the Peer Partnering network.

COURTESY JOHNSON CONTROLS

LEGO InMotion is a concept vehicle interior created by an exclusive partnership of LEGO Company & Johnson Controls, a supplier of automotive interior systems. The sports utility vehicle (SUV), designed for families, features luxurious front seat materials and bold colors and materials for the back seats, including Johnson Controls' removable AutoVision® video entertainment system DVD player with the LEGO Go Pad (a portable, hand-held digital device), and a LEGO digital camera.

SOURCES: 2002, Johnson Controls–Corporate Home, Recognition, http://www.johnsoncontrols.com, March 10; 2002, Johnson Controls, Corporate profile, http://www.johnsoncontrols.com, March 10; 2002, Johnson Controls, Johnson Controls partners with MatrixOne, http://www.johnsoncontrols.com, March 10; 2002, Johnson Controls, Peer partners, http://www.johnsoncontrols.com, March 10; 2002, Johnson Controls, *Standard & Poor's Stock Report,* http://www.fidelity.com, March 2; B. Berentson, 2001, Johnson Controls, *Forbes Best of the Web,* May 21, 70.

Alliance Network Types

An important advantage of a network cooperative strategy is that firms gain access "to their partners' partners."[123] As discussed in the Strategic Focus on page 292, JCI has access to other relationships with which Gentex, Jabil, Microchip, Philips, and Tokai Rika are involved, and those firms have access to JCI's other collaborative relationships. Having access to multiple collaborations increases the likelihood that additional competitive advantages will be formed as the set of resources and capabilities being shared expands. In turn, increases in competitive advantages further stimulate the development of product innovations that are so critical to strategic competitiveness in the global economy.[124]

The set of partnerships, such as strategic alliances, that result from the use of a network cooperative strategy is commonly called an *alliance network*. The alliance networks that companies develop vary by industry conditions. A *stable alliance network* is formed in mature industries where demand is relatively constant and predictable. Through a stable alliance network, firms try to extend their competitive advantages to other settings while continuing to profit from operations in their core, relatively mature industry. Thus, stable networks are built for *exploitation* of the economies (scale and/or scope) available between firms.[125] *Dynamic alliance networks* are used in industries characterized by frequent product innovations and short product life cycles. Believing that "no single company can hope to anticipate and fulfill all the challenges that are emerging today," Intel is involved with a number of e-business alliances in partnership with several firms, including BEA, Microsoft, i2, and BroadVision. This dynamic alliance network has been created to ". . . craft a new breed of computing solutions—open, flexible, scalable solutions that offer enterprise-grade reliability and outstanding value."[126] Thus, dynamic alliance networks are primarily used to stimulate rapid, value-creating product innovations and subsequent successful market entries, demonstrating that their purpose is often *exploration* of new ideas.[127]

Competitive Risks with Cooperative Strategies

Stated simply, many cooperative strategies fail.[128] In fact, evidence shows that two-thirds of cooperative strategies have serious problems in their first two years and that as many as 70 percent of them fail.[129] This failure rate suggests that even when the partnership has potential complementarities and synergies, alliance success is elusive.[130] We describe failed alliances in the Strategic Focus on page 294.

Although failure is undesirable, it can be a valuable learning experience. Companies willing to carefully study a cooperative strategy's failure may gain insights that can be used to successfully develop and use future cooperative strategies. Thus, companies should work equally hard to avoid cooperative strategy failure and to learn from failure if it were to occur.

As suggested in the Strategic Focus on page 294, the firm takes risk when it uses one or more cooperative strategies. Prominent cooperative strategy risks are shown in Figure 9.4.

One cooperative strategy risk is that a partner may act opportunistically. Opportunistic behaviors surface either when formal contracts fail to prevent them or when an alliance is based on a false perception of partner trustworthiness. Not infrequently, the opportunistic firm wants to acquire as much of its partner's tacit knowledge as it can.[131] Full awareness of what a partner wants in a cooperative strategy reduces the likelihood that a firm will suffer from another's opportunistic actions.[132]

Some cooperative strategies fail when it is discovered that a firm has misrepresented the competencies it can bring to the partnership. This risk is more common when the partner's contribution is grounded in some of its intangible assets. Superior

Strategic Focus

All Cooperative Strategies Aren't Made in Heaven

Firms are relying more and more on cooperative strategies as a means of achieving strategic competitiveness. To increase the probability of success, IBM is one of the growing number of firms assigning responsibility to oversee the development and use of cooperative strategies to a senior-level executive. However, in spite of all their good efforts, a number of firms find that their cooperative strategies fail. Announced with great fanfare, the Global One joint venture formed by Deutsche Telekom, Sprint, and France Telecom in 1996 is an example of a failed cooperative strategy. A senior-level executive set high expectations for this venture when he suggested that, "Global One (was) organized to respond to the customer, the technology and the marketplace (and) that no one else in the world (was) offering this unique level of service." Three years later, the partnership had ended and the venture is now run by France Telecom.

The joint venture's three-year history was filled with disagreements about many issues, including who would manage Global One's different divisions, who were its target customers, and where its headquarters should be located. Cultural differences were another issue. For example, during ". . . meetings the French would be on one side of the room, the Germans on the other. . . . ." However, cultural distinctions are to be expected when forming cooperative strategies. The most effective partners anticipate cultural differences and prepare to deal with them before they surface. Critical to this preparation is making certain that partners know how to appropriately change some of their deep-seated traditions to respect their collaborators.

Although culture differences were an issue in Global One's failure, corporate governance and control was the primary cause of it. Instead of a jointly chosen team of managers and workers who would collaborate on a day-to-day basis to successfully operate the venture, Global One was run by a high-level board of chief executives with layers of committees below it. This bureaucratic structure negatively affected decision making, particularly in response to "out-of-the-ordinary" requests from customers. The venture's decision structure forced specific customer requests ". . . to filter through layers of executives at Global One and also through executives at each parent." This centralization of decision making prevented Global One from developing the flexibility needed to use rapidly changing technologies to satisfy customers' quickly changing needs and from determining who should be responsible for meeting those needs.

The list of factors behind cooperative strategy failure is long. For example, the complexity of its strategic plan contributed to Pandesic's failure. Formed between Intel and German software firm SAP, this venture lasted only three years. Some believe that too many people were responsible for executing Pandesic's strategic plan and that the plan was too complicated, especially with respect to the venture's intended market position. Additional flexibility to those operating the venture would have allowed greater focus on meeting customers' needs rather than on executing an eloquent but overly detailed strategic plan.

In other instances, partners develop a product for which a target market of sufficient size doesn't exist. For example, Motorola and Cisco formed the joint venture Spectrapoint Wireless to become a leader in fixed wireless: "a medium where phone calls, Internet pages and television signals are beamed to a rooftop dish and then transported through the building via wires." After only a year, the partners concluded that while customers were impressed with the venture's product, they weren't willing to pay the high price necessary to buy it. As a result, the venture that started with much anticipation in 1999 was called off in 2000.

SOURCES: K. Eisenhardt, 2002, Has strategy changed? *MIT Sloan Management Review,* 43(2): 88–91; C. Ghosn, 2002, Saving the business without losing the company, *Harvard Business Review,* 80(1): 37–45; N. Hutheesing, 2001, *Forbes Best of the Web,* May 21, 30–32; L. Khosla, 2001, You say tomato, *Forbes Best of the Web,* May 21, 36; J. W. Michaels, 2001, Don't buy, bond instead, *Forbes Best of the Web,* May 21, 20.

Figure 9.4 Managing Competitive Risks in Cooperative Strategies

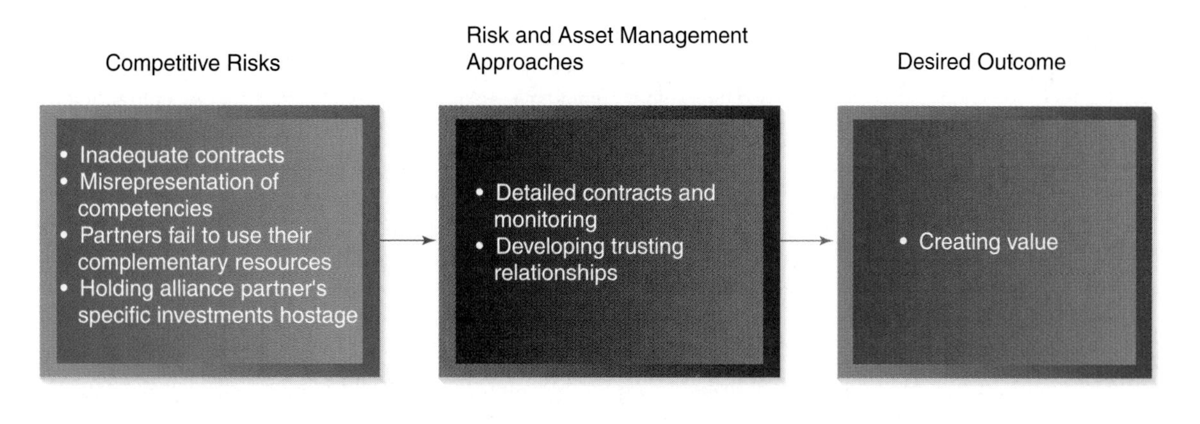

knowledge of local conditions is an example of an intangible asset that partners often fail to deliver. Asking the partner to provide evidence that it does possess the resources and capabilities (even when they are largely intangible) it is to share in the cooperative strategy may be an effective way to deal with this risk.

Another risk is that a firm won't actually make the resources and capabilities (such as its most sophisticated technologies) that it committed to the cooperative strategy available to its partners. This risk surfaces most commonly when firms form an international cooperative strategy.[133] In these instances, different cultures can result in different interpretations of contractual terms or trust-based expectations.

A final risk is that the firm may make investments that are specific to the alliance while its partner does not. For example, the firm might commit resources and capabilities to develop manufacturing equipment that can be used only to produce items coming from the alliance. If the partner isn't also making alliance-specific investments, the firm is at a relative disadvantage in terms of returns earned from the alliance compared to investments made to earn the returns.

Managing Cooperative Strategies

As our discussion has shown, cooperative strategies are an important option for firms competing in the global economy.[134] However, our study of cooperative strategies also shows that they are complex.[135]

Firms gain the most benefit from cooperative strategies when they are effectively managed. As discussed in the Strategic Focus on page 296, managing and flexibly adapting partnerships are crucial aspects of cooperative strategies.[136] The firm that learns how to manage cooperative strategies better than its competitors do may develop a competitive advantage in terms of this activity.[137] This is possible because the ability to effectively manage cooperative strategies is unevenly distributed across organizations.

In general, assigning managerial responsibility for a firm's cooperative strategies to a high-level executive or to a team improves the likelihood that the strategies will be well managed. IBM (see the following Strategic Focus), Johnson Controls, Coca-Cola, and Siebel Systems are four companies that have made such assignments. United Airlines has established an alliance division to monitor and create new partnerships and to manage the more than 100 cooperative strategies with which it is currently involved.[138]

Those responsible for managing the firm's set of cooperative strategies coordinate activities, categorize knowledge learned from previous experiences, and make

Strategic Focus

Managing Cooperative Strategies to Gain a Competitive Advantage

To date, effective alliance management skills seem to be in relatively short supply—few firms have developed a competitive advantage through the management of their cooperative strategies. A key reason is the need for the firm to simultaneously learn from its alliance partners while preventing its partners from learning too much from it. Another way of saying this is that as a partner, a company must develop the skills needed to manage the balance "... between trying to learn and trying to protect" its knowledge and sources of competitive advantages from excessive learning by partners. Finding ways to achieve this balance—a balance that is critical to developing a competitive advantage in terms of the management of cooperative strategies—seems to be difficult for most firms.

Global companies commonly compete against those with whom they are also collaborating. Toyota and General Motors, and Dell and IBM, are examples of companies that are both collaborators and competitors. While sharing some of their resources and capabilities in a partnership, firms exchange knowledge that may be related to a host of issues, including their technological skills, future plans, logistic systems, and hiring and training practices among many others. Part of the successful management of cooperative strategies is to follow procedures preventing partners from being disadvantaged in future competitions as a result of the resources, capabilities, and knowledge they share to use their cooperative strategy.

In spite of the difficulty, research findings and company experiences yield suggestions about knowledge protection and effective management of cooperative strategies. For example, assigning the responsibility to manage the firm's cooperative strategies to a group of people that reports to a senior-level official is vital. The charge to such a group is broad and should include responsibility to "... coordinate all alliance-related activity within the organization and (to institutionalize) processes and systems to teach, share, and leverage prior alliance-management experience and know-how throughout the company."

To manage its 70-plus cooperative strategies, IBM formed a strategic alliance team. Headed by an upper-level executive, the team handles all of IBM's collaborative ventures to create what it calls an alliance culture within the existing organizational structure. In the desired alliance culture, all parts of the company seek partners who could benefit from using IBM's marketing, sales, and solutions resources while leading with IBM's middleware, server platforms, and services to develop successful new market entries as outputs from each collaboration.

An important part of executing the broad charge given to teams (such as IBM's) that are expected to successfully manage their firm's cooperative strategies is their clear and detailed specification of the benefits of current cooperative strategies as well as those expected from the integration of new ones into the current set. Simultaneously, the team should closely work with all partners to specify the resources and capabilities that will be shared during the partnership and those that will not be shared. Part of this discussion must focus on knowledge that is to remain within the confines of the cooperative strategy, not leaking to other sections of the partner's organization. Collaborations based on trust have a higher probability of being successful in this effort.

SOURCES: R. D. Ireland, M. A. Hitt, & D. Vaidyanath, 2002, Alliance management as a source of competitive advantage, *Journal of Management*, in press; J. H. Dyer, P. Kale, & H. Singh, 2001, How to make strategic alliances work, *MIT Sloan Management Review*, 42(4): 37–43; A. C. Inkpen, 2001, Strategic alliances, in M. A. Hitt, R. E. Freeman, & J. S. Harrison (eds.), *Handbook of Strategic Management*, Oxford, U.K.: Blackwell Publishers, 409–432; 2001, IBM, IDC names IBM's strategic alliance program as a best practice in concept and implementation, http://www.ibm.com, December 1; D. Ernst & T. Halvey, 2000, When to think alliance, *McKinsey Quarterly*, 4, 46–55; P. Kale, H. Singh, & H. Perlmutter, 2000, Learning and protection of proprietary assets in strategic alliances: Building relational capital, *Strategic Management Journal*, 21: 217–237.

certain that what the firm knows about how to effectively form and use cooperative strategies is in the hands of the right people at the right time. Firms use one of two primary approaches to manage cooperative strategies—cost minimization and opportunity maximization[139] (see Figure 9.4). This is the case whether the firm has formed a separate cooperative strategy management function or not.

In the *cost minimization* management approach, the firm develops formal contracts with its partners. These contracts specify how the cooperative strategy is to be monitored and how partner behavior is to be controlled. The goal of this approach is to minimize the cooperative strategy's cost and to prevent opportunistic behavior by a partner. The focus of the second managerial approach—*opportunity maximization*—is on maximizing a partnership's value-creation opportunities. In this case, partners are prepared to take advantage of unexpected opportunities to learn from each other and to explore additional marketplace possibilities.[140] Less formal contracts, with fewer constraints on partners' behaviors, make it possible for partners to explore how their resources and capabilities can be shared in multiple value-creating ways.

Firms can successfully use either approach to manage cooperative strategies. However, the costs to monitor the cooperative strategy are greater with cost minimization, in that writing detailed contracts and using extensive monitoring mechanisms is expensive, even though the approach is intended to reduce alliance costs. Although monitoring systems may prevent partners from acting in their own best interests, they also preclude positive responses to those situations where opportunities to use the alliance's competitive advantages surface unexpectedly. Thus, formal contracts and extensive monitoring systems tend to stifle partners' efforts to gain maximum value from their participation in a cooperative strategy and require significant resources to put into place and use.

The relative lack of detail and formality that is a part of the contract developed by firms using the second management approach of opportunity maximization means that firms need to trust each other to act in the partnership's best interests. A psychological state, *trust* is a willingness to be vulnerable because of the expectations of positive behavior from the firm's alliance partner.[141] When partners trust each other, there is less need to write detailed formal contracts to specify each firm's alliance behaviors[142] and the cooperative relationship tends to be more stable.[143] On a relative basis, trust tends to be more difficult to establish in international cooperative strategies compared to domestic ones. Differences in trade policies, cultures, laws, and politics that are part of cross-border alliances account for the increased difficulty. When trust exists, partners' monitoring costs are reduced and opportunities to create value are maximized.

Research showing that trust between partners increases the likelihood of alliance success[144] seems to highlight the benefits of the opportunity maximization approach to managing cooperative strategies. Trust may also be the most efficient way to influence and control alliance partners' behaviors.[145] Research indicates that trust can be a capability that is valuable, rare, imperfectly imitable, and often nonsubstitutable.[146] Thus, firms known to be trustworthy can have a competitive advantage in terms of how they develop and use cooperative strategies. One reason is that it is impossible to specify all operational details of a cooperative strategy in a formal contract. Confidence that its partner can be trusted reduces the firm's concern about the inability to contractually control all alliance details.

Summary

- A cooperative strategy is one in which firms work together to achieve a shared objective. Strategic alliances, which are cooperative strategies in which firms combine some of their resources and capabilities to create a competitive advantage, are the primary form of cooperative strategies. Joint ventures (where firms create and own equal shares of a new venture that is intended to develop competitive advantages), equity strategic alliances (where firms own different shares of a newly created venture), and nonequity strategic alliances (where firms cooperate through a contractual relationship) are the three basic types of strategic alliances. Outsourcing, discussed in Chapter 3, commonly occurs as firms form nonequity strategic alliances.
- Collusive strategies are the second type of cooperative strategies (with strategic alliances being the other). In many economies and certainly developed ones, explicit collusive strategies are illegal unless sanctioned by government policies. With increasing globalization, fewer government-sanctioned situations of explicit collusion exist. Tacit collusion, also called mutual forbearance, is a cooperative strategy through which firms tacitly cooperate to reduce industry output below the potential competitive output level, thereby raising prices above the competitive level.
- Reasons firms use cooperative strategies vary by slow-cycle, fast-cycle, and standard-cycle market conditions. To enter restricted markets (slow-cycle), to move quickly from one competitive advantage to another (fast-cycle), and to gain market power (standard-cycle) demonstrate the differences among reasons by market type for use of cooperative strategies.
- There are four business-level cooperative strategies (a business-level cooperative strategy is used to help the firm improve its performance in individual product markets). Through vertical and horizontal complementary alliances companies combine their resources and capabilities to create value in different parts (vertical) or the same parts (horizontal) of the value chain. Competition responding strategies are formed to respond to competitors' actions, especially strategic ones. Competition reducing strategies are used to avoid excessive competition while the firm marshals its resources and capabilities to improve its competitiveness. Uncertainty reducing strategies are used to hedge against the risks created by the conditions of uncertain competitive environments. Complementary alliances have the highest probability of yielding a sustainable competitive advantage; competition reducing have the lowest probability of doing so.
- Corporate-level cooperative strategies are used when the firm wants to pursue product and/or geographic diversification. Through diversifying strategic alliances, firms agree to share some of their resources and capabilities to enter new markets or produce new products. Synergistic alliances are ones where firms share resources and capabilities to develop economies of scope. This alliance is similar to the business-level horizontal complementary alliance in which firms try to develop operational synergy whereas synergistic alliances are used to develop synergy at the corporate level. Franchising is a corporate-level cooperative strategy where the franchisor uses a franchise as a contractual relationship to describe the sharing of its resources and capabilities with franchisees.
- As an international cooperative strategy, cross-border alliances are used for several reasons, including the performance superiority of firms competing in markets outside their domestic market and governmental restrictions on growth through mergers and acquisitions. Cross-border alliances tend to be riskier than their domestic counterparts, particularly when partners aren't fully aware of each other's purpose for participating in the partnership.
- A network cooperative strategy is one wherein several firms agree to form multiple partnerships to achieve shared objectives. One of the primary benefits of a network cooperative strategy is the firm's opportunity to gain access "to its partner's other partnerships." When this happens, the probability greatly increases that partners will find unique ways to uniquely share their resources and capabilities to form competitive advantages. Network cooperative strategies are used to form either a stable alliance network or a dynamic alliance network. Used in mature industries, partners use stable networks to extend competitive advantages into new areas. In rapidly changing environments where frequent product innovations occur, dynamic networks are primarily used as a tool of innovation.
- Cooperative strategies aren't risk free. If a contract is not developed appropriately, or if a partner misrepresents its competencies or fails to make them available, failure is likely. Furthermore, a firm may be held hostage through asset-specific investments made in conjunction with a partner, which may be exploited.
- Trust is an increasingly important aspect of successful cooperative strategies. Firms recognize the value of partnering with companies known for their trustworthiness. When trust exists, a cooperative strategy is managed to maximize the pursuit of opportunities between partners. Without trust, formal contracts and extensive monitoring systems are used to manage cooperative strategies. In this case, the interest is to minimize costs rather than to maximize opportunities by participating in a cooperative strategy.

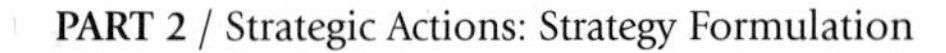

Review Questions

1. What is the definition of cooperative strategy and why is this strategy important to firms competing in the 21st-century competitive landscape?
2. What is a strategic alliance? What are the three types of strategic alliances firms use to develop a competitive advantage?
3. What are the four business-level cooperative strategies and what are the differences among them?
4. What are the three corporate-level cooperative strategies? How do firms use each one to create a competitive advantage?
5. Why do firms use cross-border strategic alliances?
6. What risks are firms likely to experience as they use cooperative strategies?
7. What are the differences between the cost-minimization approach and the opportunity-maximization approach to managing cooperative strategies?

Experiential Exercise

Cooperative Strategy Risk

Your firm manufactures fasteners for industrial applications. As the senior vice president of sales, you have developed several long-term relationships with your customers. Your main competitor has recently approached you about establishing a strategic alliance with your firm.

1. Because you are not sure if this alliance would be beneficial to your firm, you decide to bring the proposal to your firm's executive committee for a preliminary discussion. You anticipate that the committee will ask several basic questions. What information should you be able to provide?
2. After several weeks of investigating the value of an alliance, your firm decides that it would be financially beneficial, but the executive committee now wants you to present the risks that an alliance might entail and how you would suggest minimizing them. What risks do you foresee? How can they be prevented?
3. Before a contract between your firm and your competitor can be signed, you begin negotiations with one of your competitor's largest customers to provide new products based on a new technology your firm has developed. In your opinion, does the alliance raise legal or ethical issues that your firm should consider before proceeding with your negotations?

Notes

1. K. M. Eisenhardt, 2002, Has strategy changed? *MIT Sloan Management Review,* 43(2): 88–91; T. B. Lawrence, C. Hardy, & N. Phillips, 2002, Institutional effects of interorganizational collaborations: The emergence of proto-institutions, *Academy of Management Journal,* 45: 281–290.
2. J. B. Barney, 2002, *Gaining and Sustaining Competitive Advantage,* 2nd ed., Upper Saddle River, NJ: Prentice-Hall, 339.
3. W. S. Desarbo, K. Jedidi, & I. Sinha, 2001, Customer value in a heterogeneous market, *Strategic Management Journal,* 22: 845–857.
4. C. Young-Ybarra & M. Wiersema, 1999, Strategic flexibility in information technology alliances: The influence of transaction cost economics and social exchange theory, *Organization Science,* 10: 439–459; M. E. Porter & M. B. Fuller, 1986, Coalitions and global strategy, in M. E. Porter (ed.), *Competition in Global Industries,* Boston: Harvard Business School Press, 315–344.
5. M. Schifrin, 2001, Partner or perish, *Forbes Best of the Web,* May 21, 26–28.
6. J. Bowser, 2001, Strategic co-opetition: The value of relationships in the networked economy, *IBM Business Strategy Consulting,* http://www.ibm.com, March 12.
7. M. A. Hitt, R. D. Ireland, S. M. Camp, & D. L. Sexton, 2002, Strategic entrepreneurship: Integrating entrepreneurial and strategic management perspectives, in M. A. Hitt, R. D. Ireland, S. M. Camp, & D. L. Sexton (eds.), *Strategic Entrepreneurship: Creating a New Mindset,* Oxford, U.K.: Blackwell Publishers, 8.
8. J. R. Harbison & P. Pekar, Jr., 1998, Institutionalizing alliance skills: Secrets of repeatable success, *Strategy & Business,* 11: 79–94.
9. S. Ulfelder, 2001, Partners in profit, http://www.computerworld.com, July/August, 24–28.
10. Barney, *Gaining and Sustaining Competitive Advantage,* 339.
11. Y. L. Doz & G. Hamel, 1998, *Alliance Advantage: The Art of Creating Value through Partnering,* Boston: Harvard Business School Press, xiii.
12. R. D. Ireland, M. A. Hitt, & D. Vaidyanath, 2002, Alliance management as a source of competitive advantage, *Journal of Management,* in press; J. G. Coombs & D. J. Ketchen, 1999, Exploring interfirm cooperation and performance: Toward a reconciliation of predictions from the resource-based view and organizational economics, *Strategic Management Journal,* 20: 867–888.
13. P. Kale, H. Singh, & H. Perlmutter, 2000, Learning and protection of proprietary assets in strategic alliances: Building relational capital, *Strategic Management Journal,* 21: 217–237.
14. D. F. Kuratko, R. D. Ireland, & J. S. Hornsby, 2001, Improving firm performance through entrepreneurial actions: Acordia's corporate entrepreneurship strategy, *Academy of Management Executive,* 15(4): 60–71; D. Ernst & T. Halevy, 2000, When to think alliance, *The McKinsey Quarterly,* Number 4: 46–55.
15. 2002, Borrego blurs traditional lines, *Dallas Morning News,* February 24, M4.
16. 2002, Lockheed Martin, Responsive global partnerships, http:/www.lockheedmartin.com, March 17.
17. J. H. Tiessen & J. D. Linton, 2000, The JV dilemma: Cooperating and competing in joint ventures, *Revue Canadienne des Sciences de l'Administration,* 17(3): 203–216.
18. T. K. Das & B.-S. Teng, 2001, A risk perception model of alliance structuring, *Journal of International Management,* 7: 1–29; J. H. Dyer & H. Singh, 1998, The relational view: Cooperative strategy and sources of interorganizational competitive advantage, *Academy of Management Review,* 23: 660–679.
19. A. Afuah, 2002, Mapping technological capabilities into product markets and competitive advantage: The case of cholesterol drugs, *Strategic Management Journal,* 23: 171–179; A. Arino, 2001, To do or not to do? Noncooperative behavior by commission and omission in interfirm ventures, *Group & Organization Management,* 26(1): 4–23; C. Holliday, 2001, Sustainable growth, the DuPont Way, *Harvard Business Review,* 79(8): 129–134.
20. M. A. Geletkanycz & S. S. Black, 2001, Bound by the past? Experienced-based effects on commitment to the strategic status quo, *Journal of Management,* 27: 3–21.
21. S. L. Berman, J. Down, & C. W. L. Hill, 2002, Tacit knowledge as a source of competitive advantage in the National Basketball Association, *Academy of Management Journal,* 45: 13–31.
22. Tiessen & Linton, The JV dilemma, 206; P. E. Bierly, III & E. H. Kessler, 1999, The timing of strategic alliances, in M. A. Hitt, P. G. Clifford, R. D. Nixon, & K. P. Coyne (eds.), *Dynamic Strategic Resources: Development, Diffusion and Integration,* Chichester: John Wiley & Sons, 299–345.
23. 2001, Dow Jones Newswires and Bloomberg News Reports, Sprint, Virgin Group to create joint venture, *Dallas Morning News,* October 6, F3.
24. B. Orwall, 2001, Five Hollywood studios enter venture to offer feature films over Internet, *The Wall Street Journal,* http://www.wsj.com, August 17.
25. R. E. Hoskisson & L. W. Busenitz, 2002, Market uncertainty and learning distance in corporate entrepreneurship entry mode choice, in M. A. Hitt, R. D. Ireland, S. M. Camp, & D. L. Sexton (eds.), *Strategic Entrepreneurship: Creating a New Mindset,* Oxford, U.K.: Blackwell Publishers, 151–172.
26. A.-W. Harzing, 2002, Acquisitions versus Greenfield investments: International strategy and management of entry modes, *Strategic Management Journal,* 23: 211–227; S.-J. Chang & P. M. Rosenzweig, 2001, The choice of entry mode in sequential foreign direct investment, *Strategic Management Journal,* 22: 747–776; Y. Pan, 1997, The formation of Japanese and U.S. equity joint ventures in China, *Strategic Management Journal,* 18: 247–254.
27. 2002, Cott and J. D. Iroquois Enterprises Ltd. announce bottle water alliance, *Business Wire,* http://www.fidelity.com, February 26.
28. S. Das, P. K. Sen, & S. Sengupta, 1998, Impact of strategic alliances on firm valuation, *Academy of Management Journal,* 41: 27–41.
29. Bierly & Kessler, The timing of strategic alliances, 303.
30. Barney, *Gaining and Sustaining Competitive Advantage,* 339; T. B. Folta & K. D. Miller, 2002, Real options in equity partnerships, *Strategic Management Journal,* 23: 77–88.
31. J. McCullam, 2001, Polo Ralph Lauren, *Forbes Best of the Web,* May 21, 68.
32. A. C. Inkpen, 2001, Strategic alliances, in M. A. Hitt, R. E. Freeman, & J. S. Harrison (eds.), *Handbook of Strategic Management,* Oxford, U.K.: Blackwell Publishers, 409–432.
33. M. Delio, 1999, Strategic outsourcing, *Knowledge Management,* 2(7): 62–68.
34. 2002, Magna—Company information, http://www.magna.com, March 5.
35. J. J. Reuer, M. Zollo, & H. Singh, 2002, Post-formation dynamics in strategic alliances, *Strategic Management Journal,* 23: 135–151; P. Buxbaum, 2001, Making alliances work, *Computerworld,* 35(30): 30–31; Inkpen, Strategic alliances, 409.
36. D. Campbell, 2001, High-end strategic alliances as fundraising opportunities, *Nonprofit World,* 19(5): 8–12; M. D. Hutt, E. R. Stafford, B. A. Walker, & P. H. Reingen, 2000, Case study: Defining the social network of a strategic alliance, *Sloan Management Review,* 41(2): 51–62.
37. F. M. Lysiak, 2002, M&As create new competencies, *Best's Review,* 102(9): 32–33.
38. M. J. Kelly, J.-L. Schaan, & H. Jonacas, 2002, Managing alliance relationships: Key challenges in the early stages of collaboration, *R&D Management,* 32(1): 11–22.
39. A. C. Inkpen & J. Ross, 2001, Why do some strategic alliances persist beyond their useful life? *California Management Review,* 44(1): 132–148.
40. Schifrin, *Best of the Web,* 28.
41. Inkpen, Strategic alliances, 411.
42. L. Fuentelsaz, J. Gomez, & Y. Polo, 2002, Followers' entry timing: Evidence from the Spanish banking sector after deregulation, *Strategic Management Journal,* 23: 245–264.
43. K. R. Harrigan, 2001, Strategic flexibility in the old and new economies, in M. A. Hitt, R. E. Freeman, & J. S. Harrison (eds.), *Handbook of Strategic Management,* Oxford, U.K.: Blackwell Publishers, 97–123.
44. G. W. Dent, Jr., 2001, Gap fillers and fiduciary duties in strategic alliances, *The Business Lawyer,* 57(1): 55–104.
45. Ulfelder, Partners in profit, 24.
46. M. Gonzalez, 2001, Strategic alliances, *Ivey Business Journal,* 66(1): 47–51.
47. M. Johnson, 2001, Airlines rush for comfort alliances, *Global Finance,* 15(11): 119–120.
48. J. Child & D. Faulkner, 1998, *Strategies of Co-operation: Managing Alliances, Networks, and Joint Ventures,* New York: Oxford University Press.
49. J. R. Williams, 1998, *Renewable Advantage: Crafting Strategy Through Economic Time,* New York: The Free Press.
50. B. Nelson, Usinor Group, *Forbes Best of the Web,* May 21, 96.
51. V. Kumari, 2001, Joint ventures bolster credibility of new players in India, *National Underwriter,* 105(14): 46.
52. C. Hoag, 1999, Oil duo plan energy alliance, *Financial Times,* June 30, 17.
53. S. A. Zahra, R. D. Ireland, I. Gutierrez, & M. A. Hitt, 2000, Privatization and entrepreneurial transformation: Emerging issues and a future research agenda, *Academy of Management Review,* 25: 509–524.
54. Eisenhardt, Has strategy changed?, 88.

55. H. W. Chesbrough, 2002, Making sense of corporate venture capital, *Harvard Business Review,* 80(3): 90–99.
56. J. Strauss, 2001, Visa International: Creating the next generation of commerce, *Venture Capital Journal,* December 21, 40–41.
57. Ibid., 40.
58. B. Berentson, 2001, United Airlines, *Forbes Best of the Web,* May 21, 68.
59. 2002, Goodyear Tire—Press Releases, http://www.goodyear.com, March 5.
60. J. S. Harrison, M. A. Hitt, R. E. Hoskisson, & R. D. Ireland, 2001, Resource complementarity in business combinations: Extending the logic to organizational alliances, *Journal of Management,* 27: 679–699; S. H. Park & G. R. Ungson, 1997, The effect of national culture, organizational complementarity, and economic motivation on joint venture dissolution, *Academy of Management Journal,* 40: 297–307.
61. 2002, McDonald's, McDonald's USA—Oil Alliances, http://www.mcdonalds.com, March 6,
62. C. F. Freidheim, Jr., 1999, The trillion-dollar enterprise, *Strategy & Business,* 14: 60–66.
63. M. Kotabe & K. S. Swan, 1995, The role of strategic alliances in high technology new product development, *Strategic Management Journal,* 16: 621–636.
64. 2002, Caterpillar announces agreement with Mitsubishi Heavy Industries, http://www.caterpillar.com, March 5.
65. D. Clark, 2000, CSK, Advance Auto form firm to allow customers to purchase parts online, *The Wall Street Journal,* January 10, A8.
66. 2002, PartsAmerica.com Affiliate Program, http://www.partsamerica.com, March 6.
67. 2002, FedEx and KPMG join forces to deliver the next generation of global supply-chain services, http://www.fedex.com, March 7.
68. 2001, Marathon forms alliance with Russia's Yukos, *National Petroleum News,* 93(11): 10.
69. 2002, Marathon Oil Corporation outlines business strategy to security analysts, *PRNewswire,* http://www.prnewswire.com, February 28.
70. Hitt, Ireland, Camp, & Sexton, Strategic entrepreneurship, 9; R. G. McGrath, 1999, Falling forward: Real options reasoning and entrepreneurial failure, *Academy of Management Journal,* 22: 13–30.
71. 2002, Fujitsu Siemens Computers, Corporate profile,http://www. siemens.com, March 7.
72. J. Ball, 1999, To define future car, GM, Toyota say bigger is better, *The Wall Street Journal,* April 20, B4.
73. J. Ball, 1999, Five of the world's top auto makers agree to develop technology standard, *The Wall Street Journal,* April 28, B6.
74. Barney, *Gaining and Sustaining Competitive Advantage,* 339.
75. M. Freedman, 2000, Planting seeds, *Forbes,* February 7, 62–64.
76. J. M. Broder, 1997, Toys 'R' Us led price collusion, judge rules in upholding F.T.C. *The New York Times, http://*www.nytimes.com, October 1.
77. S. Jayachandran, J. Gimeno, & P. Rajan, 1999, Theory of multimarket competition: A synthesis and implications for marketing strategy, *Journal of Marketing,* 63(3): 49–66.
78. G. K. Price, 2000, Cereal sales soggy despite price cuts and reduced couponing, *Food Review,* 23(2): 21–28.
79. S. B. Garland & A. Reinhardt, 1999, Making antitrust fit high tech, *Business Week,* March 22, 34–36.
80. B. Mitchener & P. Shishkin, 2001, Price fixing by top five record companies, *The Wall Street Journal,* January 29, B1, B4.
81. G. Gari, 1999, Leveraging the rewards of strategic alliances, *Journal of Business Strategy,* 20(2): 40–43.
82. Price, Cereal sales soggy, 21.
83. Harrison, Hitt, Hoskisson, & Ireland, Resource complementarity, 684–685; S. Chaudhuri & B. Tabrizi, 1999, Capturing the real value in high-tech acquisitions, *Harvard Business Review,* 77(5): 123–130; J -F. Hennart & S. Reddy, 1997, The choice between mergers/acquisitions and joint ventures in the United States, *Strategic Management Journal,* 18: 1–12.
84. Inkpen, Strategic alliances, 413.
85. Young-Ybarra & Wiersema, Strategic flexibility, 439.
86. Folta & Miller, Real options, 77.
87. 2002, Wal-Mart Stores, Wal-Mart and Sumitomo agree to acquire strategic stake in Japan's Seiyu, http://www.walmart.com, March 16.
88. 2002, Boeing, Insitu to cooperatively develop unmanned vehicle prototype, Boeing News, http://www.boeing.com, March 8.
89. 2002, HP & Cisco, Cisco Strategic Alliances, http://www.cisco.com, March 8.
90. C. Harris & G. Cramb, 1999, Seeking wider co-operation, *Financial Times,* October 19, 20.
91. S. A. Shane, 1996, Hybrid organizational arrangements and their implications for firm growth and survival: A study of new franchisers, *Academy of Management Journal,* 39: 216–234.
92. F. Lafontaine, 1999, Myths and strengths of franchising, *Financial Times,* Mastering Strategy (Part Nine), November 22, 8–10.
93. L. Fenwick, 2001, Emerging markets: Defining global opportunities, *Franchising World,* 33(4): 54–55.
94. M. Sullivan, 2001, McDonald's, *Forbes Best of the Web,* May 21, 100.
95. R. P. Dant & P. J. Kaufmann, 1999, Franchising and the domain of entrepreneurship research, *Journal of Business Venturing,* 14: 5–16.
96. M. Gerstenhaber, 2000, Franchises can teach us about customer care, *Marketing,* March 16, 18.
97. P. J. Kaufmann & S. Eroglu, 1999, Standardization and adaptation in business format franchising, *Journal of Business Venturing,* 14: 69–85.
98. L. Wu, 1999, The pricing of a brand name product: Franchising in the motel services industry, *Journal of Business Venturing,* 14: 87–102.
99. Barney, *Gaining and Sustaining Competitive Advantage,* 110–111.
100. J. Higley, 2000, La Quinta jumps into franchising, *Hotel and Motel Management,* 215(13): 1, 54.
101. P. J. Buckley & M. Casson, 1996, An economic model of international joint venture strategy, *Journal of International Business Studies,* 27: 849–876; M. J. Dowling & W. L. Megginson, 1995, Cooperative strategy and new venture performance: The role of business strategy and management experience, *Strategic Management Journal,* 16: 565–580.
102. Ireland, Hitt, & Vaidyanath, Alliance management.
103. B. L. Simonin, 1997, The importance of collaborative know-how: An empirical test of the learning organization, *Academy of Management Journal,* 40: 1150–1174.
104. M. A. Hitt, M. T. Dacin, E. Levitas, J. -L. Arregle, & A. Borza, 2000, Partner selection in emerging and developed market contexts: Resource-based and organizational learning perspectives, *Academy of Management Journal,* 43: 449–467; M. D. Lord & A. L. Ranft, 2000, Organizational learning about new international markets: Exploring the internal transfer of local market knowledge, *Journal of International Business Studies,* 31: 73–589.
105. A. L. Velocci, Jr., 2001, U.S.-Euro strategic alliances will outpace company mergers, *Aviation Week & Space Technology,* 155(23): 56.
106. D. Kruger, 2001, Citigroup, *Forbes Best of the Web,* May 21, 71.
107. Ireland, Hitt, & Vaidyanath, Alliance management; M. A. Hitt, R. E. Hoskisson, & H. Kim, 1997, International diversification: Effects on innovation and firm performance in product diversified firms, *Academy of Management Journal,* 40: 767–798. R. N. Osborn & J. Hagedoorn, 1997, The institutionalization and evolutionary dynamics of interorganizational alliances and networks, *Academy of Management Journal,* 40: 261–278.
108. J. Hagedoorn, 1995, A note on international market leaders and networks of strategic technology partnering, *Strategic Management Journal,* 16: 241–250.
109. W. Heuslein, 2001, Coca-Cola, *Forbes Best of the Web,* May 21, 72.
110. P. Newcomb, 2001, Sony, *Forbes Best of the Web,* May 21, 84.
111. A. Gillies, General Mills, *Forbes Best of the Web,* May 21, 86.
112. M. Schuman, 1996, South Korea raises limit to 18% on foreign investment in firms, *The Wall Street Journal,* February 27, A12.
113. S. R. Miller & A. Parkhe, 2002, Is there a liability of foreignness in global banking? An empirical test of banks' X-efficiency, *Strategic Management Journal,* 23: 55–75; Y. Luo, 2001, Determinants of local responsiveness: Perspectives from foreign subsidiaries in an emerging market, *Journal of Management,* 27: 451–477.
114. A. Cane, 1999, GEC and NEC in alliance talks, *Financial Times,* May 11, 20.
115. P. Ghemawat, 2001, Distance matters: The hard reality of global expansion, *Harvard Business Review,* 79(8): 137–147.
116. J. K. Sebenius, 2002, The hidden challenge of cross-border negotiations, *Harvard Business Review,* 80(3): 76–85.
117. L. Kroll, 2001, Procter & Gamble, *Forbes Best of the Web,* May 21, 90.

118. C. B. Copp & R. L. Ivy, 2001, Networking trends of small tourism businesses in Post-Socialist Slovakia, *Journal of Small Business Management,* 39: 345–353.
119. S. S. Cohen & G. Fields, 1999, Social capital and capital gains in Silicon Valley, *California Management Review,* 41(2): 108–130; J. A. Matthews, 1999, A silicon island of the east: Creating a semiconductor industry in Singapore, *California Management Review,* 41(2): 55–78; M. E. Porter, 1998, Clusters and the new economics of competition, *Harvard Business Review,* 78(6): 77–90; R. Pouder & C. H. St. John, 1996, Hot spots and blind spots: Geographical clusters of firms and innovation, *Academy of Management Review,* 21: 1192–1225.
120. A. C. Cooper, 2001, Networks, alliances, and entrepreneurship, in M. A. Hitt, R. D. Ireland, S. M. Camp, & D. L. Sexton (eds.), *Strategic Entrepreneurship: Creating a New Mindset,* Oxford, U.K.: Blackwell Publishers, 203–222.
121. 2002, Johnson Controls, Corporate profile, http://www.johnsoncontrols com, March 10.
122. 2002, Johnson Controls, Corporate profile, http://www.johnsoncontrols. com, March 12.
123. R. S. Cline, 2001, Partnering for strategic alliances, *Lodging Hospitality,* 57(9): 42.
124. G. J. Young, M. P. Charns, & S. M. Shortell, 2001, Top manager and network effects on the adoption of innovative management practices: A study of TQM in a public hospital system, *Strategic Management Journal,* 22: 935–951.
125. F. T. Rothaermel, 2001, Complementary assets, strategic alliances, and the incumbent's advantage: An empirical study of industry and firm effects in the biopharmaceutical industry, *Research Policy,* 30: 1235–1251.
126. 2002, Intel, Strategic alliances, http://www.intel.com, March 10.
127. H. W. Volberda, C. Baden-Fuller, & F. A. J. van den Bosch, 2001, Mastering strategic renewal: Mobilising renewal journeys in multi-unit firms, *Long Range Planning,* 34(2): 159–178.
128. D. C. Hambrick, J. Li, K. Xin, & A. S. Tsui, 2001, Compositional gaps and downward spirals in international joint venture management groups, *Strategic Management Journal,* 22: 1033–1053; T. K. Das & B.-S. Teng, 2000, Instabilities of strategic alliances: An internal tensions perspective, *Organization Science,* 11: 77–101.
129. M. P. Koza & A. Y. Lewin, 1999, Putting the S-word back in alliances, Mastering Strategy (Part Six), *Financial Times,* November 1, 12–13; S. H. Park & M. Russo, 1996, When cooperation eclipses competition: An event history analysis of joint venture failures, *Management Science,* 42: 875–890.
130. A. Madhok & S. B. Tallman, 1998, Resources, transactions and rents: Managing value through interfirm collaborative relationships, *Organization Science,* 9: 326–339.
131. P. M. Norman, 2001, Are your secrets safe? Knowledge protection in strategic alliances, *Business Horizons,* November/December, 51–60.
132. M. A. Hitt, M. T. Dacin, B. B. Tyler, & D. Park, 1997, Understanding the differences in Korean and U.S. executives strategic orientations, *Strategic Management Journal,* 18: 159–168.
133. P. Lane, J. E. Salk, & M. A. Lyles, 2001, Absorptive capacity, learning, and performance in international joint ventures, *Strategic Management Journal,* 22: 1139–1161.
134. R. Larsson, L. Bengtsson, K. Henriksson, & J. Sparks, 1998, The interorganizational learning dilemma: Collective knowledge development in strategic alliances, *Organization Science,* 9: 285–305.
135. Ireland, Hitt, & Vaidyanath, Alliance management.
136. Reuer, Zollo, & Singh, Post-formation dynamics, 148.
137. J. H. Dyer, P. Kale, & H. Singh, 2001, How to make strategic alliances work, *MIT Sloan Management Review,* 42(4): 37–43.
138. Berentson, United Airlines, 68.
139. J. H. Dyer, 1997, Effective interfirm collaboration: How firms minimize transaction costs and maximize transaction value, *Strategic Management Journal,* 18: 535–556; M. H. Hansen, R. E. Hoskisson, & J. B. Barney, 1997, Trustworthiness in strategic alliances: Opportunism minimization versus opportunity maximization, Working paper, Brigham Young University.
140. Mitchell, Alliances, 7.
141. Hutt, Stafford, Walker, & Reingen, Defining the social network, 53.
142. D. F. Jennings, K. Artz, L. M. Gillin, & C. Christodouloy, 2000, Determinants of trust in global strategic alliances: Amrad and the Australian biomedical industry, *Competitiveness Review,* 10(1): 25–44.
143. H. K. Steensma, L. Marino, & K. M. Weaver, 2000, Attitudes toward cooperative strategies: A cross-cultural analysis of entrepreneurs, *Journal of International Business Studies,* 31: 591–609.
144. A. Arino & J. de la Torre, 1998, Learning from failure: Towards and evolutionary model of collaborative ventures, *Organization Science,* 9: 306–325; J. B. Barney & M. H. Hansen, 1994, Trustworthiness: Can it be a source of competitive advantage? *Strategic Management Journal,* 15(Special Winter Issue): 175–203.
145. R. Gulati & H. Singh, 1998, The architecture of cooperation: Managing coordination costs and appropriation concerns in strategic alliances, *Administrative Science Quarterly,* 43: 781–814; R. Gulati, 1996, Social structure and alliance formation patterns: A longitudinal analysis, *Administrative Science Quarterly,* 40: 619–652.
146. J. H. Davis, F. D. Schoorman, R. C. Mayer, & H. H. Tan, 2000, The trusted general manager and business unit performance: Empirical evidence of a competitive advantage, *Strategic Management Journal,* 21: 563–576; R. C. Mayer, J. H. Davis, & F. D. Schoorman, 1995, An integrative model of organizational trust, *Academy of Management Review,* 20: 709–734.

PART THREE

Strategic Actions: Strategy Implementation

Chapter 10
Corporate Governance

Chapter 11
Organizational Structure and Controls

Chapter 12
Strategic Leadership

Chapter 13
Strategic Entrepreneurship

10

Chapter Ten

Corporate Governance

Knowledge Objectives

Studying this chapter should provide you with the strategic management knowledge needed to:

1. Define corporate governance and explain why it is used to monitor and control managers' strategic decisions.
2. Explain how ownership came to be separated from managerial control in the modern corporation.
3. Define an agency relationship and managerial opportunism and describe their strategic implications.
4. Explain how three internal governance mechanisms—ownership concentration, the board of directors, and executive compensation—are used to monitor and control managerial decisions.
5. Discuss trends among the three types of compensation executives receive and their effects on strategic decisions.
6. Describe how the external corporate governance mechanism—the market for corporate control—acts as a restraint on top-level managers' strategic decisions.
7. Discuss the use of corporate governance in international settings, in particular in Germany and Japan.
8. Describe how corporate governance fosters ethical strategic decisions and the importance of such behaviors on the part of top-level executives.

Corporate Governance and CEO Pay

Top executive pay increased by 571 percent between 1990 and the end of 2000. Even in 2000, the year in which the Standard & Poor's stock index of 500 firms suffered a loss of 10 percent, this trend of increased CEO pay continued. In comparison, the average worker's pay barely outpaced inflation over this same decade; worker pay increased 37 percent versus inflation of 32 percent. In an age where pay for performance has been prominently featured in the business press, this discrepancy seems to defy logic. What caused this disparity?

The board of directors of any large publicly owned corporation makes executive pay decisions, typically through an executive compensation committee. In the 1990s, competitive benchmarking—setting standards based on those of competitors—became widespread. It is estimated that 96 percent of the companies in Standard & Poor's 500 stock index used such benchmarking to set pay. Executive compensation committees rationalize that if their CEOs do not earn as much as their peers, they may seek a position with another firm. By using this benchmarking trend instead of *directly* tying pay to performance, firms seem to be using alternative mechanisms for corporate governance. In fact, some research has suggested that this approach has led to underperforming executives getting increased pay regardless of the performance of the firm they manage.

Cash compensation for CEOs in the year 2000 increased 18 percent, while total pay increased 6.3 percent—the smallest total increase in compensation in 5 years. This increase far exceeds the 4.3 percent increase received by salaried workers in 2000, however, and the gap is even wider between the CEO and the average rank-and-file worker. Some hard-hit companies continued to increase their CEOs' pay even though the companies they managed underperformed their competitors. Net income at Walt Disney Company, for example, fell from $1.9 billion in 1997 to $920 million in the year 2000, but Disney increased Michael Eisner's salary and awarded him 2 million stock option shares valued at $37.7 million and a $11.5 million bonus.

At a minority of companies, however, the board of directors lowered a top executive's pay when the company did not perform well. For instance, at Dana Corporation, CEO Joseph M. Magliochetti had his pay reduced to $948,363 in 2000, a 63 percent drop from 1999. The auto parts maker had a poor year in 2000 as

In spite of being ranked the fifth most powerful person in Hollywood, Walt Disney chairman Michael Eisner's annual compensation for 2001 fell to $1 million in salary and no bonus at all, reflecting the economic downturn and the effect on travel and entertainment from the events of September 11. In one of Disney's strongest years, Eisner's annual compensation from salary, bonuses, and stock option came to $40 million.

AP PHOTO/BOB CHILD

sales dropped 6 percent, profits fell by 44 percent, and Dana's stock lost more than half of its value, which accordingly made Magliochetti's stock options worthless in addition to his salary decrease.

Other companies may have reduced CEO salary but have increased CEO stock options grants when the price of the stock is considerably lower than in previous years. For example, if a stock declines to $2.00 from $10.00, a firm will give significantly more stock options to meet a certain CEO compensation goal. As the economy expands, these managers will then receive a windfall thanks to a booming economy for which they were not responsible.

The bottom line is that even though mid-year 2002 found the economy and the stock market retreating from their then-recent high levels, few firms seemed willing to reduce executive pay in proportions mirroring declines in the performance of the firm for which they were responsible. Of course, it is more costly for a firm that has had performance problems to hire a top flight CEO, because it is a high-risk situation for the executive. Nonetheless, even though a firm will have to pay significantly more for a CEO for a turnaround situation, additional efforts to more closely align executive pay with firm performance appear necessary.

SOURCES: G. Colvin, 2001, The great CEO pay heist, *Fortune*, June 25, 64–70; J. Fox, 2001, The amazing stock option sleight of hand, *Fortune*, June 25, 86–92; L. Lavelle & F. F. Jespersen, 2001, Executive pay, *Business Week*, April 16, 76–80; C. J. Loomis, 2001, This stuff is wrong, *Fortune*, June 25, 73–84; D. Nichols & C. Subramaniam, 2001, Executive compensation; Excess or equitable? *Journal of Business Ethics*, 29: 339–351; R. C. Anderson, T. W. Bates, J. M. Bizjak, & M. L. Lemmon, 2000, Corporate governance and firm diversification, *Financial Management*, 29(1): 5–22.

As the Opening Case illustrates, corporate governance is an increasingly important part of the strategic management process.[1] If the board makes the wrong decision in compensating the firm's strategic leader, the CEO, the whole firm suffers, as do its shareholders. Compensation is used to motivate CEOs to act in the best interests of the firm—in particular, the shareholders. When they do, the firm's value should increase.

What are a CEO's actions worth? The Opening Case suggests that they are worth a significant amount in the United States. While some critics argue that U.S. CEOs are paid too much, the hefty increases in their compensation in recent years ostensibly have come from linking their pay to their firms' performance, and U.S. firms have performed better than many firms in other countries. However, research suggests that firms with a smaller pay gap between the CEO and other top executives perform better, especially when collaboration among top management team members is more important.[2] The performance improvement is attributed to better cooperation among the top management team members. Other research suggests that CEOs receive excessive compensation when corporate governance is the weakest.[3] Also, as noted in the Opening Case, benchmarking—basing CEO compensation on that paid to peers at other companies—appears to be a prevalent cause of excessive compensation.

Corporate governance represents the relationship among stakeholders that is used to determine and control the strategic direction and performance of organizations.

Corporate governance represents the relationship among stakeholders that is used to determine and control the strategic direction and performance of organizations.[4] At its core, corporate governance is concerned with identifying ways to ensure that strategic decisions are made effectively.[5] Governance can also be thought of as a means corporations use to establish order between parties (the firm's owners and its top-level managers) whose interests may be in conflict. Thus, corporate governance reflects and enforces the company's values.[6] In modern corporations—especially those in the United States and the United Kingdom—a primary objective of corporate governance is to ensure that the interests of top-level managers are aligned with the interests of the shareholders. Corporate governance involves oversight in areas where owners, managers, and members of boards of directors may have conflicts of interest. These areas include the election of directors, the general supervision of CEO pay and more focused supervision of director pay, and the corporation's overall structure and strategic direction.[7]

Corporate governance has been emphasized in recent years because, as the Opening Case illustrates, corporate governance mechanisms occasionally fail to adequately monitor and control top-level managers' decisions. This situation has resulted in changes in governance mechanisms in corporations throughout the world, especially with respect to efforts intended to improve the performance of boards of directors. A second and more positive reason for this interest is that evidence suggests that a well-functioning corporate governance and control system can create a competitive advantage for an individual firm.[8] For example, one governance mechanism—the board of directors—has been suggested to be rapidly evolving into a major strategic force in U.S. business firms.[9] Thus, in this chapter, we describe actions designed to implement strategies that focus on monitoring and controlling mechanisms, which can help to ensure that top-level managerial actions contribute to the firm's strategic competitiveness and its ability to earn above-average returns.

Effective corporate governance is also of interest to nations.[10] As stated by one scholar, "Every country wants the firms that operate within its borders to flourish and grow in such ways as to provide employment, wealth, and satisfaction, not only to improve standards of living materially but also to enhance social cohesion. These aspirations cannot be met unless those firms are competitive internationally in a sustained way, and it is this medium- and long-term perspective that makes good corporate governance so vital."[11]

Corporate governance, then, reflects company standards, which in turn collectively reflect societal standards.[12] In many individual corporations, shareholders hold top-level managers accountable for their decisions and the results they generate. As with these individual firms and their boards, nations that effectively govern their corporations may gain a competitive advantage over rival countries. For example, during the 1997 currency crisis in Asia, weak governance in the emerging economies resulted in asset prices falling lower than would have been the case had there been strong governance.[13]

In a range of countries, but especially in the United States and the United Kingdom, the fundamental goal of business organizations is to maximize shareholder value.[14] Traditionally, shareholders are treated as the firm's key stakeholders, because they are the company's legal owners. The firm's owners expect top-level managers and others influencing the corporation's actions (for example, the board of directors) to make decisions that will result in the maximization of the company's value and, hence, of the owners' wealth.[15]

In the first section of this chapter, we describe the relationship providing the foundation on which the modern corporation is built: the relationship between owners and managers. The majority of this chapter is used to explain various mechanisms owners use to govern managers and to ensure that they comply with their responsibility to maximize shareholder value.

Three internal governance mechanisms and a single external one are used in the modern corporation (see Table 10.1). The three internal governance mechanisms we

Table 10.1 Corporate Governance Mechanisms

Internal Governance Mechanisms

Ownership Concentration

- Relative amounts of stock owned by individual shareholders and institutional investors

Board of Directors

- Individuals responsible for representing the firm's owners by monitoring top-level managers' strategic decisions

Executive Compensation

- Use of salary, bonuses, and long-term incentives to align managers' interests with shareholders' interests

External Governance Mechanism

Market for Corporate Control

- The purchase of a company that is underperforming relative to industry rivals in order to improve the firm's strategic competitiveness

describe in this chapter are (1) ownership concentration, as represented by types of shareholders and their different incentives to monitor managers, (2) the board of directors, and (3) executive compensation. We then consider the market for corporate control, an external corporate governance mechanism. Essentially, this market is a set of potential owners seeking to acquire undervalued firms and earn above-average returns on their investments by replacing ineffective top-level management teams.[16] The chapter's focus then shifts to the issue of international corporate governance. We briefly describe governance approaches used in German and Japanese firms whose traditional governance structures are being affected by the realities of global competition. In part, this discussion suggests the possibility that the structures used to govern global companies in many different countries, including Germany, Japan, the United Kingdom, and the United States, are becoming more, rather than less, similar. Closing our analysis of corporate governance is a consideration of the need for these control mechanisms to encourage and support ethical behavior in organizations.

Importantly, the mechanisms discussed in this chapter can positively influence the governance of the modern corporation, which has placed significant responsibility and authority in the hands of top-level managers. The most effective managers understand their accountability for the firm's performance and respond positively to corporate governance mechanisms.[17] In addition, the firm's owners should not expect any single mechanism to remain effective over time. Rather, the use of several mechanisms allows owners to govern the corporation in ways that maximize strategic competitiveness and increase the financial value of their firm.[18] With multiple governance mechanisms operating simultaneously, however, it is also possible for some of the governance mechanisms to conflict.[19] Later, we review how these conflicts can occur.

Separation of Ownership and Managerial Control

Historically, the founder-owners and their descendants managed U.S. firms. In these cases, corporate ownership and control resided in the same persons. As firms grew larger, "the managerial revolution led to a separation of ownership and control in most large corporations, where control of the firm shifted from entrepreneurs to professional managers while ownership became dispersed among thousands of unorganized stockholders who were removed from the day-to-day management of the firm."[20] These changes created the modern public corporation, which is based on the efficient separation of ownership and managerial control. Supporting the separation is a basic legal premise suggesting that the primary objective of a firm's activities is to increase the corporation's profit and, thereby, the financial gains of the owners (the shareholders).[21]

The separation of ownership and managerial control allows shareholders to purchase stock, which entitles them to income (residual returns) from the firm's operations after paying expenses. This right, however, requires that they also take a risk that the firm's expenses may exceed its revenues. To manage this investment risk, shareholders maintain a diversified portfolio by investing in several companies to reduce their overall risk.[22] As shareholders diversify their investments over a number of corporations, their risk declines. The poor performance or failure of any one firm in which they invest has less overall effect. Thus, shareholders specialize in managing their investment risk.

In small firms, managers often are high percentage owners, so there is less separation between ownership and managerial control, but as these firms grow and become more complex, their owners-managers may contract with managerial specialists. These managers oversee decision making in the owner's firm and are compensated on the basis of their decision-making skills. As decision-making specialists, managers are agents of the firm's owners and are expected to use their decision-making skills to operate the owners' firm in ways that will maximize the return on their investment.[23]

Without owner (shareholder) specialization in risk bearing and management specialization in decision making that we have described, a firm probably would be limited by the abilities of its owners to manage and make effective strategic decisions. Thus, the separation and specialization of ownership (risk bearing) and managerial control (decision making) should produce the highest returns for the firm's owners.

Shareholder value is reflected by the price of the firm's stock. As stated earlier, corporate governance mechanisms, such as the board of directors or compensation based on the performance of a firm, is the reason that CEOs show general concern about the firm's stock price. For example, Cisco earned the dubious honor in 2001 of losing the most in shareholder value: $156 billion for the year. Furthermore, it lost $456 billion between March 2000 and December 2001. Although Cisco CEO John Chambers had been considered an excellent CEO, mid-2002 was a time during which the firm's losses since early 2000 as well as its possible future prospects caused some to begin questioning this belief.[24] On a more positive note, it is fair to report that over its lifetime, Cisco has created significant wealth for its investors and managers; it ranks 11th overall in regard to wealth creation.[25] Moreover, study of 2001's business landscape shows that Cisco's performance in that year was not unlike that of many other U.S. companies, which lost a combined total of $2.5 trillion in shareholder wealth.

Agency Relationships

An **agency relationship** exists when one or more persons (the principal or principals) hire another person or persons (the agent or agents) as decision-making specialists to perform a service.

The separation between owners and managers creates an agency relationship. An **agency relationship** exists when one or more persons (the principal or principals) hire another person or persons (the agent or agents) as decision-making specialists to perform a service.[26] Thus, an agency relationship exists when one party delegates decision-making responsibility to a second party for compensation (see Figure 10.1).[27] In addition to shareholders and top executives, other examples of agency

Figure 10.1 An Agency Relationship

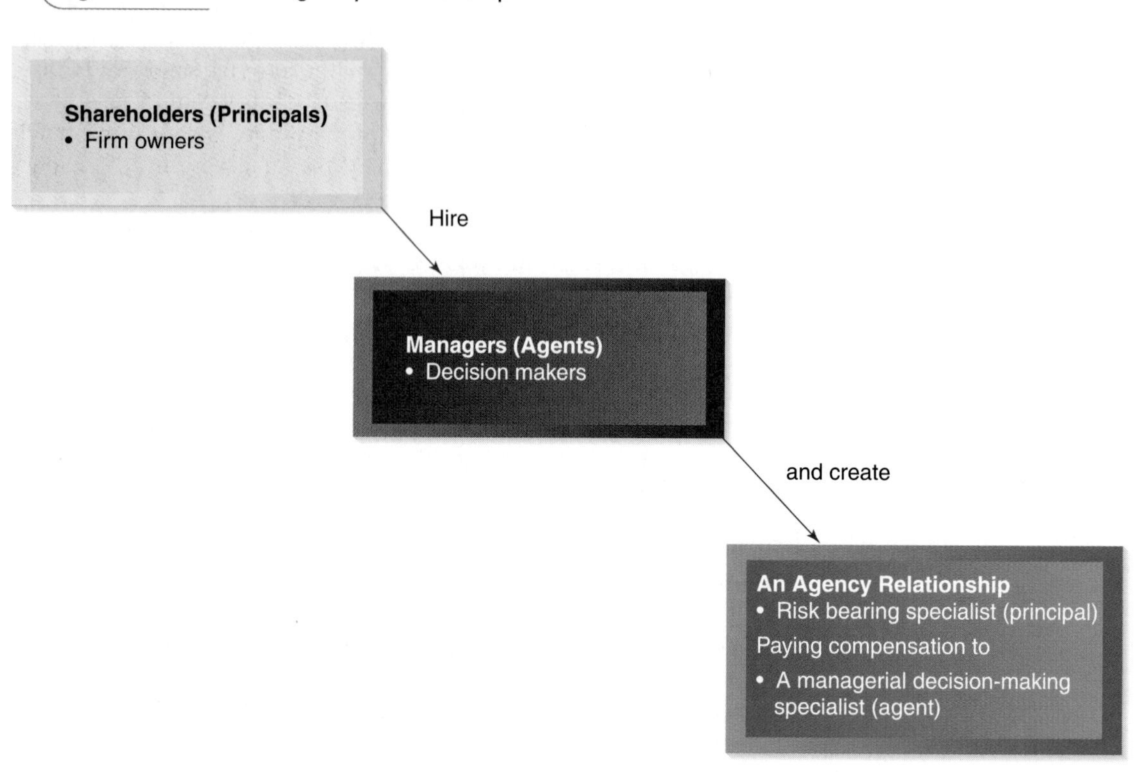

relationships are consultants and clients and insured and insurer. Moreover, within organizations, an agency relationship exists between managers and their employees, as well as between top executives and the firm's owners.[28] In the modern corporation, managers must understand the links between these relationships and the firm's effectiveness.[29] Although the agency relationship between managers and their employees is important, in this chapter we focus on the agency relationship between the firm's owners (the principals) and top-level managers (the principals' agents), because this relationship is related directly to how the firm's strategies are implemented.

The separation between ownership and managerial control can be problematic. Research evidence documents a variety of agency problems in the modern corporation.[30] Problems can surface because the principal and the agent have different interests and goals, or because shareholders lack direct control of large publicly traded corporations. Problems also arise when an agent makes decisions that result in the pursuit of goals that conflict with those of the principals. Thus, the separation of ownership and control potentially allows divergent interests (between principals and agents) to surface, which can lead to managerial opportunism.

Managerial opportunism is the seeking of self-interest with guile (i.e., cunning or deceit).

Managerial opportunism is the seeking of self-interest with guile (i.e., cunning or deceit).[31] Opportunism is both an attitude (e.g., an inclination) and a set of behaviors (i.e., specific acts of self-interest).[32] It is not possible for principals to know beforehand which agents will or will not act opportunistically. The reputations of top executives are an imperfect predictor, and opportunistic behavior cannot be observed until it has occurred. Thus, principals establish governance and control mechanisms to prevent agents from acting opportunistically, even though only a few are likely to do so.[33] Any time that principals delegate decision-making responsibilities to agents, the opportunity for conflicts of interest exist. Top executives, for example, may make strategic decisions that maximize their personal welfare and minimize their personal risk.[34] Decisions such as these prevent the maximization of shareholder wealth. Decisions regarding product diversification demonstrate these possibilities.

Product Diversification as an Example of an Agency Problem

As explained in Chapter 6, a corporate-level strategy to diversify the firm's product lines can enhance a firm's strategic competitiveness and increase its returns, both of which serve the interests of shareholders and the top executives. However, product diversification can result in two benefits to managers that shareholders do not enjoy, so top executives may prefer more product diversification than do shareholders.[35]

First, diversification usually increases the size of a firm, and size is positively related to executive compensation. Also, diversification increases the complexity of managing a firm and its network of businesses and may thus require more pay because of this complexity.[36] Thus, increased product diversification provides an opportunity for top executives to increase their compensation.[37]

Second, product diversification and the resulting diversification of the firm's portfolio of businesses can reduce top executives' employment risk.[38] Managerial employment risk is the risk of job loss, loss of compensation, and loss of managerial reputation.[39] These risks are reduced with increased diversification, because a firm and its upper-level managers are less vulnerable to the reduction in demand associated with a single or limited number of product lines or businesses. For example, Gemplus International named Antonio Perez as its CEO in 2000. With his 25-year career at Hewlett-Packard, Perez had a good reputation in the business world and his Hewlett-Packard experience seemed to be perfect preparation for his new position. Gemplus, headquartered in France, is the world's top producer of smart cards, "microchip-embedded cards used for everything from phone calls to credit-card transactions," and is very focused on a narrow product market. Perez's appointment was met with outrage by the French media over the $97 million worth of stock and options he received when he was hired. When demand for the Gemplus smart cards dropped sharply with slowing sales of mobile phones that used Gemplus chips, the company, worth approximately $3 billion in December 2000, lost more than 65 percent of its worth in the ensuing 15 months. Perez cut his own pay by 20 percent, but his decision to cut some of the company's 7,800-person workforce and the ensuing battle with Marc Lassus, company founder and chairman, led to both being forced by the firm's major shareholders to resign. Perez's employment risk was higher because the firm lacked significant product diversification, which is probably why he received significant compensation in the form of stock and options when he began his tenure with Gemplus.[40]

Another concern that may represent an agency problem is a firm's free cash flows over which top executives have control. Free cash flows are resources remaining after the firm has invested in all projects that have positive net present values within its current businesses.[41] In anticipation of positive returns, managers may decide to invest these funds in products that are not associated with the firm's current lines of business to increase the firm's level of diversification. The managerial decision to use free cash flows to overdiversify the firm is an example of self-serving and opportunistic managerial behavior. In contrast to managers, shareholders may prefer that free cash flows be distributed to them as dividends, so they can control how the cash is invested.[42]

Curve *S* in Figure 10.2 depicts the shareholders' optimal level of diversification. Owners seek the level of diversification that reduces the risk of the firm's total failure while simultaneously increasing the company's value through the development of economies of scale and scope (see Chapter 6). Of the four corporate-level diversification strategies shown in Figure 10.2, shareholders likely prefer the diversified position noted by point *A* on curve *S*—a position that is located between the dominant business and related-constrained diversification strategies. Of course, the optimum level of diversification owners seek varies from firm to firm.[43] Factors that affect shareholders' preferences include the firm's primary industry, the intensity of rivalry among competitors in that industry, and the top management team's experience with implementing diversification strategies.

As do principals, upper-level executives—as agents—also seek an optimal level of diversification. Declining performance resulting from too much product diversification increases the probability that corporate control of the firm will be acquired in the market. Once a firm is acquired, the employment risk for the firm's top executives increases substantially. Furthermore, a manager's employment opportunities in the external managerial labor market (discussed in Chapter 12) are affected negatively by a firm's poor performance. Therefore, top executives prefer diversification, but not to a point that it increases their employment risk and reduces their employment opportunities.[44] Curve *M* in Figure 10.2 shows that executives prefer higher levels of product diversification than shareholders. Top executives might prefer the level of diversification shown by point *B* on curve *M*.

In general, shareholders prefer riskier strategies and more focused diversification. They reduce their risk through holding a diversified portfolio of equity investments. Alternatively, managers obviously cannot balance their employment risk by working for a diverse portfolio of firms. Therefore, top executives may prefer a level of diversification that maximizes firm size and their compensation and that reduces their employment risk. Product diversification, therefore, is a potential agency problem that could result in principals incurring costs to control their agents' behaviors.

Figure 10.2 Manager and Shareholder Risk and Diversification

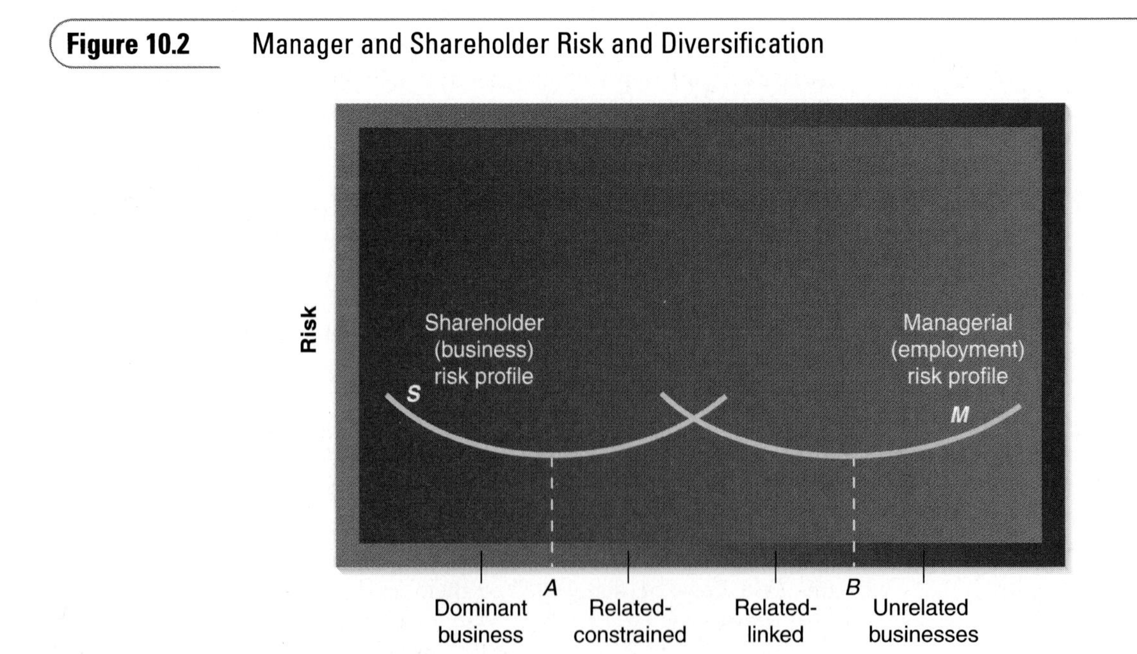

Agency Costs and Governance Mechanisms

Agency costs are the sum of incentive costs, monitoring costs, enforcement costs, and individual financial losses incurred by principals, because governance mechanisms cannot guarantee total compliance by the agent.

The potential conflict illustrated by Figure 10.2, coupled with the fact that principals do not know which managers might act opportunistically, demonstrates why principals establish governance mechanisms. However, the firm incurs costs when it uses one or more governance mechanisms. **Agency costs** are the sum of incentive costs, monitoring costs, enforcement costs, and individual financial losses incurred by principals, because governance mechanisms cannot guarantee total compliance by the agent. If a firm is diversified, governance costs increase because it is more difficult to monitor what is going on inside the firm.[45]

In general, managerial interests may prevail when governance mechanisms are weak, as is exemplified by allowing managers a significant amount of autonomy to make strategic decisions. If, however, the board of directors controls managerial autonomy, or if other strong governance mechanisms are used, the firm's strategies should better reflect the interests of the shareholders.

Recent research suggests that even using more governance mechanisms may produce major changes in strategies. Firms acquired unrelated businesses at approximately the same rate in the 1980s as they did in the 1960s, even though more governance mechanisms were employed in the 1980s. Thus, governance mechanisms are an imperfect means of controlling managerial opportunism.[46] Alternatively, other current evidence suggests that active shareholders, especially institutional investors, are more willing to try to remove the CEO leading a firm that is performing poorly. The actions taken at Gemplus International, as explained above, demonstrate this willingness.[47]

Next, we explain the effects of different governance mechanisms on the decisions managers make about the choice and the use of the firm's strategies.

Ownership Concentration

Ownership concentration is defined by both the number of large-block shareholders and the total percentage of shares they own.

Large-block shareholders typically own at least 5 percent of a corporation's issued shares.

Both the number of large-block shareholders and the total percentage of shares they own define **ownership concentration. Large-block shareholders** typically own at least 5 percent of a corporation's issued shares. Ownership concentration as a governance mechanism has received considerable interest because large-block shareholders are increasingly active in their demands that corporations adopt effective governance mechanisms to control managerial decisions.[48]

In general, diffuse ownership (a large number of shareholders with small holdings and few, if any, large-block shareholders) produces weak monitoring of managers' decisions. Among other problems, diffuse ownership makes it difficult for owners to effectively coordinate their actions. Diversification of the firm's product lines beyond the shareholders' optimum level might result from weak monitoring of managers' decisions. Higher levels of monitoring could encourage managers to avoid strategic decisions that do not create greater shareholder value. In fact, research evidence shows that ownership concentration is associated with lower levels of firm diversification.[49] Thus, with high degrees of ownership concentration, the probability is greater that managers' strategic decisions will be intended to maximize shareholder value.

Ownership concentration is a natural consequence of deregulated industries. For example, after the airline industry was deregulated in the United States, the ownership of the airlines became more concentrated.[50] A similar pattern has occurred in the banking industry, where there has been substantial consolidation through acquisitions.[51] Much of this concentration has come from increasing equity ownership by institutional investors.

The Growing Influence of Institutional Owners

A classic work published in the 1930s argued that the "modern" corporation had become characterized by a separation of ownership and control.[52] This change occurred primarily because growth prevented founders-owners from maintaining their dual positions in their increasingly complex companies. More recently, another shift has occurred: Ownership of many modern corporations is now concentrated in the hands of institutional investors rather than individual shareholders.[53]

Institutional owners are financial institutions such as stock mutual funds and pension funds that control large-block shareholder positions.

Institutional owners are financial institutions such as stock mutual funds and pension funds that control large-block shareholder positions. Because of their prominent ownership positions, institutional owners, as large-block shareholders, are a powerful governance mechanism. Institutions of these types now own more than 50 percent of the stock in large U.S. corporations, and of the top 1,000 corporations, they own, on average, 59 percent of the stock.[54] Pension funds alone control at least one-half of corporate equity.[55]

These ownership percentages suggest that as investors, institutional owners have both the size and the incentive to discipline ineffective top-level managers and can significantly influence a firm's choice of strategies and overall strategic decisions.[56] Research evidence indicates that institutional and other large-block shareholders are becoming more active in their efforts to influence a corporation's strategic decisions. Initially, these shareholder activists and institutional investors concentrated on the performance and accountability of CEOs and contributed to the ouster of a number of them. They are now targeting what they believe are ineffective boards of directors.[57]

For example, CalPERS provides retirement and health coverage to over 1.3 million current and retired public employees.[58] One of the largest public employee pension funds in the United States, CalPERS is generally thought to act aggressively to promote decisions and actions that it believes will enhance shareholder value in companies in which it invests. To pressure boards of directors to make what it believes are needed changes, CalPERS has advocated for board reform. In 1990, 66 percent of all directors on U.S. company boards were outsiders; by 2000 the level had risen to 78 percent. CalPERS believes that all but the CEO should be outsiders, "which translates into 92 percent of all company directors should be independent non-executives."[59] The largest institutional investor, TIAA-CREF, has taken actions similar to those of CalPERS, but with a less publicly aggressive stance (furthermore, as the Strategic Focus on page 318 suggests, CalPERS may not be as aggressive in regard to governance as it has been historically). To date, research suggests that these institutions' activism may not have a direct effect on firm performance, but that its influence may be indirect through its effects on important strategic decisions, such as those concerned with innovation.[60]

Shareholder Activism: How Much Is Possible?

The U.S. Securities and Exchange Commission (SEC) has issued several rulings that support shareholder involvement and control of managerial decisions. For example, the SEC eased its rule regarding communications among shareholders. Historically, shareholders could communicate among themselves only through a cumbersome and expensive filing process. Now, with a simple notification to the SEC of an upcoming meeting, shareholders can convene to discuss a corporation's strategic direction. If a consensus on an issue exists, shareholders can vote as a block. "In 2000, we saw 24 proxy fights—of those, management won 14 and dissidents won 10, which means that management was victorious in 58 percent of them and the dissident group was victorious in 42 percent."[61] Among these 24 proxy fights, management proposals receiving significant opposition from institutional investors included "executive compensation, stock options and anti-takeover devices." The Internet has also facilitated proxy battles because "the Web makes it easier and cheaper to contact and organize other investors."[62]

Some argue that greater latitude should be extended to those managing the funds of large institutional investor groups, believing that allowing these individuals to hold positions on boards of firms in which their organizations have significant investments might enable fund managers to better represent the interests of those they serve.[63] However, the actions of traditionally activist institutional investor CalPERS were potentially compromised by investments it had in Enron (see the Strategic Focus on page 332 on Enron's governance and ethics and Chapter 7's Strategic Focus on page 225 about the failed acquisition of Enron by Dynegy). Institutional activism should create a premium for companies with good corporate governance. However, trustees for these funds sometimes have other relationships that compromise their effectiveness, as apparently was the case for CalPERS. It is more often the case that large *private* pension funds, which have other business relationships with companies in their fund's portfolio, reduce effective monitoring.[64]

Also, the degree to which institutional investors can effectively monitor the decisions being made in all of the companies in which they have investments is questionable. Historically, CalPERS targeted 12 companies at a time for improvement. The New York Teachers Retirement Fund, another activist institutional investor, focuses on 25 of the 1,300-plus companies in its portfolio. Given limited resources, even large-block shareholders tend to concentrate on corporations in which they have significant investments. Thus, although shareholder activism has increased, institutional investors face barriers to the amount of active governance they can realistically employ.[65] Furthermore, at times, activist institutional shareholders may have conflicting goals.[66] Other means of corporate governance are needed.

Sam Wyly founded his first company—University Computing Company—with $1,000 in 1963. The firm went public in 1965 and earned its investors an astounding 100 to 1 return in the next four years, eventually merging with Computer Associates. Sterling Software, which he founded in 1983, was sold to Computer Associates for $8 billion in 2000.

Besides institutional owners, other owners are able to influence the decisions managers make as agents. Although other investors have significant influence, battles are not likely to be won or lost unless institutional investors are involved because they currently are such significant shareholders. Texas billionaire Sam Wyly sold his company, Sterling Software, to Computer Associates in 2000. Wyly fought to elect a new Computer Associates board that would in turn elect him to be Computer Associates chairman. He argued that Computer Associates, the fourth largest software company in the world, had not performed well since 1996 and had alienated customers and employees.[67] As part of his leadership proposal, Wyly sought to break the company into four small companies. Influential shareholders who considered it "too radical" did not support this proposal and Walter Haefner, who is the largest shareholder in the company, supported the current management. Wyly was unsuccessful in his attempt to take over the leadership of Computer Associates, but his revised plan won the support of CalPERS and other investors. Even though Wyly lost his attempt at leadership, Computer Associates will likely improve its corporate governance procedures.[68]

AP PHOTO/ED BAILEY

Corporate governance may also by affected by the recent phenomenon of increased managerial ownership of the firm's stock. There are many positive reasons for managerial ownership, including the use of stock options to link managerial pay to the performance of a firm. However, an unexpected outcome of managerial ownership has been reduced support for shareholder-sponsored proposals to repeal anti-takeover provisions. Institutional owners generally support the repeal of these provisions because shareholder wealth is typically increased if a takeover is offered, while managerial owners, whose jobs are at risk if a takeover is executed,

Strategic Focus

CalPERS, Institutional Investor Activism, and Conflict of Interest

Although large active institutional investors, such as the California Public Employees Retirement System (CalPERS), have been significant advocates of improved corporate governance and better board oversight of large corporations, they have also pursued a trend of private placement of equity investments.

CalPERS' private placement of equity in Enron partnerships may be cause for concern because of a potential conflict of interest. CalPERS' December 2000 board proceedings show that the institution was a substantial shareholder and partner with Enron in a set of private partnerships that ultimately was the impetus for Enron's failure. Because these partnerships were guaranteed by Enron stock and thus represented off-balance sheet liabilities, the investments were riskier than common shareholders realized because the accounting for these liabilities was not transparent in annual reports.

Records indicate that the CalPERS board was considering an additional proposed private equity investment in LJM3, an Enron-sponsored partnership proposed by Andrew Fastow, Enron's former chief financial officer. Although CalPERS had received a good return from previous partnerships with Enron, the CalPERS board declined to invest in this partnership. The Pacific Corporate Group, an investment advisor for CalPERS on private equity deals such as the LJM3 partnership, indicated that there were potential conflicts of interest for Fastow and others at Enron. A memo from Pacific indicated that the visibility and "duality" of Fastow's roles as a partner in the private partnership as well as serving as Enron's chief financial officer were of concern. Accordingly, Pacific alerted the CalPERS board to these potential difficulties.

Pacific reported further that "CalPERS should have been deeply concerned that the Enron board would approve something that could seriously endanger the company's reputation." CalPERS had in the past been known to actively lobby against a corporate governance issue such as this, and had symbolized such activism for shareholders. In this case, CalPERS seems to have put its own interest ahead of the shareholders of Enron because of the previous private partnership investments that CalPERS had pursued with Enron and some of its top-level managers. These earlier investments may have constituted a conflict of interest for CalPERS against protecting Enron shareholders. At the time, CalPERS simply declined to participate in LJM3 rather than going directly to the Enron board and seeking to correct the problem identified by Pacific. Because of this lapse in activism, CalPERS' board is now debating whether it should again be more proactive in board governance issues, as it had been in the past. It remains to be seen whether CalPERS will continue to be as effective as it once was in advocating board governance reforms. It appears that because of its private placement and involvement with Enron and its reduced emphasis on governance reforms, it is less proactive in pursuing shareholder rights and information disclosure.

In many ways, this conflict of interest and lack of action by CalPERS hurt other pension systems significantly. After CalPERS realized a $132.5 million profit on a $250 million investment in Enron's joint energy development investments (JEDI), it poured an additional $175 million into another Enron partnership called JEDI II, which has returned $171.7 million so far and actually expects to break even. However, other public pension funds that invested in Enron's stock (not in its private equity partnerships) have lost significant amounts. For instance, six of California's other public pension funds lost $250 million when the market devalued Enron's stock. Florida's state retirement system lost $325 million as a result of losses on Enron's stock.

CalPERS' profits from its investments in the JEDI partnerships came about because of opportunities created by measures such as deregulation in California's energy market. This windfall opportunity for Enron and its private placement partners that took advantage of high-priced energy also significantly increased California's debt and contributed to the bankruptcy proceedings of its largest utility. Although Enron was not responsible for deregulation and energy prices, it is responsible for its own corporate governance and strategic leadership, just as CalPERS is responsible for management of its assets. In both situations, an improved focus on corporate governance would have contributed to significantly lower losses and may have helped prevent the financial disaster associated with Enron's collapse.

SOURCES: M. Benson, 2002, Two large pension funds may adopt tougher corporate-governance policies, *The Wall Street Journal Interactive,* http://www.wsj.com, January 16; G. Colvin, 2002, The boardroom follies, *Fortune,* January 7, 32; J. Schwartz, 2002, Darth Vader. Machiavelli. Skilling set intense pace, *The New York Times,* http://www.nytimes.com, February 7; A. Felo, 2001, Ethics programs, board involvement, and potential conflicts of interest in corporate governance, *Journal of Business Ethics,* 32: 205–218; D. B. Henriques, 2002, Even a watchdog is not always fully awake, *The New York Times,* http://www.nytimes.com, February 5; 2002, California pension funds hurt by Enron downfall, *The Wall Street Journal Interactive,* http://www.wsj.com, January 29.

generally oppose their repeal. Thus, managerial ownership provides managers with power to protect their own interests.[69]

Board of Directors

Typically, shareholders monitor the managerial decisions and actions of a firm through the board of directors. Shareholders elect members to their firm's board. Those who are elected are expected to oversee managers and to ensure that the corporation is operated in ways that will maximize its shareholders' wealth. As we have described, the practices of large institutional investors have resulted in an increase in ownership concentration in U.S. firms. Nonetheless, diffuse ownership still describes the status of most U.S. firms,[70] which means that monitoring and control of managers by individual shareholders is limited in large corporations. Furthermore, large financial institutions, such as banks, are prevented from directly owning stock in firms and from having representatives on companies' boards of directors, although this is not the case in Europe and elsewhere.[71] These conditions highlight the importance of the board of directors for corporate governance. Unfortunately, over time, boards of directors have not been highly effective in monitoring and controlling top management's actions.[72] While boards of directors are imperfect, they can positively influence both managers and the companies they serve.[73]

The **board of directors** is a group of elected individuals whose primary responsibility is to act in the owners' interests by formally monitoring and controlling the corporation's top-level executives.

The **board of directors** is a group of elected individuals whose primary responsibility is to act in the owners' interests by formally monitoring and controlling the corporation's top-level executives.[74] Boards have power to direct the affairs of the organization, punish and reward managers, and protect shareholders' rights and interests.[75] Thus, an appropriately structured and effective board of directors protects owners from managerial opportunism. Board members are seen as stewards of their company's resources, and the way they carry out these responsibilities affects the society in which their firm operates.[76]

Generally, board members (often called directors) are classified into one of three groups (see Table 10.2). *Insiders* are active top-level managers in the corporation who are elected to the board because they are a source of information about the firm's day-to-day operations.[77] *Related outsiders* have some relationship with the firm, contractual or otherwise, that may create questions about their independence, but these individuals are not involved with the corporation's day-to-day activities. *Outsiders* provide independent counsel to the firm and may hold top-level managerial positions in other companies or may have been elected to the board prior to the beginning of the current CEO's tenure.[78]

Some argue that many boards are not fulfilling their primary fiduciary duty to protect shareholders. Among other possibilities, it may be that boards are a managerial tool: they do not question managers' actions, and they readily approve managers' self-serving initiatives.[79] In general, those critical of boards as a governance mechanism believe that inside managers dominate boards and exploit their personal ties with them. A widely accepted view is that a board with a significant percentage of its membership from the firm's top executives tends to provide relatively weak monitoring and control of managerial decisions.[80]

Critics advocate reforms to ensure that independent outside directors represent a significant majority of the total membership of a board.[81] For instance, Interpublic, a global marketing communications and marketing services company, had six inside and six outside directors when it announced a change in early 2002 to a majority of outside directors—two inside and seven outside directors, with the arrival of a new outside director, Michael I. Roth, chief executive at the MONY Group. "The interests of Interpublic shareholders will be best served by a board that is primarily made up of independent, outside directors, consistent with that of other leading public companies," said John J. Dooner Jr., Interpublic's chairman and CEO.[82]

Because successful high-tech startup firms usually operate in a dynamic environment, they often have strong entrepreneurial leaders or founders who guide them through rapid changes. However, such entrepreneurs often put together weak boards of directors. By creating strong boards with independent outsiders who can help foster the entrepreneurial spirit, such "high-flying" firms can maintain their momentum and profitability if and when their founders leave. Some examples of these strong leaders are Jeff Bezos at Amazon, Stephen Case at AOL Time Warner, and Bill Gates at Microsoft.[83]

One criticism of boards has been that some have not been vigilant enough in hiring and then monitoring the behavior of CEOs. For example, Albert Dunlap, the former CEO at Sunbeam, agreed to settle a shareholder lawsuit brought against him (and other former executives) for $15 million out of his own pocket. A number of questionable acquisitions had been made by the Dunlap team, ultimately spreading the company too thin and causing Sunbeam to file for Chapter 11 bankruptcy. Although Dunlap and his colleagues claimed that they did nothing wrong, there were significant performance problems and the accounting at the company lacked transparency.[84] The Sunbeam board must share the blame in the failure for two reasons. First, it selected the CEO. Second, the board should have been actively involved in the development of the firm's strategy—if the strategy fails, the board has failed.[85]

Other issues, in addition to criticisms of their work, affect today's corporate

Table 10.2 Classifications of Boards of Directors' Members

Insiders

- The firm's CEO and other top-level managers

Related outsiders

- Individuals not involved with the firm's day-to-day operations, but who have a relationship with the company

Outsiders

- Individuals who are independent of the firm in terms of day-to-day operations and other relationships boards. For example, there is some disagreement about the most appropriate role of outside directors in a firm's strategic decision-making process.[86] Because of external pressures, board reforms have been initiated. To date, these reforms have generally called for an increase in the number of outside directors, relative to insiders, serving on a corporation's board. For example, in 1984, the New York Stock Exchange started requiring that listed firms have board audit committees composed solely of outside directors.[87] As a result of external pressures, boards of large corporations have more outside members. Research shows that outside board members can influence the strategic direction of companies.[88] Therefore, there are potential strategic implications associated with the movement toward having corporate boards dominated by outsiders.

Alternatively, a large number of outside board members can create some issues. Outsiders do not have contact with the firm's day-to-day operations and typically do not have easy access to the level of information about managers and their skills that is required to effectively evaluate managerial decisions and initiatives. Outsiders can, however, obtain valuable information through frequent interactions with inside board members, during board meetings and otherwise. Insiders possess such information by virtue of their organizational positions. Thus, boards with a critical mass of insiders typically are better informed about intended strategic initiatives, the reasons for the initiatives, and the outcomes expected from them.[89] Without this type of information, outsider-dominated boards may emphasize the use of financial, as opposed to strategic, controls to gather performance information to evaluate managers' and business units' performances. A virtually exclusive reliance on financial evaluations shifts risk to top-level managers, who, in turn, may make decisions to maximize their interests and reduce their employment risk. Reductions in R&D investments, additional diversification of the firm, and the pursuit of greater levels of compensation are some of the results of managers' actions to achieve financial goals set by outsider dominated boards.[90]

Enhancing the Effectiveness of the Board of Directors

Because of the importance of boards of directors in corporate governance and as a result of increased scrutiny from shareholders—in particular, large institutional investors—the performances of individual board members and of entire boards are being evaluated more formally and with greater intensity.[91] Given the demand for greater accountability and improved performance, many boards have initiated voluntary changes. Among these changes are (1) increases in the diversity of the backgrounds of board members (for example, a greater number of directors from public service, academic, and scientific settings; a greater percentage of boards with ethnic minorities and women; and members from different countries on boards of U.S. firms), (2) the strengthening of internal management and accounting control systems, and (3) the establishment and consistent use of formal processes to evaluate the board's performance.[92]

Boards have become more involved in the strategic decision-making process, so they must work collaboratively. Research shows that boards working collaboratively make higher-quality strategic decisions, and they make them faster.[93] Sometimes, as the Strategic Focus on page 322 about the merger between Hewlett-Packard (HP) and Compaq illustrates, there is conflict among board members regarding the appropriate strategic direction for a company. In addition, because of the increased pressure from owners and the potential conflict, procedures are necessary to help boards function effectively in facilitating the strategic decision-making process.[94] (See also Chapter 7's Opening Case on page 213, where we consider the HP/Compaq transaction from the perspective of acquisitions and mergers.)

Strategic Focus

Hewlett-Packard Board of Directors Versus Walter Hewlett, Board Member

The merger between Hewlett-Packard Company (HP) and Compaq Computer Corp. was the largest high-tech merger in history. Almost as noteworthy, however, was the resulting battle among board members.

While industry analysts questioned the merger because of past problems in merging two large technology and computer companies, the most significant opposition regarding the transaction came from a board member. Walter Hewlett, son of Hewlett-Packard founder William Hewlett and member of HP's board of directors, fought the merger as a representative of a group who collectively represent 18 percent of HP's ownership. At the end of 2001, he filed a preliminary proxy filing with the SEC trying to block the proposed deal.

In his proxy filing, Hewlett said that the acquisition of Compaq was overpriced and unnecessarily risky. He also stated that he had expressed similar doubts since learning of the possibility of a deal in May 2001. He argued that combining the two firms would damage the value of shareholders' investments, noting that HP's market capitalization diminished by $12.3 billion from the announcement of the deal until the day he came out in opposition; that day, shares rose 7 percent, adding $5.7 billion in value. His reason for filing the proxy was to convince other shareholders to vote against the merger.

Interestingly, Hewlett had originally voted in favor of the merger when it came before the board. Carly Fiorina, HP's CEO, speaking about Mr. Hewlett's actions, said that she was surprised, and that "there [was] a big difference between an individual managing his own personal assets and the assets of the foundation and a board member going out and actively soliciting against a board's decision." She believed that the transaction would strengthen the combined firm's sales of personal computers, servers, and technology consulting, putting the company in a stronger position to compete with market leaders IBM and Dell Computer. Among the shareholders, both sides had their strong supporters. Together with Hewlett, the other heirs of HP founders, as mentioned, control 18 percent of the company's stock through foundations and came out in opposition to the merger. Board members in favor of the merger noted that the internal rate of return following the 1998 merger of DEC and Compaq was a very high 29 percent. These board members believed that this fact swayed some shareholders to their side in the shareholder vote.

The battle between the board members was fought quite publicly. Each side ran full-page newspaper ads addressed to each other and to shareholders, and both established websites to further their reach (http://www.votethehpway.com for the corporation and http://www.votenohpcompaq.com for the opposition). Following the vote on March 19, 2002, Walter Hewlett filed suit against the apparent passage of the merger, citing shareholders were allowed to change their votes and to vote twice, and records of two large institutional shareholders—Deutschebank and Northern Trust—were being investigated. However, even if these votes were thrown out, there were enough votes for the merger to pass because of a 3 percent margin of victory. With the transaction approved, the challenge for the newly created firm's board of directors is to make decisions that will maximize shareholders' wealth.

SOURCES: M. Kane, 2002, Government examining HP vote, http://www.cnet.com, April 15; S. Lohr, 2002, Hewlett's chief says count confirms victory, *The New York Times,* http://www.nytimes.com, April 18; S. Lohr, 2002, 2 computer giants hope to avoid pitfalls of past mergers, *The New York Times,* http://www.nytimes.com, January 1; S. Thurm, 2002, A lion's capital throws its support behind HP proposal to buy Compaq, *The Wall Street Journal Interactive,* http://www.wsj.com, January 21; P. Burrows & K. Rebello, 2001, Q&A: Fiorina: The deal is "the right thing for shareholders," *Business Week Online,* http://businessweek.com, December 24; C. Gaither, 2001, Hewlett heir in new action against merger, *The New York Times,* http://nytimes.com, December 28; S. Lohr, 2001, Hewlett chief battles for her deal and her career, *The New York Times,* http://nytimes.com, December 10; A. Park, 2001, Can Compaq survive as a solo act?, *Business Week Online,* http://businessweek.com, December 24; R. Sidel & M. Williams, 2001, Hewlett's opposition to Compaq deal is strong statement for board member, *The Wall Street Journal Interactive,* http://wsj.com, December 31; M. Williams, 2001, Walter Hewlett files SEC proxy materials urging deal's rejection, defending stance, *The Wall Street Journal Interactive,* http://wsj.com, December 28.

Besides being increasingly involved in important strategic decisions such as the HP/Compaq combination, boards also are becoming more active in expressing their view about CEO succession, as opposed to readily supporting the incumbent's choice. In general, however, boards have relied on precedence (past decisions) for guidance in the selection process. Also, they are most likely to consider inside candidates before looking for outside candidates.[95] Outside directors have the power to facilitate the firm's transition to a new CEO. When an internal heir apparent CEO candidate is associated with a high performing firm, outside directors are likely to help the heir apparent make the transition. However, if firm performance is problematic, outside directors are less likely to support the chosen successor and are often skeptical of someone chosen to follow in the footsteps of the former CEO.[96]

Increasingly, outside directors are being required to own significant equity stakes as a prerequisite to holding a board seat. In fact, some research suggests that firms perform better if outside directors have such a stake.[97] Another study suggests that the performance of inside directors also improves if they hold an equity position. Therefore, an inside director's knowledge of the firm can be used appropriately. Finally, an inside director's relationship to the CEO does not necessarily lead to entrenchment of that CEO if the inside director has a strong ownership position.[98] One activist concludes that boards need three foundational characteristics to be effective: director stock ownership, executive meetings to discuss important strategic issues, and a serious nominating committee that truly controls the nomination process to strongly influence the selection of new board members.[99]

Executive Compensation

As the Opening Case illustrates, the compensation of top-level managers, and especially of CEOs, generates a great deal of interest and strongly held opinions. One reason for this widespread interest can be traced to a natural curiosity about extremes and excesses. Another stems from a more substantive view, that CEO pay is tied in an indirect but very tangible way to the fundamental governance processes in large corporations: Who has power? What are the bases of power? How and when do owners and managers exert their relative preferences? How vigilant are boards? Who is taking advantage of whom?[100]

Executive compensation is a governance mechanism that seeks to align the interests of managers and owners through salaries, bonuses, and long-term incentive compensation, such as stock options.

Executive compensation is a governance mechanism that seeks to align the interests of managers and owners through salaries, bonuses, and long-term incentive compensation, such as stock options.[101] Stock options are a mechanism used to link executives' performance to the performance of their company's stock.[102] Increasingly, long-term incentive plans are becoming a critical part of compensation packages in U.S. firms. The use of longer-term pay helps firms cope with or avoid potential agency problems.[103] Because of this, the stock market generally reacts positively to the introduction of a long-range incentive plan for top executives.[104]

Sometimes the use of a long-term incentive plan prevents major stockholders (e.g., institutional investors) from pressing for changes in the composition of the board of directors, because they assume that the long-term incentives will ensure that top executives will act in shareholders' best interests. Alternatively, stockholders largely assume that top-executive pay and the performance of a firm are more closely aligned when firms have boards that are dominated by outside members.[105]

Effectively using executive compensation as a governance mechanism is particularly challenging to firms implementing international strategies. For example, the interests of owners of multinational corporations may be best served when there is less uniformity among the firm's foreign subsidiaries' compensation plans.[106] Developing an array of unique compensation plans requires additional monitoring and increases the firm's agency costs. Importantly, levels of pay vary by regions of the world. For example, managers receive the highest compensation in the United States,

while managerial pay is much lower in Asia. Compensation is lower in India partly because many of the largest firms have strong family ownership and control.[107] As corporations acquire firms in other countries, the managerial compensation puzzle becomes more complex and may cause additional executive turnover.[108] For instance, when Daimler-Benz acquired Chrysler, the top executives of Chrysler made substantially more than the executives at Daimler-Benz—but the Chrysler executives ended up reporting to the Daimler executives.[109]

A Complicated Governance Mechanism

For several reasons, executive compensation—especially long-term incentive compensation—is complicated. First, the strategic decisions made by top-level managers are typically complex and nonroutine, so direct supervision of executives is inappropriate for judging the quality of their decisions. The result is a tendency to link the compensation of top-level managers to measurable outcomes, such as the firm's financial performance. Second, an executive's decision often affects a firm's financial outcomes over an extended period, making it difficult to assess the effect of current decisions on the corporation's performance. In fact, strategic decisions are more likely to have long-term, rather than short-term, effects on a company's strategic outcomes. Third, a number of other factors affect a firm's performance besides top-level managerial decisions and behavior. Unpredictable economic, social, or legal changes (see Chapter 2) make it difficult to discern the effects of strategic decisions. Thus, although performance-based compensation may provide incentives to top management teams to make decisions that best serve shareholders' interests,[110] such compensation plans alone are imperfect in their ability to monitor and control managers.[111] Still, annual bonuses as incentive compensation represent a significant portion of many executives' total pay. For example, annual bonuses compose an average of about 60 percent of the CEO's total compensation in the United States, about 45 percent in the United Kingdom, approximately 30 percent in Canada, while only 19 percent in France.[112]

Although incentive compensation plans may increase the value of a firm in line with shareholder expectations, such plans are subject to managerial manipulation. For instance, annual bonuses may provide incentives to pursue short-run objectives at the expense of the firm's long-term interests. Supporting this conclusion, some research has found that bonuses based on annual performance were negatively related to investments in R&D when the firm was highly diversified, which may affect the firm's long-term strategic competitiveness.[113] In high tech firms, where uncertainty is higher, short-term (salary and bonus) compensation was related to innovation, but no such relationship was found in low tech firms. However, no relationship between innovation and long-term compensation was found among either high tech or low tech firms.[114]

Although long-term performance-based incentives may reduce the temptation to under invest in the short run, they increase executive exposure to risks associated with uncontrollable events, such as market fluctuations and industry decline. The longer the focus of incentive compensation, the greater are the long-term risks borne by top-level managers. Also, because long-term incentives tie a manager's overall wealth to the firm in a way that is inflexible, such incentives and ownership may not be valued as highly by a manager as by outside investors who have the opportunity to diversify their wealth in a number of other financial investments.[115] Thus, firms may have to overcompensate managers using long-term incentives, especially stock options, as the next section suggests.

The Effectiveness of Executive Compensation

The compensation recently received by some top-level managers, especially CEOs, has angered many stakeholders, including shareholders. Table 10.3 lists the compensation received by the highest-paid U.S. CEOs in the 1990s, and Table 10.4 shows the

Table 10.3 Highest-Paid U.S. CEOs, 1990–2000

Year	CEO, *Company*	Compensation (in $millions)
1990	Steven Ross, *Time Warner*	$75
1991	Roberto Goizueta, *Coca-Cola*	$61
1992	Alan Greenberg, *Bear Stearns*	$16
1993	George Fisher, *Eastman Kodak*	$29
1994	Lawrence Bossidy, *AlliedSignal*	$34
1995	Lawrence Coss, *Green Tree Financial*	$66
1996	Michael Eisner, *Walt Disney*	$194
1997	Henry Silverman, *Cendant*	$194
1998	Michael Dell,* *Dell Computer*	$94
1999	Charles Wang, *Computer Associates*	$507
2000	Steven Jobs, *Apple Computer*	$381

Note: "Compensation" includes salary, bonuses, restricted stock granted (regardless of when it vests), long-term payouts, "other" compensation, and an estimate of the present value of options grants.
*Though reported in fiscal year 1999, Dell's options were granted in March and July 1998.
SOURCE: From "The Great CEO Pay Heist" by G. Covin in *Fortune*, June 25, 2001, pp. 66–67.

largest value of stock options for CEOs for the same time period. As the tables show, in 2000, Steven Jobs, CEO of Apple Computer, had both the highest total compensation and value of stock options granted at $381 and $872 million, respectively.[116]

As Tables 10.3 and 10.4 indicate, stock and stock options are the primary component of large compensation packages. In fact, the average amount of the stock held by top executives and directors of firms reached 21 percent in the 1990s. This trend

Table 10.4 Largest Options Grants, 1990–2000

Year	CEO, *Company*	Grants (in $millions)
1990	Steven Ross, *Time Warner*	$215
1991	Leon Hirsch, *U.S. Surgical*	$170
1992	Roy Vagelos, *Merck*	$35
1993	George Fisher, *Eastman Kodak*	$67
1994	Lawrence Bossidy, *AlliedSignal*	$63
1995	Millard Drexler, *Gap*	$79
1996	Michael Eisner, *Walt Disney*	$506
1997	Henry Silverman, *Cendant*	$570
1998	Michael Dell,* *Dell Computer*	$272
1999	Joseph Nacchio, *Qwest Communications*	$257
2000	Steven Jobs, *Apple Computer*	$872

Note: These figures reflect the face value of the options at the time they were granted–that is, the then-current price of the stock multiplied by the number of shares optioned. Options, of course, don't automatically deliver wealth. For that to happen, the stock must increase in value.
*Though reported in fiscal year 1999, Dell's options were granted in March and July 1998.
SOURCE: From "The Great CEO Pay Heist" by G. Covin in *Fortune*, June 25, 2001, pp. 66–67.

has continued into the 21st century, partly because of the long-term incentive plans that compensate executives in stock options and stock.[117]

The primary reasons for compensating executives in stock is that the practice affords them with an incentive to keep the stock price high and hence aligns managers' interests with shareholders' interests. However, there may be some unintended consequences. Managers who own greater than 1 percent of their firm's stock may be less likely to be forced out of their jobs, even when the firm is performing poorly.[118] Furthermore, a review of the research suggests "that firm size accounts for more than 40 percent of the variance in total CEO pay, while firm performance accounts for less than 5 percent of the variance."[119] Thus, the effectiveness of pay plans as a governance mechanism is suspect.

© JOHN G. MABANGLO/AFP/CORBIS

Apple CEO Steve Jobs, who cofounded Apple in 1976 and returned to the firm in 1997. His business philosophy is, "It's not about the money. It's about the people you have, how you're led and how much you get it." It may also be about the options he holds, which have an estimated value of up to $1.4 billion, and the $9 million Gulfstream jet he received as his 1999 bonus.

Another way that boards may compensate executives is through loans with favorable, or no, interest for the purpose of buying company stock. If appropriately used, this practice can be a governance tool, since it aligns executives' priorities with the shareholders in that the executives hold stock, not just options on the stock. They gain or lose money along with the shareholders. "When people exercise most stock options, they pay the regular income-tax rate—close to 40 percent for executives—on the difference between the option's exercise price and the share price at that time. But if executives buy shares with borrowed money instead of receiving options, the government considers their profit to be an investment gain, not a part of their salary, and they pay only the capital-gains tax of 20 percent or less."[120]

Despite the positive benefits of providing loans for buying stock, it can also be devastating if the value of the stock falls. For example, in 1998, Comdisco lent 106 executives an average of $1 million to buy company stock; the price of the stock at that time was $20 a share. At the beginning of 2002, the stock traded at about 50 cents per share and $104 million of the original $109 million in loans is still outstanding. A loan to buy stock seems effective only when the upside is considered. But when stocks fall, and thus the executive's ability to pay back the loan decreases, companies can be seriously affected.[121]

To foster improved performances from their companies during the recessionary year 2001, many boards granted more stock options to executives than they had in the past. This trend of increasing stock options to compensate managers after a bad year seems to run counter to the concept of pay for performance. For example, Larry Ellison, CEO of Oracle, cashed in options for 23 million shares of stock worth $700 million in January 2001. To make good on these options and provide Ellison with 23 million shares, Oracle must issue that many new shares of stock, repurchase that amount from investors, or do a mixture of the two. No matter which approach Oracle takes, shareholder value or available cash decreases (this phenomenon is often called shareholder dilution).

While some stock option-based compensation plans are well designed with option strike prices substantially higher than current stock prices, too many have been designed simply to give executives more wealth that will not immediately show up on the balance sheet.[122] Research of stock option repricing where the strike price value of the option has been changed to lower than it was originally set suggests that step is taken more frequently in high risk situations. However, it also happens when firm performance was poor to restore the incentive effect for the option. But evidence also suggests that politics are often involved.[123] Again, this evidence shows that no internal governance mechanism is perfect.

Market for Corporate Control

The **market for corporate control** is an external governance mechanism that becomes active when a firm's internal controls fail.

The **market for corporate control** is an external governance mechanism that becomes active when a firm's internal controls fail.[124] The market for corporate control is composed of individuals and firms that buy ownership positions in or take over potentially undervalued corporations so they can form new divisions in established diversified companies or merge two previously separate firms. Because the undervalued firm's executives are assumed to be the party responsible for formulating and implementing the strategy that led to poor performance, that team is usually replaced. For instance, HP has performed better than Compaq recently, and the merger between the two firms described in the Strategic Focus on page 322 may turn out to be controlled by HP. Thus, when the market for corporate control operates effectively, it ensures that managers who are ineffective or act opportunistically are disciplined.[125]

The market for corporate control governance mechanism should be triggered by a firm's poor performance relative to industry competitors. A firm's poor performance, often demonstrated by the firm's earning below-average returns, is an indicator that internal governance mechanisms have failed; that is, their use did not result in managerial decisions that maximized shareholder value. This market has been active for some time. As noted in Chapter 7, the 1980s were known as a time of merger mania, with almost 55,000 acquisitions valued at approximately $1.3 trillion. However, there were many more acquisitions in the 1990s, and the value of mergers and acquisitions in that decade was more than $10 trillion.[126]

During the economic downturn of 2001–2002, unsolicited takeover bids increased. In a recession, poorly managed firms are more easily identified.[127] In a few cases, unsolicited offers may come from familiar parties. Ford made an offer to buy back at $30 per share the Hertz stock it sold to the public at $24 per share a few years ago. The stock had reached $64 per share but then fell drastically. Even though it sold a substantial amount of stock, Ford retained significant ownership control. Critics think that Ford has taken advantage of Hertz investors by offering only $30 when they felt it was worth at least $40 per share at the time. The directors of Hertz, who owned only 6,000 shares, did not have much control over whether to sell or keep the stock. In this case, minority stakeholders had little or no say in decision making because of Ford's strong ownership position.[128]

Managerial Defense Tactics

Hostile takeovers are the major activity in the market for corporate control governance mechanism. Not all hostile takeovers are prompted by poorly performing targets, and firms targeted for hostile takeovers may use multiple defense tactics to fend off the takeover attempt. Historically, the increased use of the market for corporate control has enhanced the sophistication and variety of managerial defense tactics that are used to reduce the influence of this governance mechanism. The market for corporate control tends to increase risk for managers. As a result, managerial pay is often augmented indirectly through golden parachutes (wherein a CEO can receive up to three years' salary if his or her firm is taken over).

Among other outcomes, takeover defenses increase the costs of mounting a takeover, causing the incumbent management to become entrenched, while reducing the chances of introducing a new management team.[129] Some defense tactics require asset restructuring created by divesting one or more divisions in the diversified firm's portfolio. Others necessitate only changes in the financial structure of the firm, such as repurchasing shares of the firm's outstanding stock.[130] Some tactics (e.g., reincorporation of the firm in another state) require shareholder approval, but the greenmail tactic, wherein money is used to repurchase stock from a corporate raider to avoid the takeover of the firm, does not. These defense tactics are controversial, and the research on their effects is inconclusive. Alternatively, most institutional investors oppose the use of defense tactics. TIAA-CREF and CalPERS have taken actions to have several firms' poison pills eliminated.[131]

As an example, when Alltel Corp. decided to try to take over CenturyTel Inc., a smaller competitor in the telecommunications industry, CenturyTel rejected Alltel's offer to purchase the company despite the large premium Alltel was willing to pay. For Alltel to succeed in a hostile takeover bid, it would have had to overcome many defenses. For example, CenturyTel staggered its board elections—new board members are elected on a staggered schedule, meaning a bid to take control of the board of directors could take years. In addition, company bylaws required a supermajority of shares to support a takeover bid. The company also had arranged to provide significant voting power to long-term shareholders and employees, who are expected to be more loyal to a company. Finally, CenturyTel also boasted a poison pill: as soon as a company or investor gained control of more than 15 percent of the stock, the board would automatically reject a merger. Because the board would have rejected a merger, Alltel would then need to have a shareholder vote taken and would have needed to receive 80 percent support to be successful. Thus, the bid by Alltel was not successful.[132]

A potential problem with the market for corporate control is that it may not be totally efficient. A study of several of the most active corporate raiders in the 1980s showed that approximately 50 percent of their takeover attempts targeted firms with above-average performance in their industry—corporations that were neither undervalued nor poorly managed.[133] The targeting of high-performance businesses may lead to acquisitions at premium prices and to decisions by managers of the targeted firm to establish what may prove to be costly takeover defense tactics to protect their corporate positions.[134]

Although the market for corporate control lacks the precision of internal governance mechanisms, the fear of acquisition and influence by corporate raiders is an effective constraint on the managerial-growth motive.[135] The market for corporate control has been responsible for significant changes in many firms' strategies and, when used appropriately, has served shareholders' interests.[136] But this market and other means of corporate governance vary by region of the world and by country. Accordingly, we next address the topic of international corporate governance.

International Corporate Governance

Understanding the corporate governance structure of the United Kingdom and the United States is inadequate for a multinational firm in today's global economy.[137] The governance of German and Japanese corporations, and corporations in other countries, illustrate that the nature of corporate governance throughout the world has been affected by the realities of the global economy and its competitive challenges.[138] While the stability associated with German and Japanese governance structures has historically been viewed as an asset, some believe that it may now be a burden.[139] And the governance in Germany and Japan is changing, just as it is changing in other parts of the world.

For example, shareholder activism is increasing in South Korea. Small shareholders won a lawsuit against the heads of Samsung Group, the parent company of Samsung Electronics. The suit alleged that the company was misusing funds; profits from the successful businesses in the corporation were diverted to poorly performing sister companies so as to make them appear to be more successful than they were. Although the $7 million that ten company officers must pay back to the company does not greatly reduce their personal worth, the ruling is a large victory for small shareholders in this Southeast Asian country.[140]

Corporate Governance in Germany

In many private German firms, the owner and manager may still be the same individual. In these instances, there is no agency problem.[141] Even in publicly traded German corporations, there is often a dominant shareholder. Thus, the concentration of ownership is an important means of corporate governance in Germany, as it is in the United States.[142]

Historically, banks have been at the center of the German corporate governance structure, as is also the case in many other European countries, such as Italy and France. As lenders, banks become major shareholders when companies they financed earlier seek funding on the stock market or default on loans. Although the stakes are usually under 10 percent, the only legal limit on how much of a firm's stock banks can hold is that a single ownership position cannot exceed 15 percent of the bank's capital. Through their shareholdings, and by casting proxy votes for individual shareholders who retain their shares with the banks, three banks in particular—Deutsche, Dresdner, and Commerzbank—exercise significant power. Although shareholders can tell the banks how to vote their ownership position, they generally do not do so. A combination of their own holdings and their proxies results in majority positions for these three banks in many German companies. Those banks, along with others, monitor and control managers, both as lenders and as shareholders, by electing representatives to supervisory boards.

German firms with more than 2,000 employees are required to have a two-tiered board structure. Through this structure, the supervision of management is separated from other duties normally assigned to a board of directors, especially the nomination of new board members. Germany's two-tiered system places the responsibility for monitoring and controlling managerial (or supervisory) decisions and actions in the hands of a separate group.[143] While all the functions of direction and management are the responsibility of the management board (the Vorstand), appointment to the Vorstand is the responsibility of the supervisory tier (the Aufsichtsrat). Employees, union members, and shareholders appoint members to the Aufsichtsrat.

Because of the role of local government (through the board structure) and the power of banks in Germany's corporate governance structure, private shareholders rarely have major ownership positions in German firms. Large institutional investors, such as pension funds and insurance companies, are also relatively insignificant owners of corporate stock. Thus, at least historically, German executives generally have not been dedicated to the maximization of shareholder value that is occurring in many countries.

Volkswagen (VW) made an amazing turnaround in the latter half of the 1990s. The company became much more profitable than it had been, and it appeared to be headed to new heights. Despite these promising signs, many investors had uneasy feelings about VW. The company would not release financial data including operating profits that investors wanted to examine. Plus, it was difficult to learn how VW calculates earnings. Some people wondered whether the earnings were real or "pumped-up." As a result, VW's stock price has changed little since the spring of 1997. In 2001, VW's market capitalization was less than Bayerische Motoren Werke's (BMW's), another German carmaker, in spite of the fact that VW generated twice as much revenue as BMW.

Investors suspected that VW management cared little for profit margins. This might be because the largest stakeholder in VW was the government of Lower Saxony, in which five of VW's seven German factories are located. These five factories are among the least productive in Europe. "The government of Lower Saxony . . . worries more about jobs than shareholder value."[144] Thus, the stock price of Volkswagen should have been higher, but problems with productivity (because of government ownership of stock) and investor trust kept it low.

Corporate governance in Germany is changing, at least partially, because of the increasing globalization of business. Many German firms are beginning to gravitate toward the U.S. system. For example, German drug maker Bayer experienced a 40 percent decline in its stock price on the Frankfurt Exchange throughout 2001. While some of this decline can be attributed to the failure of Baycol, a cholesterol-lowering drug that was implicated in 52 deaths, much can be ascribed to investor discontent with the company's strategy. Activist shareholders have tried to convince management to sell off under-performing parts of the company and focus on the lucrative pharmaceutical business. One London analyst indicated, "This is a classic case of a company that should be broken up to get some value out of it, but management clearly doesn't agree."[145] However, it will be difficult for Bayer not to refocus because it is listed on the New York Stock Exchange and will feel continued pressure to sell off under-performing divisions.

© TORU YAMANAKA/AFP/CORBIS

Timothy Collins (right), in 1995 founded Ripplewood Holdings LLC, named after his grandfather's Kentucky tobacco farm. In March 2000 his New-York based private equity company became the first overseas investor to buy a Japanese bank (the Long Term Credit Bank (LTCB), which it relaunched as Shinsei with Masamoto Yashiro (left) serving as its president). Ripplewood also bought the biggest share of 93-year-old Japanese music company Nippon Columbia Co. and purchased Seagaia, Japan's sprawling golf-and-beach resort.

Corporate Governance in Japan

Attitudes toward corporate governance in Japan are affected by the concepts of obligation, family, and consensus.[146] In Japan, an obligation "may be to return a service for one rendered or it may derive from a more general relationship, for example, to one's family or old alumni, or one's company (or Ministry), or the country. This sense of particular obligation is common elsewhere but it feels stronger in Japan."[147] As part of a company family, individuals are members of a unit that envelops their lives; families command the attention and allegiance of parties throughout corporations. Moreover, a *keiretsu* (a group of firms tied together by cross-shareholdings) is more than an economic concept; it, too, is a family. Consensus, an important influence in Japanese corporate governance, calls for the expenditure of significant amounts of energy to win the hearts and minds of people whenever possible, as opposed to issuing edicts from top executives. Consensus is highly valued, even when it results in a slow and cumbersome decision-making process.

As in Germany, banks in Japan play an important role in financing and monitoring large public firms. The bank owning the largest share of stocks and the largest amount of debt—the main bank—has the closest relationship with the company's top executives. The main bank provides financial advice to the firm and also closely monitors managers. Thus, Japan has a bank-based financial and corporate governance structure, whereas the United States has a market-based financial and governance structure.

Aside from lending money, a Japanese bank can hold up to 5 percent of a firm's total stock; a group of related financial institutions can hold up to 40 percent. In many cases, main-bank relationships are part of a horizontal keiretsu. A keiretsu firm usually owns less than 2 percent of any other member firm; however, each company typically has a stake of that size in every firm in the keiretsu. As a result, somewhere between 30 and 90 percent of a firm is owned by other members of the keiretsu. Thus, a keiretsu is a system of relationship investments.

As is the case in Germany, Japan's structure of corporate governance is changing. For example, because of their continuing development as economic organizations, the role of banks in the monitoring and control of managerial behavior and firm outcomes is less significant than in the past.[148] The Asian economic crisis in the latter part of the 1990s made the governance problems in Japanese corporations apparent. The problems were readily evidenced in the large and once-powerful Mitsubishi keiretsu. Many of its core members lost substantial amounts of money in the late 1990s.[149]

Still another change in Japan's governance system has occurred in the market for corporate control, which was nonexistent in past years. Japan experienced three recessions in the 1990s and is facing another one at the start of the 21st century. Many managers are unwilling to make the changes necessary to turn their companies around. As a result, many firms in Japan are performing poorly, but could, under the right guidance, improve their performance. Timothy Collins, CEO of Ripplewood Holdings LLC, is acquiring companies that he feels are greatly undervalued, which is a risky move in Japan. Among his takeovers is Shinsei Bank Ltd., formerly Long Term Credit Bank, which was one of the financiers of Japan's post-World War II recovery. This takeover has been good for the bank, which recorded a profit for the year ending March 31, 2001 of $730 million, the company's first profit in over three years.[150]

Global Corporate Governance

The 21st-century competitive landscape is fostering the creation of a relatively uniform governance structure that will be used by firms throughout the world.[151] As markets become more global and customer demands more similar, shareholders are becoming the focus of managers' efforts in an increasing number of companies. Investors are becoming more and more active throughout the world.

Changes in governance are evident in many countries and are moving the governance models closer to that of the United States. For example, in France, very little information about top executives' compensation has traditionally been provided. However, this practice has come under pressure with increasing foreign investment in French companies.[152] One report recommended that the positions of CEO and chairman of the board be held by different individuals; it also recommended reducing the tenure of board members and disclosing their pay.[153] In South Korea, changes went much further: Principles of corporate governance were adopted that "provide proper incentives for the board and management to pursue objectives that are in the interests of the company and the shareholders and facilitate effective monitoring, thereby encouraging firms to use resources more efficiently."[154]

Even in transitional economies, such as those of China and Russia, changes in corporate governance are occurring.[155] However, changes are implemented much slower in these economies. Chinese firms have found it helpful to use stock-based compensation plans, thereby providing an incentive for foreign companies to invest in China.[156] Because Russia has reduced controls on the economy and on business activity much faster than China has, the country needs more effective governance systems to control its managerial activities. In fact, research suggests that ownership concentration leads to lower performance in Russia, primarily because minority shareholder rights are not well protected through adequate governance controls.[157]

Governance Mechanisms and Ethical Behavior

The governance mechanisms described in this chapter are designed to ensure that the agents of the firm's owners—the corporation's top executives—make strategic decisions that best serve the interests of the entire group of stakeholders, as described in Chapter

Strategic Focus

The Enron Disaster: The Importance of Ethics in Governance

Enron, the large energy-trading firm, headquartered in Houston, filed for bankruptcy in late 2001. Huge losses were suffered not only by Enron's shareholders, employees, and managers, but also by other stakeholders in the energy industry. These losses were the result of a disaster created by the poor ethics of Enron's top executives and its board of directors. Not only were Enron and other energy firms affected, but the entire accounting and auditing industry was also tarnished by the misconduct of Enron's auditor Arthur Andersen and Enron executives. Beyond Andersen and Enron, any firm that has less transparent accounting practices has been called into question. The magnitude of this disaster and its effect on the U.S. economy were underscored by President Bush in his 2002 State of the Union address when he indicated that accounting reform would be on the national agenda.

© STEPHEN JAFFE/AFP/CORBIS

Kenneth Lay, former Enron CEO, was called before Congress in February 2002, but invoked his Fifth Amendment rights and did not testify. Although his wife proclaimed tearfully that "Everything we had was mostly in Enron stock. . . . We are struggling for liquidity," Lay had sold 18 million shares of Enron for $101 million between October 1998 and November 2001.

Enron's problems started with its decisions to create off balance sheet partnerships or private equity placement with pension funds, such as those mentioned in an earlier Strategic Focus about CalPERS. Andrew Fastow, Enron's former chief financial officer, formed a number of these private placements, enriching him and other Enron employees through these partnership deals. The problem was that many of these partnerships were underwritten by Enron stock and thus were potential liabilities for Enron shareholders.

Enron's board of directors should have ensured that private partnerships such as these were not approved because they represented a conflict of

1. In the United States, shareholders are recognized as a company's most significant stakeholder. Thus, governance mechanisms focus on the control of managerial decisions to ensure that shareholders' interests will be served, but product market stakeholders (e.g., customers, suppliers, and host communities) and organizational stakeholders (e.g., managerial and nonmanagerial employees) are important as well.[158] Therefore, at least the minimal interests or needs of all stakeholders must be satisfied through the firm's actions. Otherwise, dissatisfied stakeholders will withdraw their support from one firm and provide it to another (for example, customers will purchase products from a supplier offering an acceptable substitute).

The firm's strategic competitiveness is enhanced when its governance mechanisms take into consideration the interests of all stakeholders. Although the idea is subject to debate, some believe that ethically responsible companies design and use governance mechanisms that serve all stakeholders' interests. There is, however, a more critical relationship between ethical behavior and corporate governance mechanisms. The Strategic Focus on the Enron disaster illustrates the devastating effect of poor ethical behavior not only on a firm's stakeholders, but also on other firms.

interest for Fastow and other key executives. Even if Enron had a reason to pursue private placement of equity investments, the transactions and their effects for shareholders should have been transparent in accounting reports. Because they were not transparent, Enron's auditor, Arthur Andersen, shared Enron's culpability by its approval of the financial reports Enron provided to the public. An Andersen partner was fired and later prosecuted for authorizing the destruction of thousands of e-mails and paper documents related to its auditing of Enron's finances—after learning that federal regulators were probing Enron's finances and accounting practices. Thus, both Enron and Andersen employees contributed to Enron's ethical failure.

As a result of this disaster, regulatory procedures regarding financial reporting will be strengthened and enforced. Auditing firms will also tighten their reporting requirements. Another outcome will be the further separation between consulting and auditing. Even though Arthur Andersen's consulting business had broken from the firm and renamed itself Accenture as an independent firm in a highly publicized action several years earlier, Andersen continued to offer non-auditing consulting services to its clients. As such, in addition to serving as Enron's auditor, Andersen also had a significant consulting relationship with Enron—and a contributing conflict of interest with the firm. Andersen may not survive as an independent company due to this crisis.

Because ethical governance had not been implemented by Enron or by Andersen, the resulting financial disaster devastated not only Enron's stakeholders and those closely associated with them, but, by implication, many other firms—even those only remotely associated with Enron.

SOURCES: N. Byrnes, 2002, Paying for the sins of Enron, *Business Week*, February 11, 35; 2002, A chronology of Enron's recent woes, *The Wall Street Journal Interactive*, http://www.wsj.com, February 5; G. Colvin, 2002, You're on your own, *Fortune*, February 4, 42; 2002, Enron and stock market jitters; The good Lay, *The Economist*, February 2, 70; J. D. Glater, 2002, Lone ranger of auditors fellow slowly out of the saddle, *The New York Times*, http://www.nytimes.com, April 20; D. B. Henriques, 2002, Even a watchdog is not always fully awake, *The New York Times*, http://www.nytimes.com, February 5; S. Lubov & E. McDonald, 2002, *Forbes*, February 18, 56–57; A. Barrionuevo, 2001, Williams Cos. seeks stronger balance sheet among jitters concerning energy traders, *The Wall Street Journal*, December 20, B2; A. J. Felo, 2001, Ethics programs board involvement and potential conflicts of interest in corporate governance, *Journal of Business Ethics*, 32: 205–218; G. Morgenson, 2001, After Enron's failure should Calpine investors worry? *The New York Times* http://www.nytimes.com, December 9.

As the Strategic Focus about Enron demonstrates, all corporate owners are vulnerable to unethical behaviors by their employees, including top-level managers—the agents who have been hired to make decisions that are in shareholders' best interests. The decisions and actions of a corporation's board of directors can be an effective deterrent to these behaviors. In fact, some believe that the most effective boards participate actively to set boundaries for their firms' business ethics and values.[159] Once formulated, the board's expectations related to ethical decisions and actions of all of the firm's stakeholders must be clearly communicated to its top-level managers. Moreover, as shareholders' agents, these managers must understand that the board will hold them fully accountable for the development and support of an organizational culture that results in ethical decisions and behaviors. As explained in Chapter 12, CEOs can be positive role models for ethical behavior.

Only when the proper corporate governance is exercised can strategies be formulated and implemented that will help the firm achieve strategic competitiveness and earn above-average returns. As the discussion in this chapter suggests, corporate governance mechanisms are a vital, yet imperfect, part of firms' efforts to select and successfully use strategies.

Summary

- Corporate governance is a relationship among stakeholders that is used to determine a firm's direction and control its performance. How firms monitor and control top-level managers' decisions and actions affects the implementation of strategies. Effective governance that aligns managers' decisions with shareholders' interests can be a competitive advantage.
- There are three internal governance mechanisms in the modern corporation—ownership concentration, the board of directors, and executive compensation. The market for corporate control is the single external governance mechanism influencing managers' decisions and the outcomes resulting from them.
- Ownership is separated from control in the modern corporation. Owners (principals) hire managers (agents) to make decisions that maximize the firm's value. As risk-bearing specialists, owners diversify their risk by investing in multiple corporations with different risk profiles. As decision-making specialists, owners expect their agents (the firm's top-level managers) to make decisions that will lead to maximization of the value of their firm. Thus, modern corporations are characterized by an agency relationship that is created when one party (the firm's owners) hires and pays another party (top-level managers) to use its decision-making skills.
- Separation of ownership and control creates an agency problem when an agent pursues goals that conflict with principals' goals. Principals establish and use governance mechanisms to control this problem.
- Ownership concentration is based on the number of large-block shareholders and the percentage of shares they own. With significant ownership percentages, such as those held by large mutual funds and pension funds, institutional investors often are able to influence top executives' strategic decisions and actions. Thus, unlike diffuse ownership, which tends to result in relatively weak monitoring and control of managerial decisions, concentrated ownership produces more active and effective monitoring. An increasingly powerful force in corporate America, institutional investors actively use their positions of concentrated ownership to force managers and boards of directors to make decisions that maximize a firm's value.
- In the United States and the United Kingdom, a firm's board of directors, composed of insiders, related outsiders, and outsiders, is a governance mechanism that shareholders expect to represent their collective interests. The percentage of outside directors on many boards now exceeds the percentage of inside directors. Outsiders are expected to be more independent of a firm's top-level managers compared to those selected from inside the firm.
- Executive compensation is a highly visible and often criticized governance mechanism. Salary, bonuses, and long-term incentives are used to strengthen the alignment between managers' and shareholders' interests. A firm's board of directors is responsible for determining the effectiveness of the firm's executive compensation system. An effective system elicits managerial decisions that are in shareholders' best interests.
- In general, evidence suggests that shareholders and boards of directors have become more vigilant in their control of managerial decisions. Nonetheless, these mechanisms are insufficient to govern managerial behavior in many large companies. Therefore, the market for corporate control is an important governance mechanism. Although it, too, is imperfect, the market for corporate control has been effective in causing corporations to combat inefficient diversification and to implement more effective strategic decisions.
- Corporate governance structures used in Germany and Japan differ from each other and from that used in the United States. Historically, the U.S. governance structure has focused on maximizing shareholder value. In Germany, employees, as a stakeholder group, have a more prominent role in governance. By contrast, until recently, Japanese shareholders played virtually no role in the monitoring and control of top-level managers. However, all of these systems are becoming increasingly similar, as are many governance systems in both developed countries, such as France and Italy, and transitional economies, such as Russia and China.
- Effective governance mechanisms ensure that the interests of all stakeholders are served. Thus, long-term strategic success results when firms are governed in ways that permit at least minimal satisfaction of capital market stakeholders (e.g., shareholders), product market stakeholders (e.g., customers and suppliers), and organizational stakeholders (managerial and nonmanagerial employees, see Chapter 2). Moreover, effective governance produces ethical behavior in the formulation and implementation of strategies.

Review Questions

1. What is corporate governance? What factors account for the considerable amount of attention corporate governance receives from several parties, including shareholder activists, business press writers, and academic scholars? Why is governance necessary to control managers' decisions?
2. What does it mean to say that ownership is separated from control in the modern corporation? Why does this separation exist?
3. What is an agency relationship? What is managerial opportunism? What assumptions do owners of modern corporations make about managers as agents?
4. How is each of the three internal governance mechanisms—ownership concentration, boards of directors, and executive compensation—used to align the interests of managerial agents with those of the firm's owners?
5. What trends exist regarding executive compensation? What is the effect of the increased use of long-term incentives on executives' strategic decisions?
6. What is the market for corporate control? What conditions generally cause this external governance mechanism to become active? How does the mechanism constrain top executives' decisions and actions?
7. What is the nature of corporate governance in Germany and Japan?
8. How can corporate governance foster ethical strategic decisions and behaviors on the part of managers as agents?

Experiential Exercise

Corporate Governance and the Board of Directors

The composition and actions of the firm's board of directors have a profound effect on the firm. "The most important thing a board can ask itself today is whether it is professionally managed in the same way that the company itself is professionally managed," says Carolyn Brancato, director of the Global Corporate Governance Research Center at The Conference Board, which creates and disseminates knowledge about management and the marketplace. "The collegial nature of boards must give way to a new emphasis on professionalism, and directors must ask management the hard questions."

Following are several questions about boards of directors and corporate governance. Break into small groups and use the content of this chapter to discuss these questions. Be prepared to defend your answers.

1. How can corporate governance keep a company viable and maintain its shareholders' confidence?
2. How should boards evaluate CEOs? How can the board learn of problems in the CEO's performance? How does a board decide when a CEO needs to be replaced? How should succession plans be put in place?
3. Who should serve on a board? What human factors affect board members' interactions with each other, and how can those factors be used to best advantage?
4. Should independent directors meet on a regular basis without management present? Does the board have a role in setting corporate strategy?
5. What should a CEO expect of directors? How can a CEO move unproductive participants off a board?
6. What processes can be put in place to help make the board more aware of problems in company operations? How can the board be assured of receiving appropriate information? How can the board fulfill its monitoring role while relying on information provided by management and external accountants?

Notes

1. M. Carpenter & J. Westphal, 2001, Strategic context of external network ties: Examining the impact of director appointments on board involvement in strategic decision making, *Academy of Management Journal,* 44: 639–660.
2. A. Henderson & J. Fredrickson, 2001, Top management team coordination needs and the CEO pay gap: A competitive test of economic and behavioral views, *Academy of Management Journal,* 44: 96–117.
3. F. Elloumi & J.-P. Gueyie, 2001, CEO compensation, IOS and the role of corporate governance, *Corporate Governance,* 1(2): 23–33; J. E. Core, R. W. Holthausen, & D. F. Larcker, 1999, Corporate governance, chief executive officer compensation, and firm performance, *Journal of Financial Economics,* 51: 371–406.
4. A. J. Hillman, G. D. Keim, & R. A. Luce, 2001, Board composition and stakeholder performance: Do stakeholder directors make a difference? *Business and Society,* 40: 295–314; R. K. Mitchell, B. R. Agle, & D. J. Wood, 1997, Toward a theory of stakeholder identification and salience: Defining the principle of who and what really counts, *Academy of Management Review,* 22: 853–886.
5. P. Stiles, 2001, The impact of the board on strategy: An empirical examination, *Journal of Management Studies,* 38: 627–650; J. H. Davis, F. D. Schoorman, & L. Donaldson, 1997, Toward a stewardship theory of management, *Academy of Management Review,* 22: 20–47.
6. D. Finegold, E. E. Lawler III, & J. Conger, 2001, Building a better board, *Journal of Business Strategy,* 22(6): 33–37.
7. E. F. Fama & M. C. Jensen, 1983, Separation of ownership and control, *Journal of Law and Economics,* 26: 301–325.
8. R. Charan, 1998, *How Corporate Boards Create Competitive Advantage,* San Francisco: Jossey-Bass.
9. A. Cannella Jr., A. Pettigrew, & D. Hambrick, 2001, Upper echelons: Donald Hambrick on executives and strategy, *Academy of Management Executive,* 15(3): 36–52; J. D. Westphal & E. J. Zajac, 1997, Defections from the inner circle: Social exchange, reciprocity and diffusion of board independence in U.S. corporations, *Administrative Science Quarterly,* 42: 161–212; Ward, 21st Century Corporate Board.
10. J. McGuire & S. Dow, 2002, The Japanese keiretsu system: An empirical analysis, *Journal of Business Research,* 55: 33–40.
11. J. Charkham, 1994, *Keeping Good Company: A Study of Corporate Governance in Five Countries,* New York: Oxford University Press, 1.
12. A. Cadbury, 1999, The future of governance: The rules of the game, *Journal of General Management,* 24: 1–14.
13. S. Johnson, P. Boone, A. Breach, & E. Friedman, 2000, Corporate governance in the Asian financial crisis, *Journal of Financial Economics,* 58: 141–186.
14. Cadbury Committee, 1992, *Report of the Cadbury Committee on the Financial Aspects of Corporate Governance,* London: Gee.
15. C. K. Prahalad & J. P. Oosterveld, 1999, Transforming internal governance: The challenge for multinationals, *Sloan Management Review,* 40(3): 31–39.
16. M. A. Hitt, R. A. Harrison, & R. D. Ireland, 2001, *Creating Value through Mergers and Acquisitions: A Complete Guide to Successful M&As,* New York: Oxford University Press; M. A. Hitt, R. E. Hoskisson, R. A. Johnson, & D. D. Moesel, 1996, The market for corporate control and firm innovation, *Academy of Management Journal,* 39: 1084–1119; J. P. Walsh & R. Kosnik, 1993, Corporate raiders and their disciplinary role in the market for corporate control, *Academy of Management Journal,* 36: 671–700.
17. Davis, Schoorman & Donaldson, Toward a stewardship theory of management.
18. R. C. Anderson, T. W. Bates, J. M. Bizjak, & M. L. Lemmon, 2000, Corporate governance and firm diversification, *Financial Management,* 29(1): 5–22; C. Sundaramurthy, J. M. Mahoney, & J. T. Mahoney, 1997, Board structure, antitakeover provisions, and stockholder wealth, *Strategic Management Journal,* 18: 231–246; K. J. Rediker & A. Seth, 1995, Boards of directors and substitution effects of alternative governance mechanisms, *Strategic Management Journal,* 16: 85–99.
19. R. E. Hoskisson, M. A. Hitt, R. A. Johnson, & W. Grossman, 2002, Conflicting voices: The effects of ownership heterogeneity and internal governance on corporate strategy, *Academy of Management Journal,* in press.
20. G. E. Davis & T. A. Thompson, 1994, A social movement perspective on corporate control, *Administrative Science Quarterly,* 39: 141–173.
21. R. Bricker & N. Chandar, 2000, Where Berle and Means went wrong: A reassessment of capital market agency and financial reporting, *Accounting, Organizations and Society,* 25: 529–554; M. A. Eisenberg, 1989, The structure of corporation law, *Columbia Law Review,* 89(7): 1461 as cited in R. A. G. Monks & N. Minow, 1995, *Corporate Governance,* Cambridge, MA: Blackwell Business, 7.
22. R. M. Wiseman & L. R. Gomez-Mejia, 1999, A behavioral agency model of managerial risk taking, *Academy of Management Review,* 23: 133–153.
23. E. E. Fama, 1980, Agency problems and the theory of the firm, *Journal of Political Economy,* 88: 288–307.
24. J. A. Byrne & B. Elgin, 2002, Cisco: Behind the hype, *Business Week,* January 21, 56–61.
25. D. Stires, 2001, America's best & worst wealth creators, *Fortune,* December 10, 137–142.
26. M. Jensen & W. Meckling, 1976, Theory of the firm: Managerial behavior, agency costs, and ownership structure, *Journal of Financial Economics,* 11: 305–360.
27. L. R. Gomez-Mejia, M. Nunez-Nickel, & I. Gutierrez, 2001, The role of family ties in agency contracts, *Academy of Management Journal,* 44: 81–95; H. C. Tosi, J. Katz, & L. R. Gomez-Mejia, 1997, Disaggregating the agency contract: The effects of monitoring, incentive alignment, and term in office on agent decision making, *Academy of Management Journal,* 40: 584–602.
28. M. G. Jacobides & D. C. Croson, 2001, Information policy: Shaping the value of agency relationships, *Academy of Management Review,* 26: 202–223.
29. R. Mangel & M. Useem, 2001, The strategic role of gainsharing, *Journal of Labor Research,* 2: 327–343; T. M. Welbourne & L. R. Gomez-Mejia, 1995, Gainsharing: A critical review and a future research agenda, *Journal of Management,* 21: 577.
30. Jacobides & Croson, Information policy: Shaping the value of agency relationships.
31. O. E. Williamson, 1996, *The Mechanisms of Governance,* New York: Oxford University Press, 6; O. E. Williamson, 1993, Opportunism and its critics, *Managerial and Decision Economics,* 14: 97–107.
32. C. C. Chen, M. W. Peng, & P. A. Saparito, 2002, Individualism, collectivism, and opportunism: A cultural perspective on transaction cost economics, *Journal of Management,* in press; S. Ghoshal & P. Moran, 1996, Bad for practice: A critique of the transaction cost theory, *Academy of Management Review,* 21: 13–47.
33. K. H. Wathne & J. B. Heide, 2000, Opportunism in interfirm relationships: Forms, outcomes, and solutions, *Journal of Marketing,* 64(4): 36–51.
34. Y. Amihud & B. Lev, 1981, Risk reduction as a managerial motive for conglomerate mergers, *Bell Journal of Economics,* 12: 605–617.
35. Anderson, Bates, Bizjak & Lemmon, Corporate governance and firm diversification; R. E. Hoskisson & T. A. Turk, 1990, Corporate restructuring: Governance and control limits of the internal market, *Academy of Management Review,* 15: 459–477.
36. M. A. Geletkanycz, B. K. Boyd, & S. Finklestein, 2001, The strategic value of CEO external directorate networks: Implications for CEO compensation, *Strategic Management Journal,* 9: 889–898.
37. P. Wright, M. Kroll, & D. Elenkov, 2002, Acquisition returns, increase in firm size and chief executive officer compensation: The moderating role of monitoring, *Academy of Management Journal,* 45: in press; S. Finkelstein & D. C. Hambrick, 1989, Chief executive compensation: A study of the intersection of markets and political processes, *Strategic Management Journal,* 16: 221, 239; H. C. Tosi & L. R. Gomez-Mejia, 1989, The decoupling of CEO pay and performance: An agency theory perspective, *Administrative Science Quarterly,* 34: 169–189.
38. Hoskisson & Turk, Corporate restructuring.
39. Gomez-Mejia, Nunez-Nickel, & Gutierrez, The role of family ties in agency contracts.
40. C. Matlack, 2001, Gemplus: No picnic in Provence, *Business Week Online,* http://www.businessweek.com, August 6; C. Matlack, 2001, A global clash at France's Gemplus, *Business Week Online,* http://www.businessweek.com, December 21.
41. M. S. Jensen, 1986, Agency costs of free cash flow, corporate finance, and takeovers, *American Economic Review,* 76: 323–329.
42. T. H. Brush, P. Bromiley, & M. Hendrickx, 2000, The free cash flow hypothesis for sales growth and firm performance, *Strategic Management Journal,* 21: 455–472; H. DeAngelo & L. DeAngelo, 2000, Controlling stockholders and the disciplinary role of corporate payout policy: A study of the Times Mirror Company, *Journal of Financial Economics,* 56: 153–207.
43. K. Ramaswamy, M. Li, & R. Veliyath, 2002, Variations in ownership behavior and propensity to diversify: A study of the Indian corporate context, *Strategic Management Journal,* 23: 345–358.

44. P. Wright, M. Kroll, A. Lado, & B. Van Ness, 2002, The structure of ownership and corporate acquisition strategies, *Strategic Management Journal,* 23: 41–53.
45. R. Rajan, H. Servaes, & L. Zingales, 2001, The cost of diversity: The diversification discount and inefficient investment, *Journal of Finance,* 55: 35–79; A. Sharma, 1997, Professional as agent: Knowledge asymmetry in agency exchange, *Academy of Management Review,* 22: 758–798.
46. P. Lane, A. A. Cannella, Jr., & M. H. Lubatkin, 1999, Agency problems as antecedents to unrelated mergers and diversification: Amihud and Lev reconsidered, *Strategic Management Journal,* 19: 555–578.
47. David Champion, 2001, Off with his head? *Harvard Business Review,* 79(9): 35–46.
48. J. Coles, N. Sen, & V. McWilliams, 2001, An examination of the relationship of governance mechanisms to performance, *Journal of Management,* 27: 23–50.
49. S.-S. Chen & K. W. Ho, 2000, Corporate diversification, ownership structure, and firm value: The Singapore evidence, *International Review of Financial Analysis,* 9: 315–326; R. E. Hoskisson, R. A. Johnson, & D. D. Moesel, 1994, Corporate divestiture intensity in restructuring firms: Effects of governance, strategy, and performance, *Academy of Management Journal,* 37: 1207–1251.
50. S. R. Kole & K. M. Lehn, 1999, Deregulation and the adaptation of governance structure: The case of the U.S. airline industry, *Journal of Financial Economics,* 52: 79–117.
51. K.C. Banning, 1999, Ownership concentration and bank acquisition strategy: An empirical examination, *International Journal of Organizational Analysis,* 7(2): 135–152.
52. A. Berle & G. Means, 1932, *The Modern Corporation and Private Property,* New York: Macmillan.
53. P. A. Gompers & A. Metrick, 2001, Institutional investors and equity prices, *Quarterly Journal of Economics,* 116: 229–259; M. P. Smith, 1996, Shareholder activism by institutional investors: Evidence from CalPERS, *Journal of Finance,* 51: 227–252.
54. M. Useem, 1998, Corporate leadership in a globalizing equity market, *Academy of Management Executive,* 12(3): 43–59.
55. Hoskisson, Hitt, Johnson, & Grossman, Conflicting Voices; C. M. Dailey, 1996, Governance patterns in bankruptcy reorganizations, *Strategic Management Journal,* 17: 355–375.
56. Hoskisson, Hitt, Johnson, & Grossman, Conflicting Voices; Useem, Corporate leadership in a globalizing equity market; R. E. Hoskisson & M. A. Hitt, 1994, *Downscoping: How to Tame the Diversified Firm,* New York: Oxford University Press.
57. K. Rebeiz, 2001, Corporate governance effectiveness in American corporations: A survey, *International Management Journal,* 18(1): 74–80;
58. 2002, CalPERS at a glance, http://www.calpers.com, April 24.
59. 2001, The fading appeal of the boardroom series, *The Economist,* February 10 (Business Special): 67–69.
60. Hoskisson, Hitt, Johnson & Grossman, Conflicting voices; P. David, M. A. Hitt, & J. Gimeno, 2001, The role of institutional investors in influencing R&D, *Academy of Management Journal,* 44: 144–157; B. J. Bushee, 2001, Do institutional investors prefer near-term earnings over long-run value? *Contemporary Accounting Research,* 18: 207–246.
61. 2001, Shareholder activism is rising, *Investor Relations Business,* August 6, 8.
62. 2000, Now, a gadfly can bite 24 hours a day, *Business Week,* January 24, 150.
63. M. J. Roe, 1993, Mutual funds in the boardroom, *Journal of Applied Corporate Finance,* 5(4): 56–61.
64. R. A. G. Monks, 1999, What will be the impact of active shareholders? A practical recipe for constructive change, *Long Range Planning,* 32(1): 20–27.
65. B. S. Black, 1992, Agents watching agents: The promise of institutional investor's voice, *UCLA Law Review,* 39: 871–893.
66. Hoskisson, Hitt, Johnson, & Grossman, Conflicting voices; T. Woidtke, 2002, Agents watching agents?: Evidence from pension fund ownership and firm value, *Journal of Financial Economics,* 63, 99–131.
67. A. Berenson, 2001, The fight for control of Computer Associates, *The New York Times,* http://www.nytimes.com, June 25.
68. A. Park, 2001, If at first you don't succeed, *Business Week,* September 3, 39.
69. C. Sandaramurthy & D. W. Lyon, 1998, Shareholder governance proposals and conflict of interests between inside and outside shareholders, *Journal of Managerial Issues,* 10: 30–44.
70. Wright, Kroll, Lado, & Van Ness, The structure of ownership and corporate acquisition strategies.
71. S. Thomsen & T. Pedersen, 2000, Ownership structure and economic performance in the largest European companies, *Strategic Management Journal,* 21: 689–705.
72. D. R. Dalton, C. M. Daily, A. E. Ellstrand, & J. L. Johnson, 1998, Meta-analytic reviews of board composition, leadership structure, and financial performance, *Strategic Management Journal,* 19: 269–290; M. Huse, 1998, Researching the dynamics of board-stakeholder relations, *Long Range Planning,* 31: 218–226.
73. A. Dehaene, V. De Vuyst, & H. Ooghe, 2001, Corporate performance and board structure in Belgian companies, *Long Range Planning,* 34(3): 383–398;
74. Rebeiz, Corporate governance effectiveness in American corporations; J. K. Seward & J. P Walsh, 1996, The governance and control of voluntary corporate spinoffs, *Strategic Management Journal,* 17: 25–39.
75. S. Young, 2000, The increasing use of non-executive directors: Its impact on UK board structure and governance arrangements, *Journal of Business Finance & Accounting,* 27(9/10): 1311–1342; P. Mallete & R. L. Hogler, 1995, Board composition, stock ownership, and the exemption of directors from liability, *Journal of Management,* 21: 861–878.
76. J. Chidley, 2001, Why boards matter, *Canadian Business,* October 29, 6; D. P. Forbes & F. J. Milliken, 1999, Cognition and corporate governance: Understanding boards of directors as strategic decision-making groups, *Academy of Management Review,* 24: 489–505.
77. Hoskisson, Hitt, Johnson, & Grossman, Conflicting voices; B. D. Baysinger & R. E. Hoskisson, 1990, The composition of boards of directors and strategic control: Effects on corporate strategy, *Academy of Management Review,* 15: 72–87.
78. Carpenter & Westphal, Strategic context of external network ties: Examining the impact of director appointments on board involvement in strategic decision making; E. J. Zajac & J. D. Westphal, 1996, Director reputation, CEO-board power, and the dynamics of board interlocks, *Administrative Science Quarterly,* 41: 507–529.
79. A. Hillman, A. Cannella Jr., & R. Paetzold, 2000, The resource dependence role of corporate directors: Strategic adaptation of board composition in response to environmental change, *Journal of Management Studies,* 37: 235–255; J. D. Westphal & E. J. Zajac, 1995, Who shall govern? CEO/board power, demographic similarity, and new director selection, *Administrative Science Quarterly,* 40: 60–83.
80. J. Westphal & L. Milton, 2000, How experience and network ties affect the influence of demographic minorities on corporate boards, *Administrative Science Quarterly,* June, 45(2): 366–398; R. P. Beatty & E. J. Zajac, 1994, Managerial incentives, monitoring, and risk bearing: A study of executive compensation, ownership, and board structure in initial public offerings, *Administrative Science Quarterly,* 39: 313–335.
81. The fading appeal of the boardroom series. A. Bryant, 1997, CalPERS draws a blueprint for its concept of an ideal board, *The New York Times,* June 17, C1.
82. 2002, Interpublic board to add outsiders, *The New York Times,* http://www.nytimes.com, February 12.
83. A. L. Ranft & H. M. O'Neill, 2001, Board composition and high-flying founders: Hints of trouble to come? *Academy of Management Executive,* 15(1): 126–138.
84. K. Greene, 2002, Dunlap agrees to settle suit over Sunbeam, *The Wall Street Journal,* January 15, A3, A8.
85. Stiles, The impact of the board on strategy; J. A. Byrne, 1999, Commentary: Boards share the blame when the boss fails, *Business Week Online,* http://www.businessweek.com, December 27.
86. E. Perotti & S. Gelfer, 2001, Red barons or robber barons? Governance and investment in Russian financial-industrial groups, *European Economic Review,* 45(9): 1601–1617; I. M. Millstein, 1997, Red herring over independent boards, *The New York Times,* April 6, F10; W. Q. Judge, Jr. & G. H. Dobbins, 1995, Antecedents and effects of outside directors' awareness of CEO decision style, *Journal of Management,* 21: 43–64.
87. I. E. Kesner, 1988, Director characteristics in committee membership: An investigation of type, occupation, tenure and gender, *Academy of Management Journal,* 31: 66–84.
88. T. McNulty & A Pettigrew, 1999, Strategists on the board, *Organization Studies,* 20: 47–74.
89. J. Coles & W. Hesterly, 2000, Independence of the Chairman and board composition: Firm choices and shareholder value, *Journal of Management,* 26: 195–214; S. Zahra, 1996, Governance, ownership and corporate entrepreneurship among the Fortune 500: The moderating impact of industry technological opportunity, *Academy of Management Journal,* 39: 1713–1735.
90. Hoskisson, Hitt, Johnson & Grossman, Conflicting Voices.

91. A, Conger, E.E. Lawler, & D.L. Finegold, 2001, *Corporate Boards: New Strategies for Adding Value at the Top,* San Francisco: Jossey-Bass; J. A. Conger, D. Finegold, & E. E. Lawler, III, 1998, Appraising boardroom performance, *Harvard Business Review,* 76(1): 136–148.
92. J. Marshall, 2001, As boards shrink, responsibilities grow, *Financial Executive,* 17(4): 36–39.
93. C. A. Simmers, 2000, Executive/board politics in strategic decision making, *Journal of Business and Economic Studies,* 4: 37–56.
94. Hoskisson, Hitt, Johnson, & Grossman, Conflicting voices.
95. W. Ocasio, 1999, Institutionalized action and corporate governance, *Administrative Science Quarterly,* 44: 384–416.
96. A. A. Cannella, Jr. & W. Shen, 2001, So close and yet so far: Promotion versus exit for CEO heirs apparent, *Academy of Management Journal,* 44: 252–270.
97. M. Gerety, C. Hoi, & A. Robin, 2001, Do shareholders benefit from the adoption of incentive pay for directors?, *Financial Management,* 30: 45–61; D. C. Hambrick & E. M. Jackson, 2000, Outside directors with a stake: The linchpin in improving governance, *California Management Review,* 42(4): 108–127.
98. S. Rosenstein & J. G. Wyatt, 1997, Inside directors, board effectiveness, and shareholder wealth, *Journal of Financial Economics,* 44: 229–250.
99. J. Kristie, 2001, The shareholder activist: Nell Minow, *Directors and Boards,* 26(1): 16–17.
100. D. C. Hambrick & S. Finkelstein, 1995, The effects of ownership structure on conditions at the top: The case of CEO pay raises, *Strategic Management Journal,* 16: 175.
101. J. S. Miller, R. M. Wiseman, & L. R. Gomez-Mejia, 2002, The fit between CEO compensation design and firm risk, *Academy of Management Journal,* in press; L. Gomez-Mejia & R. M. Wiseman, 1997, Reframing executive compensation: An assessment and outlook, *Journal of Management,* 23: 291–374.
102. J. G. Combs & M. S. Skill, 2002, Managerialist and human capital explanations for key executive pay premiums: A Contingency, *Academy of Management Journal,* in press; S. Finkelstein & B. K. Boyd, 1998, How much does the CEO matter? The role of managerial discretion in the setting of CEO compensation, *Academy of Management Journal,* 41: 179–199.
103. W. G. Sanders & M. A. Carpenter, 1998, Internationalization and firm governance: The roles of CEO compensation, top team composition and board structure, *Academy of Management Journal,* 41: 158–178.
104. N. T. Hill & K. T. Stevens, 2001, Structuring compensation to achieve better financial results, *Strategic Finance,* 9: 48–51; J. D. Westphal & E. J. Zajac, 1999, The symbolic management of stockholders: Corporate governance reform and shareholder reactions, *Administrative Science Quarterly,* 43: 127–153.
105. Elloumi & Gueyie, CEO compensation, IOS and the role of corporate governance; M. J. Conyon & S. I. Peck, 1998, Board control, remuneration committees, and top management compensation, *Academy of Management Journal,* 41: 146–157; Westphal & Zajac, The symbolic management of stockholders.
106. S. O'Donnell, 2000, Managing foreign subsidiaries: Agents of headquarters, or an interdependent network? *Strategic Management Journal,* 21: 521–548; K. Roth & S. O'Donnell, 1996, Foreign subsidiary compensation: An agency theory perspective, *Academy of Management Journal,* 39: 678–703.
107. K. Ramaswamy, R. Veliyath, & L. Gomes, 2000, A study of the determinants of CEO compensation in India, *Management International Review,* 40(2): 167–191.
108. J. Krug & W. Hegarty, 2001, Predicting who stays and leaves after an acquisition: A study of top managers in multinational firms, *Strategic Management Journal,* 22: 185–196.
109. S. Fung, 1999, How should we pay them? *Across the Board,* June: 37–41.
110. M. A. Carpenter & M. G. Sanders, 2002, Top management team compensation: The missing link between CEO pay and firm performance, *Strategic Management Journal,* in press.
111. S. Bryan, L. Hwang, & S. Lilien, 2000, CEO stock-based compensation: An empirical analysis of incentive-intensity, relative mix, and economic determinants, *Journal of Business,* 73: 661–693.
112. C. Peck, H. M. Silvert, & K. Worrell, 1999, Top executive compensation: Canada, France, the United Kingdom, and the United States, *Chief Executive Digest,* 3: 27–29.
113. R. E. Hoskisson, M. A. Hitt, & C. W. L. Hill, 1993, Managerial incentives and investment in R&D in large multiproduct firms, *Organization Science,* 4: 325–341.
114. D. B. Balkin, G. D. Markman, & L. Gomez-Mejia, 2000, Is CEO pay in high-technology firms related to innovation? *Academy of Management Journal,* 43: 1118–1129.
115. L. K. Meulbroek, 2001, The efficiency of equity-linked compensation: Understanding the full cost of awarding executive stock options, *Financial Management,* 30(2), 5–44.
116. G. Colvin, 2001, The great CEO pay heist, *Fortune,* June 25, 67.
117. S. Strom, 2002, Even last year, option spigot was wide open, *The New York Times,* http://www.nytimes.com, February 3; C. G. Holderness, R. S. Kroszner, & D. P. Sheehan, 1999, Were the good old days that good? Changes in managerial stock ownership since the Great Depression, *Journal of Finance,* 54: 435–469.
118. J. Dahya, A. A. Lonie, & D. A. Power, 1998, Ownership structure, firm performance and top executive change: An analysis of UK firms, *Journal of Business Finance & Accounting,* 25: 1089–1118.
119. H. Tosi, S. Werner, J. Katz, & L. Gomez-Mejia, 2000, How much does performance matter? A meta-analysis of CEO pay studies, *Journal of Management,* 26: 301–339.
120. D. Leonhardt, 2002, It's called a 'loan,' but it's far sweeter, *The New York Times,* http://www.nytimes.com, February 3.
121. Ibid.
122. Strom, Even last year, Option spigot was wide open.
123. T. G. Pollock, H. M. Fischer, & J. B. Wade, 2002, The role of politics in repricing executive options, *Academy of Management Journal,* in press; M. E. Carter, L. J. Lynch, 2001, An examination of executive stock option repricing, *Journal of Financial Economics,* 2: 207–225; D. Chance, R. Kumar, & R. Todd, 2001, The 'repricing' of executive stock options, *Journal of Financial Economics,* 57: 129–154.
124. R. Coff, 2002, Bidding wars over R&D intensive firms: Knowledge, opportunism and the market for corporate control, *Academy of Management Journal,* in press; Hitt, Hoskisson, Johnson, & Moesel, The market for corporate control and firm innovation; Walsh & Kosnik, Corporate raiders.
125. D. Goldstein, 2000, Hostile takeovers as corporate governance? Evidence from 1980s, *Review of Political Economy,* 12: 381–402.
126. Hitt, Harrison, & Ireland, *Creating Value through Mergers and Acquisitions.*
127. E. Thorton, F. Keesnan, C. Palmeri, & L. Himelstein, 2002, It sure is getting hostile, *Business Week,* January 14, 28–30.
128. R. Barker, 2000, Hijacking Hertz shareholders, *Business Week,* October 16, 214.
129. Sundaramurthy, Mahoney, & Mahoney, Board structure, antitakeover provisions, and stockholder wealth.
130 J. Westphal & E. Zajac, 2001, Decoupling policy from practice: The case of stock repurchase programs, *Administrative Science Quarterly,* 46: 202–228.
131. J. A. Byrne, 1999, Poison pills: Let shareholders decide, *Business Week,* May 17, 104.
132. 2001, Reuters, Alltel bid encounters takeover defenses, *The New York Times,* http://www.nytimes.com, August 15.
133. Walsh & Kosnik, Corporate raiders.
134. A. Chakraborty & R. Arnott, 2001, Takeover defenses and dilution: A welfare analysis, *Journal of Financial and Quantitative Analysis;* 36: 311–334.
135. A. Portlono, 2000, The decision to adopt defensive tactics in Italy, *International Review of Law and Economics,* 20: 425–452.
136. C. Sundaramurthy, 2000, Antitakeover provisions and shareholder value implications: A review and a contingency framework. *Journal of Management,* 26: 1005–1030.
137. B. Kogut, G. Walker, & J. Anand, 2002, Agency and institutions: National divergence in diversification behavior, *Organization Science,* 13: 162–178; D. Norburn, B.K. Boyd, M. Fox, & M. Muth, 2000, International corporate governance reform, *European Business Journal,* 12(3): 116–133; Useem, Corporate leadership in a globalizing equity market.
138. Monks & Minow, *Corporate Governance,* 271–299; J. Charkham, *Keeping Good Company: A Study of Corporate Governance in Five Countries,* 6–118.
139. Y. Yafeh, 2000, Corporate governance in Japan: Past performance and future prospects. *Oxford Review of Economic Policy,* 16(2): 74–84; H. Kim & R. E. Hoskisson, 1996, Japanese governance systems: A critical review, in B. Prasad (ed.), *Advances in International Comparative Management,* Greenwich, CT: JAI Press, 165–189.
140. D. Kirk, 2001, Court order tells 10 executives to pay $75 million to Samsung, *The Wall Street Journal Interactive,* http://www.wsj.com, December 28.
141. S. Klein, 2000, Family businesses in Germany: Significance and structure, *Family Business Review,* 13: 157–181.
142. J. Edwards & M. Nibler, 2000, Corporate governance in Germany: The role of banks and ownership concentration, *Economic Policy,* 31: 237–268; E. R. Gedajlovic & D. M. Shapiro, 1998, Management and ownership effects: Evidence from five countries, *Strategic Management Journal,* 19: 533–553.

143. S. Douma, 1997, The two-tier system of corporate governance, *Long Range Planning,* 30(4): 612–615.
144. C. Tierney, 2001, Volkswagen, *Business Week Online,* http://www.businessweek.com, July 23.
145. K. Capell, 2002, Can Bayer cure its own headache?, *Business Week Online,* http://www.businessweek.com, January 28.
146. T. Hoshi, A.K. Kashyap, & S. Fischer, 2001, *Corporate Financing and Governance in Japan,* Boston: MIT Press.
147. Charkham, *Keeping Good Company,* 70.
148. B. Bremner, 2001. Cleaning up the banks—finally, *Business Week,* December 17: 86; 2000, Business: Japan's corporate-governance u-turn, *The Economist,* November 18, 73.
149. B. Bremner, E. Thornton, & I. M. Kunii, 1999, Fall of a keiretsu, *Business Week,* March 15, 87–92.
150. B. Bremner & J. Lichtblau, 2001, Gaijin at the gate, *Business Week Online,* http://www.businessweek.com, December 10.
151. J. B. White, 2000, The company we'll keep, *The Wall Street Journal Interactive,* http://www.wsj.com, January 17.
152. A. Alcouffe & C. Alcouffe, 2000, Executive compensation-setting practices in France, *Long Range Planning,* 33(4): 527–543.
153. J. Groenewegen, 2001, European integration and changing corporate governance structures: The case of France, *Journal of Economic Issues,* 34: 471–479.
154. C. P. Erlich & D.-S. Kang, 1999, South Korea: Corporate governance reform in Korea: The remaining issues—Part I: Governance structure of the large Korean firm, *East Asian Executive Reports,* 21: 11–14+.
155. P. Mar & M. Young, 2001, Corporate governance in transition economies: A case study of 2 Chinese airlines, *Journal of World Business,* 36(3): 280–302; M. W. Peng, 2000, *Business Strategies in Transition Economies,* Thousand Oaks, CA: Sage.

156. L. Chang, 1999, Chinese firms find incentive to use stock-compensation plans, *The Wall Street Journal,* November 1, A2.; T. Clarke & Y. Du, 1998, Corporate governance in China: Explosive growth and new patterns of ownership, *Long Range Planning,* 31(2): 239–251.
157. I. Filatotchev, R. Kapelyushnikov, N. Dyomina, & S. Aukutsionek, 2001, The effects of ownership concentration on investment and performance in privatized firms in Russia, *Managerial and Decision Economics,* 22(6): 299–313; E. Perotti & S. Gelfer, 2001, Red barons or robber barons? Governance and investment in Russian financial-industrial groups, *European Economic Review,* 45(9): 1601–1617; T Buck, I. Filatotchev, & M. Wright, 1998, Agents, stakeholders and corporate governance in Russian firms, *Journal of Management Studies,* 35: 81–104.
158. Hillman, Keim, & Luce, Board composition and stakeholder performance; R. Oliver, 2000, The board's role: Driver's seat or rubber stamp?, *Journal of Business Strategy,* 21: 7–9.
159. A. Felo, 2001, Ethics programs, board involvement, and potential conflicts of interest in corporate governance, *Journal of Business Ethics,* 32: 205–218.

11

Chapter Eleven

Organizational Structure and Controls

Knowledge Objectives

Studying this chapter should provide you with the strategic management knowledge needed to:

1. Define organizational structure and controls and discuss the difference between strategic and financial controls.
2. Describe the relationship between strategy and structure.
3. Discuss the functional structures used to implement business-level strategies.
4. Explain the use of three versions of the multidivisional (M-form) structure to implement different diversification strategies.
5. Discuss the organizational structures used to implement three international strategies.
6. Define strategic networks and strategic center firms.

Aligning Strategy and Structure at Zurich Financial Services

Zurich Financial Services was founded in Switzerland in 1872, primarily as a property and casualty insurer and re-insurer. Part of the reason for Zurich's historical success was the firm's rapid movement into markets outside its home nation. International expansion intensified during the early 1990s when Rolf Hüppi, Zurich CEO, concluded that the dynamic global economy created significant opportunities for firms to profitably sell financial products and services to customers in different regions of the world.

Convinced that acquisition was the route for Zurich to become a diversified, global financial powerhouse, Hüppi acted quickly and boldly. In 1996, Zurich gained a strong presence in the asset management business by spending $2 billion to acquire Kemper, a U.S. life insurer and asset manager. Paying an additional $2 billion one year later to buy Scudder, Stevens & Clark, a U.S. fund manager, significantly expanded Zurich's asset management position. The two acquisitions were then combined to form Zurich Scudder Investments, which became Zurich's global fund management arm. Zurich's size doubled in 1998 when it merged with the financial service arm of British American Tobacco.

Rolf Hüppi, CEO and chairman of Zurich Financial Services, announced in late spring 2002 that he would leave the firm, which reported a large loss for 2001. Huppi had urged Zurich managers to develop technology projects like a "field of one thousand flowers," resulting in heavy spending and duplication. According to a former manager, "The problem was overextension into areas which were not their core business, and undoubtedly a worry that too much scrutiny is coming its way. It can't get worse than that."

Study of Zurich's transactions shows that by 2000, the firm had become a diversified, global financial corporation with 70,000-plus employees and operations in more than 60 countries, serving more than 35 million customers. By this time, a new organizational structure was formed. This structure grouped the firm's diversified businesses into five segments: non-life insurance (e.g., property, accident, and car and liability); life insurance; reinsurance; farmers management services; and asset management. Investors responded favorably to Zurich's diversification, as shown by the company's quick growth to a $50 billion-plus market capitalization.

Hüppi touted the merits of what Zurich had become and confidently claimed that the company should be worth $100 billion because of its large, lucrative customer base. However, all was not well at Zurich. In fact, in 2001, the company surprised investors when it issued a series of profit warnings and hints of unexpected and significant losses in its fund management business unit.

Zurich's market value quickly tumbled by half to $25 billion. In response, Zurich announced plans to divest several large holdings to raise $4 billion to reduce the firm's debt and the burden of servicing that debt.

What caused Zurich's problems? How could the value of a firm that appeared to have effectively diversified its operations tumble so quickly? In the words of a business analyst, "It was not Zurich's expansion (diversification strategy) that got it into trouble. It was its failure to adapt its structure to its new incarnation (strategy)."

Throughout the time Zurich was quickly diversifying its operations, Hüppi focused on driving top line sales revenue growth, but little attention was paid to the company's organizational structure. In fact, the structure in place prior to diversification—a hybrid of centralization and decentralization designed to coordinate and control roughly a dozen business units—remained relatively unchanged as Zurich became more diversified. This structure could not accommodate the complexity of the 350 or so business units that resulted from rapid growth and diversification. Without an organizational structure that could support the firm's new and more diversified corporate-level strategy, decisions about how to best integrate Zurich's recently acquired businesses with existing units were slow in the making.

The lack of integration was particularly pronounced in the Scudder Investments division. Kemper and Scudder, Stevens & Clark were combined to form Zurich's asset management business, but the two firms had very different cultures. Well-known in the midwestern United States, Kemper sold funds through brokers and financial advisors. Scudder, on the other hand, was an old-line Boston-based money manager selling mutual funds directly to investors. The decision to have Scudder executives run the asset management unit complicated things, as these executives had little experience in convincing brokerage firms and banks to sell mutual funds. The decisions made by inexperienced decision makers appear to have contributed to former Kemper investors withdrawing $7 billion in assets in 1999 and another $5.3 billion in 2000.

Convinced that a lack of fit between its diversification strategy and organizational structure was contributing to its financial difficulties, in late 2001, Zurich's top-level managers changed their firm's structure while simultaneously reshaping its portfolio of businesses (for example, Zurich left the reinsurance business by spinning off Converium, its reinsurance operation formerly known as Zurich Re). In the new organizational structure, 11 global and regional businesses were grouped into five business units, each headed by an executive reporting directly to Hüppi. As shown in the chart, four of the units are organized across geographic lines with the fifth framed around global asset and investment businesses. An eight-member Group Executive Committee, consisting of Hüppi, the five unit heads, the chief financial officer, and the chief operating officer, considers strategic and financial issues for all of Zurich. The 25-person Group Management Board is an information and networking body working to ensure horizontal collaboration across the segments.

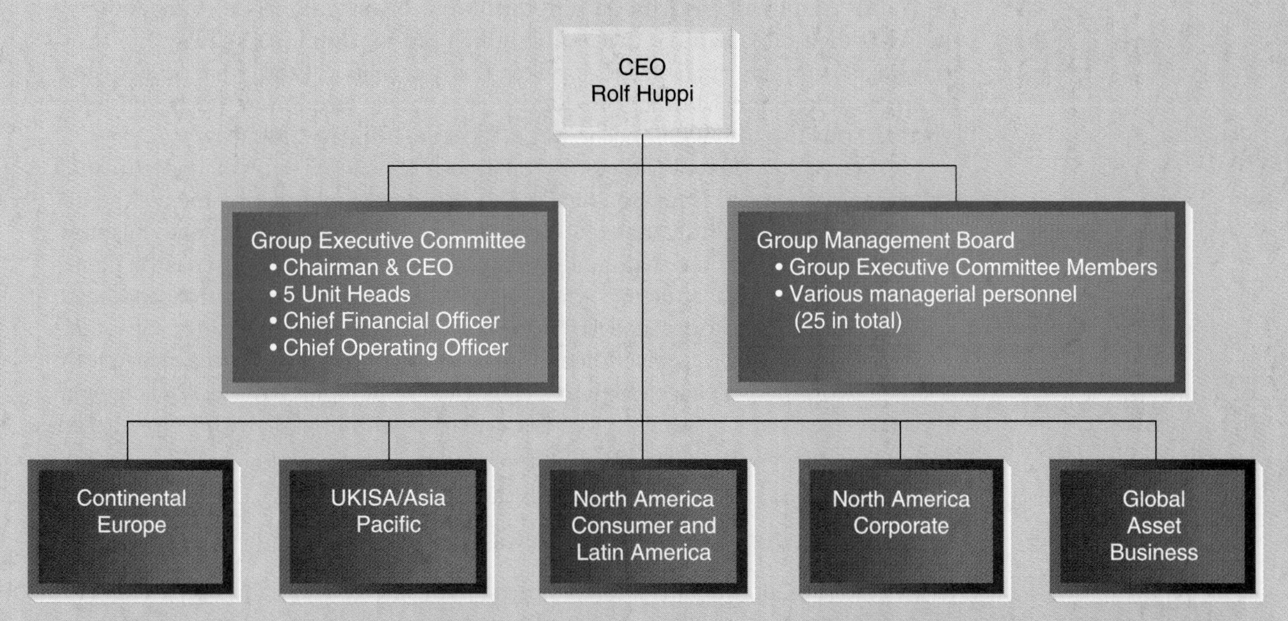

By creating these larger, regional geographic business units, Zurich intends to capitalize on economies of scale in purchasing and back office functions, and it also plans to customize its product offerings to satisfy the needs of local clientele. Scale economies should help Zurich reduce its costs, while local product customization should increase revenue. Hüppi believes in the new structure's value, suggesting that it ". . . is an important step in creating the platform for an efficient and focused development of our Group (business firm)." In mid-2002, new CEO James J. Schiro remained committed to using the structure shown here.

SOURCES: B. Rigby & T. Johnson, 2002, Zurich scraps plan to sell U.S. unit, *Reuters Business News,* http://www.fidelity.com, January 9; 2001, Zurich Financial Services and Deutsche Bank have signed definitive agreements, Zurich Financial Services, http://www.zurich.com/newsmedia, December 4; 2001, Zurich Financial Services: Refining the management structure and streamlining the organization, Zurich Financial Services, http://www.zurich.com/newsmedia, July 9; 2001, Re structure, The Swiss group badly needs a structure to fit its strategy, *The Economist,* September 8, 80–82; H. Deogun & T. Lauricella, 2001, Zurich Financial seeks a merger to reinvigorate its Scudder unit, *The Wall Street Journal,* April 23; 2001, W. Hall, 2001, Zurich financial profits fall amid fund management fears, *Financial Times,* September 6; S. Tuckey, 2001, Zurich CEO sees consolidation, *Insurance Accounting,* December 3; 2000, Analyst's day presentation, Zurich Financial Services, http://www.zurich.com/presentations, November; 2000, Zurich Financial Services Group: New organizational structure, Zurich Financial Services, http://www.zurich.com/newsmedia, October 31.

As described in Chapter 4, all firms use one or more business-level strategies. In Chapters 6–9, we discuss the other strategies that might be used (corporate-level, international, and cooperative strategies). Once selected, strategies can't be implemented in a vacuum. Organizational structure and controls, this chapter's topic, provide the framework within which strategies are used. However, as we explain, separate structures and controls are required to successfully implement different strategies. Top-level managers have the final responsibility for ensuring that the firm has matched each of its strategies with the appropriate organizational structure and that changes to both take place when needed.[1] The match or degree of fit between strategy and structure influences the firm's attempts to earn above-average returns.[2] Thus, the ability to select an appropriate strategy and match it with the appropriate structure is an important characteristic of effective strategic leadership.[3]

This chapter opens with an introduction to organizational structure and controls. We then provide more details about the need for the firm's strategy and structure to be properly matched. Critical to this match is the fact that strategy and structure influence each other.[4] As we discuss, strategy has a more important influence on structure, although once in place, structure influences strategy.[5]

The chapter then describes the relationship between growth and structural change that successful firms experience. This is followed with discussions of the different organizational structures that firms use to implement the separate business-level, corporate-level, international, and cooperative strategies. A series of figures highlights the different structures firms match with strategies. Across time and based on their experiences, organizations, especially large and complex ones, customize these general structures to meet their unique needs.[6] Typically, the firm tries to form a structure that is complex enough to facilitate use of its strategies but simple enough for all to effectively implement.[7] The chapter closes with brief discussions of alternative organizational structures and controls.

Organizational Structure and Controls

Research shows that organizational structure and the controls that are a part of it affect firm performance.[8] In particular, when the firm's strategy isn't matched with the most appropriate structure and controls, performance declines.[9] This relationship is shown in the Opening Case: the mismatch between strategy and structure contributed to Zurich Financial Services' declining performance. Recognizing this mismatch, the firm is changing its structure and controls to form a better match with strategy. Even though mismatches between strategy and structure do occur, the evidence suggests that managers try to act rationally when forming or changing their firm's structure.[10]

Organizational Structure

Organizational structure specifies the firm's formal reporting relationships, procedures, controls, and authority and decision-making processes.

Organizational structure specifies the firm's formal reporting relationships, procedures, controls, and authority and decision-making processes.[11] Developing an organizational structure that will effectively support the firm's strategy is difficult, especially because of the uncertainty about cause-effect relationships in the global economy's rapidly changing and dynamic competitive environments.[12] When a structure's elements (e.g., reporting relationships, procedures, and so forth) are properly aligned with one another, that structure facilitates effective implementation of the firm's strategies.[13]

Organizational structure influences how managers work and the decisions resulting from that work.[14] As explained in the Opening Case, in Zurich's structure prior to diversification, former CEO Hüppi's decisions were oriented to driving the firm's growth through sales volume increases. However, greater diversification created a need for Huppi and the top management team to choose a structure that facilitated coordination and integration among the firm's rapidly growing number of business units.

A firm's structure specifies the work to be done and how to do it, given the firm's strategy or strategies.[15] Supporting the implementation of strategies,[16] structure is concerned with processes used to complete organizational tasks.[17] Effective structures provide the stability a firm needs to successfully implement its strategies and maintain its current competitive advantages, while simultaneously providing the flexibility to develop competitive advantages that will be needed for its future strategies.[18] Thus, *structural stability* provides the capacity the firm requires to consistently and predictably manage its daily work routines,[19] while *structural flexibility* provides the opportunity to explore competitive possibilities and then allocate resources to activities that will shape the competitive advantages the firm will need to be successful in the future.[20] An effective organizational structure allows the firm to *exploit* current competitive advantages while *developing* new ones.[21]

Modifications to the firm's current strategy or selection of a new strategy call for changes to its organizational structure. As explained in the Opening Case, Zurich's existing structure—developed when Zurich had far fewer business units and when it was much less diversified— became incapable of supporting implementation of the firm's new corporate-level diversification strategy. However, Zurich's structure wasn't changed until the firm's performance had dramatically declined.

Research shows that Zurich's experience with strategy and structure isn't unusual. Once in place, organizational inertia often inhibits efforts to change structure, even when the firm's performance suggests that it is time to do so.[22] In his pioneering work, Alfred Chandler found that organizations change their structures only when inefficiencies force them to do so.[23] Firms seem to prefer the structural status quo and its familiar working relationships until the firm's performance declines to the point where change is absolutely necessary. In addition, top-level managers hesitate to conclude that there are problems with the firm's structure (or its strategy, for that matter), in that doing so suggests that their previous choices weren't the best ones.[24]

Because of these inertial tendencies, structural change is often induced instead by the actions of stakeholders who are no longer willing to tolerate the firm's performance. For example, continuing losses of customers who have become dissatisfied with the value created by the firm's products could force change, as could reactions from capital market stakeholders (see Chapter 2). In Zurich's case, changes were made to form a match between strategy and structure when the firm's shareholders and debt holders became quite dissatisfied with the firm's financial performance.

In spite of the timing of structural change described above, many companies make changes prior to substantial performance declines. Appropriate timing of structural change happens when top-level managers quickly recognize that a current organizational structure no longer provides the coordination and direction needed for the firm to successfully implement its strategies.[25] Effective organizational controls help managers recognize when it is time to change the firm's structure.

Organizational Controls

Organizational controls guide the use of strategy, indicate how to compare actual results with expected results, and suggest corrective actions to take when the difference between actual and expected results is unacceptable.

Strategic controls are largely subjective criteria intended to verify that the firm is using appropriate strategies for the conditions in the external environment and the company's competitive advantages.

Organizational controls are an important aspect of structure. **Organizational controls** guide the use of strategy, indicate how to compare actual results with expected results, and suggest corrective actions to take when the difference between actual and expected results is unacceptable. The fewer are the differences between actual and expected outcomes, the more effective are the organization's controls.[26] It is hard for the company to successfully exploit its competitive advantages without effective organizational controls.[27] Properly designed organizational controls provide clear insights regarding behaviors that enhance firm performance.[28] Firms rely on strategic controls and financial controls as part of their structures to support use of their strategies.[29]

Strategic controls are largely subjective criteria intended to verify that the firm is using appropriate strategies for the conditions in the external environment and the company's competitive advantages. Thus, strategic controls are concerned with examining the fit between what the firm *might do* (as suggested by opportunities in its external environment) and what it *can do* (as indicated by its competitive advantages) (see Figure 3.1). Effective strategic controls help the firm understand what it takes to be successful.[30] Strategic controls demand rich communications between managers responsible for using them to judge the firm's performance and those with primary responsibility for implementing the firm's strategies (such as middle- and first-level managers). These frequent exchanges are both formal and informal in nature.[31]

Strategic controls are also used to evaluate the degree to which the firm focuses on the requirements to implement its strategies. For a business-level strategy, for example, the strategic controls are used to study primary and support activities (see Tables 3.8 and 3.9) to verify that those critical to successful execution of the business-level strategy are being properly emphasized and executed. With related corporate-level strategies, strategic controls are used to verify the sharing of appropriate strategic factors such as knowledge, markets, and technologies across businesses. To effectively use strategic controls when evaluating related diversification strategies, executives must have a deep understanding of each unit's business-level strategy.[32]

Financial controls are largely objective criteria used to measure the firm's performance against previously established quantitative standards.

Partly because strategic controls are difficult to use with extensive diversification,[33] financial controls are emphasized to evaluate the performance of the firm following the unrelated diversification strategy. The unrelated diversification strategy's focus on financial outcomes (see Chapter 6) requires the use of standardized financial controls to compare performances between units and managers.[34] **Financial controls** are largely objective criteria used to measure the firm's performance against previously established quantitative standards. Accounting-based measures, such as return on investment and return on assets, and market-based measures, such as economic value added, are examples of financial controls.

When using financial controls, firms evaluate their current performance against previous outcomes as well as their performance compared to competitors and industry averages. In the global economy, technological advances are being used to develop more sophisticated financial controls, making it possible for firms to more thoroughly analyze their performance results.[35] Pfizer Inc.'s expectations of sophisticated financial controls are that they will: "(1) safeguard the firm's assets, (2) ensure that transactions are properly authorized, and (3) provide reasonable assurance, at reasonable cost, of the integrity, objectivity, and reliability of the financial information."[36]

Without effective financial controls, the firm's performance can deteriorate. PSINet, for example, grew rapidly into a global network providing Internet services to 100,000 business accounts in 27 countries. However, expensive debt instruments such as junk bonds were used to fuel the firm's rapid expansion. According to a member of the firm's board of directors, PSINet spent most of its borrowed money "without the financial controls that should have been in place."[37] With a capital structure unable to support its rapidly growing and financially uncontrolled operations, PSINet and 24 of its U.S. subsidiaries filed for bankruptcy in June 2001.[38]

Pfizer Inc. is a global pharmaceutical and consumer products company that discovers, develops, manufactures, and markets innovative medicines for humans, and animals. Its 2000 merger with Warner-Lambert for $90 billion made it the world's second largest pharmaceutical company.

Both strategic and financial controls are important aspects of each organizational structure, and any structure's effectiveness is determined by using a combination of strategic and financial controls. However, the relative use of controls varies by type of strategy. For example, companies and business-units of large diversified firms using the cost leadership strategy emphasize financial controls (such as quantitative cost goals), while companies and business units using the differentiation strategy empha-

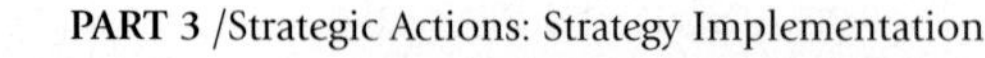

size strategic controls (such as subjective measures of the effectiveness of product development teams).[39] As explained above, a corporatewide emphasis on sharing among business units (as called for by related diversification strategies) results in an emphasis on strategic controls while financial controls are emphasized for strategies in which activities or capabilities aren't shared (e.g., in an unrelated diversification).

Relationships between Strategy and Structure

Strategy and structure have a reciprocal relationship.[40] This relationship highlights the interconnectedness between strategy formulation (Chapter 4 and Chapters 6–9) and strategy implementation (Chapters 10–13). In general, this reciprocal relationship finds structure flowing from or following the selection of the firm's strategy. Once in place, structure can influence current strategic actions as well as choices about future strategies. The general nature of the strategy/structure relationship means that changes to the firm's strategy create the need to change how the organization completes its work. In the "structure influences strategy" direction, firms must be vigilant in their efforts to verify that how their structure calls for work to be completed remains consistent with the implementation requirements of chosen strategies. Research shows, however, that ". . . strategy has a much more important influence on structure than the reverse."[41]

Regardless of the strength of the reciprocal relationships between strategy and structure, those choosing the firm's strategy and structure should be committed to matching each strategy with a structure that provides the stability needed to use current competitive advantages as well as the flexibility required to develop future advantages. This means, for example, that when changing strategies, the firm should simultaneously consider the structure that will be needed to support use of the new strategy. Moreover, a proper strategy/structure match can be a competitive advantage.[42] Based on the four criteria of sustainability discussed in Chapter 3, the firm's strategy/structure match is a competitive advantage when that match is valuable, rare, imperfectly imitable, and nonsubstitutable. When the firm's strategy/structure combination is a competitive advantage, it contributes to the earning of above-average returns.[43]

Recent actions at Charles Schwab & Co. demonstrate these issues. A premier discount broker, Schwab has been challenged by declines in its online trading volume and its overall financial performance. At least partly as a result of uncertainty created by the events of September 11, 2001, Schwab's average daily trades in the third quarter of 2001 fell 26 percent compared to the same period a year earlier. In turn, revenue declines were instrumental in the 50.6 percent fall in year-to-year (2000–2001) net income. Following analysis of these data as well as current and possible future conditions in the global financial industry, Schwab concluded that its website and discount trades could no longer be the foundation for the firm's strategy in what were rapidly changing financial markets. Supporting this conclusion was feedback indicating that an increasing number of investors want a relationship in the form of financial advice, in addition to low trading costs, when making their investment choices. This feedback is not surprising—recent evidence suggests that customers for all types of firm services want to receive them through relationships rather than through encounters.[44] Commenting about the importance of the trend of customers wanting personal relationships, one analyst noted, "If Schwab doesn't offer advice, it risks losing the customer relationship altogether."[45] As a result of Schwab's evaluation of its current situation and future possibilities, the firm decided to change its cost leadership strategy as a discount broker to an integrated cost leadership/differentiation strategy. This change was made so Schwab could offer relatively low-cost financial advice while simultaneously becoming more of a full-service brokerage house.

Schwab's decision makers recognize that the firm's structure will have to change to support the new strategy. Historically, the firm's strategy called for Schwab brokers to take orders rather than sell them. In that structure the brokers served as intermediaries between customers who had decided what they want to buy with the sellers of those products. The firm's new structure must now support brokers' efforts to find customers and sell advice and a broad array of products. Work in the previous structure was largely centralized and dictated by rules and procedures. To support a marketing, advice-driven strategy, Schwab's structure needs to be more decentralized with greater decision responsibility at the individual broker level.

Efforts are underway at Schwab to match structure with the new strategy. If that match proves to be valuable, rare, imperfectly imitable, and nonsubstitutable, the firm will have a competitive advantage based on its integration between strategy and structure.

Evolutionary Patterns of Strategy and Organizational Structure

Research suggests that most firms experience a certain pattern of relationships between strategy and structure. Chandler[46] found that firms tended to grow in somewhat predictable patterns: "first by volume, then by geography, then integration (vertical, horizontal) and finally through product/business diversification."[47] (See Figure 11.1). Chandler interpreted his findings to indicate that the firm's growth patterns determine its structural form.

As shown in Figure 11.1, sales growth creates coordination and control problems that the existing organizational structure can't efficiently handle. Organizational growth creates the opportunity for the firm to change its strategy to try to become even more successful. However, the existing structure's formal reporting relationships, procedures, controls, and authority and decision making processes lack the sophistication required to support use of the new strategy. A new structure is needed that can help decision makers gain access to the knowledge and understanding required to effectively coordinate and integrate the actions to implement the new strategy.[48]

Three major types of organizational structures are used to implement strategies: simple structure, functional structure, and multidivisional structure.

Simple Structure

The **simple structure** is a structure in which the owner-manager makes all major decisions and monitors all activities while the staff serves as an extension of the manager's supervisory authority.

The **simple structure** is a structure in which the owner-manager makes all major decisions and monitors all activities while the staff serves as an extension of the manager's supervisory authority.[49] Typically, the owner-manager actively works in the business on a daily basis. Informal relationships, few rules, limited task specialization, and unsophisticated information systems describe the simple structure. Frequent and informal communications between the owner-manager and employees make it relatively easy to coordinate the work that is to be done. The simple structure is matched with focus strategies and business-level strategies as firms commonly compete by offering a single product line in a single geographic market. Local restaurants, repair businesses, and other specialized enterprises are examples of firms relying on the simple structure to implement their strategy.

As the small firm grows larger and becomes more complex, managerial and structural challenges emerge. For example, the amount of competitively relevant information requiring analysis substantially increases, placing significant pressure on the owner-manager. Still additional growth and success may cause the firm to change its strategy. Even if the strategy remains the same, the firm's larger size dictates the need for more sophisticated workflows and integrating mechanisms. At this evolu-

Figure 11.1 Strategy and Structure Growth Pattern

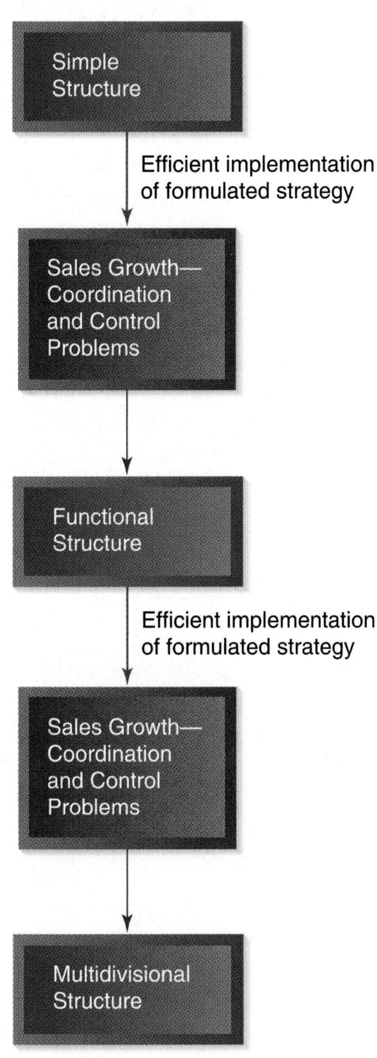

tionary point, firms tend to move from the simple structure to a functional organizational structure.[50]

This move may soon be made by Casketfurniture.com, a firm mentioned in Chapter 4 as an example of a company using the focus differentiation strategy. Family-owned and managed, this venture is a new part of MHP Enterprises Ltd.'s operations. As a small family firm, MHP has long been managed through the simple structure. In 1997, MHP decided to expand its distribution by establishing Casketfurniture.com. Using the Internet, this venture sells what it believes are creative products throughout the world. The continuing success of Casketfurniture.com could create coordination and control problems for MHP that may be solved only by the firm changing from the simple to the functional structure.[51]

Functional Structure

The **functional structure** is a structure consisting of a chief executive officer and a limited corporate staff, with functional line managers in dominant organizational areas such as production, accounting, marketing, R&D, engineering, and human resources.[52] This structure allows for functional specialization,[53] thereby facilitating active sharing of knowledge within each functional area. Knowledge sharing facilitates career paths as well as the professional development of functional specialists. However, a functional orientation can have a negative effect on communication and coordination among those representing different organizational functions. Because of this, the CEO must work hard to verify that the decisions and actions of individual business functions promote the entire firm rather than a single function.[54] The functional structure supports implementation of business-level strategies and some corporate-level strategies (e.g., single or dominant business) with low levels of diversification.

The **functional structure** is a structure consisting of a chief executive officer and a limited corporate staff, with functional line managers in dominant organizational areas such as production, accounting, marketing, R&D, engineering, and human resources.

The **multidivisional (M-form) structure** consists of operating divisions, each representing a separate business or profit center in which the top corporate officer delegates responsibilities for day-to-day operations and business-unit strategy to division managers.

Multidivisional Structure

With continuing growth and success firms often consider greater levels of diversification. However, successful diversification requires analysis of substantially greater amounts of data and information when the firm offers the same products in different markets (market or geographic diversification) or offers different products in several markets (product diversification). In addition, trying to manage high levels of diversification through functional structures creates serious coordination and control problems.[55] Thus, greater diversification leads to a new structural form.[56]

The **multidivisional (M-form) structure** consists of operating divisions, each representing a separate business or profit center in which the top corporate officer delegates responsibilities for day-to-day operations and business-unit strategy to division managers. Each division represents a distinct, self-contained business with its own functional hierarchy.[57] As initially designed, the M-form was thought to have three major benefits: "(1) it enabled corporate officers to more accurately monitor the performance of each business, which simplified the problem of control; (2) it facilitated comparisons between divisions, which improved the resource allocation process; and (3) it stimulated managers of poorly performing divisions to look for

ways of improving performance."[58] Active monitoring of performance through the M-form increases the likelihood that decisions made by managers heading individual units will be in shareholders' best interests. Diversification is a dominant corporate-level strategy in the global economy, resulting in extensive use of the M-form.[59]

Used to support implementation of related and unrelated diversification strategies, the M-form helps firms successfully manage the many demands (including those related to processing vast amounts of information) of diversification.[60] Chandler viewed the M-form as an innovative response to coordination and control problems that surfaced during the 1920s in the functional structures then used by large firms such as DuPont and General Motors.[61] Research shows that the M-form is appropriate when the firm grows through diversification.[62] Partly because of its value to diversified corporations, some consider the multidivisional structure to be one of the 20th century's most significant organizational innovations.[63]

No organizational structure (simple, functional, or multidivisional) is inherently superior to the other structures.[64] Because of this, managers concentrate on developing proper matches between strategies and organizational structures rather than searching for an "optimal" structure.

We now describe the strategy/structure matches that evidence shows positively contribute to firm performance.

Matches between Business-Level Strategies and the Functional Structure

Different forms of the functional organizational structure are used to support implementation of the cost leadership, differentiation, and integrated cost leadership/differentiation strategies. The differences in these forms are accounted for primarily by different uses of three important structural characteristics or dimensions—*specialization* (concerned with the type and number of jobs required to complete work[65]), *centralization* (the degree to which decision-making authority is retained at higher managerial levels), and *formalization* (the degree to which formal rules and procedures govern work[66]).

Using the Functional Structure to Implement the Cost Leadership Strategy

Firms using the cost leadership strategy want to sell large quantities of standardized products to an industry's or a segment's typical customer. Simple reporting relationships, few layers in the decision-making and authority structure, a centralized corporate staff, and a strong focus on process improvements through the manufacturing function rather than the development of new products through an emphasis on product R&D characterize the cost leadership form of the functional structure.[67] (See Figure 11.2). This structure contributes to the emergence of a low cost culture—a culture in which all employees constantly try to find ways to reduce the costs incurred to complete their work.

In terms of centralization, decision-making authority is centralized in a staff function to maintain a cost-reducing emphasis within each organizational function (for example, engineering, marketing, etc.). While encouraging continuous cost reductions, the centralized staff also verifies that further cuts in costs in one function won't adversely affect the productivity levels in other functions.

Jobs are highly specialized in the cost leadership functional structure. Job specialization is accomplished by dividing work into homogeneous subgroups. Organizational functions are the most common subgroup, although work is sometimes batched on the basis of products produced or clients served. Specializing in their work allows employees to increase their efficiency, reducing the firm's costs as a

Figure 11.2 Functional Structure for Implementation of a Cost Leadership Strategy

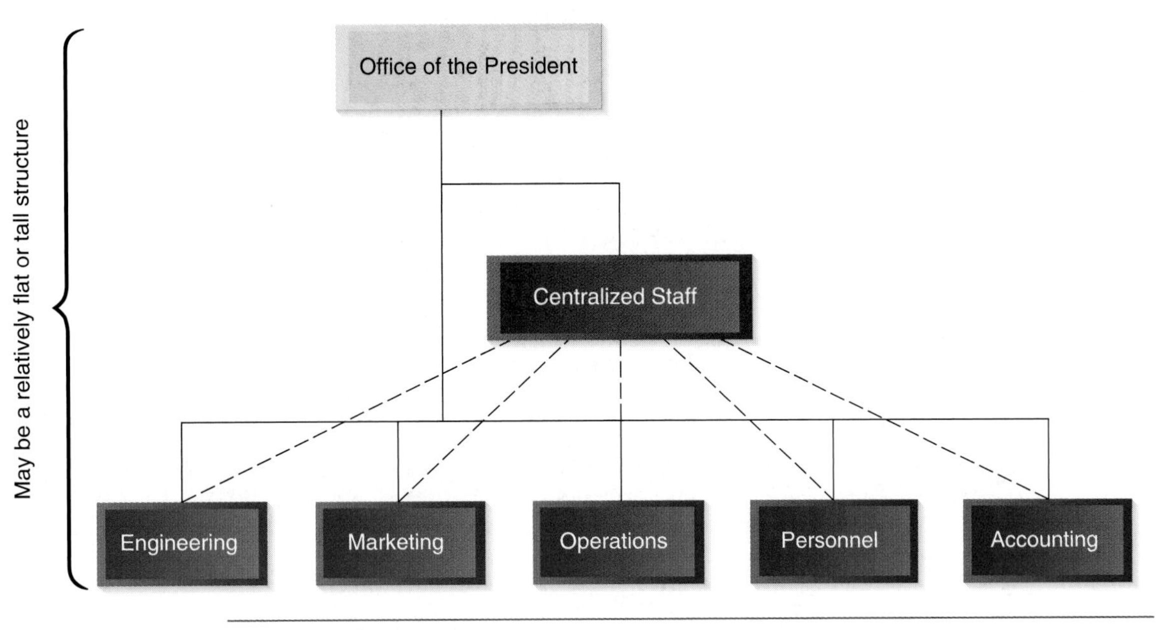

Notes:
- Operations is the main function
- Process engineering is emphasized rather than new product R&D
- Relatively large centralized staff coordinates functions
- Formalized procedures allow for emergence of a low-cost culture
- Overall structure is mechanical; job roles are highly structured

result. Highly formalized rules and procedures, often emanating from the centralized staff, guide the work completed in the cost leadership form of the functional structure. Predictably following formal rules and procedures creates cost-reducing efficiencies. Known for its commitment to EDLP ("everyday low price"), Wal-Mart's functional organizational structures in both its retail (e.g., Wal-Mart Stores, Supercenters, Sam's Club) and specialty (e.g., Wal-Mart Vacations, Used Fixture Auctions) divisions are formed to continuously drive costs lower.[68] As discussed in Chapter 4, competitors' efforts to duplicate the success of Wal-Mart's cost leadership strategies have failed, partly because of Wal-Mart's effective strategy/structure configurations in its business units.

Using the Functional Structure to Implement the Differentiation Strategy

Firms using the differentiation strategy produce products that customers perceive as being different in ways that create value for them. With this strategy, the firm wants to sell nonstandardized products to customers with unique needs. Relatively complex and flexible reporting relationships, frequent use of cross-functional product development teams, and a strong focus on marketing and product R&D rather than manufacturing and process R&D (as with the cost leadership form of the functional structure) characterize the differentiation form of the functional structure (see Figure 11.3). This structure contributes to the emergence of a development-oriented culture—a culture in which employees try to find ways to further differentiate current products and to develop new, highly differentiated products.

Continuous product innovation demands that people throughout the firm be able to interpret and take action based on information that is often ambiguous,

Figure 11.3 Functional Structure for Implementation of a Differentiation Strategy

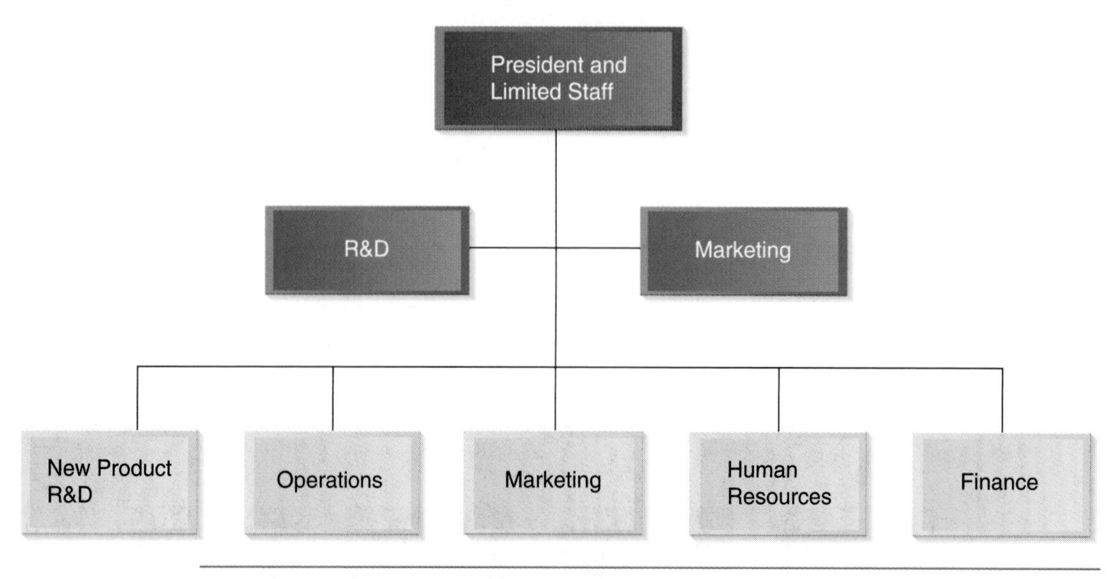

Notes:
- Marketing is the main function for keeping track of new product ideas
- New product R&D is emphasized
- Most functions are decentralized, but R&D and marketing may have centralized staffs that work closely with each other
- Formalization is limited so that new product ideas can emerge easily and change is more readily accomplished
- Overall structure is organic; job roles are less structured

incomplete, and uncertain. With a strong focus on the external environment to identify new opportunities, employees often gather this information from people outside the firm, such as customers and suppliers. Commonly, rapid responses to the possibilities indicated by the collected information are necessary, suggesting the need for decision-making responsibility and authority to be decentralized. To support creativity and the continuous pursuit of new sources of differentiation and new products, jobs in this structure are not highly specialized. This lack of specialization means that workers have a relatively large number of tasks in their job descriptions. Few formal rules and procedures are also characteristics of this structure. Low formalization, decentralization of decision-making authority and responsibility, and low specialization of work tasks combine to create a structure in which people interact frequently to exchange ideas about how to further differentiate current products while developing ideas for new products that can be differentiated to create value for customers.

Using the Functional Structure to Implement the Integrated Cost Leadership/Differentiation Strategy

Firms using the integrated cost leadership/differentiation strategy want to sell products that create value because of their relatively low cost and reasonable sources of differentiation. The cost of these products is low "relative" to the cost leader's prices while their differentiation is "reasonable" compared to the clearly unique features of the differentiator's products.

The integrated cost leadership/differentiation strategy is used frequently in the global economy, although it is difficult to successfully implement. This difficulty is due largely to the fact that different primary and support activities (see Chapter 3) must be emphasized when using the cost leadership and differentiation strategies. To achieve the low-cost position, emphasis is placed on production and process engineering, with infrequent product changes. To achieve a differentiated position, marketing and new-product R&D are emphasized while production and process engineering are not. Thus, use of the integrated strategy results when the firm successfully combines activities intended to reduce costs with activities intended to create additional differentiation features. As a result, the integrated form of the functional structure must have decision-making patterns that are partially centralized and partially decentralized. Additionally, jobs are semi-specialized, and rules and procedures call for some formal and some informal job behavior.

Matches between Corporate-Level Strategies and the Multidivisional Structure

As explained earlier, Chandler's research showed that the firm's continuing success leads to product or market diversification or both.[69] The firm's level of diversification is a function of decisions about the number and type of businesses in which it will compete as well as how it will manage the businesses (see Chapter 6). Geared to managing individual organizational functions, increasing diversification eventually creates information processing, coordination, and control problems that the functional structure can't handle. Thus, use of a diversification strategy requires the firm to change from the functional structure to the multidivisional structure to develop an appropriate strategy/structure match.

As defined in Figure 6.1 in Chapter 6, corporate-level strategies have different degrees of product and market diversification. The demands created by different levels of diversification highlight the need for each strategy to be implemented through a unique organizational structure (see Figure 11.4).

Using the Cooperative Form of the Multidivisional Structure to Implement the Related-Constrained Strategy

The **cooperative form** is a structure in which horizontal integration is used to bring about interdivisional cooperation.

The **cooperative form** is a structure in which horizontal integration is used to bring about interdivisional cooperation. The divisions in the firm using the related-constrained diversification strategy commonly are formed around products, markets or both. The objective of related-constrained firm Procter & Gamble (P&G), to "think globally, act locally," for example, is supported by a cooperative structure of five global business product units (baby, feminine and family care, fabric and home care, food

Figure 11.4 Three Variations of the Multidivisional Structure

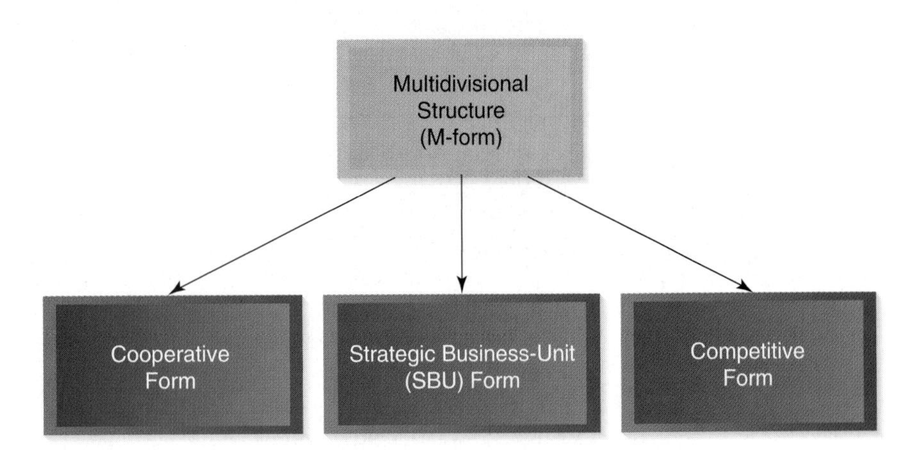

and beverage, and health and beauty care) and seven market development organizations (MDOs), each formed around a region of the world, such as Northeast Asia. Using the five global product units to create strong brand equities through ongoing innovation is how P&G thinks globally; interfacing with customers to ensure that a division's marketing plans fully capitalize on local opportunities is how P&G acts locally. Information is shared between the product-oriented and the marketing-oriented efforts to enhance the corporation's performance. Indeed, some corporate staff members are responsible for focusing on making certain that knowledge is meaningfully categorized and then rapidly transferred throughout P&G's businesses.[70]

In Figure 11.5, we use product divisions as part of the representation of the cooperative form of the multidivisional structure, although as the P&G example suggests, market divisions could be used instead of or in addition to product divisions to develop the figure. Thus, P&G has slightly modified the core cooperative form of the multidivisional structure to satisfy its unique strategy/structure match requirements.

All of the related-constrained firm's divisions share one or more corporate strengths. Production competencies, marketing competencies, or channel dominance are examples of strengths that the firm's divisions might share.[71] Production expertise is one of the strengths shared across P&G's divisions. At Halliburton Co., the world's largest oilfield services company, the firm's competence in the development and application of sophisticated technologies is shared between its two major divisions.[72]

The sharing of divisional competencies facilitates the corporation's efforts to

Figure 11.5 Cooperative Form of the Multidivisional Structure for Implementation of a Related–Constrained Strategy

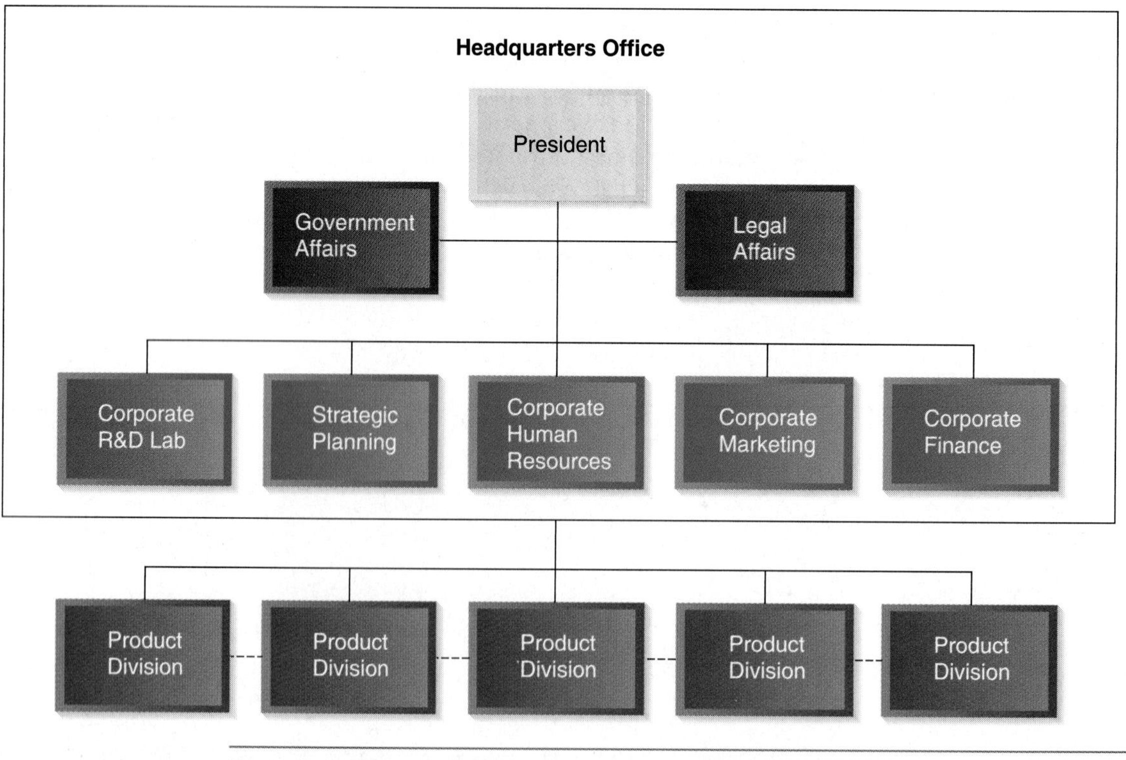

Notes:
- Structural integration devices create tight links among all divisions
- Corporate office emphasizes centralized strategic planning, human resources, and marketing to foster cooperation between divisions
- R&D is likely to be centralized
- Rewards are subjective and tend to emphasize overall corporate performance in addition to divisional performance
- Culture emphasizes cooperative sharing

develop economies of scope. As explained in Chapter 6, economies of scope (cost savings resulting from the sharing of competencies developed in one division with another division) are linked with successful use of the related-constrained strategy. Interdivisional sharing of competencies depends on cooperation, suggesting the use of the cooperative form of the multidivisional structure.[73] Increasingly, it is important that the links resulting from effective use of integration mechanisms support the cooperative sharing of both intangible resources (such as knowledge) as well as tangible resources (such as facilities and equipment).[74]

Different characteristics of structure are used as integrating mechanisms by the cooperative structure to facilitate interdivisional cooperation. Defined earlier in the discussion of functional organizational structures, centralization is one of these mechanisms. Centralizing some organizational functions (human resource management, R&D, marketing, and finance) at the corporate level allows the linking of activities among divisions. Work completed in these centralized functions is managed by the firm's central office with the purpose of exploiting common strengths among divisions by sharing competencies. The intent is to develop a competitive advantage in the divisions as they implement their cost leadership, differentiation, or integrated cost leadership/differentiation business-unit strategies that exceeds the value created by the advantages used by undiversified rivals' implementation of these strategies.[75]

Frequent, direct contact between division managers, another integrating mechanism, encourages and supports cooperation and the sharing of either competencies or resources that have the possibility of being used to create new advantages. Sometimes, liaison roles are established in each division to reduce the amount of time division managers spend integrating and coordinating their unit's work with the work taking place in other divisions. Temporary teams or task forces may be formed around projects whose success depends on sharing competencies that are embedded within several divisions. Formal integration departments might be established in firms frequently using temporary teams or task forces. Ultimately, a matrix organization may evolve in firms implementing the related-constrained strategy. A *matrix organization* is an organizational structure in which there is a dual structure combining both functional specialization and business product or project specialization. Although complicated, an effective matrix structure can lead to improved coordination among a firm's divisions.[76]

The success of the cooperative multidivisional structure is significantly affected by how well information is processed among divisions. But because cooperation among divisions implies a loss of managerial autonomy, division managers may not readily commit themselves to the type of integrative information-processing activities that this structure demands. Moreover, coordination among divisions sometimes results in an unequal flow of positive outcomes to divisional managers. In other words, when managerial rewards are based at least in part on the performance of individual divisions, the manager of the division that is able to benefit the most by the sharing of corporate competencies might be viewed as receiving relative gains at others' expense. Strategic controls are important in these instances, as divisional managers' performance can be evaluated at least partly on the basis of how well they have facilitated interdivisional cooperative efforts. Furthermore, using reward systems that emphasize overall company performance, besides outcomes achieved by individual divisions, helps overcome problems associated with the cooperative form.

Using the Strategic-Business-Unit Form of the Multidivisional Structure to Implement the Related-Linked Strategy

When the firm has fewer links or less constrained links among its divisions, the related-linked diversification strategy is used. The strategic business-unit form of the multidivisional structure supports implementation of this strategy. The **strategic**

Figure 11.6 SBU Form of the Multidivisional Structure for Implementation of a Related–Linked Strategy

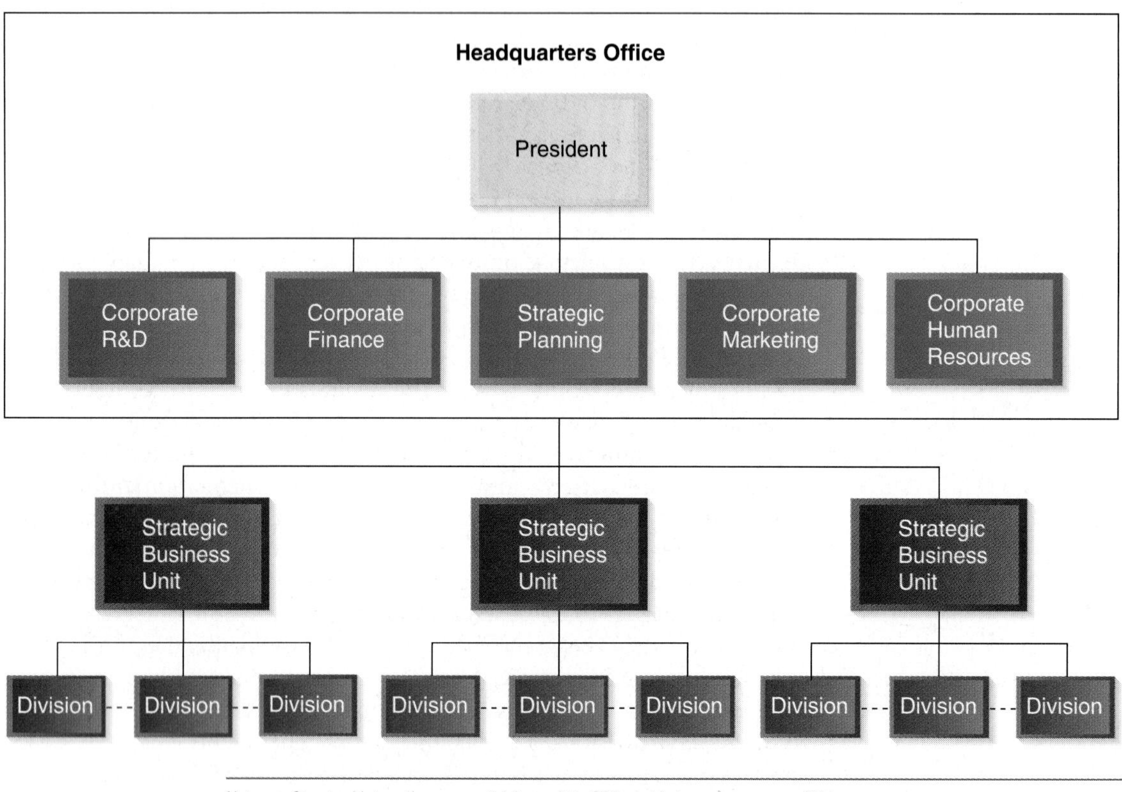

Notes:
- Structural integration among divisions within SBUs, but independence across SBUs
- Strategic planning may be the most prominent function in headquarters for managing the strategic planning approval process of SBUs for the president
- Each SBU may have its own budget for staff to foster integration
- Corporate headquarters staff serve as consultants to SBUs and divisions, rather than having direct input to product strategy, as in the cooperative form

The **strategic business unit (SBU) form** is a structure consisting of three levels: corporate headquarters, strategic business units (SBUs), and SBU divisions.

business unit (SBU) form is a structure consisting of three levels: corporate headquarters, strategic business units (SBUs), and SBU divisions (see Figure 11.6).

The divisions within each SBU are related in terms of shared products or markets or both, but the divisions of one SBU have little in common with the divisions of the other SBUs. Divisions within each SBU share product or market competencies to develop economies of scope and possibly economies of scale. The integration mechanisms used by the divisions in a cooperative structure can be equally well used by the divisions within the individual strategic business units that are part of the SBU form of the multidivisional structure. In the SBU structure, each SBU is a profit center that is controlled and evaluated by the headquarters office. Although both financial and strategic controls are important, on a relative basis, financial controls are vital to headquarters' evaluation of each SBU; strategic controls are critical when the heads of SBUs evaluate their divisions' performance. Strategic controls are also critical to the headquarters' efforts to determine if the company has chosen an effective portfolio of businesses and if those businesses are being effectively managed.

Used by large firms, the SBU structure can be complex, with the complexity reflected by the organization's size and product and market diversity. Related–linked firm GE, for example, has 28 strategic business units, each with multiple divisions. GE Aircraft Engines, Appliances, Power Systems, NBC, and GE Capital are a few of the firm's SBUs. As is frequently the case with large diversified corporations, the scale of GE's business units is striking. GE Aircraft Engines, for example, is the world's leading manufacturer of jet engines for civil and military aircraft. With almost 30 divisions, GE Capital is a diversified financial services company creating comprehensive solutions to increase client productivity and efficiency. The GE Power Systems business unit has 21 divisions including GE Energy Rentals, GE Distributed Power, and GE Water Technologies.[77]

In many of GE's SBUs, efforts are undertaken to form competencies in services and technology as a source of competitive advantage. Recently technology was identified as an advantage for the GE Medical Systems SBU, as that unit's divisions share technological competencies to produce an array of sophisticated equipment, including computed tomography (CT) scanners, magnetic resonance imaging (MRI) systems, nuclear medicine cameras, and ultrasound systems.[78] Once a competence is developed in one of GE Medical Systems' divisions, it is quickly transferred to the other divisions in that SBU so that the competence can be leveraged to increase the unit's overall performance.[79]

Eastman Kodak also uses the SBU structure. In the Strategic Focus on page 360, we describe this firm's evolution to the SBU structure. To date, it is not clear whether the diversification strategy and structure are now properly matched at Kodak. This latest structural change occurred under Patricia Russo's leadership as CEO. However, Russo departed after only 8 months at Kodak to accept the CEO position at Lucent Technologies.[80] In spite of this disruption to the firm's operations, Kodak's current leadership is confident that it has the strategy and structure in place that will lead to competitive success.

Using the Competitive Form of the Multidivisional Structure to Implement the Unrelated Diversification Strategy

Firms using the unrelated diversification strategy want to create value through efficient internal capital allocations or by restructuring, buying, and selling businesses.[81] The competitive form of the multidivisional structure supports implementation of this strategy.

The **competitive form** is a structure in which there is complete independence among the firm's divisions.

The **competitive form** is a structure in which there is complete independence among the firm's divisions (see Figure 11.7). Unlike the divisions included in the cooperative structure, the divisions that are part of the competitive structure do not share common corporate strengths (e.g., marketing competencies or channel dominance). Because strengths aren't shared, integrating devices aren't developed for use by the divisions included in the competitive structure.

The efficient internal capital market that is the foundation for use of the unrelated diversification strategy requires organizational arrangements that emphasize divisional competition rather than cooperation.[82] Three benefits are expected from the internal competition that the competitive form of the multidivisional structure facilitates. First, internal competition creates flexibility—corporate headquarters can have divisions working on different technologies to identify those with the greatest future potential. Resources can then be allocated to the division that is working with the most promising technology to fuel the entire firm's success. Second, internal competition challenges the status quo and inertia, because division heads know that future resource allocations are a product of excellent current performance as well as superior positioning of their division in terms of future performance. Lastly, internal competition motivates effort. The challenge of competing against internal peers can be as great as the challenge of competing against external marketplace competitors.[83]

Strategic Focus

Kodak Implements the Strategic-Business-Unit Form to Regain Growth

The world's largest manufacturer of photographic film, Kodak has struggled recently with intense competitive pressures from several sources. Kodak is engaged in a fierce price war with Fuji Photo Film, its biggest competitor, to maintain its market share in film sales both in the United States and in international markets. Even more potentially competitively threatening are the revolutionary changes taking place in photography with the advent of digital technology. In growing numbers, consumers are abandoning traditional film in favor of digital cameras.

Shareholder concerns about future performance pushed Kodak's stock price down from near $70 in late 2000 to the $30–$35 range in mid-2002. Contributing to shareholders' actions were recent earnings per share figures. Kodak's third-quarter 2001 earnings were $0.15 per share, significantly below the expected $0.46 per share. Although the firm's fourth-quarter 2001 earnings of $0.12 per share beat analysts' expectation of $0.09, shareholders remained unimpressed. The September 11 events may have influenced these results somewhat when consumers canceled or curtailed their travel plans (less travel leads to fewer film purchases). In addition, Hollywood studios canceled film projects and commercials, negatively affecting Kodak's entertainment business. Even Kodak's traditionally dependable medical imaging business suffered as hospitals banded together to demand lower prices from their suppliers.

For years, Kodak used the cooperative form of the multidivisional structure to implement the related–constrained diversification strategy. In this structure, primary organizational functions such as manufacturing, customer care, and strategic planning were centralized, which allowed their expertise to be shared among its seven product divisions. Consistent with the cooperative structure's mandates, headquarters personnel encouraged interdivisional cooperation. In addition to the product divisions, Kodak also maintained separate divisions organized according to geographic region.

The cooperative structure worked well for Kodak as it used the related–constrained strategy to compete in what for many years had been relatively stable markets. However, innovative technologies and increased competition disrupted these markets, making the sharing of the firm's technologies and related skills across product divisions less competitively valuable. Moreover, sharing key resources and their corresponding costs across many business units with increased competition in unstable markets made it difficult for Kodak to assess the profitability of its product divisions. The inability to pinpoint the firm's revenue and profitability sources was an issue, as Kodak had decided that it wanted to develop "anything that helps people capture, use or store images, including digital technology." However, the firm also concluded that being able to pinpoint the revenue and profitability outcomes of all new product offerings would influence these attempts to improve its overall financial performance.

Study of its external environment and its competitive advantages found Kodak concluding that it should reduce the number of links between its business units and their products and services. In October 2000, Kodak moved to the SBU structure. As shown in the figure, this structure combined seven previous product divisions into two broad customer-oriented SBUs, Consumer and Commercial. Global Operations, the third SBU included in the structure, continued to handle Kodak's supply chain and operational needs.

Although this SBU structure halved the number of direct reports to the CEO, the structure did not yield the robust feedback needed to assess products on a stand-alone profitability basis, as competencies were shared within individual SBU product divisions. Furthermore, the customer groupings were too broad to generate scope and scale economies among the product divisions. Executives concluded that another form of the SBU structure was necessary.

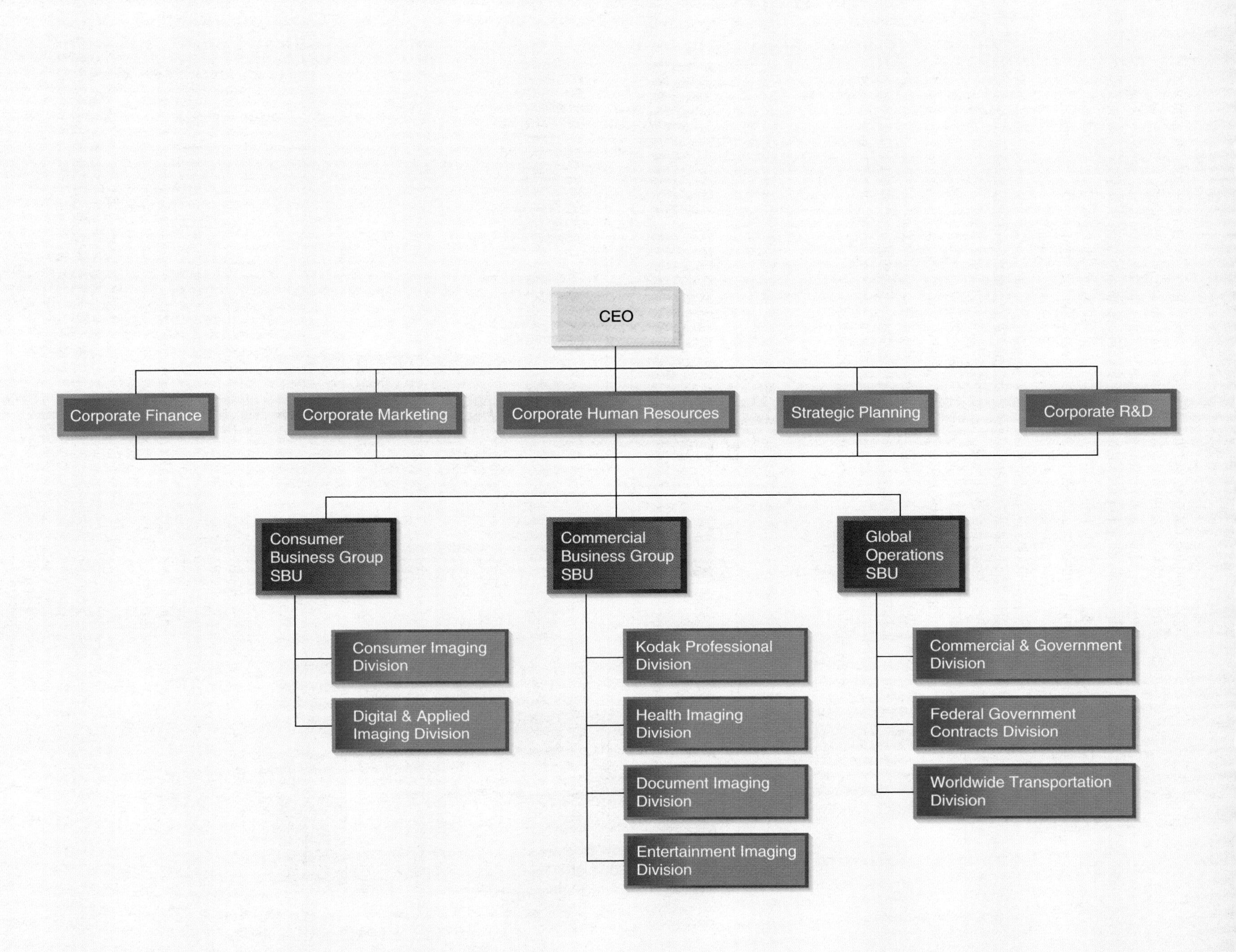
CEO
Corporate Finance
Corporate Marketing
Corporate Human Resources
Strategic Planning
Corporate R&D
Consumer Business Group SBU
Commercial Business Group SBU
Global Operations SBU
Consumer Imaging Division
Digital & Applied Imaging Division
Kodak Professional Division
Health Imaging Division
Document Imaging Division
Entertainment Imaging Division
Commercial & Government Division
Federal Government Contracts Division
Worldwide Transportation Division

Kodak completed a new version of its SBU structure in November 2001, as shown below. The firm believes that this version is a proper match with its newly selected related–linked diversification strategy and that it offers the benefits it had been seeking. Each product division is now responsible for managing all activities that affect earnings, including supply chain management, inventory, marketing, and customer service. Each product division also generates its own independent financial statements. Financial controls can be used to measure performance within divisions, creating the data required to identify the profitability of individual products and product lines. The additional autonomy this form of the SBU structure provides to division heads should allow product-related decisions to be made more quickly. The rapidly changing nature of Kodak's competitive arena affords a premium to the firm able to quickly satisfy consumers' emerging needs with new products. Finally, Kodak's product divisions should be able to realize scope and possible scale economies because they have been grouped based on a similar customer orientation, technology platform, and channel structure. Strategic controls can be used to determine the degree to which divisions are effectively sharing common competencies in terms of customers, technologies, and distribution channels.

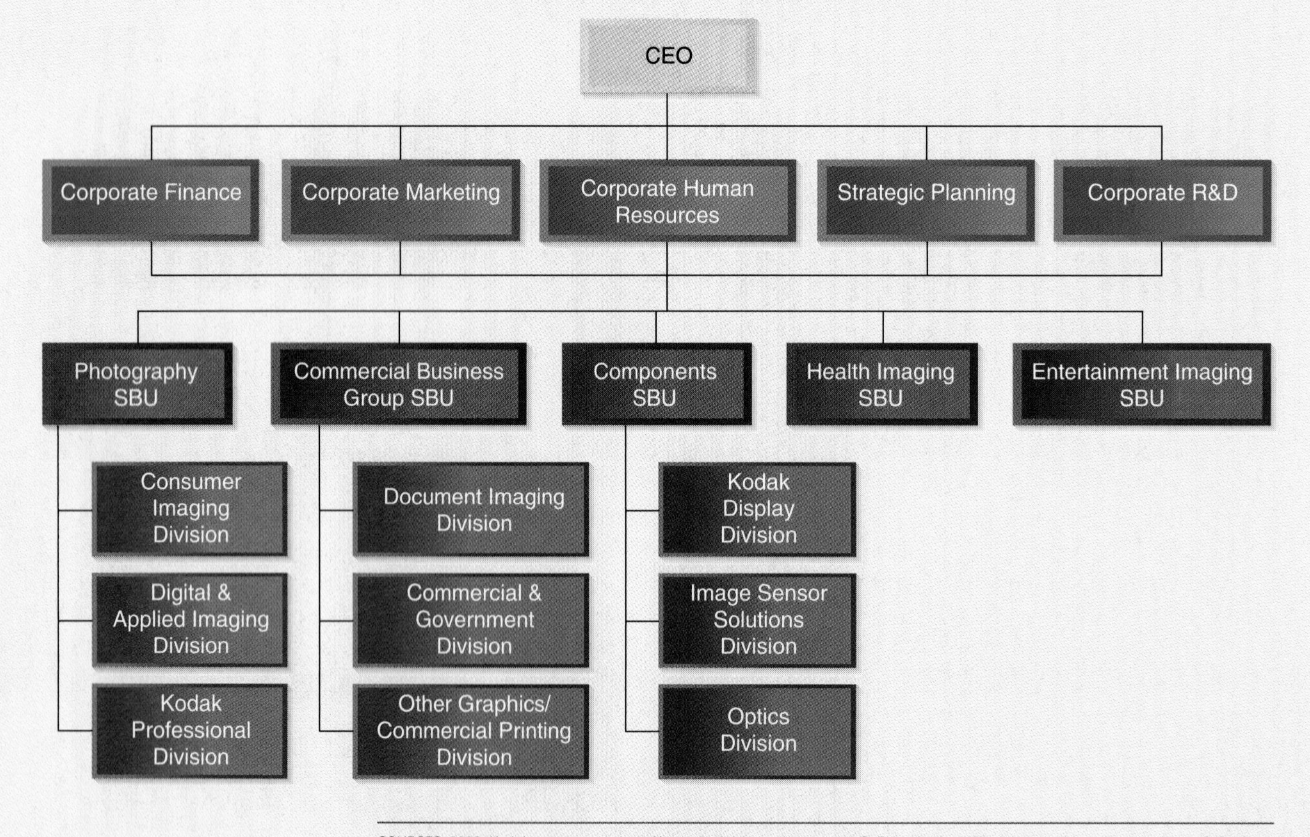

SOURCES: 2002, Kodak press center, http://www.kodak.com, January 15; S. Rosenbush, 2002, A lengthy honeymoon at Lucent? *Business Week,* January 31, 34; 2001, Kodak's Eric Steenburgh announces retirement, *Business Wire,* November 14; C. Deutsch, 2001, Kodak realigns operations as slump in demand persists, *The New York Times,* http://www.nyt.com, November 15; 2001, Eastman Kodak restructures business units, *Reuters,* November 14; A. Hill & P. Russo, 2001, Kodak puts its faith in group reorganization, *Financial Times,* http://www.ft.com, November 15; 2001, Eastman Kodak Company, *Hoovers Online,* http://www.hoovers.com, December 12; A. Tsao, 2001, Kodak: Not enough positive developments? Its shares are off their lows, but long term question marks over its transition to a digital world linger, *Business Week Online,* http://www.businessweek.com, November 26; 2001, Kodak aligns business units to focus on growth, simplification: New structure designed to improve customer satisfaction, drive growth, Eastman Kodak Company press release, http://www.kodak.com, October 23; 2001, Kodak announces new operating model, business alignment to build profitable growth, businesses given more direct responsibility for sales and profits, Eastman Kodak Company press release, http://www.kodak.com, November 14; 2001, Kodak reports third quarter 2001 sales and earnings; Operating results within expectations, economic downturn deepens, Eastman Kodak Company press release, http://www.kodak.com, October 24; D. Shook, 2000, Why Kodak is worth focusing on again: The company's plausible digital strategy could slowly start to improve its image on the Street, *Business Week Online,* http://www.businessweek.com, June 27.

Figure 11.7 Competitive Form of the Multidivisional Structure for Implementation of an Unrelated Strategy

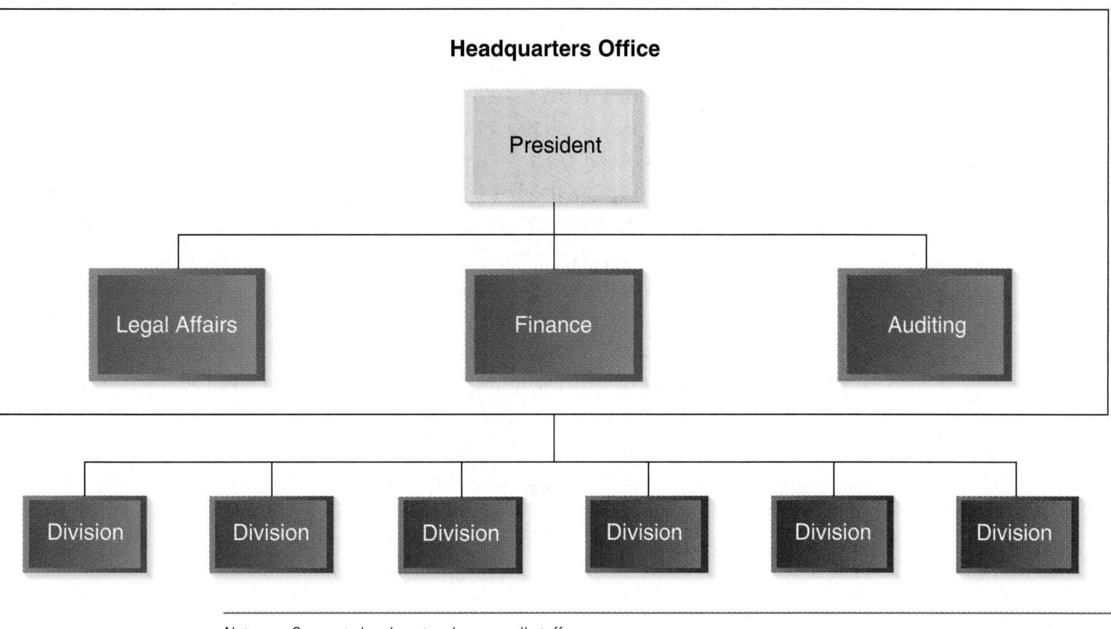

Notes:
- Corporate headquarters has a small staff
- Finance and auditing are the most prominent functions in the headquarters office to manage cash flow and assure the accuracy of performance data coming from divisions
- The legal affairs function becomes important when the firm acquires or divests assets
- Divisions are independent and separate for financial evaluation purposes
- Divisions retain strategic control, but cash is managed by the corporate office
- Divisions compete for corporate resources

Independence among divisions, as shown by a lack of sharing of corporate strengths and the absence of integrating devices, allows the firm using the unrelated diversification strategy to form specific profit performance expectations for each division to stimulate internal competition for future resources. The benefits of internal capital allocations or restructuring cannot be fully realized unless divisions are held accountable for their own independent performance. In the competitive structure, organizational controls (primarily financial controls) are used to emphasize and support internal competition among separate divisions and as the basis for allocating corporate capital based on divisions' performances.

To emphasize competitiveness among divisions, the headquarters office maintains an arms-length relationship with them and does not intervene in divisional affairs, except to audit operations and discipline managers whose divisions perform poorly. In this situation, the headquarters office relies on strategic controls to set rate-of-return targets and financial controls to monitor divisional performance relative to those targets. The headquarters office then allocates cash flow on a competitive basis, rather than automatically returning cash to the division that produced it. Thus, the focus of the headquarters' work is on performance appraisal, resource allocation, and long-range planning to verify that the firm's portfolio of businesses will lead to financial success.[84]

Textron Inc. is an industrial conglomerate using the unrelated diversification strategy.[85] Textron has grown through the "volume, geography, vertical or horizontal integration, diversification" pattern we mention earlier in the chapter. The seed for Textron was Special Yarns Corporation, a small textile company founded in 1923 with first year revenues of $75,000. Special Yarns Corporation became the world's first conglomerate. Its evolution started when the firm vertically integrated in 1943 to gain control of declining revenues and underutilized production capacity. Facing another revenue decline in 1952, the CEO received board approval to diversify the firm by acquiring businesses in unrelated industries. Today, Textron has five divisions—aircraft, automotive, industrial products, fastening systems, and finance. Return on invested capital is the financial control Textron uses as the primary measure of divisional performance. According to the firm, "return on invested capital serves as both a compass to guide every investment decision and a measurement of Textron's success."[86]

The three major forms of the multidivisional structure should each be paired with a particular corporate-level strategy. Table 11.1 shows these structures' characteristics. Differences are seen in the degree of centralization, the focus of the performance appraisal, the horizontal structures (integrating mechanisms), and the incentive compensation schemes. The most centralized and most costly structural form is the cooperative structure. The least centralized, with the lowest bureaucratic costs, is the competitive structure. The SBU structure requires partial centralization and involves some of the mechanisms necessary to implement the relatedness between divisions. Also, the divisional incentive compensation awards are allocated according to both SBUs and corporate performance.

An early Textron facility and its Providence, R.I. headquarters.

© COURTESY OF TEXTRON INC./POTOGRAPHER: FRANK GUILIANNI

Table 11.1 Characteristics of the Structures Necessary to Implement the Related–Constrained, Related–Linked, and Unrelated Diversification Strategies

	Overall Structural Form		
Structural Characteristics	Cooperative M-Form (Related–Constrained Strategy)[a]	SBU M-Form (Related–Linked Strategy)[a]	Competitive M-Form (Unrelated Diversification Strategy)[a]
Centralization of operations	Centralized at corporate office	Partially centralized (in SBUs)	Decentralized to divisions
Use of integration mechanisms	Extensive	Moderate	Nonexistent
Divisional performance appraisals	Emphasize subjective (strategic) criteria	Use a mixture of subjective (strategic) and objective (financial) criteria	Emphasize objective (financial) criteria
Divisional incentive compensation	Linked to overall corporate performance	Mixed linkage to corporate, SBU, and divisional performance	Linked to divisional performance

[a]Strategy implemented with structural form.

Matches between International Strategies and Worldwide Structures

As explained in Chapter 8, international strategies are becoming increasingly important for long-term competitive success.[87] Among other benefits, international strategies allow the firm to search for new markets, resources, core competencies, and technologies as part of its efforts to outperform competitors.[88]

As with business-level and corporate-level strategies, unique organizational structures are necessary to successfully implement the different international strategies. Forming proper matches between international strategies and organizational structures facilitates the firm's efforts to effectively coordinate and control its global operations.[89] More importantly, recent research findings confirm the validity of the international strategy/structure matches we discuss here.[90]

Using the Worldwide Geographic Area Structure to Implement the Multidomestic Strategy

The *multidomestic strategy* decentralizes the firm's strategic and operating decisions to business units in each country so that product characteristics can be tailored to local preferences. Firms using this strategy try to isolate themselves from global competitive forces by establishing protected market positions or by competing in industry segments that are most affected by differences among local countries. The worldwide geographic area structure is used to implement this strategy. The **worldwide geographic area structure** is a structure emphasizing national interests and facilitating the firm's efforts to satisfy local or cultural differences (see Figure 11.8).

The **worldwide geographic area structure** is a structure emphasizing national interests and facilitating the firm's efforts to satisfy local or cultural differences.

Because using the multidomestic strategy requires little coordination between different country markets, integrating mechanisms among divisions in the worldwide

Figure 11.8 Worldwide Geographic Area Structure for Implementation of a Multidomestic Strategy

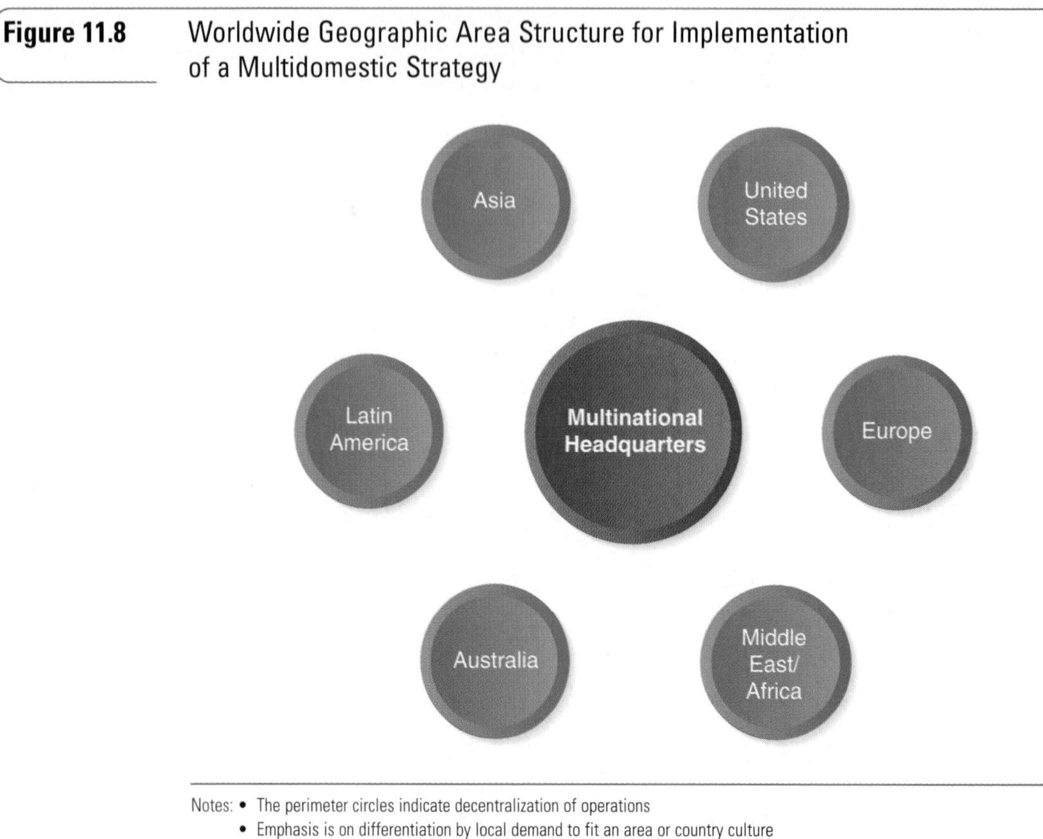

Notes:
- The perimeter circles indicate decentralization of operations
- Emphasis is on differentiation by local demand to fit an area or country culture
- Corporate headquarters coordinates financial resources among independent subsidiaries
- The organization is like a decentralized federation

geographic area structure aren't needed. Hence, formalization is low, and coordination among units in a firm's worldwide geographic area structure is often informal.

The multidomestic strategy/worldwide geographic area structure match evolved as a natural outgrowth of the multicultural European marketplace. Friends and family members of the main business who were sent as expatriates into foreign countries to develop the independent country subsidiary often implemented this type of structure for the main business. The relationship to corporate headquarters by divisions took place through informal communication among "family members."[91]

As mentioned in Chapter 6, Unilever, the giant Dutch consumer products firm, has refocused its business operations. As a result, the firm grouped its worldwide operations into two global divisions—foods and home and personal care. The firm uses the worldwide geographic area structure. For the foods division (known as Unilever Bestfoods), regional presidents are responsible for results from operations in the region to which they have been assigned. Asia, Europe, North America, Africa, Middle East and Turkey, and Latin America are the regions of the foods division. The firm describes the match between the multidomestic strategy and Unilever's worldwide geographic structure (in terms of the firm's foods division): "Unilever Bestfoods' strength lies in our ability to tailor products to different markets as well as to anticipate consumer trends and demands. This comes from our deep understanding of the countries in which we operate and our policy of listening to our customers."[92]

A key disadvantage of the multidomestic strategy/worldwide geographic area structure match is the inability to create global efficiency. With an increasing emphasis on lower-cost products in international markets, the need to pursue worldwide economies of scale has also increased. These changes have fostered the use of the global strategy and its structural match, the worldwide product divisional structure.

Using the Worldwide Product Divisional Structure to Implement the Global Strategy

With the corporation's home office dictating competitive strategy, the *global strategy* is one through which the firm offers standardized products across country markets. The firm's success depends on its ability to develop and take advantage of economies of scope and scale on a global level. Decisions to outsource some primary or support activities to the world's best providers are particularly helpful when the firm tries to develop economies of scale.

The **worldwide product divisional structure** is a structure in which decision-making authority is centralized in the worldwide division headquarters to coordinate and integrate decisions and actions among divisional business units.

The worldwide product divisional structure supports use of the global strategy. In the **worldwide product divisional structure,** decision-making authority is centralized in the worldwide division headquarters to coordinate and integrate decisions and actions among divisional business units (see Figure 11.9). This structure is often used in rapidly growing firms seeking to manage their diversified product lines effectively, as in Japan's Kyowa Hakko. With businesses in pharmaceuticals, chemicals, bio-chemicals and liquor and food, this company uses the worldwide product divisional structure to facilitate its decisions about how to successfully compete in what it believes are rapidly shifting global competitive environments.[93]

Figure 11.9 Worldwide Product Divisional Structure for Implementation of a Global Strategy

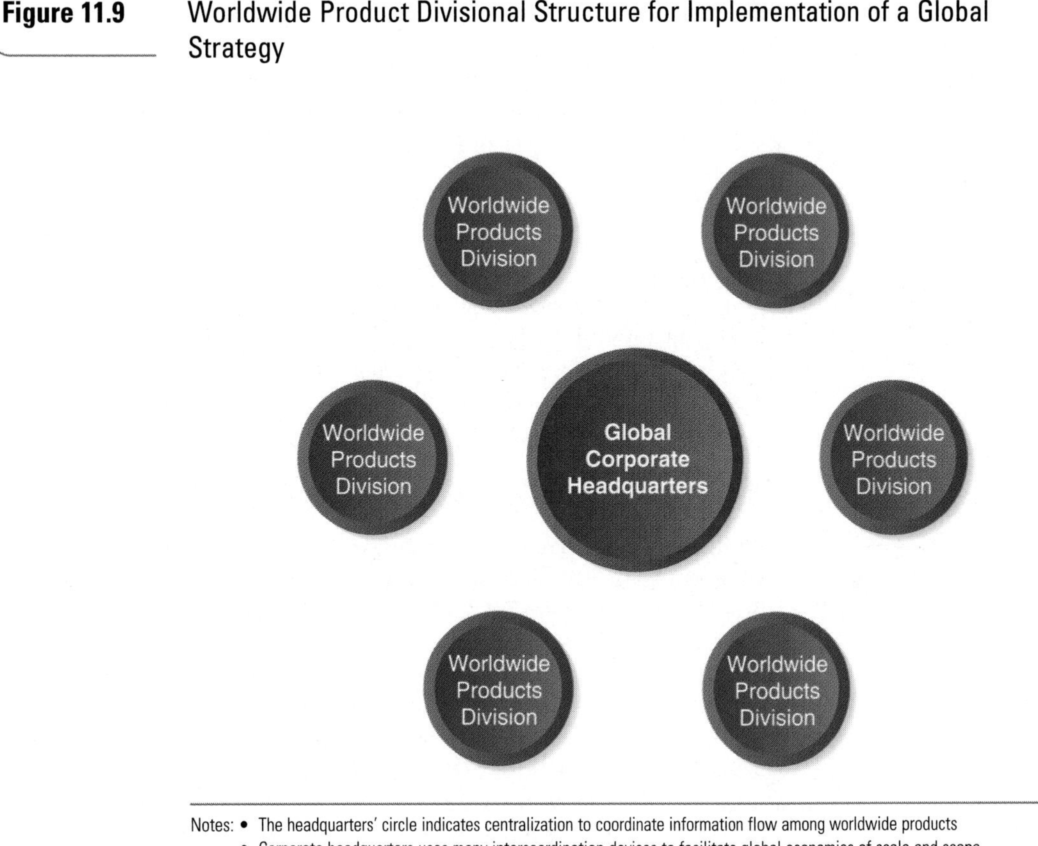

Notes:
- The headquarters' circle indicates centralization to coordinate information flow among worldwide products
- Corporate headquarters uses many intercoordination devices to facilitate global economies of scale and scope
- Corporate headquarters also allocates financial resources in a cooperative way
- The organization is like a centralized federation

Integrating mechanisms are important to effective use of the worldwide product divisional structure. Direct contact between managers, liaison roles between departments, and temporary task forces as well as permanent teams are examples of these mechanisms. One researcher describes the use of these mechanisms in the worldwide structure, "There is extensive and formal use of task forces and operating committees to supplement communication and coordination of worldwide operations."[94] The evolution of a shared vision of the firm's strategy and how structure supports its implementation is one of the important outcomes resulting from these mechanisms' effective use. The disadvantages of the global strategy/worldwide structure combination are the difficulty involved with coordinating decisions and actions across country borders and the inability to quickly respond to local needs and preferences.

Using the Combination Structure to Implement the Transnational Strategy

The *transnational strategy* calls for the firm to combine the multidomestic strategy's local responsiveness with the global strategy's efficiency. Thus, firms using this strategy are trying to gain the advantages of both local responsiveness and global efficiency.[95] The combination structure is used to implement the transnational strategy. The **combination structure** is a structure drawing characteristics and mechanisms from both the worldwide geographic area structure and the worldwide product divisional structure.

The **combination structure** is a structure drawing characteristics and mechanisms from both the worldwide geographic area structure and the worldwide product divisional structure.

The fits between the multidomestic strategy and the worldwide geographic area structure and between the global strategy and the worldwide product divisional structure are apparent. However, when a firm wants to implement both the multidomestic and the global strategy simultaneously through a combination structure, the appropriate integrating mechanisms for the two structures are less obvious. The structure used to implement the transnational strategy must be simultaneously centralized and decentralized; integrated and nonintegrated; formalized and nonformalized. These seemingly opposite characteristics must be managed by an overall structure that is capable of encouraging all employees to understand the effects of cultural diversity on a firm's operations.

This requirement highlights the need for a strong educational component to change the whole culture of the organization. If the cultural change is effective, the combination structure should allow the firm to learn how to gain competitive benefits in local economies by adapting its core competencies, which often have been developed and nurtured in less culturally diverse competitive environments. As firms globalize and move toward the transnational strategy, the idea of a corporate headquarters has become increasingly important in fostering leadership and a shared vision to create a stronger company identity.[96]

Matches between Cooperative Strategies and Network Structures

As discussed in Chapter 9, a network strategy exists when partners form several alliances together in order to improve the performance of the alliance network itself through cooperative endeavors.[97] The greater levels of environmental complexity and uncertainty companies face in today's competitive environment are causing increasing numbers of firms to use cooperative strategies such as strategic alliances and joint ventures.[98]

The breadth and scope of firms' operations in the global economy create many opportunities for firms to cooperate.[99] In fact, the firm can develop cooperative relationships with many of its stakeholders, including customers, suppliers, and competitors.[100] When the firm becomes involved with combinations of cooperative relationships, it is part of a strategic network.

A *strategic network* is a group of firms that has been formed to create value by participating in multiple cooperative arrangements, such as alliances and joint ventures. An effective strategic network facilitates the discovery of opportunities beyond those identified by individual network participants.[101] A strategic network can be a source of competitive advantage for its members when its operations create value that is difficult for competitors to duplicate and that network members can't create by themselves.[102] Strategic networks are used to implement business-level, corporate-level, and international cooperative strategies.

Commonly, a strategic network is a loose federation of partners who participate in the network's operations on a flexible basis. At the core or center of the strategic network, the *strategic center firm* is the one around which the network's cooperative relationships revolve (see Figure 11.10).

Because of its central position, the strategic center firm is the foundation for the strategic network's structure. Concerned with various aspects of organizational structure, such as formal reporting relationships and procedures, the strategic center firm manages what are often complex, cooperative interactions among network partners. The strategic center firm is engaged in four primary tasks as it manages the strategic network and controls its operations:[103]

Strategic outsourcing. The strategic center firm outsources and partners with more firms than do other network members. At the same time, the strategic center firm requires network partners to be more than contractors. Members are expected to find opportunities for the network to create value through its cooperative work.

Competencies. To increase network effectiveness, the strategic center firm seeks ways to support each member's efforts to develop core competencies that can benefit the network.

Figure 11.10 A Strategic Network

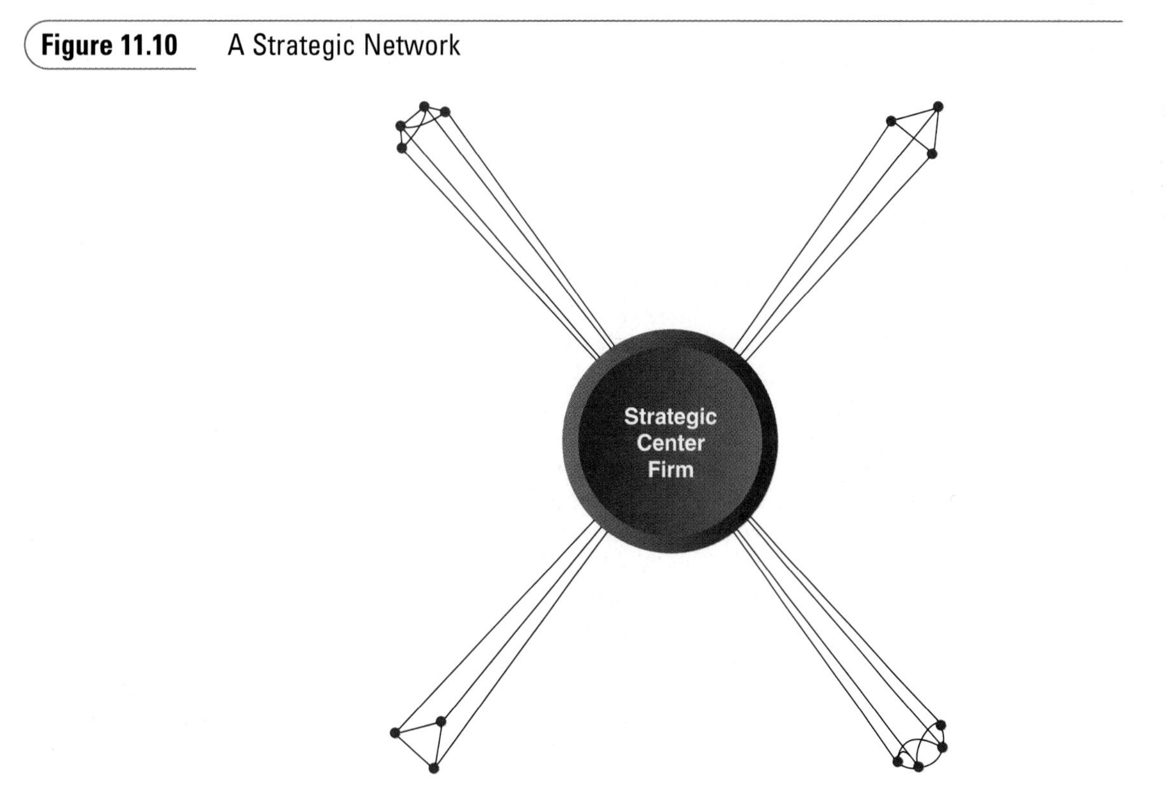

Technology. The strategic center firm is responsible for managing the development and sharing of technology-based ideas among network members. The structural requirement that members submit formal reports detailing the technology-oriented outcomes of their efforts to the strategic center form facilitates this activity.

Race to learn. The strategic center firm emphasizes that the principal dimensions of competition are between value chains and between networks of value chains. Because of this, the strategic network is only as strong as its weakest value-chain link. With its centralized decision-making authority and responsibility, the strategic center firm guides participants in efforts to form network-specific competitive advantages. The need for each participant to have capabilities that can be the foundation for the network's competitive advantages encourages friendly rivalry among participants seeking to develop the skills needed to quickly form new capabilities that create value for the network.[104]

Implementing Business-Level Cooperative Strategies

As noted in Chapter 9, there are two types of business-level complementary alliances: vertical and horizontal. Firms with competencies in different stages of the value chain form a vertical alliance to cooperatively integrate their different, but complementary skills. Firms who agree to combine their competencies to create value in the same stage of the value chain form a horizontal alliance. Vertical complementary strategic alliances, such as those developed by Toyota Motor Company, are formed more frequently than horizontal alliances. Acting as the strategic center firm, Toyota fashioned its lean production system around a network of supplier firms.[105]

A strategic network of vertical relationships, such as the network in Japan between Toyota and its suppliers, often involves a number of implementation issues. First, the strategic center firm encourages subcontractors to modernize their facilities and provides them with technical and financial assistance to do so, if necessary. Second, the strategic center firm reduces its transaction costs by promoting longer-term contracts with subcontractors, so that supplier-partners increase their long-term productivity. This approach is diametrically opposed to that of continually negotiating short-term contracts based on unit pricing. Third, the strategic center firm enables engineers in upstream companies (suppliers) to have better communication with those companies with whom it has contracts for services. As a result, suppliers and the strategic center firm become more interdependent and less independent.[106]

The lean production system pioneered by Toyota has been diffused throughout the Japanese and U.S. automobile industries. However, no automobile company has learned how to duplicate the manufacturing effectiveness and efficiency Toyota derives from the cooperative arrangements in its strategic network.[107] A key factor accounting for Toyota's manufacturing-based competitive advantage is the cost other firms would incur to imitate the structural form used to support Toyota's application. In part, then, the structure of Toyota's strategic network that it created as the strategic center firm facilitates cooperative actions among network participants that competitors can't fully understand or duplicate.

In vertical complementary strategic alliances, such as the one between Toyota and its suppliers, the strategic center firm is obvious, as is the structure that that firm establishes. However, this is not always the case with horizontal complementary strategic alliances where firms try to create value in the same part of the value chain, as with airline alliances that are commonly formed to create value in the marketing and sales primary activity segment of the value chain (see Table 3.8).

© TIMOTHY A. CLARY/AFP/CORBIS

From left: Aeromexico chairman Alfonso Pasquel, Delta Air Lines chairman Leo Mullin, Korean Air President Yi-Taek Shim, and Air France chairman Jean-cyril Spinetta announce the Sky Team alliance of their airlines.

As strategic networks, airline alliances have not been very stable. An airline may decide to change alliances, as when Delta left a network with Swiss Air and Sabena, its primary partners, to join Air France, Korean Air, and Aero Mexico to form the Sky Team alliance (Alitalia has since joined this network).[108] Or, an airline may simultaneously participate in several strategic networks. American Airlines (AA) and British Airways (BA) are members of the Oneworld alliance of eight airlines. However, BA formed another network (and serves as the strategic center firm) to provide region-specific service to customers and to extend its reach by offering a broader set of destination choices to its customers. Called Franchise Carriers, its partners (including British Mediterranean Airways, Brymon Airlines, Loganair, and Maersk Air) fly aircraft featuring the BA cabin interior and inflight service is provided by personnel wearing BA uniforms.[109] In addition, BA has a separate partnership with AA and Iberia Airlines, all of whom are also members of Oneworld.[110] Participating in multiple networks makes it difficult to select the strategic center firm and may cause firms to question partners' true loyalties and intentions. For these reasons, horizontal complementary alliances are used less frequently than their vertical counterpart.

As explained in the Strategic Focus on page 372, strategic networks have been important to Cisco Systems, Inc. The worldwide leader in networking for the Internet, Cisco provides a broad line of solutions for transporting data, voice, and video in multiple settings[111] and has been involved with a number of strategic networks in its pursuit of competitive success. Cisco recently announced that it was changing its organizational structure. Historically, the firm's structure featured three primary business units—enterprise, service provider, and commercial. In late 2001, Cisco changed its structure to create 11 technology areas.[112] Will cooperative strategies be as critical to the firm as it completes its work through the dictates of a new organizational structure? In all likelihood, this will be the case, although the evolution of strategy and structure at Cisco will ultimately decide this issue.

Implementing Corporate-Level Cooperative Strategies

Corporate-level cooperative strategies (such as franchising) are used to facilitate product and market diversification. As a cooperative strategy, franchising allows the firm to use its competencies to extend or diversify its product or market reach, but without completing a merger or acquisition. For example, McDonald's, the largest fast-food company in the world, has more than 50 percent of its almost 30,000 restaurants outside the United States and serves more than 45 million customers daily.[113]

The McDonald's franchising system is a strategic network. McDonald's headquarters office serves as the strategic center firm for the network's franchisees. The headquarters office uses strategic controls and financial controls to verify that the franchisees' operations create the greatest value for the entire network. One strategic control issue is the location of franchisee units. McDonald's believes that its greatest expansion opportunities are outside the United States. Density percentages seem to

Strategic Focus

Cisco Utilizes Strategic Networks to Achieve Success

Networks of cooperative relationships, including vertical complementary alliances, are critical to Cisco Systems, Inc. For example, Cisco long ago decided that its suppliers should be partners who were fully integrated into Cisco's supply chain. Cisco's goal was to ultimately create a "single enterprise," providing a seamless, unified front to customers despite multiple suppliers managing major portions of the firm's supply chain. To accomplish this level of mutual interdependence, Cisco removed barriers that would impede the flow of information within the strategic network that it had formed between itself and its suppliers. Cisco also encouraged its suppliers to adopt the Internet and created Cisco Online, a standardized platform across which network participants interact.

Cisco and its suppliers are able to exchange critical information about customers, products, schedules, inventories, and costs in real time, which has resulted in significant time savings for performing key aspects of the manufacturing process. For example, Cisco discovered that as many as four to five iterations, each taking one to two weeks, were required when building prototypes of new products. By automating the information-gathering process and simulating the manufacturability of a product's design, Cisco was able to reduce the number of supplier interactions by half and identify 98 percent of manufacturing problems before beginning the actual production process.

Based on its success with vertical complementary alliances, Cisco has also formed a series of "ecosystems." An ecosystem is a web of business partnerships that includes everything from product sales and distribution to e-learning. The ecosystems make it possible for Cisco to provide end-to-end solutions to its customers without expending significant resources to develop the required capabilities. Instead, Cisco relies on its partners to provide complementary products and services. Cisco also has access to a greater array of customers through leveraging its partners' business contacts. Finally, Cisco is better able to cope with the rapid evolution of new technologies by sharing knowledge and different perspectives with its partners.

Cisco's entry into the Japanese market demonstrates the firm's success with its ecosystem model. Despite a sagging Japanese economy, Cisco was able to grow its business in Japan from almost nothing in the early 1990s to nearly $1 billion in annual sales ten years later. This achievement was largely a function of Cisco's understanding that cooperative relationships were critical to its success in Japan. Thus, with full support of the Japanese government, Cisco formed cooperative ventures with 14 Japanese partners. These relationships gave Cisco the local credibility required to compete in what was a challenging economy.

Because of its positive experience in Japan as well as in other areas, Cisco has forged alliances with hundreds of companies. To enhance the benefits gained from its cooperative arrangements, Cisco works hard to ensure their success. Partners are carefully chosen, with consideration given to those with similar corporate cultures. In addition, Cisco's partners must be strongly committed to providing superior customer service. In this context, once an ecosystem has been established, Cisco assumes an active leadership role, requiring its partners to have at least one technology specialization and meet annual customer satisfaction targets. Cisco then strives to ensure that every ecosystem benefits financially as a result of its decision to partner with Cisco. The company also provides non-financial incentives such as free on-line training and marketing and sales support to partners generating high sales volume or demonstrating superior technical expertise. These measures reflect the strong commitment to building mutually beneficial relationships that has enabled Cisco to achieve success via its ecosystem strategy.

SOURCES: 2002, News @ Cisco, http://www.cisco.com, February 5; D. R. Beresford, 2002, Getting to the bottom of Cisco's numbers, *Business Week,* February 11, 18; R. Hacki & J. Lighton, 2001, The future of the networked company, *The McKinsey Quarterly,* September, 3; R. Nolan, W. Harding, K. Porter, C. Akers, & C. Darwall, 2001, Cisco Systems: Web-enablement, *Harvard Business School Case,* April 6; R. Preston, 2000, Vendor partners stand by you when things go south, *Internetweek,* http://www.internetwk.com, November 13, 9; D. Strausl, 2001, Four stages to building an effective supply chain network, *EBN,* http://www.ebnonline.com, February 26, 43; G. Anders, 2001, After the deluge, *Fast Company,* July, 100–110; L. Hooper, 2001, Chairman & CEO, Cisco, *Jericho,* November 12, 82–84.

support this conclusion. "While in the United States there are 22,000 people per McDonald's, in the rest of the world there is only one McDonald's for every 605,000 people."[114] As a result, as the strategic center firm, McDonald's is devoting its capital expenditures (over 70 percent in the last three years) primarily to develop units in non-U.S. markets. Financial controls are framed around requirements an interested party must satisfy to become a McDonald's franchisee as well as performance standards that are to be met when operating a unit.[115]

As the strategic center of its cooperative network of franchisees, McDonald's concentrates on finding ways for all network units to improve their performance. Currently, the headquarters office is developing an evaluation system to improve customer service, especially in the U.S. units. Increased training for personnel and simplification of processes used to take and deliver orders are actions that the strategic center firm is requiring all network members to take. In addition, the financial controls used to determine the bonuses for regional teams are being changed. The intent is to increase managers' accountability for the performance of units for which they are responsible.

Improving service throughout a strategic network as large as the McDonald's franchise system is challenging.[116] However, being able to do this is necessary for the strategic center firm to increase the value created by its corporate-level cooperative franchising strategy.

Implementing International Cooperative Strategies

Strategic networks formed to implement international cooperative strategies result in firms competing in several countries.[117] Differences among countries' regulatory environments increase the challenge of managing international networks and verifying that at a minimum, the network's operations comply with all legal requirements.[118]

Distributed strategic networks are the organizational structure used to manage international cooperative strategies. As shown in Figure 11.11, several regional strategic center firms are included in the distributed network to manage partner firms' multiple cooperative arrangements.[119] Strategic centers for Ericsson (telecommunications exchange equipment) and Electrolux (white goods, washing machines) are located in countries throughout the world, instead of only in Sweden where the firms are headquartered. Ericsson, for example, is active in more than 140 countries and employs more than 90,000 people. Using the SBU structure, Ericsson has five strategic business units and has formed cooperative agreements with companies throughout the world in each unit. As a founding member of an Ethernet alliance (Intel and Cisco are also members), Ericsson acts as the strategic center firm for this cooperative arrangement, which seeks to solve the wireline access bottleneck by promoting open industry standards.[120]

Jan Wareby (left), president of Ericcson Consumer Products, and Katsumi Ihara, president of Sony Digital Telecommunications Network Company are pictured here. Wareby and Ihara lead their firms' joint venture company, Sopny Ericsson Mobil Communications.

Organizational Structure and Controls: An Additional Perspective

As noted in Chapter 4, no business-level strategy is inherently superior to the others. In this chapter, we note that the same is true for organizational structures. The objective when dealing with strategy and structure is to design a way for the firm's work to be completed as called for by a strategy's focus and details. Peter Drucker's words address this matter: "There is no one right organization anymore. Rather, the task . . . is to select the organization

Figure 11.11 A Distributed Strategic Network

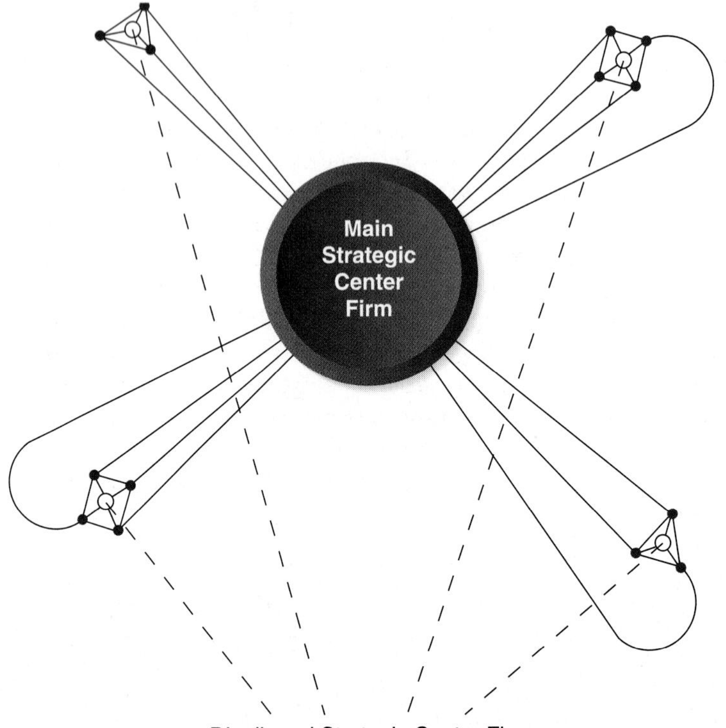

for the particular task and mission at hand."[121] In our context, Drucker is saying that the firm must select a structure that is "right" for the particular strategy that has been chosen to pursue the firm's strategic intent and strategic mission.

The increasingly competitive global economy finds firms continuously modifying the use of their strategies to improve performance. An important theme of this chapter is that once a strategy has been modified, the firm should also change how its work is to be done. Thus, 21st-century companies, especially global competitors, are in a stream of strategy and structure changes. In all cases, the outcome sought is to develop an effective match between what the firm intends to do (as indicated by strategy) with how it intends to do it (as indicated by structure).

There is no inherently superior strategy or structure, and there is no inherently superior strategy/structure match. In the Strategic Focus on page 375 about Semco, we describe an informal structure that seems to be effectively matched with a firm's strategy.

How appropriate are Semco's organizational structure and controls for other companies? For similar firms (that is, for relatively small companies committed to resource sharing across somewhat diversified product lines and markets) there are lessons to be learned. However, the primary message remains the same—firms must match strategy and structure to increase the probability of competitive success. Not set in concrete, strategy/structure matches evolve with changes in the firm's external and internal environments and should be grounded in the core matches discussed in this chapter.

Strategic Focus

Semco's Unique Organizational Structure

Semco is a diversified Brazilian manufacturing company specializing in marine and food service equipment. The firm's strategy is to grow by sharing ideas, people, technologies, and distribution channels. Thus, Semco essentially follows a dominant-business diversification strategy (one in which there is some, but not extensive product and market diversification). Supporting the use of this strategy is a unique organizational structure that appears to be effectively matched with the firm's strategy.

Semco was teetering on the brink of bankruptcy in the early 1980s when Ricardo Semler, the founder's son, became president at the age of 22. Semler thought that management control in the form of pyramidal hierarchy stifled creativity and flexibility. He believed that employees should be treated as adults and managed by common sense rather than rules, procedures, and formal decision-making processes. To implement his unconventional ideas, Semler streamlined Semco's organizational structure into an organizational "circle." Pictured here, this structure consists of three concentric circles, each representing a management level. One level is corporate and the other two are operating levels.

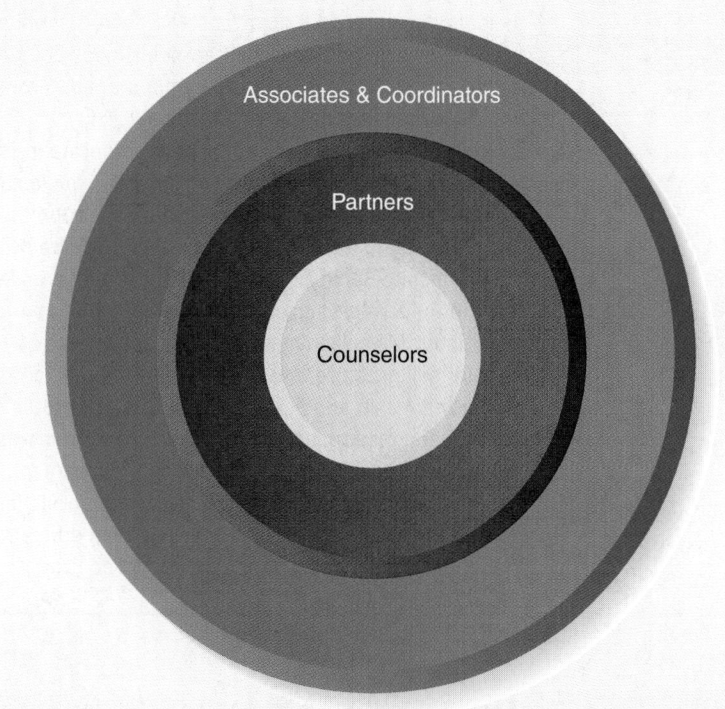

The smaller circle depicts the corporate level, containing the six individuals (called counselors) who are jointly responsible for coordinating Semco's operations. Rather than having a permanent CEO, Semco rotates each counselor into the CEO position for a six-month period. This structural characteristic allows responsibility for the firm's performance to be shared rather than isolated to one key executive. In Semler's view, "When financial performance is one person's problem, then everyone else can relax. In our system, no one can relax. You get to pass on the baton, but it comes back again two-and-a-half years later." The middle circle depicts the operating level of Semco's divisions and includes the division heads (called partners). The outer, largest circle also depicts an operating level and holds Semco's remaining employees, the majority of whom are classified as associates. Without direct reports, associates perform the research, design, sales, and manufacturing work at Semco. They select their own permanent and temporary task leaders, called coordinators, who are openly evaluated every six months. Depending on the uniqueness of their skill sets, associates often earn greater compensation than coordinators and partners. Moreover, associates can increase their corporate status and compensation through continuing excellence in their work, unlike employees at other firms, who more commonly must move into managerial positions to increase their status and total compensation.

The amount of authority and responsibility given to individual employees also differentiates Semco's structure from more traditional ones. Examples of empowerment by the firm's structure include the absence of a dress code, set work hours, assigned offices, and employee manuals. Indeed, employees determine their own hours, decide when to take holidays, and chose how they will be compensated. Staff functions such as human resources and marketing also are not part of Semco's structure. The firm feels that its turnover rate of roughly 1 percent precludes the need to allocate resources to examine personnel issues, and marketing is the responsibility of every employee. To support individuals' marketing efforts, all employees are provided cost and pricing information for the firm's products.

Semco does not hire individuals for specific jobs. Instead, it allows employees to chose their work and the location in which they'll perform it. All entry-level new hires participate in a program called "Lost in Space," in which they spend six months to a year rotating through at least 12 different business units and job functions until a preferred position is found. Employees are also encouraged to rotate positions at least every five years to "prevent boredom" and develop new skills.

Finally, Semco does not have a corporate mission and refuses to define its business. "Once you say what business you are in," explains Semler, "you put your employees in a mental straitjacket. You place boundaries around their thinking and, worst of all, you hand them a ready-made excuse for ignoring new opportunities."

Despite Semco's success, critics aren't convinced that the firm's unique structure is transferable. At present, Semco operates with approximately 1,000 employees and generates about $40 million in annual sales. This relatively small size, some argue, requires a less formal structure and fewer organizational controls compared to those needed by large organizations. In addition, its smaller size facilitates communication within the firm as well as between the firm and its stakeholders. As a privately held company with Semler holding the majority ownership position, Semco encounters minimal pressure for growth from investors. Although the applicability of Semco's ideas to mainstream businesses is debatable, Semco is an interesting example of an efficient and successful organization built and operated without conventional rules and controls.

SOURCES: G. Colvin, 2001, The anti-control freak, *Fortune,* November 26, 60; R. Semler, 2000, How we went digital without a strategy, *Harvard Business Review,* 78(5): 51–58; J. F. Wolff, 1999, In the organization of the future, competitive advantage will lie with inspired employees, *Research Technology Management,* 42(4): 2–4; R. Semler, 1994, Why my former employees still work for me, *Harvard Business Review,* 72(1): 64–74; R. Semler, 1989, Managing without managers, *Harvard Business Review,* 89(5): 76–84.

Summary

- Organizational structure specifies the firm's formal reporting relationships, procedures, controls, and authority and decision-making processes. Influencing managerial work, structure essentially details the work to be done and how that work is to be accomplished. Organizational controls guide the use of strategy, indicate how to compare actual and expected results, and suggest actions to take to improve performance when it falls below expectations. When properly matched with the strategy for which they were intended, structure and controls can be a competitive advantage.
- Strategic controls (largely subjective criteria) and financial controls (largely objective criteria) are the two types of organizational controls used to successfully implement the firm's chosen strategy. Both types of controls are critical, although their degree of emphasis varies based on individual matches between strategy and structure.
- Strategy and structure influence each other, although strategy has an overall stronger influence on structure. Research indicates that firms tend to change structure when declining performance forces them to do so. Effective managers anticipate the need for structural change, quickly modifying structure to better accommodate the firm's strategy implementation needs when evidence calls for that action.
- Business-level strategies are implemented through the functional structure. The cost leadership strategy requires a centralized functional structure—one in which manufacturing efficiency and process engineering are emphasized. The differentiation strategy's functional structure decentralizes implementation-related decisions, especially those concerned with marketing, to those involved with individual organizational functions. Focus strategies, often used in small firms, require a simple structure until such time that the firm diversifies in terms of products and/or markets.
- Unique combinations of different forms of the multidivisional structure are matched with different corporate-level diversification strategies to properly implement these strategies. The cooperative M-form, used to implement the related–constrained corporate-level strategy, has a centralized corporate office and extensive integrating mechanisms. Divisional incentives are linked to overall corporate performance. The related–linked SBU M-form structure establishes separate profit centers within the diversified firm. Each profit center may have divisions offering similar products, but the centers are unrelated to each other. The competitive M-form structure, used to implement the unrelated diversification strategy, is highly decentralized, lacks integrating mechanisms, and utilizes objective financial criteria to evaluate each unit's performance.
- The multidomestic strategy, implemented through the worldwide geographic area structure, emphasizes decentralization and locates all functional activities in the host country or geographic area. The worldwide product divisional structure is used to implement the global strategy. This structure is centralized in order to coordinate and integrate different functions' activities so as to gain global economies of scope and scale. Decision-making authority is centralized in the firm's worldwide division headquarters.
- The transnational strategy—a strategy through which the firm seeks the local responsiveness of the multidomestic strategy and the global efficiency of the global strategy—is implemented through the combination structure. Because it must be simultaneously centralized and decentralized, integrated and nonintegrated, and formalized and nonformalized, the combination structure is difficult to organize and manage successfully.
- Increasingly important to competitive success, cooperative strategies are implemented through organizational structures framed around strategic networks. Strategic center firms are critical to the management of strategic networks.

Review Questions

1. What is organizational structure and what are organizational controls? What are the differences between strategic controls and financial controls?
2. What does it mean to say that strategy and structure have a reciprocal relationship?
3. What are the characteristics of the functional structures that are used to implement the cost leadership, differentiation, integrated cost leadership/differentiation, and focused business-level strategies?
4. What are the differences among the three versions of the multidivisional (M-form) organizational structures that are used to implement the related–constrained, related–linked, and unrelated corporate-level diversification strategies?
5. What organizational structures are used to implement the multidomestic, global, and transnational international strategies?
6. What is a strategic network? What is a strategic center firm?

Experiential Exercise

Organizational Structure and Controls

As an executive board member for a successful 50-partner firm that provides accounting services to corporate clients, you are interested in expanding to offer management consulting services to these clients. Another possibility for your firm is offering both types of services to smaller clients.

Part One. You are concerned about how your organizational structure may need to change to support these services. Based on the material in the chapter, use the chart to rank each type of organizational structure against the activities—information processing, coordination, and control—that you anticipate will need to be strengthened.

	Information Processing	Coordination	Control
Simple structure			
Functional structure			
Multidivisional structure			

Part Two. You are also very concerned that there may be a potential conflict of interest if your firm provides both accounting and management consulting services to the same client. In small groups, discuss whether it is possible for a firm to use organizational structure and controls to achieve its strategic objectives but also to prevent conflicts of interest among its divisions.

Notes

1. R. J. Herbold, 2002, Inside Microsoft: Balancing creativity and discipline, *Harvard Business Review,* 80(1): 73–79.
2. R. E. Miles & C. C. Snow, 1978, *Organizational Strategy, Structure and Process,* New York: McGraw-Hill.
3. M. van Clieaf, 2001, Leading & creating value in the knowledge economy, *Ivey Business Journal,* 65(5): 54–59.
4. T. Amburgey & T. Dacin, 1994, As the left foot follows the right? The dynamics of strategic and structural change, *Academy of Management Journal,* 37: 1427–1452.
5. B. Keats & H. O'Neill, 2001, Organizational structure: Looking through a strategy lens, in M. A. Hitt, R. E. Freeman, & J. S. Harrison (eds.), *Handbook of Strategic Management,* Oxford, U.K.: Blackwell Publishers, 520–542.
6. R. E. Hoskisson, C. W. L. Hill, & H. Kim, 1993, The multidivisional structure: Organizational fossil or source of value? *Journal of Management,* 19: 269–298.
7. F. Warner, 2002, Think lean, *Fast Company,* February, 40–42.
8. T. Burns & G. M. Stalker, 1961, *The Management of Innovation,* London: Tavistok; P. R. Lawrence & J. W. Lorsch, 1967, *Organization and Environment,* Homewood, IL.: Richard D. Irwin; J. Woodward, 1965, *Industrial Organization: Theory and Practice,* London: Oxford University Press.
9. P. Jenster & D. Hussey, 2001, *Company Analysis: Determining Strategic Capability,* Chichester: John Wiley & Sons, 135–171; D. J. Teece, G. Pisano, & A. Shuen, 1997, Dynamic capabilities and strategic management, *Strategic Management Journal,* 18: 509–533.
10. B. Keats & H. O'Neill, 2001, Organizational structure: Looking through a strategy lens, in M. A. Hitt, R. E. Freeman & J. S. Harrison (eds.), *Handbook of Strategic Management,* Oxford, U.K.: Blackwell Publishers, 520–542; J. R. Galbraith, 1995, *Designing Organizations,* San Francisco: Jossey-Bass, 6.
11. Keats & O'Neill, Organizational structure, 533; Galbraith. *Designing Organizations,* 6.
12. V. P. Rindova & S. Kotha, 2001, Continuous "morphing": Competing through dynamic capabilities, form, and function, *Academy of Management Journal,* 44: 1263–1280.
13. J. G. Covin, D. P. Slevin, & M. B. Heeley, 2001, Strategic decision making in an intuitive vs. technocratic mode: Structural and environmental consideration, *Journal of Business Research,* 52: 51–67.
14. M. A. Schilling & H. K. Steensma, 2001, The use of modular organizational forms: An industry-level analysis, *Academy of Management Journal,* 44: 1149–1168.
15. Jenster & Hussey, *Company Analysis,* 169; L. Donaldson, 1997, A positivist alternative to the structure-action approach, *Organization Studies,* 18: 77–92.
16. D. C. Hambrick & J. W. Fredrickson, 2001, Are you sure you have a strategy? *Academy of Management Executive,* 15(4): 48–59.
17. G. G. Dess & G. T. Lumpkin, 2001, Emerging issues in strategy process research, in M. A. Hitt, R. E. Freeman, & J. S. Harrison (eds.), *Handbook of Strategic Management,* Oxford, U.K.: Blackwell Publishers, 3–34.
18. C. A. de Kluyver, 2000, *Strategic Thinking: An Executive Perspective,* Upper Saddle River: Prentice Hall, 52.
19. G. A. Bigley & K. H. Roberts, 2001, The incident command system: High-reliability organizing for complex and volatile task environments, *Academy of Management Journal,* 44: 1281–1299.
20. J. Child & R. M. McGrath, 2001, Organizations unfettered: Organizational form in an information-intensive economy, *Academy of Management Journal,* 44: 1135–1148.
21. T. W. Malnight, 2001, Emerging structural patterns within multinational corporations: Toward process-based structures, *Academy of Management Journal,* 44: 1187–1210; A. Sharma, 1999, Central dilemmas of managing innovation in firms, *California Management Review,* 41(3): 146–164; H. A. Simon, 1991, Bounded rationality and organizational learning, *Organization Science,* 2: 125–134.
22. B. W. Keats & M. A. Hitt, 1988, A causal model of linkages among environmental dimensions, macroorganizational characteristics, and performance, *Academy of Management Journal,* 31: 570–598.
23. A. Chandler, 1962, *Strategy and Structure,* Cambridge, MA.: MIT Press.
24. Keats & O'Neill, Organizational structure, 535.
25. C. H. Noble, 1999, The eclectic roots of strategy implementation research, *Journal of Business Research,* 45: 119–134.
26. S. Venkataraman & S. D. Sarasvathy, 2001, Strategy and entrepreneurship: Outlines of an untold story, in M. A. Hitt, R. E. Freeman & J. S. Harrison (eds.), *Handbook of Strategic Management,* Oxford, U.K.: Blackwell Publishers, 650–668.
27. J. Matthews, 1999, Strategic moves, *Supply Management,* 4(4): 36–37.
28. D. F. Kuratko, R. D. Ireland, & J. S. Hornsby, 2001, Improving firm performance through entrepreneurial actions: Acordia's corporate entrepreneurship strategy, *Academy of Management Executive,* 15(4): 60–71.
29. J. S. Harrison & C. H. St. John, 2002, *Foundations in Strategic Management* (2nd ed.), Cincinnati: South-Western College Publishing, 118–129.
30. D. Incandela, K. L. McLaughlin, & C. S. Shi, 1999, Retailers to the world, *The McKinsey Quarterly,* 3: 84–97.
31. R. E. Hoskisson, M. A. Hitt, & R. D. Ireland, 1994, The effects of acquisitions and restructuring strategies (strategic refocusing) on innovation, in G. von Krogh, A. Sinatra, & H. Singh (eds.), *Managing Corporate Acquisition,* London: MacMillan Press, 144–169.
32. M. A. Hitt, R. E. Hoskisson, R. A. Johnson, & D. D. Moesel, 1996, The market for corporate control and firm innovation, *Academy of Management Journal,* 39: 1084–1119.
33. R. E. Hoskisson & M. A. Hitt, 1988, Strategic control and relative R&D investment in multiproduct firms, *Strategic Management Journal,* 9: 605–621.
34. D. J. Collis, 1996, Corporate strategy in multibusiness firms, *Long Range Planning,* 29: 416–418.
35. K. Massaro, 2000, FTI and PeopleSoft ally to offer financial control solution, *Wall Street & Technology,* 18(11): 84.
36. 2002, Pfizer Inc., Management's report, http://www.pfizer.com, January 27.
37. S. Woolley, 2001, Digital hubris, *Forbes,* May 28, 66–70.
38. 2001, PSINet announces NASDAQ delisting, http://www.psinet.com, June 1.
39. J. B. Barney, 2002, *Gaining and Sustaining Competitive Advantage* (2nd ed.), Upper Saddle River: Prentice Hall.
40. M. Sengul, 2001, Divisionalization: Strategic effects of organizational structure, Paper presented during the 21st Annual Strategic Management Society Conference.
41. Keats & O'Neill, Organizational structure, 531.
42. K. J. Euske & A. Riccaboni, 1999, Stability to profitability: Managing interdependencies to meet a new environment, *Accounting, Organizations & Society,* 24: 463–481; D. Miller & J. O. Whitney, 1999, Beyond strategy: Configuration as a pillar of competitive advantage, *Business Horizons,* 42(3): 5–17.
43. S. Tallman, 2001, Global strategic management, in M. A. Hitt, R. E. Freeman, & J. S. Harrison (eds.), *Handbook of Strategic Management,* Oxford, U.K.: Blackwell Publishers, 464–490.
44. B. A. Gutek & T. Welsh, 2000, *The Brave New Service World,* New York: AMACOM.
45. L. Lee, 2002, Will investors pay for Schwab's advice? *Business Week,* January 21, 36.
46. Chandler, *Strategy and Structure.*
47. Keats & O'Neill, Organizational structure, 524.
48. G. M. McNamara, R. A. Luce, & G. H. Thompson, 2002, Examining the effect of complexity in strategic group knowledge structures on firm performance, *Strategic Management Journal,* 23: 153–170; J. P. Walsh, 1995, Managerial and organizational cognition: Notes from a trip down memory lane, *Organization Science,* 6: 280–321.
49. C. Levicki, 1999, *The Interactive Strategy Workout* (2nd ed.), London: Prentice-Hall.
50. J. J. Chrisman, A. Bauerschmidt, & C. W. Hofer, 1998, The determinants of new venture performance: An extended model, *Entrepreneurship Theory & Practice,* 23(3): 5–29; H. M. O'Neill, R. W. Pouder, & A. K. Buchholtz, 1998, Patterns in the diffusion of strategies across organizations: Insights from the innovation diffusion literature, *Academy of Management Review,* 23: 98–114.
51. 2002, Casketfurniture.com, About our company, http://www.casketfurniture.com, February 2.
52. Galbraith, *Designing Organizations,* 25.
53. Keats & O'Neill, Organizational structure, 539.
54. Lawrence & Lorsch, *Organization and Environment.*
55. O. E. Williamson, 1975, *Markets and Hierarchies: Analysis and Anti-trust Implications,* New York: The Free Press.
56. Chandler, *Strategy and Structure.*
57. J. Greco, 1999, Alfred P. Sloan, Jr. (1875–1966): The original organizational man, *Journal of Business Strategy,* 20(5): 30–31.
58. Hoskisson, Hill, & Kim, The multidivisional structure, 269–298.
59. W. G. Rowe & P. M. Wright, 1997, Related and unrelated diversification and their effect on human resource management controls, *Strategic Management Journal,* 18: 329-338; D. C. Galunic & K. M. Eisenhardt, 1996, The evolution of intracorporate domains: Divisional charter losses in high-technology, multidivisional corporations, *Organization Science,* 7: 255–282.

60. A. D. Chandler, 1994, The functions of the HQ unit in the multibusiness firm, in R. P. Rumelt, D. E. Schendel, & D. J. Teece (eds.), *Fundamental Issues in Strategy,* Cambridge, MA: Harvard Business School Press, 327.
61. O. E. Williamson, 1994, Strategizing, economizing, and economic organization, in R. P. Rumelt, D. E. Schendel, & D. J. Teece (eds.), *Fundamental Issues in Strategy,* Cambridge, MA: Harvard Business School Press, 361–401.
62. R. M. Burton & B. Obel, 1980, A computer simulation test of the M-form hypothesis, *Administrative Science Quarterly,* 25: 457–476.
63. O. E. Williamson, 1985, *The Economic Institutions of Capitalism: Firms, Markets, and Relational Contracting,* New York: MacMillan.
64. Keats & O'Neill, Organizational structure, 532.
65. R. H. Hall, 1996, *Organizations: Structures, Processes, and Outcomes* (6th ed.), Englewood Cliffs: Prentice-Hall, 13; S. Baiman, D. F. Larcker, & M. V. Rajan, 1995, Organizational design for business units, *Journal of Accounting Research,* 33: 205–229.
66. Hall, *Organizations,* 64–75.
67. Barney, *Gaining and Sustaining Competitive Advantage,* 257.
68. 2002, Wal-Mart stores pricing policy, http://www.walmart.com, February 2.
69. Chandler, *Strategy and Structure.*
70. 2002, Procter & Gamble corporate structure, http://www.procter&gamble.com, January 26.
71. R. Rumelt, 1974, *Strategy, Structure and Economic Performance,* Boston: Harvard University Press.
72. 2002, Halliburton Co., http://www.halliburton.com, February 1.
73. C. C. Markides & P. J. Williamson, 1996, Corporate diversification and organizational structure: A resource-based view, *Academy of Management Journal,* 39: 340–367; C. W. L. Hill, M. A. Hitt, & R. E. Hoskisson, 1992, Cooperative versus competitive structures in related and unrelated diversified firms, *Organization Science,* 3: 501–521.
74. P. F. Drucker, 2002, They're not employees, they're people, *Harvard Business Review,* 80(2): 70–77; J. Robins & M. E. Wiersema, 1995, A resource-based approach to the multibusiness firm: Empirical analysis of portfolio interrelationships and corporate financial performance, *Strategic Management Journal,* 16: 277–299.
75. C. C. Markides, 1997, To diversify or not to diversify, *Harvard Business Review,* 75(6): 93–99.
76. J. G. March, 1994, *A Primer on Decision Making: How Decisions Happen,* New York: The Free Press, 117–118.
77. 2002, GE businesses, http://www.ge.com, February 4.
78. 2002, General Electric Co., Argus Research, http://argusresearch.com, February 4.
79. J. Welch with J. A. Byrne, 2001, *Jack: Straight from the Gut,* New York: Warner Business Books.
80. S. Rosenbush, 2002, A lengthy honeymoon at Lucent? *Business Week,* January 21, 34.
81. R. E. Hoskisson & M. A. Hitt, 1990, Antecedents and performance outcomes of diversification: A review and critique of theoretical perspectives, *Journal of Management,* 16: 461–509.
82. Hill, Hitt, & Hoskisson, Cooperative versus competitive structures, 512.
83. J. Birkinshaw, 2001, Strategies for managing internal competition, *California Management Review,* 44(1): 21–38.
84. T. R. Eisenmann & J. L. Bower, 2000, The entrepreneurial M-form: Strategic integration in global media firms, *Organization Science,* 11: 348–355.
85. C. Scott, 2001, Enterprising values, *The Wall Street Journal Sunday,* December 23, D5.
86. 2002, Textron profile, http://www.textron.com, February 4.
87. Y. Luo, 2002, Product diversification in international joint ventures: Performance implications in an emerging market, *Strategic Management Journal,* 23: 1–20.
88. Tallman, Global strategic management, 467.
89. Malnight, Emerging structural patterns, 1188.
90. J. Wolf & W. G. Egelhoff, 2002, A reexamination and extension of international strategy-structure theory, *Strategic Management Journal,* 23: 181–189.
91. C. A. Bartlett & S. Ghoshal, 1989, *Managing across Borders: The Transnational Solution,* Boston: Harvard Business School Press.
92. 2002, Unilever today, http://www.unilever.com, February 5.
93. 2001, Kyowa Hakko, Semiannual report, September 30.
94. Malnight, Emerging structural patterns, 1197.
95. Barney, *Gaining and Sustaining Competitive Advantage,* 533.
96. R. J. Kramer, 1999, Organizing for global competitiveness: The corporate headquarters design, *Chief Executive Digest,* 3(2): 23–28.
97. Y. L. Doz & G. Hamel, 1998, *Alliance Advantage: The Art of Creating Value through Partnering,* Boston: Harvard Business School Press, 222.
98. A. C. Inkpen, 2001, Strategic alliances, in M. A. Hitt, R. E. Freeman, & J. S. Harrison (eds.), *Handbook of Strategic Management,* Oxford, U.K.: Blackwell Publishers, 409–432.
99. Luo, Product diversification in international joint ventures, 2.
100. R. Gulati, N. Nohira, & A. Zaheer, 2000, Strategic networks, *Strategic Management Journal,* 21(Special Issue): 203–215; B. Gomes-Casseres, 1994, Group versus group: How alliance networks compete, *Harvard Business Review,* 72(4): 62–74.
101. C. Lee, K. Lee, & J. M. Pennings, 2001, Internal capabilities, external networks, and performance: A study on technology-based ventures, *Strategic Management Journal* 22(Summer Special Issue): 615–640.
102. M. B. Sarkar, R. Echambadi, & J. S. Harrison, 2001, Alliance entrepreneurship and firm market performance, *Strategic Management Journal,* 22(Summer Special Issue): 701–711.
103. S. Harrison, 1998, *Japanese Technology and Innovation Management,* Northampton, MA: Edward Elgar.
104. P. Dussauge, B. Garrette, & W. Mitchell, 2000, Learning from competing partners: Outcomes and duration of scale and link alliances in Europe, North America and Asia, *Strategic Management Journal,* 21: 99–126; G. Lorenzoni & C. Baden-Fuller, 1995, Creating a strategic center to manage a web of partners, *California Management Review,* 37(3): 146–163.
105. J. H. Dyer & K. Nobeoka, 2000, Creating and managing a high-performance knowledge-sharing network: The Toyota case, *Strategic Management Journal,* 21(Special Issue): 345–367; J. H. Dyer, 1997, Effective interfirm collaboration: How firms minimize transaction costs and maximize transaction value, *Strategic Management Journal,* 18: 535–556.
106. T. Nishiguchi, 1994, *Strategic Industrial Sourcing: The Japanese Advantage,* New York: Oxford University Press.
107. W. M. Fruin, 1992, *The Japanese Enterprise System,* New York: Oxford University Press.
108. 2002, About Delta, http://www.delta.com, February 10.
109. 2002, British Airways' Extended Network, http:/www.ba.com, February 10.
110. 2002, Iberia's History, http://www.iberia.com, February 10.
111. 2002, News @ Cisco, http://www.cisco.com, February 10.
112. 2002, Q&A with John Chambers, http://www.cisco.com, February 10.
113. 2002, McDonald's Corp., *Standard & Poor's Stock Report,* http://www.fidelity.com, January 26.
114. Ibid.
115. 2002, McDonald's USA franchising, http://www.mcdonalds.com, February 9.
116. 2002, Argus Company Report, McDonald's Corp, http://argusresearch.com, February 10.
117. C. Jones, W. S. Hesterly, & S. P. Borgatti, 1997, A general theory of network governance: Exchange conditions and social mechanisms, *Academy of Management Review,* 22: 911–945.
118. J. M. Mezias, 2002, Identifying liabilities of foreignness and strategies to minimize their effects: The case of labor lawsuit judgments in the United States, *Strategic Management Journal,* 23: 229–244.
119. R. E. Miles, C. C. Snow, J. A. Mathews, G. Miles, & J. J. Coleman, Jr., 1997, Organizing in the knowledge age: Anticipating the cellular form, *Academy of Management Executive,* 11(4): 7–20.
120. 2002, Ericsson NewsCenter, http://www.ericsson.com, February 10.
121. M. F. Wolff, 1999, In the organization of the future, competitive advantage will be inspired, *Research Technology Management,* 42(4): 2–4.

12

Chapter Twelve

Strategic Leadership

Knowledge Objectives

Studying this chapter should provide you with the strategic management knowledge needed to:

1. Define strategic leadership and describe top-level managers' importance as a resource.
2. Define top management teams and explain their effects on firm performance.
3. Describe the internal and external managerial labor markets and their effects on developing and implementing strategies.
4. Discuss the value of strategic leadership in determining the firm's strategic direction.
5. Explain strategic leaders' role in exploiting and maintaining core competencies.
6. Describe the importance of strategic leaders in developing human capital.
7. Define organizational culture and explain what must be done to sustain an effective culture.
8. Explain what strategic leaders can do to establish and emphasize ethical practices.
9. Discuss the importance and use of organizational controls.

IBM and Strategic Leadership: Transitioning from Gerstner to Palmisano

Louis V. Gerstner left his position of CEO of IBM (remaining as chairman of the board) at the end of February 2002, and Samuel J. Palmisano, who had served as the firm's president, took over as CEO on March 1. Gerstner came to IBM as an outsider. During his 10 years as CEO, he turned the fading hardware-based company around by becoming more focused on services and software.

When Gerstner was hired as CEO, IBM's primary business of mainframe computers was slipping, and the company seemed to have lost its competitive edge. With experience as CEO for RJ Reynolds (tobacco and food) and American Express (financial services) he did not have a strong technical background, but was instead hired because of his skill in general management. IBM's board of directors had ascertained that the problem with the company was not its technology, but its culture and focus. As CEO, Gerstner guided the company away from a pure focus on hardware, particularly PCs and mainframes, and into the services market. Under his leadership, the company's stock market value increased to more than $180 billion, and profits increased more than $3.5 billion. According to one analyst, "A $10,000 investment made in IBM the day Gerstner took over is worth $92,060 today."

Unlike Gerstner, Palmisano has spent his entire 28-year career with IBM, having joined the company out of college. He is known as a strong salesman who is not afraid to take risks and push the company in new directions. With positive results being generated by using the firm's current strategies, Palmisano seems to be a good choice to follow Gerstner. He is an insider, and current performance outcomes suggest that at least in the short run, he should keep IBM focused on effectively implementing its strategies. On the other hand, he is not afraid to take risks, so he should be able to continue to promote innovation at IBM. For example, when Palmisano became head of IBM's computer servers business in 1999 he aggressively changed the way business had been done, and made it more profitable. "He assigned his top people to key bids and freed the sales staff to dazzle customers with discounts of up to 70 percent—untouchable by other computer makers." By the first quarter of 2000, IBM was number one in the servers market with a 25 percent share.

Samuel J. Palmisano (left) succeeded Lous V. Gerstner as IBM's CEO in spring 2002. One of Palmisano's first strategic actions was cutting IBM's work force to reduce costs and help the firm maintain productivity.

Palmisano's achievement in the servers business mirrored his success as head of Integrated Systems Solutions Corp. beginning in 1992; this group became the core of Global Services, now IBM's largest revenue generating unit. By changing the way people were paid—basing their commissions on the profitability instead of the size of contracts—he led the group as revenues increased from $14.9 billion in 1993 to $22.9 billion in 1996.

When Palmisano became IBM's CEO in 2002, the firm's sales and earnings were flat because of the downturn in the economy. It will be interesting to see his strategic approach. It may be a difficult challenge to find opportunities of new growth, because Gerstner did such a good job in turning IBM around and as a result of changing the firm's strategies. As Andrew Grove, former CEO of Intel, said about Gerstner, "The key to IBM's success with its services business is that it wraps things around commodity products that differentiate them. Every other computer company has now adopted as its primary objective to be more IBM-like. It's kind of interesting that this service-driven strategy, an idea that everyone else is now copying, came from an outsider to this industry."

So far, Palmisano has maintained that IBM's sectors, including computer servers, data storage devices, database software, and middleware programs, are still in good shape, but it is obvious that he will have to focus on increasing revenue. Although some insiders thought that Palmisano should make some large acquisitions in the beginning to bolster revenue growth, he made it clear such actions were not in the near future for the company. It will be interesting to see if Palmisano can boost revenues at IBM and maintain high growth levels while steering the firm towards continued success.

SOURCES: S. E. Ante & I. Sager, 2002, IBM's new boss, *Business Week,* February 11, 66–72; W. Bulkeley, 2002, As PC industry slumps, IBM hands off manufacturing of desktops, *The Wall Street Journal*, January 9, B1, B4; W. Bulkeley & J. Guidera, 2002, IBM taps its president to succeed Gerstner as CEO, *The Wall Street Journal,* January 30, B1, B4; L. DiCarlo, 2002, A successor for IBM's silent man, *Forbes,* http://www.forbes.com, January 29; D. Kirkpatrick, 2002, The future of IBM, *Fortune,* February 18, 60–64; S. Lohr, 2002, Gerstner to step down as IBM. chief, *The New York Times,* http://www.nytimes.com, January 29; B. J. Feder, 2001, Waiting to call plays for IBM, *The New York Times,* http://www.nytimes.com, August 15.

As the Opening Case illustrates, the selection of a new CEO can make a significant difference in how a firm performs. If a new leader can create a strategic vision for the firm and energize its human capital, positive outcomes can be achieved, as was the case at IBM under Louis V. Gerstner's leadership as the firm's CEO. Although the challenge of strategic leadership is significant, as it will be for Samuel Palmisano who took Gerstner's position at IBM, the outcomes of strategic leadership are potentially significant. However, it is difficult to build and maintain success over a sustained period of time.

As this chapter makes clear, it is through effective strategic leadership that firms are able to successfully use the strategic management process. As strategic leaders, top-level managers must guide the firm in ways that result in the formation of a strategic intent and strategic mission. This guidance may lead to goals that stretch everyone in the organization to improve their performance.[1] Moreover, strategic leaders must facilitate the development of appropriate strategic actions and determine how to implement them. These actions on the part of strategic leaders culminate in strategic competitiveness and above-average returns,[2] as shown in Figure 12.1.

This chapter begins with a definition of strategic leadership and its importance as a potential source of competitive advantage. Next, we examine top management teams and their effects on innovation, strategic change, and firm performance. Following this discussion is an analysis of the internal and external managerial labor markets from which strategic leaders are selected. Closing the chapter are descriptions of the six key components of effective strategic leadership: determining a strategic

Figure 12.1 Strategic Leadership and the Strategic Management Process

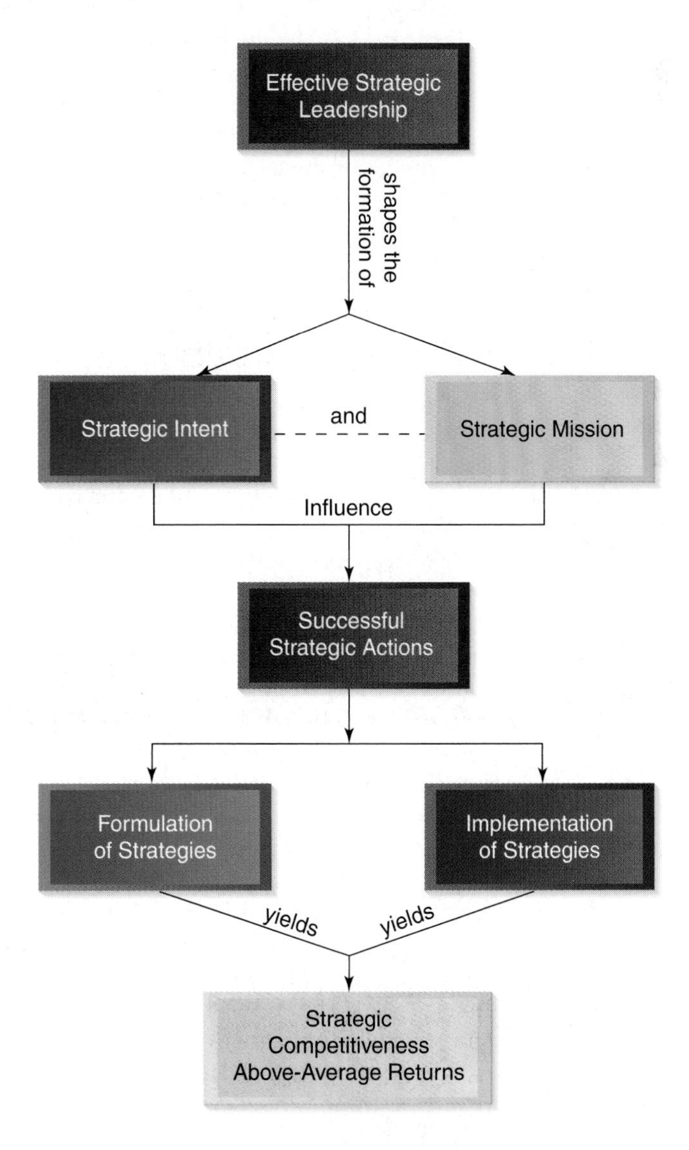

AP PHOTO/XEROX, DOUG KANTER

Xerox recently set up an independent company at the firm's Palo Alto Research Center (pictured here), where the graphical user interface and mouse were invented, to commercialize more of Xerox's non-core innovation. CEO and chairman Anne Mulcahy said, "The nature of this research is that you capitalise on some of it in your own business and some of it you don't. For as many examples of innovation that have migrated to other places, there are great examples of innovation that stays."

direction, exploiting and maintaining core competencies, developing human capital, sustaining an effective organizational culture, emphasizing ethical practices, and establishing balanced organizational control systems.

The impermanence of success is well documented by the frequent changes in leadership at Xerox. Xerox's board of directors promoted Anne Mulcahy to president in May 2000, after it ousted CEO G. Richard Thoman, who lasted 13 months. Thoman had followed Paul A. Allaire as CEO, who remained chairman of the board. Even though Xerox invented the idea of the personal computer and was the innovator of the copier machine, it was not able to capitalize on the computer and has stumbled in copiers. For example, Hewlett-Packard's division that manufactures and sells laser printers (based on the same technology as the copier) has more total revenue than all of Xerox. Even with these strategic blunders, Xerox has enjoyed significant success in its digital copiers (see the Strategic Focus on page 10 in Chapter 1).[3] However, because of significant weakness in its many businesses "the company was close to floundering after years of weak sales and high costs; employees were as disgruntled as customers."[4] Mulcahy, who was named CEO and chairman in July 2001 after several unsuccessful leaders, is trying to turn the situation at Xerox around by divesting businesses, such as financial services, and not only selling copiers and printers, but also by strengthening its services and solutions business as IBM did, as described in the Opening Case.

Strategic Leadership

Strategic leadership is the ability to anticipate, envision, maintain flexibility, and empower others to create strategic change as necessary.

Strategic leadership is the ability to anticipate, envision, maintain flexibility, and empower others to create strategic change as necessary. Multifunctional in nature, strategic leadership involves managing through others, managing an entire enterprise rather than a functional subunit, and coping with change that seems to be increasing exponentially in the 21st-century competitive landscape. Because of this landscape's complexity and global nature, strategic leaders must learn how to effectively influence human behavior in what is an uncertain environment. By word or by personal example, and through their ability to envision the future, effective strategic leaders meaningfully influence the behaviors, thoughts, and feelings of those with whom they work.[5]

The ability to manage human capital may be the most critical of the strategic leader's skills.[6] In the 21st century, intellectual capital, including the ability to manage knowledge and create and commercialize innovation, affects a strategic leader's success.[7] Competent strategic leaders also establish the context through which stakeholders (such as employees, customers, and suppliers) can perform at peak efficiency.[8] "When a public company is left with a void in leadership, for whatever reason, the ripple effects are widely felt both within and outside the organization. Internally, a company is likely to suffer a crisis of morale, confidence and productivity among employees and, similarly, stockholders may panic when a company is left rudderless and worry about the safety and future of their investment."[9] The crux of strategic leadership is the ability to manage the firm's operations effectively and sustain a high performance over time.[10]

A firm's ability to achieve strategic competitiveness and earn above-average returns is compromised when strategic leaders fail to respond appropriately and quickly to changes in the complex global competitive environment. As mentioned, the failure to respond quickly resulted in problems at Xerox. Research suggests that a firm's "long-term competitiveness depends on managers' willingness to challenge continually their managerial frames" and that global competition is more than product versus product or company versus company: It is also a case of "mind-set versus mind-set, managerial frame versus managerial frame."[11] Competing on the basis of mind-sets demands that strategic leaders learn how to deal with diverse and cognitively complex competitive situations. One author labels this ability strategic intelligence, which consists of five interrelated elements or competencies: "foresight, systems thinking, visioning, motivating, and partnering."[12]

Effective strategic leaders are willing to make candid and courageous, yet pragmatic, decisions—decisions that may be difficult, but necessary—through foresight as they reflect on external conditions facing the firm. They also need to understand how such decisions will affect the internal systems currently in use in the firm. Effective strategic leaders use visioning to motivate employees. They often solicit corrective feedback from peers, superiors, and employees about the value of their difficult decisions and vision. Ultimately, they develop strong partners internally and externally to facilitate execution of their strategic vision.[13]

The primary responsibility for effective strategic leadership rests at the top, in particular, with the CEO. Other commonly recognized strategic leaders include members of the board of directors, the top management team, and divisional general managers. Regardless of their title and organizational function, strategic leaders have substantial decision-making responsibilities that cannot be delegated.[14] Strategic leadership is an extremely complex, but critical, form of leadership. Strategies cannot be formulated and implemented to achieve above-average returns without effective strategic leaders. Because strategic leadership is a requirement of strategic success, and because organizations may be poorly led and overmanaged, firms competing in the 21st-century competitive landscape are challenged to develop effective strategic leaders.[15]

Managers as an Organizational Resource

As we have suggested, top-level managers are an important resource for firms seeking to formulate and implement strategies effectively.[16] The strategic decisions made by top-level managers influence how the firm is designed and whether goals will be achieved. Thus, a critical element of organizational success is having a top-management team with superior managerial skills.[17]

Managers often use their discretion (or latitude for action) when making strategic decisions, including those concerned with the effective implementation of strategies.[18] Managerial discretion differs significantly across industries. The primary factors that determine the amount of decision-making discretion a manager (especially a top-level manager) has include (1) external environmental sources (such as the industry structure, the rate of market growth in the firm's primary industry, and the degree to which products can be differentiated), (2) characteristics of the organization (including its size, age, resources, and culture), and (3) characteristics of the manager (including commitment to the firm and its strategic outcomes, tolerance for ambiguity, skills in working with different people, and aspiration levels) (see Figure 12.2). Because strategic leaders' decisions are intended to help the firm gain a competitive advantage, how managers exercise discretion when determining appropriate strategic actions is critical to the firm's success.[19] Top executives must be action oriented; thus, the decisions that they make should spur the company to action.

In addition to determining new strategic initiatives, top-level managers develop the appropriate organizational structure and reward systems of a firm. In Chapter 11, we describe how the organizational structure and reward systems affect strategic actions taken to implement different strategies. Top executives also have a major

Figure 12.2 Factors Affecting Managerial Discretion

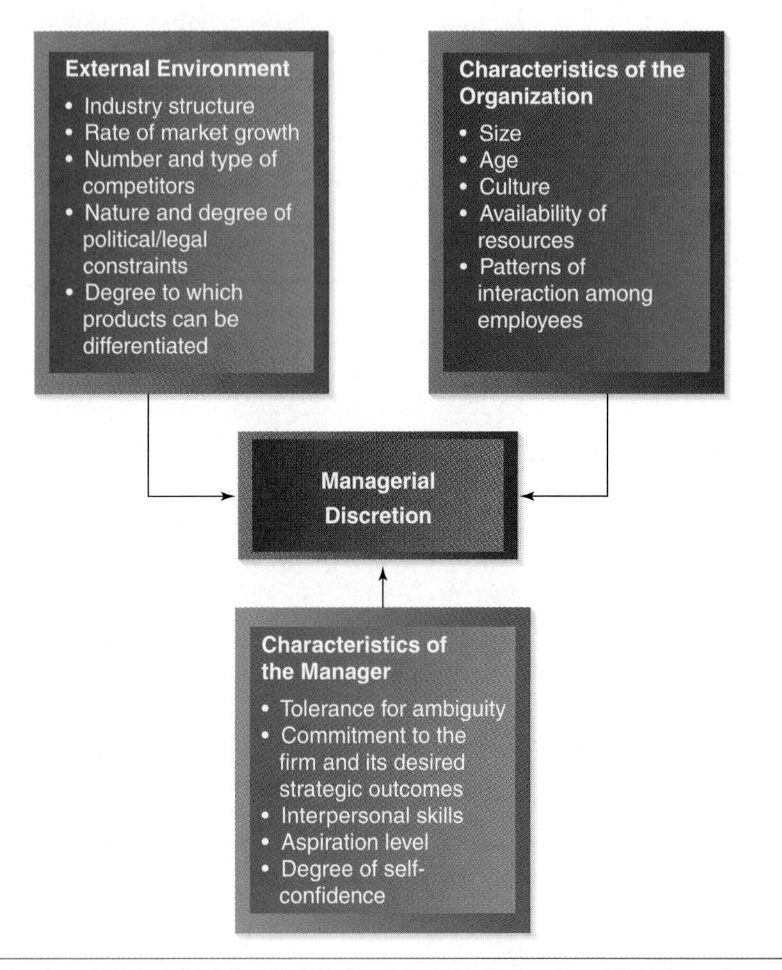

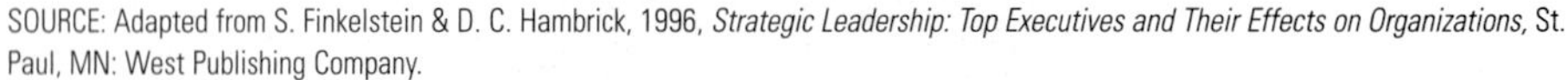

SOURCE: Adapted from S. Finkelstein & D. C. Hambrick, 1996, *Strategic Leadership: Top Executives and Their Effects on Organizations*, St. Paul, MN: West Publishing Company.

effect on a firm's culture. Evidence suggests that managers' values are critical in shaping a firm's cultural values.[20] Accordingly, top-level managers have an important effect on organizational activities and performance.[21]

The potential effect of strategic leadership is illustrated by Mitt Romney's successful turnaround of the 2002 Winter Olympic Games. When Romney took over as CEO of the Salt Lake Organizing Committee in 1999, it had a $379 million deficit resulting from the loss of sponsors following the Olympic bid scandal and allegations of bribery. Romney's ability not only to cut costs but also to attract new sponsors saved the games financially. Moreover, his approach and integrity won over many and helped heal the wounds from the bid controversy. "If we do our job well, people will go away feeling like they have had a fire lit within them or they've been inspired by the athletes and by the people they've met here and by their fellow citizens from around the world."[22] Romney's leadership was very effective in accomplishing this aspiration.

The decisions and actions of strategic leaders can make them a source of competitive advantage for the firm. In accordance with the criteria of sustainability discussed in Chapter 3, strategic leaders can be a source of competitive advantage only

© KEVIN LAMARQUE /REUTERS NEWMEDIA INC./CORBIS

Mitt Romney, pictured here with the 2002 Olympic torch, oversaw the Salt Lake Olympic Games. Following a six-year position as vice president of Boston-based management consulting firm Bain & Company, he founded Bain Capital. He later served as interim CEO of Bain & Company during a period of financial turmoil and led the firm's highly successful turnaround. In 2002, he became a candidate for governor of Massachusetts.

when their work is valuable, rare, costly to imitate, and nonsubstitutable. Effective strategic leaders become a source of competitive advantage when they focus their work on the key issues that ultimately shape the firm's ability to earn above-average returns.[23] Accordingly, managerial beliefs affect strategic decisions that in turn affect the firm's performance.[24] For example, Mitt Romney certainly believed that the 2002 Winter Olympic Games could be turned into a success. However, Romney's vision was achieved through a team of leaders.

Top Management Teams

The complexity of the challenges faced by the firm and the need for substantial amounts of information and knowledge require teams of executives to provide the strategic leadership of most firms. The **top management team** is composed of the key managers who are responsible for selecting and implementing the firm's strategies. Typically, the top management team includes the officers of the corporation, defined by the title of vice president and above or by service as a member of the board of directors.[25] The quality of the strategic decisions made by a top management team affects the firm's ability to innovate and engage in effective strategic change.[26]

Top Management Team, Firm Performance, and Strategic Change

The job of top-level executives is complex and requires a broad knowledge of the firm's operations, as well as the three key parts of the firm's external environment—the general, industry, and competitor environments, as discussed in Chapter 2. Therefore, firms try to form a top management team that has the appropriate knowledge and expertise to operate the internal organization, yet also can deal with all the firm's stakeholders as well as its competitors.[27] This normally requires a heterogeneous top management team. A **heterogeneous top management team** is composed of individuals with different functional backgrounds, experience, and education. The more heterogeneous a top management team is, with varied expertise and knowledge, the more capacity it has to provide effective strategic leadership in *formulating* strategy.

The **top management team** is composed of the key managers who are responsible for selecting and implementing the firm's strategies.

A **heterogeneous top management team** is composed of individuals with different functional backgrounds, experience, and education.

Members of a heterogeneous top management team benefit from discussing the different perspectives advanced by team members. In many cases, these discussions increase the quality of the top management team's decisions, especially when a synthesis emerges from the diverse perspectives that is generally superior to any one individual perspective.[28] For example, heterogeneous top management teams in the airline industry have the propensity to take stronger competitive actions and reactions than do more homogenous teams.[29] The net benefit of such actions by heterogeneous teams has been positive in terms of market share and above-average returns. Research shows that more heterogeneity among top management team members promotes debate, which often leads to better strategic decisions. In turn, better strategic decisions produce higher firm performance.[30]

It is also important that the top management team members function cohesively. In general, the more heterogeneous and larger the top management team is, the more difficult it is for the team to effectively implement strategies.[31] Comprehensive and long-term strategic plans can be inhibited by communication difficulties among top executives who have different backgrounds and different cognitive skills.[32] As a result, a group of top executives with diverse backgrounds may inhibit the process of decision making if it is not effectively managed. In these cases, top management teams may fail to comprehensively examine threats and opportunities, leading to a suboptimal strategic decision.

Having members with substantive expertise in the firm's core functions and businesses is also important to the effectiveness of a top management team. In a high-technology industry, it may be critical for a firm's top management team to have R&D expertise, particularly when growth strategies are being implemented.[33]

The characteristics of top management teams are related to innovation and strategic change.[34] For example, more heterogeneous top management teams are associated positively with innovation and strategic change. The heterogeneity may force the team or some of the members to "think outside of the box" and thus be more creative in making decisions.[35] Therefore, firms that need to change their strategies are more likely to do so if they have top management teams with diverse backgrounds and expertise. A top management team with various areas of expertise is more likely to identify environmental changes (opportunities and threats) or changes within the firms that require a different strategic direction.[36]

CEO Daniel Vasella, chairman of Novartis, formed through the merger of Swiss drugmakers Sandoz and Ciba-Geigy in 1996, runs the world's seventh-largest pharmaceutical company.[37] Vasella, formerly a physician, has transformed the once stodgy Swiss conglomerate into an aggressive innovator, partly by putting together an energetic but diverse top management team. One analyst noted, "Although the top executives at Novartis contain a diversity of strong personalities, their oft-used term 'alignment' rings true in their teamwork. . . . Yet, each team member carries a different charge and perspective."[38]

The CEO and Top Management Team Power

As noted in Chapter 10, the board of directors is an important governance mechanism for monitoring a firm's strategic direction and for representing stakeholders' interests, especially those of shareholders. In fact, higher performance normally is achieved when the board of directors is more directly involved in shaping a firm's strategic direction.[39]

Boards of directors, however, may find it difficult to direct the strategic actions of powerful CEOs and top management teams.[40] It is not uncommon for a powerful CEO to appoint a number of sympathetic outside board members or have inside board members who are on the top management team and report to the CEO.[41] In either case, the CEO may have significant control over the board's actions. "A central question is whether boards are an effective management control mechanism . . . or whether they are a 'management tool,' . . . a rubber stamp for management initiatives . . . and often surrender to management their major domain of decision-making authority, which includes the right to hire, fire, and compensate top management."[42]

As mentioned earlier, Xerox has stumbled, partly due to its board. *Fortune* named it one of the "dirty half dozen" in 2001: "Xerox is a textbook example of a high-profile board asleep at the wheel . . . the once proud document giant has been plagued by everything short of locusts: missed earnings estimates, plummeting stock, mounting debt, and an SEC investigation of dodgy accounting practices in Xerox's Mexican operations. What have the venerable directors done? Very little—perhaps because they were busy at other meetings (most of Xerox's directors serve on at least four other boards)."[43]

Alternatively, recent research shows that social ties between the CEO and board members may actually increase board members' involvement in strategic decisions. Thus, strong relationships between the CEO and the board of directors may have positive or negative outcomes.[44]

DaimlerChrysler Corporation President and CEO Dieter Zetsche, pictured here, believes firms should take marketing risks. "We are willing to cause just a bit of controversy, if it creates products that resonate with our customers," Zetsche said. "We also want to find ways not to be driven to middle ground, the `no man's land' of ultraconservative products ."

CEOs and top management team members can achieve power in other ways. A CEO who also holds the position of chairman of the board usually has more power than the CEO who is not simultaneously serving as chairman of the firm's board.[45] Although this practice of CEO duality (when the CEO and the chairperson of the board are the same) has become more common in U.S. businesses, it has come under heavy criticism. Duality has been blamed for poor performance and slow response to change in a number of firms.[46]

DaimlerChrysler CEO Jergen Schrempp, who holds the dual positions of chairman of the board and CEO, has substantial power in the firm. In fact, insiders suggest that he was purging those individuals who are outspoken and who represent potential threats to his dominance. In particular, former Chrysler executives are leaving the firm, although research suggests that retaining key employees after an acquisition contributes to improved post acquisition performance.[47] Thus, it has been particularly difficult to turn around the US operations.[48] Dieter Zetsche, a German who is likely next in line to be CEO at DaimlerChrysler, is leading the team that is seeking to reverse Chrysler's fortunes. Schrempp's future may depend on how Zetsche's team does. It is ironic that six of the turnaround team members are former Chrysler executives. The loss of some of these key executives, such as Thomas Stallkamp, has been blamed in part for the poor performance.

Although it varies across industries, duality occurs most commonly in the largest firms. Increased shareholder activism, however, has brought CEO duality under scrutiny and attack in both U.S. and European firms. Historically, an independent board leadership structure in which the same person did not hold the positions of CEO and chair was believed to enhance a board's ability to monitor top-level managers' decisions and actions, particularly in terms of the firm's financial performance.[49] Stewardship theory, on the other hand, suggests that CEO duality facilitates effective decisions and actions. In these instances, the increased effectiveness gained through CEO duality accrues from the individual who wants to perform effectively and desires to be the best possible steward of the firm's assets. Because of this person's positive orientation and actions, extra governance and the coordination costs resulting from an independent board leadership structure would be unnecessary.[50]

Top-management team members and CEOs who have long tenure—on the team and in the organization—have a greater influence on board decisions.[51] Long tenure is known to restrict the breadth of an executive's knowledge base. With the limited perspectives associated with a restricted knowledge base, long-tenured top executives typically develop fewer alternatives to evaluate in making strategic decisions.[52] However, long-tenured managers also may be able to exercise more effective strategic control, thereby obviating the need for board members' involvement because effective strategic control generally produces higher performance.[53]

To strengthen the firm, boards of directors should develop an effective relationship with the firm's top management team. The relative degrees of power held by the board and top management team members should be examined in light of an individual firm's situation. For example, the abundance of resources in a firm's external environment and the volatility of that environment may affect the ideal balance of power between boards and top-management teams.[54] Moreover, a volatile and uncertain environment may create a situation where a powerful CEO is needed to move quickly, but a diverse top management team may create less cohesion among team members and prevent or stall a necessary strategic move.[55] Through the development of effective working relationships, boards, CEOs, and other top management team members are able to serve the best interests of the firm's stakeholders.[56]

Managerial Labor Market

The choice of top executives—especially CEOs—is a critical organizational decision with important implications for the firm's performance.[57] Many companies use leadership screening systems to identify individuals with managerial and strategic leadership potential. The most effective of these systems assess people within the firm and gain valuable information about the capabilities of other companies' managers, particularly their strategic leaders.[58] Based on the results of these assessments, training and development programs are provided for current managers in an attempt to preselect and shape the skills of people who may become tomorrow's leaders. The "ten-step talent" management development program at GE, for example, is considered one of the most effective in the world.[59]

An **internal managerial labor market** consists of the opportunities for managerial positions within a firm.

An **external managerial labor market** is the collection of career opportunities for managers in organizations other than the one for which they work currently.

Organizations select managers and strategic leaders from two types of managerial labor markets—internal and external.[60] An **internal managerial labor market** consists of the opportunities for managerial positions within a firm, whereas an **external managerial labor market** is the collection of career opportunities for managers in organizations other than the one for which they work currently. Several benefits are thought to accrue to a firm when the internal labor market is used to select an insider as the new CEO. Because of their experience with the firm and the industry environment in which it competes, insiders are familiar with company products, markets, technologies, and operating procedures. Also, internal hiring produces lower turnover among existing personnel, many of whom possess valuable firm-specific knowledge. When the firm is performing well, internal succession is favored to sustain high performance. It is assumed that hiring from inside keeps the important knowledge necessary to sustain the performance.

Given the phenomenal success of GE and its highly effective management development program, an insider, Jeffrey Immelt, was chosen to succeed Jack Welch.[61] Similarly, as the Opening Case illustrates, an insider, Samuel Palmisano, was selected to replace Louis Gerstner, who was an outsider when he was chosen as IBM's CEO. Gerstner was selected to change the strategic direction of the firm, which was suffering at the time of his hire. Since IBM's performance has improved considerably, investors do not want a change in strategic direction. For an inside move to the top to occur successfully, however, firms must develop and implement effective succession management programs. In that way, managers can be developed so that one will eventually be prepared to ascend to the top.[62]

It is not unusual for employees to have a strong preference for the internal managerial labor market to be used to select top management team members and the CEO.[63] This preference for insiders to fill top-level management positions reflects a desire for continuity and a continuing commitment to the firm's current strategic intent, strategic mission, and chosen strategies.[64] Thus, internal candidates tend to be valued over external candidates[65] in the selection of a firm's CEO and other top-level managers. In fact, outside succession to the CEO position "is an extraordinary event for business firms [and] is usually seen as a stark indicator that the board of directors wants change."[66]

Alternatively, firms often have valid reasons to select an outsider as its new CEO. For example, research evidence suggests that executives who have spent their entire career with a particular firm may become "stale in the saddle."[67] Long tenure with a firm seems to reduce the number of innovative ideas top executives are able to develop to cope with conditions facing their firm. Given the importance of innovation for a firm's success in today's competitive landscape (see Chapter 13), an inability to innovate or to create conditions that stimulate innovation throughout a firm is a liability in a strategic leader. Figure 12.3 shows how the composition of the top

Figure 12.3 Effects of CEO Succession and Top Management Team Composition on Strategy

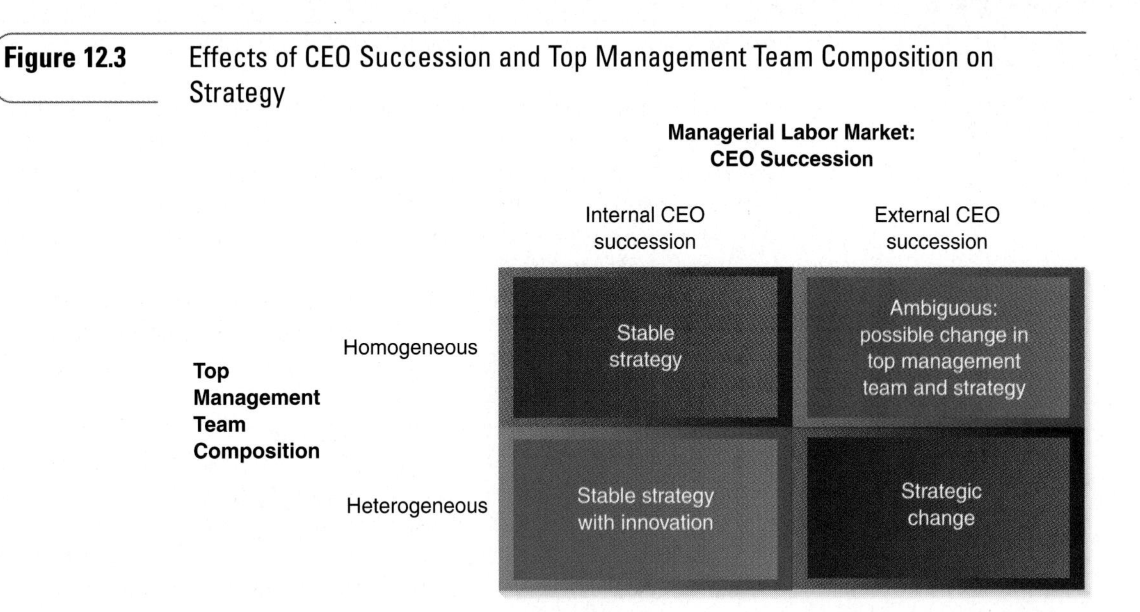

management team and CEO succession (managerial labor market) may interact to affect strategy. For example, when the top-management team is homogeneous (its members have similar functional experiences and educational backgrounds) and a new CEO is selected from inside the firm, the firm's current strategy is unlikely to change.

On the other hand, when a new CEO is selected from outside the firm and the top management team is heterogeneous, there is a high probability that strategy will change. When the new CEO is from inside the firm and a heterogeneous top management team is in place, the strategy may not change; but, innovation is likely to continue. An external CEO succession with a homogeneous team creates a more ambiguous situation.

To have an adequate number of top managers, firms must take advantage of a highly qualified labor pool, including one source of managers that has often been overlooked: women. Firms are beginning to utilize women's potential managerial talents with substantial success, as described in the Strategic Focus on page 394.

The early years of the 21st century find women being more frequently appointed to the boards of directors for organizations in both the private and public sectors. These additional appointments suggest that women's ability to represent stakeholders' and especially shareholders' best interests in for-profit companies at the level of the board of directors is being more broadly recognized. However, in addition to appointments to the board of directors, firms competing in the complex and challenging global economy—an economy demanding the best of an organization—may be well served by adding more female executives to their top management teams.

Key Strategic Leadership Actions

Several identifiable actions characterize strategic leadership that positively contributes to effective use of the firm's strategies.[68] We present the most critical of these actions in Figure 12.4. Many of the actions interact with each other. For example,

Strategic Focus

Opportunities for Women as Top-Level Managers

Is there a "glass ceiling" keeping women from becoming CEOs? Only 1.2 percent of CEOs in the *Fortune* 500 are women, while 20.6 percent of federal judges are women, as are 13 percent of U.S. senators. Women have also made significant progress in top positions in Europe. A recent *Wall Street Journal* survey of the top 25 women managers across firms in Europe found that nearly a third of the entrepreneurs starting new business are women (although Germany had no women in the CEO position).

The small percentage of women holding top-level managers' positions typically receives more media attention than do many of their male counterparts. The attention is generally positive when a woman succeeds, such as is the case with eBay's Meg Whitman. It can also be very negative when a woman fails, as did Linda Wachner, former CEO of Warnaco. Positive media attention about a woman CEO can also help a company's image, as when Carly Fiorina became head of the respected Silicon Valley firm, Hewlett-Packard. If the 2002 merger between HP and Compaq is unsuccessful, Fiorina may become another failure story, which could make it more difficult for other women to get significant corporate leadership opportunities. Each time a woman executive succeeds, all women executives seem to receive some new measure of respect, while each time one fails, the others are studied with a more critical eye.

© MIKE BLAKE /REUTERS NEWMEDIA INC./CORBIS

eBay, headed by President and CEO Meg Whitman, pictured here, has $300 exchanged every second on its website. During the late 1990s, Whitman was upstaged by the heads of other Internet firms, but eBay was profitable from the start under her disciplined management.

Lucent's new CEO, Patricia Russo, is only the ninth woman to run one of the 1,000 largest companies. She is not new to Lucent, even though she was only recently hired from Kodak. Most of her career had been spent working for a division of AT&T, which subsequently became Lucent after the AT&T break up. She had left Lucent for a position at Kodak, and she was rehired by Lucent as its CEO only eight months later, in January 2002. It was likely that Russo would have been named CEO of Kodak after a few years of service as the firm's COO (chief operating officer). Lucent has struggled in the last two years and is looking for help from its new CEO. Russo claims that she will continue to use former Lucent CEO Schacht's plan for the company. She also claims that no significant changes in management will occur. Some critics worry that this inaction could make the situation worse for Lucent and that the lack of new blood could cause the company to become stagnant. Russo will make an estimated base salary of at least $1.1 million per year, and she could receive more than four million stock options within her first year.

A study examining the gender compensation gap among high-level executives in the United States found that women, who represented about 2.5 percent of the sample, earned about 45 percent less than men. However, "as much as 75 percent of this gap can be explained by the fact that women managed smaller companies and were less likely to be CEO, chair, or company president." In fact, the gap decreases to less than 5 percent when the study results are controlled for the younger average age and lower average seniority of the female executives. Also, the gap was reduced between 1992 and 1997, the timeframe of one study, because women's participation in the top executive ranks nearly tripled and their relative compensation also strongly improved, mostly by their increased representation in larger corporations.

Still, female CEOs earned far less than their male CEO counterparts in 2000. In fact, even when compared to women executives in other positions, female CEOs earned less, partly because they cashed in fewer stock options than other female executives. Another, possibly more important, reason was that companies led by women CEOs had a rough year in 2000. Women CEOs also are found more often at so-called "old economy" companies, which do a better job of promoting women but do not consistently compensate upper-level executives as generously as have many "new economy" companies. However, the compensation practices of new economy companies is coming under increasing scrutiny as a result of the declining performances recorded by many of them in the first few years of the 21st century.

SOURCES: D. Berman & J. Lublin, 2002, Russo's goal as Lucent's new chief: Restore luster, *The Wall Street Journal*, January 8, B1, B4; A. Stanley, 2002, For women, to soar is rare, to fall is human, *The New York Times*, http://www.nytimes.com, January 13;. E. Williamson, 2002, List of leading female executives doesn't include German women, *The Wall Street Journal Interactive*, http://www.wsj.com, February 27; M. Bertrand & K. F. Hallock, 2001, The gender gap in top corporate jobs, *Industrial & Labor Relations Review*, 55: 3–21; L. Lavelle, 2001, For female CEOs, it's stingy at the top, *Business Week*, April 23, 70–71; J. G. Oakley, 2000, Gender-based barriers to senior management positions: Understanding the scarcity of female CEOs, *Journal of Business Ethics*, 27: 321–334.

developing human capital through executive training contributes to establishing a strategic direction, fostering an effective culture, exploiting core competencies, using effective organizational control systems, and establishing ethical practices.

Determining Strategic Direction

Determining the strategic direction of a firm involves developing a long-term vision of the firm's strategic intent.

Determining the strategic direction of a firm involves developing a long-term vision of the firm's strategic intent. A long-term vision typically looks at least five to ten years into the future. A philosophy with goals, this vision consists of the image and character the firm seeks.[69]

Figure 12.4 Exercise of Effective Strategic Leadership

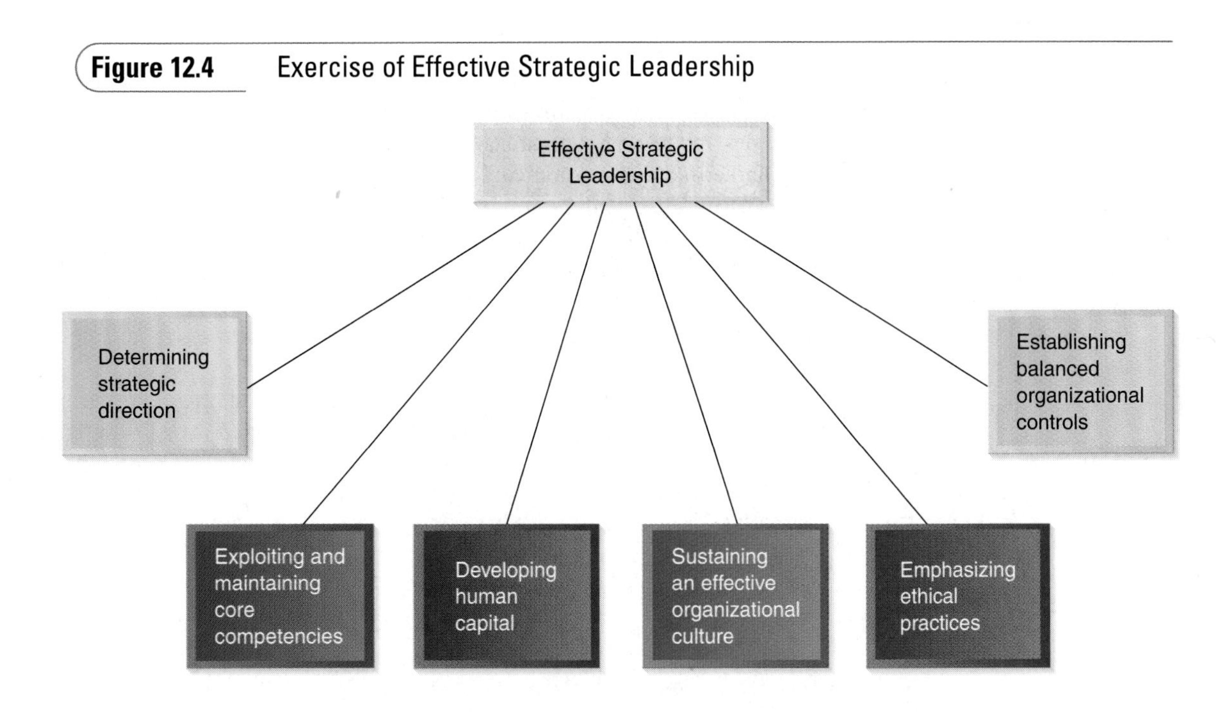

The ideal long-term vision has two parts: a core ideology and an envisioned future. While the core ideology motivates employees through the company's heritage, the envisioned future encourages employees to stretch beyond their expectations of accomplishment and requires significant change and progress in order to be realized.[70] The envisioned future serves as a guide to many aspects of a firm's strategy implementation process, including motivation, leadership, employee empowerment, and organizational design.

Matthew D. Heyman came out of Harvard Business School in 1993 with a vision of building lavish movie theaters in Mexico City, a city with 20 million inhabitants. The Mexican theater industry was in shambles because of government price controls, and so a vacuum existed for quality movie theaters. For six months, Heyman and his partners, Miguel Angel Dávila and Adolfo Fastlicht, were told by investors that their idea was too risky. After finding financial backing for their company, Cinemex, they began constructing movie theaters, but then the Mexican economy crashed. Heyman decided to push through anyway, as much of his competition disappeared as a result of the crash. He decided early on to target the largest market in Mexico City, the working poor. His theaters charged about half as much for tickets in poor areas of the city compared to the price charged by theaters in wealthy areas, even though these theaters were just as extravagant. In 2001, Cinemex was expected to generate a profit of approximately $40 million.[71] This accomplishment is largely due to Heyman's vision and the employees of Cinemex who were inspired by Heyman's leadership to implement his vision.

A charismatic CEO may foster employees' commitment to a new vision and strategic direction. Nonetheless, it is important not to lose sight of the strengths of the organization in making changes required by a new strategic direction. Most top executives obtain inputs regarding their vision from many people with a range of skills to help them analyze various aspects of the firm's operations. In addition, executives must structure the firm effectively to help achieve their vision.[72] The goal is to balance the firm's short-term need to adjust to a new vision while maintaining its long-term survivability by emphasizing its current and valuable core competencies.

Exploiting and Maintaining Core Competencies

Examined in Chapters 1 and 3, *core competencies* are resources and capabilities that serve as a source of competitive advantage for a firm over its rivals. Typically, core competencies relate to an organization's functional skills, such as manufacturing, finance, marketing, and research and development. As shown by the descriptions that follow, firms develop and exploit core competencies in many different functional areas. Strategic leaders must verify that the firm's competencies are emphasized in strategy implementation efforts. Intel, for example, has core competencies of *competitive agility* (an ability to act in a variety of competitively relevant ways) and *competitive speed* (an ability to act quickly when facing environmental and competitive pressures).[73]

In many large firms, and certainly in related diversified ones, core competencies are effectively exploited when they are developed and applied across different organizational units (see Chapter 6). For example, PepsiCo purchased Quaker Oats, which makes the sports drink Gatorade. Pepsi plans to use its competence in distribution systems to build market share outside the United States. Accordingly, Pepsi soft drinks (e.g., Pepsi Cola and Mountain Dew) and Gatorade will share the logistics activity. Similarly, Quaker Oats' healthy snacks and Frito Lay's salty snacks (already owned by Pepsi) can use this competence and be distributed through the same channels.[74]

In making a number of acquisitions, Cisco became skilled at integrating the new businesses into the firm's operating culture, especially in building its main business in routers, which was a critical part of building the Internet infrastructure. In light of new opportunities, Cisco is now trying to diversify into new businesses of "voice-over-Internet systems, wireless networking gear, storage-networking devices and optical equipment."[75] The degree to which Cisco will be able "to pluck promising technology after someone else had borne the development risk" using an acquisition strategy as the foundation for how it competes in its new business areas is unknown. Other competitors exist in these new markets with already established capabilities. Cisco's human capital will play a critical role in the firm's attempt to develop the core competencies that are required to successfully compete in the markets Cisco is now targeting.

Developing Human Capital

Human capital refers to the knowledge and skills of a firm's entire workforce.

Human capital refers to the knowledge and skills of a firm's entire workforce. From the perspective of human capital, employees are viewed as a capital resource that requires investment.[76] These investments are productive, in that much of the development of U.S. industry can be attributed to the effectiveness of its human capital,[77] leading to the conviction in many business firms today that "as the dynamics of competition accelerate, people are perhaps the only truly sustainable source of competitive advantage."[78] Human capital's increasing importance suggests a significant role for the firm's human resource management activities.[79] As a support activity (see Chapter 2), human resource management practices facilitate people's efforts to successfully select and especially to use the firm's strategies.[80]

Finding the human capital necessary to run an organization effectively is a challenge that many firms attempt to solve by using temporary employees. Other firms try to improve their recruiting and selection techniques. Solving the problem, however, requires more than hiring temporary employees; it requires building effective commitment to organizational goals as well. Hiring star players is also insufficient; rather, a strategic leader needs to build an effective organizational team committed to achieving the company's vision and goals.[81]

Increasingly, international experience has become essential to the development necessary for strategic leaders. Because nearly every industry is targeting fast-growing foreign markets, more companies are requiring "global competency" among their top managers.[82] Thus, companies trying to learn how to compete successfully in the global economy should find opportunities for their future strategic leaders to work in locations outside of their home nation.[83] When multinational corporations invest in emerging economies, they are also wise to invest in human capital in foreign subsidiaries.[84] Also, because international management capabilities are becoming important, managing "inpatriation" (the process of transferring host-country or third-country national managers into the domestic market of multinational firms) has become an important means of building global core competencies.[85]

Effective training and development programs increase the probability that a manager will be a successful strategic leader. These programs have grown progressively important as knowledge has become more integral to gaining and sustaining a competitive advantage.[86] Additionally, such programs build knowledge and skills, inculcate a common set of core values, and offer a systematic view of the organization, thus promoting the firm's strategic vision and organizational cohesion. The programs also contribute to the development of core competencies.[87] Furthermore, they help strategic leaders improve skills that are critical to completing other tasks associated with effective strategic leadership, such as determining the firm's strategic direction, exploiting and maintaining the firm's core competencies, and developing an organizational culture that supports ethical practices. Thus, building human capital is vital to the effective execution of strategic leadership.[88]

© MICHAEL NICHOLSON/CORBIS

Barclays Bank headquarters in London. Currently, Barclays is emphasizing human capital and strategic leadershp to create competitive advantages the firm believes are linked to its success.

Strategic leaders must acquire the skills necessary to help develop human capital in their areas of responsibility. This challenge is important, given that most strategic leaders need to enhance their human resource management abilities. For example, firms that place value on human resources and have effective reward plans for employees obtained higher returns on their initial public offerings.[89] When human capital investments are successful, the result is a workforce capable of learning continuously. Continuous learning and leveraging the firm's expanding knowledge base are linked with strategic success.[90]

Although Barclays Group lost its position among the world's largest banks in the 1980s (it was ranked fifth in the world in assets in the early 1980s), its prestige was rising again in 2000. Barclays' return on equity was 23 percent in fiscal year 2000, up from 15 percent in 1997, thanks to the leadership of Barclays' Matthew Barrett, named CEO in October 1999. Much of Barrett's accomplishments can be attributed to hiring significant leadership talent away from other firms to form formidable top management teams for Barclays' various business groups. For instance, he hired Robert Diamond from Morgan Stanley to lead Barclays' capital unit. Barrett has developed a new long-term vision of the firm's strategic intent by taking the position that: "I want us to be the premier European investment bank for debt finance." While competitors are downsizing, Barclays is adding key people, partly by raiding its German rival Deutsche Bank for additional talent. The firm has also hired 25 senior investment bankers for its New York unit and hired Michael O'Neill from Bank of America to be the chief executive of its long-term capital management group. In summary, Barrett is relying on Barclay's human capital to pursue the firm's newly determined strategic direction.[91]

Programs that achieve outstanding results in the training of future strategic leaders become a competitive advantage for a firm. As noted earlier, General Electric's system of training and development of future strategic leaders is comprehensive and thought to be among the best.[92] Accordingly, it may be a source of competitive advantage for the firm.

Because of the economic downturn in 2001 and early 2002, many firms are laying off key people. Layoffs can result in a significant loss of the knowledge possessed by a firm's human capital. Although it is also not uncommon for restructuring firms to reduce their expenditures on, or investments in, training and development programs, restructuring may actually be an important time to increase investments in these programs. Restructuring firms have less slack and cannot absorb as many errors; moreover, the employees who remain after layoffs may find themselves in positions without all of the skills or knowledge they need to perform the required tasks effectively.[93] Improvements in information technology can facilitate better use of human resources when a downsizing event occurs.[94]

Viewing employees as a resource to be maximized rather than a cost to be minimized facilitates the successful implementation of a firm's strategies. The implementation of such strategies also is more effective when strategic leaders approach layoffs in a manner that employees believe is fair and equitable.[95]

Sustaining an Effective Organizational Culture

An **organizational culture** consists of a complex set of ideologies, symbols, and core values that is shared throughout the firm and influences the way business is conducted.

An **organizational culture** consists of a complex set of ideologies, symbols, and core values that is shared throughout the firm and influences the way business is conducted. Evidence suggests that a firm can develop core competencies in terms of both the capabilities it possesses and the way the capabilities are used to produce strategic actions. In other words, because the organizational culture influences how the firm conducts its business and helps regulate and control employees' behavior, it can be a source of competitive advantage.[96] Thus, shaping the context within which the firm formulates and implements its strategies—that is, shaping the organizational culture—is a central task of strategic leaders.[97]

Entrepreneurial Orientation

An organizational culture often encourages (or discourages) the pursuit of entrepreneurial opportunities, especially in large firms.[98] Entrepreneurial opportunities are an important source of growth and innovation.[99] In Chapter 13, we describe how large firms use strategic entrepreneurship to pursue entrepreneurial opportunities and to gain first-mover advantages. Medium and small firms also rely on strategic entrepreneurship when trying to develop innovations as the foundation for profitable growth. In firms of all sizes, strategic entrepreneurship is more likely to be successful when employees have an entrepreneurial orientation. Five dimensions characterize a firm's entrepreneurial orientation: autonomy, innovativeness, risk taking, proactiveness, and competitive aggressiveness.[100] In combination, these dimensions influence the activities of a firm to be innovative and launch new ventures.

The first of an entrepreneurial orientation's five dimensions, *autonomy,* allows employees to take actions that are free of organizational constraints and permits individuals and groups to be self-directed. The second dimension, *innovativeness,* "reflects a firm's tendency to engage in and support new ideas, novelty, experimentation, and creative processes that may result in new products, services, or technological processes."[101] Cultures with a tendency toward innovativeness encourage employees to think beyond existing knowledge, technologies, and parameters in efforts to find creative ways to add value. *Risk taking* reflects a willingness by employees and their firm to accept risks when pursuing entrepreneurial opportunities. These risks can include assuming significant levels of debt and allocating large amounts of other resources (e.g., people) to projects that may not be completed. The fourth dimension of an entrepreneurial orientation, *proactiveness,* describes a firm's ability to be a market leader rather than a follower. Proactive organizational cultures constantly use processes to anticipate future market needs and to satisfy them before competitors learn how to do so. Finally, *competitive aggressiveness* is a firm's propensity to take actions that allow it to consistently and substantially outperform its rivals.[102]

James Farrell, CEO of Illinois Tool Works (ITW), uses an unorthodox method for creating an entrepreneurial culture among ITW's businesses, most of which were acquired. In many organizations, acquisitions are consolidated with other business units, but Farrell does not consolidate the businesses he purchases. In fact, ITW usually breaks up acquisitions into smaller units so business managers can be closer to their customers. Farrell gives these managers a large amount of autonomy, which encourages them to act like entrepreneurs. Farrell suggests that his success with acquisitions is how he focuses management on what ITW calls the "80/20 process." This means that the division should aggressively focus on the 20 percent of customers or products that provide 80 percent of sales, and forget about the rest, which are seen as a distraction. Usually, the firms ITW acquires experience an increase in their operating margin, from an average of 9 percent to an average of 19 percent.[103]

Changing the Organizational Culture and Business Reengineering

Changing a firm's organizational culture is more difficult than maintaining it, but effective strategic leaders recognize when change is needed. Incremental changes to the firm's culture typically are used to implement strategies.[104] More significant and, sometimes, even radical changes to organizational culture are used to support the selection of strategies that differ from those the firm has implemented historically. Regardless of the reasons for change, shaping and reinforcing a new culture require effective communication and problem solving, along with the selection of the right people (those who have the values desired for the organization), effective performance appraisals (establishing goals and measuring individual performance toward goals that fit in with the new core values), and appropriate reward systems (rewarding the desired behaviors that reflect the new core values).[105]

Evidence suggests that cultural changes succeed only when the firm's CEO, other key top management team members, and middle-level managers actively support them.[106] To effect change, middle-level managers in particular need to be highly disciplined to energize the culture and foster alignment with the strategic vision.[107]

As noted earlier, selecting new top management team members from the external managerial labor market is a catalyst for changes to organizational culture. This is illustrated in the Strategic Focus about Carlos Ghosn on page 401. A Brazilian-born manager working for Renault, Ghosn was charged with turning around Nissan, partially owned by Renault, which was suffering from lost market share. As this Strategic Focus about illustrates, transforming an organization and its culture is challenging. For example, William W. George, CEO until June 2001 of Medtronic, a medical device company, spent years building Medtronic into a "mission driven" company that creates long-term value for shareholders. He has built a culture that has a goal of deriving 70 percent of its revenue from products launched in the previous two years. George argues that making decisions based solely on financial considerations leads to poor market place competitiveness and customer satisfaction, because such decisions only enhance the wealth of the top officers and do not engage the rest of the employees—in fact, they create cynicism.[108] He argues that a customer-focused culture, which is mission-driven, based on a clear set of widely used values and an adaptable business strategy, has allowed Medtronic and other firms to create successful and innovation-oriented cultures.[109]

Emphasizing Ethical Practices

The effectiveness of processes used to implement the firm's strategies increases when they are based on ethical practices. Ethical companies encourage and enable people at all organizational levels to act ethically when doing what is necessary to implement the firm's strategies. In turn, ethical practices and the judgment on which they are based create "social capital" in the organization in that "goodwill available to individuals and groups" in the organization increases.[110] Thus, while "money motivates, it does not inspire" as social capital can.[111] Alternately, when unethical practices evolve in an organization, they become like a contagious disease.[112]

To properly influence employees' judgment and behavior, ethical practices must shape the firm's decision-making process and be an integral part of an organization's culture. In fact, research has found that a value-based culture is the most effective means of ensuring that employees comply with the firm's ethical requirements.[113] As discussed in chapter 10, in the absence of ethical requirements, managers may act opportunistically, making decisions that are in their own best interests, but not in the firm's best interests. In other words, managers acting opportunistically take advantage of their positions, making decisions that benefit them to the detriment of the firm's owners (shareholders).[114]

Managerial opportunism may explain the behavior and decisions of a few key executives at Enron, where stockholders lost almost all the value in their Enron stock in the firm's bankruptcy proceeding. The bankruptcy seems to have been precipitated by off-balance sheet partnerships formed by Enron managers (see the Strategic Focus on page 332 in Chaper 10).[115] Accounting firm Arthur Andersen, Enron's auditor, was

Strategic Focus

An Outsider from Brazil Facilitates Change at Nissan

In 1999, Renault assumed $5.4 billion of Nissan's debt in return for 36.6 percent of Nissan's equity, giving it a controlling stake in the Japanese automaker. The combined assets of Renault and Nissan made them the fourth largest carmaker in the world. However, Nissan was struggling with shrinking market share, both domestically in Japan and worldwide. Renault turned to Carlos Ghosn to lead a turnaround for the Japanese carmaker.

Ghosn came to Renault from Michelin's Brazilian subsidiary. He was given a complex challenge—not only did he face the difficulty of overcoming conservatism among Nissan car designers, which had allowed engineers to dominate for the past decade of slow market share loss, but he also had to face the cultural challenge of being an outsider in the homogeneous Japanese culture. Although the challenge was daunting, Ghosn was able to win over key Japanese inside managers necessary to implement his plan, as well as suppliers and labor leaders who might have been expected to resist more intensely. Furthermore, the car designs created under Ghosn's leadership had much more flare than in the recent past. As a result, in 2001, Nissan posted a profit of $2.7 billion; its largest in its 68-year history and its first annual profit in 4 years.

Nissan CEO Carlos Ghosn oversaw the development of the new Micra subcompact, a result of the Nissan/Renault partnership.

How was Ghosn, a manager who was selected from the external managerial labor market, able to accomplish this significant strategic turnaround? Although he continues to indicate that his strategic change agenda is not complete because facilitating a change in the organization culture takes time, several actions can be identified. For example, he charged Itaru Koeda with the task of drastic cost reduction with specific targets and tactics. To accomplish this reduction, Ghosn brought together a younger set of Nissan managers, "thirty-five- and forty-five-year-old managers," to participate in identifying issues to focus on in the cost reduction. Although this action may not sound that unusual outside of Japan, it was revolutionary to have "young people in the company to debate things and propose what we should do."

Next, he changed the way the supply chain was managed by reducing the number of suppliers and, at the same time, sought to create deeper partnerships with them. To fund this new way of managing the supply chain, Ghosn dismantled the cross shareholding associated with Nissan's keiretsu investments. Ghosn found that $4 billion was tied up in cross shareholdings with keiretsu partner companies, which often had no relationship with Nissan. Following this action, Nissan allowed suppliers to specialize in what they do best, and suppliers became part of cross-functional teams for new model development. Because of this fresh outside influence, the car designs have become much more sleek and exciting.

Another difficult action Ghosn took was to close a number of plants, although in Japan lifetime employment is still seen as an important labor movement objective. To facilitate closure of a plant in a Tokyo suburb, Ghosn worked with Nissan's unions to show that no matter how painful, in the long run such actions would be good for workers as well. He negotiated a generous one-time bonus of 5.2 months pay for those workers who were laid off. Because other companies were challenging the practice of lifetime employment, Ghosn's efforts had some legitimacy.

Although Nissan knew such actions were needed before it put Ghosn in charge, it needed someone like him to "push the button." Kenichi Ohmae, a Japanese management expert, has indicated that a large majority of Japanese companies face problems similar to Nissan's. However, few have the "power to heal themselves from within." In Ghosn's words, "a good corporate culture taps into the productive aspects of a country's culture,

and in Nissan's case we have been able to exploit the uniquely Japanese combination of keen competitiveness and sense of community that has driven the likes of Sony and Toyota—and Nissan itself in earlier times." A Japanese manager will likely take over Nissan after Ghosn leaves. However, he will have left a legacy of significant cultural change that will likely foster success in the future.

SOURCES: C. Dawson, 2002, Nissan bets big on small, *Business Week Online,* http://www.businessweek.com, March 4; C. Ghosn, 2002, Saving the business without losing the company, *Harvard Business Review,* 80(1): 37–45; M. S. Mayershon, 2002, Nissan's u-turn to profits, *Chief Executive,* January, 12–16; A. Raskin, 2002, Voulez-dous completely overhaul this big, slow company and start making some cars people actually want avec moi? *Business 2.0,* January, 61–67; G. S. Vasilash, 2002, Managing design; Design management, *Automotive Design and Production,* February, 34–35; C. Ahmadjian & P. Robinson, 2001, Safety in numbers: Downsizing and the deinstitutionalization of permanent employment in Japan, *Administrative Science Quarterly,* 46: 622–654; C. Dawson & S. Prasso, 2001, Pow! Bam! Zap! Meet Nissan's super hero, *Business Week,* April 30, 12; L. P. Norton, 2001, Meet Mr. Nissan, *Barron's,* November 19, 17–19.

also severely damaged by the disaster. The SEC, other federal agencies, and several different Congressional committees have investigated Enron's financial reporting. Andersen fired partner David Duncan and put two others from the firm's Houston office on administrative leave. Duncan had ordered the destruction of documents regarding accounting practices at Enron. Due to the unethical practices of both the company and the auditor, many accounting firms and other firms unrelated to Enron but with aggressive accounting methods have not only been criticized, but have lost customers or been devalued by investors.[116] Firms that have been reported to have poor ethical behavior, such as fraud or having to restate financial results, see their overall corporate value in the stock market drop precipitously.[117]

These incidents suggest that firms need to employ ethical strategic leaders—leaders who include ethical practices as part of their long-term vision for the firm, who desire to do the right thing, and for whom honesty, trust, and integrity are important.[118] Strategic leaders who consistently display these qualities inspire employees as they work with others to develop and support an organizational culture in which ethical practices are the expected behavioral norms.[119]

Unfortunately, not all people in positions of strategic leadership display the ethical approach described. The actions explained in the next Strategic Focus about Global Crossing suggests the need for vigilance in guarding against unethical actions taken by those in key managerial positions.

Strategic leaders are challenged to take actions that increase the probability that an ethical culture will prevail in their organizations. One action that has gained favor is to institute a formal program to manage ethics. Operating much like control systems, these programs help inculcate values throughout the organization.[120] Therefore, when these efforts are successful, the practices associated with an ethical culture become institutionalized in the firm; that is, they become the set of behavioral commitments and actions accepted by most of the firm's employees and other stakeholders with whom employees interact.

Additional actions strategic leaders can take to develop an ethical organizational culture include (1) establishing and communicating specific goals to describe the firm's ethical standards (e.g., developing and disseminating a code of conduct); (2) continuously revising and updating the code of conduct, based on inputs from people throughout the firm and from other stakeholders (e.g., customers and suppliers); (3) disseminating the code of conduct to all stakeholders to inform them of the firm's ethical standards and practices; (4) developing and implementing methods and procedures to use in achieving the firm's ethical standards (e.g., using internal auditing practices that are consistent with the standards); (5) creating and using

Strategic Focus

The Cost of Poor Ethical Decisions by Strategic Leaders

As Internet use expanded, telecom firm Global Crossing went public and accumulated debt to finance the expansion of its long-haul fiber optics networks across the ocean in order to carry increased traffic. The firm ran into trouble when the price of long-haul traffic dropped dramatically as companies overbuilt this capacity. An additional problem was that, although Global Crossing had a good long-haul network, there was no way to facilitate metropolitan connectivity. Only firms that had the connectivity, such as Qwest, which had acquired U.S. West, a local phone system operator with lots of local connectivity, could use its capacity effectively. Global Crossing had to sell its capacity on the unfavorable open market and was left with a very low-margin business. It could not pay the debt that had accumulated to fund the fixed assets of laying fiber optic cable thousands of feet under the world's oceans to link networks across countries.

Although there were strategic errors by Global Crossing's leaders, significant ethical issues are also a part of this story. As with Enron, some insiders at Global Crossing had enriched themselves to the detriment not only of shareholders, but also of employees. On January 28, 2002, Global Crossing declared bankruptcy. The company's stock dropped from a high of $64 to below $.30, and many workers lost nearly all of the value in their 401k accounts. Although many employees received a severance package, the company cannot pay them until it emerges from bankruptcy proceedings, as these severance packages are considered accounting liabilities. However, some Global Crossing top-level managers, including Gary Winnick, Barry Porter, Lodwrick Cook, and Joseph Clayton, sold over a billion dollars worth of stock options in the months leading to their firm's bankruptcy. Although selling these options is not a crime, it is unethical. In addition, many loans made to executives were forgiven before the firm declared bankruptcy. Because upper-level Global Crossing managers likely had knowledge about the firm's impending failure, investors were at a significant disadvantage, as were employees who weren't members of the top management team. Poor ethical behavior by executives, such as Global Crossing's, undermines the confidence of investors and employees and damages the firm's attempts to earn above-average returns.

Because of Global Crossing's bankruptcy and loss of confidence in the industry, other firms have also experienced difficulties. Level 3 Communications, Williams Communications, and 360Networks are under pressure. Because of the excess telecommunications capacity, these competitors are not only competing against each other, but also more established carriers, such as AT&T and WorldCom. The competition against the more established competitors is difficult because they are more financially stable than are firms such as Level 3 Communications, Williams Communications, and 360Networks that are concentrating on developing additional network capacity.

In addition to affecting competitors throughout an industry such as the telecommunications industry, a lapse in ethics across a number of firms creates a crisis of confidence in financial institutions. This crisis of confidence because of unethical behavior makes banks leery of lending money, makes investors leery of investing, and makes employees leery of working for firms with a reputation for poor ethical behavior. After all, if you can't trust managers as decision-making specialists (see Chapter 10) to make ethical decisions that are in stakeholders' and especially shareholders' best interests, the efficiency of separating ownership from the making of decisions in the modern corporation is undermined and governance or monitoring costs are increased for all stakeholders.

SOURCES: A. Borrus & L. Woellert, 2002, Global Crossing: Where's the outrage on Capitol Hill? *Business Week,* February 25, 53; R. Blumestein, D. Soloman, & K. Chen, 2002, As Global Crossing crashed, executives got loan relief, pension payouts, *The Wall Street Journal,* February 21, B1, B4; J. Creswell, 2002, First going for broke, *Fortune,* February 18, 24–25; L. H. LaBarba, 2002, Global blunder, *Telephony,* February 4, 25; G. Fabrikant & S. Romero, 2002, How executives prospered as Global Crossing collapsed, *The New York Times,* http://www.nytimes.com, February 11; K. Fitchard, 2002, Global Crossing bombshell creates fallout among IXCs, *Telephony,* February 4, 12; S. Romero & G. Fabrikant, 2002, Another twist at Global as chairman quits board, *The New York Times,* http://www.nytimes.com, February 23; M. Weisskopf, 2002, Equal-opportunity crisis, *Time,* February 25, 45.

explicit reward systems that recognize acts of courage (e.g., rewarding those who use proper channels and procedures to report observed wrongdoings); and (6) creating a work environment in which all people are treated with dignity.[121] The effectiveness of these actions increases when they are taken simultaneously, thereby making them mutually supportive. When managers and employees do not engage in such actions—perhaps because an ethical culture has not been created—problems are likely to occur. As we discuss next, formal organizational controls can help prevent further problems and reinforce better ethical practices.

Establishing Balanced Organizational Controls

Organizational controls have long been viewed as an important part of strategy implementation processes. Controls are necessary to help ensure that firms achieve their desired outcomes.[122] Defined as the "formal, information-based . . . procedures used by managers to maintain or alter patterns in organizational activities," controls help strategic leaders build credibility, demonstrate the value of strategies to the firm's stakeholders, and promote and support strategic change.[123] Most critically, controls provide the parameters within which strategies are to be implemented, as well as corrective actions to be taken when implementation-related adjustments are required. In this chapter, we focus on two organizational controls—strategic and financial—that are introduced in Chapter 11. Our discussion of organizational controls here emphasizes strategic and financial controls because strategic leaders are responsible for their development and effective use.

Evidence suggests that, although critical to the firm's success, organizational controls are imperfect. *Control failures* have a negative effect on the firm's reputation and divert managerial attention from actions that are necessary to effectively use the strategic management process.

As explained in Chapter 11, financial control focuses on short-term financial outcomes. In contrast, strategic control focuses on the *content* of strategic actions, rather than their *outcomes.* Some strategic actions can be correct, but poor financial outcomes may still result because of external conditions, such as a recession in the economy, unexpected domestic or foreign government actions, or natural disasters.[124] Therefore, an emphasis on financial control often produces more short-term and risk-averse managerial decisions, because financial outcomes may be caused by events beyond managers' direct control. Alternatively, strategic control encourages lower-level managers to make decisions that incorporate moderate and acceptable levels of risk because outcomes are shared between the business-level executives making strategic proposals and the corporate-level executives evaluating them.

The Balanced Scorecard

The **balanced scorecard** is a framework that firms can use to verify that they have established both strategic and financial controls to assess their performance.

The **balanced scorecard** is a framework that firms can use to verify that they have established both strategic and financial controls to assess their performance.[125] This technique is most appropriate for use when dealing with business-level strategies, but can also apply to corporate-level strategies.

The underlying premise of the balanced scorecard is that firms jeopardize their future performance possibilities when financial controls are emphasized at the expense of strategic controls,[126] in that financial controls provide feedback about outcomes achieved from past actions, but do not communicate the drivers of the firm's future performance.[127] Thus, an overemphasis on financial controls could promote organizational behavior that has a net effect of sacrificing the firm's long-term value creating potential for short-term performance gains.[128] An appropriate balance of strategic controls and financial controls, rather than an overemphasis on either, allows firms to effectively monitor their performance.

Four perspectives are integrated to form the balanced scorecard framework: *financial* (concerned with growth, profitability, and risk from shareholders' perspective), *customer* (concerned with the amount of value customers perceive was created by the firm's products), *internal business processes* (with a focus on the priorities for various business processes that create customer and shareholder satisfaction), and *learning and growth* (concerned with the firm's effort to create a climate that supports change, innovation, and growth). Thus, using the balanced scorecard's framework allows the firm to understand how it looks to shareholders (financial perspective), how customers view it (customer perspective), the processes it must emphasize to successfully use its competitive advantage (internal perspective), and what it can do to improve its performance in order to grow (learning and growth perspective).[129] Generally speaking, strategic controls tend to be emphasized when the firm assesses its performance relative to the learning and growth perspective, while financial controls are emphasized when assessing performance in terms of the financial perspective. Study of the customer and internal business processes perspectives often is completed through virtually an equal emphasis on strategic controls and financial controls.

Firms use different criteria to measure their standing relative to the scorecard's four perspectives. Sample criteria are shown in Figure 12.5. The firm should select the number of criteria that will allow it to have both a strategic understanding and a

Figure 12.5 Strategic Controls and Financial Controls in a Balanced Scorecard Framework

Perspectives	Criteria
Financial	• Cash flow • Return on equity • Return on assets
Customer	• Assessment of ability to anticipate customers' needs • Effectiveness of customer service practices • Percentage of repeat business • Quality of communications with customers
Internal Business Processes	• Asset utilization improvements • Improvements in employee morale • Changes in turnover rates
Learning and Growth	• Improvements in innovation ability • Number of new products compared to competitors' • Increases in employees' skills

financial understanding of its performance without becoming immersed in too many details.[130]

Strategic leaders play an important role in determining a proper balance between strategic controls and financial controls for their firm. This is true in single business firms as well as in diversified firms. A proper balance between controls is important, in that, "Wealth creation for organizations where strategic leadership is exercised is possible because these leaders make appropriate investments for future viability [through strategic control], while maintaining an appropriate level of financial stability in the present [through financial control]."[131] In fact, most corporate restructuring is designed to refocus the firm on its core businesses, thereby allowing top executives to reestablish strategic control of their separate business units.[132] Thus, as emphasized in Chapter 11, both strategic controls and financial controls support effective use of the firm's corporate-level strategy.

Successful use of strategic control by top executives frequently is integrated with appropriate autonomy for the various subunits so that they can gain a competitive advantage in their respective markets.[133] Strategic control can be used to promote the sharing of both tangible and intangible resources among interdependent businesses within a firm's portfolio. In addition, the autonomy provided allows the flexibility necessary to take advantage of specific marketplace opportunities. As a result, strategic leadership promotes the simultaneous use of strategic control and autonomy.[134]

Balancing strategic and financial controls in diversified firms can be difficult. Failure to maintain an effective balance between strategic controls and financial controls in these firms often contributes to a decision to restructure the company. For example, following the 1997 Southeast Asian currency crisis, Samsung Electronics, a large Korean firm, was heading into a significant crisis in its Chinese operations. It was a large diversified firm, which had businesses throughout the world. Its Chinese operations were selling everything from washing machines to VCRs. Each product division had established Chinese factories and a nationwide sales organization by the mid-1990s. However, in China, these divisions encountered significant losses, losing $37 million in 1998.

When Yun Jonong Yong took over as Samsung's CEO in 1997, he shut down all 23 sales offices and declared that each of the seven mainland factories would have to become profitable on its own to survive. Thus, he instituted strong financial controls that were to be followed to verify that each division was operating profitably. Additionally, based on market survey results, Samsung executives decided that the firm would focus on 10 major cities in China. Furthermore, the firm carefully selected products and supported them with intense marketing. Thus, the firm improved strategic controls using a "top-down marketing strategy." As a result, in 2001, Samsung sold products worth $1.81 billion in China, a fivefold increase since 1998, and profits increased over 70 percent to $228 million. A more effective balance between strategic and financial controls has helped Samsung to improve its performance and to make progress towards its goal of establishing marquee brands in China, comparable to Sony and Motorola.[135]

Summary

- Effective strategic leadership is a prerequisite to successfully using the strategic management process. Strategic leadership entails the ability to anticipate events, envision possibilities, maintain flexibility, and empower others to create strategic change.
- Top-level managers are an important resource for firms to develop and exploit competitive advantages. In addition, when they and their work are valuable, rare, imperfectly imitable, and nonsubstitutable, strategic leaders can themselves be a source of competitive advantage.
- The top management team is composed of key managers who play a critical role in the selection and implementation of the firm's strategies. Generally, they are officers of the corporation or members of the board of directors.
- There is a relationship among the top management team's characteristics, a firm's strategies, and its performance. For example, a top management team that has significant marketing and R&D knowledge positively contributes to the firm's use of growth strategies. Overall, most top management teams are more effective when they have diverse skills.
- When the board of directors is involved in shaping a firm's strategic direction, that firm generally improves its performance. However, the board may be less involved in decisions about strategy formulation and implementation when CEOs have more power. CEOs increase their power when they appoint people to the board and when they simultaneously serve as the CEO and board chair.
- Strategic leaders are selected from either the internal or the external managerial labor market. Because of their effect on performance, the selection of strategic leaders has implications for a firm's effectiveness. There are valid reasons to use either the internal or the external market when choosing the firm's strategic leaders. In most instances, the internal market is used to select the firm's CEO. Outsiders often are selected to initiate needed change.
- Effective strategic leadership has six major components: determining the firm's strategic direction, exploiting and maintaining core competencies, developing human capital, sustaining an effective organizational culture, emphasizing ethical practices, and establishing balanced organizational controls.
- A firm must develop a long-term vision of its strategic intent. A long-term vision is the driver of strategic leaders' behavior in terms of the remaining five components of effective strategic leadership.
- Strategic leaders must ensure that their firm exploits its core competencies, which are used to produce and deliver products that create value for customers, through the implementation of strategies. In related-diversified and large firms in particular, core competencies are exploited by sharing them across units and products.
- A critical element of strategic leadership and the effective implementation of strategy is the ability to develop a firm's human capital. Effective strategic leaders and firms view human capital as a resource to be maximized, rather than as a cost to be minimized. Resulting from this perspective is the development and use of programs intended to train current and future strategic leaders to build the skills needed to nurture the rest of the firm's human capital.
- Shaping the firm's culture is a central task of effective strategic leadership. An appropriate organizational culture encourages the development of an entrepreneurial orientation among employees and an ability to change the culture as necessary.
- In ethical organizations, employees are encouraged to exercise ethical judgment and to behave ethically at all times. Improved ethical practices foster social capital. Setting specific goals to describe the firm's ethical standards, using a code of conduct, rewarding ethical behaviors, and creating a work environment in which all people are treated with dignity are examples of actions that facilitate and support ethical behavior within the firm.
- Developing and using balanced organizational controls is the final component of effective strategic leadership. An effective balance between strategic and financial controls allows for the flexible use of core competencies, but within the parameters indicated by the firm's financial position. The balanced scorecard is a tool used by the firm and its strategic leaders to develop an appropriate balance between its strategic and financial controls.

Review Questions

1. What is strategic leadership? In what ways are top executives considered important resources for an organization?
2. What is a top-management team, and how does it affect a firm's performance and its abilities to innovate and make appropriate strategic changes?
3. What are the differences between the internal and external managerial labor markets? What are the effects of each type of labor market on the formulation and implementation of strategies?
4. How does strategic leadership affect the determination of the firm's strategic direction?
5. Why is it important for strategic leaders to make certain that their firm exploits its core competencies in the pursuit of strategic competitiveness and above-average returns?
6. What is the importance of human capital and its development for strategic competitiveness?
7. What is organizational culture? What must strategic leaders do to develop and sustain an effective organizational culture?
8. As a strategic leader, what actions could you take to establish and emphasize ethical practices in your firm?
9. What are organizational controls? Why are strategic controls and financial controls important parts of the strategic management process?

Strategic Leadership

The executive board for a large company is concerned that the firm's future leadership needs to be developed. Several top-level managers are expected to leave the firm in the next three to seven years. You have been put in charge of a committee to determine how the firm should prepare for these departures.

Part 1 (individual) Use the information provided within this chapter and your own perceptions to complete the following chart. Be prepared to discuss in class.

Candidates	**Internal Managerial Labor Market**	**External Managerial Labor Market**
Strengths		
Weaknesses		

Part 2 (Individually or in small groups) The firm's executive board feels that the external managerial labor market is beyond its control—the managerial resources the firm will need may or may not be available when they are needed. The board has then asked your committee to consider a program that would develop the firm's internal managerial labor market. Outline the objectives that you want your program to achieve, the steps you would take to reach them, and the time frame involved. Also consider potential problems in such a program and how they could be resolved.

Notes

1. R. D. Ireland, M. A. Hitt, S. M. Camp, & D. L. Sexton, 2001, Integrating entrepreneurship and strategic management actions to create firm wealth, *Academy of Management Executive*, 15(1): 49–63; K. R. Thompson, W. A. Hochwarter, & N. J. Mathys, 1997, Stretch targets: What makes them effective? *Academy of Management Executive*, 11(3): 48–59.
2. A. Cannella Jr., A. Pettigrew, & D. Hambrick, 2001, Upper echelons: Donald Hambrick on executives and strategy, *Academy of Management Executive*, 15(3): 36–52; R. D. Ireland & M. A. Hitt, 1999, Achieving and maintaining strategic competitiveness in the 21st century: The role of strategic leadership, *Academy of Management Executive*, 12(1): 43–57; D. Lei, M. A. Hitt, & R. Bettis, 1996, Dynamic core competencies through meta-learning and strategic context, *Journal of Management*, 22: 547–567.
3. A. Bianco & P. L. Moore, 2001, Downfall: The inside story of the management fiasco at Xerox, *Business Week*, March 5, 82–92.
4. P. A. Moore, 2001, She's here to fix the Xerox: Can Anne Mulcahy pull off an IBM-style makeover? *Business Week*, August 6, 47–48.
5. T. J. Peters, 2001, Leadership: Sad facts and silver linings, *Harvard Business Review*, 79(11): 121–128.
6. J. Collins, 2001, Level 5 Leadership: The triumph of humility and fierce resolve, *Harvard Business Review*, 79(1): 66–76; M. A. Hitt, B. W. Keats, & S. DeMarie, 1998, Navigating in the new competitive landscape: Building competitive advantage and strategic flexibility in the 21st century, *Academy of Management Executive*, XI(4): 22–42; J. B. Quinn, P. Anderson, & S. Finkelstein, 1996, Managing professional intellect: Making the most of the best, *Harvard Business Review*, 74(2): 71–80.
7. D. J. Teece, 2000, *Managing Intellectual Capital: Organizational, Strategic and Policy Dimensions*, Oxford: Oxford University Press.
8. M. F. R. Kets de Vries, 1995, *Life and Death in the Executive Fast Lane*, San Francisco: Jossey-Bass.
9. D. C. Carey & D. Ogden, 2000, *CEO Succession: A Window on How Boards Can Get It Right When Choosing a New Chief Executive*, New York: Oxford University Press.
10. M. Maccoby, 2001, Making sense of the leadership literature, *Research Technology Management*, 44(5): 58–60; T. Kono, 1999, A strong head office makes a strong company, *Long Range Planning*, 32: 225–246.
11. G. Hamel & C. K. Prahalad, 1993, Strategy as stretch and leverage, *Harvard Business Review*, 71(2): 75–84.
12. M. Maccoby, 2001, Successful leaders employ strategic intelligence, *Research Technology Management*, 44(3): 58–60.
13. Ibid.; M. Hammer & S. A. Stanton, 1997, The power of reflection, *Fortune*, November 24, 291–296.
14. S. Finkelstein & D. C. Hambrick, 1996, *Strategic Leadership: Top Executives and Their Effects on Organizations*, St. Paul, MN: West Publishing Company, 2.
15. Collins, Level 5 Leadership.
16. R. Castanias & C. Helfat, 2001, The managerial rents model: Theory and empirical analysis, *Journal of Management*, 27: 661–678; H. P. Gunz & R. M. Jalland, 1996, Managerial careers and business strategy, *Academy of Management Review*, 21: 718–756.
17. M. Beer & R. Eisenstat, 2000, The silent killers of strategy implementation and learning, *Sloan Management Review*, 41(4): 29–40; C. M. Christensen, 1997, Making strategy: Learning by doing, *Harvard Business Review*, 75(6): 141–156; M. A. Hitt, B. W. Keats, H. E. Harback, & R. D. Nixon, 1994, Rightsizing: Building and maintaining strategic leadership and long-term competitiveness, *Organizational Dynamics*, 23: 18–32.
18. M. Wright, R. E. Hoskisson, L. W. Busenitz, & J. Dial, 2000. Entrepreneurial growth through privatization: The upside of management buyouts, *Academy of Management Review*, 25: 591–601; M. J. Waller, G. P. Huber, & W. H. Glick, 1995, Functional background as a determinant of executives' selective perception, *Academy of Management Journal*, 38: 943–974; N. Rajagopalan, A. M. Rasheed, & D. K. Datta, 1993, Strategic decision processes: Critical review and future directions, *Journal of Management*, 19: 349–384.
19. W. Rowe, 2001, Creating wealth in organizations: The role of strategic leadership, *Academy of Management Executive*, 15(1): 81–94; Finkelstein & Hambrick, *Strategic Leadership*, 26–34; D. C. Hambrick & E. Abrahamson, 1995, Assessing managerial discretion across industries: A multimethod approach, *Academy of Management Journal*, 38: 1427–1441; D. C. Hambrick & S. Finkelstein, 1987, Managerial discretion: A bridge between polar views of organizational outcomes, in B. Staw & L. L. Cummings (eds.), *Research in Organizational Behavior*, Greenwich, CT: JAI Press, 369–406.
20. J. A. Petrick & J. F. Quinn, 2001, The challenge of leadership accountability for integrity capacity as a strategic asset, *Journal of Business Ethics*, 34: 331–343; R. C. Mayer, J. H. Davis, & F. D. Schoorman, 1995, An integrative model of organizational trust, *Academy of Management Review*, 20: 709–734.
21. J. J. Sosik, 2001, Self-other agreement on charismatic leadership: Relationships with work attitudes and managerial performance, *Group & Organization Management*, 26: 484–511; D. A. Waldman & F. Yammarino, 1999, CEO charismatic leadership: Levels of management and levels of analysis effects, *Academy of Management Review*, 24: 266–285.
22. J. Call, 2002, The fire within, *BYU Magazine*, Winter, 34–39.
23. J. E. Dutton, S. J. Ashford, R. M. O'Neill, & K. A. Lawrence, 2001, Moves that matter: Issue selling and organizational change. *Academy of Management Journal*, 44: 716–736.
24. W. Ferrier, 2001, Navigating the competitive landscape: The drivers and consequences of competitive aggressiveness, *Academy of Management Journal*, 44: 858–877; P. Chattopadhyay, W. H. Glick, C. C. Miller, & G. P. Huber, 1999, Determinants of executive beliefs: Comparing functional conditioning and social influence, *Strategic Management Journal*, 20: 763–789.
25. I. Goll, R. Sambharya, & L. Tucci, 2001, Top management team composition, corporate ideology, and firm performance, *Management International Review*, 41(2): 109–129.
26. L. Markoczy, 2001, Consensus formation during strategic change, *Strategic Management Journal*, 22: 1013–1031; A. L. Iaquito & J. W. Fredrickson, 1997, Top management team agreement about the strategic decision process: A test of some of its determinants and consequences, *Strategic Management Journal*, 18: 63–75.
27. C. Pegels, Y. Song, & B. Yang, 2000, Management heterogeneity, competitive interaction groups, and firm performance, *Strategic Management Journal*, 21: 911–923; N. Athanassiou & D. Nigh, 1999, The impact of U.S. company internationalization on top management team advice networks: A tacit knowledge perspective, *Strategic Management Journal*, 20: 83–92.
28. Markoczy, Consensus formation during strategic change; D. Knight, C. L. Pearce, K. G. Smith, J. D. Olian, H. P. Sims, K. A. Smith, & P. Flood, 1999, Top management team diversity, group process, and strategic consensus, *Strategic Management Journal*, 20: 446–465.
29. D. C. Hambrick, T. S. Cho, & M. J. Chen, 1996, The influence of top management team heterogeneity on firms' competitive moves, *Administrative Science Quarterly*, 41: 659–684.
30. J. J Distefano & M. L. Maznevski, 2000, Creating value with diverse teams in global management, *Organizational Dynamics*, 29(1): 45–63; T. Simons, L. H. Pelled, & K. A. Smith, 1999, Making use of difference, diversity, debate, and decision comprehensiveness in top management teams, *Academy of Management Journal*, 42: 662–673.
31. Finkelstein & Hambrick, *Strategic Leadership*, 148.
32. S. Barsade, A. Ward, J. Turner, & J. Sonnenfeld, 2000, To your heart's content: A model of affective diversity in top management teams, *Administrative Science Quarterly*, 45: 802–836; C. C. Miller, L. M. Burke, & W. H. Glick, 1998, Cognitive diversity among upper-echelon executives: Implications for strategic decision processes, *Strategic Management Journal*, 19: 39–58.
33. U. Daellenbach, A. McCarthy, & T. Schoenecker, 1999, Commitment to innovation: The impact of top management team characteristics, *R & D Management*, 29(3): 199–208; D. K. Datta & J. P. Guthrie, 1994, Executive succession: Organizational antecedents of CEO characteristics, *Strategic Management Journal*, 15: 569–577.
34. S. Wally & M. Becerra, 2001, Top management team characteristics and strategic changes in international diversification: The case of U.S. multinationals in the European community, *Group & Organization Management*, 26: 165–188; W. Boeker, 1997, Strategic change: The influence of managerial characteristics and organizational growth, *Academy of Management Journal*, 40: 152–170.
35. A. Tomie, 2000, Fast Pack 2000, *Fast Company Online*, http://www.fastcompany.com, March 1.
36. Wally & Becerra, Top management team characteristics and strategic changes in international diversification; L. Tihanyi, C. Daily, D. Dalton, & A. Ellstrand, 2000, Composition of the top management team and firm international diversification, *Journal of Management*, 26: 1157–1178; M. E. Wiersema & K. Bantel, 1992, Top management team demography and corporate strategic change, *Academy of Management Journal*, 35: 91–121; K. Bantel & S. Jackson, 1989, Top management and innovations in banking: Does the composition of the top team make a difference? *Strategic Management Journal*, 10: 107–124.
37. 2002, The top 25 managers: Daniel Vasella, *Business Week*, January 14, 58.
38. W. Koberstein, 2001, Executive profile: Novartis inside out, *Pharmaceutical Executive*, November, 36–50.

39. B. Taylor, 2001, From corporate governance to corporate entrepreneurship, *Journal of Change Management,* 2(2): 128–147; W. Q. Judge, Jr. & C. P. Zeithaml, 1992, Institutional and strategic choice perspectives on board involvement in the strategic decision process, *Academy of Management Journal,* 35: 766–794; J. A. Pearce II & S. A. Zahra, 1991, The relative power of CEOs and boards of directors: Associations with corporate performance, *Strategic Management Journal,* 12: 135–154.
40. B. R. Golden & E. J. Zajac, 2001, When will boards influence strategy? Inclination times power equals strategic change, *Strategic Management Journal,* 22: 1087–1111.
41. M. Carpenter & J. Westphal, 2001, Strategic context of external network ties: Examining the impact of director appointments on board involvement in strategic decision making, *Academy of Management Journal,* 44: 639–660.
42. J. D. Westphal & E. J. Zajac, 1995, Who shall govern? CEO/board power, demographic similarity, and new director selection, *Administrative Science Quarterly,* 40: 60.
43. M. Boyle, 2001, The dirty half-dozen: America's worst boards, *Fortune,* May 14, 249–252.
44. J. D. Westphal, 1999, Collaboration in the boardroom: Behavioral and performance consequences of CEO-board social ties, *Academy of Management Journal,* 42: 7–24.
45. Ibid., 66; J. Roberts & P. Stiles, 1999, The relationship between chairmen and chief executives: Competitive or complementary roles? *Long Range Planning,* 32(1): 36–48.
46. J. Coles, N. Sen, & V. McWilliams, 2001, An examination of the relationship of governance mechanisms to performance, *Journal of Management,* 27: 23–50; J. Coles & W. Hesterly, 2000, Independence of the chairman and board composition: Firm choices and shareholder value, *Journal of Management,* 26: 195–214; B. K. Boyd, 1995, CEO duality and firm performance: A contingency model, *Strategic Management Journal,* 16: 301.
47. D. D. Bergh, 2001, Executive retention and acquisition outcomes: A test of opposing views on the influence of organizational tenure, *Journal of Management,* 27: 603–622.
48. J. Muller, J. Green, & C. Tierney, 2001, Chrysler's Rescue Team, *Business Week,* January 15, 48–50.
49. C. M. Daily & D. R. Dalton, 1995, CEO and director turnover in failing firms: An illusion of change? *Strategic Management Journal,* 16: 393–400.
50. R. Albanese, M. T. Dacin, & I. C. Harris, 1997, Agents as stewards, *Academy of Management Review,* 22: 609–611; J. H. Davis, F. D. Schoorman, & L. Donaldson, 1997, Toward a stewardship theory of management, *Academy of Management Review,* 22: 20–47.
51. M. A. Carpenter, 2002, The implications of strategy and social context for the relationship between top management team heterogeneity and firm performance, *Strategic Management Journal,* 23: 275–284; J. D. Westphal & E. J. Zajac, 1997, Defections from the inner circle: Social exchange, reciprocity and diffusion of board independence in U.S. corporations, *Administrative Science Quarterly,* 161–183.
52. Rajagopalan & Datta, CEO characteristics, 201.
53. R. A. Johnson, R. E. Hoskisson, & M. A. Hitt, 1993, Board involvement in restructuring: The effect of board versus managerial controls and characteristics, *Strategic Management Journal,* 14(Summer Special Issue): 33–50.
54. Boyd, CEO duality and firm performance: A contingency model.
55. M. Carpenter & J. Fredrickson, 2001, Top management teams, global strategic posture, and the moderating role of uncertainty, *Academy of Management Journal,* 44: 533–545.
56. M. Schneider, 2002, A stakeholder model of organizational leadership, *Organization Science,* 13: 209–220.
57. M. Sorcher & J. Brant, 2002, Are you picking the right leaders? *Harvard Business Review,* 80(2): 78-85; D. A. Waldman, G. G. Ramirez, R. J. House, & P. Puranam, 2001, Does leadership matter? CEO leadership attributes and profitability under conditions of perceived environmental uncertainty, *Academy of Management Journal,* 44: 134–143; R. Charan & G. Colvin, 2000, The right fit, *Fortune,* April 17, 226–238.
58. A. Kakabadse & N. Kakabadse, 2001, Dynamics of executive succession, *Corporate Governance,* 1(3): 9–14.
59. R. Charan, 2000, GE's ten-step talent plan, *Fortune,* April 17, 232.
60. R. E. Hoskisson, D. Yiu, & H. Kim, 2000, Capital and labor market congruence and corporate governance: Effects on corporate innovation and global competitiveness. In S. S. Cohen & G. Boyd (eds.), *Corporate Governance and Globalization,* Northampton, MA: Edward Elgar, 129–154.
61. S. B. Shepard, 2002, A Talk with Jeff Immelt: Jack Welch's successor charts a course for GE in the 21st century, *Business Week,* January 28, 102–104.
62. D. C. Carey & D. Ogden, 2000, *CEO Succession: A Window on How Boards Can Get It Right When Choosing a New Chief Executive,* New York: Oxford University Press.
63. A. A. Cannella, Jr. & W. Shen, 2001, So close and yet so far: Promotion versus exit for CEO heirs apparent, *Academy of Management Journal,* 44: 252–270.
64. V. Kisfalvi, 2000, The threat of failure, the perils of success and CEO character: Sources of strategic persistence, *Organization Studies,* 21: 611–639.
65. Datta & Guthrie, Executive succession, 570.
66. Finkelstein & Hambrick, *Strategic Leadership,* 180–181.
67. D. Miller, 1991, Stale in the saddle: CEO tenure and the match between organization and environment, *Management Science,* 37: 34–52.
68. B. Dyck, M. Mauws, F. Starke, & G. Mischke, 2002, Passing the baton: The importance of sequence, timing, technique and communication in executive succession, *Journal of Business Venturing,* 17: 143–162.
69. J. J. Rotemberg & G. Saloner, 2000, Visionaries, managers, and strategic direction, *RAND Journal of Economics,* 31: 693–716.
70. I. M. Levin, 2000, Vision revisited, *Journal of Applied Behavioral Science,* 36: 91–107; J. C. Collins & J. I. Porras, 1996, Building your company's vision, *Harvard Business Review,* 74(5): 65–77.
71. G. Gori, 2001, An American directs Mexico City's cinema revival, *The New York Times,* http://www.nytimes.com, July 15.
72. P. W. Beamish, 1999, Sony's Yoshihide Nakamura on structure and decision making, *Academy of Management Executive,* 13(4): 12–16; R. M. Hodgetts, 1999, Dow Chemical's CEO William Stavropoulos on structure and decision making, *Academy of Management Executive,* 13(4): 29–35.
73. R. A. Burgelman, 2001, *Strategy Is Destiny: How Strategy-Making Shapes a Company's Future,* New York: The Free Press.
74. S. Jaffe, 2001, Do Pepsi and Gatorade mix? *Business Week Online,* http://www.businessweek.com, August 14.
75. J. Byrne & B. Elgin, 2002, Cisco: Behind the hype, *Business Week Online,* http://www.businessweek.com, January 21.
76. C. A. Lengnick-Hall & J. A. Wolff, 1999, Similarities and contradictions in the core logic of three strategy research streams, *Strategic Management Journal,* 20: 1109–1132.
77. M. A. Hitt, L. Bierman, K. Shimizu, & R. Kochhar, 2001, Direct and moderating effects of human capital on strategy and performance in professional service firms: A resource-based perspective, *Academy of Management Journal,* 44:13–28;
78. S. A. Snell & M. A. Youndt, 1995, Human resource management and firm performance: Testing a contingency model of executive controls, *Journal of Management,* 21: 711–737.
79. P. Caligiuri & V. Di Santo, 2001, Global competence: What is it, and can it be developed through global assignments? *Human Resource Planning,* 24(3): 27–35; D. Ulrich, 1998, A new mandate for human resources, *Harvard Business Review,* 76(1): 124–134.
80. A. McWilliams, D. D. Van Fleet, & P. M. Wright, 2001, Strategic management of human resources for global competitive advantage, *Journal of Business Strategies* 18(1): 1–24; J. Pfeffer, 1994, *Competitive Advantage through People,* Cambridge, MA: Harvard Business School Press, 4.
81. L. Gratton, 2001, *Living Strategy: Putting People at the Heart of Corporate Purpose,* London: Financial Times/Prentice Hall, London.
82. Caligiuri & Di Santo, Global competence.
83. M. W. McCall & G. P. Hollenbeck, 2001, *Developing Global Executives: The Lessons of International Experience,* Boston: Harvard Business School Press.
84. C. F. Fey & I. Bjorkman, 2001, The effect of human resource management practices on MNC subsidiary performance in Russia, *Journal of International Business Studies,* 32: 59–75.
85. M. G. Harvey & M. M. Novicevic, 2000, The influences of inpatriation practices on the strategic orientation of a global organization, *International Journal of Management,* 17: 362–371; M. G. Harvey & M. R. Buckley, 1997, Managing inpatriates: Building a global core competency, *Journal of World Business,* 32(1): 35–52.
86. C. A. Bartlett & S. Ghoshal, 2002, Building competitive advantage through people, *MIT Sloan Management Review,* 43(2): 34–41; D. M. DeCarolis & D. L. Deeds, 1999, The impact of stocks and flows of organizational knowledge on firm performance: An empirical investigation of the biotechnology industry, *Strategic Management Journal,* 20: 953–968.
87. J. Sandberg, 2000, Understanding human competence at work: An interpretative approach, *Academy of Management Journal,* 43: 9–25.
88. J. Lee & D. Miller, 1999, People matter: Commitment to employees, strategy and performance in Korean firms, *Strategic Management Journal,* 20: 579–593.
89. T. M. Welbourne & L. A. Cyr, 1999, The human resource executive effect in initial

public offering firms, *Academy of Management Journal,* 42: 616–629; J. Pfeffer & J. F. Veiga, 1999, Putting people first for organizational success, *Academy of Management Executive,* 13(2): 37–48.
90. Bartlett & Ghoshal, Building competitive advantage through people.
91. J. H. Christy, 2001, Eagle aloft, *Forbes,* August 6, 60.
92. H. Collingwood & D. L. Coutu, 2002, Jack on Jack, *Harvard Business Review,* 80(2): 88–94.
93. J. Di Frances, 2002, 10 reasons why you shouldn't downsize, *Journal of Property Management,* 67(1): 72–73; M. A. Hitt, R. E. Hoskisson, J. S. Harrison, & B. Summers, 1994, Human capital and strategic competitiveness in the 1990s, *Journal of Management Development,* 13(1): 35–46.
94. A. Pinsonneault & K. Kraemer, 2002, The role of information technology in organizational downsizing: A tale of two American cities, *Organization Science,* 13: 191–208.
95. M. David, 2001, Leadership during an economic slowdown, *Journal for Quality and Participation,* 24(3): 40–43; C. L. Martin, C. K. Parsons, & N. Bennett, 1995, The influence of employee involvement program membership during downsizing: Attitudes toward the employer and the union, *Journal of Management,* 21: 879–890.
96. A. K. Gupta & V. Govindarajan, 2000, Knowledge management's social dimension: Lessons from Nucor steel, *Sloan Management Review,* 42(1): 71–80; C. M. Fiol, 1991, Managing culture as a competitive resource: An identity-based view of sustainable competitive advantage, *Journal of Management,* 17: 191–211; J. B. Barney, 1986, Organizational culture: Can it be a source of sustained competitive advantage? *Academy of Management Review,* 11: 656–665.
97. V. Govindarajan & A. K. Gupta, 2001, Building an effective global business team, *Sloan Management Review,* 42(4): 63–71; S. Ghoshal & C. A. Bartlett, 1994, Linking organizational context and managerial action: The dimensions of quality of management, *Strategic Management Journal,* 15: 91–112.
98. D. F. Kuratko, R. D. Ireland, & J. S. Hornsby, 2001, Improving firm performance through entrepreneurial actions: Acordia's corporate entrepreneurship strategy, *Academy of Management Executive,* 15(4): 60–71.
99. T. E. Brown, P. Davidsson, & J. Wiklund, 2001, An operationalization of Stevenson's conceptualization of entrepreneurship as opportunity-based firm behavior, *Strategic Management Journal,* 22: 953–968.
100. G. T. Lumpkin & G. G. Dess, 1996, Clarifying the entrepreneurial orientation construct and linking it to performance, *Academy of Management Review,* 21: 135–172.
101. Ibid., 142.
102. Ibid., 137.
103. M. Arndt, 2001, The rules of James Farrell's game, *Business Week Online,* http://www.businessweek.com, August 6.
104. R. R. Sims, 2000, Changing an organization's culture under new leadership, *Journal of Business Ethics,* 25: 65–78.
105. R. A. Burgelman & Y. L. Doz, 2001, The power of strategic integration, *Sloan Management Review,* 42(3): 28–38; P. H. Fuchs, K. E. Mifflin, D. Miller, & J. O. Whitney, 2000, Strategic integration: Competing in the age of capabilities, *California Management Review,* 42(3): 118–147.
106. J. S. Hornsby, D. F. Kuratko, & S. A. Zahra, 2002, Middle managers' perception of the internal environment for corporate entrepreneurship: Assessing a measurement scale, *Journal of Business Venturing,* 17: 253–273; J. E. Dutton, S. J. Ashford, R. M. O'Neill, E. Hayes, & E. E. Wierba, 1997, Reading the wind: How middle managers assess the context for selling issues to top managers, *Strategic Management Journal,* 18: 407–425.
107. B. Axelrod, H. Handfield-Jones, & E. Michaels, 2002, A new game plan for C players, *Harvard Business Review,* 80(1): 80–88.
108. J. E. Garten, 2001, *The Mind of the CEO,* New York: Basic Books.
109. W. W. George, 2001, Medtronic's chairman William George on how mission-driving companies create long-term shareholder value, *Academy of Management Executive,* 15(4): 39–47.
110. P. S. Adler & S.-W. Kwon, 2002, Social capital: Prospects for a new concept, *Academy of Management Review,* 27: 17–40.
111. T. A. Stewart, 2001, Right now the only capital that matters is social capital, *Business 2.0,* December, 128–130.
112. D. J. Brass, K. D. Butterfield, & B. C. Skaggs, 1998, Relationships and unethical behavior: A social network perspective, *Academy of Management Review,* 23: 14–31.
113. L. K. Trevino, G. R. Weaver, D. G. Toffler, & B. Ley, 1999, Managing ethics and legal compliance: What works and what hurts, *California Management Review,* 41(2): 131–151.

114. C. W. L. Hill, 1990, Cooperation, opportunism, and the invisible hand: Implications for transaction cost theory, *Academy of Management Review,* 15: 500–513.
115. S. Forest, W. Zellner, & H. Timmons, 2001, The Enron debacle, *Business Week,* November 12, 106–110.
116. K. Brown, G. Hitt, S. Liesman, & J. Weil, 2002, Andersen fires partner it says led shredding of Enron documents, *The Wall Street Journal,* January 16, A1, A18.
117. W. Wallace, 2000, The value relevance of accounting: The rest of the story, *European Management Journal,* 18(6): 675–682.
118. E. Soule, 2002, Managerial moral strategies—In search of a few good principles, *Academy of Management Review,* 27: 114–124; J. Milton-Smith, 1995, Ethics as excellence: A strategic management perspective, *Journal of Business Ethics,* 14: 683–693.
119. L. M. Leinicke, J. A. Ostrosky, & W. M. Rexroad, 2000, Quality financial reporting: Back to the basics, *CPA Journal,* August, 69–71.
120. J. R. Cohen, L. W. Pant, & D. J. Sharp, 2001, An examination of differences in ethical decision-making between Canadian business students and accounting professionals, *Journal of Business Ethics,* 30: 319–336; G. R. Weaver, L. K. Trevino, & P. L. Cochran, 1999, Corporate ethics programs as control systems: Influences of executive commitment and environmental factors, *Academy of Management Journal,* 42: 41–57.
121. P. E. Murphy, 1995, Corporate ethics statements: Current status and future prospects, *Journal of Business Ethics,* 14: 727–740.
122. J. H. Gittell, 2000, Paradox of coordination and control, *California Management Review,* 42(3): 101–117; L. J. Kirsch, 1996, The management of complex tasks in organizations: Controlling the systems development process, *Organization Science,* 7: 1–21.
123. M. D. Shields, F. J. Deng, & Y. Kato, 2000, The design and effects of control systems: Tests of direct- and indirect-effects models, *Accounting, Organizations and Society,* 25: 185–202; R. Simons, 1994, How new top managers use control systems as levers of strategic renewal, *Strategic Management Journal,* 15: 170–171.
124. K. J. Laverty, 1996, Economic "short-termism": The debate, the unresolved issues, and the implications for management practice and research, *Academy of Management Review,* 21: 825–860.
125. R. S. Kaplan & D. P. Norton, 2001, The strategy-focused organization, *Strategy & Leadership,* 29(3): 41–42; R. S. Kaplan & D. P. Norton, 2000, *The Strategy-Focused Organization: How Balanced Scorecard Companies Thrive in the New Business Environment,* Boston: Harvard Business School Press.
126. B. E. Becker, M. A. Huselid, & D. Ulrich, 2001, *The HR Scorecard: Linking People, Strategy, and Performance,* Boston: Harvard Business School Press, 21.
127. Kaplan & Norton, The strategy-focused organization; Kaplan & Norton, *The Strategy-Focused Organization.*
128. R. S. Kaplan & D. P. Norton, 2001, Transforming the balanced scorecard from performance measurement to strategic management: Part I, *Accounting Horizons,* 15(1): 87–104.
129. R. S. Kaplan & D. P. Norton, 1992, The balanced scorecard—measures that drive performance, *Harvard Business Review,* 70(1): 71–79.
130. M. A. Mische, 2001, *Strategic Renewal: Becoming a High-Performance Organization,* Upper Saddle River: Prentice Hall, 181.
131. Rowe, Creating wealth in organizations: The role of strategic leadership.
132. R. E. Hoskisson, R. A. Johnson, D. Yiu, & W. P. Wan, 2001, Restructuring strategies of diversified business groups: Differences associated with country institutional environments. In M. A. Hitt, R. E. Freeman, J. S. Harrison (eds.), *Handbook of Strategic Management,* Oxford, U.K.: Blackwell Publishers, 433–463; R. A. Johnson, 1996, Antecedents and outcomes of corporate refocusing, *Journal of Management,* 22: 437–481; R. E. Hoskisson & M. A. Hitt, 1994, *Downscoping: How to Tame the Diversified Firm,* New York: Oxford University Press.
133. J. Birkinshaw & N. Hood, 2001, Unleash innovation in foreign subsidiaries, *Harvard Business Review,* 79(3): 131–137.
134. Ireland & Hitt, Achieving and maintaining strategic competitiveness.
135. M. Ihlwan, & D. Roberts, 2002, How Samsung plugged into China, *Business Week Online,* http://www.businessweek.com, March 4.

13

Chapter Thirteen

Strategic Entrepreneurship

Knowledge Objectives

Studying this chapter should provide you with the strategic management knowledge needed to:

1. Define and explain strategic entrepreneurship.
2. Describe the importance of entrepreneurial opportunities, innovation, and entrepreneurial capabilities.
3. Discuss the importance of international entrepreneurship and describe why it is increasing.
4. Describe the two forms of internal corporate venturing: autonomous and induced strategic behaviors.
5. Discuss how cooperative strategies such as strategic alliances are used to develop innovation.
6. Explain how firms use acquisitions to increase their innovations and enrich their innovative capabilities.
7. Describe the importance of venture capital and initial public offerings to entrepreneurial activity.
8. Explain how the practice of strategic entrepreneurship creates value for customers and shareholders of all types of firms, large and small, new and established.

What Makes Entrepreneurs Successful?

There is a wide variety of types of entrepreneurs, but no one formula for success. However, there are many successful entrepreneurs. For example, Marion McCaw Garrison was one of the first female accounting graduates of the University of Washington in 1939. While she was told that it was unlikely she could ever earn her CPA because she was a woman, she completed her degree in accounting anyway. At 22 years of age, she bought 40 acres of land and became a real estate developer, one of the first women to do so. After she married, she helped her husband manage their businesses, including radio and television stations and real estate. When her husband died suddenly, she took over the management of the businesses. She moved out of the radio business and entered cable television and wireless communications. The company went public in 1987, and in 1994, McCaw Cellular Communications was sold to AT&T for more than $11 billion. Garrison was successful because of her strong business knowledge and determination.

Anatoly Karachinsky originally had no thoughts of starting his own business. In 1992, he was invited to attend a conference in Arizona, where he met the CEO of EDS, Mort Myerson. After a several-hour conversation with Myerson, Karachinsky returned to Russia and took over a friend's computer consulting firm. In 1994, Karachinsky met Michael Dell and became the exclusive distributor of Dell computers in Russia. Several U.S. investors became impressed with his company, Informatsionniye Biznes Sistemy (IBS), and how he managed it, and Citigroup and AIG Brunswick Millennium Fund invested $30 million of capital in his firm. IBS has continued to grow and now controls much of the IT market in Russia. In 2001, IBS earned more than $5 million of pretax income on total revenues of $200 million. Karachinsky was successful because he had a good idea and implemented it without help from the Russian government or the "black market." He was able to obtain the critical venture capital for these reasons.

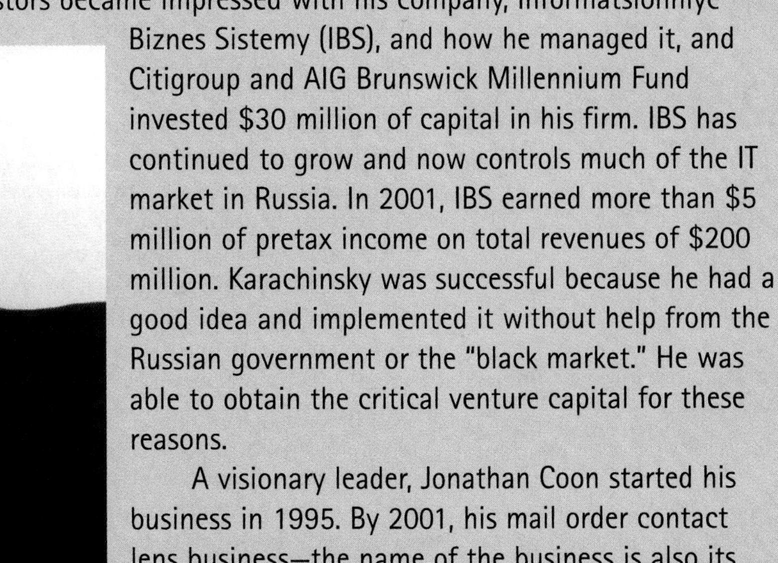

COURTESY OF IBS, HTTP://WWW.IBS.RU

Anatoly Karachinsky, CEO and founder of Informatsionniye Biznes Sistemy (IBS).

A visionary leader, Jonathan Coon started his business in 1995. By 2001, his mail order contact lens business—the name of the business is also its phone number: 1-800 CONTACTS—had become the largest direct-to-consumer contact lens business in the world. It stocks 9 million lenses, selling over 100,000 per day. Before he started the business, Coon developed an effective business plan that has produced a strong cash flow. He also has an effective distribution system and built-in repeat business because the product is disposable. Coon's employees are empowered to do whatever is necessary to satisfy customers. He also allows them to participate in developing company policies and provides stock options to all employees. Because of his firm's success, he was named the National Ernst & Young Retail Entrepreneur of the Year.

Each of these three successful entrepreneurs took some unique actions and had some special traits, but they all had a passion for the businesses they developed. According to Michael Dell, passion must be the driving force for starting a company. Dell also emphasizes the importance of identifying and exploiting opportunities. All of the entrepreneurs described identified opportunities and obviously were passionate about exploiting them.

SOURCES: T. Singer, 2002, What business would you start? *INC*, March, 68–76; 2001, Direct-to-consumer visionary Jonathan Coon of mail order giant, 1-800 CONTACTS, named Ernst & Young Retail Entrepreneur of the Year, Ernst & Young newsroom, http://www.ey.com/global, October 30; 2001, Marion McCaw Garrison: An entrepreneurial woman, *Business*, University of Washington Business School, Fall, 40; T. Kellner, 2001, Entrepreneurs, *Forbes*, April 30, 116–117.

The Opening Case provides examples of three successful entrepreneurs. While the descriptions are brief, several factors can be identified as important for each person's success. They all have a passion for their business. Furthermore, they had strong business knowledge and planned well (for example, they developed a business plan). Each identified opportunities and exploited them. Other factors, such as determination (Marion McCaw Garrison), strong values and independence (Anatoly Karachinsky), and creativity and empowering employees (Jonathan Coon) also contributed to their success.

Understanding why some entrepreneurs succeed while others fail is important to help future entrepreneurs in their efforts to be successful. Entrepreneurship is the economic engine driving many nations' economies in the global competitive landscape. Entrepreneurship and innovation have become important for young and old and for large and small firms in all types of industries. Research conducted by the Center for Entrepreneurial Leadership at the Kauffman Foundation has shown that in recent years almost 100 percent of the new jobs in the United States were created by entrepreneurial firms of less than two years of age.[1] As a result, this chapter focuses on strategic entrepreneurship. **Strategic entrepreneurship** is taking entrepreneurial actions using a strategic perspective. More specifically, it involves engaging in simultaneous opportunity seeking and competitive advantage seeking behaviors to design and implement entrepreneurial strategies to create wealth.[2] These actions can be taken by individuals or by corporations. Such activity is particularly important in the evolving 21st-century landscape.

Strategic entrepreneurship is taking entrepreneurial actions using a strategic perspective.

The competitive landscape that has evolved in the 21st century presents firms with substantial change, a global marketplace, and significant complexity and uncertainty.[3] Because of this uncertain environment, firms cannot easily predict the future. As a result, they must develop strategic flexibility to have a range of strategic alternatives that they can implement as needed. To do so, they must acquire resources and build the capabilities that allow them to take necessary actions to adapt to a dynamic environment or to proact in that environment.[4] In this environment, entrepreneurs and entrepreneurial managers design and implement actions that capture more of existing markets from less aggressive and innovative competitors while creating new markets.[5] In effect, they are trying to create tomorrow's businesses.[6]

Creating tomorrow's businesses requires identifying opportunities, as argued by Michael Dell in the Opening Case, and developing innovation. In other words, firms must be entrepreneurial and innovative. Innovations are critical to companies' efforts to differentiate their goods or services from competitors in ways that create additional or new value for customers.[7] Thus, entrepreneurial competencies are important for firms to achieve and sustain competitive advantages for a period of time.[8]

To describe how firms produce and manage innovation, we examine several topics in this chapter. To set the stage, we first examine entrepreneurship and innovation in a strategic context. Next, we discuss international entrepreneurship, a phenomenon reflecting the increased use of entrepreneurship in countries throughout the world. Internally, firms innovate through either autonomous or induced strategic behavior. After our descriptions of these internal corporate venturing activities, we discuss actions taken by firms to implement the innovations resulting from those two types of strategic behavior. In addition to innovating through internal activities, firms can gain access to other companies' innovations or innovative capabilities through strategic alliances and acquisitions. Following our discussion of these topics is a description of entrepreneurship in start-up ventures and smaller firms. This section closes both the chapter and our analysis of actions that firms take to successfully implement strategies.

Strategic Entrepreneurship and Innovation

Joseph Schumpeter viewed entrepreneurship as a process of "creative destruction," through which existing products or methods of production are destroyed and replaced with new ones.[9] Thus, entrepreneurship is "concerned with the discovery and exploitation of profitable opportunities."[10] Entrepreneurial activity is an important mechanism for creating changes, as well as for helping firms adapt to changes created by others. Firms that encourage entrepreneurship are risk takers, are committed to innovation, and act proactively in that they try to create opportunities rather than waiting to respond to opportunities created by others.[11]

Entrepreneurial opportunities represent conditions in which new products or services can satisfy a need in the market.

Entrepreneurial opportunities represent conditions in which new products or services can satisfy a need in the market. The essence of entrepreneurship is to identify and exploit these opportunities.[12] Importantly, entrepreneurs or entrepreneurial managers must be able to identify opportunities not perceived by others. Identifying these opportunities in a dynamic and uncertain environment requires an entrepreneurial mind-set that entails the passionate pursuit of opportunities.[13] Matthew Heyman and two Harvard classmates found opportunity in the chaos of Mexico City's movie theater industry. The movie theaters were all in bad shape and largely unprofitable. All of the major theater companies gave up and departed the Mexico City market. However, Heyman and his colleagues saw opportunity and started Cinemex in 1994. They received venture capital from J.P. Morgan and used it to attract other investors. After raising almost $22 million in capital, Cinemex built attractive theaters and now dominates the market with approximately 90,000 viewers and revenues of $140 million in 2001.[14] In the previous chapter, we described the long-term vision (one of the actions associated with effective strategic leadership) that supported Heyman and his partners as they started their entrepreneurial venture. As we now see, these strategic leaders were successful in their pursuit of what they recognized to be an entrepreneurial opportunity.

After identifying the opportunities, entrepreneurs take actions to exploit them and establish a competitive advantage. The process of identifying and pursuing opportunities is entrepreneurial, but this activity alone is rarely enough to create maximum wealth or even to survive over time. Actions must be valuable, rare, difficult to imitate, and non-substitutable to create and sustain a competitive advantage (as described in Chapter 3). Without the competitive advantage, success will be only temporary (as explained in Chapter 1). An innovation may be valuable and rare early in its life, if a market perspective is used in its development. However, strategic actions must be taken to introduce the new product to the market and protect its position in the market against competitors (difficult to imitate) to gain a competitive advantage. These actions combined represent strategic entrepreneurship.

Peter Drucker argues that "innovation is the specific function of entrepreneurship, whether in an existing business, a public service institution, or a new venture started by a lone individual." Moreover, Drucker suggests that innovation is "the means by which the entrepreneur either creates new wealth-producing resources or endows existing resources with enhanced potential for creating wealth."[15] Thus, entrepreneurship and the innovation resulting from it are important for large and small firms, as well as for start-up ventures, as they compete in the 21st-century competitive landscape. Therefore, we can conclude that, "Entrepreneurship and innovation are central to the creative process in the economy and to promoting growth, increasing productivity and creating jobs."[16]

Innovation

Innovation is a key outcome firms seek through entrepreneurship and is often the source of competitive success. In Rosabeth Moss Kanter's words, "Winning in business today demands innovation. Companies that innovate reap all the advantages of a first mover."[17] For example, research results show that firms competing in global industries that invest more in innovation also achieve the highest returns.[18] In fact, investors often react positively to the introduction of a new product, thereby increasing the price of a firm's stock. Innovation, then, is an essential feature of high-performance firms.[19] Furthermore, "innovation may be required to maintain or achieve competitive parity, much less a competitive advantage in many global markets."[20]

Invention is the act of creating or developing a new product or process.

Innovation is the process of creating a commercial product from an invention.

Imitation is the adoption of an innovation by similar firms.

In his classic work, Schumpeter argued that firms engage in three types of innovative activity.[21] **Invention** is the act of creating or developing a new product or process. **Innovation** is the process of creating a commercial product from an invention. Thus, an invention brings something new into being, while an innovation brings something new into use. Accordingly, technical criteria are used to determine the success of an invention, whereas commercial criteria are used to determine the success of an innovation.[22] Finally, **imitation** is the adoption of an innovation by similar firms. Imitation usually leads to product or process standardization, and products based on imitation often are offered at lower prices, but without as many features.

In the United States in particular, innovation is the most critical of the three types of innovative activity that occur in firms. Many companies are able to create ideas that lead to inventions, but commercializing those inventions through innovation has, at times, proved difficult. Approximately 80 percent of R&D occurs in large firms, but these same firms produce fewer than 50 percent of the patents.[23]

Corporate entrepreneurship is a process whereby an individual or a group in an existing organization creates a new venture or develops an innovation.

Innovations produced in large established firms are often referred to as corporate entrepreneurship. **Corporate entrepreneurship** is a process whereby an individual or a group in an existing organization creates a new venture or develops an innovation. Overall, corporate entrepreneurship is the sum of a firm's innovation, renewal, and venturing efforts. Evidence suggests that corporate entrepreneurship practices are facilitated through the effective use of a firm's strategic management

Cinemex founder Matthew Heyman saw a market in Mexico City and created Cinemex. His theaters offer moviegoers in Mexico an enjoyable experience, including luxurious facilities, as shown here, and first-run films for a reasonable price.

process and effectively using the firm's human capital.[24] Determining how to harness the ingenuity of a firm's employees and how to reward them for it while retaining some of the rewards of the entrepreneurial efforts for the shareholders' benefit facilitates the emergence of value-creating corporate entrepreneurship.[25]

Entrepreneurs and Entrepreneurial Capabilities

Entrepreneurs are individuals, acting independently or as part of an organization, who create a new venture or develop an innovation and take risks entering them into the marketplace. Entrepreneurs can be independent individuals or surface in an organization at any level. Thus, top-level managers, middle- and first-level managers, staff personnel, and those producing the company's good or service can all be entrepreneurs.

Entrepreneurs are individuals, acting independently or as part of an organization, who create a new venture or develop an innovation and take risks entering them into the marketplace.

Firms need employees who think entrepreneurially. Top-level managers should try to establish an entrepreneurial culture that inspires individuals and groups to engage in corporate entrepreneurship.[26] Apple Computer's Steve Jobs is committed to this effort, believing one of his key responsibilities is to help Apple become more entrepreneurial. And, Apple has introduced some innovatively designed products, such as its recent iMac with its 15-inch liquid crystal display attached to the base computer with a chrome swivel bar.[27] Some believe that it looks more like a desk lamp. Apple is using the new design to capture a larger share of the PC market.

Of course, to create and commercialize products such as the iMac requires not only intellectual capital, but an entrepreneurial mind-set as well. It also requires entrepreneurial competence. Returning to the Opening Case, entrepreneurial competence involves effective knowledge of the business and technology, a passion for the business, and a risk orientation.[28] In most cases, knowledge must be transferred to others in the organization, even in smaller ventures, to enhance the entrepreneurial competence of the firm. The transfer is likely to be more difficult in larger firms. Research has shown, however, that units within firms are more innovative if they have access to new knowledge.[29]

Transferring knowledge can be difficult, because the receiving party must have adequate absorptive capacity to learn the knowledge.[30] This requires that the new knowledge be linked to the existing knowledge. Thus, managers will need to develop the capabilities of their human capital to build on their current knowledge base while incrementally expanding that knowledge.[31]

Developing innovations and achieving success in the marketplace requires effective human capital. In particular, firms must have strong intellectual capital in their R&D organization.[32] However, a firm must have strong human capital throughout its workforce if employees are to be innovative. For example, Winspec West Manufacturing Inc. credits its positive market position to innovation produced by its strong employee base. In fact, the managers are very careful in hiring. Even in jobs with seemingly low challenges, they try to hire high potential employees. For one secretarial position, the managers hired a person with an MBA in finance; that person went on to serve as the acting chief financial officer.[33]

Having the intellectual talent is only part of the challenge. The management of the talent to realize its potential is critical for a firm to be entrepreneurial.[34] Managers must develop the culture and infuse it with the values espoused by successful entrepreneurs such as those discussed in the Opening Case. Additionally, managers should empower employees at all levels to act independently, as Jonathan Coon of 1-800 CONTACTS did, described in the Opening Case.[35]

International Entrepreneurship

Entrepreneurship is a global phenomenon.[36] It is at the top of public policy agendas in many of the world's countries, including Finland, Germany, Israel, Ireland, and France, among others. In Northern Ireland, for example, the minister for enterprise, trade, and investment told businesspeople that their current and future commercial success would be affected by the degree to which they decided to emphasize R&D and innovation (critical components of entrepreneurship).[37]

According to some researchers who are studying economies throughout the world, virtually all industrial nations "are experiencing some form of transformation in their economies, from the dramatic move from centrally planned to market economies in East-central Europe . . . to the efforts by Asian countries to return to their recent high growth levels."[38] Entrepreneurship can play central roles in those transformations, in that it has a strong potential to fuel economic growth, create employment, and generate prosperity for citizens.[39]

While entrepreneurship is a global phenomenon, there are differences in the rate of entrepreneurship across countries. A recent study of 29 countries found that the percentage of adults involved in entrepreneurial activity ranged from a high of more than 20 percent in Mexico to a low of approximately 5 percent in Belgium. The United States had a rate of about 13 percent. Importantly, this study also found a strong positive relationship between the rate of entrepreneurial activity and economic development in the country.[40]

Culture is one of the reasons for the differences in rates of entrepreneurship among different countries. For example, the tension between individualism and collectivism is important for entrepreneurship; research shows that entrepreneurship declines as collectivism is emphasized. Simultaneously, however, research results suggest that exceptionally high levels of individualism might be dysfunctional for entrepreneurship. Viewed collectively, these results appear to call for a balance between individual initiative and a spirit of cooperation and group ownership of innovation. For firms to be entrepreneurial, they must provide appropriate autonomy and incentives for individual initiative to surface, but also promote cooperation and group ownership of an innovation if it is to be implemented successfully. Thus, entrepreneurship often requires teams of people with unique skills and resources, especially in cultures where collectivism is a valued historical norm.[41]

Another important dimension of international entrepreneurship is the level of investment outside of the home country made by young ventures. In fact, with increasing globalization, a greater number of new ventures have been 'born global.'[42] Research has shown that new ventures that enter international markets increase their learning of new technological knowledge and thereby enhance their performance.[43] Because of these outcomes, the amount of international entrepreneurship has been increasing in recent years.[44]

The probability of entering international markets increases when the firm has top executives with international experience. Furthermore, the firm has a higher likelihood of successfully competing in international markets when its top executives have international experience.[45] Because of the learning and economies of scale and scope afforded by operating in international markets, both young and established internationally diversified firms often are stronger competitors in their domestic market as well. Additionally, internationally diversified firms are generally more innovative, as research has shown.[46]

International entrepreneurship has been an important factor in the economic development of Asia. In fact, private companies owned by Chinese families outside of China compose the fourth largest economic power in the world. Significant learning from their international ventures occurs in these businesses, and this learning enhances their success with future ventures.[47] The learning that occurs contributes to a firm's knowledge of operating in international markets.[48] It also contributes knowledge that can enhance a firm's new product development, on which we focus in the next section.

The outcomes of effective new product development are described in the Strategic Focus on page 422. These processes render outstanding and smartly designed new products, such as those chosen as the best new products of 2001.

New Product Development and Internal Corporate Ventures

Most corporate innovation is developed through research and development (R&D). In many industries, the competitive battle for the market begins in the R&D labs. In fact, R&D may be the most critical factor in gaining and sustaining a competitive advantage in some industries, such as pharmaceuticals. Larger, established firms use R&D labs to create the competence-destroying new technology and products envisioned by Schumpeter. Such radical innovation has become an important component of competition in many industries.[49]

Incremental and Radical Innovation

Firms can create incremental or more radical innovations. Most innovations are *incremental*—that is, they build on existing knowledge bases and provide small improvements in the current product lines. Alternatively, *radical innovations* usually provide significant technological breakthroughs and create new knowledge.[50]

Radical innovations are rare because of the difficulty and risk involved in developing them. There is substantial uncertainty with radical innovation regarding the technology and the market opportunities.[51] Because radical innovation creates new knowledge and uses only some or little of a firm's current product or technological knowledge, creativity is required. However, creativity does not create something from nothing. Rather, creativity discovers, combines, or synthesizes current knowledge, often from diverse areas.[52] This knowledge is then used to develop new products or services that can be used in an entrepreneurial manner to move into new markets, capture new customers, and gain access to new resources.[53] Such innovations are often developed in separate units that start internal ventures.[54]

Internal corporate venturing is the set of activities used to create inventions and innovations through internal means.[55] Spending on R&D is linked to success in internal corporate venturing. Put simply, firms are unable to invent or innovate without significant R&D investments. Because of the importance of innovation to the competitiveness of multinational firms, the effectiveness of their internal venturing process is critical.

Internal corporate venturing is the set of activities used to create inventions and innovations through internal means.

Strategic Focus

Developing the Best New Products on the Market

The best new products for 2001 range from high technology to food. They include the Apple PowerBook G4 laptop, Harmony, a new low-fat cereal for women offered by General Mills, and Visa's plastic paycheck. Using the plastic paycheck, consumers can have their pay deposited into their Visa accounts and then use their Visa card to pay for goods, similar to a debit card.

Hitachi's new DZ-MV100A camcorder can be used to edit home movies. Equator developed the Round Refrigerator that features pull-out shelves that operate similar to a "lazy susan." Listerine introduced stamp-sized strips to freshen your breath.

While the Samsung 1300 phone, combining wireless phone functions with those of a palm organizer, was selected as a best product, Nokia brought to the market the Nokia 8270a phone, named one of the "cutest" wireless phones. Nokia's phone offers code division multiple access (CDMA) technology, supports a wireless Internet browser, enables two-way text messaging, and serves as an alarm clock and calendar. Analysts believe the new fashion-sensitive phone will compete well with Samsung and Motorola products.

Intel is well known as one of the most innovative firms in any industry. Intel invests $4 billion annually in R&D and does not let up during recessions. In fact, Intel has learned that it can gain ground on competitors during recessions. Intel's laboratories are developing the semi-conductor chips of the future. Intel is now designing a new way to manufacture chips, which could not be built much smaller or faster using the firm's existing manufacturing technology. This process innovation will facilitate further product innovation.

Innovation is increasing at GM. Because of its emphasis on planning and analysis in prior years, GM autos were perceived as boring, with only incremental innovations added to new models. Its designs were "criteria-ed to death," and its market share had markedly decreased. However, Robert Lutz, formerly of Chrysler, was hired as GM's new product czar in late 2001 and has changed the system that he described as producing a lot of bunts, singles, and walks, but no home runs. Lutz is changing the culture to promote inspiration and the development of new ideas, which hopefully will lead to innovative GM products in future years.

SOURCES: G. Anders, 2002, How Intel puts innovation inside, *Fast Company*, March, 122–124; A. Hesseidahl, 2002, Nokia has fashion sense, *Forbes*, http://www.forbes.com, February 19; L. Armstrong, 2001, The best products of 2001, *Business Week*, December 17, 116–124; J. Flint, 2001, A breath of fresh air, *Forbes*, http://www.forbes.com, November 11.

As shown in Figure 13.1, there are two forms of internal corporate venturing: autonomous strategic behavior and induced strategic behavior.

Autonomous Strategic Behavior

Autonomous strategic behavior is a bottom-up process in which product champions pursue new ideas, often through a political process, by means of which they develop and coordinate the commercialization of a new good or service until it achieves success in the marketplace.

Autonomous strategic behavior is a bottom-up process in which product champions pursue new ideas, often through a political process, by means of which they develop and coordinate the commercialization of a new good or service until it achieves success in the marketplace. A *product champion* is an organizational member with an entrepreneurial vision of a new good or service who seeks to create support for its commercialization. Evidence suggests that product champions play critical roles in moving innovations forward.[56] Autonomous strategic behavior is based on a firm's wellsprings of knowledge and resources that are the sources of the firm's innovation. Thus, a firm's technological capabilities and competencies are the basis for new products and processes.[57]

Figure 13.1 Model of Internal Corporate Venturing

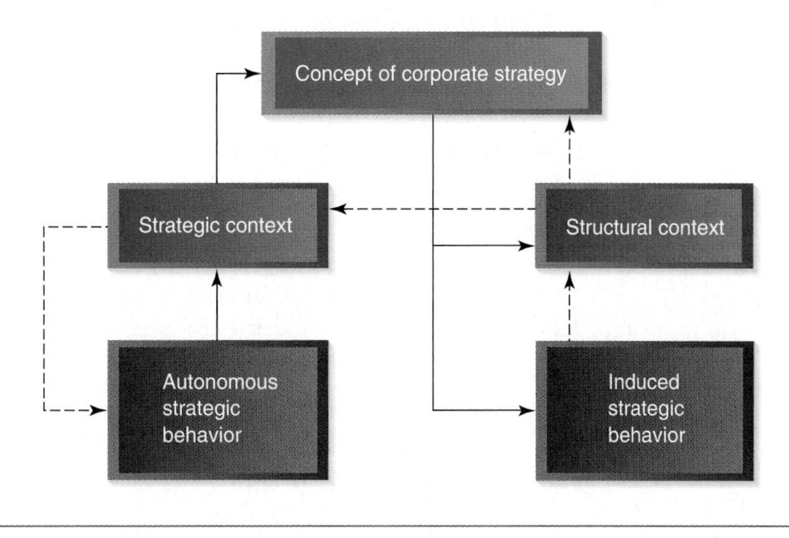

SOURCE: Adapted from R. A. Burgelman, 1983, A model of the interactions of strategic behavior, corporate context, and the concept of strategy, *Academy of Management Review*, 8: 65.

GE depends on autonomous strategic behavior on a regular basis to produce innovations. Essentially, "the search for marketable services can start in any of GE's myriad businesses. [For example], an operating unit seeks out appropriate technology to better do what it already does. Having mastered the technology, it then incorporates it into a service it can sell to others." In response to frequent crisis calls and requests from customers, GE's Industrial Systems division took six months to develop a program that uses artificial intelligence to help assign field engineers to customer sites. Quite sophisticated, the program handles thousands of constraints while making assignments. The division's customer relationship manager was a champion for this product. The manager observed that the program "reduced the average time to dispatch an engineer from 18 hours to 4 hours."[58] In addition to facilitating the operations of one of GE's units, the program is being sold as a marketable item that developed through autonomous strategic behavior.

Changing the concept of corporate-level strategy through autonomous strategic behavior results when a product is championed within strategic and structural contexts (see Figure 13.1). The strategic context is the process used to arrive at strategic decisions (often requiring political processes to gain acceptance). The best firms keep changing their strategic context and strategies because of the continuous changes in the current competitive landscape. Thus, some believe that the most competitively successful firms reinvent their industry or develop a completely new one across time as they engage in competition with current and future rivals.[59]

To be effective, an autonomous process for developing new products requires that new knowledge be continuously diffused throughout the firm. In particular, the diffusion of tacit knowledge is important for development of more effective new products.[60] Interestingly, some of the processes important for the promotion of autonomous new product development behavior vary by the environment and country in which a firm operates. For example, the Japanese culture is high on uncertainty avoidance. As such, research has found that Japanese firms are more likely to engage in autonomous behaviors under conditions of low uncertainty.[61]

GM is trying to develop a process that resembles autonomous strategic behavior as explained in the Strategic Focus on page 422 about the best new products. Robert Lutz feels GM must change its approach in order to develop more competitive products and break away from the tradition of incremental innovations. To do so, it must change older practices that are more similar to induced strategic behavior.

Induced Strategic Behavior

Induced strategic behavior is a top-down process whereby the firm's current strategy and structure foster product innovations that are closely associated with that strategy and structure.

The second of the two forms of internal corporate venturing, **induced strategic behavior,** is a top-down process whereby the firm's current strategy and structure foster product innovations that are closely associated with that strategy and structure. In this form of venturing, the strategy in place is filtered through a matching structural hierarchy. Some of the best new products described in the Strategic Focus on page 422 were developed through induced strategic behavior.

Implementing New Product Development and Internal Ventures

To be innovative and develop internal ventures requires an *entrepreneurial mind-set.* In Chapter 12, we discuss an entrepreneurial orientation that includes several dimensions, such as risk propensity. Clearly, firms and individuals must be willing to take risks in order to commercialize new products. While they must continuously attempt to identify opportunities, they must also select and pursue the best opportunities and do so with discipline. Thus, employing an *entrepreneurial mind-set* entails not only developing new products and markets but also an emphasis on execution. According to Rita McGrath and Ian MacMillan, those with an entrepreneurial mind-set "engage the energies of everyone in their domain," both inside and outside the organization.[62]

Having processes and structures in place through which a firm can successfully implement the outcomes of internal corporate ventures and commercialize the innovations is critical. The successful introduction of innovations into the marketplace reflects implementation effectiveness.[63] In the context of internal corporate ventures, processes are the "patterns of interaction, coordination, communication, and decision making employees use" to convert the innovations resulting from either autonomous or induced strategic behaviors into successful market entries.[64] As we described in Chapter 11, organizational structures are the sets of formal relationships supporting organizational processes.

Effective integration of the various functions involved in innovation processes—from engineering to manufacturing and, ultimately, market distribution—is required to implement (that is, to effectively use) the innovations that result from internal corporate ventures.[65] Increasingly, product development teams are being used to integrate the activities associated with different organizational functions. Product development teams are commonly used to produce cross-functional integration. Such coordination involves coordinating and applying the knowledge and skills of different functional areas in order to maximize innovation.[66]

Cross-Functional Product Development Teams

Cross-functional teams facilitate efforts to integrate activities associated with different organizational functions, such as design, manufacturing, and marketing. In addition, new product development processes can be completed more quickly and the products more easily commercialized when cross-functional teams work effectively.[67] Using cross-functional teams, product development stages are grouped into parallel or overlapping processes to allow the firm to tailor its product development efforts to its unique core competencies and to the needs of the market.

Horizontal organizational structures support the use of cross-functional teams in their efforts to integrate innovation-based activities across organizational functions.[68] Therefore, instead of being built around vertical hierarchical functions or departments, the organization is built around core horizontal processes that are used to produce and manage innovations. Some of the core horizontal processes that are critical to innovation efforts are formal; they may be defined and documented as procedures and practices. More commonly, however, these processes are informal: "They are routines or ways of working that evolve over time."[69] Often invisible, informal processes are critical to successful product innovations and are supported properly through horizontal organizational structures more so than through vertical organizational structures.

GM's president of North America operations and vice chairman of product development, Robert Lutz, is pictured here with the Pontiac Solstice roadster concept vehicle.

Two primary barriers that may prevent the successful use of cross-functional teams as a means of integrating organizational functions are independent frames of reference of team members and organizational politics.[70]

Team members working within a distinct specialization (i.e., a particular organizational function) may have an independent frame of reference typically based on common backgrounds and experiences. They are likely to use the same decision criteria to evaluate issues such as product development efforts as they do within their functional units. Research suggests that functional departments vary along four dimensions: time orientation, interpersonal orientation, goal orientation, and formality of structure.[71] Thus, individuals from different functional departments having different orientations on these dimensions can be expected to perceive product development activities in different ways. For example, a design engineer may consider the characteristics that make a product functional and workable to be the most important of the product's characteristics. Alternatively, a person from the marketing function may hold characteristics that satisfy customer needs most important. These different orientations can create barriers to effective communication across functions.[72]

Organizational politics is the second potential barrier to effective integration in cross-functional teams. In some organizations, considerable political activity may center on allocating resources to different functions. Interunit conflict may result from aggressive competition for resources among those representing different organizational functions. This dysfunctional conflict between functions creates a barrier to their integration.[73] Methods must be found to achieve cross-functional integration without excessive political conflict and without changing the basic structural characteristics necessary for task specialization and efficiency.

Facilitating Integration and Innovation

Shared values and effective leadership are important to achieve cross-functional integration and implement innovation.[74] Highly effective shared values are framed around the firm's strategic intent and mission, and become the glue that promotes integration between functional units. Thus, the firm's culture promotes unity and internal innovation.[75]

Strategic leadership is also highly important for achieving cross-functional integration and promoting innovation. Leaders set the goals and allocate resources. The goals include integrated development and commercialization of new goods and services. Effective strategic leaders remind organizational members continuously of the value of product innovations. In the most desirable situations, this value-creating potential becomes the basis for the integration and management of functional department activities.

Effective strategic leaders also ensure a high quality communication system to facilitate cross-functional integration. A critical benefit of effective communication is the sharing of knowledge among team members.[76] Effective communication thus helps create synergy and gains team members' commitment to an innovation throughout the organization. Shared values and leadership practices shape the communication systems that are formed to support the development and commercialization of new products.[77]

Creating Value from Innovation

The model in Figure 13.2 shows how the firm can create value from the internal processes it uses to develop and commercialize new goods and services. An entrepreneurial mind-set is necessary so that managers and employees will consistently try to identify entrepreneurial opportunities that the firm can pursue by developing new goods and services and new markets. Cross-functional teams are important to promote integrated new product design ideas and commitment to their implementation thereafter. Effective leadership and shared values promote integration and vision for

Figure 13.2 Creating Value through Internal Innovation Processes

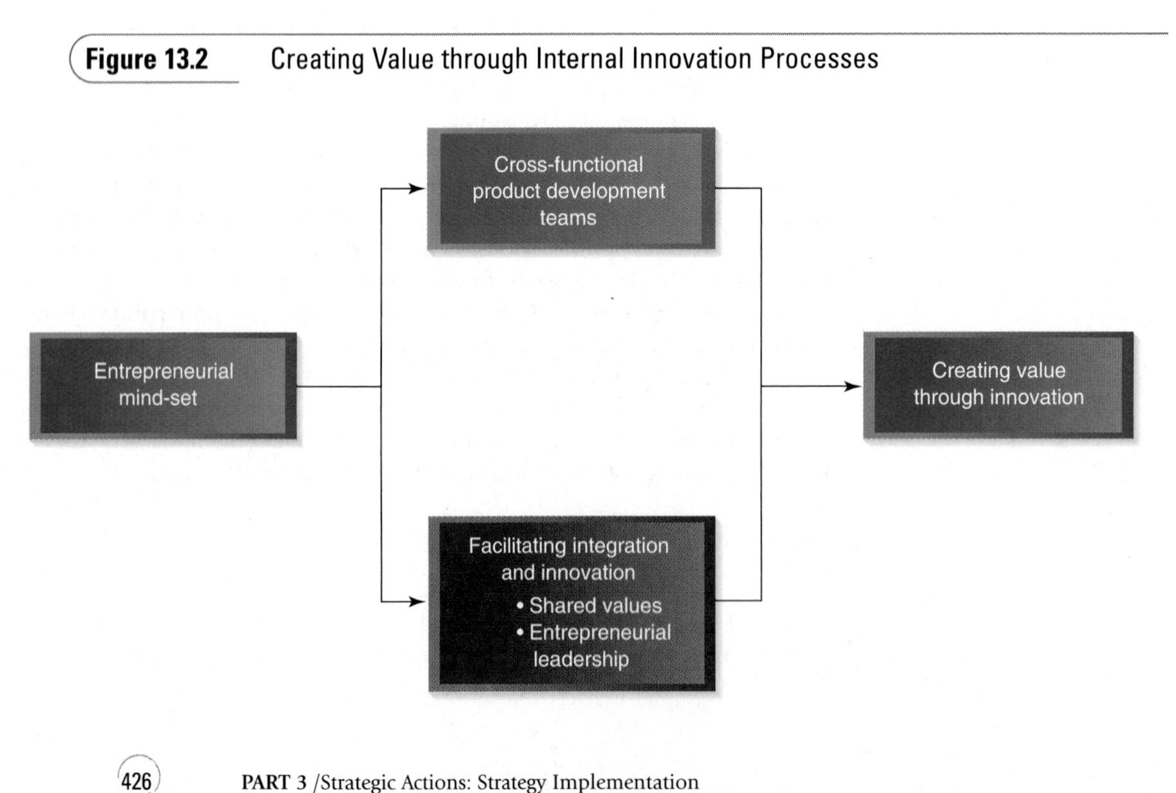

innovation and commitment to it. The end result for the firm is the creation of value for the customers and shareholders through development and commercialization of new products.[78]

Cooperative Strategies for Entrepreneurship and Innovation

It is unlikely that a firm possesses all the knowledge and resources required for it to be entrepreneurial and innovative in dynamic competitive markets. Knowledge and resources are needed to develop new products and serve new markets.[79] To successfully commercialize inventions, firms may therefore choose to cooperate with other organizations and integrate their knowledge and resources. Entrepreneurial new ventures, for example, may seek investment capital as well as the distribution capabilities of more established firms to implement a new product idea and introduce it to the market.[80] Alternatively, more established companies may need new technological knowledge and can gain access to it through alliances with newer entrepreneurial firms.[81] Alliances between large pharmaceutical firms and biotechnology companies have increasingly been formed to integrate the knowledge and resources of both to develop new products and bring them to market.[82] With increasing frequency, alliances are used to produce or manage innovations. To innovate through a cooperative relationship, firms must share their knowledge and skills.[83]

Microsoft and Intel—two corporations that have earned considerable profits from the personal computer markets with their software and computer chips, respectively— formed an alliance to develop similar innovations in the mobile phone market. They are creating the same "Wintel duopoly" that they used in the PC market in an attempt to replicate their business model for the high end of the mobile phone market. In 2002, the two companies announced that they were cooperating to provide their software and chips to allow other firms to enter the market and compete successfully against the industry leader, Nokia. Essentially, they are developing complementary new products that will make mobile phones more like computers. Through this alliance, Microsoft and Intel are combining their technological expertise (knowledge) in an attempt to develop the standard technology for cell phones. In this case, both firms are integrating their technological expertise to successfully commercialize their complementary technologically-based products for cell phones.[84]

Because of the importance of alliances, particularly in the development of new technology and in commercializing innovations, firms are beginning to build networks of alliances that represent a form of social capital to them. This social capital in the form of relationships with other firms helps them to obtain the knowledge and other resources necessary to develop innovations.[85] Knowledge from these alliances helps firms develop new capabilities.[86] Some firms now even allow external firms to participate in their internal new product development processes. It is not uncommon for firms to have supplier representatives on their cross-functional innovation teams because of the importance of the suppliers' input to ensure quality materials for any new product developed.[87]

However, alliances formed for the purpose of innovation are not without risks. An important risk is that a partner will appropriate a firm's technology or knowledge and use it to enhance its own competitive abilities.[88] To prevent or at least minimize this risk, firms, particularly new ventures, need to select their partners carefully. The ideal partnership is one in which the firms have complementary skills, as well as compatible strategic goals.[89] However, because firms are operating in a network of firms and thus may be participating in multiple alliances simultaneously, they encounter challenges in managing the alliances.[90] Research has shown that firms can become involved in too many alliances, which can harm rather than facilitate their innovation capabilities.[91] Thus, effectively managing the cooperative relationships to produce innovation is critical.

Strategic Focus

Seeking Growth through Internal Development or Acquisitions

The capital market values growth, and firms therefore seek growth in multiple ways. Creating new products through invention and commercializing them through innovation are important means of organizational growth. For example, innovation has been a primary means of growth for 3M; it has developed a reputation for being an innovative company. However, 3M CEO Jim McNerney has a goal of doubling 3M's rate of growth in sales and earnings in 10 years. He does not believe that it can be accomplished only through new products developed by 3M's 7,000-strong R&D work force that operates with an annual budget of $1 billion. McNerney suggests that he will have to make several acquisitions to supplement the innovations produced by 3M's R&D operations.

While acquisitions can be expensive, as explained in Chapter 7, R&D is costly as well. For example, Campbell Soup's CEO, Doug Conant, announced in 2002 that the company was cutting dividends to shareholders in order to increase its investment in R&D. The firm's intent is to develop new products and improve the quality of Campbell's existing product lines in soups and snacks. Analysts expressed concern with the time required for Conant's strategy to work. Computer Associates, long known for its growth through acquisitions, announced in 2002 that it was foregoing major acquisitions in order to invest more in internal development of new products.

Acquisitions can provide access to new products more quickly than additional investments in R&D. For example, Carlos Gutierrez, CEO of Kellogg, dramatically changed his firm's product mix with its acquisition of Keebler Foods for $4.4 billion. Before the acquisition, 75 percent of Kellogg's sales revenues came from cereal products. After the acquisition, 60 percent of the firm's sales came from non-cereal products. The acquisition of Keebler provided Kellogg with faster growth products along with an effective distribution system.

Merck traditionally has had a policy of growth through internally developed new products. Merck faces the expiration of patents on several of its primary drug products, which will reduce its sales revenues (and profits) if it does not introduce new drugs to replace them. Its new pain reliever drug, Vioxx, has not done as well in the market as hoped. Accordingly, in 2001–2002, Merck faced increasing pressure from its shareholders to acquire a firm with several new drugs. However, Merck CEO Raymond Gilmartin considers the firm's core competence to be the capability to "turn cutting-edge science into medical breakthroughs." Merck's future may rest on its continued ability to introduce valuable pharmaceutical innovations without making acquisitions.

SOURCES: S. Hamm, 2002, A long climb out of a deep rut, *Business Week*, February 25, 124–125; M. Kwak, 2002, Shopping for R&D, *MIT Sloan Management Review*, 43(2): 9–10; G. Dyer & A. Michaels, 2002, Merck in need of fix to get off the sick list, *Financial Times*, http://www.ft.com, January 22; M. Arndt, 2002, 3M: A lab for growth, *Business Week*, January 21, 50–51; A. Edgecliffe-Johnson, 2001, Campbell cuts to revive its brands, *Financial Times*, http://www.ft.com, July 29; J. Muller, 2001, Thinking outside of the cereal box, *Business Week*, January 15, 54–55.

Acquisitions to Buy Innovation

The Strategic Focus above describes several situations where firms have made or plan to make acquisitions to supplement their product line. One of the reasons that firms turn to acquisitions is the capital market values growth; acquisitions provide a means to rapidly extend the product line and increase the firm's revenues. 3M likely cannot achieve its growth goals without acquiring other companies. Kellogg changed its product mix quickly by acquiring Keebler. Firms can acquire firms with new products or new product development capability. Usually, investing in R&D does not produce new products rapidly. Analysts are concerned that Campbell Soup's new investments in R&D may not achieve new products and growth fast enough to satisfy the capital market.

Similar to internal corporate venturing and strategic alliances, acquisitions are not a risk-free approach to producing and managing innovations. A key risk of acquisitions is that a firm may substitute an ability to buy innovations for an ability to produce innovations internally. In support of this contention, research shows that firms engaging in acquisitions introduce fewer new products into the market.[92] This substitution may take place because firms lose strategic control and focus instead on financial control of their original and especially of their acquired business units. This outcome is evident on page 428 in the Strategic Focus description of Merck, which chose to avoid acquisitions to emphasize its R&D process to develop innovations.

We noted in Chapter 7 that firms can also learn new capabilities from acquired firms. As such, firms can gain capabilities to produce innovation from an acquired firm. Additionally, firms that emphasize innovation and carefully select companies for acquisition that also emphasize innovation are likely to remain innovative.[93]

Capital for Entrepreneurial Ventures

Venture capital is a resource that is typically allocated to entrepreneurs who are involved in projects with high growth potential. The intent of venture capitalists is to achieve a high rate of return on the funds they invest.[94] In the late 1990s, the number of venture capital firms and the amount of capital invested in new ventures reached unprecedented levels. The amount of venture capital invested in new ventures reached a high of $46.1 billion in 1999.[95] Venture capitalists desire to receive large returns on their investments and take major risks by investing in new ventures. Research has shown that venture capitalists may earn large returns or experience significant losses. For example, one study found that 34 percent of venture capitalists experienced a loss, while 23 percent gained a rate of return on their investments of 50 percent or greater.[96]

For the decade of the 1990s, the top quintile of performers in the *Standard & Poor 500* had average annual growth in revenues and earnings of 20.6 percent and 29.3 percent, respectively. Furthermore, these firms provided average annual returns to their shareholders of 34 percent.[97] Additional research showed that 90 percent of these high-performing firms had created and successfully commercialized a radical innovation or developed a fundamental new business model in an existing industry, both indicative of an entrepreneurial firm.[98]

Venture capitalists place weight on the competence of the entrepreneur or the human capital in the firms in which they consider investing. They also weigh the expected scope of competitive rivalry the firm is likely to experience and the degree of instability in the market addressed.[99] However, the characteristics of the entrepreneur or firm in which venture capitalists invest as well as the rate of return expected will vary with the type of venture in which investments are made.[100]

Increasingly, venture capital is being used to support the acquisition of innovations. To provide such support, some firms establish their own venture-capital divisions. These divisions carefully evaluate other companies to identify those with innovations or innovative capabilities that might yield a competitive advantage. In other instances, a firm might decide to serve as an internal source of capital for innovative product ideas that can be spun off as independent or affiliated firms. New enterprises that are backed by venture capital provide an important source of innovation and new technology. The amount of corporate venture capital invested grew exponentially at the end of the 1990s and in 2000. For example, it grew from about

$2 billion in 1998 to almost $11 billion in 1999. In 2000, the amount of corporate venture capital invested was slightly over $18 billion.[101]

Some relatively new ventures are able to obtain capital through initial public offerings (IPOs). Firms that offer new stock in this way must have high potential in order to sell their stock and obtain adequate capital to finance the growth and development of the firm. This form of capital can be substantial and is often much larger than the amounts obtained from venture capitalists. Investment bankers frequently play major roles in the development and offering of IPOs. Research has shown that founder-managed firms generally receive lower returns from IPOs than professionally managed firms.[102] The IPO market values experienced managers more than founders who frequently do not have substantial managerial experience. JetBlue Airways created a lot of interest from investors because of its low costs, strong customer demand, and highly experienced CEO (who also happens to be the firm's founder).[103] Investors believe that the firm with an experienced CEO is more likely to succeed. Also, firms that have received venture capital backing usually receive greater returns from IPOs.[104]

The Strategic Focus on page 431 explains that the capital for new ventures was difficult to obtain in 2001–2002, when the downturn in the stock market dried up the IPO market. Moreover, the substantial losses by venture capitalists in the high technology sector reduced the amount of capital available for investment in new ventures. Still, some capital was available, and these investors were able to obtain attractive terms for their capital investments.

Creating Value through Strategic Entrepreneurship

Newer entrepreneurial firms often are more effective than larger firms in identifying opportunities. Some believe that these firms tend to be more innovative as well because of their flexibility and willingness to take risks. Alternatively, larger and well-established firms often have more resources and capabilities to exploit opportunities that are identified.[105] So, younger, entrepreneurial firms are generally opportunity seeking, and more established firms are advantage seeking. However, to compete effectively in the landscape of the 21st century, firms must identify and exploit opportunities but do so while achieving and sustaining a competitive advantage.[106] Thus, newer entrepreneurial firms must learn how to gain a competitive advantage, and older more established firms must relearn how to identify entrepreneurial opportunities. The concept of strategic entrepreneurship suggests that firms can be simultaneously entrepreneurial and strategic regardless of their size and age.

To be entrepreneurial, firms must develop an entrepreneurial mind-set among their managers and employees. Managers must emphasize the development of their resources, particularly human capital and social capital. The importance of knowledge to identify and exploit opportunities as well as to gain and sustain a competitive advantage suggests that firms must have strong human capital.[107] Social capital is critical for access to comple-

JetBlue Airways founder and CEO David Neeleman speaks at the firm's highly successful initial public offering of stock in his firm. Neeleman, who refers to his company not as an airline but as a services company, says of his employees, "We don't want jaded people working here. If you don't like people or can't deal with rude customers, you'll be fired."

AP PHOTO/RICHARD DREW

Strategic Focus

Sources of Capital for Entrepreneurial Ventures

Early in their development, biotechnology firms received strong support from the capital market and several of them were able to raise significant capital through IPOs. When the stock market entered a downturn in late 2000 and 2001, biotech firms needing capital had to turn instead to venture capitalists. The investors obtained attractive terms from these firms to provide them with needed capital.

IPOs provided biotech firms with between $10 billion and $11 billion in 2000 but provided only about $3 billion in 2001. Alternatively, biotech firms received about $5 billion from venture capitalists in 1998-1999, but received about $17 billion in 2000-2001. Many other new venture high technology firms also received venture capital in the late 1990s and into 2000. For example, venture capitalists invested $98 billion in U.S. new ventures in 2000. Such amounts were prompted by results such as the approximately 100,000 percent return earned by venture capitalists that invested early in eBay. A McKinsey study, however, showed that in the 1990s venture capitalists earned an average return of 13.4 percent, compared to 12.1 percent earned by public equity firms. The difference is not large, considering the significant difference in risk taken by the two on their investments.

In 2001, many venture capitalists were hurting. The rapid decline in 2001–2002 of the dot.com firms in which they had invested substantial venture capital placed many venture capitalists in a crisis mode. Thus, new venture firms experienced difficulty in obtaining the necessary capital to survive and grow.

One unique form of venture capital fund is the Markle Foundation. President Zoe Baird invests the funds to create social change. The funds are invested in for-profit companies, usually as foundation investments in firms that are developing interactive media that will improve people's lives. Example investments include projects to reunite missing children with their families in West Africa and other projects in Kosovo. The foundation has invested in Global Forest Watch. This program tracks the degradation of old forests and firms working in them and posts the results on the Internet to stop companies (and governments) from cheating on the amount of trees that are cut. Another investment by the Markle Foundation supports a polling organization on issues of interest to women.

Most venture capitalists invest to earn a good return, but events beyond recessions and stock market downturns can harm the venture capital markets. For example, the events on September 11 had a negative effect on venture capital investments. The financial services firm of Cantor Fitzgerald, with its offices on the top five floors of one of the World Trade Center towers, was literally destroyed when the airliner struck the tower. This event severely harmed new ventures that were to receive venture capital from the firm, such as Livewire International. Craig Souser, the entrepreneur who started Livewire, was to receive the first payment of $1 million in cash from Cantor Fitzgerald on September 11. It did not come, and Livewire was able to persevere only by making substantial reductions in its operations.

SOURCES: A. Barrett & E. Licking, 2002, In biotech, private cash is king, *Business Week,* February 18, 90; J. Harwood & B. Gruley, 2001, How Sept. 11 upended the life and work of one entrepreneur, *The Wall Street Journal,* December 28, A4; 2001, Silicon Valley's venture capitalists face cash burn, *Financial Times,* http://www.ft.com, August 18; J. Reingold, 2001, Fast foundation, *Fast Company,* February, 124–133.

mentary resources from partners in order to compete effectively in domestic and international markets.[108]

There remain many entrepreneurial opportunities in international markets. Thus, firms should seek to enter and compete in international markets. Firms can learn new technologies and management practices from international markets and diffuse this knowledge throughout the firm. Furthermore, the knowledge firms gain can contribute to their innovations. Research has shown that firms operating in international markets tend to be more innovative.[109] Small and large firms are now regularly moving into international markets. Both types of firms must also be innovative to compete effectively. Thus, developing resources (human and social capital), taking advantage of opportunities in domestic and international markets, and using the resources and knowledge gained in these markets to be innovative, firms achieve competitive advantages. In so doing, they create value for their customers and shareholders.

Firms that practice strategic entrepreneurship contribute to a country's economic development. In fact, some countries such as Ireland have made dramatic economic progress by changing the institutional rules for business operating in the country. This could be construed as a form of institutional entrepreneurship. Likewise, firms that seek to establish their technology as a standard, also representing institutional entrepreneurship, are engaging in strategic entrepreneurship because creating a standard produces a sustainable competitive advantage for the firm.[110]

Research shows that because of its economic importance and individual motives, entrepreneurial activity is increasing across the globe. Furthermore, more women are becoming entrepreneurs because of the economic opportunity entrepreneurship provides and the individual independence it affords.[111] In future years, entrepreneurial activity may increase the wealth of less affluent countries and continue to contribute to the economic development of the more affluent countries. Regardless, the companies that practice strategic entrepreneurship are likely to be the winners in the 21st century.[112]

Summary

- Strategic entrepreneurship is taking entrepreneurial actions using a strategic perspective. More specifically, it involves engaging in simultaneous opportunity seeking and competitive advantage seeking behaviors to design and implement entrepreneurial strategies to create wealth.
- The concepts of entrepreneurial opportunity, innovation, and capabilities are important to firms. Entrepreneurial opportunities represent conditions in which new products or services can satisfy a need in the market. The essence of entrepreneurship is to identify and exploit these opportunities. Innovation is the process of commercializing the products or processes that surfaced through invention. Entrepreneurial capabilities include building an entrepreneurial culture, having a passion for the business, and having a desire for measured risk.
- Increasingly, entrepreneurship is being practiced in many countries. As used by entrepreneurs, entrepreneurship and corporate entrepreneurship are strongly related to a nation's economic growth. This relationship is a primary reason for the increasing use of entrepreneurship and corporate entrepreneurship in countries throughout the global economy.
- Three basic approaches are used to produce and manage innovation: internal corporate venturing, strategic alliances, and acquisitions. Autonomous strategic behavior and induced strategic behavior are the two processes of internal corporate venturing. Autonomous strategic behavior is a bottom-up process through which a product champion facilitates the commercialization of an innovative good or service. Induced strategic behavior is a top-down process in which a firm's current strategy and structure facilitate product or process innovations that are associated with them. Thus, induced strategic behavior is driven by the organization's current corporate strategy, structure, and reward and control systems.
- To create incremental and radical innovation requires effective innovation processes and practices. Increasingly, cross-functional integration is vital to a firm's efforts to develop and implement internal corporate venturing activities and to commercialize the resulting innovation. Additionally, integration and innovation can be facilitated by the development of shared values and the practice of entrepreneurial leadership.
- In the complex global economy, it is difficult for an individual firm to possess all the knowledge needed to innovate consistently and effectively. To gain access to the kind of specialized knowledge that often is required to innovate, firms may form a cooperative relationship such as a strategic alliance with other firms, sometimes even with competitors.
- Acquisitions provide another means for firms to produce and manage innovation. Innovation can be acquired through direct acquisition, or firms can learn new capabilities from an acquisition, thereby enriching their internal innovation processes.

- Entrepreneurial activity requires capital for development. Venture capitalists are a prime source for this capital. The amount of venture capital available increased dramatically in the decade of the 1990s. While it decreased recently due to economic problems, it remains much higher than in earlier years. Initial public offerings (IPOs) also have become a common means of obtaining capital for new ventures.
- The practice of strategic entrepreneurship by all types of firms, large and small, new and more established, creates value for all stakeholders, especially for shareholders and customers. Strategic entrepreneurship also contributes to the economic development of entire nations. Thus, entrepreneurial activity is increasing throughout the world.

Review Questions

1. What is strategic entrepreneurship? What is its importance for firms competing in the global economy?
2. What are entrepreneurial opportunities, innovation, and entrepreneurial capabilities, and what is their importance?
3. Why is international entrepreneurship important and why is it increasing across the globe?
4. What is autonomous strategic behavior? What is induced strategic behavior?
5. How do firms use strategic alliances to help them produce innovation?
6. How can a firm use acquisitions to increase the number of innovations it produces and improve its capability to produce innovations?
7. What is the importance of venture capital and initial public offerings to entrepreneurial activity?
8. How does strategic entrepreneurship create value for customers and shareholders and contribute to economic development?

Experiential Exercise

Strategic Entrepreneurship

Assume that you are a partner in a new venture energy company called Currence. You have approached an investor group for capital to fund the first three years of your operation. Following the preliminary presentation, you find that the group is very impressed by Currence and by its six start-up partners, each of whom brings unique, yet critical skills, experience, contacts, and other knowledge to the venture. Before the investor group decides to fund your company, however, it has asked for a brief presentation about how the Currence partners will be rewarded.

Part 1 (complete individually). Indicate how Currence will determine the approximate salary, fringe benefits, and shares of stock (as a percentage) each partner will be allocated upon closing the financing of your new venture. Also indicate your rationale for these amounts.

Part 2 (in small groups). Compare your responses to Part 1 with others in your small group. Reach a consensus on the criteria your small group would use to determine how to reward each partner. Appoint one small group member to present your consensus and how your team reached it to the class.

Part 3 (in small groups). Following the presentations in Part 2, discuss the following issues and indicate any important lessons and implications:

1. Why would an entrepreneurial venture such as Currence be asked to provide this type of information to an investor group?
2. What criteria did the groups use concerning salaries and stock? Why?
3. What patterns did you perceive in the approaches taken by each team?
4. Did the groups make salaries or stock equal for all Currence partners? Why or why not? What reasons would there be for providing different rewards for different partners?
5. How difficult was it for the small groups to reach a consensus?

Notes

1. S. M. Camp, L. W. Cox, & B. Kotalik, 2001, *The Hallmarks of Entrepreneurial Excellence: 2001 Survey of Innovative Practices,* Kauffman Center for Entrepreneurial Leadership, Ewing Marion Kauffman Foundation.
2. M. A. Hitt, R. D. Ireland, S. M. Camp, & D. L. Sexton, 2002, Strategic entrepreneurship: Integrating entrepreneurial and strategic management perspectives. In M. A. Hitt, R. D. Ireland, S. M. Camp, & D. L. Sexton (eds.), *Strategic Entrepreneurship: Creating a New Mindset,* Oxford, U.K.: Blackwell Publishers, 1–16: M. A. Hitt, R. D. Ireland, S. M. Camp, & D. L. Sexton, 2001, Strategic entrepreneurship: Entrepreneurial strategies for wealth creation, *Strategic Management Journal,* 22(Special Issue): 479–491; R. D. Ireland, M. A. Hitt, S. M. Camp, & D.L. Sexton, 2001, Integrating entrepreneurship and strategic management actions to create firm wealth, *Academy of Management Executive,* 15(1): 49–63.
3. R. D. Ireland & M. A. Hitt, 1999, Achieving and maintaining strategic competitiveness in the 21st century: The role of strategic leadership, *Academy of Management Executive,* 13(1): 43–57.
4. H. Lee, M. A. Hitt, & E. K. Jeong, 2002, The impact of CEO and TMT characteristics on strategic flexibility and firm performance, working paper, University of Connecticut; M. E. Raynor, 2001, *Strategic Flexibility in the Financial Services Industry: Creating Competitive Advantage Out of Competitive Turbulence,* New York: Deloitte Research.
5. G. Hamel, 2000, *Leading the Revolution,* Boston, MA: Harvard Business School Press.
6. S. Michael, D. Storey, & H. Thomas, 2002, Discovery and coordination in strategic management and entrepreneurship. In M. A. Hitt, R. D. Ireland, S. M. Camp, & D. L. Sexton (eds.), *Strategic Entrepreneurship: Creating a New Mindset,* Oxford, U.K.: Blackwell Publishers, 45-65.
7. M. A. Hitt, R. D. Nixon, P. G. Clifford, & K. P. Coyne, 1999, The development and use of strategic resources. In M. A. Hitt, P. G. Clifford, R. D. Nixon, & K. P. Coyne (eds.), 1999, *Dynamic Strategic Resources: Development, Diffusion and Integration,* Chichester: John Wiley & Sons, Ltd., 1–14.
8. T. W. Y. Man, T. Lau, & K. F. Chan, 2002, The competitiveness of small and medium enterprises: A conceptualization with focus on entrepreneurial competencies, *Journal of Business Venturing,* 17: 123–142.
9. J. Schumpeter, 1934, *The Theory of Economic Development,* Cambridge, MA: Harvard University Press.
10. S. Shane & S. Venkataraman, 2000, The promise of entrepreneurship as a field of research, *Academy of Management Review,* 25: 217-226.
11. B. R. Barringer & A. C. Bluedorn, 1999, The relationship between corporate entrepreneurship and strategic management, *Strategic Management Journal,* 20: 421–444.
12. G. D. Meyer, H. M. Neck, & M. D. Meeks, 2002, The entrepreneurship-strategic management interface. In M. A. Hitt, R. D. Ireland, S. M. Camp & D. L. Sexton (eds.), *Strategic Entrepreneurship: Creating a New Mindset,* Oxford, U.K.: Blackwell Publishers, 19–44; I. Kirzner, 1997, Entrepreneurial discovery and the competitive market process: An Austrian approach, *Journal of Economic Literature,* 35 (1): 60–85.
13. R. G. McGrath & I. MacMillan, 2000, *The Entrepreneurial Mindset,* Boston, MA: Harvard Business School Press.
14. G. Gori, 2001, An American directs Mexico City's cinema revival, *The New York Times,* http://www.nytimes.com, July 15.
15. P. F. Drucker, 1998, The discipline of innovation, *Harvard Business Review,* 76(6): 149–157.
16. P. D. Reynolds, M. Hay, & S. M. Camp, 1999, *Global Entrepreneurship Monitor, 1999 Executive Report,* Babson Park, MA.: Babson College.
17. R. M. Kanter, 1999, From spare change to real change: The social sector as beta site for business innovation, *Harvard Business Review,* 77(3): 122–132.
18. Hamel, *Leading the Revolution;* R. Price, 1996, Technology and strategic advantage, *California Management Review,* 38(3): 38–56; L. G. Franko, 1989, Global corporate competition: Who's winning, who's losing and the R&D factor as one reason why, *Strategic Management Journal,* 10: 449–474.
19. G. T. Lumpkin & G. G. Dess, 1996, Clarifying the entrepreneurial orientation construct and linking it to performance, *Academy of Management Review,* 21: 135–172; K. M. Kelm, V. K. Narayanan, & G. E. Pinches, 1995, Shareholder value creation during R&D innovation and commercialization stages, *Academy of Management Journal,* 38: 770–786.
20. M. A. Hitt, R. D. Nixon, R. E. Hoskisson, & R. Kochhar, 1999, Corporate entrepreneurship and cross-functional fertilization: Activation, process and disintegration of a new product design team, *Entrepreneurship: Theory and Practice,* 23(3): 145–167.
21. Schumpeter, *The Theory of Economic Development.*
22. P. Sharma & J. L. Chrisman, 1999, Toward a reconciliation of the definitional issues in the field of corporate entrepreneurship, *Entrepreneurship: Theory and Practice,* 23(3): 11–27; R. A. Burgelman & L. R. Sayles, 1986, *Inside Corporate Innovation: Strategy, Structure, and Managerial Skills,* New York: Free Press.
23. R. E. Hoskisson & L. W. Busenitz, 2002, Market uncertainty and learning distance in corporate entrepreneurship entry mode choice. In M. A. Hitt, R. D. Ireland, S. M. Camp, & D. L. Sexton (eds.), *Strategic Entrepreneurship: Creating a New Mindset,* Oxford, U.K.: Blackwell Publishers, 151–172.
24. J. S. Hornsby, D. F. Kuratko, & S. A. Zahra, 2002, Middle managers' perception of the internal environment for corporate entrepreneurship: Assessing a measurement scale, *Journal of Business Venturing,* 17: 253–273.
25. S. D. Sarasvathy, 2000, Seminar on research perspectives in entrepreneurship (1997), *Journal of Business Venturing,* 15: 1–57.
26. D. F. Kuratko, R. D. Ireland, & J. S. Hornsby, 2001, Improving firm performance through entrepreneurial actions: Acordia's corporate entrepreneurship strategy, *Academy of Management Executive,* 15(4): 60–71; J. Birkinshaw, 1999, The determinants and consequences of subsidiary initiative in multinational corporations, *Entrepreneurship: Theory and Practice,* 24(1): 9–36.
27. 2002, Apple unveils its latest iMac, *The Arizona Republic,* January 8, D8; P.-W. Tam, 2002, Apple unveils sleek new iMac design, hoping to revive struggling business, *The Wall Street Journal Interactive,* http://www.wsj.com, January 8.
28. T. Erickson, 2002, Entrepreneurial capital: The emerging venture's most important asset and competitive advantage, *Journal of Business Venturing,* 17: 275–290.
29. W. Tsai, 2001, Knowledge transfer in intraorganizational networks: Effects of network position and absorptive capacity on business unit innovation and performance, *Academy of Management Journal,* 44: 996–1004.
30. S. A. Zahra & G. George, 2002, Absorptive capacity: A review, reconceptualization, and extension, *Academy of Management Review,* 27: 185–203.
31. M. A. Hitt, L. Bierman, K. Shimizu, & R. Kochhar, 2001, Direct and moderating effects of human capital on strategy and performance in professional service firms: A resource-based perspective, *Academy of Management Journal,* 44: 13–28.
32. I. Bouty, 2000, Interpersonal and interaction influences on informal resource exchanges between R&D researchers across organizational boundaries, *Academy of Management Journal,* 43: 5–65.
33. 2001, Some like it hot, *Entrepreneur.com,* October 30.
34. T. W. Brailsford, 2001, Building a knowledge community at Hallmark Cards, *Research Technology Management,* 44 (5): 18–25.
35. R. G. McGrath, 2001, Exploratory learning, innovative capacity, and managerial oversight, *Academy of Management Journal,* 44: 118–131.
36. J. W. Lu & P. W. Beamish, 2001, The internationalization and performance of SMEs, *Strategic Management Journal,* 22(Special Issue): 565–585.
37. 2000, Staff reporter, Business innovation urged, *Irish Times,* 23.
38. J. E. Jackson, J. Klich, & V. Kontorovich, 1999, Firm creation and economic transitions, *Journal of Business Venturing,* 14: 427–450.
39. M. Kwak, 2002. What's the best commercialization strategy for startups? *MIT Sloan Management Review,* 43(3): 10.
40. P. D. Reynolds, S. M. Camp, W. D. Bygrave, E. Autio, & M. Hay, 2002, *Global Entrepreneurship Monitor,* Kauffman Center for Entrepreneurial Leadership, Ewing Marion Kauffman Foundation.
41. M. H. Morris, 1998, *Entrepreneurial Intensity: Sustainable Advantages for Individuals, Organizations, and Societies,* Westport, CT: Quorum Books, 85–86. M. H. Morris, D. L. Davis, & J. W. Allen, 1994, Fostering corporate entrepreneurship: Cross-cultural comparisons of the importance of individualism versus collectivism, *Journal of International Business Studies,* 25: 65–89.
42. S. A. Zahra & G. George, 2002, International entrepreneurship: The sate of the field and future research agenda. In M. A. Hitt, R. D. Ireland, S. M. Camp, & D. L. Sexton (eds.), *Strategic Entrepreneurship: Creating a New Mindset,* Oxford, U.K.: Blackwell Publishers, 255–288.
43. S. A. Zahra, R. D. Ireland, & M. A. Hitt, 2000, International expansion by new venture firms: International diversity, mode of market entry, technological learning and performance, *Academy of Management Journal,* 43: 925–950.
44. P. P. McDougall & B. M. Oviatt, 2000, International entrepreneurship: The intersection of two paths, *Academy of Management Journal,* 43: 902–908.
45. H. Barkema & O. Chvyrkov, 2002, What sort of top management team is needed at the helm of internationally diversified firms? In M. A. Hitt, R. D. Ireland, S. M. Camp & D. L. Sexton (eds.), *Strategic Entrepreneurship: Creating a New Mindset,* Oxford, U.K.: Blackwell Publishers, 290–305.
46. T. S. Frost, 2001, The geographic sources of foreign subsidiaries' innovations, *Strategic Management Journal,* 22: 101–122.

47. E. W. K. Tsang, 2002, Learning from overseas venturing experience: The case of Chinese family businesses, *Journal of Business Venturing,* 17: 21–40.
48. W. Kuemmerle, 2002, Home base and knowledge management in international ventures, *Journal of Business Venturing, 17*: 99–12.
49. R. Leifer, G. Colarelli, & M. Rice, 2001, Implementing radical innovation in mature firms: The role of hubs, *Academy of Management Executive,* 15(3): 102–113.
50. G. Ahuja & M. Lampert, 2001, Entrepreneurship in the large corporation: A longitudinal study of how established firms create breakthrough inventions, *Strategic Management Journal,* 22(Special Issue): 521–543.
51. Leifer, Collarelli, & Rice, Implementing radical innovation.
52. R. I. Sutton, 2002, Weird ideas that spark innovation, *MIT Sloan Management Review,* 43(2): 83–87.
53. K. G. Smith & D. Di Gregorio, 2002, Bisociation, discovery, and the role of entrepreneurial action. In M. A. Hitt, R. D. Ireland, S. M. Camp & D. L. Sexton (eds.), *Strategic Entrepreneurship: Creating a New Mindset,* Oxford, U.K.: Blackwell Publishers, 129–150.
54. Hoskisson & Busenitz, Market uncertainty and learning distance.
55. R. A. Burgelman, 1995, *Strategic Management of Technology and Innovation,* Boston: Irwin.
56. R. Leifer & M. Rice, 1999, Unnatural acts: Building the mature firm's capability for breakthrough innovation. In M. A. Hitt, P. G. Clifford, R. D. Nixon, & K. P. Coyne (eds.), *Dynamic Strategic Resources: Development, Diffusion and Integration,* Chichester: John Wiley & Sons, 433–453.
57. M. A. Hitt, R. D. Ireland, & H. Lee, 2000, Technological learning, knowledge management, firm growth and performance, *Journal of Engineering and Technology Management,* 17: 231–246; D. Leonard-Barton, 1995, *Wellsprings of Knowledge: Building and Sustaining the Sources of Innovation,* Cambridge, MA: Harvard Business School Press.
58. S. S. Rao, 2000, General Electric, software vendor, *Forbes,* January 24, 144–146.
59. H. W. Chesbrough, 2002, Making sense of corporate venture capital, *Harvard Business Review,* 80(3): 90–99; G. Hamel, 1997, Killer strategies that make shareholders rich, *Fortune,* June 23: 70–88.
60. M. Subramaniam & N. Venkatraman, 2001, Determinants of transnational new product development capability: Testing the influence of transferring and deploying tacit overseas knowledge, *Strategic Management Journal,* 22: 359–378.
61. M. Song & M. M. Montoya-Weiss, 2001, The effect of perceived technological uncertainty on Japanese new product development, *Academy of Management Journal,* 44: 61–80.
62. McGrath and MacMillan, *Entrepreneurial Mindset.*
63. 2002, Building scientific networks for effective innovation, *MIT Sloan Management Review,* 43(3): 14.
64. C. M. Christensen & M. Overdorf, 2000, Meeting the challenge of disruptive change, *Harvard Business Review,* 78(2): 66–77.
65. L. Yu, 2002, Marketers and engineers: Why can't we just get along? *MIT Sloan Management Review,* 43 (1):13.
66. P. S. Adler, 1995, Interdepartmental interdependence and coordination: The case of the design/manufacturing interface, *Organization Science,* 6: 147–167.
67. B. L. Kirkman & B. Rosen, 1999, Beyond self-management: Antecedents and consequences of team empowerment, *Academy of Management Journal,* 42: 58–74; A. R. Jassawalla & H. C. Sashittal, 1999, Building collaborative cross-functional new product teams, *Academy of Management Executive,* 13(3): 50–63.
68. Hitt, Nixon, Hoskisson, & Kochhar, Corporate entrepreneurship.
69. Christensen & Overdorf, 2000, Meeting the challenge of disruptive change.
70. Hitt, Nixon, Hoskisson, & Kochhar, Corporate entrepreneurship.
71. A. C. Amason, 1996, Distinguishing the effects of functional and dysfunctional conflict on strategic decision making: Resolving a paradox for top management teams, *Academy of Management Journal,* 39: 123–148; P. R. Lawrence & J. W. Lorsch, 1969, *Organization and Environment,* Homewood, IL: Richard D. Irwin.
72. D. Dougherty, L. Borrelli, K. Muncir, & A. O'Sullivan, 2000, Systems of organizational sensemaking for sustained product innovation, *Journal of Engineering and Technology Management,* 17: 321–355; D. Dougherty, 1992, Interpretive barriers to successful product innovation in large firms, *Organization Science,* 3: 179–202.
73. Hitt, Nixon, Hoskisson, & Kochhar, Corporate entrepreneurship.
74. E. C. Wenger & W. M. Snyder, 2000, Communities of practice: The organizational frontier, *Harvard Business Review,* 78(1): 139–144.
75. Hamel, *Leading the Revolution.*
76. McGrath & MacMillan, *Entrepreneurial Mindset.*
77. Hamel, *Leading the Revolution.*
78. Hitt, Ireland, Camp, & Sexton, Strategic entrepreneurship; S. W. Fowler, A. W. King, S. J. Marsh, & B. Victor, 2000, Beyond products: New strategic imperatives for developing competencies in dynamic environments, *Journal of Engineering and Technology Management,* 17: 357–377.
79. R. K. Kazanjian, R. Drazin, & M. A. Glynn, 2002, Implementing strategies for corporate entrepreneurship: A knowledge-based perspective. In M. A. Hitt, R. D. Ireland, S. M. Camp, & D. L. Sexton (eds.), *Strategic Entrepreneurship: Creating a New Mindset,* Oxford, U.K.: Blackwell Publishers, 173–199.
80. A. C. Cooper, 2002, Networks, alliances and entrepreneurship. In M. A. Hitt, R. D. Ireland, S. M. Camp & D. L. Sexton (eds.), *Strategic Entrepreneurship: Creating a New Mindset,* Oxford, U.K.: Blackwell Publishers, 204–222.
81. S. A. Alvarez & J. B. Barney, 2001, How entrepreneurial firms can benefit from alliances with large partners, *Academy of Management Executive,* 15(1): 139–148; F. T. Rothaermel, 2001, Incumbent's advantage through exploiting complementary assets via interfirm cooperation, *Strategic Management Journal,* 22(Special Issue): 687–699.
82. J. Hagedoorn & N. Roijakkers, 2002, Small entrepreneurial firms and large companies in inter-firm R&D networks—the international biotechnology industry. In M. A. Hitt, R. D. Ireland, S. M. Camp, & D. L. Sexton (eds.), *Strategic Entrepreneurship: Creating a New Mindset,* Oxford, U.K.: Blackwell Publishers, 223–252.
83. P. Kale, H. Singh, & H. Perlmutter, 2000, Learning and protection of proprietary assets in strategic alliances: Building relational capital, *Strategic Management Journal,* 21: 217–237.
84. D. Pringle, 2002, Wintel duo targets the cellphone, *The Wall Street Journal,* February 19, B1.
85. H. Yli-Renko, E. Autio, & H. J. Sapienza, 2001, Social capital, knowledge acquisition and knowledge exploitation in young technology-based firms, *Strategic Management Journal,* 22(Special Issue): 587–613.
86. C. Lee, K. Lee, & J. M. Pennings, 2001, Internal capabilities, external networks and performance: A study of technology-based ventures, *Strategic Management Journal,* 22(Special Issue): 615–640.
87. A. Takeishi, 2001, Bridging inter- and intra-firm boundaries: Management of supplier involvement in automobile product development, *Strategic Management Journal,* 22: 403–433.
88. R. D. Ireland, M. A. Hitt, & D. Vaidyanath, 2002, Strategic alliances as a pathway to competitive success, *Journal of Management,* in press.
89. M. A. Hitt, M. T. Dacin, E. Levitas, J.-L. Arregle, & A. Borza, 2000. Partner selection in emerging and developed market contexts: Resource-based and organizational learning perspectives, *Academy of Management Journal,* 43: 449–467.
90. J. J. Reuer, M. Zollo, & H. Singh, 2002, Post-formation dynamics in strategic alliances, *Strategic Management Journal,* 23: 135–151.
91. F. Rothaermel & D. Deeds, 2002, More good things are not always necessarily better: An empirical study of strategic alliances, experience effects, and new product development in high-technology start-ups. In M. A. Hitt, R. Amit, C. Lucier, & R. Nixon (eds.) *Creating Value: Winners in the New Business Environment,* Oxford, U.K.: Blackwell Publishers, 85–103.
92. M. A. Hitt, R. E. Hoskisson, R. A. Johnson, & D. D. Moesel, 1996, The market for corporate control and firm innovation, *Academy of Management Journal,* 39: 1084–1119.
93. M. A. Hitt, J. S. Harrison, & R. D. Ireland, 2001, *Mergers and Acquisitions: A Guide to Creating Value for Stakeholders,* New York: Oxford University Press.
94. J. A. Timmons, 1999, *New Venture Creation: Entrepreneurship for the 21st Century* (5th ed.), New York: Irwin/McGraw-Hill.
95. R. Amit, C. Lucier, M. A. Hitt, & R. D. Nixon, 2002, Strategies for the entrepreneurial millennium. In M. A. Hitt, R. Amit, C. Lucier & R. Nixon (eds.) *Creating Value: Winners in the New Business Environment,* Oxford, U.K.: Blackwell Publishers, 1–12.
96. C. M. Mason & R. T. Harrison, 2002, Is it worth it? The rates of return from informal venture capital investments, *Journal of Business Venturing,* 17: 211–236.
97. Amit, Lucier, Hitt, & Nixon, Strategies for the entrepreneurial millennium.
98. C. E. Lucier, L. H. Moeller, & R. Held, 1997, 10X value: The engine powering long-term shareholder returns, *Strategy & Business,* 8: 21–28.
99. D. A. Shepherd & A. Zacharakis, 2002, Venture capitalists' expertise: A call for research into decision aids and cognitive feedback, *Journal of Business Venturing,* 17: 1–20.
100. S. Manigart, K. de Waele, M. Wright, K. Robbie, P. Desbrieres, H. J. Sapienza, & A. Beekman, 2002, Determinants of required return in venture capital investments: A

five-country study, *Journal of Business Venturing,* 17: 291–312.

101. M. Maula & G. Murray, 2002, Corporate venture capital and the creation of U. S. public companies: The impact of sources of capital on the performance of portfolio companies. In M. A. Hitt, R. Amit, C. Lucier, & R. Nixon (eds.) *Creating Value: Winners in the New Business Environment,* Oxford, U.K.: Blackwell Publishers, 164–187.
102. S. T. Certo, J. G. Covin, C. M. Daily, & D. R. Dalton, 2001, Wealth and the effects of founder management among IPO-stage new ventures, *Strategic Management Journal,* 22(Special Issue): 641–658.
103. L. DeCarlo, 2002, JetBlue IPO will fly right for investors, *Forbes,* http://www.forbes.com, February, 13.
104. Maula & Murray, Corporate venture capital.
105. Amit, Lucier, Hitt, & Nixon, Strategies for the entrepreneurial millennium.
106. Hitt, Ireland, Camp, & Sexton, Strategic entrepreneurship.
107. Hitt, Bierman, Shimizu, & Kochhar, Direct and moderating effects of human capital.
108. M. A. Hitt, H. Lee, & E. Yucel, 2002, The importance of social capital to the management of multinational enterprises: Relational networks among Asian and Western firms, *Asia Pacific Journal of Management,* in press.
109. M. A. Hitt, R. E. Hoskisson, & H. Kim, 1997, International diversification: Effects on innovation and firm performance in product diversified firms, *Academy of Management Journal,* 40: 767–798.
110. R. Garud, S. Jain, & A. Kumaraswamy, 2002, Institutional entrepreneurship in the sponsorship of common technological standards: The case of Sun Microsystems and JAVA, *Academy of Management Journal,* 45: 196–214.
111. Reynolds, Camp, Bygrave, Autio, & Hay, *Global Entrepreneurship Monitor.*
112. Hitt, Ireland, Camp, & Sexton, Strategic entrepreneurship; Amit, Lucier, Hitt, & Nixon, Strategies for the entrepreneurial millennium.

Case Studies

Introduction

Preparing an Effective Case Analysis

In most strategic management courses, cases are used extensively as a teaching tool.[1] A key reason is that cases provide active learners with opportunities to use the strategic management process to identify and solve organizational problems. Thus, by analyzing situations that are described in cases and presenting the results, active learners (i.e., students) become skilled at effectively using the tools, techniques, and concepts that combine to form the strategic management process.

The cases that follow are concerned with actual companies. Presented within the cases are problems and situations that managers and those with whom they work must analyze and resolve. As you will see, a strategic management case can focus on an entire industry, a single organization, or a business unit of a large, diversified firm. The strategic management issues facing not-for-profit organizations also can be examined using the case analysis method.

Basically, the case analysis method calls for a careful diagnosis of an organization's current conditions (as manifested by its external and internal environments) so that appropriate strategic actions can be recommended in light of the firm's strategic intent and strategic mission. Strategic actions are taken to develop and then use a firm's core competencies to select and implement different strategies, including business-level, corporate-level, acquisition and restructuring, international, and cooperative strategies. Thus, appropriate strategic actions help the firm to survive in the long run as it creates and uses competitive advantages as the foundation for achieving strategic competitiveness and earning above-average returns. The case method that we are recommending to you has a rich heritage as a pedagogical approach to the study and understanding of managerial effectiveness.[2]

As an active learner, your preparation is critical to successful use of the case analysis method. Without careful study and analysis, active learners lack the insights required to participate fully in the discussion of a firm's situation and the strategic actions that are appropriate.

Instructors adopt different approaches in their application of the case analysis method. Some require active learners/students to use a specific analytical procedure to examine an organization; others provide less structure, expecting students to learn by developing their own unique analytical method. Still other instructors believe that a moderately structured framework should be used to analyze a firm's situation and make appropriate recommendations. Your professor will determine the specific approach you take. The approach we are presenting to you is a moderately structured framework.

We divide our discussion of a moderately structured case analysis method framework into four sections. First, we describe the importance of understanding the skills active learners can acquire through effective use of the case analysis method. In the second section, we provide you with a process-oriented framework. This framework can be of value in your efforts to analyze cases and then present the results of your work. Using this framework in a classroom setting yields valuable experiences that can, in turn, help you successfully complete assignments that you will receive from your employer. The third section is where we describe briefly what you can expect to occur during in-class case discussions. As this description shows, the relationship and interactions between instructors and active learners/students during case discussions are different than they are during lectures. In the final section, we present a moderately structured framework that we believe can help you prepare effective oral and written presentations. Written and oral communication skills also are valued highly in many organizational settings; hence, their development today can serve you well in the future.

Skills Gained Through Use of the Case Analysis Method

The case analysis method is based on a philosophy that combines knowledge acquisition with significant involvement from students as active learners. In the words of Alfred North Whitehead, this philosophy "rejects the doctrine that students had first learned passively, and then, having learned should apply knowledge."[3] In contrast to this philosophy, the case analysis method is based on principles that were elaborated upon by John Dewey:

> *Only by wrestling with the conditions of this problem at hand, seeking and finding his own way out, does [the student] think. . . . If he cannot devise his own solution (not, of course, in isolation, but in correspondence with the teacher and other pupils) and find his own way out he will not learn, not even if he can recite some correct answer with a hundred percent accuracy.*[4]

The case analysis method brings reality into the classroom. When developed and presented effectively, with rich and interesting detail, cases keep conceptual discussions grounded in reality. Experience shows that simple fictional accounts of situations and collections of actual organizational data and articles from public sources are not as effective for learning as fully developed cases. A comprehensive case presents you with a partial clinical study of a real-life situation that faced managers as well as other stakeholders including employees. A case presented in narrative form provides motivation for involvement with and analysis of a specific situation. By framing alternative strategic actions and by confronting the complexity and ambiguity of the practical world, case analysis provides extraordinary power for your involvement with a personal learning experience. Some of the potential consequences of using the case method are summarized in Exhibit 1.

As Exhibit 1 suggests, the case analysis method can assist active learners in the development of their analytical and judgment skills. Case analysis also helps you learn how to ask the right questions. By this we mean questions that focus on the core strategic issues that are included in a case. Active learners/students with managerial aspirations can improve their ability to identify underlying problems rather than focusing on superficial symptoms as they develop skills at asking probing yet appropriate questions.

The collection of cases your instructor chooses to assign can expose you to a wide variety of organizations and decision situations. This approach vicariously broadens your experience base and provides insights into many types of managerial situations, tasks, and responsibilities. Such indirect experience can help you make a more informed career decision about the industry and managerial situation you believe will prove to be challenging and satisfying. Finally, experience in analyzing cases definitely enhances your problem-solving skills, and research indicates that the case method for this class is better than the lecture method.[5]

Furthermore, when your instructor requires oral and written presentations, your communication skills will be honed through use of the case method. Of course, these added skills depend on your preparation as well as your instructor's facilitation of learning. However, the primary responsibility for learning is yours. The quality of case discussion is generally acknowledged to require, at a minimum, a thorough mastery of case facts and some independent analysis of them. The case method there-

Exhibit 1 Consequences of Student Involvement with the Case Method

1. Case analysis requires students to practice important managerial skills—diagnosing, making decisions, observing, listening, and persuading—while preparing for a case discussion.
2. Cases require students to relate analysis and action, to develop realistic and concrete actions despite the complexity and partial knowledge characterizing the situation being studied.
3. Students must confront the *intractability of reality*—complete with absence of needed information, an imbalance between needs and available resources, and conflicts among competing objectives.
4. Students develop a general managerial point of view—where responsibility is sensitive to action in a diverse environmental context.

SOURCE: C. C. Lundberg and C. Enz, 1993, A framework for student case preparation, *Case Research Journal*, 13 (Summer): 134.

fore first requires that you read and think carefully about each case. Additional comments about the preparation you should complete to successfully discuss a case appear in the next section.

Student Preparation for Case Discussion

If you are inexperienced with the case method, you may need to alter your study habits. A lecture-oriented course may not require you to do intensive preparation for *each* class period. In such a course, you have the latitude to work through assigned readings and review lecture notes according to your own schedule. However, an assigned case requires significant and conscientious *preparation before class.* Without it, you will be unable to contribute meaningfully to in-class discussion. Therefore, careful reading and thinking about case facts, as well as reasoned analyses and the development of alternative solutions to case problems, are essential. Recommended alternatives should flow logically from core problems identified through study of the case. Exhibit 2 shows a set of steps that can help you familiarize yourself with a case, identify problems, and propose strategic actions that increase the probability that a firm will achieve strategic competitiveness and earn above-average returns.

Gaining Familiarity

The first step of an effective case analysis process calls for you to become familiar with the facts featured in the case and the focal firm's situation. Initially, you should

Exhibit 2 An Effective Case Analysis Process

Step 1: *Gaining Familiarity*	a. In general—determine who, what, how, where, and when (the critical facts of the case). b. In detail—identify the places, persons, activities, and contexts of the situation. c. Recognize the degree of certainty/uncertainty of acquired information.
Step 2: *Recognizing Symptoms*	a. List all indicators (including stated "problems") that something is not as expected or as desired. b. Ensure that symptoms are not assumed to be the problem (symptoms should lead to identification of the problem).
Step 3: *Identifying Goals*	a. Identify critical statements by major parties (e.g., people, groups, the work unit, etc.). b. List all goals of the major parties that exist or can be reasonably inferred.
Step 4: *Conducting the Analysis*	a. Decide which ideas, models, and theories seem useful. b. Apply these conceptual tools to the situation. c. As new information is revealed, cycle back to substeps a and b.
Step 5: *Making the Diagnosis*	a. Identify predicaments (goal inconsistencies). b. Identify problems (discrepancies between goals and performance). c. Prioritize predicaments/problems regarding timing, importance, etc.
Step 6: *Doing the Action Planning*	a. Specify and prioritize the criteria used to choose action alternatives. b. Discover or invent feasible action alternatives. c. Examine the probable consequences of action alternatives. d. Select a course of action. e. Design an implementation plan/schedule. f. Create a plan for assessing the action to be implemented.

SOURCE: C. C. Lundberg and C. Enz, 1993, A framework for student case preparation, *Case Research Journal*, 13 (Summer): 144.

become familiar with the focal firm's general situation (e.g., who, what, how, where, and when). Thorough familiarization demands appreciation of the nuances as well as the major issues in the case.

Gaining familiarity with a situation requires you to study several situational levels, including interactions between and among individuals within groups, business units, the corporate office, the local community, and the society at large. Recognizing relationships within and among levels facilitates a more thorough understanding of the specific case situation.

It is also important that you evaluate information on a continuum of certainty. Information that is verifiable by several sources and judged along similar dimensions can be classified as a *fact*. Information representing someone's perceptual judgment of a particular situation is referred to as an *inference*. Information gleaned from a situation that is not verifiable is classified as *speculation*. Finally, information that is independent of verifiable sources and arises through individual or group discussion is an *assumption*. Obviously, case analysts and organizational decision makers prefer having access to facts over inferences, speculations, and assumptions.

Personal feelings, judgments, and opinions evolve when you are analyzing a case. It is important to be aware of your own feelings about the case and to evaluate the accuracy of perceived "facts" to ensure that the objectivity of your work is maximized.

Recognizing Symptoms

Recognition of symptoms is the second step of an effective case analysis process. A symptom is an indication that something is not as you or someone else thinks it should be. You may be tempted to correct the symptoms instead of searching for true problems. True problems are the conditions or situations requiring solution before the performance of an organization, business unit, or individual can improve. Identifying and listing symptoms early in the case analysis process tends to reduce the temptation to label symptoms as problems. The focus of your analysis should be on the *actual causes* of a problem, rather than on its symptoms. Thus, it is important to remember that symptoms are indicators of problems, subsequent work facilitates discovery of critical causes of problems that your case recommendations must address.

Identifying Goals

The third step of effective case analysis calls for you to identify the goals of the major organizations, business units, and/or individuals in a case. As appropriate, you should also identify each firm's strategic intent and strategic mission. Typically, these direction-setting statements (goals, strategic intents, and strategic missions) are derived from comments made by central characters in the organization, business unit, or top management team as described in the case and/or from public documents (e.g., an annual report).

Completing this step successfully sometimes can be difficult. Nonetheless, the outcomes you attain from this step are essential to an effective case analysis because identifying goals, intent, and mission helps you to clarify the major problems featured in a case and to evaluate alternative solutions to those problems. Direction-setting statements are not always stated publicly or prepared in written format. When this occurs, you must infer goals from other available factual data and information.

Conducting the Analysis

The fourth step of effective case analysis is concerned with acquiring a systematic understanding of a situation. Occasionally cases are analyzed in a less-than-thorough manner. Such analyses may be a product of a busy schedule or the difficulty and complexity of the issues described in a particular case. Sometimes you will face pressures on your limited amounts of time and may believe that you can understand the situation described in a case without systematic *analysis* of all the facts. However, experience shows that familiarity with a case's facts is a necessary, but insufficient, step in the development of effective solutions—solutions that can enhance a firm's strategic competitiveness. In fact, a less-than-thorough analysis typically results in an emphasis on symptoms, rather than problems and their causes. To analyze a case effectively, you should be skeptical of quick or easy approaches and answers.

A systematic analysis helps you understand a situation and determine what can work and probably what will not work. Key linkages and underlying causal networks based on the history of the firm become apparent. In this way, you can separate causal networks from symptoms.

Also, because the quality of a case analysis depends on applying appropriate tools, it is important that you use the ideas, models, and theories that seem to be useful for evaluating and solving individual and unique situations. As you consider facts and symptoms, a useful theory may become apparent. Of course, having familiarity with conceptual models may be important in the effective analysis of a situation. Successful students and successful organizational strategists add to their intellectual tool kits on a continual basis.

Making the Diagnosis

The fifth step of effective case analysis—diagnosis—is the process of identifying and clarifying the roots of the problems by comparing goals to facts. In this step, it is useful to search for predicaments. Predicaments are situations in which goals do not fit with known facts. When you evaluate the actual performance of an organization, business unit, or individual, you may identify over- or underachievement (relative to established goals). Of course, single-problem situations are rare. Accordingly, you should recognize that the case situations you study probably will be complex in nature.

Effective diagnosis requires you to determine the problems affecting longer term performance and those requiring immediate handling. Understanding these issues will aid your efforts to prioritize problems and predicaments, given available resources and existing constraints.

Doing the Action Planning

The final step of an effective case analysis process is called action planning. Action planning is the process of identifying appropriate alternative actions. In the action planning step you select the criteria you will use to evaluate the identified alternatives. You may derive these criteria from the analyses; typically, they are related to key strategic situations facing the focal organization. Furthermore, it is important that you prioritize these criteria to ensure a rational and effective evaluation of alternative courses of action.

Typically, managers "satisfice" when selecting courses of action; that is, they find *acceptable* courses of action that meet most of the chosen evaluation criteria. A rule of thumb that has proved valuable to strategic decision makers is to select an alternative that leaves other plausible alternatives available if the one selected fails.

Once you have selected the best alternative, you must specify an implementation plan. Developing an implementation plan serves as a reality check on the feasibility of your alternatives. Thus, it is important that you give thoughtful consideration to all issues associated with the implementation of the selected alternatives.

What to Expect From In-Class Case Discussions

Classroom discussions of cases differ significantly from lectures. The case method calls for instructors to guide the discussion, encourage student participation, and solicit alternative views. When alternative views are not forthcoming, instructors typically adopt one view so students can be challenged to respond to it thoughtfully. Often students' work is evaluated in terms of both the quantity and the quality of their contributions to in-class case discussions. Students benefit by having their views judged against those of their peers and by responding to challenges by other class members and/or the instructor.

During case discussions, instructors listen, question, and probe to extend the analysis of case issues. In the course of these actions, peers or the instructor may challenge an individual's views and the validity of alternative perspectives that have been expressed. These challenges are offered in a constructive manner; their intent is to help students develop their analytical and communication skills. Instructors should encourage students to be innovative and original in the development and presentation of their ideas. Over the course of an individual discussion, students can develop a more complex view of the case, benefiting from the diverse inputs of their peers and instructor. Among other benefits, experience with multiple-case discussions should help students increase their knowledge of the advantages and disadvantages of group decision-making processes.

Student peers as well as the instructor value comments that contribute to the discussion. To offer *relevant* contributions, you are encouraged to use independent thought and, through discussions with your peers outside of class, to refine your thinking. We also encourage you to avoid using "I think," "I believe," and "I feel" to discuss your inputs to a case analysis process. Instead, consider using a less emotion-laden phrase, such as "My analysis shows." This highlights the logical nature of the approach you have taken to complete the six steps of an effective case analysis process.

When preparing for an in-class case discussion, you should plan to use the case data to explain your assessment of the situation. Assume that your peers and instructor know the case facts. In addition, it is good practice to prepare notes before class discussions and use them as you explain your view. Effective notes signal to classmates and the instructor that you are prepared to engage in a thorough discussion of a case. Moreover, thorough notes eliminate the need for you to memorize the facts and figures needed to discuss a case successfully.

The case analysis process just described can help you prepare to effectively discuss a case during class meetings. Adherence to this process results in consideration of the issues required to identify a focal firm's problems and to propose strategic actions through which the firm can increase the probability that it will achieve strategic competitiveness.

In some instances, your instructor may ask you to prepare either an oral or a written analysis of a particular case. Typically, such an assignment demands even more thorough study and analysis of the case contents. At your instructor's discretion, oral and written analyses may be completed by individuals or by groups of two or more people. The information and insights gained through completing the six steps shown in Exhibit 2 often are of value in the development of an oral or written analysis.

However, when preparing an oral or written presentation, you must consider the overall framework in which your information and inputs will be presented. Such a framework is the focus of the next section.

Preparing an Oral/Written Case Strategic Plan

Experience shows that two types of thinking are necessary to develop an effective oral or written presentation (see Exhibit 3). The upper part of the model in Exhibit 3 outlines the *analysis* stage of case preparation.

In the analysis stage, you should first analyze the general external environmental issues affecting the firm. Next your environmental analysis should focus on the particular industry (or industries, in the case of a diversified company) in which a firm operates. Finally, you should examine the competitive environment of the focal firm. Through study of the three levels of the external environment, you will be able to identify a firm's opportunities and threats. Following the external environmental analysis is the analysis of the firm's internal environment, which results in the identification of the firm's strengths and weaknesses.

As noted in Exhibit 3, you must then change the focus from analysis to *synthesis*. Specifically, you must *synthesize* information gained from your analysis of the firm's internal and external environments. Synthesizing information allows you to generate alternatives that can resolve the significant problems or challenges facing the focal firm. Once you identify a best alternative, from an evaluation based on predetermined criteria and goals, you must explore implementation actions.

Exhibit 4 and Exhibit 5 outline the sections that should be included in either an oral or a written strategic plan presentation: introduction (strategic intent and

Exhibit 3 Types of Thinking in Case Preparation: Analysis and Synthesis

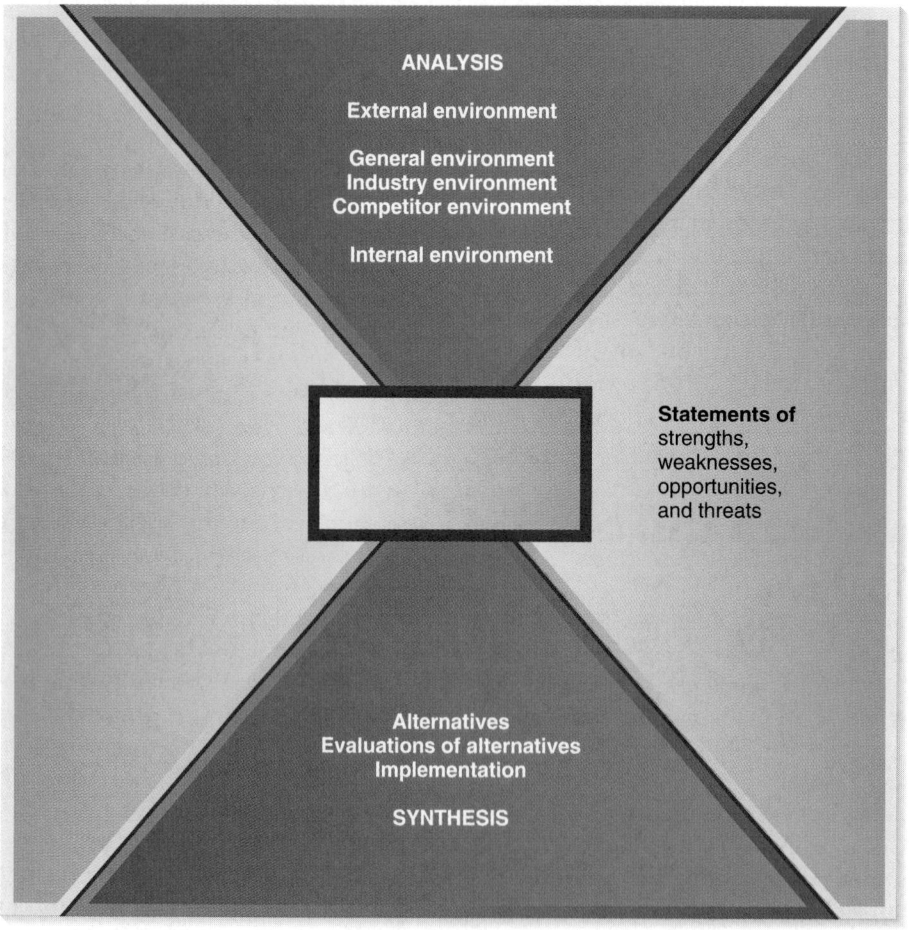

ANALYSIS

External environment

General environment
Industry environment
Competitor environment

Internal environment

Statements of
strengths,
weaknesses,
opportunities,
and threats

Alternatives
Evaluations of alternatives
Implementation

SYNTHESIS

Exhibit 4 Strategic Planning Process

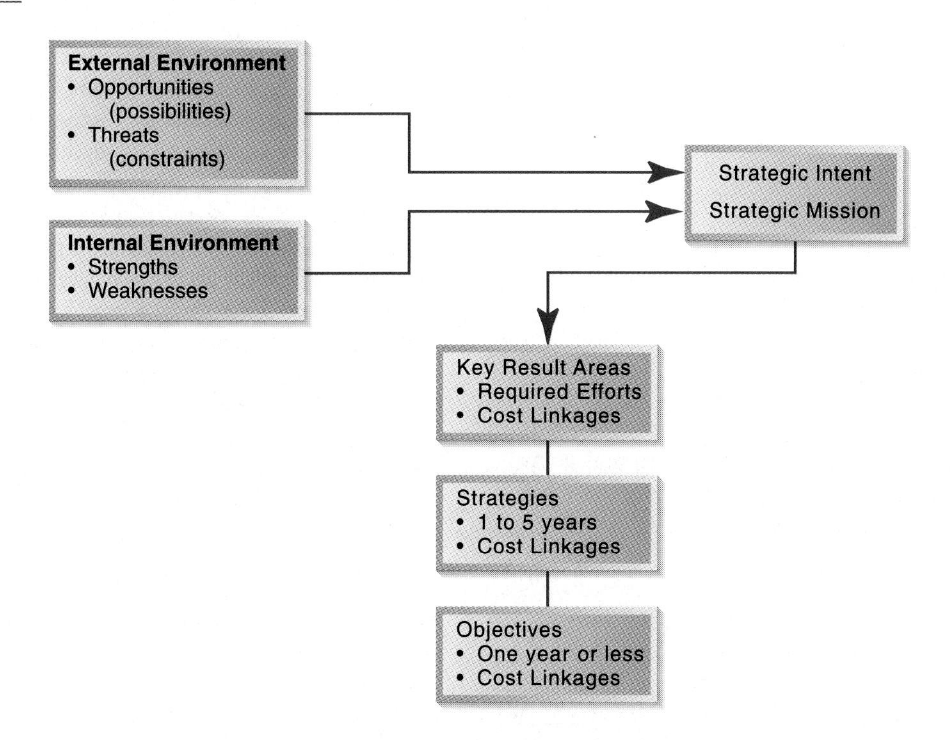

Exhibit 5 Strategic Planning and Its Parts

- *Strategic planning* is a *process* through which a firm determines what it seeks to accomplish and the actions required to achieve desired outcomes
  - ✓ *Strategic planning,* then, is a *process* that we use to determine *what* (outcomes to be reached) and how (actions to be taken to reach outcomes)
- The effective *strategic plan* for a firm would include statements and details about the following:
  - ✓ *Opportunities* (possibilities) and *threats* (constraints)
  - ✓ *Strengths* (what we do especially well) and *weaknesses* (deficiencies)
  - ✓ *Strategic intent* (an indication of a firm's ideal state)
  - ✓ *Strategic mission* (purpose and scope of a firm's operations in product and market terms)
  - ✓ *Key result areas* (KRAs) (categories of activities where efforts must take place to reach the mission and intent)
  - ✓ *Strategies* (actions for each KRA to be completed within one to five years)
  - ✓ *Objectives* (specific statements detailing actions for each strategy that are to be completed in one year or less)
  - ✓ *Cost linkages* (relationships between actions and financial resources)

mission), situation analysis, statements of strengths/weaknesses and opportunities/threats, strategy formulation, and implementation plan. These sections, which can be completed only through use of the two types of thinking featured in Exhibit 3, are described in the following discussion. Familiarity with the contents of this book's 13 chapters is helpful because the general outline for an oral or a written strategic plan shown in Exhibit 5 is based on an understanding of the strategic management process detailed in these chapters.

External Environment Analysis

As shown in Exhibit 5, a general starting place for completing a situation analysis is the external environment. The *external environment* is composed of outside (external) conditions that affect a firm's performance. Your analysis of the environment should consider the effects of the *general environment* on the focal firm. Following that evaluation, you should analyze the *industry and competitor environmental* trends.

These trends or conditions in the external environment shape the firm's strategic intent and mission. The external environment analysis essentially indicates what a firm *might choose to do*. Often called an *environmental scan*, an analysis of the external environment allows a firm to identify key conditions that are beyond its direct control. The purpose of studying the external environment is to identify a firm's opportunities and threats. *Opportunities* are conditions in the external environment that appear to have the potential to contribute to a firm's success. In essence, opportunities represent *possibilities*. *Threats* are conditions in the external environment that appear to have the potential to prevent a firm's success. In essence, threats represent potential *constraints*.

When studying the external environment, the focus is on trying to *predict* the future (in terms of local, regional, and international trends and issues) and to *predict* the expected effects on a firm's operations. The external environment features conditions in the broader society *and* in the industry (area of competition) that influence the firm's possibilities and constraints. Areas to be considered (to identify opportunities and threats) when studying the general environment are listed in Exhibit 6. Many of these issues are explained more fully in Chapter 2.

Once you analyze the general environmental trends, you should study their effect on the focal industry. Often the same environmental trend may have a significantly different impact on separate industries. Furthermore, the same trend may affect firms within the same industry differently. For instance, with deregulation of the airline industry, older, established airlines had a significant decrease in profitability, while many smaller airlines such as Southwest Airlines, with lower cost structures and greater flexibility, were able to aggressively enter new markets.

Porter's five forces model is a useful tool for analyzing the specific industry (see Chapter 2). Careful study of how the five competitive forces (i.e., supplier power, buyer power, potential entrants, substitute products, and rivalry among competitors) affect a firm's strategy is important. These forces may create threats or opportunities relative to the specific business-level strategies (i.e., differentiation, cost leadership, focus) being implemented. Often a strategic group's analysis reveals how different environmental trends are affecting industry competitors. Strategic group analysis is useful for understanding the industry's competitive structures and firm constraints and possibilities within those structures.

Firms also need to analyze each of their primary competitors. This analysis should identify competitors' current strategies, strategic intent, strategic mission, capabilities, core competencies, and a competitive response profile. This information is useful to the focal firm in formulating an appropriate strategic intent and mission. Sources that can be used to gather information about a general environment, industry, and companies with whom the focal firm competes are listed in Appendix I. Included in this list is a wide range of web sites; publications, such as periodicals, newspapers, bibliographies, and directories of companies; industry ratios; forecasts; rankings/ratings; and other valuable statistics.

Internal Environment Analysis

The *internal environment* is composed of strengths and weaknesses internal to a firm that influence its strategic competitiveness. The purpose of completing an analysis of a firm's internal environment is to identify its strengths and weaknesses. The strengths and weaknesses in a firm's internal environment shape the strategic intent and strategic mission. The internal environment essentially indicates what a firm *can do*. Capabilities or skills that allow a firm to do something that others cannot do or that allow a firm to do something better than others do it are called strengths. *Strengths* can be categorized as something that a firm does especially well. Strengths help a firm take advantage of external opportunities or overcome external threats. Capabilities or skill deficiencies that prevent a firm from completing an important activity as well as others do it are called weaknesses. *Weaknesses* have the potential to prevent a firm from taking advantage of external opportunities or succeeding in efforts to overcome external threats. Thus, *weaknesses* can be thought of as something the firm needs to improve.

Analysis of the primary and support activities of the value chain provides opportunities to understand how external environmental trends affect the specific activities of a firm. Such analysis helps highlight strengths and weaknesses (see Chapter 3 for an explanation of the value chain). For purposes of preparing an oral or written presentation, it is important to note that strengths are internal resources and capabilities that have the potential to be core competencies. Weaknesses, on the other hand, have the potential to place a firm at a competitive disadvantage relative to its rivals.

Exhibit 6 Sample General Environmental Categories

Technology	• Information technology continues to become cheaper and have more practical applications • Database technology allows organization of complex data and distribution of information • Telecommunications technology and networks increasingly provide fast transmission of all sources of data, including voice, written communications, and video information
Demographic Trends	• Computerized design and manufacturing technologies continue to facilitate quality and flexibility • Regional changes in population due to migration • Changing ethnic composition of the population • Aging of the population • Aging of the "baby boom" generation
Economic Trends	• Interest rates • Inflation rates • Savings rates • Trade deficits • Budget deficits • Exchange rates
Political/Legal Environment	• Anti-trust enforcement • Tax policy changes • Environmental protection laws • Extent of regulation/deregulation • Developing countries privatizing state monopolies • State-owned industries
Sociocultural Environment	• Increasing number of women in the work force • Awareness of health and fitness issues • Concern for the environment • Concern for customers
Global Environment	• Currency exchange rates • Free trade agreements • Trade deficits • New or developing markets

When evaluating the internal characteristics of the firm, your analysis of the functional activities emphasized is critical. For instance, if the strategy of the firm is primarily technology-driven, it is important to evaluate the firm's R&D activities. If the strategy is market-driven, marketing functional activities are of paramount importance. If a firm has financial difficulties, critical financial ratios would require careful evaluation. In fact, because of the importance of financial health, most cases require financial analyses. Appendix II lists and operationally defines several common financial ratios. Included are exhibits describing profitability, liquidity, leverage, activity, and shareholders' return ratios. Other firm characteristics that should be examined to study the internal environment effectively include leadership, organizational culture, structure, and control systems.

Identification of Strategic Intent and Mission

Strategic intent is associated with a mind-set that managers seek to imbue within the company. Essentially, a mind-set captures how we view the world and our intended role in it. Strategic intent reflects or identifies a firm's ideal state. Strategic intent flows from a firm's opportunities, threats, strengths, and weaknesses. However, the major influence on strategic intent is a firm's *strengths*. Strategic intent should reflect a firm's intended character and reflects a commitment to "stretch" available resources and strengths in order to reach what may seem to be unattainable strategies and objectives in terms of Key Result Areas (KRAs). When established effectively, strategic intent can cause each employee to perform in ways never imagined possible.

Strategic intent has the ability to reflect what may be the most worthy goal of all: to unseat the best or to be the best on a regional, national, or even international basis. Examples of strategic intent include:

- The relentless pursuit of perfection (Lexus).
- It's our strategic intent that customers worldwide view us as their most valued pharmaceutical partner (Eli Lilly).
- To be the top performer in everything that we do (Phillips Petroleum).
- To become a high performance multinational energy company—not the biggest, but the best (Unocal Corporation).
- We are dedicated to being the world's best at bringing people together (AT&T).
- Ben & Jerry's is dedicated to the creation and demonstration of a new corporate concept—linked prosperity.
- Our intent is to be better than the best (Best Products).
- The Children's Defense Fund exists to provide a strong and effective voice for the children of America who cannot vote, lobby, or speak for themselves.
- We build homes to meet people's dreams (Kaufman & Broad).
- We will be a leader in the emerging energy services industry by challenging conventional wisdom and creating superior value in a safe and environmentally responsible manner (PSI Energy, Inc.).
- We intend to become the single source of information technology for the home (Dell Computer Corporation).
- To be a premier provider of services and products that contribute to the health and well-being of people (MDS Health Group Limited).
- We seek to set the standard for excellence, leadership and integrity in the utility industry (New York State Electric & Gas Corp.).

The strategic mission flows from a firm's strategic intent; it is a statement used to describe a firm's unique intent and the scope of its operations in product and market terms. In its most basic form, the strategic mission indicates to stakeholders what a firm seeks to accomplish. An effective strategic mission reflects a firm's individuality and reveals its leadership's predisposition(s). The useful strategic mission shows how a firm differs from others and defines boundaries within which the firm intends to operate. Examples of strategic missions include:

- To make, distribute, and sell the finest quality all-natural ice cream and related products in a wide variety of innovative flavors made from Vermont dairy products (Ben & Jerry's).
- To serve the natural and LP needs of the customers in the Clearwater and surrounding Florida SunCoast area in the most safe, reliable and economical manner possible while optimizing load growth, customer satisfaction, financial return to the City of Clearwater and the equity value of the Clearwater Gas System (Clearwater Gas System).
- Public Service Company of Colorado is an energy company that primarily provides gas, electricity and related services to present and potential markets.
- Our mission is to understand and satisfy customer expectations for quality and energy and energy-related products and services and profitably serve Oklahoma markets (Public Service Company of Oklahoma).
- Children's Hospital Medical Center is dedicated to serving the health-care needs of infants, children, and adolescents and to providing research and teaching programs that ensure delivery of the highest quality pediatric care to our community, the nation, and the world (Children's Hospital Medical Center).
- To provide services and products which will assist physicians, health care institutions, corporations, government agencies, and communities to improve the health and well-being of the people for whom they are responsible (MDS Health Group Limited).
- The William Penn Foundation is a private grant making organization created in 1945 by Otto Haas and his wife, Phoebe. The principal mission of the Foundation is to help improve the quality of life in the Delaware Valley (William Penn Foundation).

Key Result Areas (KRAs)

Once the strategic intent and mission have been defined, the analysis can turn to defining KRAs to help accomplish the intent and mission. *Key result areas* are categories of activities that must receive attention if the firm is to achieve its strategic intent and strategic mission. A rationale or justification and specific courses of action for each KRA should be specified. Typically, a firm should establish no more than six KRAs. KRAs should suggest (in broad terms) a firm's concerns and intended directions.

Flowing from the nature of a firm's KRAs, *strategies* are courses of action that must be taken to satisfy the requirements suggested by each KRA. Strategies typically have a one-, two-, or three-year time horizon (although it can be as long as five years). Strategies are developed to describe approaches to be used or methods to follow in order to attain the strategic intent and strategic mission (as suggested by the KRAs). Strategies reflect a group's action intentions. Flowing from individual strategies, *objectives* are specific and measurable statements describing actions that are to be completed to implement individual strategies. Objectives, which are more specific in nature than strategies, usually have a one-year or shorter time horizon.

Strategic planning should also result in cost linkages to courses of action. Once key cost assumptions are specified, these financial requirements can be tied to strategies and objectives. Once linked with strategies and objectives, cost or budgetary requirements can be related back to KRAs.

Hints for Presenting an Effective Strategic Plan

There may be a temptation to spend most of your oral or written case analysis on results from the analysis. It is important, however, that you make an equal effort to develop and evaluate KRA alternatives and to design implementation for the chosen alternatives. In your presentation, the *analysis* of a case should not be overemphasized relative to the *synthesis* of results gained from your analytical efforts (see Exhibit 3).

Strategy Formulation: Choosing Key Result Areas

Once you have formulated a strategic intent and mission, choosing among alternative KRAs is often one of the most difficult steps in preparing an oral or written presentation. Each alternative should be feasible (i.e., it should match the firm's strengths, capabilities, and especially core competencies), and feasibility should be demonstrated. In addition, you should show how each alternative takes advantage of the environmental opportunity or avoids/buffers against environmental threats. Developing carefully thought out alternatives requires synthesis of your analyses and creates greater credibility in oral and written case presentations.

Once you develop strong alternative KRAs, you must evaluate the set to choose the best ones. Your choice should be defensible and provide benefits over the other alternatives. Thus, it is important that both the alternative development and evaluation of alternatives be thorough. The choice of the best alternative should be explained and defended.

Key Result Area Implementation

After selecting the most appropriate KRAs (that is, those with the highest probability of enhancing a firm's strategic competitiveness), you must consider effective implementation. Effective synthesis is important to ensure that you have considered and evaluated all critical implementation issues. Issues you might consider include the structural changes necessary to implement the new strategies and objectives associated with each KRA. In addition, leadership changes and new controls or incentives may be necessary to implement these strategic actions. The implementation actions you recommend should be explicit and thoroughly explained. Occasionally, careful evaluation of implementation actions may show the strategy to be less favorable than you originally thought. A strategy is only as good as the firm's ability to implement it effectively. Therefore, expending the effort to determine effective implementation is important.

Process Issues

You should ensure that your presentation (either oral or written) has logical consistency throughout. For example, if your presentation identifies one purpose, but your analysis focuses on issues that differ from the stated purpose, the logical inconsistency will be apparent. Likewise, your alternatives should flow from the configuration of strengths, weaknesses, opportunities, and threats you identified through the internal and external analyses.

Thoroughness and clarity also are critical to an effective presentation. Thoroughness is represented by the comprehensiveness of the analysis and alternative generation. Furthermore, clarity in the results of the analyses, selection of the best alternative KRAs, and design of implementation actions are important. For example, your statement of the strengths and weaknesses should flow clearly and logically from the internal analyses presented.

Presentations (oral or written) that show logical consistency, thoroughness, and clarity of purpose, effective analyses, and feasible recommendations are more effective and will receive more positive evaluations. Being able to withstand tough questions from peers after your presentation will build credibility for your strategic plan presentation. Furthermore, developing the skills necessary to make such presentations will enhance your future job performance and career success.

Appendix I: Sources for Industry and Competitor Analyses

Strategic Management Web Sites

Search Engines (may be the broadest sources of information on companies and industries)

Alta Vista—*http://www.altavista.digital.com*
Excite—*http://www.excite.com*
InfoSeek—*http://www.infoseek.com*
Lycos—*http://www.lycos.com*
WebCrawler—*http://www.webcrawler.com*
Yahoo!—*http://www.yahoo.com*

Professional Societies

Academy of Management <*http://www.aom.pace.edu*> publishes *Academy of Management Journal, Academy of Management Review, and Academy of Management Executive*, three publications that often print articles on strategic management research, theory, and practice. The Academy of Management is the largest professional society for management research and education and has a large Business Policy and Strategy Division.

Strategic Management Society <*http://www.smsweb.org*> publishes the *Strategic Management Journal* (a top academic journal in strategic management).

Government Sources of Company Information and Data

Census Bureau <*http://www.census.gov*> provides useful links and information about social, demographic, and economic information.

Federal Trade Commission <*http://www.ftc.gov*> includes discussion on several antitrust and consumer protection laws useful to businesses looking for accurate information about business statutes.

Free EDGAR <*http://www.freeedgar.com*> provides free, unlimited access to real-time corporate data filed with the Securities and Exchange Commission (SEC).

Better Business Bureau <*http://www.bbb.org*> provides a wide variety of helpful publications, information, and other resources to both consumers and businesses to help people make informed marketplace decisions.

Publication Web Sites

Business Week <*http://www.businessweek.com*> allows search of *Business Week* magazine's articles by industry or topic, such as strategy.

Forbes <*http://www.forbes.com*> provides searching of *Forbes* magazine business articles and data.

Fortune <*http://www.fortune.com*> allows search of *Fortune* magazine and other articles, many of which are focused on strategy topics.

Financial Times <*http://www.ft.com*> provides access to many *Financial Times* articles, data, and surveys.

Wall Street Journal <*http://www.wsj.com*> *The Wall Street Journal Interactive* edition provides an excellent continuing stream of strategy-oriented articles and announcements.

Abstracts and Indexes

Periodicals

ABI/Inform
Business Periodicals Index
InfoTrac (CD-ROM computer multidiscipline index)
Investext (CD-ROM)

Predicasts F&S Index United States
Predicasts Overview of Markets and Technology (PROMT)
Predicasts R&S Index Europe
Predicasts R&S Index International

Public Affairs Information Service Bulletin (PAIS)
Reader's Guide to Periodical Literature
Newspapers NewsBank
Business NewsBank
New York Times Index
Wall Street Journal Index
Wall Street Journal/Barron's Index
Washington Post Index

Bibliographies

Encyclopedia of Business Information Sources
Handbook of Business Information

Directories

Companies—General

America's Corporate Families and International Affiliates
Hoover's Handbook of American Business
Hoover's Handbook of World Business
Million Dollar Directory
Standard & Poor's Corporation Records
Standard & Poor's Register of Corporations, Directors, and Executives
Ward's Business Directory

Companies—International

America's Corporate Families and International Affiliates
Business Asia
Business China
Business Eastern Europe
Business Europe
Business International
Business International Money Report
Business Latin America
Directory of American Films Operating in Foreign Countries
Directory of Foreign Firms Operating in the United States
Hoover's Handbook of World Business
International Directory of Company Histories
Moody's Manuals, International (2 volumes)
Who Owns Whom

Companies—Manufacturers

Manufacturing USA: Industry Analyses, Statistics, and Leading Companies
Thomas Register of American Manufacturers
U.S. Office of Management and Budget, Executive Office of the President, *Standard Industrial Classification Manual*
U.S. Manufacturer's Directory

Companies—Private

Million Dollar Directory
Ward's Directory

Companies—Public

Annual Reports and 10-K Reports
Disclosure (corporate reports)
Q-File
Moody's Manuals:
Moody's Bank and Finance Manual
Moody's Industrial Manual
Moody's International Manual
Moody's Municipal and Government Manual
Moody's OTC Industrial Manual
Moody's OTC Unlisted Manual
Moody's Public Utility Manual
Moody's Transportation Manual

Standard & Poor Corporation, *Standard Corporation Descriptions*:
Standard & Poor's Handbook
Standard & Poor's Industry Surveys
Standard & Poor's Investment Advisory Service
Standard & Poor's Outlook
Standard & Poor's Statistical Service

Companies—Subsidiaries and Affiliates

America's Corporate Families and International Affiliates
Ward's Directory
Who Owns Whom
Moody's Industry Review
Standard & Poor's Analyst's Handbook
Standard & Poor's Industry Report Service
Standard & Poor's Industry Surveys (2 volumes)
U.S. Department of Commerce, *U.S. Industrial Outlook*

Industry Ratios

Dun & Bradstreet, *Industry Norms and Key Business Ratios*
Robert Morris Associates Annual Statement Studies
Troy Almanac of Business and Industrial Financial Ratios

Industry Forecasts

International Trade Administration, *U.S. Industrial Outlook*
Predicasts Forecasts

Rankings & Ratings

Annual Report on American Industry in *Forbes*
Business Rankings and Salaries
Business One Irwin Business and Investment Almanac
Corporate and Industry Research Reports (CIRR)
Dun's Business Rankings
Moody's Industrial Review
Rating Guide to Franchises
Standard & Poor's Industry Report Service
Value Line Investment Survey
Ward's Business Directory

Statistics

American Statistics Index (ASI) Bureau of the Census, U.S. Department of Commerce, *Economic Census Publications*
Bureau of the Census, U.S. Department of Commerce, *Statistical Abstract of the United States*
Bureau of Economic Analysis, U.S. Department of Commerce, *Survey of Current Business*
Internal Revenue Service, U.S. Treasury Department, *Statistics of Income: Corporation Income Tax Returns*
Statistical Reference Index (SRI)

Appendix II: Financial Analysis in Case Studies

Exhibit A-1 Profitability Ratios

Ratio	Formula	What It Shows
1. Return on total assets	$\frac{\text{Profits after taxes}}{\text{Total assets}}$	The net return on total investment of the firm
	or	or
	$\frac{\text{Profits after taxes + interest}}{\text{Total assets}}$	The return on both creditors' and shareholders' investments
2. Return on stockholders' equity (or return on net worth)	$\frac{\text{Profits after taxes}}{\text{Total stockholders' equity}}$	How effectively the company is utilizing shareholders' funds
3. Return on common equity	$\frac{\text{Profit after taxes – preferred stock dividends}}{\text{Total stockholders' equity– par value of preferred stock}}$	The net return to common stockholders
4. Operating profit margin (or return on sales)	$\frac{\text{Profits before taxes and before interest}}{\text{Sales}}$	The firm's profitability from regular operations
5. Net profit margin (or net return on sales)	$\frac{\text{Profits after taxes}}{\text{Sales}}$	The firm's net profit as a percentage of total sales

Exhibit A-2 Liquidity Ratios

Ratio	Formula	What It Shows
1. Current ratio	$\frac{\text{Current assets}}{\text{Current liabilities}}$	The firm's ability to meet its current financial liabilities
2. Quick ratio (or acid-test ratio)	$\frac{\text{Current assets – inventory}}{\text{Current liabilities}}$	The firm's ability to pay off short-term obligations without relying on sales of inventory
3. Inventory to net working capital	$\frac{\text{Inventory}}{\text{Current assets – current liabilities}}$	The extent of which the firm's working capital is tied up in inventory

Exhibit A-3 Leverage Ratios

Ratio	Formula	What It Shows
1. Debt-to-assets	Total debt / Total assets	Total borrowed funds as a percentage of total assets
2. Debt-to-equity	Total debt / Total shareholders' equity	Borrowed funds versus the funds provided by shareholders
3. Long-term debt-to-equity	Long-term debt / Total shareholders' equity	Leverage used by the firm
4. Times-interest-earned (or coverage ratio)	Profits before interest and taxes / Total interest charges	The firm's ability to meet all interest payments
5. Fixed charge coverage	Profits before taxes and interest + lease obligations / Total interest charges + lease obligations	The firm's ability to meet all fixed-charge obligations including lease payments

Exhibit A-4 Activity Ratios

Ratio	Formula	What It Shows
1. Inventory turnover	Sales / Inventory of finished goods	The effectiveness of the firm in employing inventory
2. Fixed assets turnover	Sales / Fixed assets	The effectiveness of the firm in utilizing plant and equipment
3. Total assets turnover	Sales / Total assets	The effectiveness of the firm in utilizing total assets
4. Accounts receivable turnover	Annual credit sales / Accounts receivable	How many times the total receivables have been collected during the accounting period
5. Average collection period	Accounts receivable / Average daily sales	The average length of time the firm waits to collect payments after sales

Exhibit A-5 Shareholders' Return Ratios

Ratio	Formula	What It Shows
1. Dividend yield on common stock	$\frac{\text{Annual dividends per share}}{\text{Current market price per share}}$	A measure of return to common stockholders in the form of dividends.
2. Price-earnings ratio	$\frac{\text{Current market price per share}}{\text{After-tax earnings per share}}$	An indication of market perception of the firm. Usually, the faster-growing or less risky firms tend to have higher PE ratios than the slower-growing or more risky firms.
3. Dividend payout ratio	$\frac{\text{Annual dividends per share}}{\text{After-tax earnings per share}}$	An indication of dividends paid out as a percentage of profits.
4. Cash flow per share	$\frac{\text{After-tax profits + depreciation}}{\text{Number of common shares outstanding}}$	A measure of total cash per share available for use by the firm.

Endnotes

1. M. A. Lundberg, B. B. Levin, & H. I. Harrington, 2000, *Who Learns What From Cases and How? The Research Base for Teaching and Learning with Cases* (Englewood Cliffs, New Jersey: Lawrence Erlbaum Associates).
2. L. B. Barnes, A. J. Nelson, & C. R. Christensen, 1994, *Teaching and the Case Method: Text, Cases and Readings* (Boston: Harvard Business School Press); C. C. Lundberg, 1993, Introduction to the case method, in C. M. Vance (ed.), *Mastering Management Education* (Newbury Park, Calif.: Sage); C. Christensen, 1989, *Teaching and the Case Method* (Boston: Harvard Business School Publishing Division).
3. C. C. Lundberg, & E. Enz, 1993, A framework for student case preparation, *Case Research Journal,* 13 (Summer): 133.
4. J. Solitis, 1971, John Dewey, in L. E. Deighton (ed.), *Encyclopedia of Education* (New York: Macmillan and Free Press).
5. F. Bocker, 1987, Is case teaching more effective than lecture teaching in business administration? An exploratory analysis, *Interfaces,* 17(5): 64–71.

Name Index

C

D

E

F

G

H

M

N

O

P

Q

R

S

T

U

V

W

X

Y

Z

Company Index

T

U

V

W

X

Y

Z

Subject Index

D

E

F

G

H

I

N

O

P

T